INSIGHT GUIDE

Spain

Urgent ☐

For Dr. Hill

Date 9/23/04   Time 2:4 0

While You Were Out

M

Of   //

Phone

AREA CODE   NUMBER   EXTENSION

Telephoned ☐	Please Call ☐
Came To See You ☑	Will Call Again ☐
Returned Your Call ☐	Wants To See You ☑

Message Thank you so much
for lending me this book!
It helped me out
so much. Also, thank you
for donating the orange
juice and water to the
rat fley — you're so kind

Signed _Carla afuer_

9711   ◤ ADAMS BUSINESS FORMS

Discovery CHANNEL

APA PUBLICATIONS   L

Part of the Langenscheidt Publishing Group

ABOUT THIS BOOK

Editorial

Project Editor
Helen Partington
Managing Editor
Dorothy Stannard
Editorial Director
Brian Bell

Distribution

UK & Ireland
GeoCenter International Ltd
The Viables Centre , Harrow Way
Basingstoke, Hants RG22 4BJ
Fax: (44) 1256-817988

United States
Langenscheidt Publishers, Inc.
46–35 54th Road, Maspeth, NY 11378
Fax: (718) 784-0640

Canada
Prologue Inc.
1650 Lionel Bertrand Blvd., Boisbriand
Québec, Canada J7H 1N7
Tel: (450) 434-0306. Fax: (450) 434-2627

Worldwide
Apa Publications GmbH & Co.
Verlag KG (Singapore branch)
38 Joo Koon Road
Singapore 628990
Tel: (65) 865-1600. Fax: (65) 861-6438

Printing

Insight Print Services (Pte) Ltd
38 Joo Koon Road
Singapore 628990
Tel: (65) 865-1600. Fax: (65) 861-6438

©2000 Apa Publications GmbH & Co.
Verlag KG (Singapore branch)
All Rights Reserved

First Edition 1983
Seventh Edition (Revised) 2000

CONTACTING THE EDITORS
Although every effort is made to
provide accurate information, we
live in a fast-changing world and
would appreciate it if readers
would call our attention to any
errors or outdated information
that may occur by writing to us:
**Insight Guides, P.O. Box 7910,
London SE1 1WE, England.
Fax: (44 20) 7403-0290.
insight@apaguide.demon.co.uk**

This guidebook combines the
interests and enthusiasms of
two of the world's best known information providers: Insight Guides,
whose titles have set the standard
for visual travel guides since 1970,
and Discovery Channel, the world's
premier source of nonfiction television programming.

The editors of Insight Guides provide practical advice and general
understanding about a destination's
history, culture, institutions
and people. Discovery
Channel and its Web site,
www.discovery.com,
help millions of viewers
explore their world from
the comfort of their own home and
also encourage them to explore it
first hand.

How to use this book

Insight Guide: Spain is struc-
tured both to convey an understanding of Spain and its people
and to guide readers through its
places of interest:

◆ To understand the country,
you need to know about its past.
The book's **Features** section, with a yellow bar,
covers the country's
history and culture in
a series of lively and
informative essays.

◆ The **Places** section, with a blue bar, provides a guide to the sights. Places of special interest are coordinated by number with full-colour maps.

◆ The **Travel Tips** section, with a red bar, provides a handy reference for information on travel, hotels, restaurants, etc.

The contributors

The task of coordinating the team which put together this edition fell to **Helen Partington**, assisted by **Liz Clasen**. Thoroughly revised and updated, this book builds on the first edition produced by **Kathleen Wheaton**.

The **Places** chapters were revised and updated by a team of writers based in Spain. **Vicky Hayward** updated the chapters on Galicia, Extremadura and Madrid Province and also added a chapter on Spanish food and a feature on Gypsies. She also translated the essay on flamenco by **Joaquín San Juan**.

Barcelona-based **George Semler** was well placed to update the chapter on that city, as well as chapters on Catalonia, Cantabria and Asturias, Navarre and the Basque Country. He also wrote new sections on Castilla-La Mancha and Rioja **Mark Little** turned his attention to Southern Spain and wrote the feature on gardens, while **Nick Inman** updated and expanded the chapter on Valencia and Murcia and wrote the story on Spain's festivals. **Lindsay Hunt** brought the Canary Islands, Aragón and Castile Léon up to date, and **Natalia Farrán Graves** revised Madrid and the Balearics.

The essay on Spanish painting was reworked by **Caroline Bugler**, while **Ian Chilvers** wrote the feature on Antoni Gaudí, and **Roger Williams** the story on the Guggenheim Museum.

Contributors to the previous editions include **Andrew Eames**, **Lucinda Evans**, **David Baird**, **Muriel Feiner**, **Eric Robbins**, **Ruth MacKay**, **Vega McVeagh**, **Lisa Beebe**, **Robert Crowe**, **Gil Carbajal**, **John Smith**, **Francisco Conde** and **Julian Gray**. Thanks also go to **Rachel Vermont** for proof-reading, to **Penny Phenix** for indexing and to **Ann Esden** who assembled the Travel Tips.

Map Legend

––––	International Boundary
– – – –	Regional Boundary
⊖	Border Crossing
–•–	National Park/Reserve
– – – –	Ferry Route
Ⓜ	Metro
✈ ✈	Airport: International/Regional
🚌	Bus Station
Ⓟ	Parking
❶	Tourist Information
✉	Post Office
✝ ✝	Church/Ruins
✝	Monastery
☪	Mosque
✡	Synagogue
🏰	Castle/Ruins
∴	Archaeological Site
∩	Cave
𝕴	Statue/Monument
★	Place of Interest

The main places of interest in the Places section are coordinated by number with a full-colour map (e.g. ❶), and a symbol at the top of every right-hand page tells you where to find the map.

CONTENTS

A map of Spain is also on the inside front cover, and maps of the Madrid and Barcelona metros are on the inside back cover.

The magical
Alhambra,
Granada

Insight on ...

Information panels

Places

Travel Tips

A WRITER'S READER

Ninth Edition

Donald Hall ◆ D. L. Emblen

BIENVENIDO

Spain's remarkable light and stimulating vitality are
omnipresent: all else is rich diversity

Spain. To the ancient Greeks, it was the land where Hercules'
golden apples grew; to the Arabs, it was the ground floor of
heaven; to writers such as George Orwell and Ernest Hemingway,
it was an arena where history skittered between heroic feats and
tragedy, and bullfighters flirted with death in the work of an afternoon. Few other places so dramatically stimulate the imagination.

Yet despite the steady traffic to and from its coastal resorts, Spain
has remained in the eyes of outsiders a mysterious, half-mythical
country. The Spaniards who are best known to the world are fictional
characters: Don Juan, Don Quixote and Carmen. Fiestas and
flamenco are alluring not only for their flamboyance but for their
undeniable exoticism, with influences from outside Europe.

Spain's isolation from the rest of Europe began with her peninsular
geography and is underscored by history: 700 years of Moorish
occupation were followed by a powerful empire that colonised the
New World, the failure of which led via civil war to the oppressive
regime of General Franco. But as the traveller who sets out across
Spain will discover, hundreds of years of solitude have created a
country that is anything but homogeneous. Spaniards have traditionally spoken of their land as *Las Españas*; a notion of plurality
embracing four languages and seven dialects and climates ranging
from the subtropical south, sweet with its carob and hibiscus, to the
emerald north, with its gorse and heather and plunging fjords.

Your trip will have a couple of constants. One is light: the sunshine
northern Europeans flock to bask in, the burnished red-gold that suf-
fuses whole cities, the lunar contrasts of sun and shadow, the light El
Greco, Velázquez and Picasso saw and painted by. The other is a
tremendous vitality, ubiquitous as the light, which is observed in
cafés and strolling Sunday evening crowds, in haughty urbanites and
exuberant festival dancers, or in the dignified courtesy of a stranger
on a country road, who offers to share his lunch with you and
enquires after your family.

Of all the Spains you encounter on your Spanish sojourn, surely the
most striking and intoxicating is the "new Spain" of post-Francoism:
proud parent of a young democracy, ambitious member of the European Union, a Spain that in just a couple of decades has become an
outrageous artist, uncensored journalist, idealistic politician, stage
for world events and voracious consumer of news and culture. This
Spain is joyfully dispelling a few of the darker old myths, and has
given a celebratory glow to the landscapes that await you.   ❏

PRECEDING PAGES: the Picos de Europa massif; olive plantations near Olvera;
windmills at Consuegra; Cadaqués, Spain's most easterly resort, the Costa Brava.
LEFT: a mime plays the tourist crowd, Palma de Mallorca.

Decisive Dates

11th–5th century BC Phoenicians and Greeks land around coast of the peninsula already settled by Iberians; they establish trading centres and colonies. Invading Celts intermingle with Iberians.

3rd and 1st century BC Carthaginians conquer southeast Spain. The capture of Sagunto by the Carthaginian general Hannibal leads to the Second Punic War (218–201BC). Rome triumphs and begins its 200-year conquest of Spain (Hispania).

1st century AD Christianity spreads in Spain.

409 Vandals and barbarians invade from north.

414 Visigoths conquer Swabians and Vandals and establish a monarchy. They rule Spain as a Christian nation for three centuries, with Toledo as their capital. In 589 Roman Catholicism is adopted as Spain's state religion.

711 Battle of Guadalete: the Moors invade and conquer the kingdom. They succeed in capturing most of Spain in two years.

722 Battle of Covadonga won by Christians.

756 Córdoba Caliphate established.

1085 Toledo recaptured by Christians.

THE CATHOLIC MONARCHS (1474–1516)

1474 Isabel, wife of Fernando of Aragon, succeeds Henry IV of Castile.

1478 The Inquisition introduced by papal bull.

1479 Fernando becomes King of Aragon; Christian Spain is united under one crown.

1483 Torquemada appointed Grand Inquisitor.

1492 The fall of Granada, the last Moorish stronghold, completes the Reconquest of Spain from Muslims – *La Reconquista*. Expulsion of all Jews who refuse to be baptised. Christopher Columbus discovers the New World.

1496 Juana, daughter of Isabel and Fernando, marries Philip, the son of Emperor Maximilian of Austria.

1499 4,000 Moors baptised at Toledo by order of the Catholic Monarchs Fernando and Isabel.

1504 Death of Isabel; Fernando rules in the name of Juana La Loca and later as regent for his child grandson Carlos .

HABSBURG RULE 1516–1700

1516 Death of Fernando: his grandson becomes Charles I of Spain; in 1519 he is elected Holy Roman Emperor Charles V, on the death of Maximilian of Austria.

1519 Cortés lands in Mexico.

1521–56 Charles wages war five times against the French; prevents advances of Francois I.

1532 Pizarro lands in Peru.

1556 Felipe II succeeds to the throne.

1561 Capital moved from Toledo to Madrid which becomes focus for artistic excellence.

1571 Battle of Lepanto against the Turks gives Spain control over the Mediterranean.

1588 Defeat of the Spanish Armada destroys Spain as a sea power.

1598 Felipe II dies. He leaves a huge kingdom which, despite wealth from the New World is debt-crippled after 70 years of war and massive building projects such as the Escorial.

17th century Golden age of art and literature continues under Felipe III, Felipe IV and Charles II, but Spain declines economically and politically.

1609 Expulsion of the Moors (*moriscos*).

1618–48 Thirty Years War. Treaty of Westphalia recognises the independence of the Netherlands.

1659 Treaty of the Pyrenees ends war with France. Felipe IV's daughter Mariá Teresa promised in marriage to Louis XIV.

1667–97 Further wars against France.

BOURBON RULE AND THE WAR OF INDEPENDENCE

1700 Carlos II dies without heir. He wills the crown to Philip of Anjou, grandson of Louis XIV and Maria Teresa. This offends Emperor Leopold who supports the claim of his son, Archduke Charles.

1702–14 War of Spanish Succession brings the Bourbon Felipe V to the throne.

1750–88 Carlos III rules; an enlightened despot.

1788 Carlos IV ascends throne; a weakling, he allows his wife Mariá Luisa and her favourite, Godoy, to rule.

1793 Louis XIV dies; Spain and France at war.

1804 Napoleon is crowned Emperor; Franco-Spanish rapprochement.

1805 Spain helps France in war against England. Battle of Trafalgar ends Spanish naval power.

1808 French occupation of Spain. Napoleon arrests Carlos IV and his son Fernando VII and declares his own brother Joseph King of Spain. The Madrid rising of 2 May heralds the start of the War of Independence (Peninsular War).

1811 Venezuela declares independence, and is followed by other South American republics.

1814 Ferdinand, freed by Napoleon, returns to Spanish throne and reigns as absolute monarch.

19TH-CENTURY: DISPUTES AND DISTURBANCES

1820 Liberal revolt at Cadiz.

1833 Following death of Fernando VII his brother Don Carlos disputes the right to the throne of Fernando's daughter Isabel II. This leads to the First Carlist War (1833–39).

1847–49 Second Carlist War.

1872–76 Third Carlist War.

1873 First Spanish Republic declared.

1874 Alphonso XII, son of Isabel, accedes throne. The Bourbon restoration heralds peace.

1898 Cuban independence at end of Spanish-American War; end of Spanish overseas empire.

MONARCHY IN CRISIS, THE REPUBLIC AND CIVIL WAR

1914–18 Spain is neutral during First World War. but faces growing discontent and strikes at home.

1923 General Primo de Rivera sets up dictatorship with the king's agreement. Order restored; opposition increases among working classes.

1930 Primo de Rivera goes into exile; replaced by General Berenguer.

1931 Republicans seize power in Catalonia. Republic proclaimed; certain regions are granted provincial autonomy.

1933 The Falange group, opposed to regional separation, founded by José Antonio Primo de Rivera; right-wing opposition grows; military plot against regime.

PRECEDING PAGES: 16th-century map of Iberia.
LEFT: Fernando and Isabel adorn Salamanca University.
RIGHT: detail from a 19th-century painting of Madrid's bullring by Mañuel Castellano.

1934 Catalonia proclaims its autonomy. Insurrection in the Asturias is brutally suppressed.

1936 Popular Front wins elections. General Franco leads rebellion from Morocco. Events swiftly lead to Civil War.

THE FRANCO YEARS

1938 General Franco becomes head of Nationalist Government.

1939 Nationalist victory in Civil War.

World War II Franco attempts to maintain Spain's neutrality, but supports Germany in 1941.

1953 Spain agrees to US bases in exchange for $226 million aid.

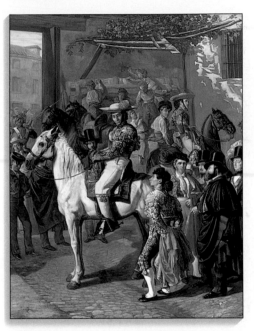

1955 Spain admitted to United Nations.

1969 Juan Carlos proclaimed heir to throne.

DEMOCRACY, REFORM, MODERNISATION

1975 Franco dies. Juan Carlos becomes king and a democratic state is established.

1978 New constitution approved.

1982 Socialists sweep into power in elections.

1985 Abortion legalised.

1986 Spain joins the European Community, later the European Union, a process completed in 1992. Referendum votes for NATO membership.

1992 Expo '92 in Seville; Barcelona hosts the Olympic Games; Madrid is the EU's Capital of Culture.

1996 Socialists voted out of office. ❑

IBERIA: BEGINNINGS

From the earliest times, foreign invaders came to Spain from beyond the Pyrenees and across the sea. Under the Phoenicians and the Greeks trading flourished

The land now covered by Spain and Portugal is a portion of the former Hercynian continent, which broke apart at Gibraltar sometime before the last Ice Age. Today the southern tip of the peninsula is 13 km (8 miles) from North Africa, but stands somewhat aloof from the main mass of Europe, jutting out into the Atlantic as far west as Ireland, and separated from the rest of the continent by the Pyrenees, whose average height of 1,500 metres (5,000 ft) exceeds that of the Alps.

Among western European countries Spain is second only to France in size, or equal to an area slightly larger than California. Most of her 39 million people live in a few densely populated cities, and her long reaches of unfarmed, uninhabited terrain enhance a sense of vastness and solitude. Traditionally in Spain people have tended to speak of Europe as if it were somewhere else.

Mountain barriers and few rivers

Within this self-contained fragment of land, two geographical facts have helped to shape Spain's history: the presence of mountains and the absence of rivers.

After Switzerland, Spain is Europe's most mountainous country: the average altitude of the peninsula is around 600 metres (2,000 ft). Mountains serve as a barrier to both Atlantic and Mediterranean air currents, dividing Spain into distinct climatic regions. To the north, in the shadow of the Pyrenees, are the wettest provinces; the eastern and southern coasts have a Mediterranean climate; the *meseta,* Spain's vast dry central plateau, suffers searing summer heat and long bitterly cold winters.

The peninsula was named Iberia – Land of Rivers – by tribes who crossed over from North Africa. To those desert people, Spanish rivers might have looked noteworthy, although in fact only two – the Ebro and the Guadalquivir – are reliably full enough to be useful in navigation

and irrigation. The Moors, who settled along the banks of the Guadalquivir, praised it to heaven, causing the French author Alexandre Dumas to write indignantly, in 1846: "French writers, never having seen it at all, believed the Arabs. True, Spanish writers could have revealed the less picturesque truth, but since it is the only

river in their country large enough to take a boat, why should they decry it? When we got there we found that between the flat and uninteresting banks rolled a mass, not of water but of liquid mud with the colour and consistency, if not the taste, of milk chocolate."

Chopped up by high, jagged mountains and lacking any unifying waterways, it was perhaps hardly surprising that Spain developed as a handful of linguistic and cultural shards; a land "without a backbone", in the words of philosopher Ortega y Gasset.

However, while Iberia's landscape encouraged internal fragmentation and isolation, her position at the mouth of the Mediterranean

LEFT: shepherds tending their flocks in Aragón.
RIGHT: dolmen near Roses, Costa Brava.

made her a natural destination for a succession of migrants, colonisers and traders.

Continental drifters

Weapons and charred bones from hunters' camps show that Neanderthal Man arrived in Spain about half a million years ago, following herds of European elephants as they migrated south. The earliest human remains have been uncovered on the *meseta*, near present-day Madrid in Soria. Neanderthal settlements, 200,000 years old, have been found at Gibraltar, leading archaeologists to argue that at least some of the earliest Spaniards were African.

paintings of the era, and presage the powerful influence that continent would have over Spanish culture for the next several thousand years.

Great waves of immigration occurred around 3000 BC, when the Iberians crossed the Strait of Gibraltar and the Ligurians descended the Pyrenees from Italy. In 900 BC, the Celts moved into Spain from France and Britain – then, as now, fleeing the northern winters and seeking the sun.

Celt-Iberians

The word Celt-Iberian, a generic term used to describe all of these groups, does not mean that

Of the abundant prehistoric remains in Spain, the most remarkable are the caves of Altamira on the northern Atlantic coast. There, Stone Age artists painted bison, stags, horses and wild boars on the stone ceilings some 14,000 years ago. Bones of the depicted animals found on the floor of the caves imply that the paintings served a ritual purpose, a sympathetic magic to make the hunting good. But their vividness and baffling technical perfection have made them the first chapter in the history of Spanish art. Other cave paintings, showing lively stick figures using bows and arrows, have been found near Valencia. Painted between 10,000 and 5,000 years ago, they are similar to African

they intermingled much. Today's fair-haired northern Spaniard, and the slighter, dark-eyed southerner, are present reminders of ancient Spanish tribalism. Territory especially belonging to the Celts included Asturias, Galicia and Portugal and the northwestern corner of the peninsula, where numerous forts, or *castros*, have been unearthed. In general, the Celts were known as violent, rustic shepherds who made good mercenaries. Their varied contributions to succeeding civilisations on the peninsula included iron and trousers.

The Iberians flourished in the south. They lived in walled cities, buried their dead in elaborate tombs, and began exploiting the rich copper deposits around Almería. These people have been characterised as peaceful farmers, who were much more receptive to foreigners and foreign ways than their inland neighbours. However, the 1st century Greek geographer Strabo found common traits among all the isolated bands living on the peninsula: hospitality, grand manners, arrogance, indifference to privation and hatred of outside interference in their community affairs. Over the centuries, historians have continued to hold up Strabo's description as a good thumbnail sketch of the Spanish temperament; it still holds good today.

> **NEW TECHNOLOGY**
>
> Greek colonisers introduced the potter's wheel as well as high artistic ideals. Sophisticated Greek ceramic vases were an inspiration to native craftsmen.

El Dorado

The Iberian skill in metallurgy attracted the attention of trading peoples from all over the eastern Mediterranean; it is thought that early Spanish metalwork taught the world to perceive gold as valuable. In 1100 BC, Phoenician traders discovered Spain's mineral wealth and set up ports of call along the coast, notably at Gadir (Cádiz), which soon became their most prosperous city. The Phoenicians brought the art of fish-salting, the Punic alphabet and music from Tyre to Spain; they left Cádiz so laden that their ships' barrels and anchors were said to be of solid silver.

Another seafaring nation anxious for trade, the Greeks, chanced upon Spain when a Greek ship was carried by a storm to Tartessos, a city which stood somewhere near Málaga. At the time, Tartessos had scarcely been touched by Phoenicians, and the Greeks returned home "with a profit greater than any Greeks before their day", according to one contemporary chronicler. They began to colonise Iberia in the 7th century BC, at Empúries (Girona) and Mainake in the south.

The Greeks added another layer of civilisation to the already cosmopolitan coast. Their contributions to the native culture included olives, wine and a stirring passion for bulls, as well as a strong influence on art. The Lady of Elche, a haughty stone statue of an Iberian

princess carved by an unknown artist some 25 centuries ago, is Spain's beloved example of the fusion of Greek and native Iberian style.

Cádiz became a melting pot of Greeks, Phoenicians and native Iberians, and by the 6th century BC the city had a reputation as a rich and sinful place, with tall (three-storey) buildings, millionaires and castanet-clicking dancers. Tartessos, according to the Greeks, was so refined that its laws were written in verse.

Spain eventually worked her way into Greek

mythology: the golden apples of the Hesperides were said to grow there, and it was one of the labours of Hercules to gather them.

Some historians have identified Tartessos as the Tarshish of the Bible, the fabulous source of "gold and silver, ivory, apes and peacocks", where Jonah was headed when he was swallowed by the whale. A case has also been made for placing the lost Atlantis at or near Cádiz.

The Romans knew the peninsula as Hispania, which is rooted in a Semitic word meaning "remote, hidden". This western land loomed large in the Mediterranean imagination, and before long it became a target of conquest as well as trade. ❑

LEFT: Iberian metalwork taught the world to perceive gold as valuable.
RIGHT: the style of dress of the Lady of Elche blends Iberian and Greek styles.

ROMANS AND VISIGOTHS

Spain became the most advanced of the Roman Empire's provinces. After 300 years
of Visigoth rule as a Christian nation, it was conquered by the Moors

The future of the Iberian peninsula was to be decided by Carthage and Rome as these two great powers jockeyed for military and economic supremacy in the western Mediterranean. Defeated by the Romans in 241 BC during the First Punic War and then driven out of the island of Sicily, the Carthaginians spent bided their time in their North African base rebuilding their armies and preparing for war.

The battle for the peninsula

Carthage made its move into Spain under Hamilcar Barca. With a vastly superior army, Hamilcar took over most of Andalusia, burning Tartessos to the ground in the process. He then proceeded up the Valencian coast, defeating those Iberian settlements foolish enough to oppose him.

To bolster the Carthaginian war machine, native Iberians were either drafted into the army or were forced to work as slaves in the gold and silver mines. Hamilcar set about fortifying Carthage's coastal settlements on the peninsula: Barcclona is named after Hamilcar Barca; the second Carthaginian city became Carthago Novo, today's Cartagena.

After Hamilcar's death, his son Hannibal, steeped in his father's hatred of the Romans, led his 60,000-man army out of Carthago Novo and headed northwards to the Pyrenees. As he took his troops up the coast, he made alliances with groups of Celts and Iberians who contributed money and manpower to his army. With his now legendary band of war elephants, Hannibal crossed into France, headed over the treacherous Alps, and swept down towards Rome from the north. In 216 BC he confronted and routed a far larger Roman army at Cannae.

But total victory was to elude Hannibal; for the next 13 years his troops moved up and down Italy, never able to defeat the Romans once and

for all. The Romans captured his brother-in-law, Hasdrubal, and in a morale-crushing gesture tossed his head into Hannibal's camp. Hannibal stayed on in Italy for four more years and was finally forced to return to North Africa in 203 BC. A year later, he was soundly defeated in battle near Carthage.

During this period Rome also had to contend with the Carthaginian base on the Iberian peninsula. In 218 BC, Publius Scipio had landed at Empúries with an expeditionary force. For several years he fought the Carthaginians and finally, in 209 BC, he captured Carthago Novo. But there were more furious battles before Scipio's army overran Gadir (Cádiz) in 206 BC, banishing Carthage for ever.

The Roman conquest

It took the Romans only seven years to subdue Gaul, but the conquest of Hispania (Spain) dragged on for nearly two centuries. The Spanish wars depleted the Roman treasury and forced

LEFT: statue of a Roman woman. Roman occupation of Spain lasted for some seven centuries.
RIGHT: Roman mosaic in Segóbriga, showing the days of the week.

the army to adopt conscription, because nobody wanted to fight in Spain. The Phoenicians and the Greeks, who came to the peninsula as traders, had found the natives to be courteous, but the invading Carthaginians and Romans encountered ferocious warriors. The Romans in Spain also had the disadvantage of overextended communications. The countryside over which they marched was hot and bleak, with little water or fodder.

The natives, on the other hand, accustomed to the harsh climate and to deprivation, defended their territory desperately. However, Celto-Iberian patriotism did not extend beyond city walls, and tribes often betrayed each other to the Romans. The Iberian lack of unity slowed Rome's conquest, since each Roman victory was simply a triumph over an isolated area.

The last stage of the Roman conquest was the Cantabrian War (29–19 BC). Seven Roman legions were forced to participate, and Augustus himself was called in to lead the final campaign in the Cantabrian Mountains. So defiant were the Cantabrians that they continued to struggle against their conquerors even after their leaders had been nailed on crosses by the Romans. Rome finally established a *Pax Romana* in 19 BC, under the reign of Augustus.

THE STUFF OF LEGEND

It took the Romans 200 years to conquer Spain, largely because of the fierce opposition they met from the native people. The most dramatic resistance was by Numancia, a city of 4,000 inhabitants in central Spain. It took a 60,000-strong Roman army several years to subdue the town and, after months of the final siege, the few citizens who had not perished through disease or cannabalism hurled themselves into the flames of their burning homes rather than submit to Roman domination. This battle took on symbolic value, and was invoked centuries later to spur Spaniards to defend their home against invaders.

Life under the Romans

During the rule of Caesar, Latin became the unifying language on the Iberian peninsula and Roman law and customs were quickly adopted. As the Carthaginians had discovered much earlier, Hispania was rich in mineral wealth and provided Rome with a seemingly endless supply of gold and silver. Also rich in livestock and agricultural goods, particularly fruit and vegetables, it became one of the wealthiest, and thus most exploited, provinces of the empire.

The extension of citizenship proved decisive in the Romanisation of Spain. At first, only colonists of Roman or Italian origin were granted citizenship. Though full citizenship was not granted to all Celto-Iberians until the Edict of Vespasian (AD 74), initial attempts to include the native population in the greater Roman Empire went a long way to establish at least the appearance of cultural cohesiveness on the peninsula.

Along with language and customs came religion: Christianity entered Spain in the 1st century AD, during the reign of Nero. It is generally believed that St Paul visited Spain – possibly Aragón – around AD 63–67, and St James, one of Christ's disciples, is said to have preached the Gospel in Spain. The Roman resistance to Christianity, however, led to the

Constantine's reign (AD 325), but it was only under Theodosius I (AD 379–395) – who was born in Spain – that Christianity became the one accepted religion in the Roman Empire.

The influence of Roman civilisation on the peninsula was enormous, particularly in the fields of construction and architecture. Roman aqueducts, bridges, roads and walls are still in use throughout Spain. Segovia's two-tiered aqueduct is among the most perfect structures of its kind. Tarragona, on the eastern coast just south of Barcelona, still has Roman arches, a three-tiered aqueduct and an amphitheatre, all in mint condition. The well preserved Roman

persecution, torture and the eventual martyrdom of many Spaniards.

Early church history in Spain is full of tales of tortured bodies redeemed by eventual sainthood. The hymns of Prudentius (AD 348–405) bring to light the tortures – no details spared – that these early Christian martyrs endured.

Yet despite persecution, Christian communities began to flourish on the peninsula. Spain was predominantly Christian by the time of

LEFT: Mérida's Roman theatre is used today to stage classical productions.
ABOVE: detail on a Roman sarcophagus in the Alcázar museum in Córdoba.

theatre in Mérida is still used for staging classical dramas. Carmona has a Roman cemetery, and the remains of mausoleums can be found in Fabara, Jumilla, Tarragona and elsewhere.

In literature and philosophy, the Roman occupation gave rise to Spain's Silver Age. Notable figures, all of them born in Spain, include the philosopher Seneca, whose Stoical ideals have had a marked effect on the evolution of the Spanish character; the historian and poet Lucan, the poet Martial and Quintilian, the master rhetorician who later became the teacher of Pliny and Tacitus. These men were all trained in the Latin schools of rhetoric and spent most of their lives in Rome penning works for Italian audiences. Only in the later work of Martial, after he had left Rome – escaping "the togas stinking of purple dye and the conversation of haughty widows" – and retired to his native Aragón, do we find verses that reflect the Spanish landscape.

Vandalism

By the 5th century, the Roman empire was in decline throughout southern Europe. The Visigoths, a warlike Germanic race under the leadership of Alaric, crossed the Alps in 401 and nine years later sacked Rome. Tribes of Seubians, Vandals and Alans swept across the Pyrenees

into Spain, and proved too numerous for the private armies of Spanish landowners. Notoriously barbaric and ruthless (the word "vandalism" can be traced to the Vandals), the warriors looted and killed as they went, effectively ending five centuries of prosperous Roman rule.

The occupation of Hispania by these Germanic tribes was almost complete by 415. Alliances were forged, power shared, until the Visigoths invaded from Gaul and established their own dynasty on the peninsula. Oddly enough, these barbarian invaders had at one time been Romanised – after having served the Romans as allies and mercenaries – so this new conquest initially brought about few changes.

The Visigoths established military rule yet permitted local culture with separate political and administrative structures, laws and religion. In theory the Hispano-Romans had their own sovereigns, and their lives proceeded so independently that marriage with Visigoths was not allowed until the reign of Leovigild (568–584).

King Leovigild did more than any other Visigothic king to unite the peninsula. Militarily, he subjugated the Basques in the north, conquered the Seubians who had managed to keep an independent kingdom in Galicia, and recovered Baetica (later to become Andalusia) from Byzantine control. He allowed Latin to become

the dominant tongue on the peninsula, and for the first time permitted Visigoths and Hispano-Romans to marry. By stressing cultural, geographical and linguistic unity, Leovigild provided Hispania with a sense of national destiny, quite independent from Rome.

Leovigild failed, however, in his attempt to convert the Hispano-Romans to Arianism, a form of natural Christianity which refuted the concept of the Trinity and subordinated the Son to the Father. He was liberal enough to allow his son Hermenegild to marry a Christian, but when Hermenegild converted to Christianity and rose up against him, Leovigild sought his revenge. He plundered churches, exacted huge sums of money from wealthy Christians, and sent many who opposed him to their deaths.

But the door had been opened. When Leovigild died, his son Recared converted to Christianity and became Spain's first Christian king. With the religious issue resolved, Hispano-Romans developed a new, strong loyalty to the Visigothic monarchy. Recared's conversion symbolised the victory of Hispano-Roman civilisation over the barbarians, and signalled the start of a new alliance between church and state on the peninsula which would last, with few interruptions, until the present century.

Drawing on Roman precedents, the Visigoths

Decline and fall

When King Witizia assumed the throne in 702, he hoped to side-step the tradition of the elective monarchy and leave the crown to his son Akhila; those nobles who opposed him were beaten and punished. But when Witizia died in 710, Akhila was in the north and Roderic, the Duke of Baetica, was acclaimed king instead by the southern Visigoths.

Witizia's family appealed to the Moors in North Africa for help. Fired by his zeal for the new religion of Mohammed, Tarik ibn Ziyad, the governor of Tangier, agreed to join in the battle. His force of 12,000 men, the majority

introduced a codified law and a workable tax system. But while they spoke Latin and emulated Roman laws, administration, customs and dress, they clung tenaciously to their belief in an elective monarchy. Visigothic society was an assembly of warriors who cherished the right to elect their king and permitted ambitious nobles to aspire to the throne. Smooth transitions to the throne were rare; in the first 300 years of Visigothic rule there were more than 30 kings, many of whom met bloody deaths.

LEFT: jewel-studied Visigothic crown in beaten gold.
ABOVE: Visigothic stone carving in the 7th-century church of Quintanilla de la Viñas, near Burgos.

of them Berbers, was ferried across the Strait of Gibraltar into southern Spain. King Roderic was routed in the Battle of Guadalete and perished by drowning.

The year was 711 and the Visigoths were without a king; they retreated to Mérida where they put up a desperate last stand in vain. Tarik should have returned home to North Africa victorious, but he was driven by two overriding desires; to carry his religion into the land of the unconverted and to seize King Solomon's legendary treasure, purported to be in Toledo. The Moors swept through Spain and by the year 714 they had established control over almost all parts of the peninsula. ❏

MOORISH SPAIN

The Muslim presence in Spain (al-Andalus) gave rise to a brilliant civilisation.

After almost eight centuries, the last Moorish bastion fell in the Reconquest

The Muslim invasion ended the cultural, linguistic and religious unity that the Visigoths had tried to achieve on the peninsula. Yet the period from 711 to 1492, when the Moors were expelled from Spain, was not one in which Moorish values flourished exclusively.

While the Moors took Seville, Mérida, Toledo and Zaragoza, Visigothic nobles regrouped in the mountains of Asturias. In the same region where 700 years earlier hardy mountaineers had held off Roman legions for 10 years, Pelayo's small Christian force confronted a more powerful invading army. Though fired up by their zeal for the new religion of Mohammed, the Moors could not prise Pelayo's men from their mountain stronghold and the Christians achieved victory at Covadonga in 722. This triumph marked the start of the *Reconquista* – the Reconquest of Spain – and assumed symbolic proportions; the Christians regarded the victory as proof that God had not abandoned his people after all.

Islam sweeps north

However, the Moors, intent on conquering all of Europe, were undeterred by Covadonga. They continued over the Pyrenees into France, until they were stopped at the Battle of Poitiers in 732 by French troops led by Charles Martel, "Charles the Hammer". This stunning defeat forced the Moors to look southwards again and to begin the difficult task of ruling over the land and the people they had recently conquered.

Unlike the Romans who established a link with a strong centralised government outside the peninsula, the Moorish invaders were only nominally the political and spiritual subjects of the Caliphate of Damascus, a distant overlord. The conquering Moors fought each other for power and control, dividing up the booty.

These early years of Moorish rule were

LEFT: A Spanish King by Alonso Cano portrays an archetypal medieval monarch.

RIGHT: under Moorish rule painting was encouraged as a courtly skill.

characterised by rebellions and frequent infighting among the Muslim kingdoms. Moreover, Spain became the nesting ground for new converts to Islam coming over from North Africa. The Berbers, for example, came from Mauritania and, after a generation of being treated like second-class citizens by the Arab nobles,

rose up against them. After years of internecine fighting, a new Moorish governor redivided the conquered lands. The Berbers were given territory in the Duero River valley but, after years of famine, many returned to North Africa.

While the Moors contended with the Berber invasions in the south, Pelayo, followed by his son Favila, set about creating a powerful Christian kingdom in the north. Later, under King Alfonso I (739–757), the Asturians occupied Galicia to the west and Cantabria to the east; under Alfonso II, they moved their capital to Oviedo, where the Asturians tried to restore the institutions of the Visigothic monarchy.

Meanwhile the Basques, usually intent on

maintaining independence, were willing to form alliances with fellow Christians. Such manoeuvrings had one aim: to expel the Moors and restore Christianity. When Charlemagne took control of Pamplona and Catalonia late in the 8th century, he set up the Spanish March, a buffer zone to keep the Moors out. The Moors had no choice but to build their base in the south, in the area now known as Andalusia.

The emirate

In 756, Abd-al-Rahman I, an Umayyad prince, came to power in Córdoba and established an emirate aligned with, but independent of, the

main seat of power in Damascus. He proclaimed himself Emir of *al-Andalus* (the Moorish name for Spain), and his ascendancy marked the dawning of the most important and advanced civilisation of the Middle Ages.

Córdoba was at the heart of this Golden Age: it became arguably the largest, wealthiest and most cultured city in all of western Europe. At its height in the mid-10th century, Córdoba's population had swelled to more than 300,000 and there were well over 800 mosques to serve the religious needs of the predominantly Muslim populace. As the Muslims performed daily ablutions as part of their religious obligations, some 700 public baths dotted the city.

The caliphs of Córdoba supported all aspects of learning. During the reign of al-Hakem II (961–976), the city library was established and soon held 250,000 volumes. Greek texts, which the Arabs had come across in their triumphant march across the Middle East, were also introduced to Europe. The works of Aristotle, Euclid, Hippocrates, Plato and Ptolemy were translated and commented upon by such noted Arabic philosophers as Avicenna and Averroës.

Poets, too, were highly regarded. They also served a political function similar to that of television commentators today. The bloodthirsty al-Mansur was reputedly surrounded by 30 to 40 poets when he marched off to battle. Poetry was written in Castilian, Galician and Hebrew, but the most powerful poetry was written in Arabic: with its fondness for metaphor this poetry would influence 15th-century Spanish lyrics and, in our own century, the sensuous *casidas* and *gacelas* of García Lorca.

Arabic influence

More than 4,000 words of Arabic origin are still in use in modern Spanish. Foods introduced by the Moors – *azúcar* (sugar), *berenjena* (eggplant), *naranjas* (oranges) and *sandías* (watermelons) – make up the daily diets of most Spaniards. Also, words connected with administration, irrigation, mathematics, architecture and medicine can be traced back to Arabic.

Many phrases still in use in Spain have their roots in Arabic culture, especially those that express courtesy – *Esta es su casa* (This is your house) and *Buen provecho* (Enjoy your meal) – and the role of God in everyday life – *si Dios quiere* (if God wills it) and the word *ojalá,* from the Arabic *wa shá' a-l-lah* (may God will it).

Córdoba also became the scientific capital of Europe during the Middle Ages. The introduction of Arabic numerals into Spain – far less cumbersome than their Roman counterparts – spurred great advances in mathematics; the Moors are thought to have invented algebra as well as spherical trigonometry. Astronomers and astrologers were numerous, and there was a significant following for the occult sciences.

New industries flourished in Córdoba. The royal factory of carpets was known throughout Spain, and Córdoba's many wonderful silk weavers increased its fame as a place where fine garments could be bought. Glass and ceramics factories were built, and the old heavy

As they were a desert people and because the Koran required daily ablutions, the Arabs were extremely fond of water. In addition to their numerous public baths, the Moors incorporated fountains and pools into their palaces and villas. This can be best appreciated in Granada's Alhambra – the Red Palace – and its neighbouring Generalife, which served as the summer residence of the caliphs. Built in the 14th and 15th centuries, towards the end of the Moorish occupation, both these structures combine water and greenery to establish a mood of elegance and relaxed splendour.

Moorish architecture

But the Moors left their most indelible stamp upon Spain with their architecture. The solid Romanesque churches of earlier centuries were far surpassed by Moorish constructions which were lighter, airier and more colourful. The cupola, the horseshoe arch and the slenderest of columns, often of jasper, onyx and marble, were all introduced by the Moors and can best be appreciated by visiting Córdoba's *Mezquita* or Mosque. As the Koran forbade the representation of human figures, Muslim artists used geometric patterns which often incorporated the graceful letters of the Arabic alphabet.

metal tableware was replaced by glass or glazed pottery. Spaniards journeyed to Córdoba to examine the latest designs by its renowned leatherworkers and silversmiths. Moorish physicians were highly prized for their ability to diagnose illnesses and for their surgical skills. The Moors used anaesthetics, and are known to have performed complicated and delicate surgeries such as cataract removal or drilling the skull to reduce pressure on the brain.

LEFT: Alfonso the Wise (1252–84) encouraged scholars to master Arab culture and translate Greek texts.
ABOVE: fresco from Galicia showing the Moors and Christians ar war.

The Jews in Spain

No story of the Moorish occupation would be complete without including the illustrious, and eventually, tragic, role played by the Jews during this renaissance of culture. Savagely persecuted by the Visigoths, the Jews were held in high esteem by the Muslim invaders for their role in bringing the invasion about. Generally speaking, they were protected by both kings and nobles for whom they worked in administrative posts. Jews were valued as merchants, ambassadors and emissaries and were taken into the confidence of Moorish and Christian rulers when their own people could not be trusted. Abd-al-Rahman III's minister of finance was a Jew, as was the vizier of the king of Granada in the 11th century.

Because of their honesty, many Jews were used as tax collectors, igniting the hatred of the labouring classes. With the arrival of the Almoravids and the Almohads, fanatical converts to Islam that came from North Africa, the Jews were either expelled to Christian lands or murdered.

Jews fared well especially under the Caliphate of Córdoba. Maimonides, the great Jew-

ish philosopher and author of the *Guide to the Perplexed*, was born in Córdoba and lived there until forced to flee to Egypt during the Almohad invasion. The Talmudic School of Córdoba attracted Jewish thinkers from all over Europe.

Jews were also held in high esteem in the Christian kingdoms; they held positions as royal treasurers and physicians, and the Catholic Monarchs came to depend upon their Jewish subjects for financial and medical advice. Alfonso X (1252–84), the "Wise King" of Castile and the founder of the University of Salamanca, created a school of translation in Toledo where Christian, Jewish and Moorish scholars worked together. The Bible, the

> **EL CID (1043–99)**
>
> Rodrigo Díaz de Vivar of Burgos battled Christian and Moorish tyrants alike. A man of courage, he was dubbed El Cid from the Arab *Sidi* (Lord). The poem *El Cantar del Mío Cid* immortalised him as a hero of the Reconquest.

Talmud, the Cabala and the Koran were all translated into Spanish at the king's behest.

Soon, however, the effect of the Crusades, which fanned hatred throughout Europe, was felt in Spain. When the plague of 1391 resulted in the deaths of hundreds of Christians, Jews were singled out as the cause. Zealous friars stirred up a wave of anti-Semitism which led to the burning of Jewish ghettos and the murder of their inhabitants. In the 14th century, the Valladolid *Ordenamientos* deprived Jewish communities of their financial and juridical autonomy. Expulsion and the Inquisition was yet to come, under Isabel and Fernando.

Reconquest

The Reconquest of Spain, which spanned 750 years, was both a battle against an invader, and a war against Islam, seen as a heretical religion that did not recognise Christ as the Messiah.

In the later 9th century, Alfonso II (866–911), taking advantage of Moorish infighting, began to colonise the Duero River valley, now abandoned by the retreating Berbers. To the east, he built many fortresses to repel Muslim attacks. These Asturians saw themselves as the heirs of Visigothic power and tradition, responsible for wrenching power from the Moors.

But when García I moved the Asturian capital from Oviedo to León in 914, the unified Moors – under the rule of the caliphs of Córdoba – wreaked great destruction upon the Christians.

Al-Mansur came to power in Córdoba in 976 and, to distract the Muslims from his own misrule, led what became almost yearly raids into the five kingdoms of Christian Spain: Asturias, León, Navarre, Aragón and Catalonia. In 985 he burned Barcelona, and its inhabitants were killed or enslaved; three years later, he plundered Burgos and León. In Santiago de Compostela he destroyed the cathedral, holiest of Christian shrines, and had its bells and doors carried by Christian slaves to Córdoba where they were used to make lamps and the ceiling for the *Mezquita*.

When al-Mansur died in battle in 1002, the Christian states counter-attacked. Count Ramón Borrell of Barcelona led troops southwards where they joined rebellious Moors. However, progress was slow: Córdoba was finally sacked in 1010, ending its pre-eminence in *al-Andalus*. Meanwhile, Sancho III became the King of Navarre (1000–35); by alliance and warfare, he came to rule over Aragón, Castile, Ribagorza, Sobrarbe and the city of León.

Civil wars and the division of territories into splinter states called *taifas* further undermined Moorish power on the peninsula. The Christian kings played one Moorish ruler off against another. By weakening the Moors, the Castilians retook Toledo, widely acknowledged as the capital of Spain, in 1085. This marked the fall of the first Muslim city and allowed the

strength, the Muslim kings sought aid from Morocco. Help came from the Almoravids – "those vowed to God" – a group of Saharan people who had recently converted to Islam and had conquered much of West Africa.

Under the leadership of Yusuf, the Almoravids brought camels and African guards to carry their weapons. In time, they captured Badajoz, Lisbon, Guadalajara and Zaragoza. Though they were repelled at the gates of Barcelona and held at bay in Toledo, the Almoravids remained in control of their territories for 50 years. By the middle of the 12th century, however, the power of the Almoravids was collaps-

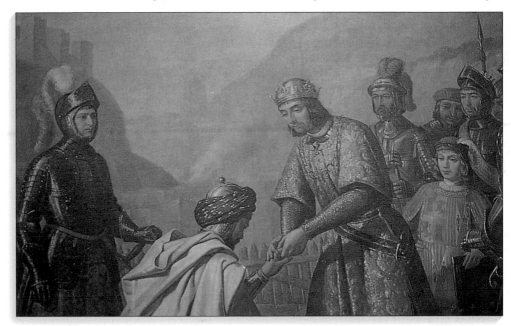

Christian forces to expand their limits to advance their southern outposts. Meanwhile, the Aragonese won Zaragoza and the Catalans retook Lérida and Tarragona. When the King of Aragón's daughter married Count Ramón Berenguer of Barcelona in 1151, Catalonia and Aragón were united under one ruler.

Holy wars

But the Moors were not going to relinquish Spain easily. To counter the growing Christian

LEFT: statue of El Cid in his home town of Burgos.
ABOVE: the Moors admit defeat before the Catholic monarchs. Granada was the last kingdom to fall.

ing and the Christians regained most of Andalusia. But then, in 1195, the Almohads, a Berber group from Morocco's Atlas Mountains, invaded Spain. They defeated and killed the Christian king of Castile at Alarcos and drove thousands of *Mozárabes* (Christians living on Moorish lands) and Jews out of Andalusia.

In response, Pope Innocent III called for a Crusade and many Christian kingdoms in Europe sent contingents of knights to wage war against the "infidel". A furious battle ensued at Las Navas de Tolosa in 1212. Alfonso VIII of Castile united troops from Navarre, Aragón and Portugal against the forces of Miramolin, the Almohad leader. Not only did the Christians achieve victory, but they were now poised for attacks on northern Andalusia.

The subjection of Muslim Spain was to follow quickly. Jaime I, the "Conqueror King", conquered Valencia and the Balearic Islands. Meanwhile, Fernando III, "the Saint", united Castile and León, thus merging their forces for further attacks. Córdoba surrendered to his troops in 1235, followed by Valencia in 1238. Many other Muslim territories futilely resisted the Christian advance. In 1246, Fernando III laid siege to Jaén which fell after months of battle. After a siege lasting over 16 months, Seville surrendered in 1248. Many of its houses were burned, vineyards destroyed, orchards set ablaze; the mosque in Seville was pulverised and only its minaret, the Giralda, was left.

With these Christian victories, Moorish domination in Spain was vastly reduced. By the end of the 13th century, only the provinces of Granada and Málaga and parts of Cádiz and Almería were still in Moorish hands. A Muslim state under Christian protection was set up in Granada; refugees from the rest of Spain settled there under the rule of the Nasrid Dynasty.

Yet, because of partisan politics and feuding, the reunification of Spain was delayed 150 years. The kings of Spain contested the throne in repeated bloody encounters. Pedro I, "The Cruel", ruled from 1350 to 1369 and left a trail of blood that included the murder of half-brothers, cousins and friends.

Fernando and Isabel

Early in the 15th century, the Aragonese took control of Catalonia and Valencia, and the House of Castile assumed charge of Murcia and Almería. Union between these two powerful kingdoms came about in 1474 when Fernando of Aragón married Queen Isabel of Castile. But this was a union of crowns, not kingdoms, for each region maintained its own leadership, government, traditions and rules of succession.

From 1483 to 1497 the *Cortes*, the assembly of nobles in court, did not convene, and the "Catholic Monarchs", Fernando and Isabel, put an end to feudalism and established an absolute monarchy. They took over the nobles' privileges and created a new upper middle class.

The Inquisition

In order to achieve Catholic unity, in 1478 Fernando and Isabel obtained a papal bull from Sixtus IV to set up the Sacred Office of the Holy Inquisition, a court at which alleged *conversos*, "false converts" to Catholicism, would be tried. Thousands were condemned and imprisoned or killed; others fled the country.

Converted Jews could stay only if their conversion was total. Many had posts both in the government and even in the Church itself. In 1483, all Jews were ordered to leave Andalusia and Fernando ordered their expulsion from Zaragoza, but both orders were largely ignored.

In the meantime, the troops of the Catholic Monarchs were laying siege to Granada. Ironically, Fernando and Isabel once more sought lands from wealthy Jews to finance the final phase of the *Reconquista*. On 2 January 1492, after 11 years of battle, the Moorish King Boabdil personally surrendered the keys of Granada to Fernando and Isabel.

Within two months of capturing Granada, the Catholic Monarchs, on the advice of Tomás de Torquemada, the first Inquisitor-General and son of a *converso* family, ordered the expulsion of all Jews who refused to be baptised. Some 170,000 Jews were expelled. They went to North Africa, Greece or Turkey. Many of these Sephardic Jews still use their Castilian speech, known as *Ladino*, today.

More than 300,000 *conversos* remained in Spain. They were treated badly and were required to show the solidity of their new faith at all times. But the Golden Century of Spain would not have been possible without them. ❑

THE SPANISH INQUISITION

Set up by Fernando and Isabel in 1480, the Inquisition was intended to unite all Spain under Catholicism. Authorised by a papal bull, it was a court, presided over by the Inquisitor General, in which suspected *conversos*, false converts to Catholicism from Jewish and Muslim faiths, were tried. The Inquisition accepted denunciations and used torture to obtain confessions. Defendants were not informed of the charges against them, were denied counsel, and were not allowed to cross-examine hostile witnesses. Those found guilty faced imprisonment, beheading, hanging or burning at the stake. The court, later directed against Protestant heretics, lasted until the 19th century.

RIGHT: enforcing the sentences of the Inquisition: *The Burning of Heretics* by Pedro Berruguete shows St Dominic seated beneath the canopy.

THE EXPANDING EMPIRE

Freed from the Muslim yoke, Spain looked abroad. Colonial expansion made it briefly, under the Habsburg kings, the greatest power on earth

Towards the end of the 15th century Portugal was the world maritime power, aggressively exploring the Atlantic coast of Africa and establishing colonies on the Azores and the Cape Verde Islands.

In 1485 Christopher Columbus, a Genoese navigator who had been in the service of Portuguese captains, approached the Catholic Monarchs Fernando and Isabel and asked for financial support to find the shortest westward route to India. He offered them new territories, abundant riches and more souls for God.

Columbus was held off for nearly seven years, but once Granada had been conquered, Spain began to concentrate its resources on overseas exploration.

Spain discovers America

On 12 October 1492, about 70 days after setting sail from Spain, Columbus and his crew landed on the island of San Salvador in the Bahamas. He claimed the new lands, which he mistook for India, for the Spanish Crown. The Papal Bull of 1494 ceded much of the New World to Spain, thereby encouraging Fernando and Isabel to finance other expeditions. In time, Spain would conquer huge empires in the Americas, notably in Peru and Mexico.

The Spaniards were driven by two equally powerful desires: to obtain gold, power and land in the Americas; and to convert and "educate" the American Indians. As Castilian money had financed the voyages, the Crown insisted that it had the right to control all trade with the colonies and that the *quinto real* – the royal fifth – of all monies should revert to the Crown.

On the more spiritual side, the Spaniards regarded themselves as missionaries bringing Christianity to distant lands, and subjugating barbaric natives who practised human sacrifice; what was before a barren landscape, would become the site of towns, cathedrals, universities. Along the way, however, several successful Indian empires were destroyed and their vast mineral wealth usurped in order to finance wars in Europe many thousands of miles away.

When Isabel died in 1504, her daughter Juana became Queen of Castile. After the sudden

death in 1506 of her husband Philip, the Archduke of Austria, she became despondent and was widely judged to be mad – thus her nickname *Juana la Loca* – and her father, Fernando took charge of Castile.

Fernando's rule was characterised by a number of struggles in which he tried to consolidate power under the Spanish Crown. Aragón held Sicily and Sardinia but, when the French intervened in Italy, Fernando went to battle; victorious, he annexed the Kingdom of Naples in 1504 and established Spain as a powerful challenger to French designs on the continent. In 1512, he annexed the Kingdom of Navarre, south of the Pyrenees, to Castile. By shrewdly

---

LEFT: *Las Meninas* by Velázquez, arguably his greatest painting.
RIGHT: the "invincible" Spanish Armada (detail), destroyed in 1588.

marrying off his children – Catalina to Henry VIII of England, Juana to Philip, the son of Maximilian, Emperor of Austria and Duke of Burgundy, and María to King Manuel of Portugal – Fernando had strengthened Spain's position with several of its European rivals.

The Habsburgs

When Fernando died in 1516, the crown devolved on his grandson Charles, the son of Juana and Philip. The heir to the Habsburg lands in Austria and southern Germany, Charles was unattractive, inexperienced and spoke no Spanish. Spain was apprehensive about being

ing of the *comuneros* or commoners; led by the town of Toledo, the *comuneros* wanted to dethrone Charles and replace him with *Juana la Loca*. They also declared that only Castilians should have administrative posts, and that the Cortes (parliament), not the king, had the right to declare war. The nobles vacillated, but when they finally aligned themselves with the court, the army crushed the rebels at the Battle of Villalar in 1521. The *comunero* leaders were executed. The power of the monarchy was restored and, in gratitude for the support of the nobles, Charles V rescinded some of his tax levies.

Charles V's rule coincided with the opening

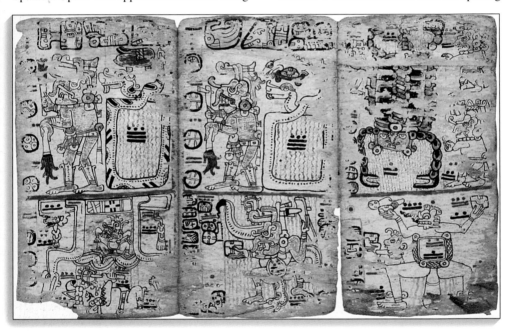

ruled by a foreigner. His arrival at Santander in 1517 and his first gestures did not quell fears. The Spanish nobility, especially, resented the King's reliance on his Flemish advisers and his unwillingness to consult with them. One unpopular decision was to appoint his own nephew to the rich prestigious Archbishopric of Toledo. To make matters worse, Charles tried to levy new taxes on both the church and nobility, as well as raise the *alcabala* or sales tax.

When his grandfather Emperor Maximilian died in 1519, Charles was elected Holy Roman Emperor as Charles V. But as he set sail for Germany, the Castilians, feeling overtaxed and ignored, rebelled. This was the infamous upris-

up of the Americas. During his reign, Hernán Cortés conquered the Aztecs and Francisco Pizarro defeated the Incas in Peru; after raiding the treasuries, both conquerors opened huge gold and silver mines in Mexico, Bolivia and Peru. Seville was placed at the centre of the burgeoning metal trade and in a few years the city doubled in size.

Debt and heretics

With peace at home and gold flowing across the Atlantic, Spain – now the most powerful country in Europe – became involved in several long and expensive wars abroad. As Charles V defended southern Italy from Turkish incursions, he became embroiled in combat with the Ottoman Empire. He also waged four wars with France, and by the end of his reign he had gone to war with almost every European nation.

Spain was forced to use the gold and silver of the Americas as collateral to secure loans from foreign bankers to finance the wars. As prices shot up, the Crown levied higher taxes and set up price controls. But as the nobles had invested much of their newly acquired wealth in land, jewellery and decorative objects rather than in industry or agriculture, Spain remained economically weak and uncompetitive. It sank deeper into debt while its European rivals developed their industries.

Another of Charles V's struggles was with the Protestant movement. As the ideas of Martin Luther took root in Germany, Switzerland and England, the Pope appealed to Charles to put an end to a heresy which claimed that "the Pope could not release souls from Purgatory on payment of a fee" and which allowed Christians to communicate directly with God without intermediaries. Charles responded by giving support to Catholic military groups, including St Ignatius Loyola's "Society of Jesus" which fought for the Papacy. In Spain itself there was a Counter Reformation in which certain books were prohibited and the popular humanist ideas of Erasmus were considered heretical.

In 1556 Charles V abdicated, retiring to the monastery of Yuste in Extremadura. His brother Ferdinand was given most of the Habsburg Empire though he left his Spanish possessions, Flanders and parts of Italy to his son, Felipe II.

Unlike his extrovert father, Felipe was withdrawn, sickly, almost bookish in his imperial pursuits. During his reign the palace, monastery and church of El Escorial was built near Madrid. It became one of his favourite retreats.

Felipe II

As his kingdom was more limited than that of his father, Felipe II generally pursued issues pertinent only to Spain and Catholicism. When the Calvinists rebelled in Holland, he had their leader beheaded and many of his followers slaughtered, thus cementing his reputation as a

---

LEFT: fragment of the Mayan Codex
RIGHT: conquistador Hernán Cortés.

> **ROYAL FANATIC**
>
> King Felipe II once said he would prefer not to rule rather than to reign over a nation of heretics.

religious fanatic and a merciless king. He even had his own son arrested and accused of treason and heresy; and ordered the Primate of Spain be deposed for having voiced his admiration for Erasmus. Felipe's cruelty was immortalised both in Schiller's *Don Carlos* and Goethe's *Egmont*.

By the 1560s Spain was, despite a surface opulence, in dire financial straits. Its industries were floundering, foreign wars were depleting her treasury and English pirates began hijacking Spanish ships returning with much-needed gold from the Americas.

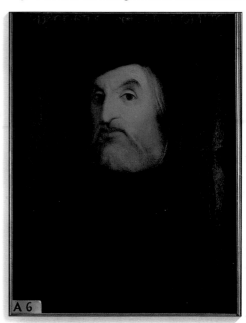

A 6

By 1575 Felipe II owed so much money to foreign banks that he was forced to suspend his debt payments.

But Felipe's aggressive religious principles dominated his economic considerations. He made the Inquisition hunt out the *moriscos*, Spaniards of Moorish ancestry, many of whom had converted to Christianity during Queen Isabel's rule but were still suspected of adhering to the Muslim faith. Spain's best farmers took refuge in the stony mountains of Andalusia until it was safe to return to their lands.

To encounter the Turks who from time to time had menaced the Spanish coastline, Felipe II formed a league with Pope Pius V, Malta and

Venice. Under the command of Felipe's brother, John of Austria, the alliance defeated – at great financial cost – the Turks in 1571 at the Bay of Lepanto, near Corinth.

Spain sinks

In Felipe II's struggle with England, however, economics and religion fused: he prepared the Spanish Armada not only because Queen Elizabeth protected the pirates who attacked Spanish galleons, but also because she persecuted English Catholics and had imprisoned his cousin Mary Stuart. But when the "Invincible Armada" confronted the more manoeuvrable

English fleet led by Sir Francis Drake in 1588, Spain lost thousands of sailors and more than half its ships. Defeat led Felipe into a long period of indecision and introspection: had God abandoned the Catholics? What was certain was that Elizabeth's victory established English maritime supremacy for decades to come.

Spain was ruled during the 17th century by the last three Habsburg kings. When Felipe III became king in 1598, his kingdom included Spain, Portugal, Flanders, much of central and southern Italy, the Americas from California to Cape Horn and the Philippines. But he was indifferent towards his responsibilities, and left the affairs of state to the Duke of Lerma who used his position to increase his wealth and to appoint relatives to important administrative posts. In 1609 he advised Felipe III to expel the *moriscos,* on religious grounds, but also to break the power of the Valencian nobles. Half a million *moriscos* were forced out, many of whom were among Spain's best farmers.

With silver production down, agriculture in disarray and corruption rife, Spain was drawn into conflict with Holland, France and England during the Thirty Years' War. Felipe IV became king in 1621 and political/military reversals during his reign brought the Empire to the verge of collapse. When in 1640 he tried to get the Catalans to pay for the maintenance of Castilian troops, they sought help from the King of France; Felipe backed down, and was forced to grant the Catalans nominal independence.

Later that same year the Duke of Braganza proclaimed himself King of Portugal which signalled that kingdom's final independence. Separatist movements were also underway in

---

THE GOLDEN AGE OF SPANISH LITERATURE

Under the Habsburg kings Spain enjoyed its greatest literary flowering. Heralding this golden age was *La Celestina* (1499) by Fernando de Rojas. Written as a play, its sense of time, plot and character development is as modern as Celestina herself, a go-between for illicit lovers.

The poet Garcilaso de la Vega, whose pastoral *Églogues* were published in 1543, revolutionised Spanish poetry with Italian verse forms. Fray Luís de León, imprisoned for five years accused of practising Judaism, wrote mostly prose, but also lyric poetry of great elegance. St Teresa of Ávila wrote with a simplicity and clarity unusual in her time, while the poetry of her disciple, the ascetic St John of the

Cross (1542–91), is deeply mystic or lyrically ecstatic. The baroque poets Luís de Gongora (1561–1625) and Francisco de Quevedo (1580–1645) had contrasting styles: Gongora lush and ornate, Quevedo dry, ascerbic, pessimistic.

Of the playwrights, Lope de Vega (1562–1635), founder of Spain's National Theatre, wrote some 1500 plays (mostly popular comedies), poetry and novels; Calderón de la Barca (1600–81) is known for his philosophical dramas.

The crowning achievement of the age is the novel *Don Quijote* by Miguel de Cervantes. An instant bestseller when published in 1605, the story of a deluded idealist battling with flawed reality still has a universal appeal.

Andalusia and Naples. The French defeated the Spanish at Rocroi in 1643, and the Peace of Westphalia (1648) marked the end of Spain's role as Europe's supreme military power.

Military defeats were not the only cause of Spain's demise. Spain failed to use gold and silver from the Americas to build strong industries at home: wool sheared in Spain was sold cheaply to Europe's northern countries where it was converted into cloth, then resold on the peninsula at exorbitant prices.

Once the *moriscos* were expelled, the best lands were given over to sheep and cattle grazing; farm goods had to be imported. The church

A regency ruled until Carlos II took the throne at 15. War with France continued for most of his rule and he was forced to surrender valuable territories in the Peace of Nimega (1678) and Ratisbonne (1684).

Carlos died without an heir and left his crown to Philip of Anjou, the grandson of Louis XIV, in the vain hope that he might keep Spain intact from further French incursions.

The Bourbons

Lacking in experience, the newly crowned Felipe V, the first Bourbon, relied on French advisers. Austria, alarmed by the prospect of

and the nobility were exempted from paying taxes, and so the poorest of merchants and peasants were obliged to support the state. The *escudo*, once accepted as currency throughout Europe, tumbled in value and Spain was unable to secure foreign loans. As a result, the vast armies of the Empire were underfed and underpaid, and morale sank.

Felipe IV died in 1665. He left an economy in shambles, deeply in debt, to his only son Carlos, a five-year-old who had yet to be weaned.

LEFT: King Felipe V painted by Hyacinth Rigaud.
ABOVE: a public spectacle in the Plaza Mayor, Madrid, around 1700.

French hegemony in Europe, declared war on France; Catalonia, Valencia and the Balearic Islands saw an opportunity to oppose Felipe V and accepted Charles, the Archduke of Austria and a Habsburg, as their ruler,

This War of the Spanish Succession lasted 13 years and, for the first time since the Reconquest, a foreign enemy marched across Castile. The Treaty of Utrecht (1713) recognised Felipe V as the King of Spain, but exacted a heavy toll on the old Spanish empire; Flanders and all of Spain's Italian possessions were lost, and Gibraltar was ceded to the British.

The ruling Bourbons embarked on a plan to unify Spain; by diminishing the role of the church, they hoped to strengthen the power of the state. By the middle of the 18th century, Spain's economy had stabilised; its army and navy had been reconstructed, and new industries, primarily in Catalonia, began to develop.

The Frenchification of Spain, both in customs and thought, was launched. The ruling kings adopted French mannerisms and clothes, believed in the Age of Enlightenment and introduced a more liberal church service. Carlos III (1759–88) was a devout Catholic but, more than that, a believer in an absolute monarchy: at his behest, church burials were forbidden, and the Inquisitor-General was expelled for drafting

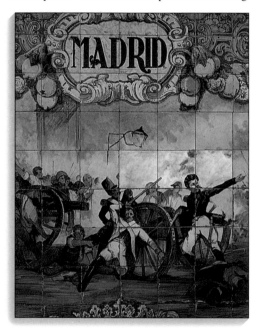

a bill without the king's authority. In 1766 he ousted the reactionary Jesuit Order from Spain because of what he perceived as their political intrigues. Unfortunately for the Bourbons, the Spanish masses were deeply conservative and suspicious of any attempt to liberalise life.

Spain truly revived under Carlos III. When he first came to Madrid, he was shocked by the squalor of the Spanish capital. During his reign, work on the Royal Palace was completed and the Prado Museum, one of the world's greatest storehouses of art, was built. He also built new canals, roads and highways. A steady rise in prices brought economic growth and prosperity.

When Louis XVI was guillotined in 1793 the Spanish king Carlos IV – a nephew of the beheaded French monarch – grew frightened of the growing liberalism on his northern border and declared war on the French. Years of war followed: Spain lost.

Napoleon

Carlos IV was a weak-minded and weak-willed ruler. His queen María Luisa and her favourite Godoy – a common soldier who rose to become Prime Minister – actually ran the state. After Napoleon gained control in France, he turned his eyes towards Spain. On the pretext of going to occupy Portugal, Napoleon brought his Imperial Army into Spain and lured the royal family to Bayonne for a meeting. By exploiting the intense factionalism among the Spanish royal family, Napoleon was able to broker an agreement: Carlos abdicated, his son Fernando was banned from Spain and Napoleon gave the crown to his own brother Joseph Bonaparte.

On 2 May 1808, the Spanish peasantry rose up spontaneously in protest; any Frenchman on the Madrid streets became a target. The crack French troops responded swiftly and brutally. Francisco Goya's *The Third of May, 1808* captures in blazing colours the execution of a group of *madrileños* who resisted. Regional uprisings followed, and France found it increasingly difficult to govern Spain. The War of Independence (also known as the Peninsular War) dragged on until Napoleon was defeated in 1814 by Wellington.

During these years of war, the liberal Spanish Cortes gathered in Cádiz to draft a constitution. In 1812 it was approved, abolishing the Inquisition, censorship and serfdom, and declaring that henceforth the king had to abide by whatever the Cortes decided.

Looking backwards

Despite this, however, Fernando VII took over the throne and was pronounced absolute monarch. He refused to pledge allegiance to the constitution, re-established the Inquisition, stifled free speech and allowed the Jesuits to return. Seeing no hope for accommodation with his despotic regime, the Spanish provinces in the Americas rebelled and established independence.

Fernando VII turned his back on the three major movements of the 18th century – the Enlightenment, the French Revolution and the Industrial Revolution – and kept Spain apart from the rest of Europe, brooding over its imperial glories and deep religious soul.

When in old age Fernando VII repealed the Salic law limiting royal succession to male heirs in favour of Isabel II, his daughter by his third wife, María Christina, a woman of liberal background, a far-right religious group that was known as the *Apostólicos* rebelled in protest. The conservatives decided to join them and threw their support behind Don Carlos, the king's brother.

The Carlist Wars were actually civil wars

water supply, dozens of nuns were slaughtered.

This internecine struggle continued until Alfonso XII, the son of Isabel II, assumed the throne in 1874, after a brief republic. By signing the Sandhurst Manifesto Alfonso tried to unite all Spaniards: "Whatever happens I shall not fail to be a good Spaniard, nor, like all my forefathers, a good Catholic, nor, as a man of this century, truly liberal."

Liberals and conservatives put down their weapons in favour of political debate and manoeuvring. Both sides agreed to adhere to

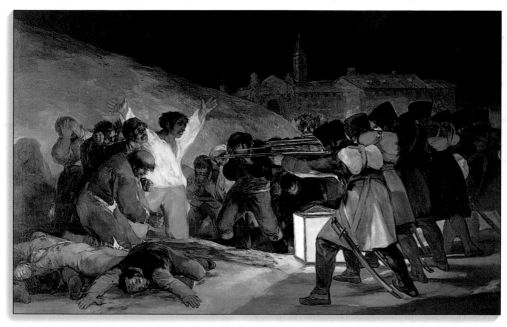

between liberals who believed in constitutional government without church domination and conservatives who favoured an alliance between church and state. The liberals were most powerful in the urban areas while the conservative Carlists drew their strength from the countryside, particularly in the northern provinces. The clergy supported the Carlists thereby stoking anticlerical fires; when it was rumoured that clerics had poisoned Madrid's

LEFT: stormy days of the Napoleonic era.
ABOVE: Goya's *The Executions of the Third of May* immortalises the *madrileños* who rose up against Napoleon in 1808.

the principle of "the peaceful rotation of the parties". The now united troops were sent off to Cuba and the Philippines where the native populations were demanding independence.

Prosperity and progress

Spain's population grew, its standard of living rose and there were great advances in transport and communications. For the first time in centuries, agriculture was revitalised. In 1890, under liberal leadership, universal suffrage with a limited electorate became law and, with the secularisation of education, schools began to improve. At the end of the century, Spain found herself hesitantly joining the rest of Europe. ❑

THE CIVIL WAR AND THE FRANCO REGIME

A period of instability and polarisation of Spanish politics led to a brief republic, the horrors of civil war and 40 years of dictatorship

The Civil War in the United States inspired an insurrection in Cuba by those seeking the abolition of slavery on the island and independence from Spain. The rebellion failed, but Cuba won a nominal degree of autonomy. In 1895, the Cuban poet and patriot José Martí resumed the struggle for independence and, after his death, the rebellion quickly spread.

Early in 1898 the United States sent the battleship *Maine* to Cuba to protect American interests; whether because of a mine or some mechanical malfunction, the ship exploded in Havana harbour. Public passion in the United States was aroused; believing that Spain had sunk the ship, President McKinley called for an armistice and the immediate release of all imprisoned rebels. Spain refused.

A series of naval battles followed in which Spain was hopelessly outmatched. The US Navy attacked Spanish ships in the Philippines and, in August, Manila surrendered. The Treaty of Paris, signed in December, granted Cuba its independence, ceded Puerto Rico to the United States as indemnity and passed the Philippines to the US for the sum of $20 million.

The end of an empire

This defeat marked the end of all Spanish pretentions to being an international power. In response, a group of writers and intellectuals, including Miguel de Unamuno, Antonio Machado and Ramón Marin del Valle Inclan – the "Generation of '98" – declared that Spain should abandon dreams of world supremacy in favour of a new, modern course. They stressed the need to revitalise the country's agriculture, reform tax structure and extend free public education to all.

PRECEDING PAGES: Picasso's *Guernica* depicts the saturation bombing of a Basque village by German planes in the Civil War.
LEFT: soldiers in war-torn Madrid.
RIGHT: King Alfonso XIII with Eduardo Dato.

It was during this period after the Spanish-American War – referred to as *El Desastre* (The Disaster) – that labour became unionised and radicalised, primarily in the industrial areas of Catalonia. Anarchism, which had attracted a

modest following during the 1870s when Bakunin's ideas were introduced, resurfaced more militantly, and in 1902 an anarchist union was formed in Barcelona which proposed general strikes.

When the liberal leader Sagasta died in 1903, both liberals and conservatives, whose leader Cánovas had been assassinated in 1897, were in disarray. The army, comprising mostly Castilian liberals opposed to the absolutist tendencies of the conservatives, was seen by all Spaniards as the traditional upholder of the existing order. But its defeat by the US in 1898 made it vulnerable to criticism, mainly by the Socialist Party and Catalan autonomists.

The people rise up

When the Spanish army found itself under siege in Morocco in 1909, Catalan reservists were called to report for duty by the ruling conservative regime. The Catalans, however, saw no need to risk their lives by clashing with Berber tribesmen. A general strike was called in Catalonia and during this so-called "Tragic Week", 200 churches and more than 30 convents were razed by the strikers and, in retaliation, the army shot dozens of strikers and passers-by.

The whole of Spain was temporarily placed under martial law. When a popular Catalan

anarchist was unjustly accused and summarily executed for his role in sparking the strikes, mass demonstrations followed. The conservatives were toppled, and the liberal José Canalejas came to power.

Being a liberal in those days simply meant that one believed in parliamentary government, not full democracy. By giving the Catalans regional control in education and over public works projects, Canalejas sought to block the growing strength of the anarchists. He went further by letting the Socialists be part of Spain's municipal governments, and he tried to woo the Far Left by attempting to limit the number of clergy. But when the railway workers went on

strike in 1912 he broke the strike militarily, arousing the hatred of many workers. Later that year he was assassinated by an anarchist.

When World War I began, Spain declared its neutrality. It was an expedient move; by continuing to trade with Allied and Axis powers alike, Spain eliminated its national debt and increased its gold reserves.

In 1917 the part-anarchist, part-socialist labour unions called for the first nationwide strike to protest against price increases and Alfonso XIII's appointment of conservatives to the cabinet. The strikes began in Barcelona and Madrid, but soon spread to Bilbao, Seville, and Valencia. The economy ground to a halt. The army crushed the strike, killing hundreds of workers and imprisoning the strike leaders.

When the wartime industrial boom came to a sudden end, thousands of workers were left without employment. With the success of the Russian Revolution fresh in their minds, the anarchists resumed their struggle in the streets. Military law was once more imposed in Barcelona.

Popular feeling against the army was strong. To make things worse, 15,000 soldiers were killed in Morocco in another attempt to subdue the Muslims. An inquiry into the army's conduct in Morocco brought down the government and García Prieto, an old monarchist who had become liberalised, came to power.

Terrorism against the church and the army intensified – the Cardinal-Archbishop of Zaragoza was assassinated – but the government refused to cede to the army's wishes for a sterner crackdown on protesters. In September 1923 the garrison in Barcelona revolted. It was followed by other rebellions throughout the country, and the civilian government collapsed. With the blessing of Alfonso XIII, Miguel Primo de Rivera, the Captain-General of Barcelona, took control of Spain.

Dictatorship

Primo de Rivera immediately suspended the 1876 Constitution and ended parliamentary rule by closing the Cortes. He made plans to restore the army, the church and the monarchy, the traditional forces of order. He placed the press under strict military censorship, rescinded Catalonia's nominal autonomy and, by favouring the Socialists within the trade union movement, neutralised the power of the anarchists.

In 1926 Spain signed a treaty of friendship with Italy. Following Mussolini's example, Primo de Rivera set up management and worker councils to resolve labour disputes and to draw up collective contracts. A period of economic expansion followed in which new railways and roads were built. But this led to huge budget deficits which became all the more critical because of the world depression of 1929. Moreover, Primo de Rivera began meddling in the army's traditional system of promotion and as a result lost

SWISS ROLE

By staying neutral during World War I, for a few short years Spain became a kind of Switzerland where international and financial issues were resolved.

The Second Republic

The elections of April 1931 were crucial. The leftist parties won overwhelming majorities and King Alfonso XIII was forced to leave Spain without formally abdicating. The Second Republic was proclaimed on 14 April, and liberal constitutionalists were installed in power. The monarchy had been overthrown without shedding one drop of blood. Briefly, it seemed as if much of Spain – industrialists, intellectuals and workers – had united for the first time.

TORO DESMANDADO EN LA GRAN VIA. 1.933.

much support. Popular feeling against the dictatorship mounted, anarchism resurfaced and there were battles between workers and the police.

In 1930 Primo de Rivera failed to rally the Captains-General behind him; under pressure, Alfonso XIII asked for his resignation. General Berenguer assumed power, but his attempts to return to a rotational Constitutional system failed. Berenguer eased censorship, reopened the universities and permitted strikes.

LEFT: satirical cartoon of "Bomb City", Barcelona.
ABOVE: snapshot (wrongly dated) taken after an unplanned *carrida* in Madrid's Gran Via.

Yet the constitutionalists were caught in the middle between a Far Right which clung to its privileges and memories of past glories and the growing anarchist unions that were opposed to any form of government. When elections were held for the Cortes, in June 1931, the Socialists and anarchists were swept into power. Six months later a new constitution was drafted in which Spain became a "democratic republic of workers of all classes". In one fell swoop Spain ceased to be a Catholic country in which the church was subsidised by the state, war was renounced as an instrument of national policy, civil marriages and divorces were to be permitted without church sanction and state-supported education was secularised. Spain had made a complete about-face.

Manuel Azaña came to power and set about expelling the Jesuits – always considered a fifth column by the Left for their allegiance to the Pope – and confiscating their property.

Other liberal measures were adopted. The Agrarian Reform Act of 1932 expropriated large estates and compensated their owners by giving them government bonds; these lands were either redistributed to the rural peasantry or reorganised on a socialist/collectivist model. Certain Spanish provinces, including Catalonia and Galicia, were granted semi-autonomy.

army; a month later more than 1,400 Asturians had been killed and several thousands injured.

When elections were held in 1936, the Left garnered the majority of the vote; though the Right was almost equal in power, the Centre had crumbled. A new wave of church burnings, coupled with new seizures of land by the peasants, followed the elections. Assassinations by the Right and the Left became the daily fare.

The Spanish Civil War

On 18 July 1936, the rightist revolt was launched: the army, supported by the National Socialist parties of Italy and Germany, decided

In the 1933 elections, the Right – Monarchists, Catholics, and José Primo de Rivera's newly formed Falange Party – achieved a small plurality. A centrist coalition was formed, but it discovered that Spain was now almost irreconcilably split between an organised but divided leftist camp and a rapidly growing Falange Party modelled on the Fascist parties of Italy and Germany. The ruling Centre had to contend with the Basques and Catalans who still sought independence, and peasants and Anarchists incensed by the government's decision to halt the expropriation of large estates.

The government was further weakened when striking miners in Oviedo rose up against the

HEROES AND EXILES

The few heroes of the Civil War were the intellectuals who defended the Second Republic. The Andalusian poet Federico García Lorca was shot by the Fascists in 1936 for simply signing a document in support of the Republic. Many writers were killed or imprisoned, but most – including Rafael Alberti, Jorge Guillén and Luis Cernuda – were exiled. Picasso's horrifying *Guernica*, inspired by the German bombing of a small Basque town, mobilised artists against Franco. The composer Manuel de Falla died in exile, heartbroken by the Civil War, and the Catalan cellist Pablo Casals refused to perform in Spain as long as Franco lived.

to seize power and put an end to the Second Republic. The Spanish Civil War had begun.

While the Republicans established their base of support in the urban areas of Madrid and Barcelona and in the provinces of Catalonia, Murcia, and Valencia, the Nationalists – as the rebels proudly called themselves – led by General Francisco Franco moved in from Morocco. They established their control in rural areas and in the more conservative provinces of Andalusia, Old and New Castile and Galicia. As the army, police and the civil guard sided with the Nationalists, the Republicans had to improvise a fighting force by arming the workers.

respect the arms embargo and in essence abandoned an ally and a legally elected government.

While the Allies pussyfooted, Germany, Italy and Salazar's Portugal poured arms and munitions into the Nationalist forces. By early 1937 Germany and Italy had recognised the Franco regime, Italian troops had taken part in the capture of Málaga and German and Italian ships were patrolling Spain's Mediterranean coast.

The Republicans, meanwhile, delivered their gold reserves over to Russia to pay for arms and support. In many countries of the world there were calls for volunteers to form International Brigades in defence of the Republic.

Franco, the former Captain-General of the Canaries, internationalised the conflict: only days after the rebellion began, Italian warplanes were in Morocco and Italian forces had secured the Balearic Islands. The French and the English responded by setting up a Non-Intervention Committee with Italy and Germany which feebly attempted to limit the flow of arms into Spain and thereby contain the conflict. The United States, for its part, also decided to

FAR LEFT: central Madrid under blitz attack in 1937.
LEFT: the bombing of Barcelona port in the Civil War by Italian aircraft loyal to Franco.
ABOVE: refugees flee to France, September 1936.

Franco's Reconquista

The Republicans, who saw themselves as opposing Fascism in Europe, were at a disadvantage from the start. In terms of military hardware, they were outnumbered by more than 10 to one. Furthermore, the Republicans were not united; some of the fiercest struggles were between the Communists, who wanted to establish disciplined cadres, and the Anarchists, whose militias were loosely organised guerrilla forces where decisions were made communally. The Anarchists gained control in Aragón and Valencia where they set up skeletal governments, burned churches and killed the hated clergy and collectivised the local factories.

But on the battlefield, the Republicans could never do more than hold off the furious Nationalist charges. The most striking Republican victory was in 1938 when they occupied Teruel. Had the Republicans been more united and had they received real support from abroad, the result might have been different.

The Nationalists, on the other hand, were well-disciplined and well-armed troops. They were led by experienced generals and had all the necessary material from abroad. Moreover, the

WHERE IS HE NOW?

Franco now lies in the Valley of the Fallen, a mausoleum near Madrid with a 135-metre (450-ft) cross, built by Republican prisoners in memory of the half-million who died in the civil war.

the Axis powers could not be denied. Franco did not want an exhausted Spain, dependent on western and mineral supplies, involved once more in war, and, when Hitler refused to accede to Franco's demand that Morocco, Tunisia and Algeria be handed over to him, he adopted a course of non-intervention. He did not give German troops permission to pass through Spain in order to attack the British at Gibraltar and, perhaps unbeknown to Hitler, he allowed thousands of Jews safe passage into

Nationalists seemed to be on a Holy Crusade to crush the infidels. The death knell for the Republicans sounded early in 1939 when Franco's forces, after weeks of siege, entered Barcelona. The remaining 250,000 Republicans withdrew, most of them crossing into France.

By 1 April, Franco had entered Madrid and the Civil War was over. In the following months thousands of Republican sympathisers were killed in mass executions and millions of others were brought in for questioning and jailed.

World War II

Franco attempted to maintain Spain's neutrality during World War II, but his indebtedness to

North Africa as they fled from the Nazis in occupied France.

Yet Spain's sympathies were unmistakable. When Germany attacked Russia in 1941, Franco sent a 17,000-man volunteer division to fight alongside the Germans.

The Franco era

When World War II drew to a close, the Allies, angered by Franco's role of professed neutrality and responsive to the clamours of thousands of Republican exiles living within their borders, blocked Spain's entrance into the United Nations and NATO and excluded itfrom the Marshall Plan. Spain, the only Fascist country left in Europe, was isolated by an economic blockade, but survived thanks to huge shipments of meat and grain from Perón's Argentina.

In 1947 a referendum was held and the Spaniards, given no other option, voted to establish a Catholic Kingdom with the knowledge that Franco would be head of state for life and would choose a successor of royal blood. Domestically, Franco stifled all dissent and ruled, supported by the church and the army, with an iron hand.

But in 1953 two important agreements were signed which signalled world rapproachment with Spain. As the Truman administration was worried about Soviet designs on Europe and North Africa, Spain's wartime role was cast aside and the United States signed a treaty giving the administration bases on the peninsula in exchange for $226 million in aid. The second agreement was a concordat signed with the Pope. Roman Catholicism was recognised as the sole religion of Spain, the church was given state financial support and the right to control education, church property was exempted from taxation and all appointments of prelates were to be agreed by the Pope and Franco. The Franco regime had been legitimised.

In 1955 Spain was admitted to the United Nations and its isolation ended. Its economy began to improve due, in large part, to the increase in tourism. As tourist dollars began to reach Spain, Franco earmarked the money for the revitalisation of industry. He also started a huge public works programme that expanded highways, built hydroelectric plants and brought cheap water to the dry central plains.

In the social sphere, social security was extended to cover all workers, free medical care was offered to those Spaniards unable to pay for it, and subsidised housing was given to the poor. Education was liberalised, and thousands of Spaniards now had the chance to attend university. A powerful upper middle class of executives, managers and technocrats developed. With a million Spaniards working abroad and sending money home, Spain was prospering.

Financial progress brought about a degree of liberalisation. Perhaps to gain access into the European Common Market, Spain passed the

LEFT: in a new political climate, General Franco and his wife welcome President Eisenhower to Madrid.
RIGHT: headlines announce the death of Franco.

Religious Liberty Act in 1967, which loosened the grip of the Catholic Church on all worship, and the Press Act of 1968 which made some effort to restrict press censorship. In 1969, Juan Carlos, the grandson of Alfonso XIII, was proclaimed heir to the throne. When Franco either retired or died, Juan Carlos would become king.

Forty years of Franco

Nearly 40 years of rule under Franco were characterised by order at the expense of freedom. Any protest against the severe restrictions on speech, press and assembly was met sternly. Moreover, the desire of both Basques and

Catalans to establish linguistic, cultural and financial autonomy through protest and, at times, violence was rapidly crushed.

Most artists and intellectuals within Spain were forced to take an obscurist path. While many writers wrote religious poems and sonnets in the style of Garcilaso de la Vega, others, including Blas de Otero and Dámaso Alonso, expressed thoughts and emotions in print that most Spaniards were afraid to even whisper.

Franco's regime, until his death in 1975, was empowered by the army, the Church and the Falange Party. But as Spain's standard of living rose, a new, more liberal bourgeoisie not haunted by memories of the Civil War came of age. ❑

DEMOCRACY AND AUTONOMY

*Spain has made remarkable strides forward in recent years, pushing
ahead unprecedented political and social reform*

During the 10 years following the death of General Franco, Spain went through political and social transformations which other countries have had the luxury to mull over for decades. The Spanish people more or less decided their own political future. They reeled back from violent threats to their new-found democratic system, they took an accelerated course in the sexual revolution and women went from wearing mostly black to wearing some of the most daring clothes ever seen on the European catwalks. There were four general elections in the course of that decade, in addition to regional and municipal elections, national referenda and regional home-rule referenda. It was a crash course in modernity, which the majority of Spaniards came through with flying colours.

A new broom

Prince Juan Carlos was crowned King of Spain on 22 November 1975, just two days after Franco died. The young King had been personally educated and trained by Franco. Few Spaniards had much hope that the dictator's chosen heir would be either able or willing to lead the country out of the system that had nurtured him. But they were proved wrong.

The last years of Francoism had given rise to illegal opposition parties whose leaders realised that Franco's end was near . There was the Communist Party (PCE), the most important of all; the Socialist Party (PSOE), which had lain dormant for years and was revived in the early 1970s by the future Prime Minister Felipe González and his young comrades from Seville; the Christian-Democrats, Social-Democrats, Liberals, Maoists and Marxist-Leninists.

There were also parties on the Right which resisted the move away from Fascism; other conservatives, notably the Popular Alliance (AP), led by the former Francoist Cabinet mem-

ber Manuel Fraga, saw that they would have to adapt themselves to the new system.

The King's task, then, was somehow to guarantee some sort of political stability at a time when inflation was nearly 30 percent, the prisons still held political prisoners, there were no institutions to speak of which could serve as

vehicles for the needed transformations and the armed forces had been recently orphaned.

Three weeks after assuming the throne, Juan Carlos charged the last Francoist president, Carlos Arias Navarro, with forming a new government. Arias lasted until July 1976, when the King, who had never got along well with him, surprised everyone by appointing Adolfo Suárez, the former head of the Falange, the only political party allowed under Franco, as the country's new Prime Minister. The King, Suárez and Santiago Carrillo, the Secretary-General of the Communist Party, are the three men generally credited with having successfully brought about Spain's political transition.

LEFT: the world came to Seville for Expo in 1992.
RIGHT: Catalan nationalists protesing for independence in Girona, 1988.

Democracy returns

In December 1976 Spaniards participated in the first democratic poll since the Civil War ended in 1939. The "Political Reform Referendum", which was overwhelmingly approved, set the wheels in motion for the first post-Franco general elections in June 1977.

But first there had to be legal political parties. One of the first tests of Suárez's experiment came in April, when the PCE was made legal. The Minister of the Navy resigned in protest and the first sabre-

tive of home-rule sentiments in northern Spain. Once the Constitution had been passed, Parliament was dissolved and new elections were held, in which the results were similar to those of 1977.

But by this time UCD was beginning to show signs of stress as the different "families" which made up the organisation began straining at the leash, jealous of each other and desirous of more power. While all this was going on, the Prime Minister inevitably felt the pressure mounting.

rattling could be heard. It would not be the last time that the military threatened to take things into their own hands.

Suárez was Prime Minister but he belonged to no political party which could return him to power. So he created the Union of the Democratic Centre (UCD), a hodgepodge of centrist parties which won 27 percent of the vote.

On 12 December 1978, Spanish voters approved the new Constitution, which had previously been passed by Parliament. It is worth pointing out that abstention was 33 percent, considered quite high, and that in the Basque Country the negative votes plus the abstentions were higher than the affirmative votes, indica-

Attempted coup

Finally, in January 1981, Suárez decided to resign as party chief and Prime Minister. But before Leopoldo Calvo-Sotelo could be invested as the country's new head of government, something happened which would shake the country as nothing else had since the death of Franco. On 23 February 1981, as the investiture roll-call vote was being taken in Parliament, a group of over 300 Civil Guards and military men, led by Lieutenant-Colonel Antonio Tejero Molina, burst into Parliament and tried to stage a military *coup d'état*. At the same time, an army general declared a state of emergency in Valencia and tanks began rolling down the city streets. Around six hours after the coup began, King Juan Carlos appeared on television and ordered the insurgents to desist. Twelve hours later they finally surrendered.

The unsuccessful putsch should not have come as a surprise to anyone who had been closely following the Spanish military in the post-Franco years. Many coup plots had been hatched, the first of them as early as 1977.

Calvo-Sotelo was invested on 25 February, and two days later an estimated one million Spaniards participated in a demonstration in Madrid in support of democracy. For the first, and possibly the last, time the leaders of all the political parties linked arms and marched together. The inherently unstable UCD was back in power but its days were numbered. In October 1982 PSOE swept into power with an overall majority – the first time since 1936 that Socialists were in the government and the first time ever that an all-Socialist government ruled Spain. In those same elections UCD virtually disappeared: its 168 deputies dwindled to a meagre 12. In contrast, the conservative Popular Coalition shot up to 106 seats from the nine it had before. Today's bipartisan system was taking shape.

This short, cluttered electoral chronology illustrates the resolution of the most pressing question following the death of Franco: rupture or reform? Was there to be a clean break with the former regime and the monarchy Franco imposed, or was there to be a gradual adaptation to modern democracy?

Spain joins Europe

The figure of King Juan Carlos was initially rejected by many people in the anti-Franco opposition who saw him as a continuation of the dictatorship. They wanted to return to the Republican system that had been violently abolished with the Civil War. These same sectors demanded that full-scale purges take place in the police, the armed forces and the judiciary once Franco had died.

None of this happened, and the voices crying out for rupture ended up accepting a slower

> **TOWARDS DEVOLUTION**
>
> Under the terms of the 1978 Constitution, Spain was divided up into 17 "autonomous communities" or regions.

reform as they saw the King was serious when he said he was the "King of all Spaniards" and not just of the victors of the Civil War, as the opposition had feared. The Left and the Right moderated their position, thus guaranteeing the stability of the new democracy.

One of the most important tasks facing the Spanish government since 1975 has been the re-establishment of Spain as a member of the international community of nations after many years of political isolation. After the Civil War, nearly all the world's countries ceased

diplomatic relations with Spain. As a result of President Eisenhower's 1953 visit, however, US military and economic aid was given to the Franco regime, enabling the beginning of an economic recovery after the very difficult post-war years.

In 1975, Spain still remained isolated. That year, only one head of state visited the country, and that was Dom Mintoff of Malta. By 1986, however, 29 heads of state had come, an indication of the degree to which Spain had gained equal standing with the rest of the world's industrialised countries.

Immediately after the death of Franco mutual diplomatic relations were reinstated with most

---

LEFT: Lieutenant-Colonel Antonio Tejero Molina attempts a military coup in parliament in 1981.
RIGHT: King Juan Carlos.

of the world's countries. Embassies in the Eastern Bloc nations were set up in 1977, and Israel was finally recognised in January 1986.

By far the most important sign of Spain's desire to become "part of Europe" was its stepped-up campaign to join the European Community (EC, now the European Union or EU) a process which was completed in 1992, and its entry into NATO, the North Atlantic defence alliance. Spain had tried on and off over a 20-year period to join the EU, but its violations of democratic principles were an obstacle to its entry. Once the constitutional governments were in power after 1978, how-

finally held after a four-year delay and a massive anti-NATO campaign by the country's peace movement. NATO membership was accepted by 52 percent of the electorate.

Economic crisis

While Spain was trying to regain its footing politically, it also had an economic crisis to face. When the international recession began to be felt in the early 1970s, other European countries were better placed to resist the blows and could transfer resources from unprofitable sectors to more profitable ones. But Spain was saddled with an outdated, over-bureaucratic,

ever, negotiations were intensified, and Spain finally took its place as a fully fledged member on 1 January 1986.

The story of Spain's accession to NATO is more complicated. The country was originally taken into the alliance in 1981 by the Calvo-Sotelo government despite the opposition of the Socialists. When the latter party came to power in 1982 it promised to hold a referendum on NATO membership. Over the course of the next four years, however, Prime Minister Felipe González and his government gradually became convinced of the virtues of NATO and began to campaign in favour of remaining a member. In March 1986 the referendum was

REGIONAL AUTONOMY

The Basque Country, Catalonia and Galicia are considered to be "historic nationalities", and have enjoyed a certain degree of autonomy or independence from central government since the unification of Spain in the 16th century. In these three regions, local languages are spoken in addition to or instead of Castilian, and the fight to get them treated on an equal basis with Castilian was a main aim of the 1970s "autonomy movement". The Basque *Euskara* language bears no relation to any other known language, and its origin is unknown; Catalan derives from the French Langues d'Oc; Galician is of Roman origin.

protectionist and paternalistic economy which had grown up in isolation over 40 years. It lacked any flexibility and when protectionist measures were dropped, businesses suffered.

The restructuring of key industries caused the loss of more than 65,000 jobs in the early 1980s. As one writer has noted, the two occasions in the 20th century when Spain began a democratic experiment, in 1931 and 1976, have coincided with world economic crises. By far the most serious economic problem facing Spanish society is unemployment.

By the early 1990s the number of people who were out of work had reached 3 million, or 22

The new federalism

One of the most salient features of Spain's democracy is the home-rule structure. In contrast to Franco's all-powerful centre which ruled with an iron fist, the new federal system has 17 "autonomous regions" with their own government and legislature, and jurisdiction over social services, housing, health, agriculture, culture, city planning and, in the case of the Basque Country, even the police.

Because Franco and his army were so fervently centralist, the anti-Franco movement believed federalism to be a more progressive stance. The creation of the federal system was

percent, of the total labour force, and the numbers continued to rise. This dramatic figure would signify social chaos in most other countries. However, the strong family structure in Spain combined with the fact that an estimated 20 percent of the GNP is produced "under the table" provide a cushion against soaring unemployment. Nevertheless, the strain is tremendous given that only around one person in three of those who are jobless receive any sort of unemployment benefit from the state.

LEFT: street demonstration, 1981.
ABOVE: an open-air session of the Andalusian Parliament on the Day of the Community.

a bumpy process, not only because of resistance from the more entrenched right-wing politicians but also because of marked differences between the regions which were seeking to gain local control.

The region best known for its separatist leanings is the Basque Country. The most obvious manifestation of this sentiment is found in the existence of ETA (*Euskadi Ta Askatasuna* – "Basque Homeland and Liberty"), an armed separatist organisation founded in the early 1960s.

Owing to the particularly harsh repression dealt out by the Franco regime to the Basque provinces, the anti-Franco struggle there became inextricably wound up in Basque nationalism. The widespread practice of torture in Basque police stations; the apparently solid voting base for Herri Batasuna, considered to be the political wing of ETA, which regularly receives around 20 percent of the vote; and the failure of the government to arrive at any effective political solution against terrorism are factors that have made Basque separatism the country's most serious problem along with high unemployment.

NEW WOMEN

Spain now has the lowest birthrate anywhere in the world: an average of 1.2 children per woman aged between 15 and 49.

Although the attempted coup of 23 February 1981 was a failure, it was a powerful reminder

to the new government that Franco's military was not prepared to let go of the reins entirely. The coup plotters were mostly given relatively light sentences, which made it unsurprising that another coup was discovered in the July of that year and yet another before the 1982 elections.

Even in the 1980s the extraordinary amount of television time given to military parades and ceremonies reflected the nervousness, thinly masked as respect, felt by the civilian government towards the country's former rulers.

Rapid change

Someone who knew Spain well during the Franco years would have a hard time recognising

things today, and a first-time visitor would have a hard time imagining that just a few years ago most aspects of cultural and intellectual life were rigidly controlled by the authorities, that superstition and clichés were a good substitute for knowledge and that personal or sexual freedom were unheard-of concepts which would have been viewed with the utmost suspicion.

The crash course in political affairs has been mirrored, in an even more visible way, by the changes in social questions which affect Spaniards' daily lives. Education, the church, family life, culture and social services – none of these emerged from the post-Franco transition unscathed. The Catholic Church's stronghold and the conservative nature of the Franco regime meant that there was little room for flexibility in family and personal relations. Divorce, birth control, abortion, homosexuality and adultery were all illegal although, one way or another, the upper classes often managed to avoid these impediments to personal happiness.

As the laws were gradually struck down during the centrist and socialist administrations, social behaviour began to resemble that of other European countries. The women's movement was launched in December 1975 and its first campaigns were largely concerned with the demand for birth control, a divorce law and an abortion law. Women would have to wait until 1985 for abortion to be legalised, but the law is often criticised for being inadequate; during its first year, only 200 women qualified for a state-sanctioned abortion while an estimated 90,000 women went abroad to have abortions.

As women now have fewer children, they have logically begun entering the workforce, although to a lesser degree than in other OECD countries. This is partly due to the high unemployment rate in general and partly due to sexism. As yet there are no laws in Spain to guarantee women equal pay for equal work, and women are often victims of labour discrimination. Nevertheless, the famed Spanish machismo is partly a myth; fathers are often seen taking their children for walks, young couples battle over the division of household tasks just as in other countries and no eyebrows are raised when women enter such professions as law, medicine or journalism.

The Church retreats

The education system, despite new reform laws, was largely incapable of responding to the needs of a new society. One indication of this is the enormous popularity of language schools; foreign languages were badly taught – if at all – during the Franco years, but given the country's isolation there was not much need to speak anything other than Castilian Spanish (the country's other languages were prohibited). With Spain's entry into the European Union, the increased living standard which permits travel and the dramatic inflow of foreign firms, there has been a rush to learn languages, especially English, and regular schools and universities have been ill-equipped to respond to the new demand.

The Church resisted some of the innovations of the education system, fearful of losing its grasp over one of the key areas of society. The Church as an institution supported the Franco regime, and was generally regarded as a bastion of conservatism rather than as a force for progress. The exceptions were mainly found in Madrid, where there was a certain "worker-priest" tradition, and in the Basque Country, where the separatists found a great deal of support from priests.

As the Church has lost battles over birth control, education and divorce, as the number of vocations has declined and as the Sunday Mass-goers have dwindled, so too has the institution lost many privileges afforded it by Franco, most importantly its financial subsidies and tax breaks. Evidence of the Church's declining role was clearest during the drafting of the 1978 Constitution. Spain's bishops fought tooth and nail even to get the Constitution to mention the Church, and it did so in a less than adulatory way: "The authorities shall take into account the religious beliefs of Spanish society and maintain appropriate relations...with the Catholic Church and the other denominations."

Media and arts

If the country's youth were to be prepared in schools for the challenges posed by this new society then the adults also needed a daily "school" to open their eyes, prepare themselves for change and to learn to think in new ways. That school for most people was the media.

Spain's many national daily papers range from extreme right-wing to left-of-centre, with one that stands out above the rest. *El País* published its first issue on 4 May 1976 and it soon became the obligatory point of reference for most political discourse, so much so that it was sometimes accused of being a mouthpiece for the Socialists. But it was also quick to report on tales of scandal in the later stages of the Socialist government which was finally voted from office in 1996. The paper has also been lambasted by film directors for its capacity to

make or break a movie, and by other journalists who complain that something just hasn't happened if it is not printed in *El País*. Despite the high number of daily newspapers and weekly news magazines, press readership in Spain is lower than in any other European country except Greece, Portugal and Ireland.

Spaniards thus rely on the radio and television for their news. Private stations introduced in the 1980s give a better balance of news, as well as giving a voice to local Basques, Galicians, Catalans and Andalusians.

The media may have blossomed but a new generation of writers has taken longer to create. It is also true that these two art forms were the

LEFT: former Socialist Prime Minister Felipe González before his second electoral victory in 1986.
RIGHT: Expo '92 brought the future to Seville.

ones most exploited for political ends under Franco and the fields most affected by the outward stream of exiles after 1939 and the postwar repression. Young writers are emerging, but they have yet to make international reputations enjoyed by their elders, such as the Nobel laureate Carmilo-José de Cela.

Spanish cinema has fared much better, perhaps because it is a relatively new art form. In fact, from the late 1970s after the Ministry of Culture was set up, "new Spanish cinema" began to attract attention from press and public alike. Films

> ### CULTURAL BIAS
> Since 1983, all museums in Spain have offered free admission to Spanish citizens.

won international prizes, and filmmakers such as Bigas Lunas and Pedro Almodóvar became known around the world.

Madrid came of its own as a cultural capital in the early 1980s when it was said that "culture was in fashion". Suddenly one had to choose between a concert, the ballet or an art exhibition. And there was more to come in the 1990s.

In fact, 1992 was the year of Spain, when three of the county's greatest cities played host to the world. In April, the first universal exposition in more than 20 years opened its doors in Seville. In July, the Olympic Games came to Barcelona, a cause of great excitement and national pride. And throughout the year, Madrid

celebrated its turn as the European Union's Capital of Culture. Spain's image among other European nations was to change for ever.

It was also, of course, the 500th anniversary of Columbus's exploratory voyage to the New World. Expo '92 in Seville was timed to begin and end on the same days as that historic journey had done, and had as its theme "the Age of Discovery". Millions visited the Exposition site on La Cartuja, an island in the Río Guadalquivir, and wandered around the dozens of pavilions crammed alongside each other like so many giant toy houses created for adults. Expo also had an ambitious arts programme.

The AVE, the new high-speed train built to link Madrid with Seville, outgrew any teething troubles, after an admittedly inauspicious start which included five breakdowns in the first 17 days of operation. Now heavily subsidised, it will carry you swiftly and cheaply to Seville, and has become the fashionable way to get there (advance reservations are essential). Long-term plans are being made for a high-speed train from Madrid to Barcelona.

Dreams that 1992 would transform Andalusia into some kind of California of southern Spain proved far-fetched, but Expo '92 did bring a new energy and stimulus, and helped to put Seville back on its feet. The city acquired a new railway terminus, a much-enlarged airport and several magnificent new bridges on the Río Guadalquivir. It is now linked by dual-carriageway, as well as high-speed train, to Madrid and by further dual-carriageway to the other major towns of Andalusia. As a result, the region as a whole has been transformed from one of the most cut-off to one of the most accessible areas of the country.

At centre stage

Despite criticisms and changes of plan, the programme for "Madrid, Capital of Culture" scheduled a total of 1,800 events throughout the year which contained many remarkable attractions. It also restored to Madrid the Palacio de Linares, superbly refurbished and subsequently a centre for Latin American culture. It led to major rethinks and improvements of the city's museums. It brought the renaissance of the Atocha railway station, made memorably exotic by a steamy tropical garden. And it was the year in which the magnificent Thyssen-Bornemisza art collection went on public view in the restored Palacio de Villahermosa, making Madrid one of the most art-rich cities anywhere in the world.

The highlight of the year, however, was the Olympic Games. If opinions were divided on Madrid's achievement, and Expo and the 500th anniversary had their detractors, no one could question the success of Barcelona. The 1992 Olympics were the first genuinely global games, with more countries participating than ever before, among them – for the first time since 1960 – South Africa.

Barcelona used the Olympics to transform itself. An ambitious urban renewal project which had been planned for years became a reality, opening up the city to the sea, getting rid of slums and creating beaches where previously there had been industrial wasteland. It gained a remodelled airport, a new ring road freeing the centre from traffic congestion and new telecommunications and sewage systems.

The Olympic installations on the hill of Montjuic have been given a further lease of life as a new "sports university". Building work continued for a further three years, when the Port Vell was transformed into a leisure area, Richard Meier's sparkling Museum of Contemporary Art opened its doors and the priceless Romanesque art collection was finally put back on show in the Palau Nacional.

Spain is different

It is impossible to deny the terrible effects of nearly 40 years under a regime that did everything it could to squash the cultural aspirations of a people who have produced remarkable artists, musicians, film directors and writers. These cultural achievements stand as a symbol of resistance during the Franco years, and the speed with which Spain is recovering its role as one of Europe's most interesting places demonstrates that political repression will never succeed in killing dreams and ideas.

In the 1960s, when Spain began to promote itself as a tourist mecca, one of the leading slogans of the publicity campaign was "Spain is Different". Today, the slogan is almost univer-

LEFT: the 1992 Barcelona Olympics.
RIGHT: a triumph in titanium: Frank O Gehry's Guggenheim Museum, Bilbo.

STIRRING STUFF

The 1992 Olympics was not one that could be said to belong to any one competitor. Rather, the Games left a series of stirring snapshots of the triumph of the human spirit over adversity.

"Magic" Johnson, of the US basketball "Dream Team", showed how courage could win out in the face of the Aids virus; and Mirsal Buric, a 22-year-old sprinter from Bosnia-Herzegovina, had fought a personal battle in order to compete, training on the battle-torn streets of Sarajevo when the firing was at its worst because "that was when the streets were empty".

sally looked down upon as symbolising the worst of the era, a clichéd celebration of bullfights, castanets and flamenco dancing that did little justice to the complexity and richness of Spanish culture.

But, in fact, Spain is different. Few countries could have achieved so much in the years following Franco's death. Political, social and cultural reforms have been implemented. Violent attempts to drag the country backwards have been repulsed. Spain's first chance at democracy was devoured by the Civil War; its second chance has proved a remarkable and - inspiring success, and now the dictator himself is almost forgotten. ❑

THE SPANISH PEOPLE

Proud, fiery and extrovert, a Spaniard is most at home in a crowd,
for where there is no noise, there is no life

Fun in Spain goes hand in hand with being in a large, noisy crowd. For many reasons, the main one being the sunny weather which keeps everyone outdoors for most of the year, gregariousness is the norm. The larger the gathering, the larger the potential audience and the opportunity for showing off. Naturally, there is a fair amount of boasting, but the pillar of Spanish *joie de vivre* is an internal self-sufficiency that needs no material support. It is expressed through wit, grandiloquence, appearance, courtesy, generosity and pride.

On the town

The best place to practise the art of self-adoration is in a bar. The "*ambiente*", or the amount of noise and people, is of utmost importance. Where there is no noise, there is no life, and a Spaniard flees from tranquillity. It is hard to determine what makes more racket in a bar, the patrons shouting at each other – for it would be a euphemism to say that they talk – or the waiters thrashing glasses about. What is certain is that the din is so deafening one can hardly hear the television perched on a shelf in the corner with its volume turned on full.

Anything goes as a subject of conversation. The Spaniard is extremely articulate, and a chat can become a literary performance punctuated with recitations. While the ratio of book readers is low by European and American standards, those who read generally choose well.

Generosity

A full third of the Spaniard's income is spent on food, drink and tobacco. Snobbishness dictates that American cigarette brands are preferable to the perfectly adequate national ones. With food, however, it is a different matter. Fast-food hamburger joints and pizza parlours are appreciated by motorcycle-driving teenagers, and

PRECEDING PAGES: dancing in a Menorcan meadow; the Alhambra, Granada, last bastion of the Moors.
LEFT: reading the news, Barcelona.
RIGHT: at Capileira, high in the Sierra Nevada.

busy office workers. But Spaniards generally prefer Spanish food. The national idea of a feast is cold *serrano* ham, sausage and shellfish, washed down by cool, dry sherry or beer. At the end of the meal, one self-satisfied-looking man flamboyantly foots the bill – which could easily add up to half his monthly salary.

The friendly generosity of the Spaniard is one of the characteristics that most astounds first-time visitors to the country. If a local and a stranger embark upon a conversation, it will at the very least end up with an invitation to a coffee or a beer. In the south, bartenders offer so many drinks on the house it is a wonder they make a profit. Young people rarely seem to buy a cigarette. They approach someone on the street to ask for one, and it is graciously given. A Spaniard will respond wholeheartedly to anything that appeals directly to his emotions. Most beggars make a living, and some have been hauled into jail for amassing a near-fortune.

A Spaniard is also politely helpful and generous with his time. If a stranger asks for an address, he will often be accompanied to his destination. But the Spaniard is also loath to disappoint, and may point down the wrong road rather than admit he does not know the way.

A large chunk of a Spaniard's monthly salary goes on clothes. The traditional style of dressing in dark colours or stark white has given way to colourful attire. In rural areas, the habit of dressing in mourning for several years after the death of a relative lingers only among the older generations, who are bound to spend the rest of their lives in black because when one term of grief ends another is likely to begin due to the

size of their families. In the cities, however, this custom has largely disappeared.

Everything under the sun

There are marked differences between people from the north, the south, the east and the centre. It has often been said that the Spanish nation is a myth, a dream of politicians and ideologues. Tourism officials coined a phrase that sums up the varied climates, landscapes and types: "Spain, everything under the sun".

Hot and perennially sunny Andalusia personifies the image foreigners tend to identify with Spain. In this vast area, where the Arab influence lingered longest, is the most pronounced joy of life coupled with a piercing tragic fatalism. The Andalusian looks and sees the parched faces of peasants mirroring parched and arid land and knows life is cruel but also exquisitely beautiful. A well-handled bullfight symbolises this particular view of existence.

By contrast the Galicians, who inhabit the green, rainy land of mist-filled valleys in the northwest, are a conservative, canny people, mostly fishermen, shepherds and farmers with a sprinkling of tobacco smugglers because of the numerous hidden coves, who speak a language close to Portuguese. They have a reputation for dourness, shared with their northern cousins, the Scots. Like them, they descend from the Celts, play the bagpipes and have emigrated in droves after generations of penury.

Further along the north coast is the land of the hardworking, heavy-drinking Basques, who have traditionally sought independence from Spain. Many are believed to be descendants of the peninsula's earliest settlers, the Iberians. Their language, Basque or Euskera, bears no relation to any other known language. And their rugged sports, such as wood-chopping and boulder-lifting, have prompted other Spaniards to view them as little more than boors.

Very different are the sophisticated Catalans, whose history is linked with the Languedoc area of France beyond the Pyrenees. They share one thing with the Basques, however: a desire to sever their ties with the rest of the country.

Fierce regionalism has been tempered by migrations from the centre and south of Spain to the rich northern and coastal lands, and from rural regions to cities. Today, the least populated parts of Europe lie just an hour's drive from Madrid.

REGIONAL RULE

Scores of rulers have attempted, by marriage or by iron fist, to unify spiritually and politically this country of 39 million individualists who speak four languages and seven different dialects. Franco went as far as to forbid the use in public of any language except Castilian and banned the christening of babies with local names.

The outburst of regionalism after Franco's death was such that today Spanish-speaking people must arm themselves with a dictionary when they visit Catalonia, Galicia or the Basque country, where regional governments actively discourage the use of Castilian in favour of the local language.

Sex and the family

The Spanish family is a large and affectionate clan in which mutual tolerance and staunch support is the norm. Take a stroll through a park on any afternoon and it is immediately evident that the Spaniard is a happy and adjusted being who will never be an outcast in his own circle. The toughest-looking ruffians are out for a walk with a grandfather leaning on one arm and a baby cousin clinging to a hand.

The honour, rights or jobs of sisters, brothers, aunts, second cousins and even in-laws are defended ferociously in Spain. The worst abuse one can hurl at a man is to insult his mother –

household and brought up the offspring, was regarded by him as something close to a saint, and certainly treated with the utmost respect.

Nowadays, men do not keep a second woman – mostly, they could not afford to – but they still have extramarital affairs. Increasingly, women now have them, too.

The new moral code

The word *noviazgo*, or engagement, referring to a state which among working-class couples used to last up to 10 years while they saved to buy a house, is rarely heard. Don Juanism has become characteristic of both sexes, who before

and at a woman, to insult her child. The children, surely the best-dressed and most pampered in the world, are good-natured and outgoing. They accompany their doting parents everywhere and stay up all hours of the night.

Spanish men are viewed as lustful, dominating macho types. Often, they are. Rarely faithful to one woman, up until recently it was acknowledged and even accepted that married men kept a mistress. The wife, who ran the

LEFT: the fiesta of San Fermin, Pamplona's week-long bull running festival.
ABOVE: young women dress up in traditional Aragonese costume.

settling into wedlock change partners with almost equal frequency and ease. The frequency of people living together without a wedding ring is indicated by the drop in the numbers of marriages, which nearly halved in the decade after Franco's death.

The changes have been largely due to the liberation of women. For many reasons, including Franco's ability to ward off progress, the pressure of the church and poverty, female liberation happened later in Spain than in the rest of the developed world. As recently as 1970, wives had to present written authorisation from their husbands to travel within the country or to open a bank account in their own name.

Perhaps most astounding has been the general acceptance of the change in sexual mores except by the most recalcitrant conservatives. But then, the largest section of society has always regarded morality as something to be broken now and then to add spice to life. Where else could the married vice president of the government have a publicly known lover and not cause righteous indignation, even after having an illegitimate child? Or a married Socialist minister date a married jet-setter and arouse only curiosity and generalised glee? Who could disapprove, when the voices of restraint are equated with the reviled dictatorship?

Religious matters

Strange as it may seem, worldly passion does not clash with religious sentiment. Religious events in Spain are celebrated with wine and dance and every excess that goes hand in hand with merriment. In the early hours of Good Friday in Seville, when Christ was on the way to his crucifixion, a huge float of the Virgin of the Macarena transported on the backs of men sets off down the tightly packed moonlit streets. Thousands of voices shatter the night with cries of "*Guapa! Guapa!*" (Beauty! Beauty!) as the band strikes up and the Virgin, despite the diamond tear in her eye, does a sensuous little dance. Lack of respect? No – just familiarity.

To the believer, God is a patient being who understands the weakness of the human flesh and easily forgives. Spaniards sometimes rely so much on his understanding that the relationship becomes one of complicity. At Mass, people act with less formality than they would in the house of a close friend. They arrive late, greet acquaintances out loud, drag chairs and at seaside resorts attend the service in bathing suits. The ceremony lasts only 20 minutes, but before the priest has given his blessing to the congregation there is a stampede for the door.

A distinction must be drawn between the Spaniard's comfortable relationship with God and his relationship with the institution of the Church. To many, the Church represents the repression of the dictatorship. After winning the Civil War, Franco sat bishops in Parliament and in the council of the realm and put the clergy in control of primary and secondary education. People who are now only 25 years old remember endless candle-bearing processions to religious shrines at dawn and being encouraged by priests at school to place small stones in their shoes for penitence. What became frustrating for educated adults was how every form of cultural expression was subject to Church censorship. The result was that upon Franco's death, pornography glutted magazine stands and cinemas.

Partly because of resentment of the control that the clergy had over their lives and partly because of new winds from abroad, the number of practising Catholics in Spain has fallen to 50 percent of the population. Only 18 percent of these attend Mass on a regular basis.

The new Spaniards

There is a tendency to classify Spaniards either according to their unique recent history or according to a modern and homogeneous Europe. They are at the crossroads of two cultures and two continents, Africa and Europe, and of two political and economic systems. Awakening from the lethargy imposed by so many years of isolationism, they are stretching and considering the situation. The man on the street is happy to have joined the European Union. He feels as if he is finally a member of an advanced society, and is proud of the way his country performed when the spotlight was on it for the Barcelona Olympics and the Expo World Fair. ❑

The Spanish Gypsies

George Borrow of the Gypsies or *gitanos* wrote: "I felt myself very much more at home with them than with the silent, reserved men of Spain ...". When he travelled with them in the 1830s they had been in Spain for over 400 years yet he found them to be foreigners in their own land, clinging to their language and culture long after they had begun to settle in the 18th century.

Today, nearly two centuries later, the Gypsies still hover on the edges of society. A few may catch the limelight as flamenco or bullfighting stars, like Joaquín Cortes or Curro Romero, but more often they are targets for everyday racism. They remain largely invisible in Spanish art, history and literature – Carmen, for example, the heroine of Bizet's opera, was the creation of Frenchman Prosper Merimée. As one Gypsy patriarch puts it, they are "one of the most unknown people in the world."

Who, then, are the Spanish Gypsies or *gitanos*? Of Hindu descent, from Rajasthan in north-western India, they left their homeland for unknown reasons – possibly an invasion– and migrated slowly westwards via Persia to arrive in Spain in the 15th century, bringing with them their language (*caló*), costume, social laws and large flocks of sheep and goats. Travelling in groups to avoid attack, they worked as blacksmiths, professional musicians, fortune-tellers, horse-dealers and sheep-shearers.

Five hundred years later there are 800,000 Gypsies in Spain and, as the population with the highest birth rate in Europe, their numbers are expected to double in the next 30 years. More than a quarter live in Andalucia. They may be antique or scrap dealers, fruit pickers, market-stall holders, horse-handlers, jewellers, flamenco musicians, or flower-sellers. In less independent jobs they often disguise their origins for fear of racism. Few have accumulated material wealth: a recent survey found that the average Andalusian Gypsy family lives on 35,000 Ptas (£150) a month. Often they are intensely religious.The Gypsy Holy Week processions are among the most moving in southern Spain, and in recent years there have been sweeping conversions to Evangelism in Madrid and in other Gypsy communities. Only a few words of *caló* are sprinkled through their speech, but they remain closely bound by private social rules, family loyalties, patriarchal authority and cultural pride.

The Gypsies' marginalised position is explained by their history in Spain. Relentless persecution from 1499 was aimed at forced assimilation through restricted movement and eradication of their culture. To quote just one of a dozen laws, Philip IV's Pragmatic of 1633 banned *gitano* language, costume, music, horse-dealing, possession of weapons, marriage and association in public as well as the use of the word Gypsy, on pain of life slavery. Even Charles III's 1783 law granting equal rights of work and residence made Gypsy "behaviour" punishable by red-hot irons or the

death sentence. It is little wonder that half a - century later Prosper Merimée found the Gypsies to be "astute, daring but naturally fearful of blows".

Settlement finally began in the 18th century in southern towns where the Gypsies had taken on jobs such as blacksmithing. But it was to be a slow process which finished only when enforced – sometimes brutally – during Franco's dictatorship.

Today the Constitution protects the Gypsies' rights, but the exclusion of *gitano* children from schools and housing schemes are everyday events. In response, Gypsy civil rights movements have grown up, they defend their culture and ways more strongly than ever – and, as in Borrow's time, keep a safe distance from Spanish society. ❑

LEFT: three generations gather for a traditional big lunch in Madrid.

RIGHT: Gypsy children during playtime at school.

A FOREIGNER'S VIEW

A seasoned visitor commends the Spanish way of life, and Spain's discovery of a genuine national pride

When I first went to Spain, in the early 1950s, travelling was far from easy: roads were very bad, accommodation sparse, comforts minimal. The sun shone however, and it was not long before sun-starved Northerners – Scandinavians, Celts, Germans – began to flock to Spain, spearheading what

provide work. The country surrendered itself to alien hordes for a period of about 20 years, something of an indignity to Spaniards, who referred to tourism as *putería*, or prostitution. The mass intrusion had a fruitful side; it put Spaniards in touch with the rest of the world and showed them other ways of being, so that,

was to become an invasion of mass tourism that reached a peak in 1974, when more than 30 million tourists, one for every native Spaniard, crossed the Spanish frontier during the year.

Broadening the mind?

The author Robert Graves, who rooted himself in the Spanish landscape for 50-odd years, gleefully told of an English secretary, newly returned from Spain, who announced to her friends that she had just been on holiday in Mallorca. "Where's that?" they asked her. "I have no idea," she replied. "I flew."

Franco, however, badly needed tourism to strengthen his foreign currency reserves and to

when the time came to make a new Spain, after Franco, Spaniards impressed everyone with their political sophistication, their native vitality and their determined optimism.

Tourism forced Spain into a whirlwind of change, grafting the trappings of modernity on to rustic foundations and often bringing the old ways and the new into sharp conflict. Tourists, however, kept to the beaten track, to the concrete meccas created for them, and much of Spain remained in rural isolation. The remote villages were sought out by sturdy souls, who found a mix of landscape, mode of being and human rhythms that existed nowhere else.

From the 1950s on, I lived for a part of every

year in a series of Spanish villages, eventually settling in one to which I would return once a year, like a pilgrim. It is in village life that Spanish qualities most reveal themselves. The elements there are so stark, so boned down, the inhabitants so separate and durable, the rituals so essential and so graceful that living in them feels like a simplification, a purification. In the remoter parts of the country, the quality that Spaniards have of being able to do with less, to wear lack with a kind of pride, often seems like a positive resistance to the trappings of civilisation. My village friends always gave off the air of being self-sufficient in their own skin, of having come to terms with their fate, with the help of the stoic proverb and the cosmic shrug. Conversations took as long as they had to, work was done in the course of time, and sometimes, sitting down to a long Spanish lunch, I could feel the world outside withdraw, giving way to the small, rich world of the table and the conversation.

> ### SURVIVAL PHILOSOPHY
>
> Spaniards' own eccentricities make them tolerant of the oddness of others, which helped them to survive tourist migrations.

From my first visit on, simply being in Spain has always brought me a sudden joy, a physical tingle, from the light, from the landscape, from the language. It springs from intense Spanish particularities: bare village cafés loud with argument and dominoes, or else sleepy and empty except for flies; sudden memorable conversations, about life and death, with total strangers; the way Spaniards have of imposing human time, so that meals and meetings decide their own duration. There is a durability about people here, an acceptance of fate that, paradoxically, sharpens their sense of the present, their spontaneity. The villages have a sparse, uncluttered look, with bare landscapes and stark interiors. The days seem wondrously long, gifts of time, and existence simplifies itself to a vocabulary of elemental acts, like drawing water and making fire.

Changing roles

Over some 25 years, I watched my own village die, in a sense, losing its agricultural self-sufficiency, when bottled gas replaced the charcoal that it had prepared from time immemorial. The population dwindled, as the men left to find work elsewhere, and the school closed when their families eventually followed them. Foreigners, in search of silence, occupied the empty houses, and the village evolved a continuing life, the remaining inhabitants playing the part of custodians, the foreigners their honoured guests.

The best of hosts

The tourist occupation of the Franco years was not a destiny that Spain wished on itself, but one which the country has survived well, and has turned to its own advantage. For me, the

great satisfaction of recent years has been in seeing the Spaniards themselves assume control of their own destiny, with flair and imagination, and with a genuine national pride. They have also taken a keen pleasure in maintaining and preserving their country, and in making it comfortably available to its own inhabitants.

Their enthusiasm makes them the best of hosts. Foreigners, consequently, who had grown used to trudging across Spain at will for so long, have now been moved towards the periphery of Spanish life, and behave more as guests to a host, a change of status desirable for Spain's sake, and has enhanced the pleasures of being in that inexhaustible human landscape. ❏

LEFT AND RIGHT: international brands and consumer values are making an increasing impact in Spain.

THE BULLS

Despite predictions about the demise of bullfighting, passionate aficionados affirm that it will exist as long as Spain does

First-time visitors to Spain are likely to approach the whole idea of bullfighting with varying mixtures of excitement, fascination and apprehension. Sitting in the stands and waiting for the initial pageantry to begin, one knows instinctively that what is about to happen is not a sport. Spanish news-

to attack anything that moves or challenges its predominance. A bull has been known to charge an express train which crossed its path.

It is, in fact, the bull's selected bloodlines, responsible for its innate bravery, nobility and proud bearing, which have kept it from the slaughterhouse and granted it an almost envi-

papers categorise the *corrida de toros* as a spectacle; ardent *corrida* advocates fiercely defend its artistic nature, and bullfighting has left its mark on painting, sculpture, music, dance and literature.

The toro bravo

Spain's brave fighting bull is a fierce, untamed animal, whose bloodlines and pedigrees have been protected over the centuries in order to maintain its purity and the characteristics which make it both fundamental and particularly apt for the *corrida de toros*.

The fighting bull is not trained to charge; this herbivorous creature is born with the tendency

able life. Pampered as a valuable thoroughbred, the *toro bravo* enjoys four to five years of splendour in the grass before it is faced with the ultimate test, its appearance in the arena.

During Spain's most glorious historic period, bullfighting was an important part of public life. For some 600 years, the aristocracy was responsible for breeding bulls and then fighting them before king and court.

The first man to turn bullfighting into a profession was the Ronda carpenter Francisco Romero, but it was his grandson, the great Pedro Romero, who is considered the father of modern bullfighting. With the *muleta* (the red cloth draped over a 2-foot-long stick) in his left hand and the sword in his right, Pedro Romero manoeuvred the animal until it was in position for placing the sword. He killed more than 5,600 bulls between 1771 and 1799, without suffering so much as a scratch. No matador since has matched his feat in terms of physical immunity.

This then was *toreo* in its most rudimentary form; the object of the "show" was to kill the bull. Today, many are the intricate and artistic manoeuvres which have been created with the cape and *muleta*, and the bullfighter is no longer merely a *matador* (killer); he is a *torero*, who expresses his sentiments and artistic ability through the art of challenging and dominating a wild beast.

The spectacle itself is filled with colour, tradition, pageantry, danger, beauty, daring, blood, excitement and sublime art, and is certainly worth a closer look. Though some view it as an unnecessarily cruel slaughter, others see in the bullfight a dramatic dance between man in all his elegant cognisance and the bull in all its natural, earthy fierceness and brutality.

Death in the afternoon

The *corrida* commences with the pageantry of the *paseíllo* or entrance parade in which the *alguacilillos*, the mounted constables in 16th-century attire, lead the march of the bullfighters into the ring to the tune of the *pasodoble*.

The *alguacilillos* are followed into the arena or *ruedo* by the three matadors who precede in turn the three rows of their respective *cuadrillas* or teams. Each matador has in his service three *banderilleros*; their role is to assist him in the handling of the bull by using the cape and also in the placing of the *banderillas*, the 60-cm-long (2-ft) crêpe paper-decorated darts.

These *banderilleros* were, in their day, aspiring matadors, though probably few progressed beyond the novice stage to the *alternativa*. This is the ceremony in which a veteran matador symbolically cedes the tools of the trade – the *muleta* and sword – to the neophyte, endowing him with the right to kill fully grown bulls and to hold the coveted title of *Matador de Toros*.

LEFT: a five-year-old fighting bull sporting the ribbons of his ranch.

RIGHT: close encounter.

> **RED RAGS AND BULLS**
>
> It is a fallacy that bulls charge only red. Bulls are colour blind, but they have an innate tendency to attack anything that moves.

The three rows of *banderilleros* are followed by the mounted picadors. Each matador will have two in his employ, one to pic each of his bulls. The *paseíllo* is completed with the no less pompous entrance of the more mundane bullring employees who will have to put in an appearance in the arena: the *monosabios*, who guide the picadors' horses, the *mulilleros*, who handle the mule team which drags out the dead bull, and the *areneros*, who tidy up the sand afterwards.

Once everyone has taken his respective post,

the President of the *corrida* will pull out his white handkerchief to signal the entrance of the first bull into the ring. This marks the initiation of the first *tercio* (third) of this live drama.

The bull will come charging into the arena through the *toril* gate which communicates directly with the *chiqueros*, the individual pens where each bull had been enclosed since the morning's *sorteo*. He will be greeted by a *banderillero*, magenta and gold *capote* (cape) in hand, or by an extremely eager matador.

The fight begins

The *torero* will effect some initial cape passes or lances directed to either of the bull's horns in order to determine the animal's natural tendencies: whether it favours one horn over the other, has a long smooth charge or swerves about rapidly, whether it sees well, and if it is strong.

As soon as the matador feels confident about the bull's condition, he will proceed to perform the most classic and fundamental of the passes, the *verónica*. A tandem of *verónicas* are linked together as the matador leads the bull gradually towards the centre of the ring. The series is concluded with a *media verónica* (half turn) in which the bull is abruptly brought about, giving the matador sufficient time and space in which to withdraw from the animal's path.

At this point, the picadors make their entrance, the least understood and appreciated aspect of the *corrida*. The picadors have a multifold purpose. First, they have the thankless task of preparing the animal for the culmination of the matador's work, the *faena*. In order for the bull to be able to follow the cape smoothly it must be slowed down, but not excessively, and its head must be lowered. To achieve this they goad the bull with lances to weaken its shoulder muscles.

The picador must also try to correct any defects in the bull's charge, such as a tendency to hook to the right or swing up its horns at the

A DRAMA IN THREE ACTS

Three is a magic number for understanding modern bullfighting. The *corrida* itself is a drama in three acts, each marked by trumpet calls.

There are three matadors, who alternate in the fighting of six bulls, which have previously been divided into three pairs of *lotes* in the *sorteo*, or drawing of lots.

The first and most senior matador is responsible for dispatching the first and fourth bulls, the second matador, the second and fifth, and the third and least experienced of the trio, the third and sixth.

Each matador has three *banderilleros*, who plant pairs of *banderillas*, or darts, in the bull's withers.

end of each pass, which could prove fatal to the matador who is unprepared for it. The picador's other important function is to determine the *toro's* bravery, for the bull is just as significant a figure in the bullfight as the matador and the public calls upon both to perform at their best. A sign of bovine bravery is the animal's repetition of buoyant and determined charges against the padding of the picador's horse.

Generally three pics or *puyazos* are administered, depending upon the animal's strength. The first *tercio* of pics is brightened by the alternating participation of the three matadors in a competitive display. With the cape known as *quites*, each matador is supposed to *quitar* or draw the bull away from the horse and perform, whenever possible, any of the many varied cape adornments, such as *verónicas, chicuelinas, gaoneras, navarras* and *delantales*.

The President will use his white handkerchief once again to mark the beginning of the second *tercio*, the *banderillas*. Some matadors are skilled in the placing of their own *banderillas*, but 80 percent of the time the public will see the assistants place the darts in the most expedient manner. This *tercio* gives the bull the opportunity to recuperate after its cumbersome struggle with the heavily padded picador's horse.

The moment of truth

The trumpet now sounds for the third and final act of the drama. Armed with his sword and the red serge *muleta*, the matador will simultaneously salute and request permission from the President to kill the bull.

The right-handed pass or *derechazo*, in which the sword is used to expand the cloth, and the left-handed *natural* are the two fundamental *muleta* passes. More importance is attributed to the *natural*, in which the *muleta* is held in its natural and more diminutive size, with the sword in the right hand. A series of smooth or tempered *naturales* is usually completed with a *remate* pass, the *pase de pecho*, taking the bull from behind the matador and leading it past and off to the right.

The matador has 15 minutes in which to bring about the death of the bull, creating his artistic masterpiece, the *faena*, In order to kill in the *volapié* fashion, the matador positions the bull, raises the sword to shoulder level and moves in to kill, using the *muleta* to guide the dangerous horns past his right hip. He must move with determination and a steady hand to ensure that the sword hits its mark, a 3-inch (7.5-cm) wide opening just between the shoulder blades. If he misses his target, he will hit bone and the *pinchazo* will not be appreciated by the public.

If the steel *estoque* is not well placed or proves to be insufficient to produce the animal's death, the matador will be obliged to make use of the *descabello*. This is a shorter sword fitted with a crossbar close to the tip. The matador directs the *descabello* to the rachidian bulb at the base of the bull's skull, which produces its instant death, if performed correctly. As soon as the bull drops to the ground, the *puntillero* rushes out with the *puntilla* or dagger to administer the *coup de grâce* to prevent any prolonged suffering.

At this point the public displays its approval – or otherwise – of the bullfighter's performance. Under satisfactory circumstances the crowd waves handkerchiefs to request the granting of an ear to the matador. Nowadays, the *orejas* (ears) and the *rabo* (tail) are sym-

bolic trophies for a good-to-excellent performance. A matador who performs well but experiences difficulty with the sword, for example, might be applauded by the crowd and invited to take a *vuelta* or lap of the ring.

As the bulls share star billing with the matadors, a brave animal that performs well is applauded as it is drawn out of the arena by the mules. It may even be granted its own turn of the ring and, in exceptional cases, a pardon. A cowardly animal will be the object of irate protests as it is dragged from the ring. The trumpet will sound again and it is time for the second bull to emerge from its dark pen into the bright sunlight of the arena.

LEFT: parading at the Fiesta of San Fermin held in Pamplona.
RIGHT: a bull charging from the gate meets a *banderillero*.

The bull has evolved from the fierce, erratic bovine faced by Pedro Romero and his contemporaries in Ronda. Years of selective breeding have produced a more tempered, noble stock, but have also led to a weakening of the caste. Additionally, the pasture areas of many ranches has been sharply reduced, and the limited area for exercise and grazing has debilitated the physical stamina of the bulls.

A cause for celebration

Every town in the country, no matter the size, celebrates its local *fiestas* on behalf of its respective patron saint, and the festivities would be incomplete without bullfighting. Madrid honours San Isidro the Farmer on 15 May with the longest bullfight fair of all: an incredible 27 consecutive days of *corridas*.

Other important *ferias* are the delightful *fallas* of Valencia in the month of March; the incomparably colourful and gay Seville Fair in April; the Corpus Christi celebrations of Granada in June; the *Sanfermines* of Pamplona in July, immortalised by Ernest Hemingway; followed by the Valencia Summer Fair; the *Semana Grande* of Bilbo in August; and the busy month of September with the Salamanca and Valladolid Fairs and the Grape Harvests of

Jerez and Logroño. The El Pilar Festivities in Zaragoza in mid-October conclude the season. *Festivales* are informal bullfights in which the *toreros* perform merely for their expenses, because the general proceeds of the *corrida* are intended for charity. In order to render these fights less dangerous, the bulls' horns are trimmed or shaved for these festivals. The bullfighters also exchange their silk and sequined *traje de luces* (suit of lights) for the *traje corto* or country costume.

Bullfighting today

Bullfighting, also referred to as the *Fiesta Nacional*, is no longer the unchallenged prime

WHEN TO SEE BULLFIGHTS

The bullfighting season officially opens on 19 March (St Joseph's Day) and ends on 12 October (Columbus' Day in America; Hispanic Day in Spain), though fights are frequently held before and after these dates.

The bullring audience sits in the *tendidos* (stalls) or the *palcos* (balcony), where the president's box is situated. Seating is normally divided into three sections: the more comfortable and expensive shady side, or *Sombra*; the cheaper sunny section, or *Sol*, where, depending upon the season, spectators suffer the summer heat; and the intermediate *Sol y Sombra*.

The *corrida* generally starts at 5pm.

national pastime. It is obliged to share the spotlight with increasingly popular soccer matches as well as with all other forms of Spanish Sunday afternoon entertainment. Ticket prices have also soared. Added to the costs involved in raising a herd of fighting bulls for four to five years (the age at which they are allowed to fight) is the fact that the *festejo* is heavily taxed.

One thing which has never changed and surely never will because it represents the very essence of the *fiesta* is the mortal danger to the

SUMMONED BY BULLS

Bulls have inspired countless writers and artists, iincluding Hemingway and Picasso. The poet Federico García Lorca called the bulls "Spain's greatest vital and poetic treasure".

ranch. The fatal gorings of these star matadors were mourned by the entire Spanish nation.

Today's crowd-pleasers include El Cordobés, who thrills his audience but is sometimes thought guilty of holding the bulls in too much disdain; Enrique Ponce, a stylish performer; Joselito, who has superb technical skills; and Jesulín de Ubrique, whose refusal to share the ring with women bullfighters has earned him support in traditional macho circles.

Such attitudes are now on the wane, how-

bullfighters. During the 1980s two top matadors died tragically in the arena. The popular Francisco Rivera, "Paquirri", married to the famous folk-singer, Isabel Pantoja, was killed by the bull "Avispado" of the Sayalero y Bandrés ranch in Pozoblanco (Córdoba) on 26 September 1984. The promising 21-year-old José Cubero, "Yiyo", died instantly in the Colmenar Viejo arena of a horn wound inflicted directly to the heart on 30 August 1985. He was a victim of "Burlero" of the Marcos Núñez

LEFT: bullfighter Espartaco executing a cape pass called *derechazo*.
RIGHT: he successfully completes a natural pass.

ever, with the emergence of star *toreras* such as Cristina Sánchez. In 1996, she gained massive popular acclaim by taking the *alternativa* at Madrid's Las Ventas bullring.

A touch of madness

The *torero* continues to be a unique human being. The profession calls for an individual with considerable courage, grace, skill, physical prowess and agility, artistic sensitivity, romanticism – and perhaps madness.

The *torero* will develop his own personalised religion or philosophy which will enable him to risk his life and regularly face death with periodic precision and serenity. ❑

SPANISH PAINTING

From early cave paintings to Picasso's "Guernica", there is

a heightened realism that characterises Spanish art

When the English writer Rose Macaulay visited Spain during the 1940s, she concluded that it "grows Roman walls and basilicas and 10th-century churches like wild figs, leaving them about in the most careless and arrogant profusion, uncharted and untended, for travellers to stumble on as they will". Today, in more enlightened and prosperous times, it is not true that Spain's artistic patrimony is, as she put it, "mouldering away". Throughout Spain there are well-catalogued museums and churches, and few important works of art are now neglected.

The majority of Spanish masterpieces were commissioned by the Church, court and higher aristocracy for Spanish eyes alone. They were meant to induce lingering contemplation on subjects such as Christ's Passion, the lives of the saints, the nobility of earthly portrait sitters and the omnipotence of the Church. An invitation to contemplation, careful observation of life as it is, directness of expression and psychological penetration are qualities that come to mind when one asks what has remained consistently "Spanish" about Spanish art.

Primitive wall paintings

The earliest Spanish masterpieces, rediscovered as recently as 100 years ago, are the prehistoric wall paintings in caves (particularly at Altamira) and early medieval wall paintings previously hidden under whitewash in Spanish churches. The cave drawings consist of marks which appear to have been primitive notational systems, and elegantly rendered bison, reindeer and other animals. The vigorous style and spiritual feeling of both cave drawings and early-Christian murals influenced 20th-century artists, notably Joan Miró and Pablo Picasso.

In the Middle Ages, pilgrims' trails and trade routes brought the stylistic influences of French and Italian, Netherlandish and German, Near

---

PRECEDING PAGES: Goya's *Marquess of Santa Cruz*.
LEFT: El Greco's *Gentleman with a Hand on his Chest*.
RIGHT: prehistoric cave painting at Altamira.

Eastern and North African art into Spain's ecclesiastical network. All artists patronised by the Church were affected by these. Thus, the decorative figures and rich colours of medieval wall paintings are also found in illuminated manuscripts in the libraries of León Cathedral, El Escorial and other cathedrals and museums.

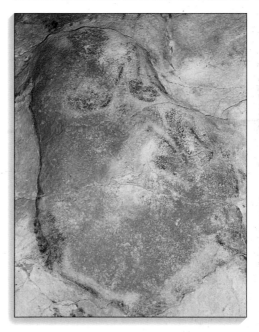

One of the most surprising ensembles of rediscovered early medieval mural paintings is in the little pre-Romanesque church known as "Santullano" (or San Julian de los Prados) in Oviedo, built in the early 9th century. Mosaics from Roman villas have been excavated near Oviedo, and Roman wall paintings similar to those preserved at Pompeii, in Italy, inspired the *trompe-l'oeil* decoration of this Asturian church. In León, south of Oviedo, the mid-11th-century Panteón de los Reyes, a royal crypt adjoining the Colegiata de San Isidro, has unusually well-preserved wall paintings dating from 1175. León is on a pilgrimage trail to Santiago de Compostela, so it is possible that

French artists painted the relatively naturalistic Christ in Majesty and scenes from the New Testament. But one of them, in which the angel appears to the shepherds, is often cited as an example of Spanish realism. Ordinary details such as a shepherd feeding his dog are found in the sacred art of other European schools, too; but in the frequency with which they occur in Spanish art, many people read a special Spanish sense of the dignity of everyday life.

Catalan Romanesque

Catalonia was the most important centre for Romanesque painting in Spain, and there are many superb examples in the Museo de Arte de Cataluña in Barcelona, where the frescoes are displayed in rooms emulating the shapes of the churches from which they have been taken. The Moors, who entered Spain from North Africa in the 8th century, had reinforced the Spanish artists' fair for flat, linear, brightly coloured stylisation. However, the oriental gift for pattern also wafted across the Mediterranean via Italy from Byzantium. The Catalan Romanesque style, in particular, shows the Byzantine influence. Its ritualistic figures are almost expressionless, even when they undergo horrifying martyrdoms. Some of the finest

paintings in this style come from the Pyrenean church of Sant Climint in Tahull, in Lérida, dedicated in 1123. Spanish anecdotal detail can be seen in the fresco in which Lazarus, propped on his crutch, is licked by an ecstatic dog.

Regional Schools

As the *Reconquista* – the recovery of Spain from the Moors – progressed, regional Spanish Schools developed. The product of their workshops was naive and at times positively homely. However, during the 14th and 15th centuries, the technical breakthroughs of the increasingly realistic northern European and northern Italian Schools profoundly affected

Spanish painting. It is unclear how many Spanish artists visited Italy or the Netherlands, but in a fresco cycle near Barcelona by the Catalan Ferrer Bassa, who is thought to have studied in Italy, there are squared, three-dimensional figures and striking narrative scenes strongly reminiscent of Giotto.

In the late 14th century, an International Gothic style spread from the Burgundian and French courts. Integrating the Flemish artists' careful drawing of meticulous detail and the Italo-Byzantine love of pattern and colour, the style was characterised by courtly elegance and a new interest in individual psychology. A

retablo, stretched out to become a wall of panels that climbed up to fill and tower over the east end of the church.

Hispano-Flemish

From around 1440 Flemish influence came to dominate Spanish painting. Lluis Dalmau, a Catalan, went to study in Bruges, and upon returning to paint in Barcelona he passed on his training to the younger Jaime Huguet. The *Virgen des Concellers*, Dalmau's impressive altarpiece in Barcelona, has a Spanish Virgin and Child on a Gothic throne in a Flemish landscape. A panel by Huguet in the same museum

superb example of this style is the Flemish painter Rogier van der Weyden's *Deposition* in the Prado, an altarpiece of around 1435 which came into the Spanish royal collection in the 16th century. Lluis Borrassa's altarpiece of Sta Clara, of around 1412, in Barcelona is a Catalan version of the International Gothic style.

The altarpiece was the most important commission for the artist of the *Reconquista*. In this lively period, Spanish fresco painting died out, the altar frontal disappeared and the retable, or

LEFT: early 12th-century painted apse, Santa Maria d'Aneu in the Catalan Pyrenees.
RIGHT: *The Last Supper* by Jaime Huguet (c1470).

contains charming Spanish anecdotal details: votive offerings hanging over the corpse of the miracle-working St Vincent, and a tiny devil escaping from the mouth of one of the cured.

The Hispano-Flemish style peaked at the centralising, art-collecting court of the Catholic monarchs Fernando and Isabel from the mid-15th and into the 16th century. Flemish or Flemish-trained artists painted his portrait (now at Windsor Castle) and hers (now in the Royal Palace, Madrid). Fernando Gallego (*Piedad* in the Prado), the outstanding Castilian master of this style, combined the decorativeness of International Gothic with the monumentality that had been developing since Giotto.

Renaissance influence

From the early 16th century a new wave of Italian influence brought the High Renaissance style to Spain. The collecting fever of the monarchy begun by Charles V, who befriended Titian, meant that Spanish painting was exposed to wider influences and lost much of its provincial character. Felipe II moved Spain's capital, from Toledo to Madrid, giving the country's artistic life a focus. A great patron of art, he also imported several Italian artists to decorate his

> ### ECLECTIC GENIUS
>
> The influences of Spanish cave drawings, early Christian church murals, Goya and Velázquez and the subject of the bullfight all find their way into Picasso's work.

from Italy to Spain hoping to find employment there. But his weird, hovering, Byzantine figures wiped with eerie bluish light did not appeal to Felipe, who had expected something very different from a pupil of Titian. Fortunately, El Greco's portraits and religious subjects, commanded an audience elsewhere in Spain. His portraits reveal an unexpected realism: in *The Gentleman with a Hand on his Chest* the dark background emphasises the features of the man's face and his aristocratic fingers. In his altarpieces for

palace at the Escorial, which consequently became a training school for Spanish painters.

But the pagan classical ideals of Italian Renaissance were not initially in tune with the prevailing ethos of priest-ridden Spain, and religious subjects continued to predominate. The Church and the Inquisition militated against the portrayal of idealised nudes and mythological subjects. Similarly, High Renaissance perspective like that in Andrea Mantegna's Italian masterpiece, *The Death of the Virgin*, in the Prado, brought to Spain by Felipe IV, was attempted by only a few Spanish artists.

Felipe II's Escorial project attracted the great Mannerist painter, El Greco, who travelled

Toledo's churches, El Greco displayed his own brand of piety and a streak of mysticism. The Inquisition was ambivalent about religious ecstasy, but the number of contemporaneous copies of his work attest to his popularity.

The Golden Age

The 17th century was a Golden Age for Spanish painting. The era was dominated by three painters from Seville: Francisco Zurbarán, Bartolomé Esteban Murillo and Diego Velázquez; and José de Ribera, a Spaniard who worked in the Spanish kingdom of Naples. Although the range of acceptable subject matter broadened to include history and mythology, religious subjects remained the most important. Paintings had to conform to Counter-Reformation ideals, which decreed that the visual arts should give clear, straightforward expositions of religious subjects to act as an aid to devotion.

This aim is most clearly realised in the work of Zurbarán, whose series of paintings featuring a single figure – usually a saint or monk – in meditation are stark, uncompromising images with violent contrasts of dark and light. Ribera also delighted in painting scenes of bloody martyrdom with the energy and verve of Caravaggio. Murillo's soft-edged treatment of religious themes was more in tune with popular taste, and his compositions were distributed in print form among the middle classes. Favoured subjects were the Immaculate Conception, the Holy Family and the Madonna and Child. Modern taste favours Murillo's pictures of children and beggars in which the vivacity of the subject is tempered by an unsentimental rendering of the reality of their circumstances.

Still Life and Velázquez

The 17th century was also a time when the Spanish love of naturalism culminated in a flowering of still-life painting. Unlike Flemish examples, Spanish still lives are often spare compositions: a few fruits, vegetables or pots arranged with austere simplicity. Lovingly delineated still-life details are often inserted into narrative paintings. This is true of the type of painting known as *bodegones* – genre scenes set in a kitchen or tavern. No-one painted these with more assurance than Velázquez, whose *Old Woman Frying Eggs* (National Gallery of Scotland, Edinburgh) is a prime example.

Velázquez enjoyed a successful career, becoming Felipe IV's favourite painter at the age of 24. His sitters ranged from the King to the court dwarves. Pope Innocent said of his portrait by the artist that it was *"troppo vero"* – too truthful. *Las Meninas*, in the Prado, records one of the royal family's visits to Velázquez' studio in the Alcázar. The bold technique, the sense of depth created by the figures in the mirror and, above all, the spontaneous snapshot quality of the royal portrait, have made this picture a masterpiece of world art.

LEFT: *The Drunkards* by Velázquez (detail) shows the artist's realism, sympathy and insight.
RIGHT: self-portrait by Goya.

Apart from *bodegones* and portraits, Velázquez made a few excursions into other fields. His monumental *Surrender of Breda* in the Prado is inspired by Rubens. Painted for Felipe IV's Buen Retiro, it recreates a gesture of magnanimity on the part of the victor and vanquished after the Spanish siege against the Dutch stronghold a few miles north of Rubens' studio in Antwerp. Velázquez's *Rokeby Venus,* one of the few paintings of the nude in Spanish art, shows his awareness of the work of Titian, who popularised the subject of Venus gazing at herself in a mirror attended by Cupid.

Goya probably took his cue from this can-

vas, which belonged to his patron the Duchess of Alba, when he came to paint his *Naked Maja* 150 years later. Like Velázquez, Goya was a court painter, and his portraits of the royal family are suffused with an astonishing realism: Ernest Hemingway claimed that he "painted his spittle into every face" in his portrait of the degenerate *Family of Charles IV* in the Prado.

Goya's realism could also descend to the horrific: following a severe bout of illness that left him profoundly deaf, a darker and highly original side emerged in his work. He produced a series of etchings, *Los Caprichos* (caprices), which took a satirical look at the follies and inadequacies of humanity, and a second series of engravings, *The Disasters of War*, which depicted atrocities committed by the French troups when they occupied Spain in the Peninsular War. This darker tendency culminated in the late "black" paintings now in the Prado, originally painted directly on the walls of his home, in which the myth of Saturn, the symbol of death and destruction, constantly recurs.

Goya was an isolated figure of genius in the 18th century, and there was no Spanish painter of comparable stature in the following century.

Yet it was then that Spanish art began to be appreciated in Europe: the French Impressionists were stunned by the realism and expressive paint-handling of Velázquez and Goya. Spain produced her own version of Impressionism, and minor masters such as Joaquin Sorolla (whose work is in Madrid's Sorolla Museum) produced paintings of great charm, characterised by fluid brushwork and high-key colour.

The 20th century

The 20th century has seen several Spanish painters of great distinction, including Pablo Picasso, who like many modern Spanish artists, spent most of his career outside Spain. With his fellow Cubist painter Juan Gris, he passed his formative years in Paris, and he spent most of the rest of his life in France. But his work retained its Spanish links. As Gertrude Stein put it, he "had in him not only Spanish painting but Spanish Cubism which is the daily life of Spain". His most famous painting, *Guernica*, was inspired by his distress at the bombing of a town during the Spanish Civil War. The Picasso Museum in Barcelona has an unrivalled collection of his early works. Salvador Dalí, too, lived most of his life in exile in Paris and the USA, and there is a Dalí museum at his birthplace, Figueras. A Catalan like Picasso and Miró, he took up the thread of realism, but turned it to Surrealist ends, to produce what he called "hand-painted dream photographs".

Joan Miró, on the other hand, after an initial period in Paris, lived mainly in and around his native Barcelona before moving to Majorca. His Surrealism was of an entirely different complexion to Dalí's: he chose to work from imagination rather than external reality, blending elements of primitivism, personal mythology and abstraction to create an enchanted dream world. The graphic quality of his work is inspired by the rhythmical forms of traditional Catalan art. The Miró Foundation in Barcelona includes his paintings, sculptures and prints.

Also in Barcelona is the Tàpies Foundation, housing the work of Antoní Tàpies, Spain's most important post-war painter. Initially influenced by Miró, among others, he developed an abstract style in the 1950s, using mixed media to produce works of startling originality.

Interest in contemporary art has increased recently, judging by the number of new museums. Barcelona's contemporary art museum, opened in 1995, is dedicated to avant-garde Catalan artists. Bilbo's Guggenheim, housed in a titanium-clad building designed by Frank Gehry, opened in 1997. It contains the world's biggest gallery space – its main gallery is over 100 metres (330 ft) long – and provides a forum for works that are too large to exhibit elsewhere. ❏

LEFT: drawing of Picasso aged 20 by Barcelona artist Ramon Casas.
RIGHT: Miro's *The Wine Bottle* is indebted to past Spanish masters.

WILDLIFE

From the high Pyrenees to low-lying marshlands: travel slowly in Spain's
unspoiled countryside and you will find wild creatures everywhere

Bullfights and beaches, *fiestas* and flamenco. These are the highlights of Spain for the millions of international tourists who crowd the *costas* every year. Too few people realise that Spain, with its vast areas of unspoiled scenery, is host to a wide range of fascinating wild animals and birds.

The country now has more than 200 nature reserves including 11 national parks. The principal highland parks are Covadonga National Park in the western Picos de Europa, home to the European brown bear as well as to wolves, wild boar and chamois; the Ordesa and Monte Perdido National Park in the Aragonese Pyrenees; and the Aigües Tortes and San Mauricio Lake National Park in the Catalan Pyrenees.

In southwest Spain, flanking the estuary of the Guadalquivir river, is the huge wetland area of Doñana National Park, habitat of six world-protected species including the imperial eagle, and the winter retreat of thousands of migratory aquatic birds. For years Doñana was under threat as its fragile environment suffered assault from developers and commercial pressure groups. Now its future seems assured. The smaller marshland area of Tablas de Daimiel in La Mancha also supports a wealth of birdlife.

So extensive is the country's list of rare and exotic creatures that, for some naturalists, Spain is Europe's last Eden. Enthusiasm and concern starts at the top. King Juan Carlos has declared: "Nature conservation is one of the great public endeavours of our age."

Imperial Eagle

Yet with varying attitudes and policies across Spain's autonomous regions, from dedicated and protectionist to indifferent or even antagonistic, conservationist ideas may have come too late. Itself a regal symbol, the Spanish imperial eagle, for example, has been reduced by habitat destruction and heedless development

---

LEFT: an imperial eagle feeds a snake to its young.
RIGHT: a well concealed Spanish lynx in the Coto Doñana. An agile tree climber, it also swims well.

to isolated pockets of existence. But with patience and luck, you can see, high above the coastal heathland in southwest Spain, pairs of these magnificent eagles in flight, displaying their remarkable mating behaviour.

It starts with a series of elegant circlings, wings and pinions fully extended. After soaring

together for a few minutes, one bird takes the initiative and dives at its mate. Male and female then perform a display of aerial swoops and chases. One bird eventually rolls on its back in mid-air and presents its unsheathed talons to the other. Finally, they plunge earthward, interlocked, then level out and fly apart a few hundred feet above ground.

The large ramshackle nest this couple will build on top of a cork-oak tree is made up of branches, twigs, dried grass and ferns. Two or three eggs produce plump balls of white fluff. After a month, the young can be left for spells as both parents go out hunting. At two months, the young eagles, now with cinnamon-brown feathers, learn to soar and to dive at prey. Within a year, with adults ready to mate again, juveniles are on their own.

Glimpse of a lynx

It could be even harder to see, in this southwestern region, one of the shyest of exclusively Iberian creatures. But if a cat with the look of a leopard cub streaks across the road in front of you, you will have had a rare glimpse of the Spanish lynx. Weighing around 12 kilos (30lb), it has markings even more pronounced than its first cousin, the European lynx. The lynx is king of Spain's wildcats, a family that includes

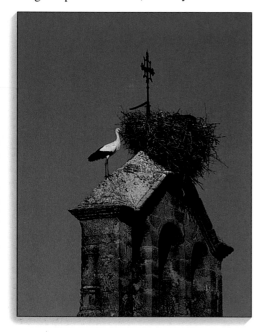

the slender genet with its characteristic long banded tail. Fur pattern apart, the lynx is distinguished by large and tapering ears, topped with tufts of black hair. These act as antennae, sensitive to air currents during up-wind stalking and to the slightest rustle in the undergrowth. Monitoring sounds inaudible to a human ear, they also compensate for a weak sense of smell. Strong, padded paws, a surprisingly short tail, exploratory white whiskers and a mottled-ochre coat – perfect camouflage in sun-dappled vegetation – complete the picture.

So lithe as to appear boneless, the lynx is a nocturnal hunter in sandy scrubland bushes, tangled heather and juniper clumps. An agile tree-climber, it is also an expert swimmer. With eyes that can be green or amber, it has ultrasensitive sight – enabling it to spot its supper at a considerable distance on a moonless night.

Living in coverts that can be flooded by rain or chilled by snow, the lynx stays active as a matter of survival. A female lynx with kittens will leave her lair to hunt across exposed areas. Desperation is the lynx's driving force, skill and cunning its protection.

Black storks

Relax under an oak in rural Spain and you might hear the unexpected sound above you of a saw cutting wood. Look carefully for the carpenter. It could just be a black stork or *Cigüeña negra*, back in Spain from its winter sojourn in Africa. A big bird with jet-dark plumage, it returns to the same large, untidy nest as the previous year.

Unlike the large white stork visible in nests on bell towers and tall chimneys throughout Spain, the black species prefer lonely elm or oak woods, river cliffs or rocky platforms in the *sierras*. A true stork for all its ebony features, the *Cigüeña negra* is a solitary bird, flying alone or in small groups during migration.

Averse to using their heavy wings, the storks do plenty of gliding, and need thermal upcurrents to maintain altitude. As there are few thermals over large expanses of water, they seek short crossings, like the Straits of Gibraltar, for their north and southbound journeys.

The black stork shares a curious habit with its white counterpart. On emerging from the egg, the nestling lays its head on its back and makes rapid snapping movements with its bill to signal it is hungry. Though silent at first (the infant

---

ON THE NATURE TRAIL

Spain's mountain parks are snow-filled from mid-November to mid-April. The best time to visit the Ordesa or Covadonga National Parks is mid-summer. Aigues Tortes can be visited in May, though the highest peaks will still be avalanche-prone. To see migratory birds on the move, visit the wetlands of Doñana and the Tablas de Daimiel in spring or autumn. Spain also has many nature reserves (*parques naturales*). Cazorla, in southwest Spain, is home to many protected bird species including the golden eagle. Monfragüe, in Extramadura, is a favoured breeding place for the black stork, the black vulture and the black-winged kite.

stork's bill is soft), in this way begins the bird's lifelong characteristic clacking. And if, in an adult, the habit looks like a warning of attack, it can also signal excitement and love.

Male and female black storks look alike, but the male's courtship – preening of wings, leaping into the air, seizing nest-sticks – signals his sex and intentions to other storks. The demonstration attracts a mate, and the pair, heads thrown back, engage in a riot of mutual bill-clapping. When eggs appear, male and female share responsibility for the hatching and, once chicks emerge – three to five of them, with snowy white feathers – the storks are faithful

fiercely protective of their engagingly-striped piglets, and they have been known to attack.

To see anything of the brown bear families of the Cantabrian mountains of northwest Spain you could do with wings or a stargazer's telescope. Even scientists trying to study them may find only one or two of the shaggy giants (at about 2.1 metres/7 ft tall, they are among the largest land animals). But a shrunken colony of bears *is* there, forced from the foothills to take refuge in forests near the peaks after centuries of persecution by hunting parties.

Once these brown bears numbered in hundreds. Today some 80 or fewer survive in the

parents. So much so that if the female dies or is killed, the male will remain alone at the nest to guard the eggs and rear the chicks.

Boar and bear

If you're planning a walk through thick forest, watch out for wild boar. The same animal that featured prominently in medieval banquets is still the curse of farmers, whose crops it raids, and target of not always legal hunters.

The boar are understandably shy but are also

LEFT: white stork and bell-tower nest.
RIGHT: the Cantabrian mountains are the last refuge of Spain's brown bears; only about 100 remain.

mountain range. In winter the bears disappear entirely, holed up in caves and crevices for their long hibernation, a prolonged light sleep on a bed of leaves, during which respiration sinks to some five breaths every couple of minutes. Heartbeats slow down accordingly, though body temperatures drop only about 10 percent. Females which have given birth lie in the den, making a warm circle for their hairless cubs.

Since 1973 Spanish bears have been legally protected. Hunting or killing carries fines of millions of pesetas, possibly imprisonment. You still might hear farmers boasting of a trophy, though the kill will be claimed as self-defence or the protection of lambs.

Flamingos

In contrast to the secretive bears, greater flamingos are eminently visible – particularly in the large Fuente de Piedra lagoon north of urban Málaga, or on the mud-flats of the Guadalquivir River estuary in Doñana and the shallow coastal lakes, floodwaters and salt marshes of the south – a sub-tropical climate where there is normally a good food supply of algae, molluscs and crustaceans. The rose-pink and white flamingos, wading or in serried flight, are an

> **BIZARRE BIRD**
>
> Spain is the last European stronghold of the Great Bustard. This "goose with eagle's wings" is almost grotesque on the ground yet spectacular in flight.

summer will shrink or dry up water habitats. Lakes become salt-pans and the birds can breed there only irregularly. Even trigger-happy hunters can be a threat.

Great Bustard

Turning from one leggy bird to another, on the plains of Spain you may see the fascinating great bustard. Weighing about 12 kilos (30lb), it has a moustache of white bristles, an ostrich type head and legs and barks like a dog when excited. One of the world's largest flying birds, it is legally pro-

ornithological treasure. Their stilt-like legs and long necks allow them to "graze" the shallow water for nutritious algae, feeding with their heads upside-down.

Totally gregarious, greater flamingos "talk" to their companions with much trumpeting and, when flying in formation, goose-like gabbles. They breed in company, building circular, mud-heap nests a few inches above brackish water . By April, each has produced a single egg, which hatches after about a month .

The puny greyish-brown chicks struggle to keep up in the water with their elders as they feed. But in the warm places they favour lies danger to the flamingo populations. A searing

tected. The courtship of great bustards, in spring often performed by dozens of birds in open spaces, is quite a spectacle. Uttering gruff barks, the males (or *barbons*) attract the assembled females with displays of their gorgeously-striped plumage and fan-tail, and showy and prolonged dancing rituals. After the ball is over, the female seeks long grass or a field of cereals for her nest. The principal enemy to her hatchlings is the raven.

Other birds

The friendly little hoopoe is found searching the grass for insects all over Spain. If you walk extensively in Spain, you are likely to see its unmistakable fanned crest of black and pale gold, pinkish-brown plumage and barred black-and-white wings. The hoopoe's singularity and its seemingly playful ways give it a considerable charm.

Spain is rich in wild birds, particularly woodpeckers. A rare prize would be a glimpse of the swamp-dwelling purple gallinule. The lovely, egg-thieving azure-winged magpie of the Coto Doñana is also a notable character which, apart from Spain, inhabits only China and east Asia.

Another striking bird, the Spanish imperial heron, is the most exalted of its species, a dramatic figure with a black crest and long, graceful, boldly striped neck. It nests and breeds in colonies, hidden in beds of dense reeds. The question arises why this bird, *Ardea purpurea,* with its dark plumage, is "imperial" in Spain when elsewhere it is simply a purple heron. The answer may lie in subtleties of sheen or colouring, but the Spanish name seems appropriate – one that is very different, moreover, from the truly purple, red-legged, red-billed gallinule. Virtually all that the two have in common is that they are secretive dwellers of the wetlands.

Two other vastly different creatures inhabit the high Pyrenees: the bearded vulture with its 3-metre (9-ft) wingspan and the odd, mole-sized Desman, one of the rarest animals on earth. Related to the mole, the Desman is a sightless nocturnal rodent with a long, flattened, red-tipped snout, clawed front feet, large webbed hind feet and a rat-like tail.

Visually unappealing, rarely photographed – and unknown to science before the 19th-century – there's nothing like it in the animal kingdom. Peasants joke that "God's hand shook when He created the Desman". An aquatic mammal, it feeds on caddis, the larva of mayfly and stone flies, probing icy river beds with its sensitive proboscis. Water pollution has driven it ever higher into the mountains; for all its unwholesome appearance, the Desman can only survive in the purest water.

Vulture and toad

The bearded vulture (or lammergeyer) is in decline due in part to shooting by hunters and its unfortunate habit of eating poisoned meat

put down by shepherds for wolves. Its main diet is the remains of wild or domestic animals. As the garbage collectors of the mountains, the birds play a vital role in the scheme of nature.

Splendid gliders, bearded vultures will stay aloft for many hours, scanning the landscape in search of food. Carrion creatures though they are, the birds' flight silhouette is not unlike the falcon's. Lacking the long, bare neck that gives other vultures a repulsive image, the birds in flight are impressive and beautiful.

The bearded vulture supplements its food by a neat trick. Its wings extended – primaries outstretched like slim fingers – it will soar over

rocky ground strewn with bones left by predators. Swooping down, it picks up a bone, flies up, then drops it from a height so that the bone cracks, exposing a tasty morsel of marrow. Thus their Spanish name *quebrantahuesos*, or bone-breakers.

Travel slowly and you will see wild creatures virtually everywhere – including, near ponds, the strange little Spanish midwife toad, its eggs on its back. You are unlikely to see any of the few remaining Iberian wolves, mainly in the west, but you could be luckier with the striking Iberian Ibex in the Gredos mountains near Madrid and, in Galicia, the heathlands' wild horse, the Garrano. ❑

LEFT: Iberian ibex.
RIGHT: the friendly hoopoe with its distinctive fanned crest can be seen almost anywhere in Spain.

FLAMENCO

*A powerful artistic expression of the sorrows and joys of life, flamenco offers
a window on the soul of Andalusia – and touches our deepest emotions*

Jazz genius Miles Davis once said: "Sometimes, when I hear flamenco, I fall on my knees." Flamenco's synthesis of song, music and dance moves audiences the world over, yet its musical complexities and emotional depth are rarely understood. What is it that gives flamenco its enormous power and has made it the art-form so closely identified with Spain?

A music and a way of life

Although deeply rooted in southern Spanish folklore, flamenco is now a complex intertwined art form. Its song, music and dance have developed separately and responded together to changes in the world at large. In the past 40 years waves of emigration from southern to northern cities and the mushrooming of dance schools all over Spain have all left their mark. Yet for all its sophistication flamenco remains eminently popular. The majority of its artists and enthusiasts come from the poorer fringes of society, where life's experiences have taught them to be fiercely independent, proud and sceptical. Above all, they share a profound sense of suffering.

These are the powerful emotions that audiences feel expressed in flamenco, even if they cannot understand its lyrics. Sparing with words and rich in metaphor, the lyrics strike directly at the emotions. As anthropologist William Washabaugh put it, they share "a rustic poetic style that operates like a psychic key to open up floodgates of passion".

Ancient art, religious roots

Flamenco's roots lie in the distant past. The hedonistic Tartessans (4th–6th century BC), thought to have come from Africa, were famed for their music and primitive dance, and later, in Roman times, dancing girls from Cádiz were

shipped off to the imperial capital where they earned a reputation for rhythmic virtuosity and sensuality close on the lascivious. The Greeks contributed the oriental patterns of Byzantine liturgical chant forms.

The cultural mix of the centuries of Muslim rule also contributed. Fragments of Jewish reli-

gious song survive in the *saetas* sung during Holy Week processions, and 11th-century *andalusí* music shaped southern folk dances such as the *fandango, jarcha* and *zambra,* which provided flamenco's formal framework. *Ziriab*, a music that originated from the Damascan caliphate, may be the source of flamenco's use of repetition to build to a cathartic emotional climax. One Arabic account tells of a fish-seller driven to such ecstatic frenzy by Ziriab that he ripped open his shirt, just as Gypsy audiences once did in moments of uncontrollable emotion.

After the Reconquest of Spain was completed with the fall of Granada in 1492, the

LEFT: even at its most flamboyant, the essence of flamenco is sorrow and loss.
RIGHT: Doré etching of the Gypsy camps at Sacromonte, Granada.

plaintive oriental sounds of Gregorian plain-song – derived from Visigothic Byzantine chants – filtered right through the Spanish folk tradition. The singer Enrique el Mellizo created one flamenco song-style after sitting outside Málaga cathedral and listening to the monks singing Mass.

Gypsy song

Professional musicians long before their arrival in Spain in the 15th century, the Gypsies (*see page 75*) were vital catalysts in the creation of flamenco. It was born – alongside bullfighting and banditry – in the rich hybrid culture of the

and Seville. A few, like Giacomo Casanova, noted it in their diaries, leaving some of the first written evidence of flamenco's existence.

In search of black sounds

Song remains flamenco's essential form of expression. Its voices are dark and wailing, hoarse and deep, capturing the pain at the heart of flamenco. When flamenco is good, it is said to pinch the listener. The singers, or *cantaores,* shift from a gravelly whisper to an intense musical shout and slide from top to bottom notes within a few seconds in search of what the singer Manuel Torres once called "black

semi-nomadic frontier world they shared with converted Muslims and those who had been left landless by the Reconquest. The word flamenco may have its roots in the Arabic *felag-mengu*, meaning wandering peasant.

As the Gypsies learned southern folksong, they added complex rhythms, expressive vocals and, above all, their innate sense of suffering. At *ferias*, cattle fairs and horse markets, they sang for money, using the lyrics of Castilian Renaissance romances, or narrative verse epics.

In the 18th century, flamenco also took root in southern towns as Gypsies' persecution became less acute. From the 1760s travellers began to chance upon flamenco in Cádiz, Jerez

MAJOR FLAMENCO FESTIVALS

Festival de Madrid (Feb): themed performances, theatre spaces.Ciclo del Centro Cultural de la Villa de Madrid (Feb–Mar): mixed performances in theatre space. Certamen Nacional de Córdoba (May): biennial national contest plus other performances. Festival Nacional del Cante de las Minas, La Union, Murcia (Aug): contest showcasing young singing talent plus performances by leading artists. Bienal de Sevilla (Aug–Sep): high quality flamenco in concert halls etc. Fiesta de la Buleria de Jerez (Sep): weekend of Jerez flamenco held in the bullring; large crowds. Apart from these major events, there are open-air festivals all summer in Andalusia.

sounds". But brilliant effect remains secondary to the singers' courage in pushing their voices and emotions to the limits.

Behind this uninhibited emotional power is a strict underlying musical discipline: a canon of more than 50 song-styles (*palos*), each defined by a different rhythmic pattern (*compás*) and mood. Each style is further subdivided into as many as 30 different variants. Mastery of these is the base from which all flamenco artists work, and a basic understanding is important for the audience, whose "*Olés*" give a live show its two-way electricity. Often, in live performances, each piece is introduced by its song-style.

Two early song-styles with Gypsy roots remain fundamental today. One is the *seguiriya*, the most tragic style of *cante jondo*, or deep song, which expresses anguish in the face of despair. Its rhythmic pattern illustrates flamenco's complexity: each line of its four-line stanzas has seven syllables, except for the third, which has 11, and on to this is grafted a 12-bar rhythm, with the emphasis on the off-beat.

The second early song-style that is still widely performed today, the *soleá*, has generated more variants than any other. It explores themes from the everyday to the dramatic, filtering them through the wisdom and irony of experience.

A third group of song-styles, *tonas* from the forge and prison, are a surviving example of old flamenco song stripped back to its essential form of the naked voice.

Dancing out emotions

Flamenco dance also emerged as a fusion of earlier forms, among them folk dances and courtly boleros. It was always marked out by its sensuality. "The fandango is an excitation to lust when danced by Gypsies," noted the minutes of Cádiz council in 1761. By 1800 it had found its way from the Gypsy quarters of Cádiz, Seville and Granada via taverns and variety theatres to dance academies.

The physical tension between discipline and freedom of movement, which so powerfully

> **LOST AND FOUND**
>
> During the 1950s, romance lyrics that had been lost for centuries were rediscovered in a few Gypsy families who had handed them down by word of mouth.

evokes a sense of caged desire, can still be strongly felt today. The dancers, or *bailaores*, do not follow any choreography or story-line. Instead, anchored by the rhythmic pattern of each song-style, they dance out their emotions. Beauty of form is less important than expression of feeling, which can produce lightning switches from moments of contained inner absorption to unleashed energy in flamenco's furious rhythmic stamping called *zapateo*.

Flamenco dance has always flirted with other

forms, thereby producing hybrid theatrical versions. Operas staged in bullrings at the turn of the century, and Antonio Gadés' films, made in the 1980s, of *Carmen* and *Blood Wedding* as well as Joaquín Cortés' dance shows today all fall within that tradition.

The cafés cantantes

From 1850 onwards flamenco found its way to wider paying audiences via *cafés cantantes*, singing cafés with small stages.

It was in the *cafés cantantes* that performances took their present-day form, with each artist coming forward at various points for solos. Here, too, the guitar finally emerged as an ele-

---

LEFT: *cante*, or song, is the heart of flamenco. Singers push their voices and emotions to the limits.
RIGHT: Paco de Lucia, top flamenco guitarist.

ment in its own right. A hybrid of two earlier stringed instruments – one Arab and the other Christian, the first plucked and the second strummed – it was initially used as basic accompaniment to dance and song. But simple early technique quickly gave way to more intricate tremolos and arpeggios as well as varied personal interpretations.

However, virtuosity is second in importance to depth of feeling. The strong rhythmic base-line, warmth of tone and vast array of chords used give flamenco guitar its particular human quality. Listening to recordings by some of the great concert guitarists of different generations – Paco

Into the modern age

Flamenco's fortunes have fluctuated since the decline of the *cafés cantantes* at the beginning of the century, but today its audience is wider than ever. Despite being passed over by the record industry, radio play lists and government cultural policy, it has shown remarkable resilience and vitality.

In the 1920s, when intellectuals such as poet Federico García Lorca believed flamenco was a dying art form, the myth grew up that only unpaid flamenco was authentic. But in fact, ever since the early cattle fairs, flamenco's paid artists have also been its creative innovators.

el de Lucena, Javier Molina, Ramón Montoya, Niño Montoya, Sabicas and Paco de Lucía, to name but a few – it is extraordinary to think that none of them could read sheet music.

Songs of life

As Gypsy and Andalusian folk singers performed alongside one another in the *cafés cantantes*, the crossover of styles gave rise to new song-forms which remain the base of flamenco's repertoire. Thus the range widened to include the *fandango* and all its variants, *malagueñas, granainas,* and the mining songs which sprung up at the end of the century.

SO MANY SONG STYLES

The *cantiñas* of Cadiz province – including *alegrías, romeras, caracoles* – grew around the Aragonese *jota* brought south by troops during the Napoleonic war of independence. *De ida y vuelta* (literally, round-trip) are folk songs taken to Latin America, brought back with new influences then flamencoised. Some song-styles focus on working life: *livianas* and *serranas* reflect the preoccupations of peasant life in the Andalusian sierras; *cantes mineros* – including *tarantos, tarantas* and *mineras* – stem from eastern Andalusia's mining communities in the late 1800s. Two other song forms, *tangos* and *bulerías,* are closely linked to the fiestas.

So, for example, in new dance forms like the *seguiriya, martinete* or *rondeña* invented by individual dancers such as Antonio. Another important influence was Carmen Amaya (1913–63), whose footwork revolutionised both men's and women's dance. Fortunately she was captured on film in *Los Tarantos* (1962), a Gypsy version of *Romeo and Juliet.* Today's key younger figures divide into two distinct groups: those who have moved back to flamenco from a classical training – like Joaquín Cortés or Antonio Canales – and others, such as Joaquín Grilo or Eva La Yierbabuena, who are stretching the boundaries of flamenco from within.

> **THRILLING FINALE**
>
> Skilled performers can graft *bulerías*, flamenco's liveliest and most vibrant form, on to any other song-style: you will often see them in the *fin de fiesta*.

Each generation has also produced great voices. Antonio Mairena and Fosforito marked the revival of unadorned Gypsy and *payo* (non-Gypsy) styles in the 1950s, and in the following generation Camarón de la Isla took *cante jondo* to a far wider Spanish and international audience than ever before. His early death in 1992, aged 42, casts a huge shadow over flamenco today. Although there are widely admired singers of great technical breadth and creativity – among them Enrique Morente, El Lebrijano, José Mercé, Carmen Linares and Mayte Martín – none has acquired his status as an idol.

This is also considered a golden age for guitar. Paco de Lucía, who accompanied Camarón de la Isla, remains a towering influence, through developing fusion styles which command the respect of the flamenco community (most do not). He also introduced the *cajón* – or percussion box – after a trip to Peru, and it has now been generally absorbed into flamenco.

A flamenco evening

Live flamenco today has been shaped not only by the artists but also by its new performance spaces. In the south, there are open-air festivals throughout the summer in Andalusian town plazas, bullrings and stadiums, while the autumn Seville biennial is regarded as a showcase of the best quality flamenco. But however artistically brilliant flamenco may be when per-

formed in a theatre or concert hall, it often loses its essentially improvisational spirit.

In this sense flamenco is at its best in intimate spaces in late night-sessions. In Andalusia there are still several hundred *peñas,* or membership clubs, where you may be allowed in as a paying guest. Members get up to sing among friends; and there is a complete rapport between the artist and audience. Then there are the *tablaos,* which range from tourist traps to reliable if expensive venues.

In Madrid, now generally considered to be flamenco's capital, you can find flamenco all year round. The city was the birthplace of *nuevo flamenco* – a bouncy wall of sound mixed in with salsa and rumba. Meanwhile Barcelona has produced some exceptionally gifted pure flamenco artists. Even in Jerez, the bastion of pure flamenco, young artists today experiment with every kind of fusion from rap and African to oriental music.

Yet the essence of flamenco as a vehicle for our deepest emotions has not changed. One thing is certain: as long as there is love and despair, innocence and loss, injustice and the search for freedom, there will be flamenco. ❑

LEFT: art in action.
RIGHT: regularly scheduled flamenco shows have somewhat changed the nature of this spontaneous musical form.

FOOD

Enriched by Roman and Moorish influences and discoveries from the New World,
the regional diversity of Spain's food tantalises the tastebuds

Spain is the last large European country in which cuisine *really* varies from province to province," wrote the French historian Jean-Francois Revel in 1982. Travellers in Spain today will quickly see what he means. The choice in municipal markets, cake-shops, pork-butchers and even lorry-drivers' cafes varies not only between regions but also between neighbouring towns and villages. And even within the same town each restaurant or *tapas* bar has its own specialities.

A jigsaw of cuisines

Spaniards talk proudly of their regional cuisine. But in reality the map is a far more complicated jigsaw. Along the coast the cooking of each region or province splits between *montaña y mar*, or mountain and sea. Inland there are similar divides between the mountains, river valleys and plains – and all of these are criss-crossed by another map of the traditional shepherds', muleteers'and harvesters' routes along which dishes like *gazpachos* (game stews with flatbread) and *ajo-arrieros* (braised salt-cod) can be found. Finally there are a few areas, such as the Empordá in Catalonia, El Bierzo in Castile Leon or the Maestrazgo in the Levante, and cities such as Segovia, Cuenca or San Sebastián (Donostia) which have nurtured their local cooking into a gastronomy.

Today these local flavours are found not only in the seasonal set menus served in *casas de comida* (eating houses), *tascas* (taverns) and *ventas* (roadside inns), but also in Spain's top restaurants. Basque chefs led the way in the 1970s with *nueva cocina* and today a brilliant younger generation of chefs around the country such as Ferran Adriá of El Bulli (Girona) and Martín Berasategui (Guipuzkoa), who won the 1989 Grand Prix as the world's most promising young chef, have kept a firm sense of their roots alongside dazzling creativity.

LEFT: leading chef Iñaki Izaguirre.
RIGHT: traditional *churros*, delicious strips of fried dough, often served with chocolate.

For all the variety of Iberian cuisine, it has a certain character which sets it apart. Surprisingly perhaps, the influence of French cooking is hardly felt, as the author Alexander Dumas noted in the 1840s. Instead, Moorish and New World flavours are close to the surface, and underlying Roman influences are still present.

Moorish and New World flavours

The impact of the Muslim centuries is most apparent in a crescent swinging south through Valencia, Murcia and Andalusia. Here you will find honey and almond pastries, cumin and aniseed spiced breads, and a vast family of rice dishes and cooling sherbets (*granizadas*).

On the other hand, the vegetables which arrived in Europe as seeds brought back by Columbus, conquistadors and missionaries are staples everywhere. Kidney beans (*alubias*) and potatoes (*patatas*) appear in regional *cocidos* (one-pot stews) while tomatoes and sweet peppers, as well as *pimentón* (paprika) from the peppers, have splashed their fiery red right across Spanish cooking. In the Canary Islands, a stop-off point between Europe and the New World, try *papas arrugadas* – barbecue-grilled potatoes with red *mojo,* a thick dipping sauce.

Roman legacies

Bread, olive oil and wine have accompanied meals since Roman times. The quality and range of both Spanish olive oil and wine have improved in the past 20 years and it is worth trying the lesser known wine denominations which are hard to find abroad: Galicia's white Albariño, or reds from Priorato, the Ribera del Duero, Toro, Somontano and Jumilla.

culture and identity; the table is a gathering place, whether at home, in male gastronomic societies, at grills (*asadores*), restaurants, cooking competitions or open-air communal meals during fiestas.

Fish cookery is superb here, and there are clusters of Michelin-starred restaurants in San Sebastián (Donostia) and Bilbao (Viscaya). In fact, such is the reputation of Basque chefs that you will find them running the kitchens of top restaurants throughout the whole of Spain.

Further west, Asturia has sturdy country dishes like bean stew (*fabada*), caramelised rice pudding (*arroz con leche*), more than 20 farm-

Fish has also been a staple since Roman times, but often in salted and dried form. Today, Spaniards are prepared to pay for the freshest fish, and lorries rush from the ports to supply markets across the country within hours of the catches being landed. Madrid has the world's second largest wholesale fish market and many Spaniards say there is no better place to eat fish as its wholesalers and restaurants claim the very best from the Atlantic and Mediterranean ports.

Around the regions

It is often said that in the north of Spain you live to eat rather than eat to live. For the Basques food and cooking are a fundamental part of their

house cheeses and dry cider. Galician cooking has cleaner flavours with excellent beef and a wealth of fish and shellfish, sturdy *empanadas* (flat pies), *lacón con grelos* (boiled ham with turnip greens) and paprika-laced dishes.

The inland cuisines of the Rioja, Navarre and Aragon share the produce of the fertile Ebro valley: peaches and pears preserved in red wine, spring vegetables braised in *menestras,* and sweet and spicy red peppers, which, along with tomatoes, are key ingredients of *chilindrón* – lamb, poultry or game stew. Red peppers also go into *patatas a la Riojana*, a potato stew, which the French chef Paul Bocuse pronounced a work of art.

Meseta and the Mediterranean

Further south the dishes of the central *meseta* – wood-roast meat such as baby milk-fed lamb (*cordero lechal*), messy dishes of tripe (*callos*), sheep's milk Manchego cheese and wonderful garlic soups (*sopas de ajo*) – have a decidedly medieval air, while those of the Mediterranean seem distinctly contemporary. Sun-drenched salads, roasted vegetables (*escalivada*), fish baked in salt or turned into soups make for delicious healthy eating.

Catalan cooking has a literary tradition dating from the 14th century. Classics include *romesco* (almond and pepper sauce) served with fish or grilled spring onions, *zarzuela* (seafood stew) and *escudella* (pot-au-feu). Each of the Balearic Islands has its own specialities: Menorca is known for its lobster and Mallorca for its spiral *ensaimada* pastries.

Valencians are justifiably famous as consummate rice cooks. What we think of as *paella* is a kind of synthesised technicolour version of the hundreds of rice dishes on menus in this area – some cooked until dry in the wide flat paella dishes, and others left wet and soupy in earthenware casseroles. Valencians are also great makers of ice-cream and sherberts (*granizada*): the most original of these is *horchata*, a sublime tiger-nut milk.

Andalusia, often much maligned for its food, also has classics. Its chilled *gazpacho* soups come every which way; the original version is not tomato-based, but a refreshing white almond soup (*ajo blanco*). This is the home of *pescaito frito* (mixed dry-fried fish), hams and *potajes* or bean stews. In the sierras you may be lucky enough to find one of the old country dishes which tell of a poorer past: *migas*, made from fried breadcrumbs or flour spiced up with bits of meat, fish or fruit, garlic and herbs. Andalusia and neighbouring Extremadura are also the principal producers of *jamón ibérico,* cured ham made from black-hooved pigs which graze free-range on acorns and chestnuts.

Wherever you go there are plenty of edible souvenirs: dried peppers, farmhouse cheeses, crimson saffron, convent sweets, a huge range of honeys and finally – strictly for the dedicated gourmet who does not mind a heavy suitcase – whole cured hams.

TRADITIONAL CURES

Native black-hooved pigs produce Spain's superb but expensive *jamon iberico,* known as the king of hams. Other cured hams, made from white pigs, are called *jamón serrano.*

Terrific tapas

Tapas, small snacks that are served with drinks in bars, have come a long way from their simple Andalusian origins as a mouthful of cured ham or cheese on a saucer used as a lid to keep the dust off a glass of wine. These days every region, town and bar has its own *tapas*

and the selection of dishes can stretch the length of the bar. Wherever you are, though, the basic rules are the same.

To *tapear* in the Spanish style you keep moving from one bar to the next, picking up just a couple of *tapas* in each place. There are three portion sizes – a *pincho* (bitesize), *tapa* (snack) and *ración* (plateful) – and a fork will come for each person to graze from the same dish. You can order one *tapa* at a time – in some places, such as San Sebastián, you help yourself from the bar, but you never pay until the end. And finally, if you want to merge with the natives, chuck your olive stones, napkins and toothpicks on the floor. ❏

LEFT: Basque specialities at the Zalacain, a leading Madrid restaurant.
RIGHT: *tapas* bars allow you to sample many dishes.

A YEAR-LONG ROUND OF FIESTAS

Spain celebrates the great feast days of the Catholic Church and other special days of the year with an unbridled intensity and passion

Even the tiniest village in Spain downs tools for at least one fiesta a year in honour of its patron saint. Whether it is a day of communal pilgrimage (*romería*) to a local shrine or a week of parades, a fiesta always offers the populace a chance to dress up in costume, dance through the night, let off firecrackers or run with bulls. Some celebrations are an excuse for fun while others are solemn acts of worship or preserve pagan fertility rites, albeit overlaid with Christian symbolism.

BAROQUE EXCESS

The most bizzare rituals have a distinctly medieval flavour but many Spanish fiestas are pure baroque in their excess and ostentation. The greatest number of celebrations take place at Epiphany (the arrival of the Three Kings on 6 January); at Carnival (in February or March); during Easter Week (March or April); on the first few days of May; at Whitsun and Corpus Christi (both in either May or June); on Midsummer Eve (also called St John's Night (23–24 June) and around the feast of the Assumption (15 August).

The picture at the top of this column shows a scene from mainland Spain's biggest carnival, held in Cádiz. It is characterised by flamboyantly dressed groups of revellers who wander the streets singing satirical songs.

◁ **CARNIVAL CAPERS**
The days before Lent are a time for licentious behaviour, above all for dressing up in outrageous masks

△ **THE *FALLAS***
Hundreds of papier-mâché monuments (*fallas*) are filled with fireworks and set alight at midnight in Valencia on 19 March.

◁ **HOLY WEEK**
Processions of hooded penitents can be seen in towns and cities all over Spain during the week leading up to Easter Sunday.

△ **EASTER RITES**
Barefoot *picaos* beat themselves on the back on Holy Thursday and Good Friday in San Vicente de la Sonsierra (La Rioja).

SEVILLE'S FAMOUS FERIA

Seville's springtime fair may have started off on the 19th century as a gathering of farmers and businessmen but it has since evolved into a gigantic party with no purpose other than pleasure. For six days and nights the purpose-built fairground, made up of over 1000 *casetas* (booths – most of them private), reverberates to the sound of Seville's own brand of flamenco music, the *sevillana*. Both men and women dress to the nines for the occasion – the latter in stunning flamenco-style dresses – and parade up and down on horseback or seated in carriages. Bullfights in Seville's Plaza de la Maestranza are also an essential ingredient of the occasion. The other major cities of Andalucía have their own, smaller but similar fairs.

△ **DRUM CHORUS**
The incessant beat of masses of drums creates a solemn mood on Good Friday in the towns of the province of Teruel.

▽ **MAY IN MADRID**
Events during the capital's main fiesta, around 15 May, in honour of St Isidore (San Isidro), range from folk dancing to rock concerts.

△ **HUMAN TOWERS**
Southern Catalonia is the home of teams of *castellers*, who compete to build their daring structures as high as possible.

▷ **FLAMENCO FINERY**
The summer fairs in southern Spain's towns are an opportunity for women to wear the typical Andalucían dresses.

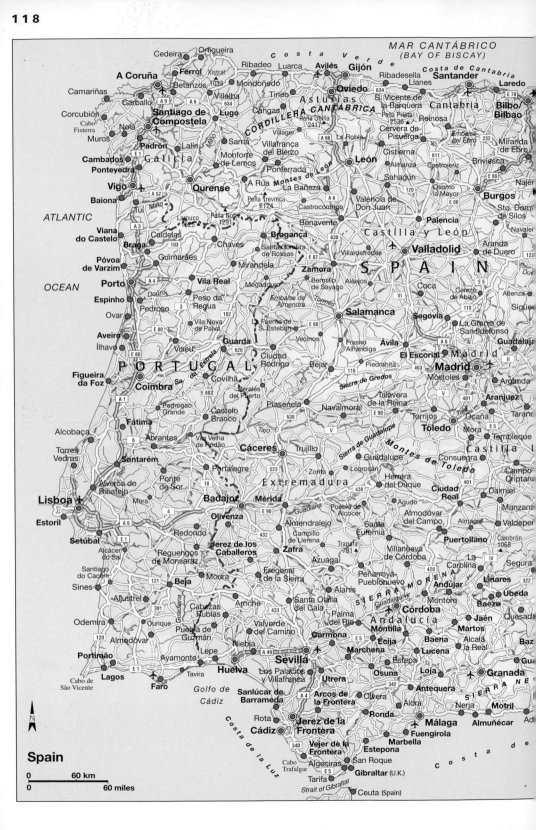

Spain

0   60 km

0   60 miles

Mont-de-Marsan
Jegun
Graulhet
Bédarieux
Dax
Aire
s-l'Adour
Auch
Toulouse
Mazamet
Montpellier
Biarritz
Cappbreton
Orthez
Masseube
Beziers
Donostia/
n Sebastián
A 64
Salies-
de-Béarn
Tarbes
Carcassonne
Narbonne
ais
asco
uskadi
Cambo-
les-Bains
933
Lourdes
St. Gaudens
Foix
Quillan
Port-Barcarès
Cauterets
St. Lary-
Soulan
Bagnères-
de-Luchon
Tarascon
Estagel
Perpignan
Iruña/
Pamplona
Jaca
Vielha
ANDORRA
Font-
Romeu
Port-Vendres
asteiz/
itoria
Navarra
240
138
Benasque
Andorra
la Vella
Roses
Logroño
Sos del Rey
Católico
Sabiñánigo
Campo
230
Ripoll
Figueres
Olot
L'Escala
ioja
Tafalla
Eja de los
Caballeros
Huesca
Graus
Berga
Girona
Torroella
de Montgrí
ebolera
142
Tudela
Barbastro
Tremp
Vic
Palamós
Soria
Tarazona
Monzón
Cataluña
Sant Feliu de Guíxols
Almazán
A 68
Aragón
240
Lleida
Manresa
Terrassa
Blanes
Lloret de Mar
Ciria
Zaragoza
Fraga
Igualada
Sabadell
Calatayud
330
Herrera
1346
Barcelona
Daroca
Gaspe
Flix
Mora la
Nova
Sitges
Reus
L'Hospitalet
de Llobregat
aranchón
211
Retuena
1491
Alcañiz
L'Espina
1182
Cambrils
de Mar
Tarragona
aorejas
Monreal
del Campo
234
Calanda
E 15
Tortosa
Mar de
astilla
S. Alta
1856
Palomera
1498
Cañada de
Benatanduz
Vinaròs
Costa Daurada
Mogorrit
1862
Jávalón
1605
Teruel
Benicarló
Peñíscola
Islas Baleares
Menorca
Ciutadella
Cuenca
Collado Bajo
1833
234
Javalambre
2020
A 7
Pollença
Maó/
Mahón
Entredichos
1062
Cuerda
1401
Onda
Benicàssim
Port de
Sóller
Inca
320
Javalambre
2020
Segorbe
Castelló
de la Plana
Mallorca
Mancha
111
Valenciana
Liria
Golfo de
Sagunt/
Sagunto
Palma de
Mallorca
Manacor
Embalse
de Alarcón
A 3
Valencia
Campos
Villanueva
de la Jara
322
Requena
Valencia
La Roda
Júcar
Almira
Ibiza
301
Albacete
Xàtiva/
Jàtiva
Gandia
S. Antoni
Eivissa
322
Almansa
Xàbia/
Jávea
430
Pozo
Cañada
Villena
E 15
Formentera
Alcaraz
Losa
1038
Tobarra
Benidorm
Altea
412
Hellín
Elda
La Vila Joiosa/
Villajoyosa
Elx/
Elche
Alacant/
Alicante
Cieza
Segura
Caravaca
de la Cruz
Mula
Orihuela
M E D I T E R R A N E A N
S E A
uéscar
Vélez
Blanco
Murcia
301
San Javier
Totana
Lorca
Cartagena
Cúllar
Baza
E 15
Águilas
Albox
Cuevas del
Almanzora
344
Mojácar
Almería
s o l

PLACES

A detailed guide to the entire country, with principal sites clearly cross-referenced by number to the maps

The territory covered by Spain's 50 provinces is vast and breath-takingly mountainous. It is a land of illusions: in the clear, bright air the windmills on the horizon seem close enough to touch, and nearly every journey is longer than it appears on a map.

This following section of the book divides Spain into its four main climatic zones, beginning with the central plateau, or *meseta*. At its heart is Madrid, home to the Prado Museum and the opulent Royal Palace. Toledo and El Escorial, both near the capital, offer insights into Iberia's mixed cultural past and the stern Catholicism that fuelled its empire. Extremadura, the *meseta* region running southwest to Portugal, is an arid, hilly country which has traditionally bred con-quistadors and brave fighting bulls. Less known in this area are the intact medieval towns, windswept and stork-filled in their isolation.

The second zone is Andalusia, the Spanish South. This is the sunny Spain of legend and travel brochures, with its Moorish architecture and passion for flamenco. In addition to the three great cities of Seville, Córdoba, and Granada, Andalusia is sprinkled with lovely white villages. Another Andalusian highlight is the Coto Doñana, a wildlife refuge for migrating birds.

In the Levant, the zone along the Mediterranean coast, the weather is mild and humid and the soil, deposited by mountain runoffs, is the most fertile in Spain. For more than 1,000 years, the city of Valen-cia has been prospering from agriculture made possible by Moorish irrigation. North of Valencia are the spectacular coastlines called the Costa Daurada and the Costa Brava. Between them lies Barcelona, the capital of Catalonia which itself offers trout fishing, hiking and skiing in the Pyrenees.

Finally, the Spanish North is the most geographically and cultur-ally varied part of the country. Navarre and Aragón offer rugged alpine vistas, Romanesque churches and the splendid festivities of San Fermín and El Pilar. The Basque Country, with its lush hills and gentle coast, is Spain's gastronomic paradise and home to a blue-eyed people with a prehistoric past. Cantabria's wide beaches draw well-heeled holiday-makers from Madrid, while Galicia remains somewhat hidden behind her mist-shrouded mountains. ❑

PRECEDING PAGES: Castilian plain; Arcos de la Frontera; an Andalusian village, dominated by its church. **LEFT:** Festival of San Fermin, Pamplona.

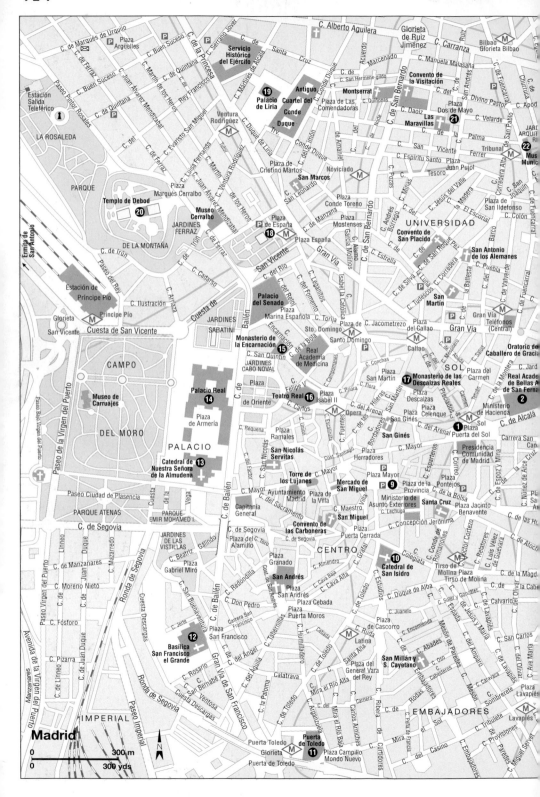

Madrid

0 _____ 300 m
0 _____ 300 yds

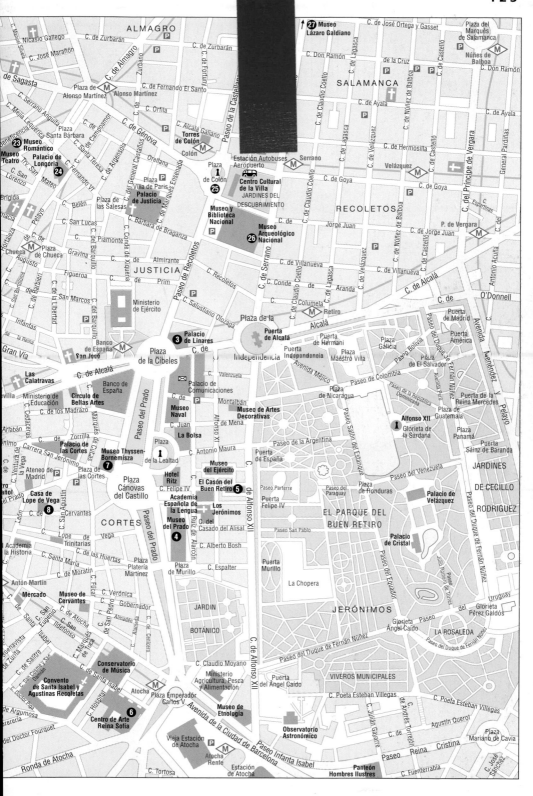

MADRID

The charm of the old quarters, the exquisite blue of the skies, the colour of the street life and the vibrance of the long, long night: these are a few of the attractions of Spain's capital

Map on pages 124–5

Think of Paris or Rome, and familiar images spring to mind. But Madrid is more elusive, and a city which takes getting to know. With so many other destinations in Spain to lure the holidaymaker, it may well be Europe's most undervalued capital. In the past few years, democracy has brought a new dynamism to the capital which was created on the caprice of a king in 1561, and the landmark year of 1992 added further attractions.

The city's evolution

Sixteenth-century Madrid was a placid farming community within sight of the **Sierra de Guadarrama**. The high terrain with its clear, dry air and the dense surrounding forests had once attracted the Moors, who built a fort called *Magerit* on a rise over the **Río Manzanares**. It was captured by the Christians in 1083, but the two religions coexisted in relative tranquillity, remote from the politics and fervour of other Castilian cities.

When Felipe II proclaimed Madrid the capital, reluctant courtiers speculated that it was simply because the town was convenient to his royal palace at El Escorial. Nevertheless, noble houses, convents and monasteries were hastily assembled in order to be near the new circles of influence. As the city grew, uncontrolled cutting of forests for construction led to erosion, drought and an increase in temperature.

After the Habsburgs, the Bourbons were horrified by the state of the 18th-century capital. The streets were filthy and crime-ridden; the housing squalid; the churches gave no sign of the artistic treasures within. The Bourbons set about putting that right.

Civic improvements weren't always received gratefully by *madrileños*. Carlos III believed that the long capes and broad-brimmed hats worn by Spaniards were conducive to Madrid's many cloak-and-dagger incidents, but his decree that citizens wear European short capes and tricorner hats caused a mutiny ending in bloodshed. Joseph Bonaparte initiated a programme of trees and open spaces, but he had been brought to power by a revolutionary invasion, and his beautification efforts earned him the nickname of "*Rey Plazuelas*" – the Courtyard King.

By the turn of this century, imposing bank buildings along the **Calle de Alcalá** marked the capital's growing financial power. Sweeping boulevards and monumental fountains had given Madrid a truly majestic appearance, yet she couldn't quite shake off her cow-town reputation. Basque novelist Pío Baroja called Madrid "an overgrown village of La Mancha".

Officially, this city of almost 4 million inhabitants is still called by its Habsburg title of "Village and Court", and in spite of Madrid's avant-garde arts scene

PRECEDING PAGES: view of Madrid from atop the Hotel Plaza. **LEFT:** Don Quixote and Sancho Panza in the Plaza de España. **BELOW:** the Retiro park as studio.

TIP

The midday sun can be intense, so it's a good idea to retreat indoors at 2pm for lunch and a nap, as the Spanish do. The lovely long *tarde* – strolling, café-sitting and people-watching – starts at 5.30 in the evening and lasts until around 10pm.

BELOW:
the neoclassical
Puerta de Alcalá.

and sophisticated nightlife, many regard it still as a mass of villages. *Madrileños* are known for being open and unaffected, and those very traits have eased the city's rapid political and cultural transformation.

On top of the world

At 600 metres (2,000 ft) above sea level, Madrid is the highest capital in Europe. Pollution from the city's 2 million vehicles and the continuing use of heating oil have made the air rather less champagne-like than it was said to have been in the 19th century, when European princesses often came to Madrid to give birth, but on a clear day the Sierra de Guadarrama seems within walking distance.

The heart of it all is the **Puerta del Sol ❶**, an oval plaza surrounded on all sides by cream-coloured 18th-century buildings. It's Spain's Kilometre 0 and the centre of most metro and bus lines; the bronze bear statue in the middle is the city's most obvious spot for a rendezvous. At midnight on New Year's Eve *madrileños* gather here to eat the traditional 12 grapes, washed down with plenty of fermented grape juice, in time to the striking of the clock.

Less festive public gatherings in the Puerta del Sol included a bloody battle with Napoleon's Egyptian forces, depicted in Goya's *Charge of the Mamelukes*, and an 1830 uprising against Madrid's friars, rumoured to have poisoned the city water supply. The Second Republic was declared here in 1931, and in the 1980s the Puerta del Sol was the centre of demonstrations against NATO; in 1997 more than 1 million *madrileños* gathered here to protest against terrorism.

Feeding into the Puerta del Sol from the north is **Calle de Preciados**, where you'll find lots of shops, including Madrid's largest department store, **El Corte Inglés**, which stays open all day.

Following the Calle de Alcalá to the northeast, you'll pass the **Real Academia de Bellas Artes de San Fernando ❷** (open daily; closed Sat–Mon pm; entrance fee). It houses paintings by artists of the Spanish School, including Goya's *Burial of the Sardine*, a portrayal of a mock-tragic funeral for a fish which takes place in Madrid on Ash Wednesday.

Alcalá intersects the **Paseo del Prado** at the spacious Plaza de la Cibeles, graced by a fountain dedicated to the goddess Cybeline. The white building opposite resembling a wedding cake is the **Palacio de Comunicaciones**, also known as Correos (the central post office). Facing it on the northeast corner of the plaza is the aristocratic **Palacio de Linares ❸** (open Tues, Thur, Fri 9.30–11.30am, Sat and Sun 10am –1.30pm; entrance fee). Neglected for years, this was restored for 1992 and now houses a centre for Latin American culture. Guided tours, some in English, reveal its fantastic 1870s interiors, the walls groaning with gold leaf, silk and marble. There are murals in the grand manner, lowering mirrors and burgeoning chandeliers. Further along Alcalá is the **Puerta de Alcalá**, built as a triumphal archway for Carlos III in 1778.

Madrid's art treasures

The **Pasco del Prado**, the southern stretch of the Castellana boulevard, has become home to a "Golden Triangle" of art collections. But of the three, the **Museo del Prado ❹** (open Tues–Sat 9am–7pm, Sun 9am –2pm; entrance fee) remains in a class of its own. If it were Madrid's sole attraction, it would still be worth the trip. Ironically, it was Joseph Bonaparte who put forth a plan to make Spanish works of art available to the Spanish public. Fernando VII completed the project. In 1819 the collection was opened in a building originally designed

Map on pages 124–5

The Infanta Margarita in Velázquez' "Las Meninas".

BELOW: looking up at Velázquez' statue outside the Museo del Prado.

TIP

Entry to the Prado and
Reina Sofía is free on
Saturday afternoons
and Sundays.

to hold a natural science museum. As notions of what public morals could bear became more enlightened, pictures such as Titian's *Venus* and Rubens' *Three Graces* were unveiled. Today the museum owns more than 7,500 paintings, less than a sixth of which are on permanent display there.

Head for the upper floor first to see the 17th- and 18th-century Spanish masters. Diego Velázquez (1599–1660), the greatest of Spain's Golden Age artists, produced outstanding royal portraits, notably *Las Meninas* (1656), depicting the Infanta Margarita among her courtiers but also including a Velázquez self-portrait. Also on the first floor are paintings by El Greco (1541–1614) and Francisco de Goya (1746–1828), noted for his brilliantly unflattering portraits of Carlos IV and his family. Also not to be missed on the first floor is the extensive collection of Italian paintings, with works by most of the great Italian masters. The ground floor, which includes Goya's "black" paintings, carried out towards the end of his life, has Flemish, Dutch and German masterpieces and earlier Spanish works. Don't miss the roomful of paintings by Hieronymus Bosch. Entry to the Prado includes a visit to the museum's annexe, **El Casón del Buen Retiro ❺**, which houses the collection's 19th-century works.

The Casón was for years the home of *Guernica*, Picasso's disturbing allegory of the bombing of the Basque town of that name during the Spanish Civil War. But in 1992, amid fierce controversy, the painting was moved to Madrid's new showcase for modern art, the **Centro de Arte Reina Sofía ❻** (open Wed–Sat 10am–9pm, Sun 10am–2.30pm; entrance fee), on Calle de Santa Isabel just off the Paseo del Prado at its southern tip. Controversy has dogged the Reina Sofía since its opening in 1986. Satirically referred to as "El Sofidú" in allusion to the Pompidou Centre in Paris, it has undergone seemingly endless

BELOW: emulating a master's strokes in the Prado.

renovations. The gallery is housed in the 18th-century former General Hospital of Madrid, its formidable exterior jazzed up by futuristic transparent lifts.

But perhaps controversy is appropriate to a setting for innovators like Picasso, Dalí, Miró and Juan Gris. There is a room devoted to each of these artists on the second floor, while *Guernica*'s enormous canvas, surrounded by Picasso's many preparatory sketches, has a room to itself. The Reina Sofía has a lively programme of temporary exhibitions on the second floor. Also worth a stop are the café and gift shop on the ground floor.

The Thyssen trove

The collection of art at the **Museo Thyssen-Bornemisza ❼** (open Tues–Sun 10am–7pm; entrance fee) came to Spain in 1993, amid hot competition from other countries, for an initial period only. But now it will be staying for good, its treasures on view in the Palacio de Villahermosa, almost across the road from the Prado. The lion's share of the art collection of Baron Hans Heinrich Thyssen-Bornemisza, reckoned the greatest in private hands after that of Britain's Queen Elizabeth, was bought by the Spanish state for 44,100 million pesetas (£230 million/US$375 million). The collection, spanning the centuries from 1290 to the 1980s, is notable for its 17th-century Dutch Old Masters; 19th-century North American paintings; 20th-century Russian Constructivists and German Expressionists.

Sunday in the park

Originally, **El Parque del Buen Retiro** was conceived as a park where the Spanish nobility could retire from the unpleasantness of the 17th-century Madrid streets. Inside the wrought-iron gates, garden parties reached lascivious heights

Map on pages 124–5

*For a refreshing antidote to Madrid's art treasures, the **Museo del Ejército** (Army museum) and **Museo de Artes Decorativas**, both just a short stroll from the Prado, offer a taste of the city's past glory (both open Tues–Sun; entrance fees).*

BELOW: boating in El Parque del Buen Retiro.

during the reign of Felipe IV. Fountains, statues and the delicate **Palacio de Cristal** (open Tues–Sun; entrance fee) still give the Retiro the air of a royal garden. Joggers and roller skaters are now a part of the landscape, but for most *madrileños*, a day in the park is a dress-up affair, from dapper old gentlemen in black suits to little girls scuffing white shoes through the dirt.

The nearby **Jardín Botánico** (open daily; closed Aug; entrance fee) was created in 1774 by Carlos III. Even if you can't tell a Japanese maple from a dahlia, these gardens are a shady and aromatic retreat. Outside the southern wall of the garden is the **Cuesta de Moyano**, a year-round outdoor book fair. Sunday morning is the peak browsing time for bestsellers and the odd rare edition.

On other mornings of the week, literary pilgrims can follow the **Calle Cervantes** from the Paseo del Prado to the **Casa de Lope de Vega** ❽ at No.11 (open Tues–Sat am; entrance fee). Here the great playwright created his most important works. The furnishings and personal effects are not his, but they show how a 17th-century Spanish household might have looked.

Returning to the Puerta del Sol along the Carrera San Jerónimo, you'll pass the parliament building, the **Palacio de las Cortes**. The bronze lions in front are made of melted-down cannons captured in the war with the Moroccans in 1860.

Old Madrid

South of the Puerta del Sol is one of Madrid's oldest and most colourful neighbourhoods: a tangle of narrow cobbled streets lined by adobe apartment houses with wrought-iron balconies and chilly, musty foyers. In this area, the prudent will give calles **Cruz** and **Espoz y Mina** a miss, since both have seen better days. Madrid, like other big cities, has its share of street crime, much of it

*Just up the street from the parliament building on Carrera San Jerónimo is the **Museo del Jamón** (open daily until midnight), a delicatessen with artful displays of Spanish ham and sausage. Be sure to try serrano, a tender, cured ham.*

BELOW: the pedestrianised Plaza Mayor.

drugs-linked. Most of the drug markets are on the outskirts of town but also take care around the Puerta del Sol and the Gran Vía. Notoriously bad for muggings is the area directly to the north of the Gran Vía, especially around Calle Ballesta. If you plan extensive wanderings on foot through the downtown area (Centro), leave your jewellery, vital documents and large amounts of cash in the hotel strongbox. It makes sense to take precautions.

Madrid's **Plaza Mayor** ❾ or main square, west of the Puerta del Sol, is a 17th-century beauty superbly restored, even if it is no longer the centre of town as it was in ages past, when *autos de fe*, bullfights and coronations took place there. The wide cobbled square is closed to traffic and is a pleasant spot to have coffee and make plans, since the main tourist office is located here. Just west of the Plaza Mayor is the **Mercado de San Miguel** enclosed in a lacy turn-of-the-century ironwork building. Redolent with *chorizo* and voluptuous heaps of fruit, a Madrid market will also give you an idea of why this city is sometimes called the best seaport in Spain. Fish and shellfish are flown into Castile daily.

Further along Calle Mayor is the **Plaza de la Villa**, a pretty pedestrian square which is a showcase of Madrid architecture from the 15th to the 17th centuries. The main attraction is the baroque Casa de la Villa, or town hall. Also worth noting is the Torre de los Lujanes, with horseshoe arches and a gothic portal. It is one of the few examples of 15th-century secular architecture in the ca

On a Sunday morning, head south to the **Catedral de San Isidro** ❿ daily; free) on Calle de Toledo. Its gloomy interior houses the rema Madrid's peasant patron saint. Just beyond the church, people say, M becomes Magerit again – the **Rastro,** an enormous open-air bazaar, fills the streets for several blocks in all directions. Clothes, furniture and animals can all

Map on pages 124–5

TIP

Old Madrid's best known bars are in and around Plaza Santa Ana. Try Cervecería Alemana, Viva Madrid or Los Gabrieles.

BELOW: combing the Rastro for the best bargains.

Dancers celebrate the Fiesta de La Paloma in old Madrid.

BELOW LEFT: the new Catedral de Santa María.
BELOW RIGHT: the 18th-century Palacio Real.

be haggled for, as well as specialised items such as rings of skeleton keys, old liquor stills and Fascist memorabilia. (Beware pickpockets here.)

In this area of the city, Madrid's throaty urban accent is at its thickest; this is the pulse point of the August fiesta de la Virgen de La Paloma, when women in colourful kerchiefs and flounced skirts dance through the streets with their waist-coated partners to alternate blasts of traditional *chotis* and rock music. Just to the south in the **Puerta de Toledo ⓫**, the old fish market has been transformed into a tasteful, triple-decked complex with small, upmarket, fashion, crafts, antique and food shops.

Fit for an angel

The neoclassical **Basilica de San Francisco el Grande ⓬** (open daily; free) was built in the southwest of the city centre on the site of a 13th-century monastery purportedly founded by St Francis during a pilgrimage to Spain. The rotunda was first designed by a monk named Francisco Cabezas, but the plans were discovered to be structurally unsound and the building was eventually completed by the Italian architect Sabatini in 1784. The interior is mostly decorated in florid 19th-century style; one mural shows an apparition of St James in the act of killing Moors. There is also an early fresco by Goya, which contains a bright-eyed self-portrait.

The capital's long wait for its cathedral came to an end on 15 June 1993 when Pope John Paul II consecrated the **Catedral de Nuestra Señora de la Almudena ⓭**, alongside the Palacio Real. The church houses the image of the Virgin of the Almudena, patroness of Madrid. Work on the building had started in 1883: indeed, King Alfonso XII hoped it would be the burial place of his

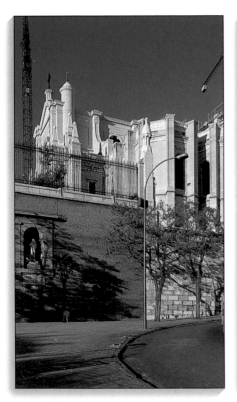

Map
on pages
124–5

beloved first wife, María de las Mercedes. A devotee of the Virgin of the Almu-dena, she had died aged 18 in 1878, and could not be interred in the Royal Pantheon at El Escorial as she had not produced heirs. A century later Madrid has its completed cathedral, but María de las Mercedes is buried at El Escorial.

The Palacio Real

For its spectacular location and opulent interior, the **Palacio Real** ⓮ (open daily; closed Sun pm; entrance fee) is the second most dazzling tourist attraction in Madrid. On Christmas Eve, 1734, the Habsburg Alcázar burned to the ground, enabling Felipe V to build a palace more suited to the requirements of a Bourbon monarch. Designed by Italian masters Sacchetti and Sabatini, it was so lavish that Napoleon claimed his brother Joseph had better lodgings than his own at the Tuileries in Paris. Inside are the Farmacia Real, with glass cases full of the exotic medications of centuries past, and the Armería Real, containing the swords of Cortés and Fernando the Catholic as well as full suits of armour. The royal apartments are a truly grand affair; it's hard not to be overwhelmed by the lavish decoration and sumptuous furnishings as you wander around the Dining Room, Throne Room and Gasparini Rooms.

Alfonso XIII was the last inhabitant of the palace. The present royal family prefers less elaborate quarters outside town and the palace is now used only for official functions. The stately **Campo del Moro** gardens are also open to the public.

The **Monasterio de la Encarnación** ⓯ (open Tues–Sun; entrance fee) was once connected to the royal palace by a passageway. Apparently the convent was meant to be a refuge for the women of the royal family, "in case of some novelty", as its founder, Queen Margaret of Austria, hinted darkly in a letter. The

BELOW: the popular King Juan Carlos.

SPAIN'S ROYAL FAMILY

When Juan Carlos came to the throne after General Franco's death, he did so in the uncomfortable knowledge that Spaniards had a well-established tradition of unseating Bourbon monarchs they did not like. The whole of the king's reign has been aimed at convincing Spaniards of his commitment to democratic politics and a just society. No one can doubt that, against all the odds and predictions, he has succeeded.

He has also helped set the tone of a new Spain free of the formality that so constricted his country in the past. His easy-going manner – more evident in private than in public – has won over many a lifelong Republican. A keen sportsman – he sailed for Spain in the 1972 Olympics – Juan Carlos's hearty image is complemented by the gentler personality of his wife. Queen Sofía's principal cultural enthusiasm is classical music, especially Bach.

Increasingly now, Spaniards' attention is turning towards the children: Elena, an accomplished horsewoman, who teaches English in Madrid; Cristina, a talented yachtswoman, who works for a cultural foundation in Barcelona; and Crown Prince Felipe. Immensely tall – almost 2 metres (6½ ft) – the heir to the throne appears to combine practicality with his mother's sensibility.

TIP

La Bola restaurant, just beside the Monasterio de la Encarnación, is an ideal place for those in search of an authentic taste of Madrid.

cloister houses royal portraits, including one of an illegitimate daughter of Felipe IV being received into heaven. The church is a splendid example of 18th-century Madrid architecture by Ventura Rodríguez. In the reliquary is a vial of a saint's blood which is said to liquefy every year on 27 July.

A grand reopening

The **Teatro Real** ⓰ (tel: 516-06 60 for information), opposite the royal palace, opened as an opera house in 1850 – due to a string of delays, it had taken 38 years to build. Legend has it that the cast of one production included live elephants. In October 1997, after lengthy renovations, the building reopened and is now one of the most spectacular and technically advanced opera houses in Europe, seating 1,800 spectators. The surrounding streets have been pedestrianised, making it very pleasant to walk around this area of Madrid.

Nearby in Plaza de San Martín is the **Monasterio de las Descalzas Reales** ⓱ (open Tues–Sun; entrance fee), founded by Juana, youngest daughter of Carlos V. It contains a number of art treasures donated by blue-blooded nuns' families. Many of the works of sacred art have children as their theme. For the Golden Age painters they represented the triumph of life over death.

The centre of the western end of Madrid is the **Plaza de España** ⓲, where larger-than-life bronze statues of Don Quijote and Sancho Panza ride toward the sunset. The square lies at the end of the Gran Vía. Just north of the Plaza de España is the **Palacio de Liria** ⓳ (send requests for visits to: Don Miguel, Calle de la Princessa 20, 28008 Madrid), the magnificent 18th-century home of the Duchess of Alba. Designed by Ventura Rodríguez, who worked on the royal palaces of Madrid and Aranjuez, the house contains an outstanding collection

BELOW: Goya frescoes in the Ermita de San Antonio.

of furniture, miniatures and European paintings. The Duchess of Alba comes from a venerable line of art patrons, including the 13th Duchess Cayetana, the beautiful and lively friend of Goya. She was long rumoured to have posed for Goya's *Naked Maja*, but art historians generally agree that the gleaming, idealised female body must have been painted from the artist's imagination.

Exquisite painting by Goya is one of two good reasons for making a pilgrimage down to the Paseo de la Florida to visit the neoclassical **Ermita de San Antonio** (open 10am–2pm, 4–8pm Tues–Fri, 10am–2pm Sat and Sun; entrance fee). In 1798, after completing this frescoed ceiling showing St Anthony raising a murdered man from the dead, Goya was appointed first painter to the court, despite the fact that the fresco's portrayal of scrofulous street people was a startling departure in church art. Goya died in 1828 and the little chapel is now his mausoleum. The popularity of the shrine – St Anthony is the patron of disappointed lovers and lost objects – has necessitated the construction of a replica chapel next door.

Other sights in this part of town include the **Templo de Debod ㉑** (open Tues–Sun; closed pm; entrance fee), which was given to Spain by Egypt in gratitude for helping with the construction of the Aswan Dam. It was originally sited on land flooded by the dam, and was built by the Pharaoh Zakheramon in the 4th century BC.

Nearby, you can board a cable car and sail over the **Parque del Oeste** and the Río Manzanares to the Casa de Campo, an enormous informal park which is sometimes used as a venue for rock concerts, with an amusement park, swimming pool and a zoo. Among the pines below your cable car you can see traces of Civil War trenches from the city's three-year siege.

Map on pages 124–5

Views over Madrid from the cable car.

BELOW: the Parque del Oeste.

The archway in the Plaza Dos de Mayo, commemorating those killed in the 1808 uprising against the French.

BELOW: serving drinks in a Malasaña bar.

Madrid's rebel roots

Madrid's centre for the counterculture element is the area known as **Malasaña**, between Calles San Bernardo and Fuencarral south of Calle Carranz**a**. By day this area is redolent of old Madrid, with local people going about their lives. Storefronts attract customers with brightly coloured 19th-century mosaics. A former pharmacy on the corner of Calles **San Andrés** and **San Vicente Ferrer** has memorable tiles advertising early 20th-century miracle cures.

But when night falls the neighbourhood changes character. Bars resound with rock 'n' roll, grunge, garage, hip-hop and jazz. The streets are filled with lively people looking for a good time – although there is some drug dealing there are always plenty of people around and the streets are well lit, so it's generally safe. The centre of the neighbourhood, the **Plaza Dos de Mayo ㉑**, was the scene of a fierce battle with Napoleon's forces in 1808; citizens rushed into the streets with whatever weapons they could lay their hands on. The civilians lost but casualties on both sides were heavy; the archway in the middle of the plaza commemorates the fallen. The plaza has been cleaned up recently and now has a number of good bars and pizzerias. Some years ago, when plans were made to tear down the old houses and put up new apartment blocks, the neighbours once again mobilised in defence of the *barrio*. This time Malasaña was saved without bloodshed and it continues as a fashionable bohemian district.

The **Museo Municipal ㉒** (open Tues–Sun; closed Sat and Sun pm and weekday pm in Aug; entrance fee) on nearby Calle Fuencarral, is installed in a former poorhouse with an ornate late-baroque façade. During the 19th-century rage for neoclassical design, the building was held up as the embodiment of bad taste. The exuberant mouldings and statuary are restored and are now historic

rather than merely out-of-date. The museum contains exhibits on the history of Madrid from the Palaeolithic period to the present day. Among its attractions are Goya's *Allegory of the City of Madrid*, an exquisite 1830 model of the capital and photographs dating from 1850.

The **Museo Romántico** ㉓ (open Tues–Sat 10am–3pm, Sun and public hols 10am–2pm; entrance fee) nearby at Calle San Mateo 13 is housed in a mansion formerly belonging to the Condes de la Puebla del Maestre, and made into a museum by the Marqués de Vega Inclán. Most of the furniture and pictures date back to the reigns of Fernando VII and Isabel II; objects which one associates with the peculiarities of the 19th century include a pair of duelling pistols instrumental in the death of satirist José de Larra, scatological moving pictures and a water closet with a velvet seat, which once belonged to Fernando VII.

While in this area, enthusiasts of the work of the Antoní Gaudí should see the **Palacio de Longoria** ㉔ (closed to the public) on Calle Fernando (at the corner with Calle Pelayo). Designed in 1902 by the Catalan architect José Grases Riera, of the Gaudí School, it is one of the best of the few examples in Madrid of Catalan Modernism. The building is the headquarters of the Society of Authors, which has restored it to its original splendour.

Upmarket Salamanca

A few blocks east, the **Plaza de Colón** ㉕ – which translates as "Columbus Square" – alongside the **Jardines del Descubrimiento** is graced by a statue of the discoverer on a carved neo-gothic column erected in 1885. On the other side of the square are four enormous concrete sculptures which resemble large decayed teeth; they, too, commemorate Columbus, with inscriptions describing

TIP

If you're looking for stylish new clothes, head south of Plaza de Colón for Calle de Almirante, a showcase for Spain's newest fashions.

BELOW: the *barrio* de Salamanca.

Map on pages 124–5

Mail box at the main post office on Cibeles.

BELOW: strolling along Paseo de la Castellana.

the discovery of America. At the western end of the square, an attractive, noisy waterfall guards the entrance to the Centro Cultural de la Villa, an arts complex with a theatre, concert hall and exhibition space.

Alongside this plaza is a monolithic Hellenic structure enclosing the **Biblioteca Nacional** (open Tues–Sun; closed Sun pm; free) facing west and the **Museuo Arqueológico Nacional**  (open Tues–Sun; closed Sun pm; entrance fee) facing east. The library, inaugurated in 1892 to mark the 400th anniversary of Columbus's voyage, contains manuscripts dating from the 10th century. The Museuo Arqueológico has rich displays from prehistoric Spain, Iberian treasures such as the mysterious, impassive Lady of Elche, Roman statues and mosaics and a Visigothic crown studded with jewels. In the garden are reproductions of the Altamira cave paintings in a reconstructed cave.

The *barrio* of **Salamanca** was constructed in the late 19th century for the Spanish aristocracy who wanted to move away from the noise and congestion of the city centre. The project was bankrolled by the Marqués de Salamanca, a soldier, politician and entrepreneur who made and lost three fortunes and whose picaresque business dealings once forced him to flee to France in disguise. Today the neighbourhood is the soul of respectability. While there are few outstanding individual examples of architecture, notice the seigneurial touches to the buildings: the ornate glassed-in balconies, the doorways cut wide enough to allow the entrance of carriages. Many of the mansions are now foreign embassies, but the area is still a comfortable enclave of the well-to-do, evidenced by the exquisite delicatessens and well-stocked antique shops.

The main shopping street is **Calle Serrano**, where French and Italian boutiques now make room for Spanish names such as **Loewe** and **Adolfo Domínguez**. Prices for shoes and leather goods are no longer low, but the quality is unsurpassed. In a nearby street the club/café complex within the trendy **Teatriz**, a converted theatre, is worth a glimpse for the architecture alone. Further north, just before Serrano crosses Calle María de Molina, is one of Madrid's loveliest museums, the **Lázaro Galdiano**  (open Tues–Sun 10am–2pm; entrance fee). The early 20th century Italianate palace and lush garden was the private residence of a publisher who bequeathed his art collection to the Spanish government in 1948. On the first floor are medieval enamels, silver and gold chalices and reliquaries, a 12th-century ivory Virgin and a small head of San Salvador. On floors above are armour and ceramics as well as paintings from Spanish and Flemish primitives to Constable and Turner.

Elegant boulevard

The **Paseo de la Castellana** bisects the city between the Atocha train station to the south and the Chamartín station to the north. Most of the 19th-century palaces along the Paseo are now banks, or have made way for new architecture of glass and chrome, but it's still a delightful promenade. Traffic islands shielded by potted palms and privet make oddly intimate outdoor cafés, since the swoop of cars is loud enough to keep conversations private. In summer the open-air *terrazas* are popular night-spots. ❑

Café Life

Most of us think of a café as a place to have a cup of a coffee and a sinful pastry. But not so to the Spaniards. To them a café is variously a place to watch the world go by, an academic arena, a setting for cultural input or a therapeutic refuge from the world beyond its velvet curtains. The 19th century was the heyday of the Madrid café. The repression inflicted by Franco stifled much of the political and philosophical rhetoric that were the mainstay of the capital's cafés before the Spanish Civil War; but the cafés at least provided a welcome refuge from the winter cold. As indoor plumbing and central heating became more common in the 1960s and '70s, the old-world café became almost extinct. But it has made a comeback since the rebirth of democracy.

To experience the Spanish café at its traditional best, visit the **Café Gijón** on the Paseo de Recoletos. More than a century old, this is the *grande dame* of the café as cultural institution. The group at the next table may be immersed in a *tertulia* – a lengthy discussion usually on some artistic or political issue, though the exigencies of modern life are putting an end to this traditional pursuit. Probably no café in Madrid goes back as far as the Gijón. The delightful Art Nouveau-style decor of **El Espejo**, also on Recoletos, is deceptive. Its tiled pictures and huge mirrors date from 1978, while the pavilion extension, a seemingly turn-of-the-century confection of glass and tiles, appeared only in 1990. Another comparative new entry in the old style is the **Café de Oriente**, opposite the royal palace. Draped with velvet, padded with plush and trimmed with lace, the café has a very versatile menu but specialises in exotic coffees and homemade patisseries.

In Spain, patronising one café over another is not just a matter of convenience and taste: it is a question of personal conviction. There are right-wing cafés and left-wing cafés; cafés for the literati, for yuppies, for the film crowd, for the *outré* and progressive. At the **Círculo de Bellas Artes**, near the Puerta del Sol at Alcalá 42, you'll see the pale-faced girls and Balzacian types you'd expect at the Fine Arts Circle. The café's fabulous interior – columns, chandeliers, painted ceilings and a magnificent sprawling nude as you walk in the door – dates from 1926.

Late in the evening at the **Café Central** (Plaza del Angel 10) you can listen to great jazz played live in an Art Deco setting, while in the next street, the **Salón del Prado** (Calle Prado 4) offers live classical music on its small stage lateish on Thursday nights (not Jul–Sept). **Libertat 8** is a favoured venue for the popular revival of *cantautores* (singer-songwriters) and *cuentacuentos* (storytellers), although it's more a bar than a café.

A range of stylish modern cafés catering to a varied clientele has recently appeared on the Madrid scene. You can surf the net or e-mail your friends at **The Net Café** (Calle San Bernardo 81), listen to small ensemble concerts at **La Fídula** (Calle Huertas 57) or dance the night away at **Star's** (Calle Marqués de Valdeiglesias 5); and trendy **La Sastrería**, at Calle Hortaleza 74, is especially popular with gay couples. ❏

RIGHT: bidding a fond farewell on the pavement outside the Gafé Gijon.

MADRID PROVINCE

Some magnificent royal palaces, as well as historic towns and villages, are easily visited from Madrid. El Escorial, in the foothills of the Sierra de Guadarrama, is the highlight

Map on page 144

The "eighth wonder of the world", a "monotonous symphony of stone", and an "architectural nightmare" are just three of the ways that **San Lorenzo de El Escorial ❶** (tel: 91-890 59 02; open Tues–Sun 10am–5pm (Apr–Sept 6pm); closed public hols; entrance fee), Felipe II's most enduring legacy to Spain and the world, has been described since it was completed in 1584. This combination monastery-palace-mausoleum is only an hour away from Madrid in the foothills of the **Sierra de Guadarrama**. There are frequent trains from Madrid's Chamartín station, via Atocha, or you can drive along the NVI and turn left on the C-600.

The origin of El Escorial is most likely 10 August 1557, the day Felipe II's armies defeated the French at the Battle of St Quentin, in Flanders. In honour of Saint Lawrence (San Lorenzo), whose feast day it was, Felipe decided to build a tribute to the saint. The King sent two architects, two doctors and two stone masons out to seek a site for the new monastery that was to be neither too hot nor too cold nor too far from the new capital. Philosophers and astrologers were also consulted to find a suitable meeting place for land and sky.

The stony monarch

Felipe II was an introverted, melancholy, deeply religious and ailing man who wanted a place to retreat to from his duties as king of the world's mightiest empire. He wanted to be surrounded by monks, not courtiers; besides being a royal residence, the king intended El Escorial to be primarily a monastery for the Order of Jeronimo monks.

Felipe did not permit anyone to write his biography while he was alive, but in fact he left it himself, written in stone. The battles he won and lost, the glories and defeats of the empire, the succession of deaths and tragedies and his obsession for learning, art, prayer and order are all reflected in El Escorial. The location of the enormous church in the centre of the complex reflected his belief that all political action should be governed by religious considerations.

Construction began in 1563 and took 21 years to complete. The chief architect was originally Juan Bautista de Toledo, a disciple of Michelangelo, but after he died the task was picked up in 1569 by Juan de Herrera, who is credited with having provided the inspiration for the final design.

Statistics give some idea of El Escorial's monumental scale. Built of grey granite, it measures 208 by 162 metres (683 by 531 ft). It has 15 cloisters, 16 patios, 13 oratorios, 300 cells, 86 stairways, nine towers, nine organs, 2,673 windows, 1,200 doors and a collection of more than 1,600 paintings. Some historians

LEFT: San Lorenzo de El Escorial.
BELOW: portrait of Felipe II.

believe that the shape of the building is like an upside-down grill, a reminder of the martyrdom of St Lawrence, who was grilled alive.

The northern and western sides of the monastery are bordered by huge patios called *la lonja,* while the southern and eastern sides are the site of gardens with excellent views of the monastery's fields and orchards and the Madrid countryside beyond. In fact, there is a statue of Felipe II there doing just that, looking out beyond the **Jardín de los Frailes**, where the monks rested from their labours. Below the garden on the right is the **Gallery of Convalescents**.

Architecture and painting at El Escorial

Visits are unaccompanied, although guides are available. The route currently starts in two small new museums (**Nuevos Museos**), the first of which explains the building's architectural history through drawings, plans, tools and scale models. Exhibits include intriguing bits of machinery dreamed up by Herrera to cope with technical problems.

Flights of stairs then lead up to nine rooms of magnificent 15th to 17th century paintings. As in the Prado, the range and quality – from Bosch to Veronese, Tintoretto and Van Dyck, as well as the Spanish School – illustrate why the Spanish Habsburgs were the greatest patrons of art of their time. The Flemish School, collected by Felipe's grandmother Isabel, and Titian, court painter to his father Carlos V, are especially well represented.

The first room of the Habsburg living quarters belonged to Felipe II's favourite daughter, Isabel Clara Eugenia, who took care of him when he was dying. The austerity is broken only by the important collection of paintings and the Talavera ceramic skirting on all the walls in this section of the palace. The

The word "palace" seems inappropriate for the living quarters at El Escorial. Felipe II himself said that he wanted to build "a palace for God and a shack for the King".

BELOW:
inside El Escorial.

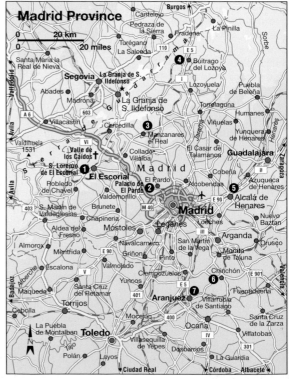

simplicity continues in the Sedan Room, where you will find the unadorned wooden chair in which the king was carried from Madrid once his gout was bad. In the adjacent Portrait Room, so-called for its portraits of the Spanish Habsburg dynasty, you can also see the chair on which Philip rested his painful leg.

A hallway leads on to the Walking Gallery, whose old leaded windows give the best views out over the gardens. The doors, made of 17 different types of wood – surprisingly splendid – were a present from Maximilian of Austria in 1567. This leads through to the Ambassadors' Salon, or waiting room, and, finally, the King's Bedroom, adjacent to the main altar of the church, so that Felipe II could hear Mass from his bed. When his gout permitted, he would walk through a small door that leads directly from his room to the church.

Stairs and corridors lead round to the four Chapter Rooms, where the monks once held their meetings. Now the walls are hung with paintings, among them Velázquez's masterpiece, *Joseph's Tunic*, in the first room and Bosch's *Garden of Pleasures* in the last.

Royal remains

One of Felipe II's motivations for building El Escorial was to construct a mausoleum for his father, Emperor Carlos V, whose remains were brought here in 1586. But it was not until the reign of Felipe III, in 1617, that this splendid bronze, marble and jasper pantheon began to be built directly below the main altar of the church. The remains of all the kings of Spain since Carlos V lie here, with the exception of Felipe V, who could not bear the gloom of the place and asked to be buried at Segovia, and Fernando VI, whose tomb is in Madrid. The queens who produced male heirs are also buried here, while across the

Portrait of Felipe II's favourite daughter, Isabel Clara Eugenia.

BELOW: elegant Bourbon apartments in the otherwise austere El Escorial.

way in the 19th-century **Princes' Pantheon** lie the remains of princes, princesses and queens whose children did not succeed to the throne.

Church and library

While some illustrious visitors have praised the church's perfect grandeur – the French writer Alexandre Dumas referred to the Kings' Courtyard as "the entrance to eternity" – others have complained about its oppressive size. French writer and intellectual Théophile Gautier wrote: "in the El Escorial church one feels so overwhelmed, so crushed, so subordinate to a melancholy and inflexible power that prayer appears to be entirely useless". The frescoes on the ceilings and along the 43 altars were painted by Spanish and Italian masters. The retable was designed by architect Juan de Herrera himself. On either side of the retable are the royal stalls and the sculpted figures of Carlos V and Felipe II.

In autumn 1997 the El Escorial library was closed indefinitely for restoration. Second only to the Vatican library, it holds the writings of St Augustine, Alfonso the Wise and Santa Teresa. It has the largest collection of Arabic manuscripts in the world, illuminated hymnals and works of natural history and cartography from the Middle Ages. It is the only library in the world to store its books facing backwards, a measure taken to preserve the ancient parchment.

Pope Gregory XIII ordered the excommunication of anyone who stole a manuscript from here. The ceiling, painted by Tibaldi and his daughter, represents the seven liberal arts: grammar, rhetoric, dialectics, arithmetic, geometry, astronomy and music.

During the reign of the Bourbons, part of the living quarters were converted and two small palaces were built near the monastery to be used as hunting

An empty tomb in the mausoleum is reserved for Don Juan, father of the present King Juan Carlos and the first non-monarch to be honoured by burial here. Spaniards believe that his defence of democracy under Franco deserves this final mark of respect.

BELOW:
the Royal Pantheon at El Escorial.

lodges and guest houses. **The Prince's Pavilion** (Lower Pavilion; closed for restoration), around a half-hour's walk down toward the train station, is a showpiece of Pompeian ceilings, Italian painting, bronze, marble and porcelain. **The Upper Pavilion**, located 3 km (2 miles) along the road leading to Ávila, is closed at present. Continuing along the Ávila road a bit, and then taking a fork to the left, leads to **La Silla de Felipe II** (Philip II's seat), a group of large boulders up on a hill from where the king supposedly gazed out over his monstrous monastery as it was being built.

In the summer months El Escorial's small, sedate town fills up with *Madrileños* escaping the city heat. If you stay overnight, you may be lucky enough to catch a performance in the **Teatro Real Coliseo**.

The cross above the basilica at Valle de los Caídos.

North from Madrid

The joy of escaping north from the capital is that the Sierra de Guadarrama is almost always in view. The peaks, which reach almost 2,500 metres (8,000 ft), can be snow-covered until early summer. There are three routes: the N-VI which cuts through the mountains by means of a tunnel; the C-607/601, which goes via the Navacerrada Pass and is the most picturesque; and the main N-I which goes through the Somosierra Pass. In winter, signposts on the main roads warn you in good time whether or not the passes are open. The Madrid side of the passes still retain many beauty spots, and you may see Castilian shepherds come past, driving their herds.

Just outside the city limits, approximately 15 km (9 miles) northwest of central Madrid, is the **Palacio de El Pardo ❷** (open daily; closed Sun pm; entrance fee), a former royal hunting lodge surrounded by forests of holm oak. Inside sev-

BELOW: the crypt of Santa Cruz del Valle de los Caídos.

THE VALLEY OF THE FALLEN

Just 13 km (8 miles) from El Escorial, on the road back to Madrid, is Santa Cruz del Valle de los Caídos, Franco's memorial to those who died in the Civil War and subsequently his own burial place (open Tues–Sun 10am–6pm Oct–Mar, 9.30–7pm Apr–Sept; entrance fee). Once you have your entry tickets you are obliged to drive along the approach road to the basilica and are not allowed to stop en route. For those without their own vehicle there is a bus to the site which leaves daily from El Escorial.

A total of 40,000 Republican and Nationalist soldiers lie buried here. Built by the sweat of left-wing prisoners of war between 1940 and 1958, the concrete basilica is a chilling sight. Few fail to be impressed by its engineering, however, carved as it is several thousand metres into the rock. Opposite Franco's tomb is that of Falange leader José Antonio Primo de Rivera, son of the 1920s dictator Miguel Primo de Rivera. He was assassinated and, some say, martyred by the Republicans in 1936.

The tombs lie directly below a massive, 150-metre (490-ft) high cross, which can be seen for miles around. If you wish, you can drive up to the base of the cross, from where there is a splendid view of the surrounding countryside.

eral hundred tapestries are on display, including some designed by Goya. General Franco lived here for a time, as did Juan Carlos I, but the palace is now used mainly for entertaining royal guests.

A little further north and a good place for a picnic stop is the pretty town of **Manzanares el Real ❸**. The 15th-century **Castillo de los Mendoza** (open Tues–Sun 10am–2pm and 4–7pm (5pm in winter); free) dominates the town. Just beyond it is Pedriza Park, which has walking trails and climbing routes among its granite rocks.

The walled town of **Buitrago del Lozoya ❹** lies just off the N-I highway about 14 km (9 miles) shy of the Somosierra Pass. In the basement of the *ayuntamiento* (town hall) in the Plaza de Picasso is the **Museo Picasso** (open Wed–Mon; free). The collection belonged to his hairdresser and, as Picasso was bald for half his life, the collection is thin!

Alcalá de Henares

The old university town of **Alcalá de Henares ❺**, 35 km (20 miles) east of Madrid on the N-II highway, is well worth visiting for lunch and the afternoon. The entrance from Madrid is unpromising: smoke-stacks and rows of high-rises. But once inside, the charm of its university buildings, convents and churches obliterates that impression.

Founded in 1508 by Cardinal Francisco de Cisneros, the university soon rivalled Salamanca as one of the great seats of learning. It was built at the peak of Plateresque, and many of its courtyards and edifices are fine examples of this style, so called because it resembles beaten and worked silver. The most exciting is the façade of the university building designed by Rodrigo Gil de Honañón.

Miguel de Cervantes Saavedra (1547–1661), the genius of Spain's Golden Age of literature, was born in Alcalá de Henares. He published his masterpiece, "Don Quixote", in 1605.

BELOW: Chinchón's rustic Plaza Mayor.

Alcalá de Henares was also the birthplace of the great writer Cervantes; on the corner of Calle Imagen and Calle Mayor is the **Museo Casa Natal de Miguel de Cervantes** (open Tues–Sun; closed public hols; free), which is dedicated to his life.

Map on page 144

South from Madrid

Within very easy reach of Madrid, 52 km (32 miles) to the southeast – is the picturesque town of **Chinchón ❻**. It is famous for two things. The first is its splendid and historic **Plaza Mayor**, which has been used for bullfights since at least 1502. Surrounded on three sides with three storeys of wooden galleries, it is both rustic and elegant.

Chinchón's other claim to fame is a strong aniseed drink which takes its name from the town and is drunk all over the country as a bump-start before work. One place to taste it, to have lunch or to stay the night is the **Parador Nacional**, set in a former 17th-century convent.

Aranjuez ❼ lies just off the N-IV highway 45 km (27 miles) south of the capital. The baroque18th-century **Palacio Real** (open Tues–Sun 10am–6pm; 5pm in winter; guided tour compulsory; entrance fee) was inspired by Versailles and is stuffed with royal portraits, porcelain, stucco and wooden carving. The setting, beside the confluence of the Ríos Tajo and Jarama, is probably the reason why most visitors choose to linger here. There are 300 hectares (740 acres) of royal gardens, including the Jardín de la Isla, close to the palace, and the extensive Jardín del Principe. The latter contains two museums: the **Casa de Marinos**, housing former royal riverboats; and the **Casa del Labrador**, a royal pavilion built by Carlos IV in response to the Petit Trianon at Versailles. ❑

ABOVE: porcelain detail in the Palacio Real. **BELOW:** view of Aranjuez.

CASTILE-LEÓN

*The architectural splendours of Salamanca, Segovia, León,
Ávila and Burgos give way to timeless mountain scenery and the
villages of the vast Castilian plain*

F or centuries Old Castile has been the geographical and spiritual heart of
Spain. Most of the great notions of Spanish history germinated here: the
unification of the ancient Iberian kingdoms, the *Reconquista* and the exploration and conquest of the New World. Felipe II chose the dead centre of Castile as the vantage point from which to rule his empire. The empire in turn grew
and then gradually disintegrated as a result of the mismanagement and short-
sightedness of Castilian governments. This process caused Ortega y Gasset to
lament, in 1921, that "Castile made Spain and Castile has been her undoing".
General Franco increased the force of the Castilian centrifuge by decreeing that
castellano was to be the nation's only legal language.

Deadpan and dignified, Castilians themselves often express mixed emotions
about their landscape. "Nine months of winter and three of hell", is their wry
assessment of the climate. The poet Antonio Machado described the rocky terrain, "crossed by the shadow of Cain", with a blend of affection and weary
despair. A visitor could well conclude that Castilians protest too much. The
winters are mild; autumns are long and richly coloured. The sierras are stark but
beautiful, the wide plains are windswept and intense.

LEFT: the monu-
mental walls of
Ávila. **BELOW:** the
Castilian costume.

Ancha es Castilla

"Wide is Castile", says the plain-spoken Castilian
proverb. After the democratic government granted
autonomous status to Spain's various regions, in 1983
Old Castile became the Autonomous Community of
Castile-León, a territory covering one-fifth of the
nation, or 94,150 sq. km (36,350 sq. miles), and including the provinces of Ávila, Burgos, León, Palencia,
Salamanca, Segovia, Soria, Valladolid and Zamora,
each with a capital of the same name. The fragrant
native scrubland of ilex, thyme and *jara* of past centuries has in large part been replaced by wheat fields,
vineyards and olive groves; most of the provincial
capitals are developing smog-producing industry.

While many Castilian villages are ancient, they cannot be described as quaint. Built as outposts against
the Moors, they still have a frontier feeling. Some,
too, are virtually ghost towns with a steadily declining
population, as young people leave to look for work.

Ávila

Sealed within its perfectly preserved medieval walls,
Ávila ❶ has been compared by poets to both a cof-
fin and a crown. It lies 113 km (70 miles) northwest of
Madrid. At 1,131 metres (3,710 ft), it is the highest
city on the peninsula. Hercules was the city's legendary founder, although it is probably older than the
Greek invasion of Spain: stone carvings of pigs and

Shrines to Sta Teresa abound in Ávila. Nuns of various orders walk the streets, and egg yolk confections called "yemas de Santa Teresa" are sold as souvenirs.

bulls found in the area point to a Celto-Iberian origin. Ávila was passed back and forth between Moors and Christians until Alfonso VI claimed it definitively in 1090. He promptly transferred his best knights from the northern kingdoms to the city, and they began constructing fortifications. The walls, which average 10 metres (33 ft) in height and 3 metres (10 ft) in width, have 88 round towers and nine fortified entrances. Over a mile of walls stretch round the old city. In the gardens next to the **Parador Nacional Raimundo de Borgoña**, you can climb the walls and look out across the surrounding plains.

Knights and nuns

The city has been a magnet for pilgrims since the late 16th century, as the birthplace of Santa Teresa, an outspoken nun who founded a reformed religious order and wrote about the presence of God in her life in distinctly physical terms. Teresa de Cepeda y Ahumada was born in 1515 to a noble family with Jewish roots who, possibly to keep their daughter out of the way of the Inquisition, sent her to a convent school. About the day she later left her father's house to enter

the Carmelite Order, at her own choice but with misgivings, Teresa wrote: "I did not think the day of my death would be more upsetting", but as a nun she thrived. She began to have face-to-face conversations with Christ, beginning with an encounter with the child Jesus on the convent stairs.

Her objections to the opulent lifestyle of the Carmelites spurred her to begin her own order, the Barefoot Carmelites. Her insistence on austerity made her unpopular with the nuns of her own city, and her unorthodox writings did bring the eye of the Inquisition upon her, but she was canonised in 1622, 40 years after her death. "Ávila of the Knights" is the city's nickname, yet within the stone walls Teresa's personality dominates.

Ávila's **catedral** (open daily 8.30am–2pm, 4–7pm; free) is set into the city walls, and has a matching military air. This is the oldest Gothic church in Spain. Inside is the mottled red-and-white stonework characteristic of churches throughout the city. Of particular artistic merit are the choir stalls, by the Dutch artist Cornelius, and the retable, painted with scenes from the life of Christ. Of interest to literary pilgrims is the chapel of San Segundo, where playwright Lope de Vega was chaplain.

Follow **Calle Santo Tomás** southeast to the **Monasterio de Santo Tomás** (open daily; entrance fee), founded by Fernando and Isabel in 1482. Its adornment includes carvings of pomegranates, or *granadas,* to commemorate the recapture of Granada in 1492. The church has a retable considered to be the masterpiece of Pedro Berruguete, depicting scenes from the life of St Thomas Aquinas. Here also is the tomb of Prince Juan, son of the Catholic Monarchs. His death at the age of 19 was a tragedy from which his parents never recovered.

Santa Teresa's relics

Enter the town again through **Plaza de Santa Teresa**. The white statue of Santa Teresa was built in honour of the Pope's visit in 1982, at which time she was named Doctor of the Church, the first woman to hold the title. Nearby, the **Convento de Santa Teresa** (open daily; entrance fee), built over the site of her childhood home. Her finger is among the objects on display in the **Convento de San José** (also known as the Convento de las Madres; open daily 10am–2pm, 4–7pm; entrance fee) east of the city walls, the first convent she founded. The more appealing relics in this museum include her saddle, her toy drum and a letter written in her fine handwriting.

North of the city walls, is the **Convento de La Encarnación**, where Teresa spent nearly 30 years. Guided tours take visitors to her cell, and the **locutorio** where she carried on animated conversations with her confessor and fellow mystic, San Juan de la Cruz. In her memoirs Teresa describes a scene in which she and "my brother Juan" became so ecstatic during a theological exchange that they levitated, each on opposite sides of the wooden screen. Today the cloistered nuns at Encarnación follow Teresa's dictates, and only leave the convent in cases of personal illness, or to vote.

The southern part of Ávila province is traversed by the **Sierra de Gredos** ❷, a weekend retreat beloved

Map on page 152

In the late 1970s, Ávila refused to be nominated a National Historical Artistic Monument, but capitulated five years later when the commercial advantages of such a title became impossible to ignore.

BELOW: landscape of the Sierra de Gredos.

of *madrileños* for its fresh air, pine woods and ski slopes. The Gredos is full of picturesque stone villages, such as **Arenas de San Pedro**, with its 15th-century castle and Gothic bridge. Part of the region is a scenic nature reserve containing Spain's first parador, opened in 1928. Two other lovely alpine hamlets are **Guisando** and **El Arenal**. Driving north of Ávila, an interesting historical detour is **Madrigal de las Altas Torres**, featuring the ruins of the palace where Queen Isabella the Catholic was born.

Salamanca – seat of learning

The honey-coloured sandstone university town of **Salamanca ❸** "is the pinnacle; the greatest triumph and honour Spain has ever had", wrote a historian in the court of Fernando and Isabel. Salamanca was an important Iberian city 2,000 years before the university was founded in 1218. It was Hannibal's westernmost conquest, and a Moorish town until it was captured by the Christians in 1085. The victors filled the city with churches: San Julián, San Martín, San Benito, San Juan, Santiago, San Cristobal and the Catedral Vieja all date from a century of feverish Romanesque construction.

Historians suspect that Alfonso IX of León established the university in response to the foundation of one in Palencia by his cousin and rival, Alfonso VIII of Castile. Salamanca quickly absorbed the latter school, and less than 30 years later the Pope, Alexander IV, proclaimed it one of the four best universities in the world, ranking alongside Oxford, Paris and Bologna.

The Inquisition put an end to the university's reputation as a haven for new ideas and thinkers, and during Felipe II's reign Spanish students were forbidden to study abroad. By the end of the 19th century the colleges were decimated by

LEFT: Salamanca's Old Cathedral.
RIGHT: the Casa de las Conchas.

war and neglect, although the 20th century brought another brief moment of triumph when the philosopher and novelist Miguel de Unamuno became University Rector. Unamuno's *Tragic Sense of Life* is a lucid, poetic exploration of the Spanish soul. Unamuno died driven mad by the atrocities of the Civil War, and the Franco period saw Salamanca, like other Spanish universities, fall into a long sleep. Now, however, it is regaining its reputation for Spanish literature.

A tour of the university

Salamanca has three universities, but the entrance to the original **Universidad** (open Mon–Fri 9.30am–1.30pm, 4–7.30pm, Sun am only; entrance fee) can be found in the **Patio de las Escuelas**. The Plateresque façade contains likenesses of the Catholic Monarchs surrounded by a jungle of literary, pagan and religious symbols.

Downstairs are several historic lecture halls, including the one where Hebrew scholar Fray Luis de León, after five years in the prisons of the Inquisition, began his first lecture with: "As we were saying yesterday…" Upstairs, the **Library** has over 40,000 rare volumes plus valuable ancient manuscripts. Across the Patio are Plateresque doors leading to the **Escuelas Menores**. One of the old classrooms here has a ceiling painted with the signs of the zodiac, a reminder that Salamanca once had a Department of Astrology.

The **Plaza de Anaya** is a graceful quadrangle surrounded on three sides by university buildings from several epochs and dominated by the **Catedral Nueva** (open daily; free). This imposing Gothic church was begun in 1513, when Salamanca's fame was such that the smaller Catedral Vieja would no longer do. It contains a magnificent gate and choir stalls by Alberto Churriguera. The **Catedral Vieja** (open daily; entrance fee), which leans against the new one like a chick under the wing of a hen, is now a museum. It is the more attractive church of the two, with its Byzantine dome and Romanesque frescoes.

In the adjacent **cloister** is the **Capilla de Santa Barbara**, where students were quizzed while touching the tomb of a bishop for luck. Exam results were made public, and a crowd of townspeople waited outside to pelt with rubbish those who failed. Those who passed were carried triumphantly around, and painted the word "Victor" on the walls of the university in bull's blood. Franco, who never attended a class here, also painted his "Victor" on the wall in 1939.

While there are those who will argue that Seville and Santiago are prettier cities, no one disagrees that Salamanca's **Plaza Mayor** is the most magnificent in Spain, for both architecture and ambience. The square, designed in 1729 by Churriguera, is bordered by an arcaded walkway lined with fashionable boutiques and voluptuous pastry shops. A *paseo* in the Plaza is a tradition beloved by students and locals alike.

Close to the Plaza Mayor is the odd-looking **Casa de las Conchas**, a noble mansion decorated all over with carved scallop shells, now the main tourist office. Following the Calle San Pablo from the Plaza Mayor leads you past the Casa de la Salina, where the unpopular Bishop Fonseca took revenge upon his enemies

Map on page 152

TIP

For a cheap snack in Salamanca, try the student bars in Plaza del Mercado, which serve delicious sausages called *farinato*.

BELOW: Salamanca's Plaza Mayor.

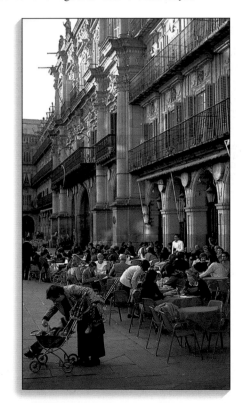

by caricaturing them in gargoyles. Further down the same street are two gorgeous examples of the Plateresque style at its zenith: the 16th-century **Convento de las Dueñas** (open daily; entrance fee), and the **Monasterio de San Esteban** (open daily; entrance fee), as delicate as spun sugar. Continue downhill as far as the river and cross over on the **Puente Romano** for a splendid look at the city rising above the bank.

Historical detours

Southwest of Salamanca, 90 km (55 miles) along the N-620, stands the handsome town of **Ciudad Rodrigo ❹**, its ramparts and lovely buildings tinged gold towards sunset. Scene of a famous battle during the War of Independence, when the Duke of Wellington captured the town from French forces, marks of shellfire are still visible on the cathedral belfry. Inside the **catedral** (open daily; free), the cloisters sporting Romanesque capitals and the racy choir-stalls by Rodrigo Alemán are worth inspecting.

The 14th-century castillo overlooking the Río Agueda now houses a pleasant parador, and the old town is crammed with Renaissance palaces – don't miss the main post office! – and interesting churches. Spend time walking the ramparts, and wandering the narrow streets around the Plaza Mayor. On the square itself is a wonderful old pharmacy and an even more amazing ice-cream shop. The surrounding countryside makes fascinating touring through vast and lonely estates where bulls destined for the *corrida* graze peacefully beneath ilex trees.

Zamora ❺ lies on the banks of the **Río Duero** 60 km (37 miles) north of Salamanca by the N-630. The town has a 12th-century **catedral** which makes it well worth a stop. The Byzantine dome of the cathedral is a striking addition

BELOW: Gaudí's extraordinary Casa de Botines in León.

to the Romanesque-Gothic structure. Inside, it is easy to see why Spaniards call the dome a half-orange. The cathedral contains a painting of *Christ in Glory* by Fernando Gallego, and 15th-century choir stalls whose carvings are spiced up by lewd satires of monastic life.

Outside the cathedral are the remains of Zamora's walls. The city was the site of centuries of bitter struggles between Moors and Christians. Sancho II was treacherously murdered here, and the spot is commemorated by the Postigo de la Traicíon (Traitor's Gate) in the ruined **castillo**.

Map
on page
152

León

Cool, regal **León** ❻ is in many respects a gateway city, with ancient ties both to Castile and to the green regions of Asturias and Galicia to the north. Its location at the base of the Cantabrian Mountains, 314 km (195 miles) from Madrid, makes it one of the less-travelled peninsula cities, yet both Spanish and foreign travellers return from a chance visit exclaiming over its dignified medieval beauty. The city's proudest century was the 10th, when Ordoño II moved his court here. León became a model of reasonable, civilised medieval government, and the assault and burning of the city by the Moor Almansor in 996 is an event still spoken of with regret. The city was recaptured in the 11th century, and was for a time capital of Spain as well as the seat of the Reconquest.

A visit to León should begin with the **catedral** (open Mon–Sat, closed Sat pm; entrance fee for museum), which has nearly 1,800 sq. metres (20,000 sq. ft) of magnificent stained-glass windows. Construction was begun in 1258, in the Romanesque style, but the soaring upper portions are Gothic at its best. In the morning and afternoon the splendid rose windows should be seen from the

TIP

Try to visit León's cathedral at least twice, at different times of day, to see the effect of the changing light on the stained glass.

BELOW: otained glass in León cathedral.

Carving in the Monasterio de Huelgas, Burgos.

inside, while at night the illumination turns the exterior into a glittering jewel box. Inside are several thousand-year-old sepulchres, including the delicate and ornate tomb of Ordoño II. The late-Gothic **cloister** and the **cathedral museum**, containing many Romanesque treasures, may be visited with a guide.

The **Colegiata de San Isidoro** (open daily; free) is a shrine dedicated to San Isidoro of Seville, whose remains were brought here to escape desecration by the Moors. Adjacent to the Romanesque and Gothic church is the **Panteón de los Reyes** (Kings' Pantheon; compulsory guided tour; entrance fee), which holds the tombs of early royalty of León and Castile. The frescoes in the pantheon are generally described as "The Sistine Chapel of Romanesque art". The old city around León's Plaza Mayor, an attractive quarter of winding cobbled streets and wrought-iron balconies, has become the domain of the younger crowd, and nearly every block has a bar or pub offering jazz and quirky decor.

A palatial prison

The **Hostal San Marcos**, on the **Río Bernesga**, is worth a visit even if you aren't a guest at the five-star parador inside. It was built in 1168 as a hospital for pilgrims on the road to Santiago. The ornate Plateresque façade, by Juan de Badajoz, was added in 1513. The hostel subsequently became a political prison (the poet Quevedo was the most illustrious guest). The cloister and sacristy house the **Museo de León** (open daily; closed Sun pm; entrance fee). Of particular note are the 11th-century ivory Christ and a 10th-century *mozarabic* cross.

BELOW: strolling on the Paseo del Espolón, Burgos.

West of León, the Roman town of **Astorga** has a huge **catedral** (open Mon–Sat; entrance fee for museum and Palacio Episcopal) with some remarkable features, including an altarpiece from the School of Michelangelo), and an interesting museum. Even more striking, however, is the **Palacio Episcopal** (Bishop's Palace) designed by the Catalan architect Antonio Gaudí. The bizarre building caused a great stir, and the horrified bishop who commissioned it refused to live there; today it houses a museum on the Santiago pilgrimage.

Burgos

Situated in the middle of the high plains of Old Castile, **Burgos** has been a Spanish crossroads for a thousand years. Founded in 884 as a fortification against the Moors, it is a relatively young city. Most of the landmarks have to do with its beloved native son, Rodrigo Díaz de Vivar, better known as El Cid. El Cid (from *Sidi,* Arabic for leader) pursued his own zealous campaign against the Moors, eventually capturing the city of Valencia in 1094.

Burgos **catedral** (open daily; free), begun in 1221, is considered to be El Cid's mausoleum. Described as "the work of angels" by Philip II, the gunmetal Gothic building dominates the city. Perhaps no other cathedral has so many curios, as well as artistic treasures. Visitors are usually as anxious to see the marionette clock **Papamoscas** and the life-size Christ made of animal skin and human hair as they are to admire the **Golden Staircase** by Diego de Siloe, the opulent Isabeline **Capilla del Condestable** and the **Capilla de Santa Ana**, with its magnificent retable

showing the Virgin's family tree. The **cloister** (entrance fee) contains a similar mixture of art and folklore. Here you may see a parchment bearing El Cid's promise of gifts to his future wife Jimena, and the coffer which he filled with sand to trick Jewish moneylenders (the legend adds that he repaid them with interest). The Cid and his wife are buried in the middle of the cathedral transept.

As an antidote to the still, dark air of the church, cross the Plaza Santa María to the esplanade along the Río Arlanzón. The turreted **Arcos de Santa María** was part of the 11th-century city walls and was decorated in the 16th century as a tribute to a visit from Charles V. The sculptures show the king surrounded by El Cid and other local heroes. Enter the city again at the **Plaza Primo de Rivera**, passing the statue of the Cid with his cape billowing around him.

Just west of the city centre, the **Monasterio de Las Huelgas** (open Tues–Sun; free) is a 12th-century nunnery where only women from the highest rank of society were admitted. The abbess was second in rank to the Queen of Spain, and it was said that if the Pope were allowed to marry only the abbess of Las Huelgas would be worthy of the honour. In addition to tombs of many early monarchs of Castile, there is a **Museo de Telas Medievales** (Museum of Medieval Textiles), containing brocades and jewellery from some of the tombs.

The roads around Burgos

The **Cartuja de Miraflores** (open daily; free), less than 3 km (2 miles) east of Burgos, was built by Queen Isabel as a memorial to her parents. The sculptures of Juan II and his queen are considered to be the most elaborate tombs in Europe. Here also is a tomb with a kneeling statue to Don Alfonso, whose early death made Isabel's succession possible.

Map on page 152

TIP

If you're touring the area, Burgos is a good place to stop for lunch. Try the local suckling pig, *morcilla* (blood sausage) or bean stew.

BELOW: Burgos cathedral, a mausoleum to the town's hero, El Cid.

The Visigothic chapel at Quintanilla de` las Viñas.

Ten km (6 miles) southeast of Burgos is the **Monasterio de San Pedro de Cardeña** (open daily; free), from where El Cid went into exile after being banished from Castile by Alfonso VI. He asked to be buried here along with his wife and his horse Babieca, but the human remains were spirited away to Burgos cathedral during the Peninsular War.

The small provincial capital of **Palencia**, just off the N-620 70 km (42 miles) southwest of Burgos, has a distinguished pedigree as a royal residence and the site of Spain's first university. The main sight is the **catedral** (open Mon–Sat; free), known as *La Bella Desconocida* (the Unknown Beauty) and stuffed with exquisite works of art, notably the retrochoir, altarpieces, the tomb of the tragic princess Doña Urraca, and a Visigothic crypt. Southwards 12 km (7 miles), the tiny church of **San Juan Bautista** at **Baños de Cerrato** is one of the earliest still standing. It is believed to date from 661, and contains Visigothic carvings.

Villages of Burgos

The province of Burgos is full of villages which strongly evoke the days of chivalry. A detour from the N-I highway takes in two particularly haunting spots. Some 4 km (2½ miles) east of **Quintanilla de las Viñas** is the ruin of a 7th-century Visigothic chapel, which is one of the earliest Christian edifices in Spain. Only a square apse and transepts remain of the original church, which may be visited in the company of a guide from the village. The squat building, alone on a desolate plain, is decorated with emblems of the sun and moon.

Passing the ruins of the **Monasterio de San Pedro de Arlanza** leads you to the village of **Covarrubias**, with its 10th-century tower where Doña Urraca, one of Spain's most tragic princesses, was imprisoned. The Colegiata contains the

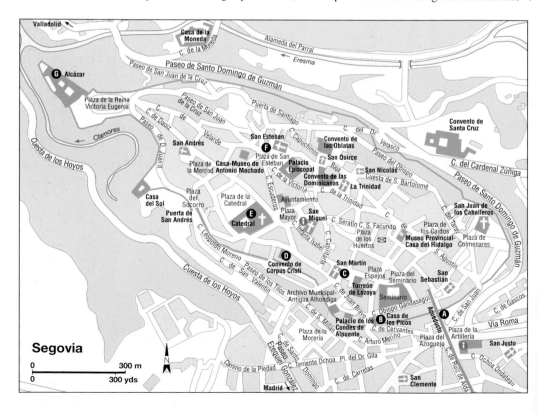

Segovia

Maps:
Area 152
City 160

tombs of the Doña's parents. Catching up with the N-I at **Lerma** ❽ allows a stop at this town rising like a mirage over the Río Arlanza. The grandiose baroque buildings here were built by the Duke of Lerma in 1605. The town's fortress-like appearance is peculiar considering the time it was built, and is testimony to 17th-century Spain's longing for the glory of the Middle Ages.

About 12 miles (20 km) southeast of Covarrubias, the **Monasterio de Santo Domingo de Silos** ❾ (open daily; free) is famed for two things: its magnificent 12th-century Romanesque cloister, and its community of Benedictine monks who hit the classical charts in 1994 with their recorded version of Gregorian chant. Visitors can hear live plainsong at the church services – it is a dignified and moving experience. The monks spend the rest of their time gardening, studying and bee-keeping. There are guided tours of the splendidly carved and tranquil cloisters; don't miss the fascinating old pharmacy, containing gorgeous Talavera jars and antique distilling equipment.

Following the N-234 southeast brings you to the small, friendly provincial capital of **Soria** ❿, which attracts comparatively few visitors. The **Museo Numantino** (open Tues–Sun; closed Sun pm; entrance fee) on Calle El Espolón displays archaeological finds from the Celtiberian settlement of Numancia, located just north of the town. The ruined Templar **Monasterio de San Juan de Duero** (open Tues–Sun; closed Sun pm; free), beside the Río Duero east of the town centre, has a memorable cloister of mudéjar arches.

The scenery of flat-topped red hills around Soria is striking. Northwest of the town, tarns glisten against the green wooded hills of the Sierra de Urbión, a popular spot for excursions.

Valladolid

Architectural glories stud the otherwise unappealing city of **Valladolid** ⓫. It is an important academic and industrial centre with interesting historical associations, but sprawling and confusing for motorists. The church of **San Pablo** to the north of the town centre, and its neighbour the **Colegio de San Gregorio**, have magnificent examples of Plateresque and Isabeline façades, spectacularly ornate and inventive styles of stone-carving which flourished during the 15th and 16th centuries. The latter houses the wonderful **Museo Nacional de Escultura** (open Tues–Sun; closed Sun pm; entrance fee), a crash course in the sculpture of the Spanish Renaissance, including works by the great masters Juan de Juni, Alonso de Berruguete and Diego de Siloé.

Valladolid's **catedral** is in the sombre Herreran style. South of the centre, the **Museo Oriental** (open daily; entrance fee), housed in an Augustinian college, has a fine collection of decorative objects from China and the Philippines.

BELOW: a painting in the ancient Monasterio Santo Domingo de Silos.

City of poets

Of all the cities of Castile, **Segovia** ⓬ may be the one whose charms are most evident at first sight. Only 92 km (57 miles) from Madrid on the N-VI and N-603 highways, Segovia fills up with *madrileños* every weekend, who come to admire the Roman aqueduct and the fairytale Alcázar, and feast on the cuisine for which the province is famous. The city has been compared to a ship sailing between the Ríos Clamores and Ledesma, or the aqueduct to a harp made of stone.

Model of Segovia's famous Roman aqueduct.

Segovia became important under the Romans, who built the aqueduct in the 1st century AD. The city was long favoured by Castilian royalty, and Isabella the Catholic was proclaimed Queen here in 1474. In 1480 it became the headquarters of the dreaded Inquisitor Torquemada.

Economic recession, war and a 1599 plague nearly brought Segovia to ruins, but it rose again under the Bourbons, who built their summer palace at La Granja nearby. It became a city known for its writers and artists, the most famous of whom was the early 20th-century poet Antonio Machado. The elegant **Parador Nacional**, on a hill overlooking the city, is now a favourite retreat of film directors, actors and other luminaries of the Madrid arts scene.

Roman marvel

All roads to Segovia lead to the **acueducto Ⓐ**. One of the largest Roman constructions still standing in Spain, it carried water until the 20th century. Its 165 arches rise as high as 29 metres (96 ft) over the **Plaza del Azoguejo**. The huge granite blocks stay in place without mortar, which may have fed the medieval legend that the Devil built the aqueduct in one night. Recently the granite was found to be crumbling and traffic was banned from passing beneath.

From the Plaza del Azoguejo, follow the Calle de Cervantes uphill to the old city, past the **Casa del los Picos Ⓑ** (closed to the public), a noble house decorated in the 15th century with diamond-shaped blocks of stone. A few steps beyond is the **Plaza de San Martín**, with the beautiful Romanesque **Iglesia de San Martín Ⓒ** (open daily; free) and a circle of Renaissance mansions. In the middle of the plaza is a statue of Segovian hero Juan Bravo, who led the citizens in their disastrous resistance against the army of Carlos V in 1520.

BELOW:
Segovia's Alcázar.

The **Convento de Corpus Cristi** ⬤ (open daily; free), consecrated in 1410, was once the largest synagogue in Segovia. The old Jewish Quarter, or *judería*, along Calle San Frutos, still has houses with tiny windows which allowed the inhabitants ventilation, but not a view of the street.

On **Plaza Mayor** stands the late-Gothic **catedral** ⬤ (open daily; entrance fee), designed by Juan Gil de Hontañón and his son Rodrigo. The Isabeline cloister was transplanted here from the old cathedral, which was burned during the insurrection against Charles V. It contains the tombs of the architects and that of María del Salto, a Jewish woman wrongly accused of adultery. She was flung from a cliff and saved by the Virgin, whom she prayed to as she fell. In the Capilla Santa Catalina is the tomb of Prince Pedro, who slipped from his nurse's arms from a balcony to his death at the Alcázar.

Of the 18 Romanesque churches in Segovia, the most beautiful is **San Esteban** ⬤ (open daily; free), behind Plaza Mayor, with its golden arcaded tower.

Fairytale castle

The **Alcázar** ⬤ (open daily; entrance fee) stands at the western end of the city, the prow of the Segovian ship. Destroyed by fire in the 19th century, its 1882 restoration combines reconstruction of some mudéjar elements with contemporary taste in castles, and the result looks like a child's dream of a castle. Two of the most interesting rooms are the **Sala de Reyes**, containing wooden carvings of the early Castilian, Leonese and Asturian kings, and **Sala del Cordón**, decorated with a frieze of the Franciscan cord. According to legend, Alfonso the Wise once ventured the heretical opinion that the earth moved around the sun. A bolt of lightning followed this remark and, terrified, he wore the penitential cord for the rest of his life. The arduous climb up the **Torre de Juan II** is rewarded by sweeping views of the Segovian countryside and Sierra de Guadarrama.

Little Versailles

The French-style palace of **La Granja de San Ildefonso** ⓭ (tel: 921-47 00 19; open Tues–Sun; entrance fee), lies 11 km (7 miles) southeast of Segovia. It symbolises the vast differences between the Bourbon monarchs who built it and their dour Habsburg predecessors. As if it were a portent, the old Habsburg retreat in these mountains burned to the ground after a visit from Carlos II, the imbecilic end of the Habsburg line. Felipe V of Bourbon bought the farm and commissioned a palace suitable for the retirement of an enlightened 18th-century despot.

A team of French and Italian architects built something along the lines of a modest Versailles, the royal residence outside Paris. The palace has interesting collections of marbles, paintings, furniture, lamps, clocks, porcelains, carpets and Flemish tapestries, with the inevitable Spanish touch of a chapel full of saints' bones and teeth. The most splendid part of San Ildefonso, however, are the gardens and fountains. You can usually catch the fountains on summer weekends at 6pm, but the gardens are especially pretty in autumn, when the yellow linden and elm trees are reflected in the pools. ❏

Maps
Area 152
City 160

During the Segovian festival of Santa Agüeda in February, women dress in traditional costume and take over the running of the provincial villages. Some say it's time this ritual was no longer treated as a joke.

BELOW: detail from La Granja de San Ildefonso.

CASTILLA-LA MANCHA

Maps:
Area 166
City 168

*_is region is the quintessential Spain – immense rolling plains,
studded with windmills and castles, fill the landscape,
_rrupted by olive groves, vineyards and dusty medieval villages*

O riginally part of New Castile, so-named when the northern Castilian kings wrested the area from Moorish control in 1085, La Mancha is, in turn, centred around Toledo, capital of Visigothic Spain and national treasury of art and architecture. Cuenca, with its Gothic and Renaissance quarter, unique *Casas Colgadas* (Hanging Houses) and Museo de Arte Abstracto is the area's second urban attraction, followed by Albacete, Guadalajara and Ciudad Real. Picturesque towns and villages are everywhere – Tembleque, Segóbriga, Sigüenza, Brihuega, Almagro, Ocaña and many more.

Natural phenomena, from the wetlands of the Tablas de Daimiel to the peaks of the Sierra de Alcaraz and the forests and meadows of the Parque Nacional de Cabañeros, are abundant and varied. The medieval castles at Belmonte, Calatrava la Nueva, Alarcón and Sigüenza provide another theme for exploring La-Mancha, as does the Don Quixote trail, from the windmills at Campo de Criptana to the village of El Toboso and the Lagunas de Ruidera, all identifiable in episodes of Cervantes' great opus, universally recognised as world literature's first modern psychological novel.

"*En un lugar de la Mancha de cuyo nombre no quiero acordarme*" (In a place in La Mancha, the name of which I do not wish to recall), the opening line of *Don Quijote de la Mancha*, is the most famous sentence in Spanish letters, just as Spain's dead centre, south of Madrid, may well be the most quintessentially Spanish portion of the Iberian Peninsula.

Toledo – Spain in a nutshell

Toledo ❶ is La Mancha's and Spain's historical and cultural heart, former Spanish capital and still today the religious seat of the nation. A natural fortress occupying high ground with the Río Tajo protecting all but its northern flank, the Roman city of Toletum was founded in AD 192. Little is left of the Roman occupation; a **Circo Romano** off the Avenida de la Reconquista, and a few mosaics and reconstructed buildings. By the 6th century the Visigoths had set up court in Toledo. The Visigothic Councils, the name given to the meetings between the Visigothic king and his advisers, were held on the site where the Mezquita Cristo de la Luz now stands.

In AD 711, the city was taken over by the Muslims, and became capital of Christian Spain in 1085 under Alfonso VI. By the 12th century, Toledo was also Spain's most important Jewish centre with over 12,000 Jewish citizens. During the 13th century under Alfonso X el Sabio (the Wise), Toledo became a cultural forum within which Muslims, Jews and Christians lived in mutual tolerance and collaborated in a school of translators responsible for introducing much

LEFT: Castilian shepherd. **BELOW:** windmill country.

of Arabic and Greek science and philosophy into the early Spanish Romance and, from there, into the budding European Renaissance.

This tolerance left its mark on the city's architecture and art. The mozarabic style of architecture was developed by Christians living under Muslim domination, while mudéjar style, well displayed in the **Taller del Moro** mudéjar palace (open Tues–Sun; entrance fee) behind the cathedral, was the work of Muslims who remained in the areas reconquered by Christians. Less apparent are the remains of Jewish influence in the city. Of the ten synagogues, only two managed to survive the Jewish progroms. The 1492 Expulsion decree was a blow to Toledo's fortunes. In 1561 Felipe II moved the Spanish court to Madrid, and by the middle of the 17th century Toledo's population was half what it had been 100 years before.

Today, Toledo is a small regional capital (pop. 62,000), but such is her beauty and history that the entire old city is a national monument, and also listed as part of the UN's World Heritage. The city lies 72 km (45 miles) south of Madrid. The unusual neo-mudéjar train station is a good starting point for a visit. Just outside

Rich, sweet marzipan, a Toledo speciality found in shops and cafés around the city, is a reviving snack or portable souvenir.

the station, the city's majestic patrician profile rises above the Río Tajo gorge. Cross the river on the **Puente de Alcántara** , the oldest bridge leading into town. It was built by the Romans, then refurbished successfully by the Muslims and the Christians. On the hill opposite the city is the **Castillo de San Servando**, built by the Romans to protect the bridge.

The main entrance to the city is by the **Puerta de Bisagra**, the most impressive of the nine toll-collecting gates along the old city walls. In the **Puerta de Cambrón**, at the west end of the city, you can still read the medieval plaque advising gatekeepers that Toledo residents need not pay.

Churches, synagogues and mosques

Visible from quite a distance on the *meseta*, the **catedral** (open daily; entrance fee) itself is testament to Toledo's long history as Spain's spiritual capital long after the Royal court moved to Madrid. The Goths worshiped on the site before the Muslim invasion, when the church was converted to a mosque. The present Spanish Gothic structure, with five broad naves around a central choir, was begun in 1226 and finished 300 years later, during which time mudéjar, baroque and neoclassical elements were added. The large polychrome retable depicting the life of Christ; the famously excessive baroque and neoclassical Transparente altarpiece, built to allow in natural light; the sacristy with its collection of paintings by El Greco, Titian, Goya and Van Dyck; the sumptuous walnut and alabaster choir stalls and mudéjar ceiling in the chapterhouse are just a few of the wealth of details here. Allow one to two hours to enjoy a complete and leisurely visit.

The **Mezquita Cristo de la Luz** (open daily am only; free) is possibly one of the oldest buildings in the city; Alfonso VI held mass here when he conquered Toledo in 1085. There is a pleasant garden behind the church which leads to the top of the **Puerta del Sol**, the old Moorish gate. The church was used as a mosque for 400 years, hence its name. To get a sense of the Visigothic presence in Toledo, visit the **Iglesia de San Román** (open Tues–Sun; entrance fee), where the Visigothic Culture and Councils Museum has been installed. In the museum are copies of the stunning Visigothic crown jewels.

The major synagogue which survived the 14th-century programs is known today as the **Sinagoga de Santa María la Blanca** (open daily; entrance fee), located on Calle Reyes Católicos. The most striking feature of the synagogue are the capitals, which reflect a Byzantine or Persian influence. The iris, symbol of honesty, and the Star of David play prominent roles in the synagogue's interior ornamentation. Except for the three chapels at the head of the building, added in the 16th century, the synagogue is much as it was before it was converted into a church in the latter half of the 15th century. The other surviving synagogue is **El Tránsito** close by, a simpler 14th-century structure, with superb Almohad-style plasterwork on the walls, which today houses the **Museo Sefardi** (open Tues–Sun; entrance fee).

The other major Catholic structure in Toledo, after

Maps:
Area 166
City 168

TIP

Ideally, try to spend the night in Toledo to catch the city's magic when empty of tourist crowds. Also bear in mind that most monuments close for lunch.

BELOW: festival time in Toledo.

the cathedral, is **San Juan de los Reyes** (open daily; free), located in what is left of the *judería*, the old Jewish quarter. The Gothic monastery, with a lovely cloister and church, was built by the Catholic Monarchs, Fernando and Isabel.

El Greco

Detail from El Greco's "Agony in the Garden". Trained and influenced by Italian masters, El Greco imbued his work with a freshness and vigour that makes his paintings seem alive and contemporary even today.

Toledo is permanently and inextricably associated with the painter Domenikos Theotocopoulos, known as El Greco, born in Crete in 1541. El Greco lived and worked in Toledo from 1577 until his death in 1614. His paintings are spread throughout the city. One of his masterpieces, *The Burial of the Count of Orgaz*, is in the **Iglesia de Santo Tomé** (open daily; free) on Calle Santo Tomé. The complexity, the blend of the temporal and spiritual and the inclusion of many supposed portraits, including El Greco's own, are just some of the ingredients that make this painting so memorable.

El Greco lived in the Jewish section of the city just behind El Tránsito. His house is no longer standing but a nearby 16th-century dwelling known today as the **Casa-Museo de El Greco** (closed for restoration) contains several paintings including the famous *View of Toledo* – painted from the north of the city – and some of the artist's possessions. The **Museo de Santa Cruz** (open daily; entrance fee), just off the central plaza, holds fine El Greco paintings as well as several rooms of typically Toledan crafts, armour and damascened swords. The building itself is beautiful, particularly its Plateresque entrance and staircase and the splendid mudéjar wooden ceilings.

Outside the city walls, the **Hospital de Tavera** (open daily; free), built in the 16th century, holds El Greco's *The Holy Family*, *The Baptism of Christ* and several important portraits of saints. One of the few Renaissance interiors which

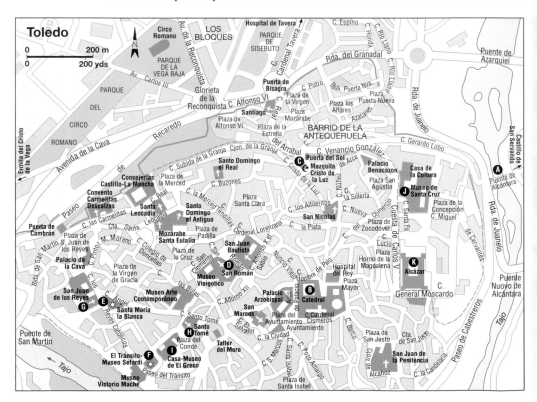

has kept intact much of an original art collection, it also has fine paintings by Caravaggio, Titian and Tintoretto.

The **Alcázar**  (open Tues–Sun; entrance fee) dates back to the era of El Cid, and its occupants, architects and purposes have been numerous. From the patio you can get a good sense of the strategic importance of the place. The Alcázar is the result of the work of Spain's finest 16th-century architects, though now heavily restored. It was burned and sacked by both English and French invaders and was the site of a famous siege during the Civil War. Today, the museum inside, dedicated to Franco's triumph over the "Communist hordes" of the Second Republic, as the commemorative plaque says, is due for overhaul as the future home of the Museo del Ejército.

The best known crafts in the city are the very striking damascene (black enamel inlaid with gold, silver and copper wire), steel knives, swords and the fine ceramic work from nearby **Talavera de la Reina** ❷. Here, the **Museo Ruiz de Luna** (open Tues–Sun; entrance fee) near Plaza de San Pedro is the place to see ceramics of all kinds, while the **Ermita de La Virgen del Prado** (open daily; free) houses traditional ceramic murals depicting religious themes. Talavera has an extraordinary old quarter featuring a 15th-century bridge and Roman ramparts. From here it is a short walk to the **Colegiata** (open daily; free), known for its rose window, and the best of the town's four churches.

The charming small town of **Oropesa** ❸, 32 km (20 miles) west of Talavera de la Reina on the N-V, has an excellent 14th-century **castillo** (open daily; entrance fee), part of which is now a parador, as well as several fine medieval and Renaissance buildings.

Covering an area of approximately 1,000 sq. km (400 sq. miles) to the south

Maps:
Area 166
City 168

BELOW: view of Toledo and the Río Tajo.

of Talavera and Toledo are the **Montes de Toledo** ❹, a low mountain range stretching west towards Extremadura. Travelling along the northern edge of the range on the C-401 and turning south onto the C-403 will bring you to the **Parque Nacional de Cabañeros**, consisting mainly of evergreen woodland and sheep pasture. You can take a guided tour of the park in a four-wheel drive vehicle, during which you may well see wild boar, stag and imperial eagles.

Southern La Mancha

Approximately 100 km (60 miles) south of Toledo on the C-401 is the old provincial capital of **Ciudad Real** ❺. Within the ringroad, the streets trace the line of the medieval ramparts and have bustling, boisterous bars, cafés and restaurants. The city is accessed from the north via the 14th-century Puerta de Toledo. The 13th-century **Iglesia de Santiago** and the **catedral** are the city's most interesting architectural features. It is in the countryside around the city, however, that some of La Mancha's greatest treasures can be found. The **Parque Nacional Tablas de Daimiel**, just northeast, is one of Spain's most important wetlands, a national park on the Río Guadiana and rallying point for migratory waterfowl from all over Europe. The town of **Almagro** ❻, southeast of Ciudad Real, is the site of an unusual stone Plaza Mayor with wooden porticoes and green painted balconies. At No.17 is a 16th-century Corral de Comedias (outdoor theatre) where an annual summer theatre festival is held.

Calatrava la Nueva ❼ (open Tues–Sun; entrance fee), on the CR-504 approximately 35 km (20 miles) south of Almagro, is a spectacular sight. This immense castle-monastery, which was founded in 1217 by the military Order of Calatrava, is visible for miles around. It was later used as a monastery

BELOW: beloved Don Quixote and Sancho Panza.

THE QUIXOTE TRAIL

A tour of central La Mancha is an ideal opportunity for fans of Don Quixote to trace key points from various chapters of Cervantes' novel – the world's first bestseller. El Toboso, on the N-301 between Albacete and Ocaña, was the village of Dulcinea, Don Quixote's fantasized true love and damsel for whom he was to risk all. A local house (Casa de Dulcinea, open Tues–Sun; entrance fee), thought to be that of the woman Cervantes had in mind, has been restored to its 16th-century appearance. The town hall has copies of Don Quixote in some three dozen languages. Puerto Lápice, 20 km (12 miles) southeast of Consuegra, matches Cervantes' description of the inn where Don Quixote officially swore in as a knight errant.

Nearby Campo de Criptana and its fleet of windmills arranged in on-line formation look ominously like the ones that made Quixote's day back in 1605, while Cueva de Montesinos, near the San Pedro lake in the Lagunas de Ruidera valley, is the very cave in which our hero was treated by Montesinos himself to elegiac visions of other bewitched knights errant and of his beloved Dulcinea.

The nearby village of Argamasilla de Alba is a firm candidate, among several, to be the place where it all began: "*En un lugar de la Mancha ...*".

until it was ruined by an earthquake in 1802. The triple-naved church has since been restored.

Nearby **Viso del Marqués** is the site of the 16th-century Renaissance colossus, **Palacio del Viso** (open Tues–Sun; entrance fee), built by the Marqués de Santa Cruz don Álvaro de Bazán, the most famous admiral in Spanish naval history, who defeated the Turks at the battle of Lepanto in 1571. The sumptuous interior is decorated with lovely Italian frescoes. **Valdepeñas**, just across the N-IV motorway, is the centre of Spain's most productive vineyards. There is an excellent wine-tasting museum, the **Bodega Museo**, at Calle Cristo 102 (tel: 926-31 17 21; open daily; free).

Windmills and castles

Consuegra ❽ is known for its windmills, its 13th-century castle and the late October saffron harvest, during which one or more of the windmills are set in motion. **Tembleque**, a little further north and so-named for "trembling" victims of medieval banditry, is built around one of Spain's most beautiful central squares, a triple-tiered, porticoed gem occasionally used as a bullring. Closer to the capital, and just off the N-401 between Madrid and Toledo, **Illescas** was the site of one of Felipe II's summer residences. Its 16th-century **Hospital de la Caridad** (open daily; entrance fee) is well worth visiting since it still houses five El Greco paintings.

Eighty km (50 miles) east, **Belmonte** ❾ has a splendidly preserved 15th-century **castillo** (open daily; entrance fee), originally built by the Marquis de Villena, Juan Pacheco, to defend the domains he is alleged to have accumulated through a series of adroit court intrigues.

Map on page 166

BELOW: the windmills at Consuegra.

Albacete ⑩, at Castilla-La Mancha's southeastern corner, famous for cutlery since Moorish times, has an excellent parador and, in the Parque Abelardo Sanchez, a **Museo Provincial** (open Tues-Sun; entrance fee) with some good Iberian and Roman objects. The nearby town of **Chinchilla de Monte Aragón** is built around a pretty Plaza Mayor, which has some lively bars and restaurants. The 15th-century castle above the town offers sweeping views south over the plains to the picturesque **Sierra de Alcaraz,** where the mountain peaks and fertile green valleys give way to spectacular gorges and little-explored villages. The town of **Alcaraz** ⑪, with its twin Renaissance towers in the attractive Plaza Mayor, is a good place for an overnight stay if you want to tour this area.

The rather singular village of **Alcalá del Júcar**, 50 km (30 miles) northeast of Albacete, literally juts out over the Júcar gorges, with houses excavated into the limestone. Some of the houses even have balconies over the far side, reached via long corridors.

Northeast Castilla-La Mancha

Lying just to the west of the main N-320 to Cuenca, the fortified town of **Alarcón** ⑫ is one of Spain's best examples of medieval military architecture. Almost completely encircled by the Río Júcar, the triangular castle, now converted to a Parador Nacional, is defended by three defensive ramparts. A Muslim stronghold, the town was subjected to a nine-month siege in 1184 before finally succumbing to the Christian conquerers.

Approximately 55 km (34 miles) to the north is the city of **Cuenca** ⑬. The old part of town, with mainly Gothic and Renaissance buildings, lies north of the modern city at the top of a steep hill. The **Casas Colgadas** (Hanging Houses)

BELOW:
strange rock
formations at
Ciudad Encantada,
northeast of
Cuenca.

Map on page 166

teetering on the edge of the cliff over the Río Huécar are the old town's most emblematic feature. Inside one of these houses is the **Museo de Arte Abstracto** (open Tues–Sun; entrance fee), with one of the best collections of abstract art in Spain, including works by Chillida, Tàpies, Saura, Zobel, Cuixart, Sempere, Rivera and others. The 18th-century **Plaza Mayor** and the mainly Gothic **catedral** (open daily; free), built on the site of a mosque between the 12th and 16th century, are other key sights. The **Serranía de Cuenca**, to the northeast of the city, is an area of pleasant, rolling hills and grassy meadows – a refreshing antidote to sun-baked countryside of much of the interior. One of the most unusual sights in this region is the Ciudad Encantada (Enchanted City), east of Villalba de la Sierra, named for its strange, twisted limestone formations.

West of Cuenca, just off the N-III motorway to Madrid, are the remains of the Roman settlement of **Segóbriga** ⓮ (open Tues–Sun; entrance fee). The ruined city includes a 2,000-spectator capacity theatre dating to the 3rd century which is still sometimes used to stage plays.

In the region's far northeastern corner, **Guadalajara's** ⓯ flamboyant Gothic-mudéjar **Palacio de los Duques del Infantado** (open daily; entrance fee), with its exquisitely carved façade, is the city's most notable structure. The **catedral** at nearby **Sigüenza** ⓰ is the site of the strikingly lifelike El Doncel, tomb of Martín Vázquez de Arce, a page of Isabel of Castile's who was killed in the taking of Granada in 1486. **La Alcarria**, the area east of Guadalajara around the so-called Mar de Castilla (Castilian Sea) formed by two reservoirs has ancient villages such as **Pastrana**. **Drihuega**, 30 km (18 miles) northeast of Guadalajara, has a picturesque medieval centre notable for its narrow streets, aristrocratic houses and for its Plaza Mayor. ❑

BELOW: the Casas Colgadas in Cuenca.

EXTREMADURA

Walk through the honey-coloured old section of an Extremaduran town and step back in time to a land of conquistador gold and baroque palaces

Map on page 176

Madrid

Bordered to the west by Portugal and to the north and south by granite mountain ranges, the arid plains and hills of Extremadura are sweet with the scent of wild thyme and eucalyptus. Cattle- and sheep-raising are traditional occupations here, while forests of cork oaks provide rooting grounds for the native black pigs which are turned into superb cured hams. A complex network of dams built since the 1960s irrigates newer market gardens and vineyards, and provides water and power to large areas of Spain.

"Land of the conquistadors, land of the gods", is a refrain travellers to this region may hear. You might also come across the apocryphal remark attributed to a French soldier, who declared that Extremaduran cooking made Spain worth invading. *Extremeños* are hospitable, expansive, horse-loving, straightforward and independent, the legacy of centuries of poverty and isolation.

Archaeological evidence, including cave paintings and Europe's only known Tartessan site, point to an extensive prehistoric settlement of the area. Mild winters and generally fertile soil made it the site of several Roman towns, most notably Mérida, which became a kind of luxury retirement colony for distinguished soldiers. Subsequent invasions of Visigoths and Moors disturbed the *Pax Romana*, however, and during the Reconquest the region became a noman's frontier land between Muslims and Christians. From the 13th century the victorious Christian military religious orders, such as Knights Templar, were granted huge tracts of land to resettle. Rural life in a vast, lonely territory is said to have helped shape the intrepid character of the conquistador.

About a third of the Spaniards who set out to explore and conquer America came from Extremadura; those who survived and triumphed named New World settlements and returned to build magnificent palaces in their home towns. Some of the houses are still inhabited by their descendants; others have become hotels or public buildings, or been abandoned to overwintering storks. Money and glory passed quickly through this land, leaving it as remote as ever when economic decline began in the 16th century.

LEFT: Trujillo's main square. **BELOW:** a local farmer.

Shrine and spiritual heart

Perched amid wooded sierras, 214 km (133 miles) southwest of Madrid, the town of **Guadalupe** ❶ is a striking point of entry to the region. Since the late-13th century, when a shepherd chanced upon a buried image of the Virgin Mary purportedly carved by St Luke, Guadalupe has been an important place of pilgrimage. Alfonso XI dedicated a battle to this Virgin in 1340; when she brought him victory he ordered the construction of a splendid monastery in which to house her. Christopher Columbus brought the first

In 1531, the Guadalupe Virgin appeared to Mexican peasant Juan Diego. More than 100 cities in the New World bear her name and, today, she is a symbol of "hispanidad", drawing thousands of pilgrims every year from the Spanish-speaking world.

Indians to be baptised to Guadalupe, where the rite was performed at the town fountain in 1496. Over the next few centuries wealthy pilgrims enriched the monastery's order of Hieronymite monks and donated funds for additions to the original building, which served as a combination palace, church, fortress and royal lodgings (the latter now a hotel).

By the 15th century the shrine was known as the "Spanish Vatican" and possessed hospitals, schools of fine arts, grammar and medicine, 30,000 head of cattle and what was possibly the world's best library. Guadalupe was also a renowned centre for the treatment of syphilis, and had a hospital specialising in the "sweat cure". The old Hospital San Juan Bautista, with a graceful 16th-century patio, is now the Parador Zurbarán, across the street from the monastery.

Such became the wealth and power of the monastery that a popular refrain went: "Better than count or duke, to be a monk in Guadalupe." The place was sacked by the French in 1809 and in 1835, when the Spanish government ordered the sale of monastic property, the Hieronymites fled. Today, however, it is once again the region's spiritual heart.

The Virgin's treasures

Presently the **Monasterio de Guadalupe** (open daily 9am–1pm, 3.30–6.30pm; entrance fee; tel: 927-154128) is inhabited by Franciscan monks, who provide both lodging for visitors and a tour of Guadalupe's treasures. A visit begins in the 14th-century Gothic *mudéjar* **cloister**, with its two-tiered horseshoe archways and lovely fountain surrounded by a miniature temple. The old **refectory** houses a dazzling collection of priests' robes, embroidered with gold threads and encrusted with pearls. Of further interest is the collection of illuminated choir

BELOW: the Guadalupe Virgin.

Map on page 176

books, and a room containing the Virgin's own rich wardrobe, necklaces and crowns, given to her by kings, presidents and popes.

The artistic highlight of the tour is the **sacristy**, nicknamed the Spanish Sistine Chapel, where portraits of monks by 17th-century master Zurbarán are set against lavishly decorated walls. Finally, up a red marble staircase is the **camarín**, where the Virgin resides. Around her in the room are statues of the eight strong women of the Bible. The famous iron grille in the **church,** entered separately off the plaza, is said to be made from the chains of freed slaves.

The cobbled streets of the town wind among traditional Extremaduran slate houses, their wooden balconies full of potted geraniums. In addition to devotional souvenirs and pottery, you can also take home a bottle of *gloria*, a local drink made of *aguardiente*, grape juice and herbs.

Crossing the **Sierra de Guadalupe** south takes you through the mountain villages of **Logrosán** and **Zorita**, the former boasting the remains of a pre-Roman town on a nearby hillside. Catch up with the main highway, the N-V, at **Miajadas**. From there you can take a 28-km (17-mile) detour to **Medellín**, birthplace of the conqueror of Mexico, Hernán Cortés. Climb up to the ruined **castle** and survey the **Río Guadiana** shimmering below. Medellín is a pleasant, quiet village, noted for its outsize bronze statue of Cortés in the town square – a rare representation, since there are no statues of him in Mexico.

Roman city, modern capital

Formerly known as Emeritus Augustus, **Mérida** ❷ lies 127 km (79 miles) south of Guadalupe, on a sluggish bend of the Guadiana. Founded in 25 BC, the city became a prosperous capital of the Roman colony of Lusitania, and Roman

The hands and face of the Guadalupe Virgin are dark brown after her 700 years underground and, according to the Franciscan guide, because the Moors tried to set her on fire.

BELOW: classical drama at Mérida's Roman theatre during its summer festival.

Roman mosaic depicting grape harvest celebrations.

TIP

It's worth buying a combined ticket for entry to all the Roman sites in Mérida. Ask at the tourist office by the gates of the Teatro Romano.

BELOW: the Milagros Aqueduct.

ruins are Mérida's pride today. Naturally, it is a mecca for archaeologists. Yet this lovely city, whose buildings and hedges of myrtle and hibiscus give a flavour of the Spanish south, also dreams of modernity. Since becoming capital of the autonomous region in 1981 its skyline has been reshaped by largely brash new development, although Calatrava's sleek Lusitania bridge and Rafael Moneo's stunning museum are both strokes of genius.

In July, Mérida hosts a classical theatre festival, which attracts Spanish and international companies and directors. Performances are held in the **Teatro Romano** and **Anfiteatro**, which seat 6,000 and 14,000 spectators, respectively. Nearby are the hippodrome, formerly used for chariot races, and the **Casa Romana del Mithraeo**, which was actually a small palace. Of particular interest are the mosaic floors depicting the four seasons, and the remains of a sauna. The **Casa del Anfiteatro** also has exceptionally good mosaics and the remains of some paintings (all sites open daily, 9am–1.45pm and 4–6.15pm; 5–7.15pm in summer; entrance fee).

Modern museum

Across the street from the theatres is the brick **Museo Nacional de Arte Romano** (1989), designed by Rafael Moneo, a superb building which holds the largest collection of Roman artefacts outside Italy (open daily 10am–2pm, 4–6pm (5–7pm Apr–Sept); entrance fee). The main hall of the museum, with its high archways and dramatic use of natural light, has the feeling of a cathedral nave, and is an impressive backdrop for the colossal statues. Two storeys of galleries built around the main hall are dedicated to theme exhibits, such as rare painted friezes, jewellery and glass, replicas of which are on sale nearby.

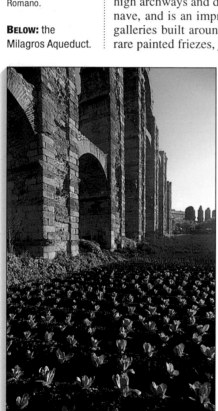

The **Arco de Trajano**, just off the Plaza de España, measures 15 metres (50 ft) by 9 metres (30 ft), dwarfing the narrow street and nearby houses. A short walk away in Calle Romero Leal is the **Templo de Diana** (1st century AD but with Renaissance additions) and the 9th century riverside **Alcazaba**, with ruins inside it. On the edge of town are the **Puente de Guadiana**, with its 60 granite arches (now open only for pedestrian traffic), and the **Milagros Aqueduct**, which brought water to Mérida until quite recently. The aqueduct leads from the La Prosepina Reservoir, which is now used for windsurfing.

Badajoz

The capital of Extremadura's southern province, Badajoz ❸ is just 6 km (3½ miles) from the Portuguese border. Originally a Roman town named Pax Augustus, it rose to prominence as Batalajoz, capital of a taifa, and once dominated half of Portugal, including Lisbon. It was captured from the Muslims in 1229, but its strategic location made it the site of many bloody sieges over the centuries.

In August 1936 it was captured by Nationalist forces, and, in one of the darkest moments of the Civil War, many Republican defenders (possibly several thousand but the exact figure is unknown) were herded into the bullring and shot. The poverty which made the city a Republican stronghold has been partially

Map on page 176

alleviated by the Badajoz Plan, a government programme of land expropriation and irrigation, begun in the 1960s.

Badajoz is now the largest city in Extremadura, and her stolid post-war appearance is given limited spark by the monuments suggesting its lost Muslim and medieval splendour. On a hill called **Orinace**, 60 metres (200 ft) over the Río Guadiana, the Moorish kings built their castle, the **Alcazaba**. Many of the original ramparts and towers remain standing, the most interesting of which is the octagonal **Espantaperros**, so called because the vibrations of its ancient bell were at a pitch that terrified dogs. The Alcazaba has pretty gardens and palm trees left over from Arab times, and the keyhole doorways are particularly evocative of the city's greatest moment. Inside is an interesting **Museo Arqueológico** (open Tues–Sun; free).

Also worth a look in Badajoz are the **Puerta de Palmas**, the old city gate, designed by Herrera, and the Gothic **Catedral,** which has impressive Renaissance choir stalls, paintings by Morales and Zurbarán, and a stunning tiled cloister.

South of Badajoz by the N-432 and N-435, is the whitewashed town of **Jerez de los Caballeros**, seat of the Knights Templar and birthplace of Nuñez de Balboa, who discovered the Pacific Ocean. Fountains, churches and heraldic shields are found at every turn in the narrow, sloping streets. The town is famous for its Easter Processions and is also a good place to try the local ham.

Noble hotheads

Cáceres ❹, the capital of the northern Extremaduran province, is a city lifted out of the pages of an illuminated book of chivalry. Over the centuries, Cáceres has been miraculously spared the sieges and bombardments which destroyed

Discovered in 1978 near Zalamea de la Serena in southeastern Extremadura are the remains of a 6th-century BC temple-palace, Cancho Ruano, the world's only known Tartessan monument. Enquire at Zalamea's town hall (tel: 924-78 00 32) to visit the site.

BELOW: the Museo Nacional de Arte Romano, Mérida.

TIP

The best time to wander around Cáceres is at dusk, as the street lights come on. Tip the porter and you may be allowed a peek into the patios of some of the inhabited palaces.

parts of other Extremaduran cities, and its old quarter was one of the first in Spain to be declared a national monument in 1949. The old city is separated from the new by well-preserved walls and towers originally built in Muslim times, and is best approached on foot from the **Plaza Mayor**. For the most dramatic ascent, climb the steps leading through the **Arco de la Estrella**.

During the Middle Ages the atmosphere was rather more hectic. When Alfonso IX took the city from the Moors in 1229, it became the seat of a brotherhood of knights called the *Fratres de Cáceres,* who eventually became Spain's most noble order, the Order of Santiago, and a wealthy centre of free trade. At one time there were 300 knights in the city, their palaces just a few steps from one another. Each *solar*, or noble house, had its own defensive tower, and the continual factions and rivalries meant that there was always a small war in progress somewhere around town. In the interests of peace Ferdinand and Isabella ordered the destruction of most of the towers in 1476, save those belonging to their favourites. Of the few which are left, the most striking is perhaps the **Torre de las Cigüeñas**, or Stork Tower, in the **Plaza San Mateo**.

Palaces and patios

Directly opposite is the **Casa de las Veletas**, a baroque palace built on the site of the Moorish castle (open Tues–Sun 9.30am–2.30pm; entrance fee). In the basement is an enormous arcaded *aljibe*, or cistern, which looks like a flooded mosque. Upstairs is the **Museo Provincial** containing artifacts from prehistoric Cáceres, Roman coins and local handicrafts and costumes. There are also reproductions of the cave paintings in the nearby caves of **Maltravieso** and contemporary Spanish art on display. Close by is the Jewish quarter, recently restored.

BELOW: buttercups in an olive grove, Extremadura.

To the left of the museum is the church of **San Mateo**, with a beautiful bell tower, and the **Convento de San Pablo**, inhabited by cloistered nuns who sell their famous *yemas* (candied yolks) through a screened dumbwaiter to avoid showing their faces to the world.

While the old town's palaces range in architectural style from Gothic to Plateresque, they blend harmoniously together through their sober grey-gold sandstone and granite façades. Palaces of particular note include the **Casa de los Solís**, with its coat of arms in the shape of a sun, and the **Casa del Mono** (monkey), now a library. Near the 16th-century church of **Santa María la Mayor** are the **Bishop's Palace**, the **Palace of Ovando**, with its lush green patio, and the **Casa Toledo-Moctezuma**, once inhabited by the descendants of the conquistador Juan Cano and Aztec Emperor Moctezuma's daughter.

Behind Santa María is the **Casa de los Golfines de Abajo**, a house belonging to a family of French knights invited here in the 12th century to help fight the Muslims. They ended up terrorising Muslims and Christians alike, so that, according to a contemporary chronicler, "even the king cannot subject them, though he has tried". It is believed that the Spanish word *golfo*, meaning "scoundrel", is derived from this family's surname.

Northwest of Cáceres on the C-523 is Alcántara, where the impressive Roman bridge is still in use. A cookbook supposedly stolen from the monastery here is said to be the source of recipes used in French haute cuisine.

Cradle of conquerers

Crowning a dusty hill surrounded by pastureland, **Trujillo ❺** is 47 km (30 miles) east of Cáceres on the N-521. Its number of extraordinarily beautiful monuments make it well worth a two-day visit. The town's long and dramatic history is said to have begun with its founding by Julius Caesar, but the city's proudest moment was clearly the conquest of Peru by native son Francisco

BELOW: statue of Pizarro in Trujillo's Plaza Mayor.

CONQUERORS OF THE NEW WORLD

The conquistadors of the Americas were not, as they are sometimes depicted, village louts but often the second or illegitimate sons of aristocrats, with grand surnames and the military training to go with it, but limited expectations in Spain. Francisco Pizarro, for example, was the bastard son of a minor nobleman from Trujillo who, together with his two half-brothers, set out to capture the fabled wealth of Peru. Even in that delirious time the expedition was widely known as *de los locos* – of the mad men – and did not fail to live up to expectations.

During one desperate moment in the jungle, Pizarro drew a line in the sand with the point of his sword and dared his comrades to cross it and head home. All but 13 did. However, the inroads made by those 13 men convinced Carlos V to give Pizarro the ships and armies he so desperately wanted, and with which he was able to conquer the Inca. A few years later, however, Pizarro was assassinated; his body is buried in Lima cathedral.

Other notable conquistadors from Extremadura include Hernán Cortés, who captured Mexico City, capital of the Aztec empire, in 1521; Hernando de Soto, who discovered the Mississippi in 1540; and Francisco de Orellana, who charted the waters of the Amazon.

Pizarro. His bronze equestrian statue dominates the **Plaza Mayor** (probably Europe's most beautiful car park), and palaces built with wealth from Inca treasures are sprinkled throughout the city.

The **Palacio del Marqués de la Conquista** (open daily; free), built by Pizarros's brother, Hernando, stands across the plaza from the statue. On the ornate façade are busts of Francisco Pizarro and his wife Inés Yupanqui, sister of the Inca emperor Atahualpa. Above them is the coat of arms ceded to them by Charles V. Behind the equestrian statue is the 15th-century church of **San Martín**, whose bell and clock towers provide ample nesting ground for several storks. Inside the church the most valuable work of art is a Baroque crucifixion, known as the *Cristo de la Agonía*.

Military miracles

Across the street from the church is the **Palacio de los Duques de San Carlos** (open daily 10.30am–1pm, 4.30–6.30; entrance fee), a 16th-century palace with a striking Baroque façade and a clutch of chimneys inspired by Inca temples. The house is now inhabited by nuns, who are happy to give a tour of the patio and staircase, as well as tell the story of miracles which occurred in Trujillo.

A few steps outside the plaza's southwest corner is the **Palacio Orellana-Pizarro** (open daily 10.30am–2pm, 4.30–6.30pm; free) also run by nuns, boasting an exquisite Plateresque patio. Francisco de Orellana was a Pizarro cousin, and the first European to navigate the Amazon. He claimed the river for Spain, and eventually perished along its banks.

Each step uphill in Trujillo is a step further back into the past. Follow the **Cuesta de Santiago** past the **Torre del Alfiler** (Needle Tower) up to the Muslim **castillo** (open daily; free). Pause for breath at **Santa María la Mayor**, a 15th-century church containing the tomb of Diego Paredes, the "Samson of Spain". As a young child he was said to have carried the stone baptismal font from the church to his mother's bedside, and Cervantes wrote that as an adult soldier, Diego "defeated the entire French army and held them at the end of a bridge". His tomb, however, is the normal small size of a medieval man. Further up is the **Casa-Museo de Pizarro** (open Tues–Sun 11am–2pm, 4.30–8pm; entrance fee), with exhibits documenting the exploits of the Pizarro family.

From the castle walls there is a panoramic view of the town and surrounding countryside. Upstairs is a chapel dedicated to the Virgin who enabled the Christian armies to take the castle from the Muslims by illuminating a dark fog which had enveloped them. A coin-operated machine allows the visitor to illuminate the granite statue of the Virgin; her bright light can be seen from the Plaza Mayor below.

The two-ton virgin

An attractive town on the banks of the Río Jerte, **Plasencia ➏** is 43 km (27 miles) north of Trujillo by the C-524. Settled by the Berbers, it was conquered by Alfonso VIII, who in 1189 granted it a coat of arms with the title *Placeat Deo et hominibus* (Pleasing to God and Man). Up until 1492 the city continued to

Pizarro's family played an important role in regaining possession of Trujillo during the Reconquest. Their reward was to be allowed to build their home, now the Casa-Museo de Pizarro, within the old city walls.

BELOW: carving in Plasencia's cathedral.

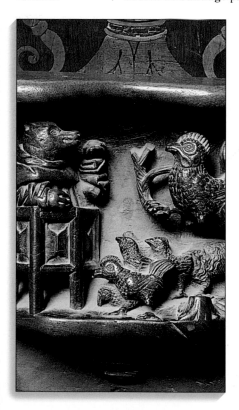

Map on page 176

have large Jewish and Arab populations, reflected by the narrow, winding streets in which they lived, as well as by street names, such as **Calle de las Morenas** (Street of the Dark Women). Try to arrive in Plasencia on a Tuesday, when the market takes place in the **Plaza Mayor**, as it has for 800 years.

Plasencia has an impressive **catedral** (open daily 9am–2.30pm, 4–6pm; closed Sun pm; free), which is actually parts of two cathedrals joined together. The first is 13th–14th-century Romanesque, with some touches of Gothic, while the second is 15th–16th-century Gothic with a Plateresque façade. The older cathedral, reached via a cloister with stone-carving, houses an exceptional collection of religious art including the 2,000-kg (2-ton) stone Virgen de Perdón.

The choir stalls are some of the most beautiful in Spain; the carving represents both sacred and, on the backs of the seats, profane subjects. The sculptor, Rodrigo Alemán, declared that even God couldn't have made such a masterpiece, a blasphemy that got him locked into a nearby castle tower. According to legend, he ended his days by falling from the tower, flapping home-made wings.

Aristrocratic homes

There are several palaces in Plasencia, the grandest of which is the **Palacio del Marqués de Mirabel**, in the Plaza de San Vicente. The house is occupied by the present marquis, but the porter will give an impromptu tour of the Italian-style patio and several of the downstairs rooms if the marquis is out. Nearby, the **Convento de los Dominices** is being converted into a *parador*, and the 14th-century Provincial Hospital on Plazuela Marqués de la Puebla now houses the wonderful **Museo Etnográfico y Textil** (open Wed–Sun 11am–2pm; free), with some vivid exhibits including regional costumes and traditional crafts.

BELOW:
clouds over Trujillo.

To the south of Plasencia is the **Parque de Monfragüe** , a 500 sq. km (200 sq. mile) national park on the Río Tagus. The name comes from the Roman "Mons Fragorum" and its Mediterranean woodland and scrub protects a wealth of wildlife, including over three-quarters of Spain's protected bird species – the imperial eagle nests here. The information centre at **Villareal de San Carlos** (tel: 927-45 51 04; open daily) on the C-524 between Plasencia and Trujillo makes a good starting point, and has information on walking trails through the park, including the best lookout points.

Coria, 33 km (20 miles) west of Plasencia, was one of Spain's earliest bishoprics (AD 589). The splendid cathedral quarter – surrounded by the best preserved medieval walls in Europe – dwarfs today's town. A good time to visit is during the June fiestas when the gates in the wall are kept shut to allow the after-dark bull-running.

Las Hurdes is known for the production of high-quality honey, and beehives are in evidence in many villages in the area.

Cherry blossom

Extremadura's northern sierras and valleys offer an unexpected mosaic of contrasting landscapes. To the north of Coria, the **Sierra de Gata**'s hamlets and green fields border on the **Las Hurdes'** ❽ slaty black slopes and beehives, caught by Luis Buñuel in his classic documentary *Tierra Sin Pan* (*Land Without Bread,* 1932).The cramped stone dwellings built into the hillsides give a sense of the terrible poverty endured in the villages of this region before new access roads were built in the 1950s. Approaching on the C-512 from the west, you'll cross the Río Hurdano at Vegas de Coria where a road turns off, following the river valley to some of the most atmospheric "black villages" of the region. The road continues all the way back to the C-512 at Riomalo de Abajo.

BELOW: in the Jewish quarter, Hervás.

To the east rise the **Sierra de Gredos'** peaks, sliced through by the lush green Ambroz, Vera and Jerte river valleys. Tobacco, asparagus, paprika peppers and cherries all flourish in the region's gentle climate. In spring the sight of the snowy cherry blossom in the Jerte valley is unforgettable.

Hervás ❾, a mountain village in the Ambroz valley, has one of the best-preserved Jewish quarters in Spain. It is thought that Hervás became a predominantly Jewish settlement in the early Middle Ages, as the Jews fled Christian and Muslim persecution of the larger cities. Perhaps because of the remoteness of the area, Hervás escaped the massive pogroms and fires of 1391. When the Jews were expelled from Spain in 1492, their neighbourhood was left intact, and their possessions ceded to the local Duke of Béjar. Its textile industry flourished until the 18th century, and today its breezy mountain location is turning it into a popular spot for *chalets*, or vacation homes.

Intricate, maze-like streets make this village an intimate one. It is not unusual for neighbours to bring their chairs outside and sit together in the sunshine. There is little sign of the town's former inhabitants, although a plaque marks the house thought to be the old synagogue in Calle Sinagoga.

An interesting side trip from Hervás, approximately 22 km (14 miles) west on the other side of the N-630, is the restored village of **Granadilla**, uninhabited since the 1960s when the Embalse de Gabriel y Galán reservoir was created on its doorstep. It now operates as an education centre (open daily).

Map on page 176

Over the pass

Leading out of Hervás, there is a narrow but spectacular road, not to be attempted in bad weather, that crosses a portion of the **Sierra de Gredos** and which soars to a height of 2,100 metres (7,000 ft). The summit is treeless and the view over the wooded La Vera valley and beyond is breathtaking. It still fits George Borrow's 1836 description in *The Bible in Spain*: "I proceeded down the pass, occasionally ruminating on the matter which had brought me to Spain, and occasionally admiring one of the finest prospects in the world. Before me out-stretched lay immense plains, bounded in the distance by huge mountains, whilst at the foot of the hill which I was now descending, rolled the Tagus, in a deep narrow stream, between lofty banks; the whole was gilded by the rays of the setting sun." The same journey was made by Carlos V in 1556, when he chose to retire to La Vera's benign climate. There is now a 28-km (17-mile) walking trail along part of the route, from Tornavacas (just off the main N-110 road) to the village of **Jarandilla de la Vera**. The Castillo de los Condes de Oropesa, where he stayed, is now a *parador*.

Carlos V soon had his own lodgings built at the **Monasterio de Yuste ❿** (open daily 9.30am–12.30pm (1.30 Sun) and 3–6pm; entrance fee), 10 km (6 miles) to the southwest of Jarandilla. Here he tended to his clock-mending and watched mass from his bed until he died in 1558. It is the unforgettable setting – above a small lake and the picturesque timbered village of **Cuacos de Yuste** – and the monastery's simplicity that make it so beautiful today. ❑

BELOW: collecting honey in Las Hurdes.

AMONG THE CASTLES OF IMPOSSIBLE DREAMS

Imperious, impervious, fantastic, steeped in history and dripping romance — it's no wonder that castles in Spain are an unattainable dream

Castile is the high, arid heart of Spain, Castilian is the country's spoken language. Both derive their names from *castillo* (castle), the building that for years was the most dominant feature of this part of Spain. Castile was where the first significant advances were made against the Moors, a Wild West of adventurers and pioneers. Frontiers were marked along the Duero, Arlanzón and Ebro rivers where there were no walled cities, monasteries or manorial estates to run to in times of trouble. Strongholds were established about 100 years after the Moorish conquest, notably under Fernán Gonzáles (910–970), first Count of Castile, and over the next 400 years of fighting, castles appeared all over the countryside.

MOORISH CASTLES

The Moors were great castle builders, too. At Berlanga de Duero the Moors constructed a fortress with a massive curtain wall and drum towers with a commanding view (*pictured above*).

As the lands became safer, Castles were adopted as glorified homes. The Fonseca family's Castillo de Coca in Segovia, for example, displays some fine Mudéjar military architecture, but it was never intended to be put to the test.

After the Moors had been driven out in 1492, castle building was forbidden, but by then some 2,000 had altered Spain's landscape forever.

△ **CASTILLO DE GUADALEST**
Alicante's eyries have commanding views. The coast needed protection from pirates.

◁ **PONFERRADA**
On the pilgrim route to Santiago de Compostella, Ponferrada was run by the Knights Templar.

◁ SEGOVIA ALCAZAR

The castle where Fernando and Isabel were proclaimed is the ultimate fairytale fortress. It stands on an 80-metre rocky outcrop.

△ TORRE DE HOMENAJE

Segovia's keep has unusual candlestick-and-snuffer towers. This was the residential and social hub of the castle.

ARISTOCRATIC LODGINGS

The picture above is of the interior of the Parador at Zamora, a 15th-century castle and former home of the counts of Alba y Aliste on the banks of the Duero. The word Parador (from the Arabic *waradah*, meaning "halting place") had been in use for many centuries before 1928 when the government instigated this chain of state-run hotels in restored historic buildings. Designed to be no more than a day's journey apart, there are around 90 altogether. They are all relatively inexpensive and have a reputation for good service and good food. As a matter of policy, they have always served the best local dishes, and even if you don't stay in one, they are worth a visit for a meal, or a coffee, just to have a look around.

△ PEÑAFIEL

One of a number of early Castilian castles built on the banks of the Duero, Peñafiel dates from the 10th century, but is mostly 15th-century.

◁ VALENCIA DE DON JUAN

The most arrogant castle in León, Valencia de Don Juan has high walls and lofty towers looming above the River Esla, near Coyança.

▽ CASTILLO DE SANTA CATALINA

This 13th-century castle in Jaén was built by Ibn-al-Ahmar, who ceded it to Ferdinand III in 1245 in return for control of Granada. The castle is now a parador.

SEVILLE

*Aside from Seville's immense cultural heritage, its convivial,
fun-loving atmosphere makes the city an ideal place to
experience Andalusia's sultry nightlife*

Map
on page
192

Seville. Córdoba. Granada. A resounding triumvirate of southern (Andalusian) Spanish cities whose very names roll from the tongue with a hint of arrogance. Flashy, flamboyant, proud. Warm of weather, attractive of scenery and easily accessible by sea, Andalusia proved vulnerable to the successive settlements of the Phoenicians, Greeks, Romans, Visigoths and Moors. But it was the Arab and Berber presence that bequeathed Andalusia the richly sensuous medieval culture of silver filigree and ornate mosques that bewitches visitors to the region today.

Under the Moorish dominion, Andalusia was the centre of the most highly developed civilisation of the Middle Ages. But its reputation for riches and flair for hospitality hark back to an even earlier incarnation as the Roman province of Baetica, when Andalusia purveyed all make and manner of luxuries to the connoisseurs and *cognoscenti* of imperial Rome.

Such 19th-century visitors as Washington Irving, George Borrow and Richard Ford were inspired to record its charms in their various travel chronicles and thus helped to convert the salient features of Andalusia into the universal Spanish stereotype. Sherry wines, well-disciplined horses, brave bulls and flamboyant flamenco were the stuff of Andalusia. And who from a colder and soggier climate could resist the promise of 3,000 hours of sunshine annually and a mere 30 cm (12 inches) of rain? Generally, Andalusia's winters are mild and its summers scorching. Throughout, the climatic catchword is "dry", as evidenced by the number of bridges spanning parched riverbeds, some of which are under cultivation.

Fellow *Andaluces*

Until the Reconquest of Granada by the Catholic Monarchs Fernando and Isabel in 1492, Andalusia had rarely been united under one ruler. Internecine strife among the *emirs* and *taifas* of Córdoba, Jaén, Granada and Seville undermined Moorish domination until the increasing pressure of Spain's northern Christian kingdoms ultimately vanquished it.

Today Andalusia is Spain's most populous region, tallying 87,270 sq. km (33,695 sq. miles), 6 million inhabitants and comprising Spain's eight southernmost provinces. Comparable in size to Portugal, it stretches from that country in the west to Murcia in the east. Its northern reaches are marked by the Sierra Morena and its southern boundaries by the Atlantic Ocean and Mediterranean Sea.

The people of the provinces of Almería, Granada, Jaén, Córdoba, Málaga, Cádiz, Seville and Huelva, each with a provincial capital of the same name, are at once fellow *Andaluces* and individual *Almerienses*,

PRECEDING PAGES:
festival gear.
LEFT: in the Parque
de María Luisa.
BELOW: Torre del
Oro, which houses
Seville's Maritime
Museum.

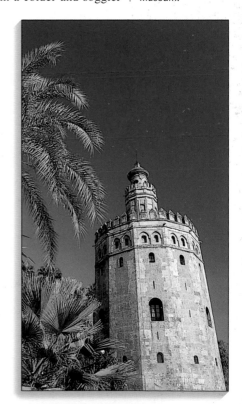

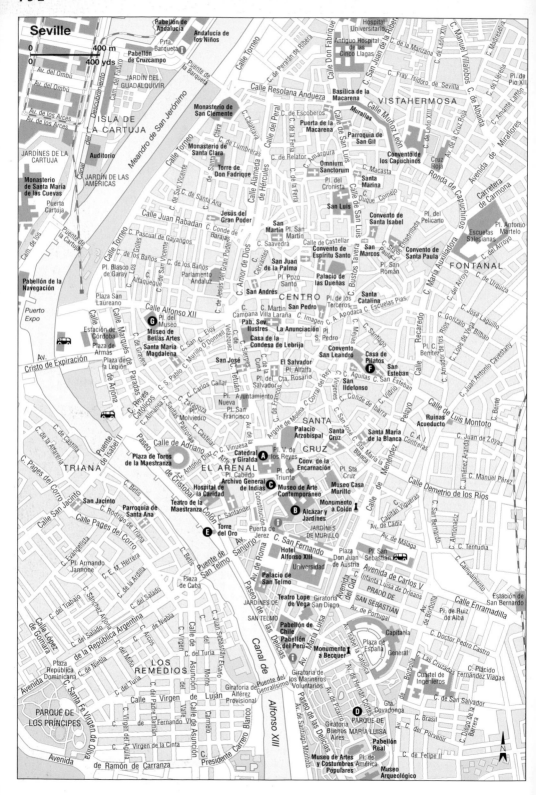

Granadinos, Cordobeses and *Sevillanos*. Says one Seville taxi driver: "Seville is different from the rest. Here we are more *simpático* and more polite in everything. We all call ourselves *Andaluces* because we share the same flag. Of course, Cádiz is somewhat similar to Seville, but the *Granadinos* are coarse fellows, as if they weren't even *Andaluces*." These provincial rivalries have their roots in a not-so-playful past of seesawing fortunes among the former Moorish kingdoms of Granada, Seville and Córdoba.

Map on page 192

Southern outlook

For a long time foreigners and fellow countrymen from Spain's industrialised north have characterised the *Andaluces* as lethargic and fond of their afternoon siesta. But at the same time all consider them to be spontaneous and witty, balancing an exaggerated sense of tragedy with a robust sense of humour. "Here are two classes of people to whom life seems one long holiday, the very rich, and the very poor", writes Washington Irving in *Tales of the Alhambra*, "one, because they need do nothing, the other, because they have nothing to do; but there are none who understand the art of doing nothing and living upon nothing better than the poor classes of Spain. Climate does one half and temperament the rest… Talk of poverty! With (a Spaniard) it has no disgrace. It sits upon him with a grandiose style, like his ragged cloak. He is an *hidalgo* even when in rags." Witness today the supreme cleanliness of even the sorriest of Andalusian streets and the smallest of its white houses – it is a matter of personal dignity.

A 19th-century sketch of Seville.

A southern farmer said this about his native *tierra*: "This is a land boiling over, yes, but here the fiestas and other things are born and die; what is important is the ephemeral, the fleeting, paper lanterns and flashes, but one doesn't build, one doesn't put cement to anything. What delights is the arrival of the heat to signal the siesta."

BELOW: a good-looking city.

Historic leap

It is true that ever since the Christians eclipsed the Moors in Andalusia, the Spanish south has been largely poor. Not the overt, searing poverty of the Third World, but rather an undercurrent of rural poverty not readily detected by the casual tourist. Fortunately, Andalusia's reputation as "a rich land inhabited by poor men" is declining. While unemployment remains high (well over 20 percent), official statistics tell only part of the story as there is a thriving underground economy and rural workers, long neglected, now enjoy an unheard-of range of social services.

The 1980s brought unprecedented prosperity to Andalusia. Spain's entry into the European Union in 1986 spurred development, which was further boosted by the investment in infrastructure for Expo '92, the world fair in Seville celebrating Columbus's voyage to the New World. Having Seville native Felipe González as prime minister was helpful, too. Four-lane highways now connect Andalusia with Madrid and the rest of Europe and the AVE high-speed train has halved travelling time from Madrid to Seville.

Abundant sunshine and fertile farmland are two enduring resources. The sunshine has converted the coast, particularly the Costa del Sol, into a favourite

Young women in flamenco costume, a manifestation of an exuberant culture.

TIP

Seville is best avoided during July and August, when the heat becomes unbearable.

BELOW: decorative tiles in the Alcázar.

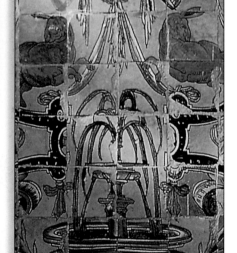

vacation and residential area for Northern Europeans, but efforts are underway to open up less-known areas inland to attract hikers and wildlife *aficionados*. Modern methods are being applied to farming, and thousands of acres of what once was desert in Almería Province have been transformed into plastic-covered greenhouses, where export crops, from melons to carnations, flourish all year.

Flirtatious Seville

Seville, Spain's fourth largest city and Andalusia's capital, is the most coquettish of the three grand cities of the south. Says an old Spanish refrain: *Quien no ha visto Sevilla, no ha visto maravilla.* (He who has not seen Seville, has not known marvel.) George Borrow, author of *The Bible in Spain*, considered it "the most interesting town in all Spain (beneath) the most glorious heaven…"

Even through a rare veil of fine December rain Seville is pretty. In the bright Andalusian sunshine, she is dazzling. A fitting setting for Byron's Don Juan, Bizet's Carmen, and Rossini's barber to play out their fictional lives. Some of the real lives that got their start here are those of the poets Gustavo Adolfo Bécquer (1836–70) and Antonio Machado (1875–1939), and the painters Diego de Velázquez (1599–1660) and Bartolomé Esteban Murillo (1618–82).

Romance has apparently always coursed through the city's veins. The Muslim historian Al-Saqundi, captivated by its charm, once proclaimed: "If one asked for the milk of birds in Seville, it would be found." St Teresa was so taken with its beauty and boldness that she confessed she felt that anyone who could somehow avoid committing sin in Seville would be doing very well indeed. Unfortunately, today's visitors are too often sinned against themselves as wallets disappear from pockets and purses from restaurant tables.

Roman rule

"Hercules built me; Caesar surrounded me with walls and towers; the King Saint took me." This terse recapitulation of Seville's multi-tiered history was carved long ago on the Jerez Gate. Later, Seville's port would bustle with New World activity as Spain built a lustrous but short-lived overseas empire.

In the era of discoverers, when the Netherlands, England and Spain were fighting for supremacy at sea and in the New World colonies, Seville was one of the richest cities in the world. But it had already known previous fame and fortune. Founded by the Iberians, it was usurped by Julius Caesar for Rome in 45 BC. Made an assize town and named *Hispalis*, it was given the title of *Colonia Julia Romula* and became one of the leading towns of the flourishing Roman province of Baetica, roughly corresponding to present-day Andalusia. There followed several lacklustre centuries under the Vandals and Visigoths, the latter having Seville report to their capital at Toledo.

Glory days

Then in 712 came the Moors, who renamed it *Ishbiliya*. Later, as part of the Caliphate of Córdoba, Seville rivalled that capital in material prosperity and as a seat of learning. When the Caliphate broke up in the 11th century, Seville pursued an independent course. Beginning in 1023, it saw the successive rule of the Abbadites, Almoravids (1091) and Almohads (1147). Under this last dynasty a new period of prosperity reigned that left behind many of Seville's fine buildings, including the Giralda. In 1248, Seville was reconquered for Christianity by Fernando III, the King Saint, who died and was buried here.

Map on page 192

The wave of New World discoveries that raised Seville to the crest of its fortunes in the 16th century also dashed it in its wake when the empire ebbed a century later. In 1519, Magellan set sail from here to circumnavigate the globe. But Seville's moment of glory was all too fleeting, and decline set in again in the early 17th century, subsequently hastened by maritime competition from Cádiz, the snowballing loss of the Spanish colonies that had brought so much trade, the troubled state of 19th-century Spain and a brief French occupation lasting from 1808 to 1812. Its historic momentum lost, Seville strolled into the 20th century trailing a tarnished heritage that nevertheless stirred great feelings of pride among *Sevillanos*. Seized early in the Civil War by the Nationalists, Seville served as a base for attacks on the rest of Andalusia. Emerging from the war physically starving and spiritually spent, the city gradually regained its legendary *alegría* under the entrenched Franco dictatorship. But for a long time its gypsy bravado resounded with a tragic note.

AVE high-speed train at Seville's Estación de Santa Justa.

From 1940 to today, Seville's population has almost doubled to the current 650,000. With the granting of regional autonomy, Seville – as capital – received a boost in importance. But Expo '92 brought an influx of professionals from other regions and countries to shake up the status quo in a community where class barriers and conservative attitudes seemed immovable. They brought new money and fresh ideas to a city frozen in its ritualistic ways.

BELOW: the world came to Seville for Expo '92.

ISLA DE LA CARTUJA

The site of Expo '92, on the west bank of the Río Guadalquivir, was once a boggy wasteland with only one building, the 15th-century **Monasterio de Santa María de las Cuevas**. Restored for the universal exposition, the monastery can now be visited (open Tues–Sun; entrance fee). The western part of the island has been developed into a high technology research area. Visitors are still able to view the Expo '92 pavilions but, since most are now in private ownership, they are not open to the public. La Cartuja is also home to the 35-hectare (88-acre) **Isla Mágica** theme park (open Mar–Oct daily; entrance fee), which opened in 1997 with rides, outdoor entertainment, cafés, bars and restaurants.

On the section of the island closest to the centre of the city is the **Puerta de Triana** (open Tues–Sun; entrance fee for individual sites), which includes the Navigation Pavilion and maritime museum. Here you can see multimedia displays on Seville's role in sea exploration and models of historical ships, including a faithful replica of Magellan's ship *Victoria*. Also on the Puerta de Triana site is the IMAX Space Theatre, which has a huge semicircular screen showing specially created films on space travel as well as the history of terrestrial exploration.

Seville's monumental catedral, with the Giralda tower rising behind.

Expo also transformed Seville physically, with splendid results. Scores of old buildings were restored, half a dozen new bridges now span the Guadalquivir, fine walkways run along the riverside and Seville finally has an opera house. A new railway station accommodates the AVE high-speed train, the airport has been enlarged and a bypass sweeps around the city.

On a huge scale

Virtually everything in Andalusia is of a human scale – with the exception of Seville's **Catedral** (open daily; closed Sun pm; entrance fee). Some 116 metres (380 ft) long and 76 metres (250 ft) wide, it is the third largest Christian church in the world (after St Peter's in Rome and St Paul's in London) and the largest Gothic one. Built between 1402 and 1506 on the site of a former mosque, it contains five spacious aisles, a large main chapel with a wrought-iron screen and vaulting that towers 56 metres (184 ft) above the transept. Allegedly it was the chapter's aim in 1401 "to construct a church such and as good that it never should have its equal. Let Posterity, when it admires it complete, say that those who dared to devise such a work must have been mad."

Hidden in its sombre shadows are many relics and treasures, including paintings by Murillo, Zurbarán and Goya; a cross said to be made from the first gold brought from America by Columbus; and a funerary monument claimed to hold the explorer's remains. In fact, he almost certainly reposes in Santo Domingo, capital of the Dominican Republic. His leaden tomb was taken from Seville to Santo Domingo Cathedral in 1544, and were supposedly returned more than three centuries later. But somewhere there was a mix-up and it is believed that the bones in Seville may be those of his son Diego.

BELOW: the tomb of Columbus in Seville's Catedral.

Adjacent to the cathedral, the chequerboard **Patio de los Naranjos** was the court of the city's main mosque, a shaded oasis of orange trees and sparkling fountains used for the ritual ablutions of Islam. Exiting through the **Puerta de Oriente**, you are at the base of Seville's trademark **Giralda**, a slender, rectangular tower rising to 93 metres (305 ft). Erected between 1184 and 1196, it is the remaining minaret of the mosque which was destroyed a century later.

Across the **Plaza del Triunfo** from the cathedral stands a Moorish fantasy in filigree: the **Alcázar** Ⓑ (open daily; closed Sun pm; entrance fee). Built between 1350 and 1369, it is a mudéjar elaboration of an original Moorish citadel and palace. For nearly seven centuries, it was the palace of Spanish kings. Most notorious among them was Pedro the Cruel, who had his half-brother Fadrique assassinated in 1358 and murdered his guest, Abu Said of Granada, for his jewels. The skulls painted over Pedro's bedroom door supposedly suggest the fate of five unjust judges who crossed him during his reign.

Though less grandiose and expansive than Granada's Alhambra, Seville's Alcázar has a special cosiness and charm derived from its sense of intimacy and its careful attention to polychrome detail. Its fanciful floors, ceilings and walls are intricate works of art, reaching heights of richness in Charles V's room and the **Salón de Embajadores**. The **Patio de las Doncellas** is noted for its friezes, *azulejos* (tiles) and stucco work. Well-manicured gardens, redolent of orange groves, palm trees and roses, contribute to the sense of a summer sanctuary.

The Jewish quarter

Stretching beyond the walls of the Alcázar is the **Barrio de Santa Cruz**, the former Jewish quarter turned fashionable neighbourhood. The walls are so white,

**Map
on page
192**

TIP

If you're driving in Seville, be aware of the web of one-way streets. Also watch out for cars parked on the curbs of already too-narrow streets.

BELOW: relaxing in the Barrio de Santa Cruz.

the flowers so bright and the iron everywhere so exquisitely wrought that you quite expect a *señorita* in full flounce to come around the corner any minute, castanets clicking. Guitar-packing gypsies also regularly flock to the local taverns. In the off season they often play until dawn for local *aficionados* at clubs, bars and private gatherings, for flamenco is a child of the night.

Amid the chic shops and rustic restaurants of this *barrio*, you can see many traditional Andalusian homes. Open-work, wrought-iron gates mark the entrance porch and iron gratings the windows. A square inner courtyard, cool and inviting with its abundant greenery, dado of Moorish tiles and central fountain is covered with an awning in the summer and used as the living-room; in winter the family retreats upstairs.

Near the cathedral, the shelves of the **Archivo de Indias ⓒ** (open weekday mornings; free) sag with the weight of history. Since 1785, it has been accumulating the heavy tomes that contain 36,000 files of documents chronicling the adventure of discovery, the trails of colonisation, colonial administration and minutiae of trade that recall a 16th-century Seville that was the headquarters for New World trade and, as a result, one of the richest cities in the Old World.

Park and plaza

The **Parque de María Luisa ⓓ** (open daily dawn–dusk; free) and the **Plaza de España** to the south of the centre have the feel of a bygone Seville. The Plaza de España is marked by a long semicircular series of arches bearing ceramic crests of all the provinces of Spain. Several ceramic-and-brick bridges span the small, concentric stream that flows through this expansive plaza. The park itself is dotted with buildings left over from the Spanish-American exhibition of

TIP

Save your feet by hiring one of the horse-drawn carriages outside the cathedral to tour the Parque de María Luisa.

BELOW:
Plaza de España.

1929. One of these now houses the **Museo Arqueológico** (open Tues–Sat; entrance fee). Artefacts from the Moorish palace at Medina Azahara (*see page 223*) are on display here. The museum also has an excellent collection of mosaics and statuary from the well-preserved ruins of Itálica, 12 km (7 miles) north of Seville.

Map on page 192

The river

Seville straddles the banks of the **Río Guadalquivir**. Known by the Romans as "Baetis" and the Moors as the "Wadi el Kebir" ("great river"), frequent droughts now render this river less than impressive, but to citizens of Seville, it is every bit as revered as the Amazon. Once upon a time in Seville you could be born on the "wrong side of the river". Over there, across the river from the cathedral, the bullring and the up-and-coming Barrio de Santa Cruz was the nefarious **Barrio de Triana**, haven of violence and vice. Today, though, it is largely a residential suburb fast becoming every bit as respectable as its neighbours across the water.

Back on the "right" side of the river, you'll see along the Paseo de Cristobal Colón the 13th-century, 12-sided, battlemented **Torre del Oro ❸** (open Tues–Sun; closed pm; entrance fee). In times of danger the tower held one end of a chain that stretched across the river to a companion tower, now vanished, on the other side. The tower now houses a small maritime museum.

The ruined Roman amphitheatre at Itálica (site open Tues–Sun; entrance fee), just off the N630 north of Seville.

Pilate's house

This 16th-century **Casa de Pilatos ❹** (open daily; entrance fee), just north of the Barrio de Santa Cruz, was indeed named after the famous Biblical magistrate whose house in Jerusalem inspired some of its features. Also incorporated

BELOW: courtyard of the Casa de Pilatos.

Map on page 192

in this mansion of the first Marquess of Tarifa are mudéjar and Renaissance elements rendered in remarkable *azulejos* and moulded stucco.

A day in the life

Late morning, Seville begins to stir. Along the **Calle de las Sierpes**, a pedestrian thoroughfare winding from **La Campana** to the **Plaza de San Francisco**, friends meet to do business and just generally pass the time. At No. 52 once stood a prison that quartered the not-yet-prominent Cervantes, author of *Don Quixote*. After dinner (9pm to 11pm), the bars of both Santa Cruz and Triana come explosively alive. Also in the neighbourhood is the **Museo de Bellas Artes** ⑥ (open Tues–Sun; closed Tues am and Sun pm; entrance fee), housed in a former friary and with works by Murillo, Zurbarán, Velázquez and El Greco.

Feria de Abril

Every April Seville dresses to the nines and lets down her hair in a confluence of Andalusian stereotypes: wine, bulls, horses and flamenco. The day begins around noon with a parade of horses and riders: men in leather chaps with scarlet cummerbunds, short jackets, and broad-brimmed hats and women riding pillion wearing full-skirted flamenco dresses. Amid all the rejoicing, dancers perform the classic *sevillanas*, a light-hearted form of flamenco.

Pavilions, arranged in rows and decorated with flowers, flags and paper lanterns, fill the **Prado de San Sebastián**. Between them, the roadway is carpeted with golden sand. In the late-afternoon the bullfights begin, in an atmosphere of great excitement. Beneath the floodlights and fireworks of night, the flirtatious merriment continues until dawn. ❑

BELOW: parading at Seville's April Fair.

Holy Week

The week preceding Easter is Semana Santa, a time of national ritual in Spain. In every corner of the country processions snake their way, day and night, from the local parishes to the main cathedrals and back again. In the larger cities there may be more than 30 different processions in any 24-hour period. Depending on the size of the municipality and its economic means, each day is marked by regalia of varying colour, elaborate floats showing scenes from the Passion and centuries-old music. Since the 16th century, this has been the Spanish way of commemorating Holy Week.

These celebrations attain a feverish pitch of pageantry and colour in the south. From Palm Sunday to Easter Sunday the communities focus on the trials of Christ and the tears of the Virgin. It has often been alleged that the Andaluces are more demonstrative in their faith because of a need to live down the Muslim-Moorish legacy.

In Seville, a fervent "thunder" fills the cathedral on Wednesday with the rending of the veil of the temple and resounds again on Saturday just before all join in singing "Gloria in Excelsis" and ringing every bell. In Córdoba, on the afternoon of Good Friday, mass is celebrated in the church within the mosque with a full symphony orchestra and a massive chorus. In Granada, mantilla'd ladies all in black dripping with jewellery and rosaries march through the city among the floats.

For everywhere *pasos*, or floats, are a fixed feature of Semana Santa. They bear life-size and extremely lifelike polychrome and gilded figures depicting every Passion scene from the Last Supper and the Garden of Olives to the Descent from the Cross. The figures wear wigs and real costumes that may cost millions of pesetas.

As the proud parishioners watch their particular Virgin pass by they may weep, applaud, sing, or even throw her some saucy compliments. Some admirers are so moved by a particular *paso* that they spontaneously sing the traditional, melancholy saeta.

The trappings of the processions are solemn. Penitents wear robes gathered with belts of esparto grass and tall, pointed hoods covering their faces except for two slits for the eyes. Called *capuchones*, these are the hoods of the Spanish Inquisition and the equally insidious Ku Klux Klan.

But the strong Andalusian sense of fun cannot be long suppressed. The processional ranks are constantly broken as people cross through the parade to greet friends and share a beer or a *boccadillo* (sandwich).

In the side streets off the parade route tables and chairs are set up to provide rest and sustenance. Torrijas, a fried, milk-soaked confection, and flamenquines, deep-fried slices of veal wrapped around snow-cured ham and cheese, are traditional snacks.

Almost everywhere in Spain, the end of Semana Santa signals the beginning of the bullfighting season. In Arcos de la Frontera a local version of the "running of the bulls" takes place on Easter Sunday, and in Málaga you can go straight from the last Easter mass to the season's first *corrida*. ❑

RIGHT: polychrome figure of Christ on the cross made for Seville's Holy Week.

Map
on page
202

- Madrid
- Córdoba

CÓRDOBA

*The walls of the Mezquita dominate the town, while
the alleyways of Córdoba's old Jewish and Muslim quarters, with
their overflowing pots of geraniums, are a delight to explore*

H andsome, honourable and forthright, Córdoba is harsher than Seville and without the benefit of a marked gypsy grace note to soften its keen masculine edge. In its no-nonsense streets there is no sense of the benign chaos that chokes rush-hour Seville, nor is there in the town centre a subtle layering of eras as in Granada.

There are just the old and the new, clearly demarcated by an intermittent, well-tended Moorish wall. To one side are the twisted ancient alleys, to the other wide, straight streets with a 20th-century purpose. Just look at a map of Córdoba and you'll see the old quarter meandering down to the banks of the wide, shallow Guadalquivir in a maze of tiny alleyways doubling back on themselves or sometimes leading nowhere. These will test the mettle of even the most seasoned navigator.

Visitors are advised to leave their cars outside the old quarter and go on foot with good reason. Most of the roads are barely wide enough to accommodate the most fuel-efficient of vehicles, and you might well find yourself suddenly backing a hasty retreat down a one-way street under the reproachful gaze of an impatient horse, tourists in tow, eager to return its carriage to the shaded queue outside the Roman walls.

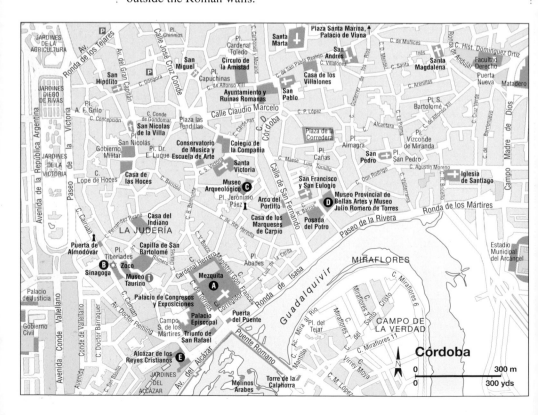

Patrician colony

Looking at Córdoba today, it is hard to imagine the truly heady heights this city achieved in earlier epochs. The history of Córdoba, like that of Granada and Seville, is a dizzying account of soaring success and dismal failure.

Like Seville, Córdoba was an important Iberian town. In 152 BC its fate passed to Roman hands when the consul Marcus Marcellus made it a colony favoured with the title *Colonia Patricia.* As the Roman "Corduba", it became the capital of *Hispania Ulterior;* and under Augustus, it came into its own as the prosperous capital of Baetica Province and Spain's largest city at the time. At this stage in its life it sired Seneca the Elder (55 BC–AD 39) and his son, Lucius Seneca (4 BC–AD 65), noted philosopher and preceptor to Nero. His statue now stands by the **Puerta de Almodóvar**, the principal entrance to the old town.

From the 6th to the 8th centuries Córdoba was ruled by the Visigoths, who gave it its first taste of Christianity. The Moors entered some two centuries later. With the help of the city's disaffected Jewish residents, harassed by the Visigoths, the invaders quickly established their supremacy and ultimately raised Córdoba to the pinnacle of prestige and prosperity.

The Caliphate

At the beginning of the 8th century, emirs from the Damascus Caliphate had already established themselves in the city; but with the arrival of Abd-al-Rahman I in 756, a discernible dynasty was founded capable of consolidating the power to rule over all of Muslim Spain, which the Moors called *al-Andalus.* Under Abd-al-Rahman III (912–61) and his successor Hakam II (961–76), the blessings of the Caliphate of Córdoba rained down on the city. Its overstuffed coffers, luxurious appointments and richly brocaded cultural achievements defied even the hyperbole that was second nature to the Moors and is a lingering trait among their present-day Andalusian offspring.

Córdoba was then possibly Europe's most civilised city. In the 10th century it founded a university of great renown. Literature and science were encouraged, schools of philosophy and medicine were strongly promoted and libraries were established. The city's inhabitants, numbering around half a million, were served by 3,000 mosques, 300 public baths and 28 suburbs. At its supreme moment of glory Córdoba was surpassed only by the city of Baghdad.

Disintegration and decline

But bad news was just around the corner. At the beginning of the 11th century internal dissent and revolt laid a foundation for its downfall. In 1031, the powerful Caliphate split up into petty kingdoms called *taifas,* and some 40 years later Córdoba itself was subsumed by the kingdom of Seville until its recapture by Fernando III in 1236. Many inhabitants fled and the Christians were indifferent to the industry, trade and agriculture that fed the city's affluence. For centuries Córdoba wallowed in the doldrums, but over the last 50 years its spirit has been steadily reviving. Since 1950 its population has grown by over 50 percent to more than 250,000.

TIP

To see Córdoba at its liveliest, visit during the Patio Fiesta, held in the second week of May, or the *Feria,* in the last week of May.

BELOW: view from the Mezquita.

The intricately deco-rated dome of the Mezquita's mihrab.

Córdoba's mosque

Whether you see it as a travesty or a triumph, the **Mezquita** (open 10am–6pm Mon–Sat, 3.30–5.30pm Sun; entrance fee) is a product and a symbol of the grafting of Christianity on to Muslim Spain. As the great mosque of the Umayyad caliphs, it enjoyed such profound artistic and religious stature that it saved the city's inhabitants the arduous pilgrimage to Mecca, whose mosque was the only one of greater size and importance. Begun in 785, the mosque was two centuries in the building, expanding with the city's population before reaching its full size of 174 by 137 metres (570 by 450 ft).

Inside, a forest of about 850 columns produces a repetitive motif of criss-crossing alleys not unlike the effect of a hall of mirrors. Uneven in height (average 4 metres, or 13 ft), and varying in material and style, these pillars support an architectural innovation of the time: two tiers of candy-striped arches that lend added height and spaciousness.

Most notable and memorable among the Moorish flourishes is the *mihrab,* or prayer recess, along the wall facing Mecca. The workmanship is a masterpiece of Moorish mosaic art. Interlaced arches sprout from the marble columns surrounding the vestibule; and, more exquisitely decorated still, is the octagonal *mihrab* itself topped by a shell-shape dome.

Newly Christian Córdoba soon claimed the mosque as its own Church of the Virgin of the Assumption, building chapels against the interior walls and closing up the open northern façade to allow access only through the **Puerta de las Palmas**. But construction of the cruciform church in the centre of the mosque did not begin until 1523. Massive as the church is, you are not immediately aware of its looming presence upon entering the mosque. Only after consider-

BELOW: columns and arches inside the Mezquita.

able slaloming beneath the arches do you suddenly stumble upon a 55-metre (180-ft) long Renaissance structure with a choir, a **Capilla Mayor**, a 15-metre (50-ft) wide transept and a lavishly adorned ceiling.

Its hodgepodge of styles (Gothic, Renaissance, Italian and baroque) required nearly a century of construction; and when Charles V, who had given his unthinking permission for the building, first saw the architectural and artistic disfigurement it caused, he reproached those responsible for the transformation. "You have built here what you or anyone might have built anywhere else", he said, "but you have destroyed what was unique in the world." It is still unique, but in a rather freakish way.

Outside the mosque but within its surrounding battlemented walls is the requisite **Patio de los Naranjos** entered through the **Puerta del Perdón** at the base of the distinctive 93-metre (305-ft) Christian belfry that replaced the Moorish minaret. From the nearby **Calleja de la Flores** (Alley of the Flowers), you can see the belfry framed in postcard splendour between the flower-studded walls of this narrow street. In true Córdoban fashion the flower pots are attached to the walls with wrought-iron rings.

Religious persecution

The site and size of Córdoba's **Judería** (Jewish Quarter) indicates that here, as elsewhere, the Jews were long considered a race apart. And like elsewhere, they were a learned, accomplished and wealthy breed that seemed never to be allowed to prosper between periods of persecution.

Disgruntled with their lot under the Visigoths, the Jews of Córdoba aided and abetted the Moorish victory; they subsequently enjoyed a welcome period of peace and prosperity under the tolerant Caliphate.

Córdoba itself was at one time home to the distinguished Moorish physicist, astrologer, mathematician, doctor and philosopher Averroës (who lived here from 1126 to 1198) and to Moses Maimonides (1135–1204), noted Jewish physician and philosopher. In the Calle Maimonides today stands his monument, along with the remains of a 14th-century **Sinagoga** ❸ (open Tues–Sun; closed Sun pm; entrance fee) built in the mudéjar style.

Córdoba's museums

Heirlooms deposited in the environs of Córdoba by the various tiers of its history are beautifully displayed in the **Museo Arqueológico** ❻ (open 10am–2pm, 6–8pm Tues–Sat, 10am–2pm Sun; entrance fee) in the Plaza de Jerónimo Páez. Housed in a Renaissance palace of the same name, the extensive collection contains prehistoric, Roman, Visigothic, Moorish and Gothic remains. Particularly striking among them are a bronze stag from nearby Medina Azahara (*see page 233*), Iberian sculptures reminiscent of Chinese temple dogs and an original Roman foundation upon which the building rests. The museum also contains the world's largest collections of lead sarcophagi and Arabic capitals.

The 17th-century **Plaza de la Corredera** a little to the north, and so named because of its earlier use for

Map on page 202

BELOW: shopping in the Jewish Quarter.

Looking up at the crucifix of El Cristo de los Faroles, north of the town centre.

bullfights, is undergoing restoration. The four-square, three-tiered structures marking its perimeter have a sagging, B-western-movie quality, though there is a lively morning food market, as well as a flea market held on most days. In contrast, the **Plaza del Potro** has remained vigorous since the days when Cervantes allegedly stayed at the *posada* in this square and wrote a part of *Don Quixote*. The square's fountain-statue of a colt is mentioned in the book.

The **Museo Provincial de Bellas Artes** (open Tues–Sun; closed Sun pm; free), in an old hospital on this square, has a large collection of paintings, including several by Murillo, Zurbarán and Goya. Just across the courtyard is the **Museo Julio Romero de Torres** (open Tues–Sun; closed Sun pm; entrance fee), which is devoted entirely to the Córdoban-born artist (1874–1930). The large collection here includes many sensual studies of Córdoban women.

Arts and crafts

Everywhere in the town, you'll notice shops offering Córdoba's prime crafts in trade: silver filigree and stamped leather. Since the time of the Moors these crafts have flourished here, but in the 16th and 17th centuries the latter in particular flourished through a prevailing fashion dictating that all walls and seats should be covered with leather, properly embossed, tooled, tinted and gilded.

The Alcázar

BELOW: looking across the rooftops of Córdoba.

Just west of the Mezquita, near the much-restored **Puente Romano** (Roman bridge) spanning the Río Guadalquivir, is the old **Alcázar de los Reyes Cristianos** (open Tues–Sun; closed Sun pm; entrance fee). Built under Alfonso XI in 1328, it was the residence of Fernando and Isabel during their campaign

against the Moors in Andalusia. Moorish patios and extensive Arabic gardens, with pools and shaded with cypresses, offer a respite from the summer heat. Inside is a museum housing impressive Roman mosaics.

Map on page 202

The original Roman bridge has in fact been rebuilt many times but retains its Roman foundations. At its southern end is the 14th-century **Torre de la Calahorra.** Inside the tower is a museum with interesting sound and light displays which explain how Christians, Jews and Muslims co-existed in 10th-century Córdoba. Also on display are impressive models of the Alhambra in Granada (*see pages 211–214*) as well as Córdoba's Mezquita.

To the northeast of the city centre, on Plaza de Don Gome, is the **Palacio de Viana** (open Thur–Tues; closed pm; entrance fee), an elegant 17th-century aristocratic home which is now a museum. It is packed with artworks and antiques, porcelain and tapestries, but perhaps the most pleasing aspects are the 12 interior courtyards and the delightful garden stocked with a variety of plants, including citrus and roses.

Nearby is the **Plaza Santa Marina** and its monument to Manolete. Born Manuel Rodríguez in 1917, Manolete was a local boy who found fame and fortune in the bullrings. Unfortunately, he encountered an untimely death by goring in 1947. The equally famous *torero* El Cordobés was actually born Manuel Benítez in 1936 in the town of Palma del Río 58 km (36 miles) west of Córdoba.

If you walk a little further west from Plaza Santa Marina, crossing Calle Alfaros, you will see the well-known crucifix **El Cristo de los Faroles**. It stands starkly in a hidden plaza surrounded by wrought-iron lanterns. A return visit at night is highly recommended, when the lanterns are alight and the crucifix can be seen in all its glory. ❑

The defensive Torre de la Calahorra on the Puente Romano.

BELOW: the Puente Romano at sunset.

GRANADA

"There is no pain in life so cruel as to be blind in Granada" is inscribed on the ramparts of the Alhambra. These words address the unique beauty of Granada

Map on page 210

Nature was generous in Granada, endowing the city with much greenery and placing it at the foot of three mountain spurs, from which it gracefully stretches up towards luminous blue skies against the blue-green backdrop of the Sierra Nevada to the southeast. To the west of the city is a broad, fertile *vega* (plain). To the north, the dainty Darro, a mountain stream, flows through the city between two of its three picturesque hills, those of the **Alhambra** and the **Albaicín**. The third hill, **Sacromonte**, is due north of the Alhambra. After the relative flatness of Seville and Córdoba, Granada's hills are a welcome change of scenic pace. For almost all year you can see snow on the Sierra Nevada, a popular winter retreat for skiers.

While Seville sprawls open-ended under the abundant Andalusian sunshine and Córdoba goes about its business with a minimum of fuss, Granada savours in its municipal valleys the romantic promise of the three hills that are the pillars of its tourism trade and the core of its own unique character.

Early history

Granada, the last stronghold and longest running kingdom of the Moors in Spain, began life as the obscure Iberian settlement of Elibyrge in the 50th century BC. From there it went on to become the equally obscure Illiberis of the Romans and Visigoths.

It is to the Moors, then, that it owes a debt of gratitude for its current national and international stature. Its name derives from the Moorish "Karnattah" and not from the Spanish word for pomegranate (*granada*), which it has nevertheless adopted as the city arms. While Seville and Córdoba both tasted wealth and glory under the Romans, Granada first knew grandeur as a provincial capital during the time of the Caliphs of Córdoba. As Córdoba's prominence waned with the fall there of the Umayyads in 1031, Granada's political stock began to rise. For some 60 years the city was the capital of an independent kingdom, but inroads by the Almoravids eventually resulted in its integration into the kingdom of Seville.

When Jaén fell to the Christians in 1246 under the relentless assaults of Ferdinand III, Ibn al-Ahmar moved his capital to Granada and, as Mohammed I, founded the Nasrid Dynasty that ruled for 250 years.

A golden age of prosperity

During this "golden age" under the Moors, the Jewish presence in Granada was important and strong. In fact, for a time Granada was known as the "City of the Jews". Here, as elsewhere in Muslim Spain, the Jews were doctors and philosophers and even diplomats and generals. Politically, however, Mohammed I

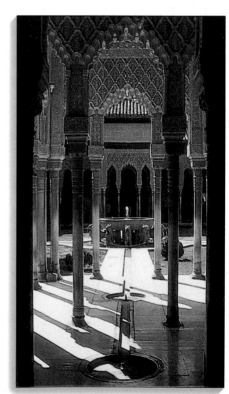

LEFT: the exquisitely decorated Alhambra.
BELOW: the Patio de los Leones (Patio of the Lions), part of the royal living quarters.

found it expedient to remain on friendly terms with Christian Castile, and even went so far as to help Fernando III capture Seville, which little helped the *granadinos* ingratiate themselves hereinafter with the *sevillanos*.

For the first time in its life, Granada was indisputably on top. In the wake of successive Christian victories in Córdoba, Seville and elsewhere throughout *al-Andalus*, Muslim refugees flocked to Granada, contributing to the trade and commerce of this up-and-coming kingdom. As surrounding Muslim kingdoms failed, Granada reaped an unprecedented prosperity. The fertile *vega* to the west enjoyed elaborate irrigation. Science, arts and the humanities flourished. Out of this impressive synergy of material, intellectual, and spiritual well-being was born the greatest triumph of Moorish art, the Alhambra.

During this period Granada's population swelled to 200,000, over four times that of the London of its day and just shy of its current headcount.

A fateful love affair

Then under Muley Hassan (1462–85) it all started to unravel over a family affair. Hassan fell in love with a Christian and entertained thoughts of repudiating his queen Ayesha, mother of his son Boabdil, for the beautiful Zoraya. Conjugal jealousy and concern for the regal inheritance of her son caused Ayesha to flee the city, which was already torn by feuds between the Abencerrajes, in support of her, and the Zegris, in support of Zoraya.

Mother and son soon returned, however, to dethrone Hassan and his brother, weakening the kingdom. Preying upon this weakness, Ferdinand V of Aragón captured Boabdil, the Boy King (*El Rey Chico*), offering him liberty at the price of remaining passive while the Catholic Monarchs gobbled up more and more

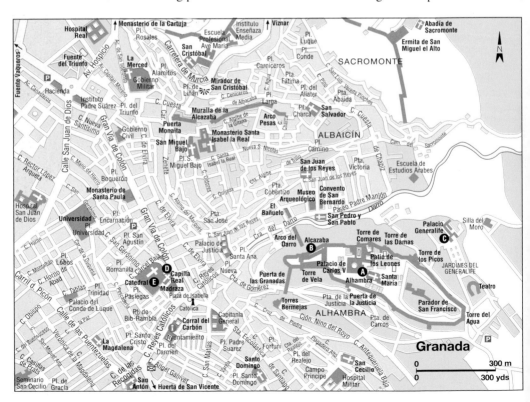

of the Moorish territory. When in late 1491 Fernando and Isabel beat down the door of Granada, the city's spirit had already been broken and Boabdil put up but a token resistance. By 2 January 1492, the capture of the sole remaining stronghold of Muslim Spain was complete.

Map on page 210

As the cross and banner of Castile cast their first Christian shadows across the 9th-century Alcazaba, Boabdil and his followers retired to the Alpujarras mountains. As Boabdil turned for a final look at the flickering glory of Granada, his mother allegedly reproved him, saying: "You weep like a woman for what you could not hold as a man." To this day that very spot is known as the *Suspiro del Moro*, the Moor's Sigh.

Unfortunately, the resounding God-speed that reverberated throughout Christendom with the fall of Granada never came to fruition. Religious intolerance culminating with the expulsion of the *moriscos* in 1609 drained the city of its most enterprising citizens and the glory they had wrought. By 1800, its population had dropped to just 40,000.

But like the rest of Andalusia, Granada is again enjoying a new prosperity resulting from improved irrigation and intense agricultural activity. Also important are the visitors who enthuse over the artistic legacy that, after 781 years of rule, was the swan-song of the Moors.

Moorish motifs decorate the pillars

The Alhambra

The **Alhambra ❹** (open daily; combined entrance fee for the Alhambra, Alcazaba and Palacio Generalife; ticket reservations tel: 958-22 09 12), the only surviving monument of Moorish Granada's great artistic outpouring, sits on a scarped ridge crowning a wooded hill. No amount of description can prepare

BELOW: the majestic beauty of the Alhambra.

Stunning symmetry of the Patio de los Arrayanes (Patio of the Myrtles).

you for its great playfulness or do justice to its exquisite delicacy and proportions. Proclaimed one of the unofficial wonders of the world, it is the epitome of Moorish imagination and artistry, the consummate expression of a sophisticated culture. For many, it serves as a kind of bridge between the Oriental and Western minds, a personal point of contact with the magical world found in the tales of the *Arabian Nights*.

Its pleasing splendour resides not in the architectural structures themselves, but in the masterful ornamentation that makes them seem almost an apparition, in the intricate delicacy of its carved wooden ceilings, the lace-like reliefs of its plaster walls, the repeated motifs of interlaced arabesques and the finely perforated tracery of the arched arcades on slender columns of white marble.

The royal apartments

Knowing a good thing when they saw it, the Catholic Monarchs had the Alhambra repaired and strengthened after their 1492 conquest and used it whenever they were in town. Subsequently, Carlos V, who had given the uninformed nod to the construction of the church inside Córdoba's mosque, deemed it insufficiently magnificent for him and pulled part of it down to make way for the palace he taxed the Moors to build here in the 16th century. Beautiful in its own right as an example of the Italian Renaissance style, his palace is nevertheless incongruous in its Aladdin's lamp setting.

BELOW: a tranquil scene in the Alhambra gardens.

The royal residence of the Moors within the Alhambra is highlighted by the **Patio de los Arrayanes** (Patio of the Myrtles), and the **Patio de los Leones** (Patio of the Lions). The former is an open court measuring 37 metres by 23 metres (121 ft by 75 ft) bisected by a narrow fishpond tucked between hedges

Map on page 210

of myrtle. At either end, within the arcaded alcoves, you can see fine stalactite vaulting. Off the northern end of this court is the lofty **Salón de los Embajadores**, the audience chamber of the Moorish kings. A dado of *azulejos* underscores the intertwining polychrome patterns and inscriptions stamped upon the stucco. Pairs of horseshoe windows admit enchanting views of Granada. And topping it all off is a domed ceiling of cedarwood.

Leading off the southern end is the Patio of the Lions (measuring 28 metres by 15 metres, or 90 ft by 50 ft), built around a massive antique fountain resting on the backs of 12 diminutive grey marble lions. Off its northern end is the **Sala de las Dos Hermanas** (Hall of the Two Sisters), containing the most elaborate of the Alhambra's honey-comb cupolas, said to comprise over 5,000 cells.

East of the royal apartments are the terraced **Partal Gardens** and charming **Torre de las Damas**.

Washington Irving

Some 19th-century writers were fortunate enough to spend some time in the Alhambra. During his three-month stay in 1829, Washington Irving began his *Tales of the Alhambra,* a collection of romantic sketches of the Moors and Spaniards that continues to sell well in Granada's souvenir shops. Richard Ford, author of the *Hand-Book for Travellers in Spain,* paid the palace a visit in the summers of 1831 and 1833; and George Borrow, author of *The Bible in Spain*, visited in 1836.

The **Alcazaba** ❸ at the western extremity of Alhambra Hill was a 9th-century Moorish citadel. Today, its vista takes in the palace, the Generalife, the Albaicín and Sacromonte sections of Granada, and the Sierra Nevada.

BELOW: geranium decked balconies in the Albaicín.

Tombs of the Catholic Monarchs in the Capilla Real.

Gardens of seduction

Adjoining the Alhambra and overlooking both it and the city are the grounds of the former summer palace of the sultans, the **Palacio Generalife C**, dating from 1250. Blessed with gardens that far outclass the sparse beauty of its restored buildings, this palace is cool and green and full of restful pools and murmuring fountains. Known in Arabic as *Jennat al-Arif*, meaning "garden of the architect" (who remains unknown), it is filled with statuesque cypresses, diminutive shrubs, orange trees, hedges and flowers. Rumour has it that Boabdil's sultana kept trysts with her lover Hamet in the enclosed **Patio de los Cipreses**. Who can blame them? This garden is a veritable invitation to indiscretion.

The **Patio de la Acequia** (Court of the Long Pond), within the gardens, has pretty pavilions at either end linked on one side by a gallery and on the other by the palace apartments. At some point be sure to pass along the **Camino de las Cascadas**, where runnels of water cascade down a series of conduits. Every summer from mid-June to the first week in July, the International Music and Dance Festival is staged in the grounds of the Generalife.

Royal tombs

Proud of their conclusive victory over the Moors, the Catholic Monarchs wished to be buried in the city where Muslim Spain met its final demise. So a decorative **Capilla Real D** (open daily; closed 1–4pm; entrance fee) was built between 1506 and 1521, and Fernando and Isabella now share this mausoleum with their daughter Juana "The Mad" and her husband Felipe the Handsome. Many of their royal accessories, such as Isabel's crown and Fernando's sword, are on display, and hanging in the sacristy are many works from Queen Isabel's personal art collection, containing Flemish, Spanish and Italian paintings of the 15th century.

BELOW: flamenco dancer performing in the Sacromonte quarter of the city.

The **Catedral E** (open daily; closed 1–4pm; entrance fee) adjoins the Royal Chapel. Begun in 1523 in the Gothic style and continued in 1528 in the early-Renaissance style, it has been described as "one of the world's architectural tragedies, one of the saddest of wasted opportunities". Not finished until 1714, it is a rather awkward structure.

Taking a break

Sightseeing in Granada always seems to be more intense, more all-consuming than in either of the other grand cities of the south. Perhaps it's the desire to drink in every last detail of the Alhambra, or to spend an afternoon just smelling the flowers of the Generalife.Whatever it is, there just doesn't seem to be enough time left to give the cafés and bars of Granada their proper due. Especially good value is the Spanish custom of dropping into a bar or three for *tapas*. Wine bars specialising in Andalusian vintages serve a drink popular with *granadinos* called *follaza*, a mixture of sweet Málaga wine and soda water.

In the heart of the city are also any number of cafés outfitted with marble columns and counters that evoke images of handlebar moustaches and pomaded hair, but in reality they are frequented by little old ladies in floral-printed dresses aggressively fanning themselves

in summer alongside black-leather-clad punks sipping their *café con leche* (coffee with milk). In the evening, crowds congregate at the **Plaza Bibrambla**, which was once the site of medieval jousts and bullfights.

Map on page 210

Albaicín and Sacromonte

The Albaicín quarter, the oldest part of Granada, covers a slope facing the Alhambra on the north side of the Río Darro. It was home to the first fortress of the Moors and the haven to which they fled when the Christians reconquered the city. Today it offers the typical tangle of Andalusian alleys and simple whitewashed homes. Often the area's long walls signal some luxuriant gardens discreetly enclosed. If you climb up the hill, the **Mirador de San Nicolás** offers a postcard view of the Alhambra. Farther up, beyond the ruins of the Moorish walls, is the **Mirador de San Cristóbal**.

The Sacromonte hillside opposite the Generalife has long been a gypsy enclave. Its character is changing and most gypsy families have moved away but every evening gypsies stage flamenco shows in their caves. It is strictly tourist fare, but among the performers there could be one destined for international fame as more than one flamenco great has started his career here.

Fuente Vaqueros, a village 16 km (10 miles) west of the city, was the birthplace of Federico García Lorca, one of the 20th century's greatest Spanish poets and dramatists. The house where he lived is now a **museum** (open Tues–Sun; closed pm; entrance fee). The Huerta de San Vincente, an old farmhouse on Granada's southern outskirts where he wrote several famous works, is also open to the public (Tues–Sun; closed pm; entrance fee). It contains interesting memorabilia, including Lorca's desk, and is surrounded by a peaceful park. ❑

BELOW: poet and dramatist Federico García Lorca.

FEDERICO GARCÍA LORCA

Born in 1898 in a village not far from Granada and raised in the city, poet and dramatist García Lorca portrayed the gypsy as exemplifying the most profound elements in the Andalusian psyche. *Gypsy Ballads*, published in 1928, brought him national fame. His plays, such as *Blood Wedding* and *Yerma*, were often based on folk themes and tended towards surrealism. But his political views – and his homosexuality – made him many enemies in his home town.

Fatefully, he was in Granada in 1936 at the start of the Spanish Civil War and was arrested with hundreds of others and summarily executed by the Nationalists. A granite block in a memorial park near Viznar, 8 km (5 miles) northeast of the city, marks the spot where he is believed to have been killed. His body was never found, and it was only after the return to democracy that it became possible to speak freely of Lorca's murder and for his work to receive the attention it deserved. His plays are now widely produced and some have been filmed.

Lorca often left Granada, but always yearned to return. He said of these leave-takings: "It will always be like this. Before and now. We must leave, but Granada remains. eternal in time, but fleeting in these poor hands ...".

THEY CAME, THEY SAW, THEY PLANTED

From the intimacy of the patios to the spectacular gardens of the Generalife in Granada, Andalusia is a magnet for gardeners from all over the world

Fertile soil and abundant sunshine make Andalusia a gardener's paradise, and the region is home to some outstanding gardens including Seville's María Luisa Park and the gardens of the Generalife in Granada.

For the Moors, gardens were intimate places which aimed to appeal to all the senses. Aromatic plants such as mint and basil were key elements, as was the soothing sound of running water. Moorish homes were arranged around interior courtyards which provided a scented refuge from the heat, of which the patios of Córdoba are a living example. After the Moors departed, the reigning style was the Italian garden of the Renaissance, designed to impress with proportioned layout, manicured aspect, statues and fountains. The Generalife gardens we see today owe more to this style than to the Moors.

COLOURFUL IMPORTS

Each subsequent lot of settlers brought with them their preferred plants. The Phoenicians, Greeks and Romans introduced olive trees, date palms and grape vines. The Moors brought orange trees and a great many herbs and flowers native to Asia. Explorations of new continents added to this botanical wealth. Geraniums, for instance, came from southern Africa, while mimosas are originally from Australia, wisteria from Asia and bougainvillea from South America.

◁ MODEL LION
A statue in the Jardín de los Leones (Lions' Garden) in Seville's María Luisa Park recalls the famous Patio of the Lions in the Alhambra, which served as the model.

△ TILED FEATURES
Pigeons congregate around a tiled fountain in the María Luisa Park's Plaza de América. This Seville park was donated to the city by Princess María Luisa de Orleans in 1893.

◁ **MOORISH LEGACY**
The gardens of El Partal in the Alhambra. Moorish gardens were designed to appeal to all the senses, and pools and channels of water were key ingredients.

▽ **ITALIAN INFLUENCE**
The Generalife in Granada is Spain's most famous garden. Originally a Moorish royal summer residence, its present layout owes more to Italian influences.

THE WONDER OF WATER

Thanks to their talent as engineers, the Romans tapped Andalusia's water resources, and their canals and aqueducts turned the region into the breadbasket of the empire. But it was the Moors who, adapting and improving on the Roman irrigation system, regarded water as an aesthetic element as well. Fountains, pools and elaborate channels, such as the "water stairway" in the Generalife gardens, filled the air with soothing sound and helped keep summer temperatures down. Water had a symbolic significance for the Moors. Gardens were divided into four sections separated by channels of water representing the four Rivers of Life.

Taking a leaf from the Moors' gardening book, Christian landscapers capitalised on water's use for dramatic visual effect, especially with exquisite fountains, such as in the Patio de la Madama in the 17th-century Palacio de Viana in Córdoba (*above*).

▽ **COOL OASIS**
Potted flowers adorn a patio in Córdoba. These cool, intimate spaces are a legacy of Moorish times. The Moors, coming as they did from the desert, were especially fond of gardens.

△ **NATURALISATION**
Geraniums are often considered the quintessential Andalusian flower. Yet, like so many of Andalusia's plants, it is an introduced variety; it was originally from South Africa.

△ **EXOTICA**
Cupola in La Concepción botanical gardens in Málaga. The garden has a unique collection of palm trees and other exotica.

THE ANDALUSIAN HEARTLAND

There is so much more to discover in the southernmost region of Spain than the Costa del Sol and the three main draws of Seville, Córdoba and Granada

Map on page 220

Within the irregular triangle defined by Seville, Córdoba, Granada and the Mediterranean Sea lies much to be seen that is little known to the general tourist population. This is Andalusia (Andalucía), the province of the *pueblo* where the spice of life is simplicity, peace and home hospitality.

Whether you spend your holiday vagabonding from village to village or simply make inland excursions from the coast, you will marvel at the spontaneous beauty and variety of Spain's landscape. Like set changes in the theatre, Andalusia's villages and vistas seem to spring suddenly out of thin, dry air. Now you *don't* see it, now you *do*.

The only redundant element in this ever-shifting scene is the ubiquitous olive tree. The first hundred groves are interesting; the first thousand, a curiosity. But when it seems that you've seen tens of thousands, the novelty begins to wear thin. Fortunately, at one turning in the road they grace plains; at the next, gentle slopes; then suddenly you will see them clinging to a steep mountainside.

Dunes and wetland

The **Parque Nacional de Doñana** ❶ (open daily; book guided tours in advance, tel: 959-43 04 32) is Spain's biggest national park, straddling more than 50,000 hectares (125,000 acres) of the Huelva and Seville provinces. Most of the park is a special reserve but organised tours in four-wheel drive jeeps, starting from the visitors' centre at **El Acebuche**, leave twice a day for a five-hour journey through the inner areas of the reserve.

The route follows the beach, where oystercatchers, dunlins and sanderlings scurry among the broken waves, and sandwich terns and black-eyed gulls swoop low across the sand. Once at the Guadalquivir estuary, the convoy swings towards the centre of the park, through pine forest and Mediterranean brush. As you travel, guides helpfully point out red stag deer, fallow deer and boars; and even the shy lynx may show itself occasionally.

At the edge of the lakes and marshes, you may see flocks of pink flamingoes, grey-lags and spoonbills. The rare imperial eagle may also be spotted, surveying his empire from the topmost branches of a pine. The vehicles then turn back towards the ocean, through more pines to the dunes; these moving mountains of sand are slowly burying part of the pine wood. Over the crest of a dune, the sea appears again.

The outskirts of the park may be explored on foot only via a choice of self-guided paths. A pollution scare in spring 1998 threatened a large area of the park; although it was quickly brought under control, environmentalists fear many species will be affected.

LEFT: the Tajo bridge, Ronda.
BELOW: stork nesting in the Parque Nacional de Doñana.

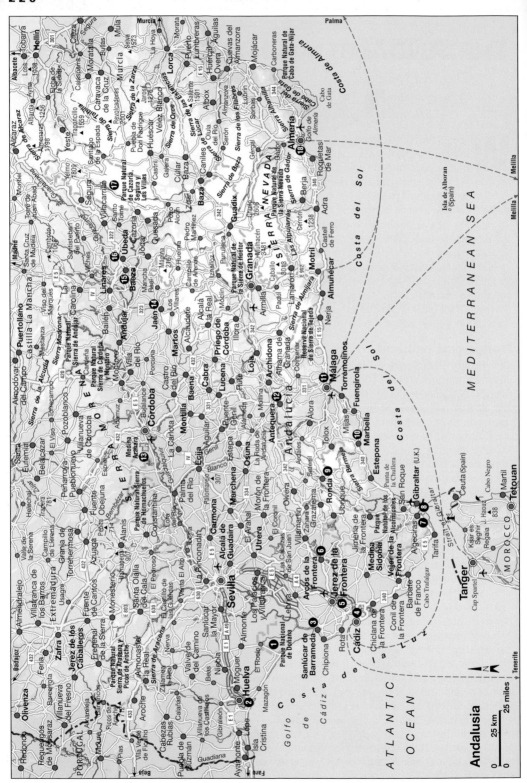

Andalusia

0   25 km
0   25 miles

Map on page 220

On the Columbus trail

The small town of **Huelva ❷** lies 80 km (48 miles) west of **Seville** (Sevilla, *see pages190–201*) along the A-49. It has been somewhat spoilt by industrial development but nevertheless retains a refreshingly innocent small-town atmosphere, especially along its Gran Via. The **Museo Provincial** (open Tues–Sat; free) has exhibits celebrating Columbus's voyage to the New World in 1492; he set sail from Palos de la Frontera, just across the Odiel estuary, on 3 August that year.

The 13th-century **Monasterio de la Rábida** (open Tues–Sun; free), 4 km (2½ miles) north of Palos, is a complete contrast to the industry around it. This is where Columbus met the Friars Antonio de Marchena and Juan Pérez, who took his case to Queen Isabella and persuaded her to back the venture. Inside are the Columbus murals painted by Vázquez Díaz in 1930, which give a simplified picture history of the "Discovery" of America.

The coast of light

Andalusia's breezy **Costa de la Luz**, stretching south from Huelva all the way to Cádiz and beyond to Tarifa, is a paradise for windsurfers. **Sanlúcar de Barrameda ❸**, best known for its production of *manzanilla*, a light, dry sherry, is a flourishing resort and fishing port less than an hour's drive from Seville on the A4 and C441 turn-off. The town looks out across the mouth of the Guadalquivir to the Coto Doñana marshlands. The **Iglesia de Nuestra Señora de la O** is noteworthy for its fine mudéjar doorway. **Chipiona**, a pleasant small resort further along the coast, has a fine beach which is popular among Spanish vacationers. The coast here is golden sand all the way to **Rota**, a Spanish naval base.

On the other side of the bay lies **Cádiz ❹**, whose safe inner harbour first attracted the Phoenicians. They established "Gadir" as early as 1100 BC. Known to the Greeks as "Gadeira", its prime stocks in trade in the 7th century BC were tin and amber. In 501 BC came the Carthaginians, followed later by the Romans under whom the city of "Gades" grew rich. When Rome fell, so did Gades, which for the succeeding Visigoths and Moors was little more than an insignificant port of entry.

With the discovery of America, Cádiz rose again to become the wealthiest port in western Europe and, as a result, the target of attack for the Barbary corsairs and the envious English naval fleet. Sir Francis Drake burned ships at anchor here in 1587, delaying the sending of the Armada and boasting afterwards that he "had singed the King of Spain's beard".

With shipbuilding in decline, Cádiz has been forced to attract other industries, including car-manufacturing. Fishing is important and fish farms have been established around the bay. Not surprisingly, the city is famed for its fresh seafood. The **catedral** (open Tues–Sat; entrance fee), a grandiose structure capped by a dome of golden tiles, was described by Richard Ford as "a stranded wreck on a quicksand". An impressive collection of church treasures can be viewed and in the crypt lies the tomb of composer Manuel de Falla, a Cádiz native, whose music is evocative of the magic of Andalusia.

A little to the south of Huelva at Punta del Sebo is the Monumento a Colón. This 34-metre (112-ft) statue sculpted by Gertrude Vanderbilt Whitney was a gift from the US in honour of the discoverers of America.

BELOW: the richly decorated mudéjar doorway of Nuestra Señora de la O, Sanlúcar de Barrameda.

The Ministry of Tourism publishes a useful map of the white towns. If you need a room for the night, just enquire at the local bar.

BELOW: the late Don José Ignacio Domecq, who was popularly known as "the Nose".

In the **Oratorio de la Santa Cueva** on Calle Rosario (open Mon–Fri; entrance fee) are some fine Goya paintings depicting the Miracle of the Loaves and Fishes, the Guest at the Wedding and the Last Supper. The **Iglesia de San Felipe Neri** (open daily; entrance fee), on Calle Santa Inés, is a place of pilgrimage for democracy-loving Spaniards, since it was here that parliament gathered in 1812 to proclaim a liberal constitution.

Despite its vacillating fortunes and the ramshackle appearance of some quarters, the *gaditanos* love their town and have a reputation for being among the liveliest of Andalusians. Many leading flamenco artists hail from the Bay of Cádiz and the city runs wild every year during the crazy days of Carnival.

The white towns

The white towns are the innumerable small villages of the Andalusian hinterland whose sparkling whitewashed houses cap the mountaintops or slide down their slopes like wilting whipped cream topped with burnt-orange cherries.

Common to all these towns nowadays is a very special brand of serenity. But it wasn't always so. You'll notice that many of the white towns share the tag *de la frontera* ("of the border"), because often throughout Andalusia's history they found themselves on the contentious frontier between Christianity and Islam.

Sherry country

The rolling landscape between **Jerez de la Frontera ❺** and the Atlantic, known as The Sherry Triangle, is ideally suited to raising the grapes that the wineries of Jerez convert into extraordinary sherries and brandies. Tours and tastings are informative and readily intoxicating.

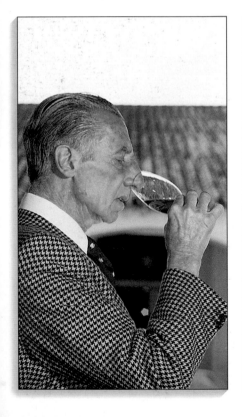

ANDALUSIA'S SHERRY DYNASTIES

Almost 250 years ago the Gordons, a Catholic family from Scotland, arrived in Cádiz and set themselves up in the wine trade. Not long afterwards, several Frenchmen established wine businesses in the area. Their names are still synonymous with sherry: Domecq, Pemartín, Lustau, Lacave and Delage. In 1765, Juan Vicente Vergare y Dickinson, the son of a Basque father and an English mother, arrived in Puerto de Santa María and entered the wine trade. His great-great-grandson, Javier Vergara, still markets sherry under the label of Juan Vicente Vergara.

Despite the foreign origins of a great many of the sherry families, they developed over the decades into a very Spanish aristocracy. Scions became scholars, priests, poets, painters, politicians, and even bullfighters.

Today's aristocrats are a more subdued breed than their predecessors, however. With big multinational companies controlling most of the *bodegas*, they have to be extremely businesslike – the polo grounds at the Chapín Club, where José Ignacio Domecq used to play in Jerez, have not seen a match in years. Manuel Zarraluqui Arana, managing director of Croft Jerez SA, is an economist and one of a new breed typical of leading figures in sherry today, being highly skilled in marketing and finance.

Map on page 220

The city's annual *Feria del Caballo* (Horse Show) at the start of May follows on the heels of Seville's *Feria de Abril*. Proud of its pure-bred line of Carthusian horses, Jerez shows them off in racing, dressage and carriage competitions. All year round these handsome Arabian animals can also be seen strutting their stuff at the **Real Escuela Andaluza de Arte Ecuestre** (open Mon–Fri; entrance fee). Performances take place on Thursdays, but visitors can watch practice sessions between 11am and 1pm. Nearby on Calle Cervantes is the **Museo de Relojes** (open Mon–Sat; entrance fee), with an impressive collection of clocks. Also in Jerez are the bare-bones remains of an 11th-century *alcázar*.

Arcos de la Frontera ❻, a sizeable town of some 25,000 inhabitants, sits on a sharp ridge above a loop of the Río Guadalete. Steep streets lead up to the panoramic parador looking out across the mottled browns and greens of Andalusia's farmland and the blue of a large lake.

Back on the coast road (N-340) south from Cádiz, you'll pass through **Vejer de la Frontera** and **Tarifa,** both having a more North African than Spanish feel to them because of their proximity to Morocco just across the Strait of Gibraltar. The ugly industrial chaos around **Algeciras ❼** is almost unavoidable. It is the main Spanish ferry port for the North African destinations of Ceuta and Tangier and on the main route if you're heading for Gibraltar and the Costa del Sol.

The Rock

Since the border between Spain and **Gibraltar ❽** was reopened after the 1969 Spanish blockade, only a passport and valid car insurance are required to allow you to cross on to the limestone rock over the airport runway that bisects the narrow isthmus. If anyone stops you in **La Línea** as you approach the border and offers, for a small commission, to facilitate your getting an insurance card, drive on. All rental cars are insured, and anyone driving into Spain requires proof of valid car insurance before crossing the border.

Since 1704 Gibraltar, one of the ancient Pillars of Hercules, has been a bone of contention between Britain and Spain. But before that it had been passed back and forth between the Spaniards and the Moors, who first took it in 711 under the Berber leadership of Tariq ibn Zeyad and gave it its name "Gebel Tarik", the mountain of Tariq. The Moor's Castle, now in ruins, was his legacy. In 1462, the Spanish regained it one last time before the British seized it in 1704.

Peaking at 425 metres (1,396 ft), Gibraltar measures less than 7 sq. km (3 sq. miles) and is home to 30,000 people. The strategic strait it controls links the Atlantic and Mediterranean and is 58 km (35 miles) long and 13 km (8 miles) wide at its narrowest point.

Wildlife

This seemingly barren rock enjoys some fame for its wildlife. The origin of its distinctive Barbary apes is not known, but they are not found on the Spanish mainland. Among the variety of birds that stop here on their annual migrations to Europe are honey buzzards, griffons, black storks and short-toed eagles.

BELOW: Gibraltar's Key Ceremony.

A curious military feat are the **Upper Galleries** (open daily; entrance fee) tunnelled into the rock at the time of the Great Siege by France and Spain between 1779 and 1783. By the end of this war the tunnel measured 113 metres (370 ft). Curious, too, is the evident cultural mixture on the Rock. Arab women in full-length dress and modified *chador* cross paths with British officers, Spanish-speaking merchants and dark-skinned descendants of the Moors. Equally mixed are the linguistics. In a local bar the TV plays in Spanish, the radio in English and the bartender speaks with a hybrid accent.

Legend has it that the British will remain in Gibraltar as long as the Barbary apes survive. When extinction threatened them in 1944, Churchill ordered reinforcements.

BELOW: the Plaza de Toros in Ronda, which opened in May 1784.

Bandido country

Heading inland from the coast on the C-369 towards **Ronda ❾**, the countryside gradually grows wilder. In the 19th century, travelling here meant taking your life in your hands. The hills were full of highwaymen. During and after the Civil War, the more remote of these villages harboured Republican refugees.

To reach **Castellar de la Frontera**, a side road climbs up a rocky hillside, passing through private yards and public chicken crossings along the way. The archetypal castle stands crumbling, deserted, devoid of all purpose, like a splendid wedding gown yellowing forgotten in an attic. The next castle, too, sits on its own hilltop, crumbling. At its feet, the town of **Jimena de la Frontera** spills like white paint down the hillside where mules graze below on the steep, grassy slopes. Between Jimena and Ronda, a distance of about 56 km (35 miles), stop somewhere by the roadside and indulge your senses. The scent of herbs perfumes a silence smooth as silk.

Whether you approach Ronda from the north or south, you are given no clues that you are about to enter a bustling town of 30,000 perched on a rocky bluff

Map on page 220

with sheer walls falling away a dramatic 180 metres (600 ft) on three sides. A deep ravine some 90 metres (300 ft) wide divides the old and new sections. Near the **Puente Nuevo** that links the old and new towns a path leads down to a fine view of this bridge that spans the vertiginous gorge. Built in the 18th century, it is beautifully unobtrusive in design, allowing the magnificent scenery to shine through. Thanks to its auspicious position, Ronda was virtually impregnable, remaining the capital of an isolated Moorish kingdom until 1485.

The 18th-century **Plaza de Toros** (open daily; entrance fee) in the new town is one of the oldest bullrings in Spain and contains an interesting museum displaying suits of lights, documents, photos, posters and Goya prints pertaining to this uniquely Spanish art.

It was in Ronda that bullfighting on foot first began early in the 18th century when a noble and his horse were upended by a bull's charge. A bystander leaped into the ring and, using his hat as a lure, managed to draw the bull away from the hapless rider.

Cut-throat den

Throughout the Serranía de Ronda, the mountain range surrounding the city, are more storybook white towns. **Grazalema**, 32 km (20 miles) west of Ronda, boasts that it gets more rain than anywhere else in Spain. Long a haunt of smugglers and brigands, it was described by Ford as a "cut-throat den". Nowadays it is somewhat more welcoming, with a municipal swimming pool, hotel and camp site, and is the gateway to the nature reserve that bears its name. Set up in 1984, the reserve extends from **El Bosque**, where there is a small information centre, to Benaoján in the east and Cortes de la Frontera to the south. Much of the Mediterranean forest of holm oak and Montpelier maple still survives, but some areas have been converted to open ranges or brush. Here mountain goats and a superb range of birds of prey can be seen, including buzzards, griffon vultures and Bonelli's booted and short-toed eagles.

BELOW: landscape around Ubrique and Grazalema.

The **Cueva de la Pileta** (guided tours from 10am–1pm and 4–5pm daily; entrance fee), with some remarkable prehistoric animal paintings, is signposted from the MA-501 about 4 km (2½ miles) south of Benaoján. The paintings were discovered by a local farmer in 1905 while he was out looking for *guano* (bird droppings) to manure his fields. Perhaps the most impressive painting is one depicting a huge fish which seems to have swallowed a seal.

Not far away, through wild, pine-clad sierras, at the foot of a mountain, lies **Ubrique**, a *pueblo* specially noted for its leatherwork. Most of these villages have spectacular settings, but that of **Zahara** ("de la Sierra" to distinguish it from Zahara de los Atunes on the Costa de la Luz) is truly breathtaking. A brilliant beacon of white, it stands on a steep crag northwest of Ronda. Neat and whiter than white, it offers another ancient castle and superb views. In contrast, much of the village of **Setenil** huddles in a chasm, its houses built right under menacing lips of rock.

Costa del Sol

Most of the Sunshine Coast is in Málaga province, running from east of Gibraltar to the province of Granada. Development has been heavy – often excessive – all along the coast. However, there are still some nooks and crannies where you can avoid the crowds, as in the western section between Gibraltar

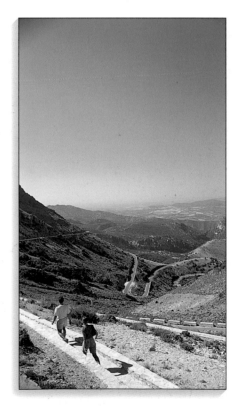

and San Pedro where resorts are relatively scattered. **Estepona**, the most westerly of the Costa's swollen fishing villages and now a large town, has so far avoided too many high-rises and remains Spanish, with an old quarter of narrow streets and bars. From here on the pace quickens and the crowds thicken, with lush golf courses interspersed with luxury villas.

The area between the flashy marina Puerta Banus and **Marbella ⑩** is known as the Golden Mile and is the playground of celebrities, sheikhs, millionaires, royalty and bullfighters. Expensive restaurants, a casino, signs in Arabic and a mosque testify to the presence of Middle East oil money. In the centre of Marbella, the old town remains unspoilt, with the Plaza de los Naranjos as its showpiece. On a hot summer night this plaza becomes one vast open-air restaurant and, lit by an orange glow, it can delight even hardened Costa-watchers.

The coast goes down-market approaching **Fuengirola**. From there to Málaga tourist traffic is intense. High-rise hotels and apartment blocks crowd the water's edge, summer beaches are packed with bodies and discos and bars compete raucously, reaching a climax at **Torremolinos**, which was a poor fishing village until the early 1960s when it was "discovered". This grotesquely overgrown village, with its hundreds of bars, lush vegetation and overhead walkways, is like some Hollywood director's concept of what a Spanish resort should be.

Just west of Málaga, at Cerro del Villar, archaeologists have recently unearthed the largest Phoenician settlement discovered so far on the Iberian peninsula and dating to at least the 8th century BC.

Donkey taxis

Up in the mountains, 8 km (5 miles) above Fuengirola, the white town of **Mijas**, once a quaint mountain village, now uses its donkeys for photo opportunities rather than for farming and seems to have more shops than residences. Despite this, there is fresher air up here and fine views down to the coast.

Málaga ⑪ (pop. 550,000) boasts it is the capital of the Costa del Sol. However, it is not a resort but a bustling port founded by the Phoenicians. Its citizens sided briefly with Carthage before becoming a Roman municipium (a town governed by its own laws). In 711 it fell to the Moors within a year of their invasion of Spain and was the port of the Kingdom of Granada until 1487, when it was taken by the Christians after a four-month siege.

Málaga's historical ruins can be found mainly on the high ground at the eastern end of the city. The Moorish **Alcazaba** (open daily; entrance fee) is a maze of pretty gardens and courtyards. It is connected to the ruined 14th-century Moorish **Castillo de Gibralfaro** (open daily; free) by a formidable double-walled rampart, while a rocky path climbs beside it. At one point a *mirador* gives a view over the harbour and down on to Málaga's bullring.

The 16th-century **catedral** (open daily; free), designed by Pedro de Mena, is further west on Calle Molina Lario, towards the dry river bed of the Río Guadalmedina. The cathedral's east tower was never completed, giving it the nickname La Manquita – "the one-armed one". Between the Alcazaba and cathedral, at Calle San Agustín 8, is the **Palacio de Buenavista**, which is being converted into a new Picasso Museum scheduled to open in 2000. A short walk north from here is the **Casa Natal de Picasso** (open

BELOW: regimented beach loungers stretch along the Golden Mile.

Mon–Fri; free) at Plaza de la Merced 15, where the artist spent his first years. The Picasso Foundation now based here organises lectures on various aspects of Picasso's work, and promotes contemporary art.

For a peaceful haven away from Málaga's careering traffic, go to the **English Cemetery**, which lies beyond the bullring, approached along avenues of orange trees. Founded in 1830, it was Spain's first Protestant cemetery. In a walled enclosure near the summit are the tiny shell-covered graves of a dozen children.

Map on page 220

Dolmens and caves

About 50 km (32 miles) north of Málaga on the N-331, **Antequera** ⑫ is an attractive town with innumerable churches and convents. Seek out the Moorish **castillo**, near the 16th-century Iglesia de Santa María la Mayor, for a fine view. To the east you will see a curiously shaped rock, the Peña de los Enamorados, which looks like a face in profile. It gets its name from a legend of two thwarted lovers who hurled themselves off the top.

Antequera's most unusual attractions are three dolmens, or ancient burial chambers, which were constructed with huge slabs of rock around 2000 BC. The **Cuevas de Menga** and **Viera** (open Tues–Sun; free) are close together on the edge of town, while the Cueva de Romeral is down the road near a defunct sugar factory, where a guardian is on duty.

Back on the coast, east of Málaga, **Nerja** is one of the larger resorts on this part of the coast and offers some vast caves nearby. On display inside are some of the Palaeolithic remains discovered on this site along with photos of the excavations. Also, over 500 cave paintings have been uncovered here, but will be accessible only to researchers until study of them has been completed.

Málaga's harbour seen from the Castillo de Gibralfaro.

BELOW: Moorish-influenced modern architecture of Torremolinos.

A 2-km (1¼-mile) path leads through the colourfully lit caverns. As yet, the full extent of this underground wonderland remains unknown. But what there is, is wonder enough. It is like an underground cathedral in an abstract Gaudí style with stalactite pipe organs and stalagmite spires. Every July these bizarre natural sculptures are the backdrop for a festival of music and ballet.

Medina Azahara

Eight km (5 miles) northwest of **Córdoba** (*see pages 202–7*) stand the emerging remains of **Medina Azahara** ⑬ (tel: 957-32 91 30; open Tues–Sun; entrance fee), an extensive palace complex begun around 936 by Abd-al-Rahman III to satisfy the caprices of his favourite wife Zahara (meaning "flower").

The new city stretched up the Sierra de Córdoba foothills of the Sierra Morena, adapting itself gracefully to the terraced terrain. Its area of approximately 110 hectares (275 acres) is divided into three levels. The highest, which has seen the greatest amount of excavation to date, contains the **Alcázar**; the middle, the gardens and orchards; and the lowest, the mosque and city proper.

The account of its construction, as rendered by Arab historian El-Makkari, gives some impression of its scale. Ten thousand men, 2,600 mules and 400 camels worked for 25 years, he reports, to erect the palace, gardens, fish ponds, mosque, baths and schools. The royal entourage included some 12,000 men, 4,000 servants and 2,000 horses. There were hanging gardens, aviaries, zoos, streams, courts, gold fountains and a quicksilver pool. But the life of the city was as fleeting as its very being was fantastic. In 1010, just 74 years after its conception, the Berbers attacked and burned it. From that moment on, it was systematically plundered to become part of other Islamic structures.

BELOW: ruins of the once-glorious Moorish palace of Medina Azahara.

Two important historical towns lie between Córdoba and Seville. **Carmona**, on the main N-IV route, was an important Roman centre. Its well-laid out **Necropolis Romana** (open Tues–Sun; entrance fee) on the western extremity of the town shows the walls of the crematorium still discoloured by the heat of the fire. **Ecija**, 56 km (34 miles) east, is built in a valley bowl and consequently has no summer breeze to relieve the heat. The town is littered with (crumbling) Baroque church towers echoing the Seville Giralda, the most notable being that of the **Iglesia de Santa María** (open daily; free). The covered market is colourful, and Calle Caballeros (north of the main square) has several rambling and ornate merchants' houses, including the **Palacio de Peñaflor** (courtyard open daily; free), with a very unusual curved balcony.

Jaén province

A massive undulating area of 150 million olive trees, Jaén province has always suffered from being a place to drive through rather than to stay. The north-south artery, the N-323, which brings you into the province takes you directly to the provincial capital, **Jaén** . Perched above the western plain with its back to the sierras, the city has surprisingly few monuments. But what it lacks in quantity it makes up for in scale.

The **catedral** (open daily; free) is a massive pile built over three centuries, with a wonderful mixture of Gothic to baroque styles. The 11th-century **Baños Arabes** (open Tues–Sun; entrance fee), superbly excavated and restored, are among the largest and best preserved in Spain. The city streets, in both the commercial zone and the old town stacked against the hillside, have a zip and energy you find only in such self-possessed Spanish provincial cities.

Olive trees dominate the landscape in Jaén province.

BELOW: peaks of the Parque Natural de Cazorla.

Map on page 220

Ubeda's Parador Condestable Davalos, housed in a 16th-century Renaissance palace.

BELOW: the hillside town of Cazorla.

Baeza , 40 km (25 miles) northeast of the provincial capital, is an architectural gem, its honey-coloured palaces, churches and civic buildings dating chiefly to the 15th–17th centuries. Star features include the studded **Palacio de Jabalquinto** and nearby, on Plaza Santa María, the **Santa Iglesia Catedral** (open daily; free), which was largely rebuilt in the 16th century. The real focus of interest, however, is the **Plaza de los Leones** to the west of the centre, which is clustered with splendid Renaissance architecture. Overlooking the fountain in the middle of the square are the **Puerta de Jaén** and the adjoining **Arco de Villalar**. On the north side of the square you can see the **Antigua Carnicería**, a 16th-century butcher's shop. A few steps away, on Paseo Cardenel Benavides, is the **Ayuntamiento** (Town Hall; open Mon–Fri am only; free), a magnificent Plateresque building that was once a courthouse and jail.

Only 10 km (6 miles) further north along the N-316 is the larger town of **Ubeda** ⑯, another Renaissance jewel. The **Plaza de Vázquez de Molina** – an architectural set-piece in a class of its own – is unmissable. The rectangular plaza runs down from the stunningly rich domed **Capilla del Salvador**, which was built as a family pantheon and is still privately owned by the Duques de Medinaceli. As it widens out, the plaza reveals a balanced, beautifully proportioned sequence of austere palaces unbroken by modern additions considered by many to be the purest architectural expression of the Renaissance in Spain.

At the far end is the church of Santa María de los Reales Alcázares, built on the site of the old mosque. Also worth seeking out are the **Iglesia de San Pablo** for its impressive Plateresque tower, and the **Hospital de Santiago**, designed by Andrés de Vandelvira and now a cultural centre (open daily; free), which is sometimes compared to El Escorial for its severity of style.

CAZORLA'S FLORA AND FAUNA

One of Spain's most beautiful natural parks, the Parque Natural de Cazorla, Segura y Las Villas (to give it its full name) is a vast protected area in the northeast of Jaén province. Designated a natural park in 1986, it covers more than 200,000 hectares (500,000 acres) of dense forests and mountain peaks. More than 500, 000 people visit every year on walking or driving trips, and to sample the immense natural attractions of the park.

The best times to visit, especially if you plan to do much walking, are spring and early or late summer, when the Andalusian climate is not so intensely hot. In spring, hikers can see primroses and the dwarf violets unique to Cazorla. At any time of year visitors may see hawks, eagles, bearded vultures, deer, boar and ibex (mountain goats) – the remoteness of the area means that the wildlife is unusually visible. An especially popular spot in the south of the reserve is the small spring where the Río Guadalquivir starts its course, when it is unceremoniously spat out from the depths of a mountain.

The sierras in the reserve are spectacular and rise to more than 2,000 metres (6,500 ft). The main driving route through the park hugs the river bed for much of the way, before reaching the Embalse del Tranco reservoir.

The town of **Cazorla**, to the east of Ubeda, is a good access point for the **Parque Natural de Cazorla** ⓱ (information and maps at Cazorla's Oficina del Parque Natural, Calle Martínez Falero 11, tel: 953-71 01 02). Buses are scarce, so to get the best from a visit here you'll need a car or, better still, be prepared to walk – undoubtedly the best way to see the abundant wildlife and spectacular scenery the park has to offer. There is a modern parador and several camp-grounds in the park as well as plenty of accommodation in Cazorla.

The **Sierra Nevada** range southeast of **Granada** (*see pages 208–15*), is also excellent for walking but most visitors come here to ski at the 2,100-metre (6,890-ft) resort of Solynieve, the southernmost ski resort in Europe. The skiing facilities are first-class and were much expanded in 1996 when the World Alpine Ski Championships were staged here.

Almería

For much of the 20th century, Almería's harsh landscape of sun-scorched sier-ras and rocky plains was dismissed as a forgotten corner. But now the desert-like climate powers a massive agricultural business spreading over 20,000 hectares (50,000 acres) of the coastal plain.

At the centre of the southern coast sits the provincial capital of **Almería** ⓲, still dominated by the 11th-century **Alcazaba**, its severe Moorish architecture overlaid by the more grandiose Catholic upper courtyard. The coast to the east of Almería runs south to the volcanic headland of **Cabo de Gata**, a protected area since 1980 for its flora, fauna and underwater life. Small resorts and villages line this stretch of coast, culminating at **Mojácar**, which until the 1960s was a quiet white village but is now overrun with chintzy bars and boutiques. ❏

Map on page 220

BELOW: Almería's coast is Europe's winter garden.

VALENCIA AND MURCIA

*Together, these two regions are often known as the Levant.
Between them they enjoy more than half of Spain's
eastern coastline, stretching from Catalonia to Almería*

J ust 3 km (2 miles) from the Mediterranean and straddling the Río Turia, the city of **Valencia ❶** has an enviable site. It lies in the middle of one of Europe's most densely developed agricultural regions. The fields surrounding the city can yield three to four crops a year. Orange and lemon trees line the roads. Rice grows alongside sweet corn. Shimmering canals weave their way through the land, giving it life. This is the *huerta*, a cultivated and irrigated plain that was considered by the Moors to be heaven on earth. Even the Spanish hero El Cid was taken by it. On his entry into Valencia he proclaimed: "From the day when I saw this city I found it to my liking, and I desired it, and I asked God to make me master of it."

The city he so desperately wanted had already seen the glories of past empires. It had been founded as Valentia by the Romans in 138 BC and became known as a retirement town for old soldiers. Chosen for its mild year-round temperatures, the Romans took advantage of the sunshine and the runoff from the surrounding mountains to turn the rich soil into some of the most efficiently irrigated farmland in their domain.

Earthly paradise

The Visigoths and Moors knew a good thing when they saw it, and continued to improve the complex system of canals and channels. To the Moors it was a paradise, and one that could effectively feed their people. They controlled the land for 500 years and built a city impressive enough to draw El Cid's attention. He conquered Valencia in 1094 but after his death it fell back under the jurisdiction of the Moors. In 1238 the city was finally wrestled from Moorish domination and incorporated into the kingdom of Aragón by Jaume I, *El Conquistador*.

The 15th century saw Valencia blossom into its Golden Age as it overtook Barcelona as the financial capital of this Mediterranean empire. Aside from its agricultural riches and its burgeoning port, the city held claim to a growing ceramic and silk industry and set up the nation's first printing press in 1474.

The city continued to prosper until 1609, when it was dealt a disastrous blow by Felipe III – the expulsion of the *moriscos* from Spain. No arca was as hard hit as Valencia, which lost one-third of its people, most of them farm labourers. Its importance further declined in the early 18th century when the kingdom of Valencia was reduced to a province dependent on Madrid. And during the Spanish Civil War, the city was hard hit as one of the last Republican strongholds.

Valencia recovered much of its prestige when it became the capital of the Comunidad Valenciana, one

PRECEDING PAGES: ceramic-covered house at Manises. **LEFT:** Alicante's Seafront. **BELOW:** orange harvest in Valencia's fertile *huerta*.

of the new autonomous regions of Spain, in 1982. Since then this city of almost 800,000 inhabitants, the third largest in Spain after Madrid and Barcelona, has been feverishly reinventing itself – laying out wide new avenues and investing in daring architectural projects.

Valenciano is actually a dialect of Catalan and today is widely, though not exclusively, spoken in the city.

The natural place to begin a tour of the city is the main square. Like most main squares, the **Plaza del Ayuntamiento** lies in the centre of the city and is the location of the city hall, post office, and bus stops. For some years, this triangular plaza was called the "Plaza of the Valencian Nation". While their separatist feelings are not as strong as the Catalans' or the Basques', Valencians do not forget that the city gained its importance long before it was joined to Castile, and are proud of their own traditions and language, *valenciano*.

The history of this nation is told in a small **museum** (open Mon–Fri 9am–2pm; free) housed on the second floor of the **Ayuntamiento** Ⓐ (City Hall). Unfortunately, there is nothing here regarding El Cid, since most of the exhibits date from the time of Jaume I of Aragón, who is considered by Valencians as the true saviour of the city from the Moors. Of special interest is the first map of the city drawn at a time when Valencia, with a population of 80,000, was bigger than Barcelona, Madrid and Genova. The map, drawn in 1704, took five years to complete as the cartographer, Padre Tosca, measured the city street by street with a tape. It's still one of the most accurate city maps in existence.

City of ceramics

BELOW:
view over Valencia.

Valencians are known for their individualism, sensuality, creativity, a desire to show off, and their pride in the natural abundance of the water on which their city is built. For evidence of this you need look no further than the railway sta-

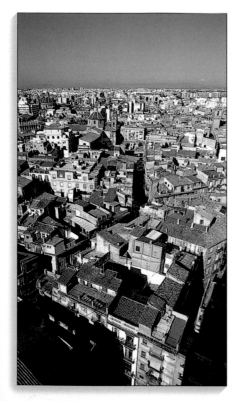

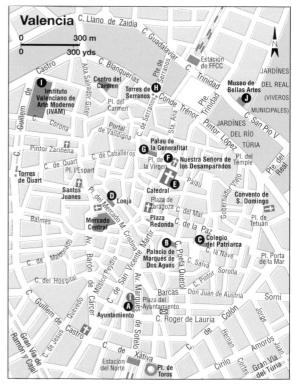

Map on page 236

tion, which is decorated on the outside with bunches of sculpted oranges and inside with stained glass and ceramic mosaics.

The craft which Valencia developed into a fine art, ceramics, is represented in the **Palacio de Marqués de Dos Aguas** ❸ on Calle Rinconada García Sanchís, which houses the **Museo Nacional de Cerámica** (closed for restoration). The industry dates back to the 13th century, when ceramic work came into use as a means of home decoration. Tapestries, which were used in colder climates to help retain heat, were never needed in Valencia and the use of *azulejos* (coloured tiles) became popular.

The oldest pieces in the museum come from two towns in the *huerta*, Paterna and Manises. Their porcelain was once much sought-after by European royal families. Today only Manises keeps up its potteries. The palace itself appears to be made of ceramic. Its grey and rust marble façade is in perfect Churrigueresque style: on either side of the alabaster entryway is a carved muscled Greek pouring water from an urn, illustrating the Marques' name.

Round the corner from the Ceramic Museum is the Real Colegio de Corpus Cristi, which is commonly known as the **Colegio del Patriarca** ❸ (open daily 11am–1.30pm; entrance fee), in honour of its founder, the 16th-century archbishop and viceroy of Valencia, St John de Ribera. Grouped around its renowned two-storey Renaissance patio are a church whose walls and ceilings are covered with frescoes and a museum housing an important collection of works of art by Spanish and foreign masters.

Glorious food

To the north of the Plaza del País Valenciano is the **Plaza del Mercado** (open Mon–Sat), site of the central market. The brick and tile market is a veritable cathedral to food. The domed building with stained-glass windows and ornate doorways is over 8,030 sq. metres (9,600 sq. yards) which makes it one of the largest markets in Europe.

Across the street is the **Lonja** ❹, the old commercial exchange, built in the 15th century for the ever-increasing mercantile industry. The prosperity is reflected in the elegant Transactions Hall. High-ceilinged and supported by eight twisted columns, the hall's delicately traced windows allow the sun to cast shadows across the red and black tiled floor.

Behind the Lonja a maze of narrow streets and squares lead to the Plaza de Zaragoza, on which stands the cathedral. On the way, you may stumble across the charming **Plaza Redonda**, a circular covered market whose stalls sell a mixture of haberdashery, clothes and crafts.

The **catedral** ❺ (open daily; free), built on the site of a Roman temple to Diana and later a mosque, was begun in 1262 in traditional Gothic style. In the 1700s its interior was covered over with a neoclassical façade, which has been removed. The west side, facing the Plaza de Zaragoza, is Italian baroque while the south door is Romanesque. The focal point of the structure is the unfinished 15th-century octagonal bell tower known as the **Miguelete** (open daily; entrance fee), or *Micalet* in *valenciano*. From the top is a fine

BELOW: the Miguelete tower.

view of the glazed tile domes of the city and a glimpse of the *huerta* stretching beyond it to the nearby hills. Inside the cathedral is a chapel containing a small purple agate cup purported to be the Holy Grail.

Water power

The cathedral's **Door of the Apostles**, a 14th-century portal adorned with statuary, gives on to the **Plaza de la Virgen**. It is in this antique doorway that once a week, without fail, the ancient Water Tribunal of Valencia meets, in which the proceedings are as they have been for hundreds of years.

Taking up the east side of the plaza and connected to the cathedral by a small bridge is the **Basílica de Nuestra Señora de los Desamparados ❻** (Our Lady of the Abandoned, open daily; free), the patron saint of the city since the 17th century. The image of the Virgin displayed above the altar was carved in 1416 for the chapel of Spain's first mental institution.

Across from the basilica is the **Palau de la Generalitat ❼**, housing the regional government (visits by prior arrangement only; tel: 96-386 61 00; free). This Gothic palace was built in the 15th century but skilfully extended in the 1950s. It is arranged around a handsome inner courtyard, off which is an exquisite reception room, the Salón Dorado, named for its ornate, gold-coffered ceiling. Upstairs is the assembly hall of the ancient *cortes*, the Valencian parliament.

Calle de Caballeros, running north from the palace, is the old main street. Its commercial importance has waned but its former glory can be seen in the Gothic residences that are interspersed with restaurants, bars and cafés. Most of the houses here have retained their beautiful patios, the sure sign of 15th-century Valencian success.

BELOW LEFT and **RIGHT:** the Palacio de Marqués de Dos Aguas.

IVAM and the Museum of Fine Arts

The maze of streets that branch off from Caballeros towards the river form the oldest part of the city, the **Barrio del Carmen**. As late as 1762, Valencia was still a network of 428 narrow streets held within fortified city walls. In 1777 the dangers of these dark alleyways gave rise to the establishment of the first corps of *serenos*, or night watchmen, who later became a standard feature of most Spanish towns. For decades, the Barrio del Carmen lay in ruins but is being rapidly refurbished and is now full of trendy Spanish pubs.

Calle de Serranos leads from the Palau de la Generalitat to the **Torres de Serranos** ❸ (open Tues–Sun; closed Sun pm; free but a tip appreciated), a city gate built in the 1390s and one of two left standing. (The other is the **Torres de Quart** at the end of Caballeros.) The tower is a massive fortification that once formed part of the city walls, torn down in 1865. The walls, broken by 10 gateways, followed the boundaries set by the present-day streets of Calle Guillem de Castro and Calle de Colón, and the bank of the Río Turia.

Calle Guillem de Castro is now the site of the **Instituto Valenciano de Arte Moderno** ❶ (IVAM, open Tues–Sun 10am–7pm; entrance fee), considered to be Spain's most dynamic contemporary art gallery. The Valencian artists, sculptor Julio González and painter Ignacio Pinazo, are well represented here. The institute also has a lively programme of temporary exhibitions.

The Torres de Serranos looks out across the dry bed of the Río Turia to the city's largest gardens, the **Jardines del Real** (open 8am–sunset daily; free). Beside them stand the **Museo de Bellas Artes** ❶ (open Tues–Sun; closed Sun pm; free), one of the most important provincial galleries in Spain. Housed in a former seminary with a stunning blue dome, the museum's most interesting

Map on page 236

Valencia suffered a disastrous flood in 1957, after which the Río Turia was diverted along an artifical channel lying outside the city.

BELOW: Water Tribunal judge.

THE WATER TRIBUNAL

Valencia's *Tribunal de las Aguas* (Water Tribunal) has been meeting every Thursday at noon for an estimated 1,000 years, making it not only one of the world's most curious legal institutions but also one of the oldest.

There are eight judges presiding, each of whom is dressed in black and each representing one of the great *acequias* or irrigation canals of the *huerta* – the 930 hectares (2,300 acres) of cultivated land which surrounds the city. These canals were originally built by the Romans over 2,000 years ago, and are still used to distribute water among the farmers of the area. Any questions regarding the intricate system of channels, canals and drains must be brought before the Water Tribunal. Every farmer is told precisely on which days and for exactly how long he can irrigate his fields. If he exceeds his quota – whether through negligence or greed – he is likely to be challenged in public before the tribunal.

The judges, who are farmers themselves, conduct their business in *valenciano*. They rarely need to discuss a case in any detail but usually pass judgement immediately and impose a fine on any farmer who is found guilty of a misdemeanour. The Water Tribunal may be ancient but it represents swift and efficient justice.

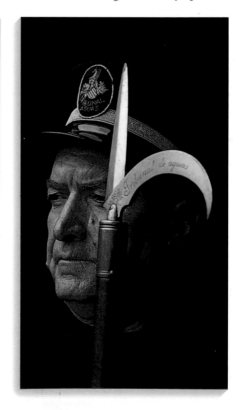

works include the 14th- and 15th-century altarpieces by so-called Valencian "primitive" painters. Also worth seeing are the late 19th/early 20th century Valencian artists who were inspired by the sea, the colours of the *huerta* and the year-round Mediterranean sunshine. The best known of them is the Impressionist Joaquín Sorolla.

Papier-mâché giants celebrating the annual fallas.

Following the river to the sea

The redundant course of the Río Turia has been turned into an attractive feature of the city, as an elongated ribbon of parks and sports fields crossed by a mixture of old and new bridges. On the bank downstream stands Valencia's main concert hall the **Palau de la Musica**, and beyond it, in the bend of the river, lies a giant figure of **Gulliver** (open 10am–8pm daily; free) for children to play on.

Further towards the port is the city's most ambitious project to date, the **City of Arts and Sciences** (tel: 96-352 55 07 for current information). Largely designed by Valencian architect Santiago Calatrava, it will consist of four main spaces. The hemispheric OMNIMAX cinema was the first part to open. The other parts of the complex – a hall for the performing arts, a science museum and an oceanographic park – are due to open in 2000.

A pleasant tram ride from the Pont de Fusta station (near the Museo de Bellas Artes) brings you to the beach, which is lined by a wide promenade stretching from the port past the old fishing quarters of El Cabañal and La Malvarrosa. A string of restaurants along Playa de las Arenas (near the penultimate tram stop) serve excellent *paella*. The most well-known of Spanish dishes, *paella* has its origins in the rice paddies south of the city around the Albufera (*see page 243*). Replete with saffron-seasoned rice, *paella* contains a variety of meats,

BELOW: young girls weep at the end of the *fallas* fiesta.

seafood and vegetables, depending on the cook's taste. Valencian drinks include fresh orange juice and *horchata*, a refreshing summer cooler which tastes faintly of almonds.

Maps:
city 236
Area 243

The fallas

Look on almost any old building in the centre of Valencia for the small plaque guaranteeing that the structure is insured against fire. Fire insurance is essential in the city with the most explosive fiestas in Spain: the *fallas*.

The custom dates back to the Middle Ages when Valencia's carpenters burned their accumulated wood shavings in huge bonfires on the eve of 19 March, the feast of St Joseph, patron of woodworkers. Over the years, the traditional woodchips were replaced with papier-mâché figures lampooning politicians, local customs and current events. For a week, 350 of these temporary works of art are on display throughout the city. The moment of truth, the *cremá*, arrives on 19 March, and the streets, plazas and balconies fill up with citizens, tourists and, most importantly, firemen. One by one the colourful images are put to the match, so that at midnight the entire city, illuminated with an orange glow, appears to be burning down.

Confusingly, the name Valencia is used in English to refer to three distinct entities: the capital city, the province that surrounds it, and the autonomous region of the Comunidad Valenciana.

The Comunidad Valenciana

The 23,300 sq. km (9,000 sq. miles) of the Comunidad Valenciana is split into three provinces: Valencia, Castellón and Alicante. This region approximately follows the boundaries of the old Kingdom of Valencia which was captured from the Moors in the 13th century by an army of Catalans, who left their language here in the form of the *Valenciano* dialect.

BELOW; Valencia's inferno-culmination of the fiesta.

Valencia, according to the paso doble which has become the region's unofficial anthem, "is the land of flowers, light and love." Thanks to an equable Mediterranean climate, all good things seem in abundance here. Sunshine saturates its many attractive beaches and warm temperatures make for an active outdoor life day and night, almost all year round.

Wooden rowing boats at the Albufera Lake.

Castellón

Away from the coast both Valencia and Murcia are mountainous. One of the most picturesque upland areas is **El Maestrazgo** (Maestrat), which straddles the border between Castellón and Teruel. The crags and flat-topped summits form a backdrop to stout medieval towns built in impregnable locations. The most impressive of these is **Morella** ❷, the "capital" of the Maestrazgo, which clings to a protruding bulge of rock. **Ares del Maestre** is also spectacularly sited. Other places that are particularly worth visiting are the two towns **Cinctorres**, **La Iglesuela del Cid**, and the extraordinary shrine of **La Balma**, in a cave half-way up a cliff.

Descending to sea level, the coast of Castellón could not come as more of a contrast. It is aptly named the **Costa del Azahar**, the orange blossom coast, after the citrus groves that cover the coastal plain and emit a sweet perfume in spring. The main resorts are **Vinaròs, Benicarló, Orpesa, Benicàssim** and **Borriana** but the most appealing one to visit is **Peñíscola** ❸. The **Castell del Papa Luna** (open daily; entrance fee), at the heart of this fortified town built on a rocky headland, was the refuge of the renegade Pedro de Luna, elected Pope Benedict XIII in the late 14th century during the Great Schism that split the Christian Church, but later deposed.

BELOW: the town of Manises, famed for its ceramic productions.

The provincial capital **Castelló de la Plana** ❹ centres on a 16th-century bell tower, El Fadrí. Other than that its most interesting monuments are the **Museo Provincial de Bellas Artes** (open Mon–Fri; Sat am; free), the **Convento de las Madres Capuchinas**, which houses a collection of paintings thought to be by Francisco de Zurbarán (open daily, pm only; free) and the **Planetarium** (open Tues–Sat; Sun am; entrance fee) near the beach.

Valencia Province

The interior of Valencia is not unmissable but it is worth exploring if you have the time. There are several beauty spots in the valley of the Río Turia (the **Alto Turia**), a destination for hikers, including the remains of a Roman aqueduct near **Chelva** ❺. **Alpuente**, somewhat out of the way, has a tiny town hall crammed into a tower above a 14th-century gateway. **Requena**, to the south of the Turia, is Valencia's principal wine town. Sensation-seekers make a pilgrimage to **Buñol** in late August for the extraordinary phenomenon of La Tomatina, a free-for-all tomato-throwing fiesta.

Continuing down the coast you come to **Sagunt** (Sagunto) ❻, the Roman town of Saguntum, which was sacked by the Carthaginian general Hannibal in 219 BC, leading to the Second Punic War and the Roman subjugation of Spain. The **theatre** that the

Romans built into the hillside above the town in the 1st century AD has been restored for performances of plays and music. The **castle** above it (open Tues–Sat; entrance fee) incorporates remains from all the races to have passed this way, from the Iberians to the Moors.

The coast of Valencia province has few resorts or sights, but there are two places south of the capital city worthy of a detour. The first is **L'Albufera** ❼, a freshwater lake separated from the sea by a sandbar. You can learn about the Albufera's birdlife in the visitor's centre at Racó de l'Olla or take a boat trip from the village of El Palmar. El Palmar is also a good place to eat paella: it stands on the edge of a maze of paddy fields.

The other place worth a stop is **Gandia** ❽. In the centre of town stands the **Palacio Ducal** (Duke's Palace, open Mon–Sat; guided tour obligatory; entrance fee), the home of St Francis Borja (1510–72) in which sumptuous chambers surround a Gothic patio. The palace is now owned by Jesuits.

The most historic town of inland Valencia is **Xàtiva** (Jativa) ❾ with a superb **castle** (open Tues–Sun; free) running along the ridge above it. This was the first European city to manufacture paper – under the Moors in the 12th century – but its prosperity came to an abrupt end during the War of the Spanish Succession when it was all but burned to the ground by Felipe V. As a reminder of this episode, Felipe's portrait hangs upside down in the **Museo Municipal** (open Tues–Sun; free).

Alicante province

Getting around inland in this mountainous region can be slow going and the main roads stay close to the coast. A short way beyond Gandia you enter the province of Alicante, whose shoreline has become famous as the **Costa Blanca**. Although some parts of it are dominated by high-rise hotels and seas of whitewashed villas built for expatriate residents, it is an attractive stretch

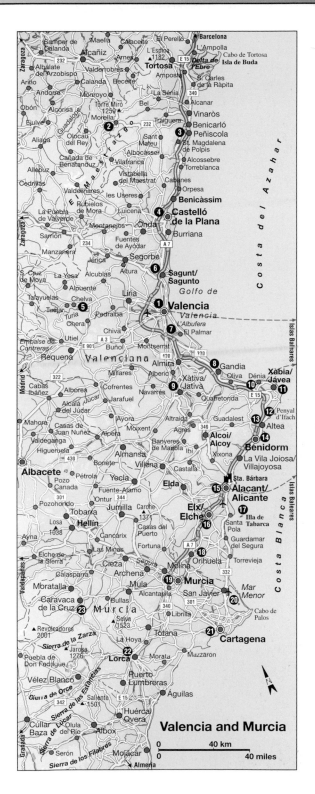

Valencia and Murcia

0   40 km
0   40 miles

of coast with enough sandy beaches, hidden coves, cliffs and headlands to keep anyone happy for a couple of weeks' holiday. The first two resorts you come to along this stretch of coast, **Dénia** ❿ and **Xábia** (Jàvea) ⓫, could not be more dissimilar, although both are worth seeing. They are separated by the distinctive hump of Mount Montgó. Dénia was originally a Greek settlement. Its main monument is the largely Arab **castle** (open daily; entrance fee) which looks down on the fishing port. Xàbia, built around an unusual, fortified church and with many of its buildings made from local Tosca sandstone, is the more attractive of the two.

The northern Costa Blanca is dominated by a huge, natural feature, the **Penyal d'Ifach** (Peñón de Ifach) ⓬, a limestone crag which juts into the sea and towers above the resort of **Calp** (Calpe). It can be climbed from the visitors' centre at its base for tremendous views.

The rise of Benidorm

A rocky gorge separates Calp from the next resort, **Altea** ⓭, whose old town is a picturesque jumble of white houses, narrow streets and steps. The Costa Blanca's most famous resort now looms on the horizon. With its innumerable tower-block hotels, **Benidorm** ⓮ looks like a mini-Manhattan set down beside two bays of golden sand. If you can penetrate past the cut-price hotels and restaurants, and the bronzing flesh, it has quite a pleasant old town centre. From the Balcón del Mediterráneo you get a good view of the whole resort.

If you want more authentic local flavour than Benidorm can offer, **La Vila Joiosa** (Villajoyosa), to the south, is a better choice. From Benidorm it is a short excursion into the nearby hills to **Guadalest**, the Costa Blanca's most

As recently as the 1950s, Benidorm was an obscure fishing village. For much of the year it is now overrun with sun-seeking tourists, and its summer club scene is quickly gaining notoriety.

BELOW: bulls at the seaside in Dénia.

scenic spot. You have to go through a pedestrian tunnel to enter the old village, at the top of which are the remains of a castle. On an adjacent rock sits the church's quaint belfry. Despite the coach loads of tourists that regularly leave Benidorm for Guadalest, it remains attractive and relatively unspoiled.

Map
on page
243

Southern Costa Blanca and the interior

Continuing south along the coast brings you to the resort town of **Alacant** (Alicante) **⑮**, a busy port and the capital of the province, which is also overlooked by a castle, the **Castillo de Santa Bárbara** (open daily; entrance fee). To avoid the long walk to the top you can take a lift from sea level. Other sights worth seeing in Alicante are the Baroque **city hall** and the **Casa de la Asegurada** (open Tues–Sun; free), which houses a collection of modern art including works by Dalí, Miró and Picasso.

Approximately 50 km (32 miles) inland from Alicante on the N-340 the landscape changes dramatically. The industrial city of **Alcoi** (Alcoy) is worth visiting in April for its famous Moors and Christians fiesta, but it is also the centre of a beautiful mountain area. Above the city itself is the wooded nature reserve of Font Roja. Not far away is the Sierra de Mariola, which is best approached through the village of **Agres**.

The lobster catch on the Illa de Tabarca.

Returning towards the coast, **Elx** (Elche) **⑯** is renowned for its palm groves, many of which have been enclosed in a garden, the **Huerto del Cura** (open daily; entrance fee). Apart from palm trees, Elx is best known for the Dama de Elche, an enigmatic Iberian sculpture (although the original is in Madrid there are several replicas in Elx) and the Misteri d'Elx, a singular piece of liturgical theatre performed in August in the 17th-century **Basílica de Santa María.**

South of Alicante, the Costa Blanca continues but is less spectacular than before. The **Illa de Tabarca ⑰** makes a pleasant day-trip from either Alicante or the fishing port of **Santa Pola** (tel: 96-669 22 76 for ferry information). Santa Pola is also distinguished by its salt pans, which attract flamingos and are particularly worth stopping to see at sunset. There are more salt pans as you near **Torrevieja**, at the southern end of the Costa Blanca, which grew exponentially during the 1980s as estates of cheap villas were sold to northern Europeans looking for their own piece of the sun.

Orihuela ⑱, inland on the N-340 and to the south of Elx, is a smaller town which prospered in the 15th century. It has some handsome churches, especially the Gothic **catedral** (open daily; free) with an elegant two-storey patio attached to it.

BELOW: the Moors and Christians fiesta at Alcoi.

Murcia: the old frontier

Covering just 11,317 sq. km (4,369 sq. miles), Murcia is one of Spain's smallest *comunidades*. Compared with its larger neighbours, Andalusia and the Comunidad Valenciana, Murcia is little known but it has its superlatives too.

Murcia ⑲, the capital, stands inland in a fertile agricultural region. At the heart of the city is the **catedral** (open daily; free), built in stages on the foundations of a former mosque between the 14th and 18th centuries. Notable features of the cathedral include its great baroque façade and two exquisite side chapels. The cathedral museum is also worth a visit for its Gothic altarpieces and Roman frieze.

A more recent building is Murcia's **Casino** (open daily, by permission; tip appreciated), a private club not a gambling den. This late 19th-century caprice is full of details, particularly the mudéjar-style entrance patio and the paintings on the ceiling of the ladies' cloakroom.

Murcia's taste for extravagance can also be seen during Easter Week when a series of baroque *pasos* (floats) are taken in procession. They are the work of the sculptor Francisco Salzillo and can be admired during the rest of the year in the **Iglesia de Jesús** (open Tues-Sat; entrance fee; free on Sun). If you want something more down to earth, at **Alcantarilla**, just outside the city, is a giant water-wheel and folk museum (open Tues–Sun; free).

Quiet Costa Cálida

While the **Costa Cálida** (the "Warm Coast") is not as developed or populous as the Costa Blanca, it possesses one unique natural feature in the **Mar Menor ⓴**, a large, calm lagoon popular for swimming and other water sports where the water is usually several degrees warmer than the Mediterranean. On the sheltered landward shore are the old-fashioned resorts of Los Alcázares and Santiago de la Ribera, which still have quaint wooden boathouses on their beaches. These small towns look across the lagoon at a futuristic vision of La Manga de Mar Menor, a narrow line of high-rise hotels and apartment blocks marching along the sand strip which all but cuts off the Mar Menor (literally "the Smaller Sea") from the Mediterranean. On a low hill overlooking the Mar Menor is the exclusive sports and hotel complex of La Manga Club.

BELOW: Murcia's cathedral by night.

South of Cabo de Palos, where La Manga is attached to the mainland, the Costa Cálida passes through some fairly inhospitable scenery before reaching the resort of **Águilas**, at the border with Andalucía.

Map on page 243

Cartagena and inland Murcia

On the way down the coast you pass through **Cartagena ㉑**, the region's seaport, which in ancient times was the principal Carthaginian city in Spain. A sign of its ancient history is the excavated stretch of the **Muralla Bizantina** (Byzantine Wall, open Tues–Sat; free) which was built in the 6th century. The **Museo Nacional de Arqueología Submarino** (Underwater Archaeology Museum, open Tues–Sun; entrance fee), also explores Spain's early history, with exhibits on maritime trade dating from Phoenician times.

The old frontier between Murcia and Andalusia is guarded by the town of **Lorca ㉒**, overlooked by a ruined castle. The **Colegiata de San Patricio** and the town hall, in the handsome Plaza de España, were erected at the height of Lorca's prosperity in the 17th and 18th centuries. Lorca's immensely popular Good Friday procession is typical of Valencia and Murcia fiestas in its love of finery and show; indeed, it typifies the Levant itself.

Further inland, there are only scattered sights to see. The northeast corner of Murcia is a wine region centring on the town of **Jumilla**, while **Caravaca de la Cruz ㉓** is well-known in Spain for the double-armed cross named after it. This is said to have appeared miraculously in 1231 in what is now the **Santuario de la Vera Cruz** (Sanctuary of the True Cross), a Renaissance and baroque church superimposed on a Templar castle. Other places worthy of a lazy detour are the pretty village of **Moratalla** and the spa of **Archena**. ❑

On the evening of Good Friday, the town of Lorca stages one of the most extraordinary processions in Spain, involving thousands of people dressed as Biblical characters.

BELOW: windmills in the sunset, Murcia.

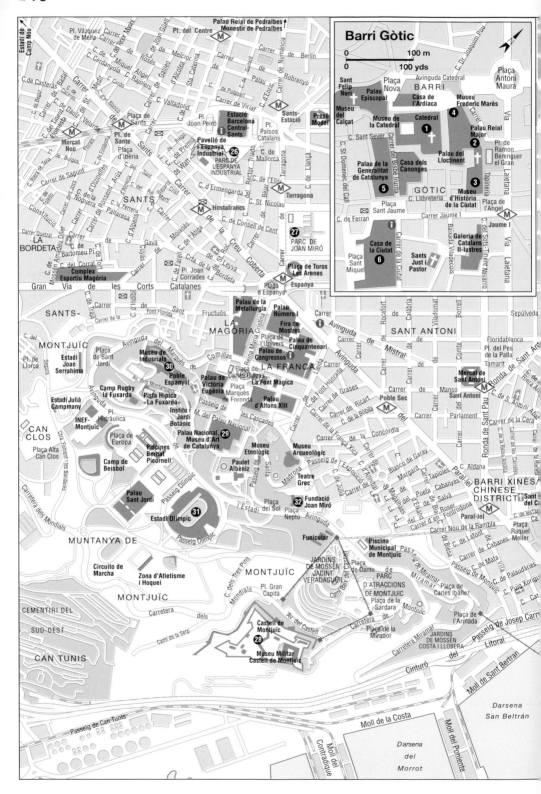

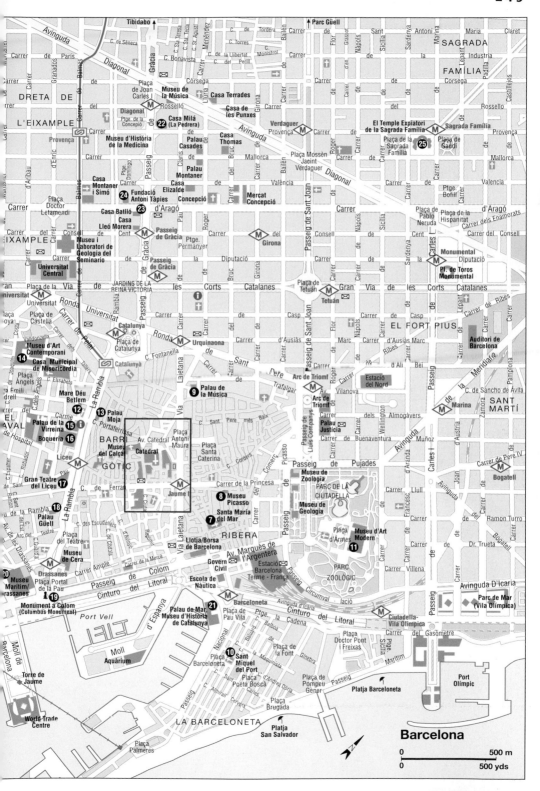

Tibidabo

Parc Güell

SAGRADA

FAMÍLIA

DRETA DE

L'EIXAMPLE

Plaça de Joan Carles I

Museu de la Música

Casa Terrades

Casa de les Punxes

Verdaguer

El Temple Expiatori de la Sagrada Família

Sagrada Família

Diagonal

Casa Milá (La Pedrera)

22

Museu d'Història de la Medicina

Palau Casades

Casa Thomas

Provença

Plaça de la Sagrada Família

Plaça de Gaudí

25

Provença

Palau Montaner

Casa Montaner i Simó

Casa Elizalde

València

Fundació Antoni Tàpies

24

Concepció

Mercat Concepció

d'Aragó

Plaça de Pablo Neruda

Plaça de la Hispanitat

d'Aragó

Casa Batlló

23

Casa Lleó Morera

Passeig de Gràcia

Monumental

IXAMPLE

Museu i Laboratori de Geologia del Seminari

Passeig de Gràcia

Girona

Pl. de Toros Monumental

Universitat Central

Gran Via de les Corts Catalanes

Gran Via de les Corts Catalanes

EL FORT PIUS

Universitat

Tetuán

Auditori de Barcelona

Ronda

Catalunya

SANT MARTÍ

Museu d'Art Contemporani

14

Catalunya

Estació del Nord

Marina

Casa Municipal de Misericòrdia

Arc de Triomf

Mare Déu Betlem

12

Palau Moja

13

Palau de la Música

9

Arc de Triomf

Bogatell

EL VAL

Palau de la Virreina

15

Boqueria

16

BARRI

Museu del Calçat

Catedral

Palau Justícia

Liceu

GÒTIC

Museu de Zoologia

Gran Teatre del Liceu

17

Jaume I

PARC DE LA CIUTADELLA

Museu Picasso

8

Museu de Geologia

Palau Güell

18

Museu de Cera

Santa María del Mar

7

Plaça d'Armes

Museu d'Art Modern

11

Drassanes

RIBERA

Llotja/Borsa de Barcelona

Museu Marítim/rassanes

0

Monument a Colom (Columbus Monument)

19

Govern Civil

Escola de Nàutica

PARC ZOOLÒGIC

Port Vell

Palau de Mar Museu d'Història de Catalunya

21

Barceloneta

Avinguda D'Icaria

Parc de Mar (Vila Olímpica)

Aquàrium

Sant Miquel del Port

10

Ciutadella-Vila Olímpica

Torre de Jaume

Platja Barceloneta

Port Olímpic

World Trade Centre

LA BARCELONETA

Platja San Salvador

Barcelona

0   500 m

0   500 yds

BARCELONA

*As well as being the largest city on the Mediterranean,
it's one of Europe's most brilliant centres, at the
forefront of modern architecture, fashion and design*

Map
on page
248–9

The capital of Catalonia and a key Mediterranean port, Barcelona is a bilingual city, its citizens speaking both Castilian Spanish and Catalan. With one foot in France and the other in traditional Spain, in many respects, the city seems almost as close to Paris and Rome as it is to Madrid, and has long been Iberia's link to the rest of Western Europe.

The city most characterised by the *modernista* architect Antoni Gaudí has also produced other world-figures in the arts – Pablo Picasso, Joan Miró, Pablo Casals, Josep Carreras and Montserrat Caballé, for instance. For the 1992 Olympic Games, it was given an enormous facelift. Many fine medieval buildings were renovated, modern, new structures put up, a ring road created, and the port and waterfront districts comprehensively overhauled and renovated.

Catalonia's relationship with Spain

Understanding Barcelona requires some insight into the Catalan-Spanish duality. Although about half of Greater Barcelona's 3 million inhabitants have emigrated from other parts of Spain, Barcelona is historically and culturally a Catalan city, the capital of Catalonia and the seat of the Generalitat, the Catalan autonomous government.

Catalonia was an independent nation with a parliament – the Council of 100 – well before the formation of the Spanish State. Catalonia became a commercial power in the Mediterranean during the 14th and 15th centuries, developing a merchant class, banking and a social structure significantly different from the feudal model which continued in most of Spain. Later, while the rest of Spain colonised, mining New World wealth, Catalonia industrialised, becoming the world's fourth manufacturing power by 1850.

Catalan, a Romance language derived from the speech of the occupying Romans, is closely related to the Provençal and Langue d'Oc French spoken in southern France. The strength of Catalan culture has fluctuated with the region's political fortunes. After uniting with the kingdom of Aragón in the 12th century, Catalonia found itself part of a new nation – Spain – when Fernando II of Aragón married Isabel I of Castile in 1469. Centuries-old privileges and institutions were suppressed by Castilian centralism over the next 300 years, most notably in 1714 when the newly installed Spanish King Felipe V, grandson of Louis XIV of France, militarily seized Barcelona and abolished all local autonomous privileges.

During the 19th century Catalonia's industrial success fostered new independence movements and a *renaixença* (renaissance) of Catalan nationalism. But in 1939 its last experiment in autonomy was crushed

LEFT: *castellers* perform in Sant Jaume square during the Fiestas de la Merced.
BELOW: a carved door at Gaudí's Casa Batlló.

Picasso fresco on Barcelona's Chamber of Architects.

by Franco's victory in the Spanish Civil War. Since Franco's death in 1975, Catalonia has undergone a spectacular cultural resurgence. Catalan, a forbidden language for 36 years, is once again taught in schools, published in books and newspapers and accepted as the co-official language. There is, as well, Catalan radio, television and cinema. The Barcelona Olympics was a high point of this new cultural golden age, with Catalan accepted as an official language. Since 1992, Catalonia and its language have continued to flourish.

Bordered by the sea on one side and by the Collserola hills to the west, Barcelona is intersected by great avenues such as the **Diagonal** and the **Passeig de Gràcia**, and punctuated by open spaces of parkland which provide welcome relief from the city's human and architectural density. The two promontories of Montjuïc (by the port) and Tibidabo (behind and inland) tower over the city's chaotic sprawl.

In the second half of the 19th century Barcelona broke out of the old Gothic city into the **Eixample**, the orderly grid of wide avenues planned by Idelfons Cerdà, which occupies the middle ground between the old city and its backdrop of hills. This grid system was extended down to the sea front on the northeast side of town when the old industrial area of **Poble Nou** was pulled down to build the 2,000 apartments of the Olympic Village and the new leisure port.

A tour of the Gothic Quarter

BELOW: on the steps of the Palau Reial Major.

Barcelona's old city, known as the **Barri Gòtic** or Gothic Quarter, is a stunning display of solid stone, sprinkled with small shops, cafés, taverns and gourmet restaurants. Although most of the major architecture was completed between the 13th and the 15th centuries, there are still traces of Roman civilisation.

Barcelona's acropolis – the highest elevation in the Barri Gòtic – was originally the Iberian village of Laia. The Romans conquered the town in 133 BC, erected the Temple of Augustus and fortified their *Mons Taber* with defensive walls in the 4th century.

The itinerary which best clarifies the city's archaeology and history begins facing the **Catedral ❶** (open Mon–Fri and Sat am; museum open 10am–1pm daily; entrance fee) at Plaça Nova, crosses to the left in front of the cathedral steps and continues round to the right down Carrer Tapineria to the Plaça de Ramon Berenguer el Gran, which was the eastern limit of the Roman walls. After another section of Carrer Tapineria, cross through Plaça de l'Angel and along the **Carrer Murallas Romanes** where original sections of the Roman walls can be seen. After cutting in behind the wall to Plaça Sant Just and doubling back up to Carrer Llibreteria, the Carrer Veguer leads up to the Plaça del Rei, and the royal buildings of the Catalonia's sovereign count-kings.

The **Palau Reial Major ❷** (open Tues–Sun; entrance fee) and the Capella de Santa Agata are located beneath the tower of St Martí, which is entered through the chapel and gives a good view down over the old city. Santa Agata is an extraordinarily pure example of Catalan Gothic construction and was the chapel of the Royal Palace, the residence of the Counts of Barcelona, who became kings of Aragón in 1137. The **Museu d'Història de la Ciutat ❸** (open Tue–Sat and Sun am; entrance fee) is a part of this complex, built over Roman foundations still visible in its basement. The impressive Saló del Tinell, the early Gothic Great Hall of the Royal Palace, and the adjacent Palau del Lloctinent complete the buildings around this regal square, widely considered the Barri Gòtic's loveliest.

Nearby, on Plaça de Sant Lu is the **Museu Frederic Marès ❹** (open Tues–Sat and Sun am; entrance fee). The collection comes from a donation made by the sculptor in 1940, with pieces from the Middle Ages to the 19th century.

The cathedral

Begun in 1298 in a transitional style, Barcelona's cathedral, known as La Seu (the "seat" of the Bishopric), was completed over the next two centuries, with the exception of the main façade which was not finished until towards the late 19th century. The two octagonal bell towers are, perhaps, the cathedral's most monumental features, while the interior cloister with its magnolias, palms, orange trees and geese is one of the city's most beautiful spots.

The Canonja, Degà and Ardiaca houses which ring the square outside the cathedral, as well as the Capella de Santa Llucia at the corner of Carrer del Bisbé, are also important architectural gems and should not be missed before moving up the Carrer del Bisbé towards the Plaça Sant Jaume. There are often guitarists or flautists along the way – usually music students – playing medieval compositions echoed and amplified by the acoustics of stone.

Catalonia's seat of government

Down Carrer del Bisbé and to the right emerging into Plaça Sant Jaume is the **Palau de la Generalitat de Catalunya ❺** (open by appointment only; write in

Map on page 248–9

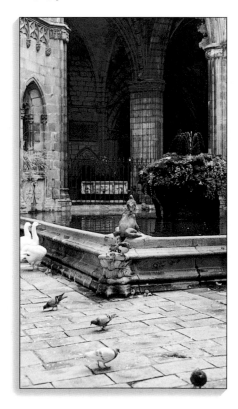

BELOW: a tranquil courtyard in old Barcelona.

advance for permission), the seat of the autonomous Catalan government since the 14th century. Any lingering doubts about Catalonia's view of herself as a nation are quickly laid to rest with a tour of the stunningly ornate Generalitat building. Constructed from the 15th to the 17th century, the main points of interest are the Gothic patio with its exterior staircase, the Sant Jordi chapel, the Patí dels Tarongers (Patio of the Orange Trees) and the Saló Daurat (Gilded Room), with its lovely murals of Catalonia's mountains, valleys, plains and beaches.

The Plaça Sant Jaume itself, originally part of the Roman forum, is a striking work of art. The neoclassical façade directly across the Plaça Sant Jaume from the Generalitat is the **Casa de la Ciutat** ❻ (open by appointment only; write in advance for permission) or town hall. Inside the building, a black marble staircase leads to the main floor, the Saló de Cent (Hall of the Hundred), which was the meeting place for one of Europe's first Republican parliaments.

The mariner's church

The **Barri de Santa Maria** is the area around the superb basilica of **Santa Maria del Mar** ❼ (open daily; free), a supreme example of Mediterranean Gothic architecture. Begun in 1329, Santa Maria del Mar was the centre of Barcelona's new seafaring and merchant community and the crowning glory of Catalonia's hegemony in the Mediterranean. "Santa Maria!" was one of the war cries of the Catalan sailors and soldiers as they stormed into Sicily, Sardinia and Greece. The church is one of the simplest and most elegant structures in the city. The three naves are vast and of similar height, reducing interior support to the bare minimum. The church's massively tall stone columns, rose window, two bell towers and virtually all of the side chapels and stained-glass windows are

The El Born area on the eastern side of Santa Maria del Mar was the site of jousts and tournaments from the 13th to the 17th century, and became the central marketplace for maritime Barcelona. The area is now popular with artists.

BELOW: religious icons, a speciality of Barcelona.

striking, with graceful, pure lines. The acoustics are also worthy of note – they produce a six-second delay which is capable of converting a dulcet medieval melody into a polyphony of powerful echoes and overtones.

An immediate left turn leaving the east end of Santa Maria del Mar leads to Carrer Montcada, one of Barcelona's most aristocratic streets in the 14th century and one of the most beautiful today. Nearly all of the 14th-century palaces on this street are in perfect shape. One of these, the Palau d'Aguilar, houses the **Museu Picasso** ❽ (open Tues–Sun; entrance fee). The building is, in fact, almost as interesting as its contents. The museum provides an insight into the early evolution of the artist's talent. From caricatures of his teachers in school texts to studies of anatomy as an art student and including his first great paintings in the styles of the Masters – Goya, Velázquez, El Greco – Picasso's extraordinary vitality comes through.

Carrer Corders leads up to the **Plaça de la Llana**, another typical medieval space. From there, continue along the narrow alleys to the stupendous **Palau de la Música** ❾ (tel: 93-268 10 10; open for concerts or guided tours by appt). Erected in 1908 by the *modernista* architect Domènech i Montaner, this explosion of form and colour is the city's prime concert hall and the flagship of Barcelona's rich endowment of Art Nouveau architecture.

Barcelona's beaches and Olympic port

The best finale to a morning of wandering through the Gothic Quarter is to head for the beach in colourful **Barceloneta**. The narrow alleys here have the feel of a southern European fishing town, with brightly painted balconies and houses, laundry hanging over the pavement, and delicious aromas of fresh

Map
on page
248–9

The artist's signature at the Museu Picasso entrance.

LEFT: the Olympic Village seafront.
BELOW: diners at the Olympic port.

Snowflake, the star of Barcelona's zoo.

seafood from its specialist restaurants. From the church of **Sant Miquel del Port** ❿, (open daily; free) which stands in a lovely square just off Passeig Joan de Borbó, it's a 15- or 20-minute meander out to the beach and the start of the new 4-km (2-mile) waterfront, encompassing seven beaches, which is a lasting legacy of the Olympic Games. The new marina, Port Olímpic, is lined with restaurants, music bars and cafés which fill with people every night, especially in summer. The Olympic Village complex nearby comprises 2,000 flats, which are now privately owned. On the port side of Barceloneta, near the beach, is the tower station for the cable car that crosses to the hill of Montjuïc, providing a spectacular panorama of the city.

Ciutadella Park

Felipe V built a citadel here in reply to Barcelona's long and bitter resistance in the siege of 1714. Some 1,162 houses were torn down in the waterfront district known as the Barri de la Ribera to make way for the fortress which became a focal point of subsequent anti-centralist resentment. It was finally razed in 1888. The **Parc de la Ciutadella** is now the site of the **Parc Zoològic** (its star is an albino gorilla), the Museu de Zoologia and Museu de Geologia, a botanical garden, a children's library and the **Museu d'Art Modern** ⓫ (open Tues–Sat and Sun am; entrance fee). This excellent collection includes works by the Catalan painters Casas, Miró, Nonell and Sert.

La Rambla and the port

Barcelona's famous **Rambla**, its lively, mile-long pedestrian thoroughfare, has something for everyone. Originally a seasonal riverbed, the Rambla runs from

BELOW LEFT:
the restored Gran Teatre del Liceu.
BELOW RIGHT:
strolling on the Rambla.

Plaça Catalunya down to the Christopher Columbus monument at the port, and now extends across a wooden walkway to the shopping and leisure complex (including the Aquarium and IMAX theatre), somewhat ironically called the Port Vell (Old Port).

Map on page 248–9

Across the street from the top of the Rambla, where the city's Metro surfaces, is the Café Zurich, a handy place to have coffee in the sun, read the paper and meet friends. The section of Rambla at **Font de les Canaletes**, around a cast-iron drinking fountain, is a traditional gathering point for soccer enthusiasts passionately debating the fortunes of Barcelona's *fútbol* club. The next section of the Rambla, the **Rambla dels Estudis**, has the renovated **Mare Déu Betlem** ⓬ church on the right and, on the left, the **Palau Moja** ⓭, an 18th-century palace now used by the Generalitat as a bookshop. Turning off the Rambla at Carrer Elisabets, you'll come to the impressive white slab of the new **Museu d'Art Contemporani** ⓮ (open daily; entrance fee), which has large abstract work, sculpture and installations.

The **Rambla de las Flors** or **Rambla de Sant Josep** is the next section of the main promenade, lined with flower stalls and overlooked by the **Palau de la Virreina** ⓯ and the spectacular **Boqueria** ⓰ market. The 18th-century Virreina Palace, named after the widow of the Viceroy of Peru, is a brilliant Louis XIV-style structure, richly endowed with sculptured ornamentation. It now houses the city's information centre. The Boqueria is Barcelona's largest open market, covered by a high-roofed, steel-girdered hangar. The arrangements of fruits and vegetables under bright lighting, the fresh salt and iodine fragrance of the seafood and the busy din of the marketplace, with its marble-countered bars, make the Boqueria market one of the city's most exhilarating and refreshing places to visit. Ramon Casas, Catalonia's first Impressionist painter, is said to have discovered his best model and, subsequently, his wife among the beautiful flower-sellers of the Rambla.

The **Rambla del Centre** or **Rambla dels Caputxins** begins at the small square – which has a pavement mosaic by Joan Miró – in front of Barcelona's famous opera house, the **Gran Teatre del Liceu** ⓱ (1862), destroyed by fire in 1992 but reopened in 1999. The Café de l'Opera across the way from the Liceu is a well-frequented meeting spot. Just off the Rambla on Carrer Nou No. 3, is the **Palau Güell** ⓲ (open Mon–Sat; entrance fee), designed in 1890 by Antoni Gaudí. This palace, with its mighty balcony, is one of the finest works which Gaudí constructed for his patron, Count Güell. Gaudí was also responsible for the interior decoration; the wooden and metal decorations are particularly impressive.

Back on the Rambla, at No. 45, is the Hotel Oriente, one of the few surviving former convents that once lined this side of the Rambla. It was originally the Franciscan Sant Bonaventura convent. The **Rambla de Santa Mònica** is the next and final part of the Rambla, extending from the entrance to Plaça Reial down to the port. The Plaça Reial, with its palm trees and uniformly porticoed 19th-century façades, is one of Barcelona's most appealing spots. The beer halls and cafés surrounding the square, tucked in under the

BELOW: the Boqueria market.

columns, are cosy places for beer, *patatas bravas* (potatoes with hot sauce) and *calamares* (squid). The bottom of the Rambla is flagged by one of the city's most famous landmarks, the **Monument a Colom ⑲** (Columbus Monument), designed by Gaietà Buïgas for the Universal Exhibition of 1888. A lift takes visitors up to the top of the 60-metre (200-ft) column. This was the former landing point for the city; today small tour boats, *goldrinas* (swallows), explore the port.

On the right (south) side at the end of the Rambla is the **Museu Marítim/ Drassanes ⑳** (open Tues–Sun; entrance fee), in the vast Gothic shipyards that once turned out 30 war galleys at a time. The exhibits include small models, life-size replicas, sea maps, documents, galleon figures and nautical instruments. The focal point is the replica of the *Galera Real*, the flagship of the Christian fleet which, under Don John of Austria, defeated the Turks at the Battle of Lepanto in October 1571. To the north is the refurbished harbour promenade, Moll de Fusta, with a jokey lobster on top of the Gambrinus restaurant overlooking the yacht clubs.

The Rambla continues over a walkway, so you can stroll all around the **Port Vell**, admiring the yacht club's vessels. Among the attractions in this leisure complex is the imaginative aquarium with sea life from local waters and beyond. On the quayside on the adjacent quay is the Palau de Mar, with a battery of restaurants downstairs and the **Museu d'Història de Catalunya ㉑** (open Tues–Sat; Sun and hols am only; entrance fee) above. Opened in 1996, this state-of-the-art museum takes you from Catalan prehistory to 1980, with lots of hands-on exhibits that will appeal especially to children. Information panels are mostly in Catalan but this shouldn't put you off trying your hand at a medieval joust or experiencing the terror of a civil war air-raid.

BELOW: the new walkway at the modernised Port Vell.

Map on page 248–9

Gaudí's Barcelona

Few architects have marked a city as Gaudí has Barcelona. Born in nearby Reus in 1852, Antoni Gaudí i Cornet created revolutionary forms which coincided with the Art Nouveau or *modernisme* artistic movements. For more information on the *modernisme* movement, *see pages 264–265*). The young Gaudí's work can be found in Pere Fontserè's Cascada in the Ciutadella Park where, as a student and Fontserè's assistant, he designed the rocks of the cascade. The Plaça Reial lamp posts are also early Gaudí products.

His 1889 **Casa Vicens**, in the **Gràcia** neighbourhood (24–26 Carrer de les Carolines), was his first major project and the debut of totally polychromatic architecture. Gaudí's most important works in Barcelona are Güell Park, Casa Batlló, Casa Milá (also known as La Pedrera) and, of course, his extraordinary temple of the Sagrada Família.

Parc Güell was commissioned by the Barcelona financier Eusebi Güell as an urban project: a combination of gardens and living spaces in the upper part of the city, above Gràcia. Between 1900 and 1914 Gaudí designed a covered market, a large central square, a series of paths across the side of the mountain and the plots for the construction of houses, of which only two were finally built. The wall surrounding the park, decorated with a ceramic mosaic, is the first notable feature of Güell Park, followed by the two houses near the entrance with their bizarre shapes, multicoloured roofing and wild, mushroom-like towers.

The market is known as the Sala de les Cent Columnes (Hall of the Hundred Columns). There are actually 86 Doric columns supporting an undulating ceiling decorated with mosaics. The dream-like, leaning arcade upstairs to the left leads around to the park's entrance. The central square, surrounded by ingeniously decorated benches, uses a wide range of found objects, tiles and rubble, all spontaneously mixed and built into the ceramic finish. A serpentine pathway winds up the mountainside above Gaudí's dream-like walls, across fantastic bridges, eventually leaving the park at La Farigola.

Casa Milá (La Pedrera) ㉒ (open daily for guided tours; entrance fee) and **Casa Batlló ㉓** (tel: 93-204 52 50; visits by appt only) are apartment houses on the **Passeig de Gràcia** in the Eixample. Casa Batlló (at No. 43) forms part of the famous "mançana de la discordia" (city block of discord), so-named for the contrasting architectural styles of the three neighbouring buildings designed by the city's greatest 19th-century architects. Apart from Gaudí's Casa Batlló, there is Puig i Cadafalch's 1900 Casa Ametller at No. 41 and Domènech i Montaner's 1905 Casa Lleó Morera at No. 35. Casa Milá, at No. 92, is a more natural fantasy by Gaudí – repetitions of sandcastle waves, shadows, elaborate wrought-iron balustrades. Even the mouldings, the door knobs and the window casings of the apartments were designed or inspired by Gaudí. Close by, at Carrer de Provença 261, is **Espai Gaudí** (open daily; entrance fee), a spectacular Gaudí-designed attic and rooftop which reveals yet more of the great master's designs and techniques.

Round the corner at Carrer d'Aragó 255 is another astonishing building, this time designed by Domènech

BELOW: chimneys of Gaudí's La Pedrera.

i Montaner between 1881 and 1886. Since 1990 it has housed the **Fundació Antoni Tàpies** ㉔ (open Tues–Sun; entrance fee), set up by the artist himself to promote modern art and culture. Some of Tàpies' own abstract works, which are noted for their use of innovative new materials such as sand, rubbed marble and varnish as well as iron and concrete, are displayed here, along with work by other modern artists. There is a small shop at the entrance, selling books on Tàpies and his work.

El Temple Expiatori de la Sagrada Família ㉕ (The Expiatory Temple of the Holy Family; open 9am–6pm daily; entrance fee), on the north side of the Avinguda Diagonal, was begun in 1882 as a neo-Gothic structure under the direction of Francesc P. Villar. In 1891 Antoni Gaudí took over, completed the crypt and designed an enormous project which would reach a height of over 150 metres (500 ft).

Gaudí worked on the Sagrada Família until his death in 1926. Conceived as a symbolic construction, the cathedral features three gigantic façades: the Nativity Facade to the east, the western side representing Christ's Passion and Death and the southern façade – the largest – portraying His Glory. The four spires of each façade symbolise the 12 apostles; the tower over the apse represents the Virgin Mary; the central spire (as yet unbuilt), dedicated to Christ the Saviour, is surrounded by four lesser towers representing the Evangelists: Matthew, Mark, Luke and John. The decorative sculpture and ornamentation covering the different elements of the structure are of extraordinary quality and density. Work is still in progress here, but much of the site can be visited.

BELOW: west façade of the Sagrada Família.

Notable in Gaudí's buildings is the extent to which the architect attempted to integrate the shapes and textures of nature. The influence of the peaks and

heights of Montserrat (*see page 275*), Catalonia's religious retreat near Barcelona, is certainly evident in the Sagrada Família.

A deeply religious man and a mystic, Gaudí, when struck by a trolley car at the age of 74, was so unassuming in physical appearance that he was unidentified for some time and died in paupers' accommodation at the Hospital de la Santa Creu, the early medieval hospital behind the Boqueria market. His body is buried in the crypt of the unfinished temple which was virtually his life's work, and which continues to grow around his tomb even today.

Just beyond the Sagrada Família is Plaça de les Glòries Catalanes where the city's big flea market, Els Encants, takes place every Monday, Wednesday, Friday and Saturday morning. The Teatre Nacional de Catalunya, designed by the trendy Barcelona architect Ricardo Bofill (as is the nearby Plaça de les Arts) is to open as the Auditori de Barcelona in 1999.

Pedralbes

From Glòries the Diagonal traverses the city to the upper part of town not far from the smart residential area of Pedralbes. The **Palau Reial de Pedralbes**, which lies on the north side of the thoroughfare, was built by the city council for Alfonso XIII in 1925 and part of it houses a fine **Museu Ceràmica** (open daily; Sat & Sun am only; entrance fee). The main focus is on contemporary works, and ceramic creations by Miró, Picasso and others are displayed to good advantage in the stylish palace. A dragon wrought-iron gate by Gaudí on the road up to the right of the palace is a clue that this was all once part of the Güell farm estate. Continue past it to reach the beautifully preserved **Reial Monestir de Pedralbes** (open Tues–Sun, am only; entrance fee), where early masterpieces from the collection of Baron Thyssen-Bornemisza are the icing on the cake in this lovely triple-tiered cloister. The bell tower, cloister and Sant Miquel Chapel are perfect examples of Catalan Gothic architecture.

Above Pedralbes is **Sarrià**, a small town swallowed up by the city, which has managed to maintain its special flavour, some of its peace and quiet and a sense of community. Occasionally a hunter carrying a basket of wild mushrooms from the Collserola hills appears at the station heading downtown. Near the station is the Plaçeta de Sant Vicens, a picturesque spot which still has the air of a village square.

On the south side of the Diagonal, below Pedralbes Palace, is the famous FC Barcelona, where visitors can see the trophies and have a look at the field from the Presidential box. Designed in 1957 by Francesc Mitjans, **El Camp Nou** stadium (open Tues–Sun, entrance fee) has a capacity of 150,000 and is considered one of the most beautiful soccer stadiums in the world. Fútbol Club Barcelona, for 40 years the *only* means of expressing Catalan nationalism, is a monolithic organisation with top professional and amateur teams competing for every amateur national championship from ice hockey to baseball.

Between here and the hill of Montjuïc is **Sants**. The area around Sants was one of several that benefited from the Olympic Games. The station was redesigned with the **Parc de l'Espanya Industrial**  in front of

Map on page 248–9

Enjoy historic and contemporary ceramics at the Palau Reial de Pedralbes.

BELOW: cloister of the Reial Monestir de Pedralbes.

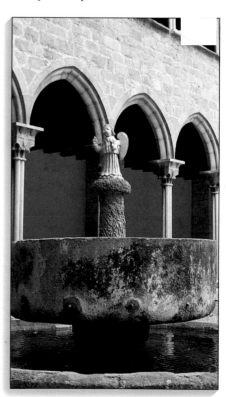

it, where boats may be hired on the small lake. Beyond it on the Carrer D'Aragó is **Parc de Joan Miró** ㉗ dominated by the artist's colourful 22-metre (70-ft) statue *Woman and Bird*.

Gràcia, the district above the Diagonal at the top of the Passeig de Gràcia, has a young, radical and traditionally working-class tradition and ambience. Mercé Rodoreda's moving novel, *La Plaça del Diament* (translated as *The Time of the Doves* by David Rosenthal), gives an excellent account of life in Gràcia during the 1930s and 1940s. La Torre de Rellotge (the clock tower) at Plaça de Rius i Taulet is one of the centres of life in Gràcia, which has the most vibrant of the city's local fiestas every August.

The 1992 Olympic site

Barcelona's sea-front hill, **Montjuïc**, overlooks the port and was the main site of the 1992 Olympic Games. Attractions include the **Castell de Montjuic** ㉘, which guards the entrance to the harbour, an amusement park, the **Parc d'Atraccions de Montjuïc** (open summer: Tues–Sun; winter: weekends and public hols; closed Nov), track and field facilities, baseball and rugby fields, an amphitheatre and several museums.

Start at **Plaça d'Espanya** and walk up between the exhibition pavilions past a series of fountains, in particular La Font Màgica (Magic Fountain), which spurts water every evening in summer, towards the imposing Palau Nacional, which houses one of the finest collections of Romanesque art in the **Museu d'Art de Catalunya** ㉙ (open Tues–Sun; entrance fee). Most of the murals come from the Catalan Pyrenees and date from the 10th to 12th centuries. The museum's Gothic collection is also superb.

BELOW:
the ultra-modern
Estadí Olímpic.

To the right of the Magic Fountain is Mies van der Rohe's restored **Pavilion**, built originally for the International Exhibition of 1929 which was the reason why the Palau Nacional and most of Montjuïc's grand edifices came to be here. Most eclectic and most popular of these projects is the **Poble Espanyol** ㉚ (open 9am–midnight Tues–Sun; entrance fee), where a collection of buildings were erected to show the different styles of all the regions of Spain. Today it is flourishing as a tourist centre, where craftsmen work and sell their wares. It is a popular place for a day or evening out, with a good selection of bars and restaurants. A double decker bus runs free of charge every half hour from Plaça d'Espanya to the Poble Espanyol. One of the city's most famous nightclubs, Torres de Avila, is at the entrance gates, its interior the work of the city's two best-known designers, Alfredo Arribas and Javier Mariscal (who was responsible for creating the Olympic mascot, Cobi).

Behind the Palau Nacional are the principal Olympic sites: the brown sandstone **Estadi Olímpic** ㉛ enlarged from Pere Domènech i Roure's 1927 original, and beside it on the Plaça Europa, a wide and elegant terrace overlooking the delta of the Llobregat and the sea, are the modern lines of Irata Isozaki's **Palau Sant Jordi**, one of the largest sports halls in the world.

On the opposite, city side of the hill, on the way up to the amusement park and the hill-top castle, is the **Fundació Joan Miró** ㉜ (open Tues–Sat and Sun am; entrance fee), one of Europe's finest modern galleries built in 1988 by the artist's friend Josep Luís Sert. More than 150 paintings, sculptures and over 5,000 drawings are on display in the airy rooms, covering each of the artist's surrealist creative periods. Works from Miró's contemporaries can also be seen, and special exhibitions are devoted to up-and-coming artists.

"The Hunter" by Joan Miró.

BELOW: thrills and spills at the Parc d'Atraccions.

Hill-top spectacular

Barcelona's other hill, **Tibidabo**, the highest point of the Collserola hills behind the city, derives its name from the Devil's temptation of Christ as reported by Saint Matthew: *Haec omnia tibi dabo si cadens adoraberis me* (I will give you this if you adore me). Catalans say that the view from the 518-metre (1,700-ft) peak, towering over the city of Barcelona on one side and looking out over the interior of Catalonia to the north and west, was the most diabolical temptation imaginable. Part of the charm of a visit to Tibidabo is the process of getting there via train, tram and funicular. Barcelona's Tibidabo train line ends at the top of Carrer de Balmes. From this point the blue tramway still runs up to the funicular where there is an excellent restaurant, **La Venta**, with outside tables for warm weather.

The **Temple Expiatori de Sagrat Cor** (Church of the Sacred Heart) with its famous boys' choir, the Hotel Florida and the amusement park are all points of interest at the top of Tibidabo, but the panorama is the main reason for being up there. The tremendous views of the city and the Mediterranean on one side, the fields of Catalonia and the jagged peaks of Montserrat (*see page 275*) on the other and, to the north, the snowcaps of the Pyrenees are, a tempting display of the city's and Catalonia's riches. ❑

THE FANTASTIC VISION OF ANTONI GAUDÍ

Antoni Gaudí's amazing buildings in Barcelona established him as the most original European architect in the early years of the 20th century

Antoni Gaudí (1852–1926) was born at Reus, Catalonia, the son of a coppersmith, and spent almost all his career in Barcelona. He was a patriotic Catalan and is said to have insisted on using the Catalan language even when talking to the King of Spain. The other major forces that shaped his life were a devotion to his work and a devout Christian faith. In 1878 he graduated from the Escuela Superior de Arquitectura, Barcelona, and soon afterwards met Eusebio Güell (1847–1918), a wealthy industrialist and Catalan nationalist who became his main patron, commissioning the Parc Güell (*above*) and other works.

A BIZARRE STYLE

Gaudí's work was influenced by various sources, including Gothic and Moorish architecture, and it has features in common with the Art Nouveau style fashionable at the time. However, his buildings have a sense of bizarre fantasy that sets them apart from anything else in the history of architecture. Walls undulate as if they were alive, towers grow like giant anthills, columns slant out of the vertical, and surfaces are encrusted with unconventional decoration, including broken bottles.

Gaudí died after being hit by a trolley bus. He cared so little for material success that – in spite of his great reputation – he was mistaken for a tramp and taken to a paupers' ward in hospital.

▷ **RAISING THE ROOF**
The undulating roof of the Casa Batlló, with its overlapping scale-like tiles, has been compared to the writhing of a dragon.

◁ **VIBRANT DECORATION**
Richly coloured ceramic decoration in playful, abstract designs typifies Gaudí's work at Parc Güell.

△ PARC GUELL
The Parc Güell is part of a garden suburb that Gaudí worked on for his patron Eusebio Güell from about 1900 to 1914 but never completed.

▽ COLOURED FACADE
Gaudí used blue-green ceramic material on the facade of the Casa Batlló; the artist Salvador Dalí compared it to "the tranquil waters of a lake."

RESIDENTIAL BUILDINGS

In 1904–06 Gaudí remodelled a house for José Batlló y Casanovas, a Barcelona textiles manufacturer. The house had been built in the 1870s and was elegant but unremarkable. Gaudí completely transformed the exterior, adding an extra storey, topping it with a spectacular roof, and adorning the windows with flowing frames and balconies. Inside the house, the subtle interplay of forms continues (*above*). Immediately after the Batlló house, Gaudí designed an apartment block (1906–10) for Don Pedro Milá, Batlló's partner. The Casa Milá has been aptly nicknamed "*la pedrera*" (the quarry) because the curving facade looks like a strange cliff-face. The sense of movement and fantasy continues on the roof, where the chimneys and ventilation stacks are a riot of exuberant shapes – see the example below.

◁ SLOW EVOLUTION
Gaudí began work on his masterpiece, the church of the Sagrada Familia (Holy Family), in 1883, but the huge building is still unfinished.

▽ DRAGON GUARDIAN
The dragon gate linking two entrance lodges (1884–88) for Eusebio Güell's estate on the outskirts of Barcelona is one of Gaudí's finest pieces of ironwork.

CATALONIA

Covering the area from the Pyrenees in the north to the Mediterranean in the east and the Ebre valley in the southwest, this region offers diverse scenery and attractions

Map on page 268

atalonia appears to have everything: rocky coasts, sandy beaches, lush plains, steppe, foothills and high sierra, all within a couple of hours of the major European metropolis of Barcelona (*see pages 251–258*). There are historic cities and towns, tiny fishing villages, mountain hamlets, some 1,000 Romanesque chapels, Roman bridges, centuries-old stone farmhouses, vineyards, wheat fields, orchards, trout streams and wild boar – all in this one autonomous community. The presence of so much variety and density within such a small area, which has struggled to keep its own identity and language, is a continual surprise, even to longtime admirers of this corner of the earth.

Catalonia's 31,910 sq. km (12,320 sq. miles) comprise 6 percent of Spain's share of the Iberian peninsula, and are divided into four provinces, Barcelona, Girona, Lleida and Tarragona, and 38 *comarques*, or counties. But the most obvious components of Catalonia for the visitor are the Mediterranean, the Pyrenees and the interior.

The Costa Brava

The term *Costa Brava* (sheer, bold, rocky coast) was originally coined by the Catalan journalist Ferran Agulló in 1905 and initially only referred to part of the rough coastline north of Barcelona. It is now taken to include all of the seafront which is in Girona Province, from **Blanes** ❶, which has one of the Costa Brava's longest beaches, all the way up to the French border. Also at Blanes is the **Jardí Botànic Mar i Murtra** (open daily; entrance fee), in a spectacular setting on the cliffs above the town, with a fantastic collection of Mediterranean and tropical plants. All along the coast, a series of *cales* or inlets, with small, intimate beaches, restaurants and hotels punctuate rocky cliffs rising out of the blue-green Mediterranean. Passenger boats ply their way from one inlet to another, picking up and dropping off travellers.

The hermitage of Santa Cristina, and the two beaches just below, lie between Blanes and **Lloret de Mar** ❷. Santa Cristina is the closest Costa Brava inlet to the city of Barcelona – barely an hour by coast road – and, though exquisite, can also be crowded. Above the populous and busy Lloret de Mar are the beaches at Canyelles and the Morisca inlets. Further north are the extraordinarily wild and unspoiled *cales* of Bona, Pola, Giverola, Sanlionç and Vallpregona. Close by, **Tossa de Mar** ❸ has a pretty old town as well as a lovely beach. A little further north, **Canyet de Mar** ❹ is a delicious inlet typical of this piney, rocky coastline. The coast road from Lloret de Mar to **Sant Feliu de Guixols** ❺ or the local ferry boat are the best ways to see the breathtaking coastal scenery.

LEFT: the monastery at Montserrat.
BELOW: fishing boats along the Costa Brava.

Beautiful scenery can be enjoyed along the coast at Begur.

Further north are S'Agaro, the smart 1920s resort, and the small town of **Platja d'Aro**, which has a big disco scene. **Palamós ⑥** is the next main town along the coast; founded in 1277, the town had its heyday in the Middle Ages and is now a resort and an important cork-exporting harbour. Further north still are a series of lonely beaches and *cales* which rank among the simplest and purest stretches on the Costa Brava. S'Alguer is a tiny fishing inlet with boat houses on the sand and natural rock jetties, and Tamariu is a particularly cosy little *cala*. Aiguablava's Parador Nacional is just over the top from Tamariu, although many maps don't show this road. Aiguablava's sheer cliffs high over the water are among the Costa Brava's most spectacular sights.

There is a really good view out across the sea from **Begur ⑦**, which is situated 200 metres (650 ft) above the steep coastline. Distinctive features of Begur are its ruined 15th-century castle and also its medieval watchtowers, which served as a defence against pirates.

About 8 km (5 miles) south of Begur and a little inland, the Sunday markets at **Palafrugell ⑧** are always festive and refreshing. **La Bisbal ⑨**, the area's most important commercial centre, has held its Friday markets since 1322. Earthenware products of all kinds, as well as the School of Ceramics, are traditional specialities. Nearby, the busy market town of **Pals** has an attractive medieval centre which can only be entered on foot.

Cultural centre

The city of **Girona ⑩** (Gerona in Castilian), originally a Roman settlement, is strategically located at the intersection of four rivers. Completely surrounded by walls up until modern times, Girona was so regularly besieged that it became known as "the city of a thousand sieges". Its famous Jewish quarter is one of Catalonia's most interesting examples of early Mediterranean architecture. The former monastery of **Sant Pere de Galligants** lies to the north of the old town beside the Riu Galligants and now houses an archaeological museum (open Tues–Sat and Sun am; entrance fee), where the highlight is the collection of Jewish gravestones. Across the river, the **Banys Arab** were built in 1295 not by Arabs but by Christians.

Girona's **catedral** is famous for its Gothic nave, the widest in the world. Construction of this superb basilica began in 1312 and took over four centuries to complete; several architectural styles, including Renaissance and Romanesque, have left their mark on it. Opposite the main entrance is the **Museu Capitular** (open Tues–Sun; entrance fee), which has a fine collection of ecclesiastical treasures, including medieval tapestries and manuscripts.

Dalí's legacy

The northernmost section of the Costa Brava stretches from the town of **L'Escala** across the **Golf de Roses** and north to France. Heading back to the coast from Girona, stop at the **Castell de Púbol ⑪** (phone the Girona tourist office: 972-22 65 75 for opening times) a Gothic and Renaissance castle owned by Dalí and just off the C-255 between Flaçà and Parlavà. Inside,

Costa Brava

0 — 25 km
0 — 25 miles

Map on page 268

the rooms are furnished in Dali's outlandish surrealist style. Dalí lived here between 1982 and 1984, but a fire which broke out in the blue bedroom almost killed him and he subsequently abandoned the castle.

Heading back to the coast on the road to **L'Estartit**, you will pass through the lovely old town of **Torroella de Montgrí ⑫**, dominated by the 300-metre (985-ft) rocky outcrop of Santa Catarina and by the Castillo de Montgrí. The old part of the town is enclosed by a wall, and two of the former six gates still exist. Just north of L'Escala, the (mostly) Greek ruins at **Empúries ⑬** (open Tues–Sun; entrance fee) are an impressive glimpse into the area's rich history. The site is extensive and includes the Greek Temples of Jupiter Serapis and Asklepios, a market place and assembly hall, as well as the remains of two Roman villas and an amphitheatre. **Roses**, an important fishing port across the bay, and neighbouring Empúria-brava are busy resorts.

Figueres ⑭ is the area's main town, known for its 18th-century **Castell de Sant Ferrán**, its important role in the development of the *sardana* – Catalonia's national dance – and, more recently, for its **Teatre-Museu Dalí** (open Tues–Sun, also Mon Jul–Sept; entrance fee). This houses a startling collection on five floors of some of Salvador Dalí's most extraordinary creations. Dalí, who was born in Figueres in 1904, converted the former theatre building himself in the 1960s and early 1970s. Among the most memorable exhibits are the Sala de Mae West on Level 3 and an extraordinary confection of Cadillac car (awash with water on the inside), fishing boat and statue called *Taxi Plujós* (Rainy Taxi) on Level 1. The museum is understandably popular, so be prepared to queue.

Cadaqués ⑮, which was Dalí's home for many years, is a sparkling, white port town heavily populated with artists and *literati*, especially in summer. **Cap**

Dalí's emotional ties to Figueres were strong. He moved into a tower adjoining his theatre-museum in 1984, living there until his death in 1989. He is also buried in the museum.

BELOW: white-washed houses along the seafront at Cadaqués.

*Fortified bridge in
medieval Besalú.*

de Creus, 8 km (5 miles) north of Cadaqués, is a wild and refreshing trip especially if the prevailing wind, known as the *Tramuntana*, is blowing. Further north still is the fishing town of **Port de la Selva**, much celebrated by Catalan poets. The monastery of **Sant Pere de Rodes** overlooks the Gulf of La Selva, the ruins an eery testimony to bygone times set against the immense panorama of the bright coastal towns and the sweep of the Mediterranean below.

A worthwhile trip from Figueres is to the outstanding medieval village of **Besalú** ⑯, 20 km (12 miles) further inland along the N-260. The village, now a national monument, is set beside the Riu Fluvía, and was once the capital of an enormous county covering present-day Barcelona and Girona provinces. It has many beautiful Romanesque buildings and a striking fortified bridge.

The Golden Coast

The coast south of Barcelona, known as the **Costa Daurada** or "Golden Coast", becomes progressively wider, wilder and lonelier. Even in August you can walk

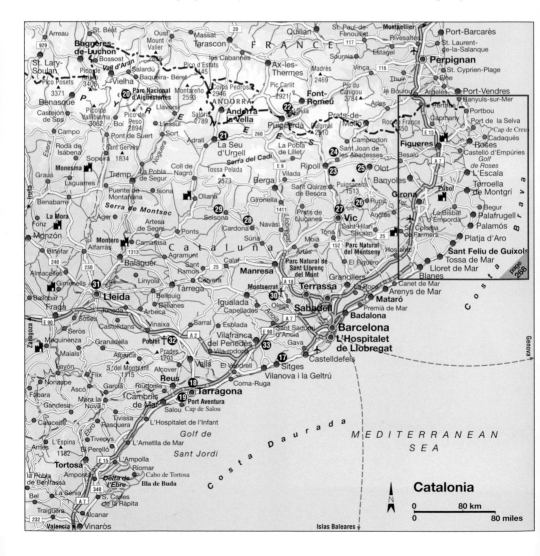

Map on page 270

for miles over strands in the **Delta de l'Ebre** with barely a glimpse of another human. If the Costa Brava *cales* are intimate and cosy, the southern beaches of Catalonia are the opposite: vast and empty spaces of sand, sea, sky and sun.

Castelldefels and **Sitges** ⑰ are the two beaches closest to Barcelona – good party value but slim on natural assets. The **Museu Cau Ferrat** (open Tues–Sun; entrance fee) in Sitges has a fine collection of Modernista objects donated by artist Santiago Rusiñol on his death in 1931. Between Sitges and Tarragona are long, open beaches with fine sand, clear water and plenty of fresh seafood.

Tarragona ⑱ itself is rich in Roman art and archaeology. It also has an impressive 12th-century **catedral** and a provincial freshness which, all together, create a unique blend of past and present, town and country. Roman remains of the **Aqüeducte de les Ferreres** and the **Arc de Berá** are located on the city's outskirts. The **Passeig Arqueològic**, a walk through the city's ancient walls, including massive boulders set in place in the 3rd century BC, is one of Tarragona's most spectacular sights. The ruins of the **Amfiteatre**, built near the beach in order to use the natural incline of the shore, are also well preserved. Tarragona's **Rambla**, an elegant, broad walkway down to the sea, is a key spot.

South from Tarragona, there are miles of sandy beaches – **Salou** is the most developed and best known, and home of the **Port Aventura** ⑲ theme park (open daily Apr–Oct; entrance fee). The thrills and spills include the Dragon Khan roller-coaster, Wild-West shoot-outs and Chinese acrobats. The park has its own train station,with several services daily from Barcelona and Tarragona.

Cambrils, further south, is an excellent fishing port and marina, especially known for superb seafood served in the restaurants of the harbour. **L'Ametlla de Mar** and **L'Ampolla** are excellent beaches to the south, approaching the Delta de l'Ebre. In the Delta itself, known for its wildlife and rice paddies, El Trabucador and La Punta de la Banya are two of the wildest stretches of sand anywhere on the Iberian peninsula.

The Catalan Pyrenees

The lush peaks and valleys of the Pyrenees provide skiing, climbing, hunting, fishing and nature's full measure, surrounded by thousands of years of civilisation. Roman bridges span trout streams, and gourmet restaurants welcome skiers at the foot of ski lifts.

The **Vall d'Aran** is Catalonia's northwest corner. "L'Aranès", the language of the valley, is a linguistic branch of Gascon French. **Baqueira-Beret**, where Spain's royal family spends Easter Week, is one of the country's best ski resorts. There are mountain trails and superb views to be found on foot or horseback in the summer, on skis in winter. The peculiar mountain architecture of the Vall d'Aran, like Alpine or Tyrolean high country design – steep, slate roofs – seems to reflect the stone *cordillera* which surround these Pyrenean dwellings. The 12th-century church at **Bossost** is one of the most extraordinary religious monuments of the valley. The 12th/13th-century church at **Salardú** houses the crucifix, the "Sant Crist de Salardú", one of the treasures of Pyrenean art.

The best route east from the Vall d'Arán would be to start south, passing through the **Tunnel de Vielha**

BELOW:
Romanesque church in the Boí Valley.

Illuminated manuscript at the Museu Diocesà, La Seu D'Urgell.

and drive down to the **Vall de Boí**, which connects to the **Parc Nacional d'Aigüestortes** ⑳ and Espot. The Boí Valley's set of churches is the most important collection of Romanesque architecture in the Pyrenees. Aigüestortes National Park, Lake Mauricio and the Vall d'Espot are all spectacular, as is the Vall d'Assua and its Llessui ski area, accessible from the town of **Sort**.

East from Sort is **La Seu d'Urgell** ㉑ and its important medieval **Catedral de Santa María y Museu Diocesà** (open Jun–Sept: Mon–Sat am only; entrance fee), which includes the cathedral cloister as well as sculptures, altarpieces and illuminated manuscripts. The cathedral is an outstanding example of the Romanesque architecture found everywhere here. The eastern Pyrenees extend almost to the Mediterranean sea. **La Cerdanya** is an especially luminous east–west running valley, which history has divided between France and Spain.

Sun and snow

Solar energy projects, solar-powered bakeries, and year-round tennis are a few results of the Cerdanya's record number of annual sun-hours. About 45 minutes from **Puigcerdà** are a dozen ski resorts in three countries: Spain, France and Andorra. Boar, chamois and wild mushrooms are hunted in the autumn, while in spring and summer the **Riu Segre** is one of Europe's premier trout streams. Hiking and camping in the upper reaches of the Pyrenees (the Pirinéos Orientales), which reach heights over 2,900 metres (9,500 ft), are superb. **Llívia** ㉒, a Spanish enclave within French territory – thanks to the wording of the 1659 Treaty of the Pyrenees ceding certain "villages" to France (Llivia was a "town") – has ancient stone streets and buildings, Europe's oldest pharmacy, and one of the area's best restaurants (**Can Ventura**) located in a farmhouse in the centre

BELOW: the rushing waters of the Riu Segre offer excellent trout fishing.

of town. La Cerdanya abounds in things to do: skiing, hiking, horseback riding, hunting, fishing or just browsing through tiny villages. **Guils**, **Aja**, **Vilallovent** and **Bellver de Cerdanya** have retained the rustic Pyrenean flavour of the early mountain towns. La Cerdanya is open and lush, brilliant and broad compared to the Vall d'Aran's steep, angular pitch.

Map on page 270

Cradle of Catalonia

East of La Cerdanya, the "*cremallera*" (zipper) or cogwheel train from Ribes de Freser up to Núria, one of Spain's earliest winter sports stations, is a spectacular excursion. The **Vall de Camprodon**, the most eastern valley in the Pyrenees, is east of **Ripoll** ㉓, an important medieval capital known as the *bressol* or "cradle" of Catalonia. The carved portal of Ripoll's **Santa María** monastery church is among the best Romanesque works in Spain. Also in the Vall de Camprodon, there is a ski area at Vallter and two fine Romanesque churches at **Molló** and **Beget**.

East of Ripoll on the C-151 is the little town of **Sant Joan de les Abadesses** ㉔. The main attraction here is the **Iglesia de Sant Joan** (open daily; closed weekdays Nov–mid-Mar; entrance fee), which was originally part of a Benedictine monastery founded in the 9th century. The highlight is the Calvary on the main altar, a masterpiece of Romanesque carving dating to 1250.

La Garrotxa, east of Camprodon, is a volcanic area which encompasses **Castellfollit de la Roca**, a town perched on a cone of basalt rock. From here, it isn't far to **Olot** ㉕, known for its 19th-century school of landscape artists. Between Olot to Figueres and around **Banyoles**' blue lake the terrain smooths out into the moist and fertile lowlands of the **Empordà**.

BELOW: the richly decorated portico of Santa María in Ripoll.

Lleida's Old Cathedral, looking more like a castle than a church, was used for many years as a military barracks.

BELOW: the Monestir de Poblet, which is once again run by monks.

The interior

Most Catalans take it for granted that one lifetime isn't enough to browse through everything the provincial towns of Catalonia have to offer.

Montseny, north from Barcelona, is a series of peaks – smooth, placid, massive heights from which there are excellent views out on to the coastal plain of Catalonia. **Rupit** ㉖, 20 km (12 miles) south of Olot, is a stunning medieval town built over a clear stream. Well-populated with restaurants specialising in the renowned *Patata de Rupit*, a potato stuffed with herbs, duck, lamb and veal, Rupit is an architectural and gastronomic gem in a wild area.

The roads around Barcelona

An hour north of Barcelona is the thriving provincial capital of **Vic** ㉗ with a lovely central square, **La Plaça Major**, and a cathedral famous for the energetic murals of Catalan painter Josep María Sert. Sert's work was destroyed by anticlerical vandals at the beginning of the Civil War in 1936, but was restored by the painter himself before his death in 1945. Many of the faces are said to be satirical representations of fascist leaders, although Franco failed to catch on when he toured the cathedral.

Cardona ㉘, 50 km (30 miles) to the west, is notable for its Parador Nacional at the site of the ancient castle and church which overlook the Vall de Cardoner. The **Salt Mountain**, a 150-metre (500-ft) hill of almost pure salt, is one of the most extraordinary geological curiosities in Catalonia, a resource exploited by the Romans and still mined today. **Solsona** ㉙, further northwest, a town steeped in medieval mystery – silence, stone, tiny streets – is known for its **catedral** and its **Museu Diocesà** (open Tues–Sun; entrance fee), where you can view local

archaeological finds. The two main squares are fine examples of early provincial architecture. Solsona's principal attraction, however, is the *feel* of the place – the sense of time, the depth of the serenity in that antique granite world. There's even a town crier.

Map on page 270

The Black Virgin of Montserrat

Every visitor to Catalonia should see the **Monestir de Montserrat** ⑳ (tel: 93-835 02 51; open 10.30am–2pm daily; closed last three weeks of Jan; entrance fee) just 45 minutes by car, train or bus from Barcelona. It is a Catalan religious shrine of great power and mystery. For many years, Montserrat performed the only marriage ceremony and celebrated the only masses in the Catalan language. *La Moreneta*, Catalonia's beloved Black Virgin, presides over the church nestled among the natural stone spires which rise up from the valley floor.

Lleida (**Lérida** in Castilian) ㉛ 75 km (45 miles) west of Montserrat, is an ancient city, perched on the edge of Spain's flat, central plateau, with an excellent **Old Cathedral** (La Seu Vella), high on a hill above the old part of the city. **La Paeria** (the town hall), on the Carrer Major, and the Gothic **Hospital de Santa María,** with pretty, arcaded inner courtyards, are two of Lleida's best early structures. The church of **Sant Llorenç,** in a square of the same name, represents the transition from Romanesque to Gothic. The delicate, octagonal bell tower, 76 metres (250 ft) high, is particularly striking.

Cava – the Catalan answer to champagne.

The **Monestir de Poblet** ㉜ (open daily; entrance fee), 40 km (25 miles) north of Tarragona, was a key link in the reconquest of Catalonia from the Moors. Surrounded by a 1.8-km (1-mile) long wall, the complex of buildings is more reminiscent of a secular royal residence than a monastic refuge. Ramón Berenguer IV, Count of Barcelona, completed his drive from Lleida, via the Segre and then the Ebro, to the sea and made the initial donation for the founding of the monastery in 1150. Surrounded by rough, austere country, Poblet reflects this severity in its sober, powerful architecture. A self-sufficient unit, the monastery has always controlled vast tracts of land. It was ransacked in 1835 but subsequently rebuilt.

BELOW: vineyard near Vilafranca.

Celebrating with wine

The seat of Catalonia's famous *cava* industry is at **Vilafranca del Penedès** ㉝, about 40 km (25 miles) west of Barcelona. *Cava* is a champagne-like white wine – 90 percent of it made from grapes grown in nearby **Sant Sadurni d'Anoia**.

Vilafranca is the commercial centre at the eye of the grape hurricane. A town with an aristocratic architectural presence, Vilafranca has plenty to offer visitors: Its **Museu del Vi** (Wine Museum, open Tues–Sun; entrance fee) on Plaça Jaume I also covers local archaeology and geology.

Also worth seeing at the right time of year are the **Fira del Gall** (fowl market) just before Christmas, human architecture – *Els Castellers* – erected by teams of "castlers" who construct human towers, and *La Calçotada* in February – a feast of new onions and *romesco* sauce. All of it accompanied by plenty of good *cava*, of course. ❏

ARAGÓN

Map on page 278

The towns and cities of this little-known region offer a feast of mudéjar architecture. In sharp contrast are the dramatic landscapes and ski slopes of the Parque Nacional de Ordesa

Many Spaniards know Aragón only as the region one must drive through when going from Madrid to Barcelona, or the home of the *jota*, the country's best-known folkloric music and dance. In winter, skiers race up the region's major roads in search of the perfect slopes in the Pyrenees, passing by mudéjar and Romanesque churches, villages that are dying from lack of attention and walled cities that hide wonders of mudéjar architecture.

Home of kings

The Romans founded Caesaraugusta, known today as Zaragoza, in 25 BC. Not much evidence of their presence remains today. Aragón was invaded along with the rest of Spain by the Moors in 714. Resistance to the occupation began around 100 years later; in 1035, Ramiro I, the bastard son of Sancho III of the neighbouring kingdom of Navarre, inherited the kingdom of Aragón, which was united with Castile in 1469. At its height it included parts of France, the Balearic Islands, Naples and Sicily, and stretched as far south as the southeasterly region of Murcia.

Zaragoza was recaptured by the Christian armies at the orders of Alfonso I in 1118. But, despite the Reconquest, Christians and Moors lived well side-by-side for centuries. The word "mudéjar" comes from *mudayyan*, Arabic for "subject". But these subjects were privileged and esteemed ones; at the beginning of the 16th century it is estimated the *moriscos*, or Moors living under Christian domination, comprised 16 percent of the region's population. But in 1502 all Moors were ordered to convert or leave the country, and the definitive expulsion order made in 1609 by Felipe III put an end to the cohabitation.

Although Fernando II was from Aragón (his marriage to Isabel of Castile in 1469 marked the unification of Spain), he was not overly sensitive to the social realities of his home region. Ignoring the protests of his lords, he imposed the Inquisition, with the unpleasant result of having his Inquisitor-General murdered in the Seo Cathedral in Zaragoza in 1485. The swords supposedly used to commit the crime can be seen today next to the altar.

Geographically, Aragón is divided into three areas which roughly correspond to its three provinces: the Pyrenees (Huesca), the Ebro River Valley (Zaragoza) and the Iberian mountains (Teruel). It is the least densely populated of Spain's regions.

Zaragoza province

There are fine examples of mudéjar architecture throughout the province of Zaragoza. **Tarazona ❶**, 72 km (45 miles) northwest of the capital, is known as

LEFT: snow-covered peaks of the Parque Nacional de Ordesa. **BELOW:** slate roof typical of the Aragón region.

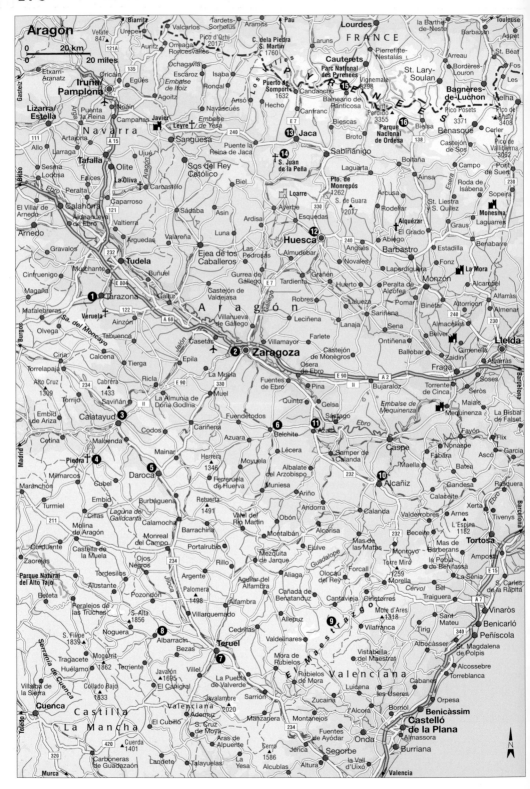

Aragon

0   20 km
0   20 miles

"The Mudéjar City" and offers a spectacle of Moorish and Sephardic history. The cloisters of the 12th-century brick-domed **catedral** (closed for restoration), have some particularly fine Moorish tracery. The twisting, cobbled streets, crossed by mudéjar arches, of the old Jewish district (located behind the Palacio Episcopal) are worth exploring on foot. Not to be missed are the 8th-century Iglesia de Santa María Magdalena and the marvellously decorated town hall.

Map on page 278

The capital of the region, **Zaragoza ❷**, has a population of around 600,000. The visitor will find few monuments indicating the city's past grandeur since time, neglect and two terrible sieges suffered during the Napoleonic Wars (1808–09) destroyed a great deal. The old part of town, on the south bank of the Río Ebro, is the place to head for first – it contains most of the sights and plenty of hotels as well as lively bars and restaurants.

The city has two cathedrals: the **Seo** (closed for restoration), which was consecrated in 1119 on the site of the old mosque, and **El Pilar** (open daily; free), built in honour of Spain's patron saint, the Virgin of Pilar, who supposedly appeared there atop a pillar to St James in AD 40. The Parroquieta chapel's mudéjar wall and ceiling, the Gothic altarpiece and the baroque choir stalls are the Seo cathedral's most outstanding features.

The Basílica de Nuestra Señora del Pilar, with its 11 domes, is the most distinctive feature of the city. The present building, dating from the 17th and 18th centuries, is the third on the site. Massive pillars split the church into three bays, some of the frescoes on the cupolas being the work of Goya. But the focal point is the Lady Chapel. There you will see the legendary marble pillar which supports the much-venerated Virgin, a tiny wooden image encrusted in silver, whose rich mantle is changed every day. The altarpiece in the basilica is alabaster. The day of El Pilar, 12 October, a national holiday, is attended by lavish celebrations in Zaragoza, with city processions of cardboard giants.

Francisco Goya y Lucientes, born in Fuendetodos in 1746, rose to become court painter to Carlos IV.

BELOW: rooftops of El Pilar cathedral.

Moorish pleasure palace

The **Aljafería** (open daily; closed Sun pm; free) to the west of the old town, has now been fully restored. It was first built in the 11th century by the ruling Moorish king and could well have been taken from the *Arabian Nights*, according to testimonies of the time. The Catholic Monarchs transformed part of the palace into their headquarters; it was later used by the Inquisition, and then as an army barracks in the 19th century. Ferdinand and Isabella's throne room, with its remarkable ceiling, and the Moorish chapel are the best-preserved parts of the interior. Outside, Santa Isabel's courtyard, adjacent to the main courtyard, has some splendid mudéjar arches.

The **Museo Camón Aznar** (open Tues–Sun; entrance fee), on Calle de Espoz y Mina, has a wide-ranging collection of Spanish art, including contemporary works, but the main draw are the fine etchings by Goya, on the top floor of the building. Goya was born in the village of **Fuendetodos**, 50 km (30 miles) directly south of Zaragoza. The house where he was born is now also a **museum** (open Tues–Sun; entrance fee), after being abandoned for years. The rooms are furnished in a simple style appropriate to the period.

Calatayud ❸, 60 km (35 miles) southwest of Zaragoza on the N-II, is justly famous for its mudéjar towers, the best example of which rises above the Colegiata de Santa María. Nearby is the **Monasterio de Piedra ❹** (open daily; entrance fee), founded by Alfonso II in 1195 and now an oasis of gardens, lakes and waterfalls around a 12th-century Cistercian monastery.

Also in the southern part of Zaragoza province is the beautiful but rather neglected town of **Daroca ❺**. Surrounded by nearly 3 km (2 miles) of walls with more than 100 towers, Daroca appeared in the annals of the Greek voyagers. The walls are now in ruins, although some of the towers have been restored. Visitors who want to understand Spain's more recent history would be well advised to visit **Belchite ❻**, 40 km (25 miles) southeast of Zaragoza. This town was the site of one of the most ferocious battles of the Civil War, and its ruins have been preserved as a reminder of the horrors of war. A new town, completed in 1954, was built alongside the original devastated site.

Of the three Aragonese provinces, Teruel is the least known, and the capital city of **Teruel ❼** is the least populated of all Spain's provincial capitals. It is a province in which mudéjar architecture abounds, both in the capital itself and in towns so far off the beaten track that most Spaniards don't know they exist.

Lovers of Teruel

The **catedral** (open daily; free) is justly famous for its remarkable ceiling, a masterpiece of the 14th century in which daily life in the Middle Ages is portrayed in portraits painted on wood. Another outstanding mudéjar monument is the **Iglesia de San Pedro** (mausoleum open Tues–Sun; entrance fee) on the eastern side of the former Jewish quarter, which has a beautiful 16th century altarpiece.

BELOW: restored towers in Daroca's medieval walls.

It is best known for housing the tombs of the Lovers of Teruel, a tragic couple immortalised in poems and plays, whose fame in Spain outdoes that of Romeo and Juliet. A relief by Juan de Avalos depicts the lovers and, if you peer into the tomb, you can see the mummified bodies. Diego Marcilla and Isabel Segura were in love, the story goes, but their parents opposed the marriage. Diego left to make his fortune, and thus endear himself to his lover's father. He came home in 1217 a rich man, only to find his beloved walking down the aisle with another. He died of heartbreak the next day and Isabel kissed the cadaver and passed on to a better world with her Diego.

Visitors should also stop to admire the twin mudéjar towers of San Martín and El Salvador, supposedly the result of a contest between two Moorish architects in love with the same woman. The winner won his love and the loser (who built San Martín) jumped off the tower.

Of all the mountain villages in Teruel, **Albarracín 8** is the best preserved, so much so that in the 1980s it won a European competition for historical preservation. Located 30 km (18 miles) west of Teruel, it is a place to stroll through, admiring the town walls, the towers, the harmony between land and construction and the architectural magic of a fortified town rising high above a river.

Moving southeast of Teruel, to the harsh mountains and spectacular gorges of **El Maestrazgo 9**, stop at **Mora de Rubielos** to see its immense castle, built between the 13th and 15th centuries, and the nearby **Rubielos de Mora** (they shouldn't be confused). The truth is that nearly any road through the mountains of Teruel will lead to mudéjar towers, castles, city walls or outstanding churches. **Alcañiz 10**, to the northeast of Teruel, is famed for its castle, with murals depicting the history of the Calatrava Order, and the Colegiata de Santa María, with its great baroque portal. North of Alcañiz, towards Zaragoza on the N-232, is **Azaila 11**, which has been declared a national monument due to the discovery of an ancient Celtic-Roman *castro*.

Romanesque region

If the dominant architectural or historical motif in Zaragoza is mudéjar, moving north to the province of Huesca, the traveller is surrounded by Romanesque buildings. The stream of pilgrims on their way to Santiago during the Middle Ages encouraged the construction of churches from Catalonia to Galicia, of which Jaca's cathedral is one of the most important. In addition to offering literally hundreds of well-preserved examples of the Romanesque style, Huesca is paradise for hikers, skiers, walkers and climbers.

The capital of the province is **Huesca 12**, whose age of splendour was the 13th century. Pedro IV founded the University of Huesca in the 14th century, but it was abolished in 1845, by which time the city had been reduced to the status of an unimportant provincial capital. Huesca's **catedral** (open daily; free) is 15th and 16th century, built on earlier foundations on the site of the old mosque. Of particular interest is the alabaster Renaissance altarpiece by Damián Forment. Nearby is the **City Hall** (1578) with a mural depicting the story of "The Bell of Huesca", one of the bloody legends of Spanish history: Ramiro

Map on page 278

TIP

To explore El Maestrazgo, which straddles southern Aragón and Valencia, you need to hire a car – few buses serve the area.

BELOW: tomb in the Iglesia de San Pedro, with the clasped hands of the Lovers of Teruel.

Saint's statue adorning Jaca cathedral.

II, a former monk who ruled Aragón in the 12th century, was disturbed by his nobles' refusal to submit to his rule. After consulting with the abbot of his former monastery, Ramiro II summoned his nobles to a banquet to celebrate the casting of a new bell which the king said would be heard throughout Aragón. When they arrived, they were assassinated. Ramiro had them all beheaded, piling up their heads in the form of a large bell, and order was restored.

The other major city in the province is **Jaca** ⓭, whose **catedral** is one of Spain's treasures of Romanesque architecture. The beautifully restored **Museo Diocesano** (open Tues–Sun; entrance fee) contains a remarkable collection of Romanesque frescoes. **La Ciudadela**, a fortress built by Felipe II, is currently under the jurisdiction of the army but is open for guided tours.

Soon after the kingdom of Aragón was established, King Sancho Ramirez founded the **Monasterio de San Juan de la Peña** ⓮ (tel: 974-36 25 21; open daily; entrance fee), which became the point of religious inspiration for the Christian Reconquest campaign. Located 27 km (17 miles) southwest of Jaca, the monastery is wedged between enormous boulders and under a sheer rock cliff. It contains an extraordinary Romanesque cloister and a 10th-century church, the monks' sleeping quarters and the Nobles' Pantheon, containing the tombs of early Aragonese kings.

West of Jaca are **Los Valles**, a series of valleys which eventually lead to Navarre and which maintain the old architectural, linguistic and cultural traditions of Aragón. The villages of **Hecho** and **Ansó** feature houses with odd-shaped chimneys which distinguish one town from another, and the windows are outlined in white. Another showcase town worth a detour in northwest Aragón is **Sos del Rey Católico**, birthplace of Fernando (the "Catholic King") and one

BELOW: cathedral nave, Jaca.

of the Five Towns (Cinco Villas) honoured by Felipe V for their support during the War of the Spanish Succession. The entire town is a monument of grand stone mansions and quaint, flower-decked houses. The frescoed Iglesia de San Esteban and the Gothic Lonja (exchange building) are worth tracking down. The town's parador makes a comfortable touring base.

Mountaineering

North of Hecho is the Los Valles National Reserve, and directly north of Jaca is the **Puerto de Somport** marking the border with France and the starting point for many trails into the high country. To the northeast of Jaca lies the **Viñamala National Reserve**. To get there you pass through the towns of **Sabiñánigo** and **Biescas**, as well as a host of tiny towns along the C-136 road that contain Romanesque churches and usually little else. Branching off the road leads you to **Balneario de Panticosa** ⓯, with a lake, hotel facilities and stores where you can stock up on provisions, buy a trail map and head off into the wild. The highest peaks in this area are over 3,000 metres (9,800 ft).

Further to the east is one of Spain's most famous national parks, **Ordesa** ⓰, which is actually part of a chain of reserve areas that can lead hikers across the border to France or east into the Catalonian Pyrenees. The park is a paradise of gorges, forests, waterfalls and dramatic cliffs. Many species of flora and fauna thrive here, including the endangered Ordesa ibex (mountain goat). The weather here can be unpredictable – the best time for hikers is between June and September. The Pyrenees in winter are, of course, taken over from the hikers by the skiers. **Candanchú** and **Canfranc**, on the road from Jaca to Somport, the town of **Panticosa** and **Formigal**, north of there, are all major ski resorts. ❑

Map on page 278

BELOW: the strategically located Monasterio de San Juan de la Peña.

Map on page 288

Madrid

THE BASQUE COUNTRY

Peaceful green river valleys set against dour peaks form the backdrop to the lively fishing ports, resorts and sandy beaches of the Basque Country

Mountain chains, like "bones showing through skin" as one historian has described them, extend along the Bay of Biscay west of the Pyrenees, separating much of the rolling farmland of the Basque Country from the rest of Spain. In this clearly defined geographical area, known locally as Euskadi, the Basques and their shadowy ancestors have lived since the end of the last Ice Age.

A world apart

Basques live on either side of the Pyrenees; in the French region of Pyrénées-Atlantiques, Spanish Navarre and the three Spanish provinces which have made up the autonomous Basque community since 1980: **Guipúzcoa** and **Vizcaya** on the coast and **Álava** on the plateau. In addition to possessing physical characteristics which have led some anthropologists to believe they are directly descended from Cro-Magnon Europeans, the Basque language, *Euskera*, sets this people apart from their French and Spanish countrymen.

Of Western Europe's living languages, only *Euskera* does not belong to the Indo-European family. It has fascinated linguists since the Middle Ages, when scholars traced it to Tubal, the grandson of Noah who settled the peninsula after The Flood. More recently, philologists comparing the Basque words for axe, *aitzor*, and stone, *aitz* have raised the possibility that the language dates from a time when tools were made of stone.

Basque was mostly preserved among rural families during the Franco years and possesses a very small written literature. It is now taught along with Castilian in Basque schools and at night courses, although it takes the average adult some 500 hours of study to be able to carry on a conversation. Road signs in Basque can confuse visitors, thus Donostia stands for San Sebastián, Bilbo for Bilbao, and Gasteiz (of Visigothic origin) for Vitoria.

Indomitable

Fiercely proud of their ancient past, Basques like to say they have never submitted to outside conquerors, including Moors and Romans. Guipúzcoa and Vizcaya possess prehistoric caves and dolmens, but are notably lacking in Roman and early-Christian remains. However, both the Romans and Christianity made inroads into the mountain strongholds, and the Basques' Catholicism has stood firm ever since. They are considered the most religious people in Spain. Appropriately, Ignacio de Loyola, the warrior who founded the influential Society of

PRECEDING PAGES: the Valle de Atxarte in Vizcaya.
BELOW: inline skaters, Santander.

Jesus or Jesuits, was born in this region, near Azpeitia, 52 km (32 miles) from Donostia (San Sebastián). On his saint's day, 31 July, large crowds flock to the massive monastery with its basilica topped by a lofty cupola.

To a certain extent it was religious feeling which brought the Basques into the 19th-century Carlist Wars. But, ironically, it was mainly to protect their *fueros* that they chose what turned out to be the losing side in both the Carlist and the Civil Wars, thus losing their independence. The terrorist incidents for which the Basque Country has become known since the 1970s – seen by radical separatists as a continuation of the struggle for the restoration of self-rule – have never been directed at tourists.

Relatively few non-Basques make a comprehensive tour of the interior of the region. Visitors typically spend the summer on the mild and misty Basque coast, as Spaniards and an increasing number of French have done since the 19th century, when the point of resort life was to rest in the shade.

Guipúzcoa

The smallest province on the peninsula and one of the most densely populated corners of Europe, **Guipúzcoa** has had close cultural connections with the other side of the Pyrenees since prehistoric times. More recently, the fortified Basque ports a few miles from the frontier have been easy targets for the French in wartime.

Eugenie de Montijo, the beautiful daughter of a Spanish nobleman who fought on the French side in the Peninsular War and the Empress of Napoleon III, is credited with setting the style for summering on the Basque coast. Soon after she introduced the Emperor to Biarritz in the French Basque Country, other royals, including Queen Victoria, arrived. By the end of the 19th century, the Spanish and South American aristocracy had made **Donostia** (San Sebastián) ❶ their favourite summer watering place.

BELOW: La Concha Beach, San Sebastián.

From this period date the **Casa Consistorial** (town hall), formerly the Gran Casino, the royal family's Tudor-style **Palacio Miramar**, dividing the two long curving beaches, and the high-style **Puente Zurriola** over the canalised Río Urumea. Casino gambling is now confined to the **Hotel Londres y Inglaterra** nearby.

Although it is now a city of 200,000 with a diverse economy, San Sebastián is still one of the most beautiful resorts in Europe: elegant and cosmopolitan during the jazz and film festivals, favoured by the Spanish aristocracy – including the king – during the warm autumn months, but still humming with street life in the old town. If you happen to arrive in the morning, proceed to the efficient tourist bureau by the Parque Alderdi Eder south of the Casa Consistorial. The beaches lying beyond a windbreak of tamarisks on the elegant **Paseo de la Concha** will rarely be full. This would be a good time to take the inexpensive funicular or to drive to the top of **Monte Igueldo**, the westernmost of the wooded promontories overlooking the Bay of La Concha.

San Sebastián is famed for its gourmet restaurants.

On 31 August, as the summer ends, a torchlight procession in the **Parte Vieja**, or Old Quarter, at the foot of Monte Urgull commemorates the virtual destruction of San Sebastián during the Peninsular War. Among the surviving structures belonging to the old walled port, are the cavernous 18th-century **Basilica of Santa María del Coro**, with its apsidal portal deeply recessed to protect the sculptures from hard winters and its graceful statue of the city's namesake in a niche, and the 16th-century Dominican monastery of **San Telmo** in the Plaza de Zuloaga. This has been converted into a wonderful museum (open Tues–Sun; free), devoted mainly to Basque culture and art but also including works by artists such as El Greco.

Part of the ethnographic collection is devoted to the history of the seafaring Basques. The Spanish colonisation of America depended on the skills of Basque navigators and shipbuilders with their experience in deepsea fishing. Other exhibits introduce *pelota*, the Basque national sport, and traditional Basque cuisine, costume and customs. In this tradition-

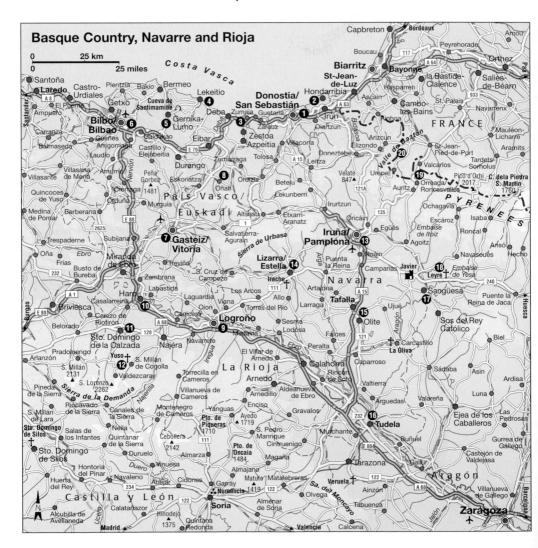

ally rainy country, the matriarchal kitchen and adjoining stable, reconstructed in the museum, became the most important rooms of the Basque farmhouse, the stone-and-timber *caserío*. The Fine Arts collection ranges from Hispano-Flemish to contemporary. Occupying a place of honour, the Basque painter Ignacio Zuloaga's best-known work shows three hearty Basque men enjoying a meal.

Map on page 288

Eating clubs

Private, men-only gastronomic societies *(txokes)* were founded here in the Parte Vieja in the 1870s. Basque cookery, with its fresh vegetables, dairy products and fish from the Bay of Biscay, seasoned with subtle sauces, is generally acknowledged to be the best on the peninsula.

The neoclassical **Pescadería** (fish market), a short walk south of the Plaza de Zuloaga near the arcaded **Plaza de la Constitución**, has, appropriately, one of the grandest façades in the Parte Vieja. At the nearby market ask for Idiazabal, cheese from the long-haired Laxa sheep which has been cured and smoked, and *txakoli*, the thin white Basque wine drunk with shellfish.

The Basque coast

East of San Sebastián, the fishing port and seaside resort of **Hondarribia ②** (Fuenterrabía in Castilian) lies just across the border with France and, over the centuries, has consequently suffered many attacks by the French. Its charming old town, entered through the **Puerta Santa María**, has somehow survived and still has many old houses with splendidly carved wooden balconies. The town's fine beach is backed by good fish restaurants.

BELOW: surfing the waves at Getaria.

A pleasant way to see this stretch of coast is to drive west all along the hilly coast of Guipúzcoa and Vizcaya, stopping whenever you feel like visiting one of the family beaches or enjoying a freshly caught fish dinner. Typical port resorts have at least one old church near the water, several good restaurants and sandy beaches. **Zarautz**, with its nice long beach, and **Getaria**, which has a smaller one, are two of the best-known producers of *txakoli*. This part of the coast may be the best place in Spain to order *chipirones en su tinta* (squid in its own ink) or *besugo* (sea bream).

In Getaria, formerly a whaling port, is a monument to Juan Sebastián Elcano, Magellan's Basque navigator, and skipper of the round-the-world voyage after Magellan was killed in the Philippines. Also born in Geteria was the man who may prove to be the 20th century's greatest couturier, Cristobal Balenciaga (1895–1972).

Past Getaria is the pretty resort of **Zumaia ③**, where the painter Ignacio Zuloaga's summer villa and studio, in a former convent, was turned into the excellent **Museo Zuloaga** (Carretera de San Sebastián, open Jan–Sept: Wed–Sun; free) after his death. Zuloaga was an important collector, and the museum includes one of El Greco's many versions of Saint Francis receiving the stigmata, a painting by Morales il Divino and two by Zurbarán, who

*Gernika,
photographed
shortly after the air
raid in 1937.*

came from a Basque family. After Zumaia the craggy shoreline of the **Cornisa Cantábrica** begins. Although it does not look far on the map, **Lekeitio** , one of the most interesting ports on the Basque coast, is a full half-day's drive from San Sebastián. The 15th-century church at Lekeitio with its flying buttresses and baroque tower is a few yards from a pretty beach where, in the morning, you may see fishermen painting their boats, or groups of children being given swimming lessons. From Lequeitio it is only a short drive south to Gernika.

Gernika (Guernica)

The bustling modern market town of **Gernika-Lumo** ❺ is sacred to the Basques for its associations with their ancient tradition of self-government. At least since the early Middle Ages, their representatives met here to elect a council of leaders and witness the titular monarch's oath to uphold their *fueros*. An event of enormous consequence for today's Basques, the election of José Antonio Aguirre at the **Casa de Juntas** (open daily; free), the parliament building, in the 1936 election, revived this tradition. Members of his government were sworn in under the **Gernikako Arbola**, the symbolic oak of Gernica. (The original oak which had stood for centuries was evidently destroyed by the French in the Peninsular War. The present one, it is claimed, grew from the original tree's acorn or sapling.)

BELOW: the symbolic oak of Gernika.

The declaration of an independent Basque state was met with swift retribution by the Nationalists under General Mola. Miraculously, the Casa de Juntas, the oak and the neighbouring **Iglesia de Santa María** (begun in the 15th century) survived the almost total destruction of Gernika on Monday 26 April 1937, the most infamous episode of the 1936–39 Spanish Civil War.

Mondays, then as now, were market days and the narrow streets were crowded with farm families and refugees. A third of the civilian population was killed in the attack, and many more were wounded, when German aircraft dropped 100,000 pounds of bombs, then flew low to shoot at the Basques fleeing into the fields. *Caseríos* in the hills were also bombed. "In the night these burned like candles", one of the dazed correspondents covering the war wrote in *The Times* of London. International outrage probably discouraged the use of such air attacks again in Spain.

The very word "Gernika" became synonymous with the horrors of war, symbolised in Picasso's famous painting *Guernica*, which now hangs in Madrid's Reina Sofía Museum. "General Franco's aeroplanes burned Gernika and the Basques will never forget it", predicted *The Times* correspondent. Repression under the Franco regime only stiffened resistance to domination by the central government and on the night of the dictator's death Basques danced in the streets. The 1979 Statute of Gernika finally gave the 2 million Basques autonomous government, although significant pressure continues for a greater degree of self-rule. Oddly enough, some of the most fervent Basque nationalists are young descendants of non-Basques who migrated to the region's industrial cities in Franco's time.

The rebuilt town of Gernika-Lumo is not handsome. However, be sure to notice the murals with their tranquil scenes of Basques at work, under the eaves of the **Casa de Ahorros Municipal de Bilbao** at the intersection of the Gran Vía and the Calle Adolfo Urioste between the tourist bureau and the Casa de Juntas. The castellated country house at Arteaga, 8 km (5 miles) to the north of here, where the Empress Eugenie spent part of her early life, is seen in one of them. Eugenie's castle is visible from the highway, but the principal attraction on the outskirts of Gernika-Lumo, to the northeast, is the **Cueva de Santimamiñe** (open Mon–Fri; free) and its prehistoric wall paintings, first discovered in 1916.

Post-Guggenheim Bilbao

The stunning new **Museo Guggenheim de Arte Contemporáneo** (Muelle Evaristo Churruca 1; tel: 94-423 27 99) has managed to relaunch **Bilbao** (Bilbo) ❻ and, in the opinion of many, the entire Basque Country into a *fin-de-siècle* rebirth of general optimism about the future. (For more information about the museum and its collection, *see pages 296–7*). As a result of the excitement caused by the Guggenheim, Bilbao has become one of Spain's hottest tourist destinations. Book well ahead – Bilbao is booming.

Bilbao's history has had its ups and downs. In 1300 the then small fishing and ironmongering village received *villa* status from Diego López de Haro. His statue stands on a high plinth sometimes hung with the *Ikurriña*, the red, white and green Basque flag inspired by the Union Jack, at the foot

Map on page 288

BELOW: the now metro at Bilbao.

of the pink and black Banco de Vizcaya tower in the **Plaza Circular** near the **Puente de la Victoria**. This is the main bridge joining old Bilbao on the east bank of the **Ría Nervión** and the newer bourgeois quarter which grew up on the west bank in the 19th century. Once you locate the **Gran Vía de López de Haro**, the main traffic artery running east to west from the Plaza Circular to the large **Parque de Doña Casilda Iturriza**, or the smart new Metro designed by Norman Foster, it is easy to get around this industrial centre, which is Spain's largest port.

Despite the air pollution and a wide ring of discouraging working-class apartment blocks, the city has a good deal to offer visitors. If you are here in August, it is worth staying for the *Semana Grande*, the biggest of the week-long festivals in the three provincial capitals. The events usually range from heavy culture to heavy metal to Basque folk music and traditional contests of stamina and strength.

Early Bilbao

The earliest settlements here are said to have been made near the present 15th-century Iglesia de San Antón in the Atxuri district along the Ribera east of the Siete Calles, the "Seven streets" of the **Casco Viejo**, or Old Town. The prosperous Casco Viejo was pillaged by the French during the Peninsular War, and much of it was destroyed in the Carlist Wars. But narrow streets and a number of pre-19th-century structures remain.

The **Museo Arqueológico, Etnográfico e Histórico Vasco** (open Tues–Sun; free) is in a converted Jesuit monastery in Calle de la Cruz which was once attached to the baroque Iglesia de los Santos Juanes. Along with prehis-

BELOW: a new route into the city.

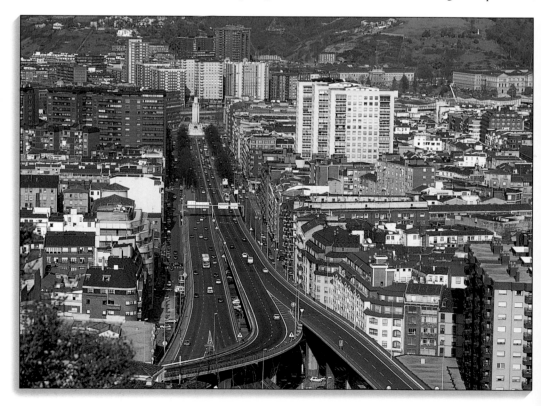

Map on page 288

toric exhibits, it contains a copy of an important piece of Basque folk art, the Kurutziaga Cross from Durango.

You can look down on the Casco Viejo from the terrace of the **Sanctuario de Nuestra Señora de Begoña** (*circa* 1511 and later). To get there, take the elevator in Calle Esperanza Ascoa behind the 15th and 18th-century **Iglesia de San Nicolás de Bari**, the original Father Christmas and patron saint of Bilbao's children, sailors, prisoners and prostitutes.

Industry and art

In the 1870s, at the end of the Second Carlist War, Bilbao began to exploit its natural iron deposits and industrialise in a big way. By the end of the century, half the Spanish merchant fleet came from Basque shipyards, much of its steel industry was located near Bilbao, and Basque bankers and businessmen wielded great financial power. The **Teatro de Arriaga** (1890) on the Paseo del Arenal, the **Ayuntamiento** (1892) at the bend in the river north of the Puente de la Victoria, and the **Palacio de la Diputación** (1897) were built, and a ground-swell of popular sentiment for going it alone and declaring a Basque State developed.

The wealthy, cosmopolitan aspect of Bilbao is reflected in the excellent **Museo de Bellas Artes** (open Tues–Sun; free) in Iturriza Park. It contains the most important collection of paintings in northern Spain. In addition to its Flemish, Catalan and classical Spanish holdings, it has a modern wing with some pieces showing the influence of various international art movements on the generation of artists who grew up under Franco, including Isabel Baquenado, Juan José Arqueretta, Andrés Nagel and Javier Morras.

BELOW: Bilbao's industrial port.

The Basques are proud of their musical traditions.

The interior

The capital of Álava, **Gasteiz (Vitoria)** is the largest and least Bascophone of the three Basque provinces and the seat of the autonomous Basque government. While Vitoria is best known for the bloody battle of 1813 in which Wellington defeated the French general Jourdan, it received its name as early as 1181 when Sancho the Wise founded a walled city here.

The narrow, concentric alleyways of the old town, some named for the crafts which flourished here – Zapatería, Cuchillería, Pintorería, Herrería – underwent a certain amount of urban renewal in the mid-19th century when medieval arcades were demolished and all the widening and airing-out possible performed to make them salubrious. But this quarter, with its three Gothic churches, town houses decorated with escutcheons and carved doorways, and shops and cafés, still imparts an authentic feeling of the prospering commercial town of the Middle Ages and Renaissance.

The **Feria de la Virgen Blanca** in August pays homage to the "White Virgin", standing in her jasper niche in the porch façade of the 14th-century **Iglesia de San Miguel** (open daily; free). The Gothic sculpture is of high quality. The city's protector, she overlooks the miradors of the busy Plaza de la Virgen Blanca and the monument erected in 1917 to commemorate the Battle of Vitoria. Inside the church is a retable by Gregorio Fernández, an important Golden Age sculptor. Notice the bagpipe player in his *Adoration of the Shepherds*.

The adjacent **Plaza del Machete**, named for the large knife on which oaths to uphold the town's *fueros* were sworn, marks the southern end of the old town. Walk north, stopping to admire the sculpture in the porch and on

BELOW:
Vitoria's old town, viewed from the air.

Map on page 288

the column capitals of the **Catedral de Santa María** (closed for restoration), to the **Museo de Arqueología** (open Tues–Sun; free). This well-designed small museum, in a 15th-century merchants' house in the **Correría**, distinguished by half-timbering and horizontal brickwork, is a wonderfully sensitive adaptation of an historic structure. The tens of thousands of years of local history to which it is devoted range from the Lower Paleolithic era through to the Middle Ages.

To the south, in a neighbourhood of large private houses between the Jardines de la Florida and the 19th-century park called El Prado, is the **Museo de Bellas Artes** (Paseo Fray Francisco, 8; open Tues–Sun; free). Its varied holdings include a Crucifixion by José de Ribera and a Virgin by the irascible Sevillan painter and sculptor Alonso Cano (1601–67), one of the most picaresque personalities in Spanish art. There are paintings and sculptures by Basque artists and a growing modern collection featuring the work of Miró, Picasso and Antonio Tápies (born 1923), the best-known Spanish abstract painter.

Basque seat of learning

About 30 km (20 miles) from Gasteiz along the GI-627 is the lovely town of **Oñati ❽**, where the **Universidad de Sancti Spiritus** (tel: 94-378 34 53; open Mon–Fri for guided tours; entrance fee) is a Renaissance gem. Built in the 16th century, the university taught a range of subjects, including law and medicine, until its closure in 1902. A stroll around the town reveals other architectural jewels, especially the Gothic Iglesia de San Miguel, with a cloister that spans the river, and the Baroque *ayuntamiento* (town hall). ❑

A small part of the Rioja winegrowing district lies inside the Basque Country. The narrow streets of the fortified town of Laguardia are lined with bodegas (wine cellars) offering tastings and tours.

BELOW: shrimp bar in Gasteiz.

THE GUGGENHEIM IN BILBAO

Bilbao's latest museum is the talk of the art world. This spectacular "Metallic Flower" beside the River Nervión has certainly given the city new life

The Guggenheim Museum in Bilbao opened in 1997 to a blaze of publicity. The city's $100-million investment in the spectacular titanium "Metallic Flower" had paid off: the story was in all the world's press; the city was on the international cultural map. Matched by Bilbao's other recent architectural triumphs – Norman Foster's metro, Santiago Calatrava's airport – the gallery confirmed the Basques as a people of vision and taste (as well as volatility: two days before it opened, a policeman was shot dead outside by ETA members attempting to deliver a bomb).

HELP FROM AEROSPACE

Set by the River Nervión and incorporating a busy vehicle bridge, the museum was designed by the Californian architect Frank O. Gehry. It is made up of inter-connected blocks, clad in limestone and topped with a shimmering titanium roof. Light floods through glass walls and a skylight in the 50-metre (165-ft)-high central atrium (pictured above) and from here walkways, lifts and stairs lead through the blocks that house the 19 spacious galleries on three floors. Many of the galleries have been designed to take large modern installations, notably the vast boat-shaped gallery built beneath the bridge. For the design of the 24,290-sq-metre (257,000-sq-ft) building, Gehry employed a computer programmme called Catia, which had been developed by the aerospace industry for mapping curved surfaces.

The Basque administration and the Solomon R. Guggenheim Foundation, based in New York, jointly administer the museum, the Guggenheim providing curatorial and administrative expertise as well as the core art collection and programming.

△ **THE COLLECTION**
The permanent collection has works from international artists from 1960 onwards. Site-specific work has also been specially commissioned.

▷ **VIEW FROM THE STREET**
The startling titanium "Metallic Flower" looms up in the heart of the town. It is designed to have a "sculptural presence" reflecting the waterfront, downtown buildings and surrounding hills. Within walking distance are the town hall and the city's existing fine art museum.

▷ **ARTS CENTRE**
The museum has a book shop, café and restaurant, and a 300-seater auditorium with multi-media technology. Note it closes on Mondays.

◁ **THE ARCHITECT**
Frank O. Gehry, the California-based architect, was attracted to the city's "tough aesthetic appeal".

MODERN MUSEUMS FOR MODERN ART

The Guggenheim is just one of a number of spectacular museums and galleries to open its doors in the last decade of the 20th century. The events of 1992 – the Seville Expo, the Barcelona Olympic Games and Madrid as cultural city of Europe – concentrated the minds of planners, architects and visionaries into turning the cities' leisure areas into modern temples for high art. There was no xenophobia: competition brought top architects from all over the world. And there was no lack of imagination: modern was set against medieval; boldness won the day.

Spain is not short of gallery space: vast halls and monumental buildings are dotted everywhere, and many have been enlisted for imaginative development. A prime example is the four-storey 18th-century General Hospital in Madrid, which reopened in 1992 as the magnificent Centro de Arte Reina Sofía, to house the city's 20th-century art collection. More daring is the 1997 Galician Centre of Contemporary Art, a blazingly modern building by Alvaro Siza Viera in the medieval centre of Santiago de Compostella in Galicia.

Another bold gallery is the Museu d'Art Contemporani in the Raval District of Barcelona. Designed by Richard Meier, this pristine slab (*pictured above*) opened in 1996 to general acclaim.

◁ **RIVERSIDE SIGHT**
The building occupies an 4.2-hectare (8-acre) site on a bend in the River Nervión, by the busy Puente de la Salve. It used to contain a factory and parking lot in an old dockland area. Another renowned architect, Cesar Pelli, has designed the adjacent waterfront development.

▽ **THE LONG GALLERY**
"Snake", by Richard Serra, is a centrepiece in an exhibition of modern American art in the 130-metre (427-ft), column-free "volume" running under the Puente de la Salve.

NAVARRE AND LA RIOJA

Map on page 288

The medieval kingdom of Navarre has an abundance of monuments, and its capital, Pamplona, hosts the world-renowned bull-running fiesta. La Rioja's vineyards produce the best red wine in Spain

Madrid

I n the year 778, the mighty Charlemagne, King of the Franks, made an unsuccessful attempt to conquer the lands to the south. As he headed home with his tired army, he was ambushed at Roncesvalles by Basques, who annihilated the rearguard. There died Roland, later to be immortalised in the *Chanson de Roland*, with the Basques conveniently replaced by Moorish attackers. Soon afterwards, a group of Basque warlords declared themselves independent, and the state they founded was destined eventually to become the kingdom of Navarre. Navarre was only finally demoted to the status of province in 1841. The greatest of its kings was Sancho III, El Grande, one of a line of Sanchos that ran from the 10th to the 13th century. Sancho III doubled Navarre's territories through astute politics, military campaigns and marriages and introduced the beginnings of a modern legal system and a process of church reform.

Fueros and Carlism

The period immediately following his death in 1035 marked an enormous advance for Navarre, as the prosperous and secure kingdom initiated the *fueros*  system, or the guarantee by the monarchy that towns and cities could enjoy a certain autonomy with their customary laws. Beginning in the 13th century, Navarre was ruled by a succession of French dynasties. But due mainly to a series of weak rulers, the Duke of Alba was able to seize the kingdom in 1512 in the name of King Fernando.

Navarre was no longer independent but it did have its *fueros*, and the monarchs in Madrid were obliged to uphold them. This system made Navarre into a very pro-monarchist region, and it is not surprising that the new ideas of liberalism, republicanism and anti-clericalism penetrating Spain in the late-18th and 19th centuries were not well received in Navarre. The centralist tendencies these movements implied meant that Navarre's autonomy was threatened.

When Fernando VII died in 1833, there was some question as to who should succeed him, his daughter Isabel or his brother Carlos. Navarre threw in its lot with Carlos, in the hope that a strong ruler like him would restore its traditions. The last of the Carlist wars ended in 1876 but the Carlists resurfaced during the Civil War, when they actively participated with Franco and played a crucial role in the coup that began the war. Franco, in fact, praised Navarre after a visit in 1936 as "the cradle of the nationalist movement".

This set Navarre off from the neighbouring Basque Country, with which it has so many ties. Even though Northern Navarre is Basque-speaking and shares a common past and many customs, the more industrial provinces of Vizcaya, Álava and Guipúzcoa threw in

LEFT: a quiet street in Pamplona.
BELOW: hard at work in a Rioja vineyard.

The best Rioja wines come from the fertile Rioja Alta. The Rioja region takes it name from the Río Oja, part of the river system draining this mountainous area.

their lot with the Republic, and lost. As the Basque nationalist movement began to grow in the early 20th century, there were vain attempts to unite with Navarre, but the centuries-old *Navarrismo* of the more conservative sectors has always impeded unity.

Vineyards of La Rioja

La Rioja has been ruled by Gascons, Romans, Moors, Navarrans and Castilians. From 573 to 711 this area, separated by the Río Ebro from the Basque country to the north and Navarre to the east, was part of the Duchy of Cantabria. The Asturian kings reconquered La Rioja in 1023, but by 1076 Alfonso VI had made it part of the crown of Castile. From the 15th–17th century, the region was divided between Castile and Navarre. When Spain became 52 provinces in 1822, one of them was Logroño, including all 8,000 sq. km (3,200 sq. miles) of the natural area of La Rioja. Fernando VII revised the map of Spain the following year, however, reducing Logroño to just over 5,000 sq. km (2,000 sq. miles) as part of the historic region of Old Castile. La Rioja only regained its name in 1980, and was recognised as an autonomous community in 1982.

The Rioja Alta is the moist and mountainous western part, and the Rioja Baja the flat and arid eastern half. **Logroño ❾**, its busy capital, lies between the two zones. The old quarter, bordered by the Ebro and the medieval walls, has the most charm. Traditionally a centre for pilgrims, many monuments, such as the **Puente de Piedra** and the **Iglesia de Santiago El Real** (open daily; free), with its equestrian statue of Saint James over the main door, are pilgrimage-connected. The twin baroque towers of Logroño's **Catedral de la Redonda** (open daily; free) are easily distinguished among the narrow streets.

BELOW: the grape harvest near Haro.

Haro , 35 km (22 miles) northwest of Logroño, is the undisputed wine capital of La Rioja. The flamboyant gothic, single-naved **Iglesia de Santo Tomás** (open daily; free), constructed in 1564, is the town's main monument. The old quarter is filled with taverns and cafés where you can sample local wines. Many of the town's manufacturers offer guided tours and tasting visits, which can be arranged at the tourist office (Plaza de la Paz 1; tel: 941-31 01 05).The Batalla del Vino festival on 29 June is a Bacchanalian free-for-all when participants hurl wine at one another as well as drinking it!

Leaving Logroño on the main N-120 west brings you to **Nájera**, once court of the Kings of Navarre. Here you will find their royal pantheon at the **Monasterio de Santa María La Real** (open Tues–Sun; entrance fee). Not to be missed are the 11th-century Gothic cloister, the Claustro de los Caballeros and the Plateresque windows over the grassy patio. Twenty km (12 miles) further west is **Santo Domingo de la Calzada** ⓫, a town dedicated to the Santiago pilgrimage route. The Romanesque-Gothic **catedral** in the medieval quarter houses the 11th-century Santo Domingo's tomb.

San Millán de la Cogolla ⓬, about 10 km (6 miles) south of Nájera, is the site of the Monasterio de Yuso, where a 10th-century manuscript on texts by Saint Augustine, the *Glosas Emilianenses*, contains the first words to have been written in Castilian Spanish.

Navarre

The Roman city of Pompaelo (the city of Pompey), **Iruña** (Pamplona) ⓭ was from the 10th to the 16th century the capital of the Kingdom of Navarre. Since the Civil War, the conservative, religious and hard-working Navarrese have

Map on page 288

TIP

Great for entertaining children is Spain's "Jurassic Park", near Enciso in the Rioja Baja. Dinosaur footprints from 150 million years ago are embedded in the rocks here.

BELOW: the twin towers of Pamplona's cathedral, with the snowy Pyrenees as a backdrop.

The running of the bulls in Pamplona appealed to Ernest Hemingway. By making its particulars universal in "The Sun Also Rises", he changed it for good by drawing the thousands of visitors who now come every year to the fiesta.

BELOW: watching the bulls from a safe distance.

transformed their ancient citadel into a prosperous industrial city. High-rise apartment blocks, manicured boulevards and factories form a protective ring around the lovely old city which perches on the banks of the **Río Arga**.

The centre of this area is the **Plaza del Castillo**, lined with outdoor cafés. Novelist Pío Baroja once said of the *paseo* in this plaza that the varying degrees of aristocracy were as evident as if they were separate floors of a building. Industry and democracy may have made a difference here, but the city's noble past is close at hand in the **Palacio de Navarra** (visits by appointment only; tel: 948-10 70 00) at the western end of the plaza. The building contains a magnificent throne room decorated with portraits of the kings of Navarre.

Most of Pamplona's historical buildings are located north of the Plaza del Castillo. Near the old city walls, in the Plaza Santa María La Real, is the 14th-century **catedral** (open Tues–Sat; entrance fee), with an 18th-century façade by the neoclassical architect Ventura Rodríguez. Inside are the lovely alabaster tombs of Carlos III of Navarre and his wife Leonor. The adjoining Gothic cloister is considered to be the best of its kind in Spain. The **Museo de Navarra** (open Tues–Sun; entrance fee), situated in a 16th-century hospital at Calle Jaranta, has interesting pieces of Navarrese archaeology, frescoes taken from Romanesque churches around the province and Goya's portrait of the Marquis of San Adrián.

Beginning at the south end of the Plaza del Castillo, the tree-lined **Paseo de Sarasate**, named after the native violinist, is Pamplona's main promenade. It runs past the Monument to the Fueros and the 13th-century **Iglesia de San Nicolás**, skirting the grassy Ciudadela, a fortress built by Felipe II and now the site of outdoor concerts in warm weather. The Paseo finishes in the **Parque de la Taconera**, a park resplendent with tame deer, fountains and monuments to Navarrese heroes. The **Iglesia de San Lorenzo**, located in the middle of the park, has a chapel dedicated to the city's world-famous saint, San Fermín.

The fiesta

There is a measured, middle-European air to Pamplona much of the time. Native *pamplonicas*, proud of their industriousness, look down upon such Spanish pastimes as flamenco, although the younger generation lead a fast and furious bar life. But at noon on 6 July, the Eve of San Fermín, a *chupinazo* (rocket) fired from the balcony of the 16th-century **Ayuntamiento** (town hall) puts an end to the order which has made the city flourish. For the next week, Pamplona becomes delirious. It has been said that this wildest of wild fiestas is an extension, rather than an aberration, of the Navarrese personality. The festival isn't about flowers or gorgeously dressed Virgins but sheer endurance. It might be true that a certain amount of stoical Basque blood is necessary to produce a celebration where the revellers drink, dance and sing for seven days, then, once worn down by exhaustion, throw themselves in front of a herd of charging bulls.

Since there's no place in the city where a visitor can merely stand and watch, everyone who arrives has no choice but to put together a semblance of the

Map on page 288

red and white costume and join in the dance. Occasionally, the *Sanfermines* are the scene of human, as well as taurine mayhem, and by the end of the week the heat, filth and broken glass will make the merriment seem less like the pages of a children's storybook come to life.

Lest you become too seduced by the prevailing fiesta mood, it ought to be pointed out that fatal gorings occur almost every year at the morning running of the bulls. It's a much better idea to watch an *encierro* from behind a grille. You will undoubtedly find that vicarious terror, or a confused bull charging the barricade you are peering through, is thrilling enough. Only the foolhardy subscribe to the *pamplonica* theory that the large number of *encierro* survivors proves that a well-timed prayer to San Fermín is all one really needs, and that, with luck, in a few days you'll be singing the "*pobre de mí*" (poor me) with the rest of the fiesta stragglers.

The southwest countryside

Navarre province is enormously varied, ranging from the western Pyrenees to vineyards near Rioja to the desert-like Bardenas Reales north of Tudela. Pilgrims on their way to Santiago from France were obliged to travel through Navarre, with the result that Romanesque churches abound. It is a province to take one's time in, drive slowly (or better yet, ride a bike) and allow plenty of time to sit down and eat, for among the many things that makes Navarre a Basque province is its fine cuisine.

Southwest of Pamplona is **Lizarra** (Estella) ⓮, one of the Navarre's most monumental cities and the closest thing to a holy city for the Carlists. Among the splendid Romanesque churches in Lizarra are **Santa María Jus del Castillo** (which used to be a synagogue), **San Pedro** and **San Miguel**, while the 12th-century **Palacio de los Reyes** is a rare example of secular Romanesque architecture.

Not far southwest of Lizarra, at the foot of **Montejurra**, site of an historic Carlist victory over the Republican troops in 1873, is the **Monasterio de Irache** (open daily 10am–2pm; free), which had its own university in the 16th century. And further down the N-111 highway is **Viana**, founded in 1219 by Sancho the Strong. The Crown Princes of Navarre held the title of Prince of Viana until they assumed the throne. In the **Iglesia de Santa María** you can see the tomb of Cesare Borgia, who died in battle here in 1507.

The C-132 road takes you to **Tafalla**, where the Iglesia de Santa María has a beautiful Renaissance altarpiece. Before reaching Tafalla, veer to the left to visit **Artajona**, a fortified town that rises up in the distance like a ghost from the Middle Ages.

Olite

South from Tafalla is **Olite** ⓯, the former residence of the kings of Navarre from the 15th century. Their castle has been restored – *too* restored, in the opinion of some – and is used for theatre and music festivals, as well as a government-run parador). Two side trips from Olite are well worth the time: the village of **Ujué** has barely been touched since the Middle Ages and has miraculously survived intact; and the **Monasterio**

BELOW: the medieval village of Ujué.

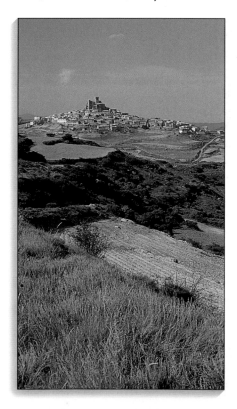

The parador in the 15th-century castle at Olite is a comfortable base if you're touring the area.

de la Oliva (open daily; free), used today by Trappist monks, was founded in 1134 by King García Ramírez.

Tudela

South of Olite on the A-15, **Tudela** ⑯ is one of those remarkable Spanish cities that illustrate the harmony in which Christians, Moors and Jews lived for several centuries. It was founded in 802 by the Moors, the remains of whose mosque can be seen today inside the **catedral**, a brilliant example of the transition from Romanesque to Gothic. The Last Judgement doorway in the main façade is a sculpted vision of the rewards and punishments supposedly awaiting us all. Tudela's old Jewish district, or *aljama*, is one of the best known in Spain. It is situated between the cathedral and the junction of the Ríos Queiles and Ebro.

Northeast from Tudela, just before you reach the N-240, is **Sangüesa** ⑰, located at the start of the Navarre Pyrenees. This is another 11th-century town, founded by Alfonso I, the Warrior, with another **Iglesia de Santa María**. This one has one of Spain's most beautiful Romanesque porticoes.

Nearby, above the Yesa Reservoir and surrounded by rugged mountains, is the **Monasterio de Leyre** ⑱ (open daily; guided tours only; entrance fee), Navarre's spiritual centre in the 11th century and pantheon of Navarre kings. Consecrated in 1057, it features beautiful Romanesque architecture, including a magnificent vaulted crypt. Abandoned in the 19th century, the monastery has been restored by Benedictine monks and now includes a hotel for those in search of tranquillity. Between here and Sangüesa is the 16th-century **Castillo de Javier**, dedicated to San Francisco Xavier, the great Jesuit

BELOW: Tudela's Plaza de los Fueros, at the heart of the the old town.

Map on page 288

missionary who was born in a house on this site. Pilgrims still visit the castle to pay homage to Xavier, and they say that one of the crucifixes there bled the day the saint died in 1552.

A tour of the valleys

By this time the traveller is entering the Valle de Roncal, one of a series of beautiful green valleys dotted with small villages that extend west to Guipúzcoa and east to Huesca and the High Pyrenees. These valleys have few monuments *per se* to offer, although there are isolated Romanesque churches and hermitages, but rather stand out more for their setting and traditional architecture. **Roncal** and **Isaba** are two of the major villages in the Roncal Valley, which is surrounded by peaks reaching as high as 2,000 metres (6,500 ft).

North of Ochagavía in the **Salazar Valley** is the **Irati Forest**, one of Europe's densest and largest beech forests, supplier of masts for the invincible *Armada* and said to be inhabited by witches. Continuing west you reach **Orreaga** (Roncesvalles) ❶, where pilgrims coming from France would stop for the night at one of the most important hostelries along the road to Santiago. Today it is an Augustine monastery. Also in Orreaga you can see the **Colegiata Real**, an overly restored Gothic construction in whose chapterhouse lies the enormous tomb of Sancho VII, the Strong (1154–1234), and his queen.

Smugglers and witches

Down the road from Orreaga to **Valcarlos** is the steep canyon where the famous ambush of 778 featured in the *Chanson de Roland* took place, and you can understand how Charlemagne's men didn't stand a chance against the Basque warriors perched high on either side. This is smugglers' country, and Valcarlos has more than a few families who have made small fortunes carrying merchandise back and forth over the French border, as do all the mountain villages in this area.

The last of the valleys before entering Guipúzcoa is the beautiful **Valle de Baztán** ❷, with its 14 villages of stone houses, many of them with noble coats-of-arms. There are a good deal more heraldic crests in Navarre than most other provinces, where an estimated 20 percent of the population during the heyday of the kingdom belonged to a noble family.

The capital of the Baztán is **Elizondo**, a resort town and residence of many *indianos* – Basques who went off to the New World, made money and returned to live out their days in their villages. North of Elizondo is **Arizcun**, one of the villages partially inhabited by *cagotes*, who suffered centuries of persecution due to their supposed descent from lepers, Jews, Moors, Visigoths or even Albigensians, depending upon whichever version one chooses to believe. Further north still is **Zugarramurdi**, where witches reputedly used to gather in caves to hold their *akelarres*, or covens. The caves were already inhabited in the Neolithic period, but their fame as the site of witches' gatherings arose from an Inquisition trial in Logroño in 1610, when 40 unfortunate women were accused of witchcraft and 12 of them were burned at the stake. ❑

BELOW: stone houses by the river in Elizondo.

CANTABRIA AND ASTURIAS

Map
on pages
308–9

*Few parts of Spain have greater natural beauty than
Cantabria and Asturias, where sandy beaches and rocky headlands
are backed by the soft greens and greys of the rugged landscape*

Madrid

The autonomous regions of Cantabria and Asturias lie between the Basque Country and Galicia along the Bay of Biscay or *Mar Cantábrico*. Each region consists of one narrow province: Santander and Asturias, respectively. A formidable mountain chain, the **Cordillera Cantábrica**, separates the coast and its narrow strip of fertile valleys from the *meseta*.

There are 72 beaches in Cantabria, stretching east to west from Castro-Urdiales to San Vicente de la Barquera, while the 290 km (180 miles) of coastline in Asturias is a succession of beaches, estuaries and promontories. From the 91-metre (300-ft) **Cabo de Peñas**, north of Gijón and Avilés, you can see a large part of it. On rainy days you may see the tiny figure of a solitary fisherman on a long stretch of sand at the foot of an immense weatherbeaten cliff. On a sunny day, the same spot will be filled with bathers and beach tents.

Even in summer there is snow on the **Picos de Europa**, which rise to over 2,640 metres (8,660 ft). The highest mountains in the Cordillera, they begin in Cantabria and almost completely cover Asturias. They are made up of the Cornión, Urrieles and Andorra massifs. The region containing the mountains which are the source of the rivers flowing into the Cantabrian Sea has long been called *La Montaña*.

LEFT: in the medieval village of Santillana del Mar. **BELOW:** the Iglesia de Santa María above the harbour in Castro-Urdiales.

From prehistory to modern times

Small nomadic bands of hunters and food-gatherers belonging to the Stone Age cultures decorated the walls and ceilings of the limestone caves in this region with pictures of the migratory animals they followed. The similarity between the decorated prehistoric caves in the limestone area of southern France and those of northern Spain led to the designation of a prehistoric "Franco-Cantabrian" cultural area, which includes a number of sites in the foothills of the Pyrenees in the Basque Country and in Asturias.

Castro-Urdiales ❶, the old Roman settlement of Flavio Briga, is the easternmost and one of the oldest ports on the coast of Cantabria. The **Playa de Brazomar** and the **Playa de Oriñón** at the mouth of the Ría Agüera are characteristically long, sandy Cantabrian beaches, a short walk from both summer resort facilities and an old quarter with medieval remains. From the small fortified peninsula, a ruined Templars' hostel, the "Castle " of Santa Ana and the Gothic **Iglesia de Santa María**, with French sculptures, flying buttresses and uncompleted towers reminiscent of Notre Dame in Paris, overlook the photogenic harbour filled with fishing boats.

The most important medieval pilgrimage trails led to Santiago de Compostela and, in the opposite direction, to Rome and on to Jerusalem. The powerful, rich

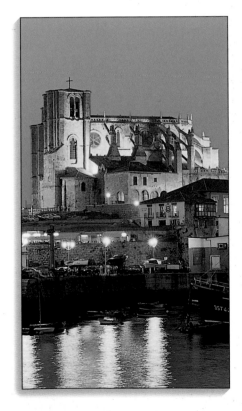

A splendid coast for sailing.

military Order of Knights Templars, ascetic monks in arms distinguished by their white habits embroidered with the red Crusaders' cross, was founded in 1120 to protect pilgrims on their way to Palestine. At Castro-Urdiales the Templars ministered to the pilgrims of St James and recruited suitable members for their main work in the Holy Land.

At **Laredo ❷**, the long, sandy beach attracts so many summer visitors that the off-season population of something over 10,000 will have multiplied by a factor of 10 by mid-August. This explains the highrises and summer houses that follow the curve of the beautiful beach.

In the Castilian Golden Age that followed the Reconquest, this part of the coast was the administrative centre of Cantabria, and Old Castile's only outlet to the sea. The size of the Cantabrian fleet which operated here increased dramatically in the 16th century. The ports on the Bay of Biscay were, according to a contemporary Venetian, the jewels in the Spanish emperor's crown. They were the basis of Spain's superior maritime capability. Ships carrying Spanish wine and wool sailed from San Sebastián, Laredo, Santander and La Coruña to Flanders and England, or into the Mediterranean through the Strait of Gibraltar. All along this coast churches were enhanced by the massive building campaign of the Catholic Monarchs as well as from their location on the pilgrim trail. In Laredo, for example, a 16th-century doorway was added to the 13th-century Gothic **Iglesia de Nuestra Señora de la Asunción**.

In 1556 Carlos V, having abdicated in favour of his son Felipe II, sailed into Laredo from Flanders on the way to his Hieronymite monastery in Extremadura. With him arrived his sister, Mary of Hungary, ruler of the Netherlands, and the art treasures accumulated by both these great Habsburg collectors. The Spanish

BELOW: beach life in Santander.

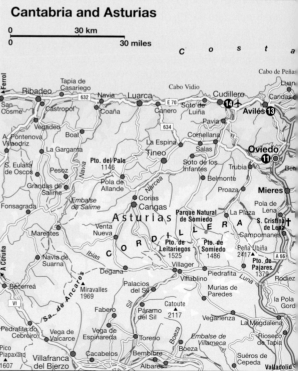

Cantabria and Asturias

public collections still hold most of the priceless works of Flemish art carried across Spain from Laredo more than 400 years ago.

Across **Santoña Bay** from Laredo is the port and resort of **Santoña ❸**. It has another church begun in the 13th century and several beaches, including the splendid 2-km long **Playa de Nueva Berria**.

Castilian summer retreat

The important modern port of **Santander ❹** has been the provincial capital since the 18th century, when the French depredated the coastal area to the east. The city centre, rebuilt after much of it was destroyed by a fire in 1941, looks south across a beautiful protected bay. On a clear day you can see the Cordillera Cantábrica from the busy quay.

There are nice beaches (El Camella, La Concha, La Primera and La Segunda, all joined at low tide) facing out to sea in the older residential and resort quarter, **El Sardinero**. Here, too, are the Gran Casino del Sardinero, the International Menéndez Pelayo University, which offers summer courses to foreign students, and the large old-fashioned resort hotel, the Hotel Real. On the **Península de La Magdalena** is the neo-Gothic summer palace of the royal family, an imitation of Balmoral built by Alfonso XIII in 1912 for his English queen. It is now part of the International University.

On a rainy day, visit the **Museo de Bellas Artes** (open Mon–Sat; free) on the Calle Rubio west of the Plaza Porticada. It shares a building with the library donated by the Santander writer, Marcelino Menéndez y Pelayo (1856–1912), whose statue is in the garden leading to the house. The museum has an interesting small collection ranging from Zurbarán to contemporary Cantabrian artists

Map below

TIP

A good time to visit Santander is during July or August, when the town hosts an international festival of music, dance and drama.

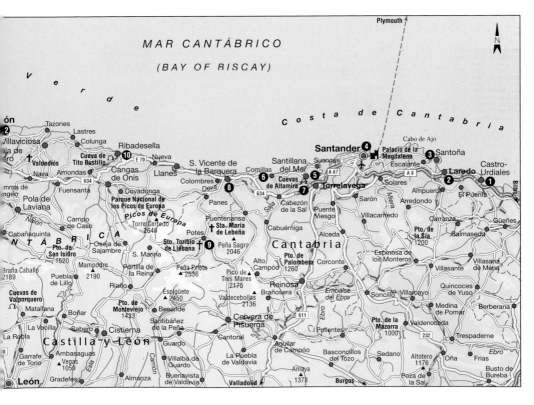

and roomy galleries for temporary exhibitions. Here hang portraits of three of Spain's less-beloved rulers: Fernando VII, Isabel II, deposed in 1868 while summering in the Basque Country, and General Franco. The portrait of Fernando, one of several painted by Goya of this weak and cruel king, is believed to have been commissioned by the city of Santander. Nearby Goya's four famous series of etchings are displayed: the *Caprichos*, the *Disasters of War*, the *Tauromaquía* and the *Disparates* or *Proverbios*.

The **Museo de Prehistoria y Arqueología** (open Tues–Sun; free) in the Diputación Provincial near the Puerto Chico, where fishing boats are moored, provides an introduction to the Late-Paleolithic cave art found in this region.

Medieval to *modernista*

The resorts of **Santillana del Mar ❺** and **Comillas ❻** on the coast west of Santander are crowded in summer with well-heeled Spaniards from further south. This is an agreeable area of first-rate beaches, pretty farms overlooking the sea, medieval and Renaissance churches and balconied, galleried and escutcheoned granite Golden Age palaces or town houses.

Santillana is an amazingly well-preserved medieval village, with fine stone mansions and cobbled streets. The 12th to 13th-century Romanesque **La Colegiata** contains the bones of one of the virgin saints, the 4th-century St Juliana. "Santillana" is derived from the Latin *Sancta Juliana*. The Colegiata itself, like many other churches in the French-influenced Romanesque style, was designed to serve as a roomy reliquary entered through the elegant round-arched west portal. Despite the cosmopolitanism it has acquired over a thousand years or so, Santillana has been able to preserve the character of a market town. The Para-

BELOW: Gaudí's handiwork in Comillas.

dor Nacional Gil Blas on the main square, one of the most popular paradors in Spain, is named for the picaresque hero of *Gil Blas de Santillane*, a novel by the 18th-century French satirist Alain-Rene Le Sage, and later a verse play by Victor Hugo. Both attacked social problems in France while pretending to write about Spain.

In Comillas, follow the signs to **El Capricho**, the summer house built to the designs of the Catalan architect Gaudí in 1883–85. At El Capricho, Gaudí combined references to the squat Romanesque columns, the minaret, mudéjar brickwork, the traditional Spanish iron balcony, the pink neo-Gothic **Palacio Sobrellano** adjacent to it, and – most imaginatively of all – the shapes and colours of the Cantabrian countryside and seashore.

Map on pages 308–9

Cave art from 12,000 BC

Altamira ❼ is about 1.5 km (less than 1 mile) south of Santillana del Mar. The "Sistine Chapel" of cave art was the first, and arguably is still the finest, Palaeolithic-decorated cave identified. Altamira's authenticity was not generally accepted until the early years of the 20th century, when other caves, to which the entrances had been blocked – ruling out any possibility of a hoax – were discovered. Ironically, the quality and precise detail of figures such as the pregnant bison were the greatest impediment to Altamira's acceptance.

The Costa Verde

Looking down for a change instead of up, the view of **San Vicente de la Barquera** ❽, 10 km (6 miles) west of Comillas, is one of the nicest surprises on the Cantabrian coast. As you travel west, the little harbours on which the old ports

BELOW: polychrome painting of a bison, Altamira.

PREHISTORY AT ALTAMIRA

In 1879 Don Marcelino de Sautuola, who lived in a villa near the site and who had seen some small engraved Paleolithic art objects which were accepted as genuine at the Universal Exposition in Paris the year before, realised by their similarity that the paintings at Altamira were prehistoric. The bison, hinds, wild boar, horses and other animals on the ceiling at Altamira are the largest known group of "polychromes", that is, figures which were painted using several colours of pigment (ochres, manganese oxides, charcoal, iron carbonate). The three most important polychrome sites in the world are Altamira, Tito Bustillo (in Asturias) and Lascaux in Perigord, France (the last of which cannot be visited). Some of these sophisticated figures of 15,000 years ago are large – over 2 metres (6 ft) long – while the ceiling is low, so the best way to view them is by lying on your back.

To preserve the paintings' condition, visitor numbers are strictly controlled – to see the cave paintings you must book at least ten months ahead by writing to **Museo de Altamira**, 39330 Santillana del Mar, Santander, specifying the number of people in your party and naming a date. The museum itself, with exhibits explaining the significance of the paintings, is open Tues–Sun (am only) and is free.

were built become wider, the river valleys look greener and the mountains are higher. The fortified walls and castle, and the 13th to 16th-century **Iglesia de Santa María de los Angeles** (open daily; free) on the pine-clad headland, are reflected in the inlet spanned by the 17th-century **Puente de la Maza**, a stone bridge with 28 arches. The beach, the **Sable de Merón**, is almost 3 km (2 miles) long and as much as 100 metres (328 ft) wide when the tide is out.

The Picos de Europa form the biggest national park in Europe. The limestone mountain range offers excellent climbing and hiking trails. Good roads through the park also make the spectacular scenery accessible by car.

Mozarabic art

Leave the coast at San Vicente and take the road that follows the **Ría Deva** valley to **Panes**, and then up into the eastern end of the **Picos de Europa** in the direction of the village of **Potes ❾**.

The narrow Desfiladero de la Hermida may be slow going as it criss-crosses the Santander-Asturias border, but it widens north of Potes to form the austere mountain setting for one of the jewels of mozarabic architecture, the **Iglesia de Santa María de Lebeña**. Founded by Alfonso, Count of Liébana (924–63), and his wife Justa, possibly immigrants from Andalusia, it combines the architectural concepts of the mosque with the forms of local pre-Romanesque Asturian churches, with its small agglomerative compartments and tunnel vaults, which had developed independently north of the Cordillera Cantábrica from the 8th century, based to some degree on Visigothic prototypes. Like the Asturian churches, Santa María was completely vaulted over.

Entered by a side door, the church has the feeling of a mosque, due in part to its horseshoe arches. Its 15th-century red, white and blue Virgin is now part of an 18th-century retable. A stone stele re-used by a 9th-century builder is carved with Visigothic designs in roundels. A primitive human figure in the lower left

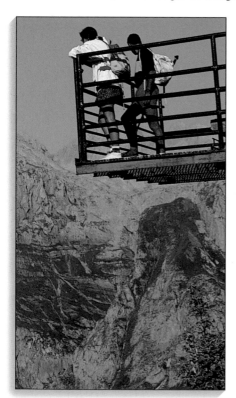

corner of the stele was painted, it is said, with a mixture of blood and ashes. At the time Santa María was built, this remote area had been a centre of monastic culture for several centuries. It was in the monastery of **Santo Toribio de Lebaña**, a few miles south, that the 8th-century monk Beatus wrote his commentaries on the Apocalypse and the Book of Daniel. The *Beatos*, as they were called, were illuminated in the scriptoria of various monasteries in the following centuries. As examples of mozarabic art, they are as important as Santa María. Santo Toribio also possesses what is claimed to be the entire right arm of Christ's wooden cross.

The Fuente Dé Parador west of Potes is located at the source of the Ría Deva and surrounded by high peaks. It is open all year, and climbers use it as a base. The view from the **Mirador del Cable**, reached by a cable car which runs all year from Fuente Dé, takes in Potes, the Deva Valley, the nearby wildlife reserves and the mountains.

Asturias

Returning to the coast and entering the kingdom of Asturias, you will find yourself on an increasingly irregular shoreline. Sandy beaches and port resorts lie between high promontories. Pretty **Llanes** has a cliff walk, the **Paseo de San Pedro**, and 30 small beaches. Ask when the charming Asturian folk dance called

El Pericote is to be performed. A prehistoric menhir carved with an anthropomorphic figure called Peña Tu is at Vidiago close by; at **Colombres** is one of the more important decorated caves, El Pindal.

Ribadesella ❿ occupies the east bank of the estuary of the Río Sella. One of the most important Franco-Cantabrian caves, **Tito Bustillo** (open May–Sept: Tues –Sun; entrance fee), is west of the port across the bridge over the estuary. The original entrance has been lost, so that it is uncertain whether the paintings here were exposed to daylight. On a red ochre-painted wall overhanging the habitation site, more than 20 animals were painted in other colours and then engraved with flint tools. The size of these well-observed animals is considerable, averaging over 2 metres (6 ft). They include at least one reindeer, a species rarely encountered in Cantabrian Palaeolithic art. To prevent deterioration of the paintings, the number of visitors per day is strictly limited, so be sure to arrive early, especially in high season.

Sea and cider

An overwhelming mural painting by the Uria Aza brothers, depicting the horrors of modern war in the church at Ribadesella, is worth a sobering look, as is the view of mountains and port life from the quay.

In any of the fishing villages here, you can eat excellent *caldereta* (fish stew), hake in cider or locally caught shellfish such as sea urchins. Cider, the traditional Asturian drink, is aerated by being poured from a bottle held some distance from the glass. Visitors tend to spill a lot, but it does not seem to matter. You may be treated to the local folk songs; Asturian voices are said to have both the depth of the mountain valleys and the lilt of the sea.

Map on pages 308–9

Asturian cider advert dating from the late 19th century.

BELOW: the grandeur of the Picos de Europa.

From Ribadesella it is a pleasant excursion to **Covadonga** in the Parque Nacional de los Picos de Europa. In a green, tree-shaded valley lies the important national shrine of Covadonga, where in the 8th century Pelayo, an Asturian warrior, crushed a Muslim force, thus becoming a symbol of Christian resistance to the invaders. A statue of Pelayo stands near a neo-Romanesque church. Continuing into the park, you reach two glacier-formed lakes, Enol and La Ercina. In the background are the snow-capped peaks of the Picos.

Oviedo – the capital of Asturias

Unless you are able to make an extended visit to Asturias, you should go first to **Oviedo** ⓫ (population about 200,000), the provincial capital of the kingdom of Asturias. It is on a plain of meadows, surrounded by fields of maize, apple orchards and small prosperous towns.

Orient yourself by the large park in the city centre, the **Parque de San Francisco**. With the tall grey post office tower on your left, walk straight ahead to the old ecclesiastical district much damaged in the anti-Fascist uprising of working-class parties led by the miners in 1934 and in the Civil War soon afterwards. The tourist office, with its models of Asturian churches, is on the Plaza Alfonso II El Casto, next to the remains of the pre-Romanesque **Iglesia de San Tirso** built by that king. The flamboyant Gothic cathedral, the **Basilica del Salvador** (open Mon–Sat; entrance fee), its perforated spire damaged in the 1930s and subsequently restored, contains the Pantheon of the Asturian Kings and the Cámara Santa, their reliquary chapel.

Behind the cathedral is a burial ground for pilgrims to Santiago de Compostela and a superb **Museo Arqueológico** (open Tues–Sun; free) in the Monas-

ABOVE: the region's traditional footwear.
BELOW: Santa María de Naranco as night falls.

terio de San Vicente. The museum's treasures include prehistoric artefacts, Roman mosaics and pre-Romanesque artwork.

Several of the finest pre-Romanesque Asturian buildings can be found in Oviedo, including the basilican church of San Julián de los Prados (*circa* 830) with illusionistic wall paintings. It was built in the reign of Alfonso II to adjoin one of the king's palaces. On **Mount Naranco,** the barrel-vaulted Santa María de Naranco, originally a royal hall built for Ramiro I in the mid-9th century, and the incomplete San Miguel de Lillo of the same period, are close together on the same hillside.

Mountain views and fishing villages

It is only an hour's drive directly south to Puerto de Pajares (1,379 metres/4,524 ft), a pass in the Picos on the border between Asturias and León. At **Mieres**, a steelworkers' town along the way, the Socialist Republic was proclaimed on 5 October 1934. Past Mieres, and accessible only by doubling back through **Pola de Lena**, the single-naved early 10th-century pre-Romanesque **Iglesia de Santa Cristina** is perched on a hill and visible from the highway.

Heading back towards the coast, the fishing-port resorts around **Gijón** with their folkloric festivals, and all of the pre-Romanesque churches in the area, are within easy driving distance. Gijon itself is an industrial port and the biggest Asturian city, with a population of 271,000. The old part of town is located on a narrow isthmus, centring around the arcaded **Plaza Mayor.**

Avilés ⑬, further west, also has a charming old town concealed within its industrial shell. The area around the Plaza de España is ancient and intimate, and filled with bustling bars and restaurants. Continuing approximately 20 km (12 miles) further west along the N-632 brings you to **Cudillero ⑭**, one of the most extraordinary Asturian fishing villages, with houses hanging from steep rock walls over the ramp leading down to the harbour. Restaurants serving fresh sardines and cider line either side of the dramatic ravine.

Luarca is really not much more than a cluster of slate-roofed houses but is a lively village and a good place to stay the night if you are touring this section of the Costa Verde. Just beyond the nearby village of Navia, a left turn up the AS-12 leads to the Celtic castro at **Coaña**, a cluster of circular stone foundations dating from the Iron Age.

Less than 20 km (12 miles) inland from the coast along the N-634 is the memorable old quarter of **Salas**, where the Valdés Salas castle, former residence of the Marquis of Valdés Salas, a leader of the Inquisition, is now a hotel and restaurant. From the Espinass Pass, which has a superlative 360-degree view, descend south to **Tineo** on the AS-216. Tineo is known for its ham industry and for the 14th-century García-Tineo and 16th-century Meras palaces.

The **Parque Natural de Somiedo**, southwest of Oviedo, surrounds the Teverga and Quirós valleys, extending into the peaks of the neighbouring province of León. The park is populated by wolves and European brown bears, and more than a dozen glacial lakes dot the landscape. ❑

Map on pages 308–9

TIP

Delicious Asturian specialities include *fabada*, a rich white bean stew. The local pork and sausages are also good, as are cheeses such as the pungent *Cabrales* and spicy *Los Beyos*.

BELOW: lush pastures in the Parque Natural de Somiedo.

GALICIA

Spain's green northwestern corner keeps a spectacular coastline. Inland, historic pilgrimage routes cut across empty sierras to meet at Santiago de Compostela

Map on page 318

Criss-crossed by myriad rivers and mountain ranges, the most northwestern region of Galicia is a land of unforgettable vistas and ocean-chiselled coastline. Across this nature-blessed region can be found treasures that are a legacy of the Celts, the Seubi, the Romans and the Visigoths who conquered and settled it. Isolated from the rest of Spain by a bulwark of mountains on the east and south and bounded to the north and west by the tumultuous North Atlantic, Galicia's natural formations include craggy mountains, long, loping valleys and distinctive *rías* or estuaries.

Half of its area lies between altitudes of 400 to 600 metres (1,300 and 2,000 ft) and less than one-fifth at altitudes lower than 400 metres. Mountains ring the interior, separating the region from the Spanish provinces of Asturias, León and Zamora to the east and Portugal to the south. Galicia is a *Finisterre*, or Land's End, as the Romans named its westernmost point. Despite occasional blasts from Atlantic storms and an average rainfall of 102 cm (40 inches). Galicia's winters are mild enough for residents of the regional capital, Santiago de Compostela, to term their city "the place where rain is art".

In spring and summer a striking palette of colours – deep green, yellow and orange – blooms, and the milder weather attracts thousands of tourists to its beaches. Lining the 380 km (240 miles) of its bold, indented coastline are quaint fishing villages, busy resorts and the major ports of Vigo and A Coruña. The *rías* in the north are known as the **Rías Altas** and those along the southwest as the **Rías Baixas**.

LEFT: modern-day pilgrims on the road to Santiago. **BELOW:** fisherman putting out to sea in the Ría de Coruña.

Celtic roots

Galicia and its people retain many traces of the Celts, who swept through from 900–600 BC and established a hold on this windswept, rain-soaked land that they did not relinquish until the arrival of the Romans in 137 BC. The region's name is derived from "Gallaeci", the name by which the Celtic tribes were known to the Romans; they coexisted for three centuries, the golden age of Celtic culture. Hundreds of ruined hilltop *castros*, or fortified Celtic settlements, survive: those at Viladonga (Lugo) and Monte Tecla (Pontevedra) are especially worthwhile.

Centuries before the Celts invaded, the indigenous people lived in *pallozas*, conical-shaped stone houses with thatched roofs. In isolated inland areas, such as Os Ancares in Ourense Province and parts of Lugo Province, some peasants lived in *pallozas* together with their animals until recently, but now Os Ancares (O Piornedo village) is a tourist sight. The people of Galicia have never lived in large numbers in towns and even today the population of 2.7 million is scattered among the region's 40,000 parishes.

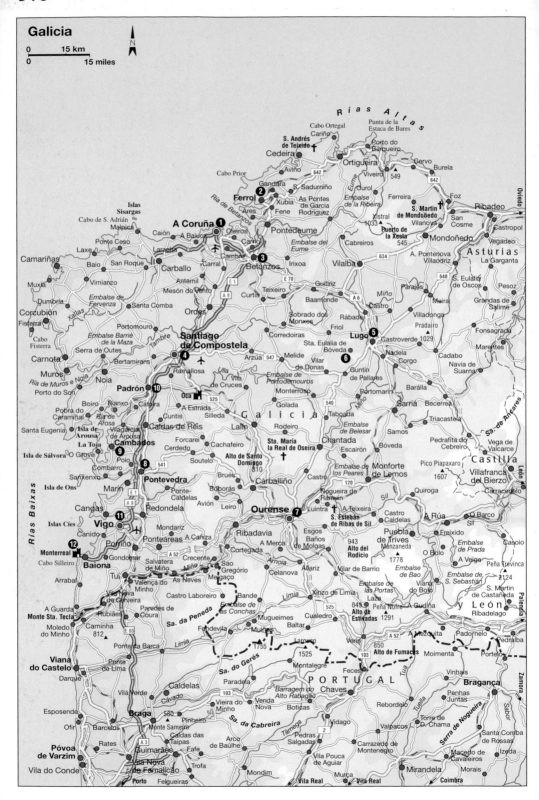

Galicia

0 15 km
0 15 miles

N

Rías Altas

Cabo Ortegal
Punta de la
Estaca de Bares
Cariño
Porto do
Barqueiro
S. Andrés
de Teixido
Cedeira
Ortigueira
Cervo
Burela
Aviño
Viveiro
549
Cabo Prior
Gandara
S. Sadurniño
Ourol
Embalse
de la Ribeira
Ferreira
Foz
Islas
Sisargas
Ferrol ②
Xubia
Fene
As Pontes
de García
Rodríguez
Ares
Pontedeume
Cabreiros
Xistral
1033 ▲
**S. Martín
de Mondoñedo**
Vilanova
San
Cosme
Ribadeo
Cabo de S. Adrián
Malpica
A Baiuca
Oleiros
Cambre
A Coruña ①
Carrio
Embalse del
Eume
**Puerto de
la Xesta**
545
Mondoñedo
Castropol
Vegadeo
Asturias
Ponte Ceso
Caión
Laracha
Irixoa
634
A. Pontenova
Villaodriz
La Garganta
Laxe
San Roque
Carral
Betanzos ③
Villadonga
640
S. Eulalia
de Oscos
Pesoz
Camariñas
Baio
Carballo
Antemil
Teixeiro
Baamonde
Miño
Castro
Pradairo
Grandas de
Salime
Muxía
Vimianzo
Mesón do Vento
Curtis
Vilalba
Meira
Embalse de
Fervenza
A 9
E 70
Guitiriz
A 6
Villadonga
Fonsagrada
Dumbría
Santa Comba
Ordes
Corredoiras
Sobrado dos
Monxes
Rábade
Friol
Castroverde 1029
Cadabo
Navia de
Suarna
Corcubión
Fisterra
Portomouro
**Santiago
de Compostela** ④
Melide
Sta. Eulalia
de Bóveda
Lugo ⑤
Nadela
Corgo
Marentes
Cabo
Fisterra
Embalse Barrié
de la Maza
Arzúa
547
Vilar
de Donas
⑥
Guntín
de Pallares
Barálla
Carnota
Serra de Outes
Bertamirans
Ramallosa
Ulla
de Cruces
Vila
de Cruces
Monterroso
Portomarín
Sarria
Becerreá
Muros
Noia
Oca ♠
A Estrada
Embalse de
Portodemouros
540
Taboada
Samos
Triacastela
Ría de Muros e Noia
Porto do Son
Padrón ⑩
Catoira
525
Cuntis
Silleda
Golada
Rodeiro
Embalse
de Belesar
Bóveda
Pedrafita do
Cebreiro
Vega de
Valcarce
Pobra do
Caramiñal
Rianxo
Boiro
Galicia
Chantada
Castilla
Santa Eugenia
Isla de
Arosa
Ría de
Arosa
Vilagarcía
de Arousa
Caldas de Reis
Forcarei
Cerdedo
Cachafeiro
Alto de Santo
Domingo
810
Lalín
Sta. María
la Real de Oseira ✝
Escairón
Embalse de
los Peares
**Monforte
de Lemos**
Pico Piapaxaro
1607
**Villafranca
del Bierzo**
La Toja
O Grove
Cambados ⑨
Poio
Combarro
Soutelo
Brués
Boborás
Carballiño
Castro
120
Nogueira de
Ramuín
Quiroga
Carracedelo
Isla de Sálvora
Sanxenxo
⑧
Pontevedra
541
Marín
Ponte-
Caldelas
Avión
Leiro
Ourense ⑦
A Teixeira
S. Esteban
de Ribas de Sil
Castro
Caldelas
A Rúa
O Barco
Isla de Ons
Cangas
Redondela
Mondariz
Ribadavia
Esgos
Baños
de Molgas
943
Alto del
Rodicio
Puebla
de Trives
Manzaneda
O Bolo
Freixido
Sil
Casoio
Vigo ⑪
Canido
Ponteareas
A Cañiza
A Merca
Amoia
Celanova
Allariz
1778
Embalse
de Bao
A Veiga
Embalse de
Prada
Islas Cíes
Porriño
Cortegada
Vilar de Barrio
Viana
do Bolo
Embalse de,
S. Sebastián
Peña Trevinca
2124
Monterreal ⑫
Baiona
Cabo Silleiro
Gondomar
Salvaterra
de Miño
Crecente
São
Gregório
Melgaço
Castro Laboreiro
Límia
Xinzo de Limia
525
Laza
849
Alto de
Estivadas 1291
Peña Nofre
1291
A Gudiña
S. Martín
de Castañeda
Ribadelago
Arrabal
Tui
Vila Nova
de Cerveira
As Neves
Bande
Mugueimes
Cualedro
A Mezquita
Padornelo
Pedralba
A Guarda
Monte Sta. Tecla
Rubiães
Paredes
de Coura
Sa. da Peneda
Embalse de
las Conchas
Baltar
Verín
850
Alto de Fumaces
Moimenta
Portelo
Moledo
do Minho
Caminha
812
Fendevila
Muiños
1755
Larouco
A 52
y León
Ponte da Barca
Límia
1525
Montalegre
Feces
103
Bragança
**Viana
do Castelo**
Ponte
de Lima
Sa. do Gerês
Portugal
Chaves
Tua
Vinhais
Darque
Vilá Verde
Paradela
Barragem do
Alto Rabagão
Rebordelo
Penhas
Juntas
Esposende
Caldelas
103
Vieira do
Minho
Venda
Nova
Boticas
Yidago
Valpaços
Torre de
D. Chama
Santa Comba
de Rossas
Ofir
Barcelos
Pinheiro
Monte Sameiro
580
Tâmega
2
Pedras
Salgadas
Rebordelo
Sabor
Izeda
**Póvoa
de Varzim**
Rates
Braga
Caldas das
Taipas
Arco
de Baúlhe
Sa. da Cabreira
Vila Pouca
de Aguiar
Carrazedo de
Montenegro
Murça
Macedo
de Cavaleiros
Morais
Vila do Conde
A 3
Guimarães
Fafe
Mondim
Mirandela
**Vila Nova
de Famalicão**
Trofa
Porto
Felgueiras
Vila Real
Vila Real
Coimbra

Rías Baixas

An independent land

Galicia remained relatively free of Muslim influence and developed a distinct cultural personality. Linguists place the beginning of the Galician language in the early 11th century, by which time it had been an independent kingdom for 500 years, albeit ruled from Asturias and León between the 8th and 11th centuries. The Galician culture showed greater affinity for Portuguese culture than for that of Spain until the final separation of the two countries in 1668. But by the time Galicia came under the rule of the Catholic Monarchs, who established the *Junta* of the kingdom of Galicia in 1495, the region had firm economic and religious ties to the central kingdom because of the importance of Santiago de Compostela as a pilgrimage destination.

Abundant rainfall gives Galicia the appearance of a bucolic paradise, but it is not so much the agricultural blessing one might suppose. Excessive rain causes severe erosion and the soil retains little moisture. Uneven terrain also makes the mechanisation of farming nearly impossible in large parts of the region, while the division of the land into small family farms, known as *minifundio*, which average just 250 sq. metres (300 sq. yds) stymies political attempts to bring about reforms leading to industrial-type farming. Everyone has some land and no one wants to give up his small parcels, which are usually spread apart, because of the way land has been passed down through inheritance.

Recent government efforts to join plots belonging to different families have failed, largely because of suspicions that the new plans would benefit the investors rather than the locals. Yet three out of ten Galician families still live off the land, the highest proportion of any European region. A regional herd of a million dairy and beef cattle provide superb quality meat and milk. The latter is used to make local farmhouse cheeses such as breast-shaped *tetilla*.

Map opposite

The Celts have a genius for poetry and music, and a deep love of what they call "Terra Nosa" (Our Land). Today, this is expressed in everything from Celtic rock music to the revival of the local "galego" language.

BELOW: the Torre de Hércules lighthouse near A Coruña.

A Coruña

A good point of departure for travellers planning to tour the Rías Altas is the port city of **A Coruña ❶** in the very northwestern corner of Spain. It has been a key shipping centre for nearly 2,000 years. Julius Caesar entered it by way of Gaul (France) in AD 60 to re-establish Roman rule in several rebellious towns nearby. The old part of the city (La Ciudad Vieja) rises from a narrow strip of land pointing out into the Atlantic, while the new section (La Pescadería) rests on the edge of the mainland and an isthmus. Because of its position near a great sea route between northern Europe and South and Central America, A Coruña continues to play an important role as a major Atlantic port with a large fishing fleet and oil refinery.

The city's showpiece is its **Torre de Hércules** (open daily), the world's only Roman-era lighthouse, which stands on the northernmost edge of the isthmus, 10 minutes by car or tram from the city centre. It dates from the time of the Celtic chieftain Breogan and was rebuilt during the reign of Trajan, the Roman Emperor born in Spain in AD 98. It looks down on the wreck of the *Mar Egeo* oil tanker, a chilling reminder of the ecological disaster caused when it ran aground on the rocks in 1992.

The characteristic enclosed glass balconies (*miradores*) of the pretty white buildings lining the seafront permit residents to admire the bay while protecting them from stiff ocean winds. The open nature of its people have made A Coruña known as "the city where no one is a stranger".

Although a native son of Galicia, Franco viewed regional loyalty as anti-Spanish, and prohibited the teaching and official use of the Galician language.

To take in the sun, cross the old city and stop at the downtown beach, **Riazor**, or take a short cab ride towards the mainland and swim at **Santa Cristina** beach on the isthmus. In the old section, pass along the gardens lining **Avenida de la Marina** and then walk over to the grandiose **Plaza de María Pita**, named after the heroine who courageously gave the alarm alerting citizens of an attack by the English admiral, Sir Francis Drake, in 1589. A few streets south is the **Castelo de San Antón**, once a prison and now an archaeological museum with a varied collection of Roman, Visigothic and even Egyptian artefacts (open Tues–Sat; also Sun, Apr–Sept; entrance fee).

The churches of **Santiago** (12th century), **María del Campo** (13th century) and **Santo Domingo** (17th century) are in the city's old section, as is the stunning **Museo de Arte Sacro** of religious silver (open Tues–Fri and Sat am; entrance fee). Just south of the old section and overlooking the harbour is the **Jardín de San Carlos**, an enclosed garden containing the granite tomb of Sir John Moore, the Englishman who died in 1809 while helping to defend the city against the French during the Peninsular War.

Franco's birthplace

An hour's drive east along the coast from A Coruña leads to the major upper *ría* on whose edge lies the city of **O Ferrol ❷**, founded during the Middle Ages. The large estuary, 6 km (4 miles) wide, forms a near-perfect, protected deep-water port where one of Spain's principal naval bases has existed since the 18th century. Shipbuilding flourished here till the closure of the yards in the 1980s, since when the town has struck hard times.

General Francisco Franco was born and grew up here, the son of a navy supply clerk. During his rule the city was officially known as *El Ferrol del Caudillo* (of the Leader). A huge equestrian statue of Franco still dominates the **Plaza de España**. Among Spaniards, Galicians are known as a conservative, cunning people. It is said that if a Galician is seen on a staircase it is hard to determine whether he is going up or down. Perhaps this is why they make such astute politicians; the rosta includes Fidel Castro, the Cuban president; Pablo Iglesias, the Founder of Spanish socialism; and Raul Alfonsín, the Argentine president.

The roads to Santiago

Cutting across Galicia from all points of the compass are the roads which pilgrims travelled to Santiago; the original Cantabrian *camino* from the Asturian coast; the French *camino* from the Pyrenées and via the Benedictine monastery at **Samos**; the so-called English *camino* from A Coruña and Betanzos; the Portuguese coastal route via Tui and Pontevedra; and, finally, the route up from Central Spain via Ourense.

Betanzos ❸ lies at the mouth of a *ría* easily reached (20 minutes east by car) from A Coruña. The city reached its apogee in the 14th and 15th centuries when the nearby **Las Marinas Valley** provided wheat for the entire A Coruña province. Three impressive but small Gothic churches, **Santa María del Azogue** (founded late 1300s), **San Francisco** (1387) and **Santiago**, have been well-preserved and serve as an illustration of the town's best moments.

The pilgrimage capital

An hour's drive south from A Coruña through high mountain passes on the smooth A-9 toll highway is a panorama of rustic Galician beauty. A feeling of entering the heart of this country, **Santiago de Compostela ❹**, is confirmed by the sight of the twin baroque towers of the city's **catedral** (open daily 7am–9pm), which shelters the tomb of St James, patron saint of Spain.

After the discovery of the tomb of St James between AD 812 and 814, immediate support from the Asturian king and his successors and later the offering – *voto de Santiago* – of the Spanish monarchs created within an otherwise turbulent province a bustling town and then a cosmopolitan city that eventually became the "light of the Christian world in the Middle Ages". Over the saint's tomb, King Alfonso II of Asturias ordered the erection of an earthen temple, later replaced by a stone church under the rule of Alfonso III. In 997, al-Mansur Abu Jafar (military commander of the Caliphate of Córdoba) destroyed the entire town except for the tomb. But in 1075 work began on the present cathedral by order of King Alfonso VI of León and Castile.

The Romanesque building (consecrated in 1211) occupies the east end of the **Praza do Obradoiro**. Its baroque façade by Fernando Casas y Novoa has graced the entrance to the cathedral since 1750. The interplay of curved and

Map on page 318

TIP

From O Ferrol, take a train ride along the wildest stretch of the Rías Altas to the magically atmospheric headland of Cabo de Bares.

BELOW: the harbour at Betanzos.

St James looks out from the cathedral.

BELOW:
the shrine of St James in Santiago de Compostela.

straight lines on the carvings appears to culminate in flickers of flame at the height of the two slender towers. Walk around the cathedral's contrasting four plazas, unique in Spain, for views back on to the building. Inside the baroque façade is *El Pórtico da Gloria*, the tripartite porch depicting the Last Judgment by Maestro Mateo, considered one of the greatest masterpieces in the Romanesque style.

The well-travelled path of thousands of pilgrims through Navarre and Galicia became known as *El Camino de Santiago* (Road to Santiago). The number of pilgrims increased dramatically after Pope Calixto II conceded the Roman Catholic Church's greatest privileges to the See of Santiago de Compostela and designated as Holy Years those in which the day of St James fell on a Sunday. Pilgrims who reached Santiago in those years obtained a plenary indulgence and absolution for one year. The shrine became the greatest place of Christian pilgrimage after Rome and Jerusalem. The cathedral inspired the design of numerous others. The city itself emerged as one of Europe's most brilliant, attracting outstanding artists, scholars and silver and goldsmiths. Santiago is still a bustling pilgrimage city; an estimated 3 million visitors now visit during a Holy Year. It is also a major university town and the region's administrative capital.

The cathedral

Inside the cathedral, the high altar is dominated by a sumptuously attired 13th-century statue of St James. Some pilgrims mount the stairs behind the altar to kiss the saint's mantle. Below the altar, a crypt constructed in the foundations of the 9th-century church holds the remains of the saint (which went missing from 1589–1879) and two of his disciples, St Theodore and St Athanasius.

THE SANTIAGO LEGEND

According to legend, a Spanish peasant led to a field by a shower of stars – *campus stella* – discovered the tomb of the Apostle of Jesus. St James had been martyred in Jerusalem in AD 44 but his remains are said to have returned by boat with his followers to Spain, where he supposedly travelled and evangelised.

The discovery became a focus of unity for Christians who were then separated politically and spread across a narrow strip of northern Spain. It inspired Christian efforts to carry out the Reconquest which would eventually force Muslims off the Iberian peninsula. Historians now dispute whether St James ever visited Spain, but there is no doubt that the idea of the possession of the sacred remains of the saint aroused tremendous passion and pride, and emboldened the Christians. As their battle cry, the Christian soldiers shouted "*Santiago y cierre España!*" (St James, and close Spain!") to urge their brethren to defeat the Muslims. Christian fighters also gave their patron the name of *Matamoros* (Slayer of Moors).

Historians have passed on numerous testimonies by Spanish champions who said they were spurred on by "visions of a white knight on horseback brandishing a fear-inspiring sword and wearing a vengeful grimace".

Map
on page
318

Other obligatory stops include the *Puerta de las Platerías* (Silversmith's Door), a Romanesque doorway so named because it led outside on to a plaza lined by silversmith shops, and the *Puerta Santa* (Holy Door), opened during Holy Years.

Across the Praza do Obradoiro from the cathedral stairs, the **Pazo de Raxoi**, a severe but impressive 18th-century mansion designed by French architect Charles Lemaur, serves as City Hall. It is capped by a bronze sculpture of Santiago the Moor Slayer in battle gear, riding a charging stallion. At the plaza's south end is the **Colegio de San Jerónimo**, a 17th-century building attractive for its 15th-century-style gateway. The north side of the plaza is occupied by the **Hostal de los Reyes Católicos**, begun in 1501 under orders of Ferdinand and Isabella as an inn and hospital for pilgrims. It is now a very luxurious hotel, forming part of the state-run *parador* chain. The building's façade features an ornate Plateresque doorway of great beauty, and the wrought-iron work and carved columns in a chapel inside are of exceptional artistic merit.

A formidable fireworks display at midnight on 25 July each year initiates the week-long festivities dedicated to Santiago.

Tourists and pilgrims

Heading out of the plaza between the cathedral and the Colegio de San Jerónimo, turn into the **Rua do Franco**, where university students, tourists and pilgrims mingle among bars, shops and colleges. The **Colegio de Fonseca** (finished in 1530) has a remarkable Renaissance doorway. While in the old section of the city, visit the Colegio de San Clemente (1601) and the **Convento de San Francisco**, said to have been founded by St Francis of Assisi in 1214 when he made a pilgrimage. The **Monasterio de San Martiño Pinario**, now a seminary, was founded in the 10th century and rebuilt in the 17th century. The monastery's church, just behind it, has a wonderful baroque retable.

BELOW: Santiago Cathedral.

Just outside the Porta do Camiño in the northeast of the old city, the **Museo do Pobo Galego** (open Mon–Sat; free) has a wide-ranging display of Galician life and culture, including arts and crafts, musical instruments and traditional costumes. The adjacent **Centro Galego de Arte Contemporánea** (open Tues–Sat; free) has temporary exhibitions of modern art. To tour the **University of Santiago de Compostela**, walk from the Praza do Obradoiro along descending cobblestoned streets. The university was established in 1532, although its present building dates from 1750. Before leaving Santiago, stroll to the southeast of the old city to the **Paseo de la Herradura**, once a fairground and now a park on a wooded hill not far from the university. The view of the cathedral's façade enveloped in the green mantle of surrounding hills is magnificent.

It is estimated that in the last 500 years one in three Galician men left his homeland. Most went to Cuba, Argentina, Uruguay or Venezuela – perhaps the most famous immigrant's son is Cuban President Fidel Castro.

Inland to Lugo and Ourense

Lugo ❺ is 95 km (60 miles) east of Santiago on the N-547 highway that twists and turns through jagged mountains. The drive is worth the effort, for circling this former Roman capital in the region is one of the best-preserved Roman walls to be found anywhere in the world. The massive schist walls are 2 km (1¼ miles) long and 10 metres (33 ft) high and date from the 3rd century; the walk around the top takes just 30 minutes.

Lugo's position on the French road to Santiago explains the strong French influence in the Romanesque parts of its **cathedral**, begun in the 12th century (open daily; free). It was expanded in the Gothic period and enlarged in the 18th century. The **Capilla de Nuestra Señora de los Ojos Grandes** (Virgin of the Big Eyes), a chapel at its east end, containing the pre-Christian figure of the Virgin, features an exquisite baroque rotunda, which contrasts with the Roman-

BELOW: the Roman walls of Lugo.

Map on page 318

esque carving on the north and south doors. Across from the north door on the lovely Praza de Santa María is the18th-century **Palacio Episcopal**, a typical *pazo*, or Galician manorhouse, one storey high with stone walls and elaborate iron balconies. The newly expanded **Museo Provincial** (open 10am–2pm and 4.30–8pm daily; free) houses a large mixed collection representing provincial history and includes a country cottage kitchen and Roman mosaics discovered while building a city-centre car park.

In summer you can join the largely local crowds who flock to Lugo's coast and its relaxed fishing ports turned beach resorts; **Viveiro** and **Ribadeo** both have lovely old towns. Alternatively, head southwest towards Ourense, the other inland provincial capital. A good choice for a brief stop is **Santa Eulalia de Bóveda ❻**, a palaeo-Christian monument unearthed early in the 20th century, which consists of a vestibule open to the sky and a rectangular chamber with a basin and round-arched niche. Lovely frescoes of birds and leaves of early Christian origin remain intact here.

For hundreds of years, Ourense has attracted visitors who come to sample the mineral waters from three springs in Praza das Burgas. The water emerges at a temperature of 67°C (153°F).

Feudal remnants

The highways and byways of Lugo and Ourense, the two eastern inland provinces, provide an insight into Galician history. Old men with weatherbeaten and wrinkled faces plough small plots with the help of a pair of oxen. Old women in the rigorous black of widowhood trudge along roads, their long-handled scythes on their shoulders as they follow carts piled high with long grass.

Farming methods here vary little from the strip farming done in the Middle Ages. In fact, a semi-feudal society continues to exist. Dominant *caciques* (bosses) maintain great influence and power over peasants in villages in many areas where communication by road off the major highways remains difficult despite recent improvements. The provinces of Lugo and Ourense have the lowest income per capita in all Spain and their population is falling dramatically through emigration to cities and the seaboard. The other side of the same coin are the region's weatherbeaten castles and *pazos*, or manorhouses, built with the rents or *foros* paid by the local aristocracy. An outstanding example of their distinctive architectural and gardening style is the **Pazo de Oca**, south of Santiago on the N-525.

Ourense ❼ is said to have received its name because of the gold that legend says was mined by the Romans in the Valdeorras hills of the Sil valley. Although it is now a busy commercial town, Ourense retains some wonders of its Roman origin, including the **Puente Romano** that was rebuilt on its original foundations in the 13th century. In the **Museo Arqueológico** (closed for restoration), just behind Praza Maior, prehistoric, pre-Roman and Roman-era specimens are kept. The Fine Art departments hold Romanesque Virgins, baroque altarpieces and a 17th-century woodcarving of the Stations of the Cross.

Close by, the **Catedral de San Martiño** is heavily influenced by Santiago cathedral. The richly carved Romanesque Pórtico del Paraíso (Paradise Door) inside the west front illustrates the 24 Old Men of the Apocalypse and still has its medieval colouring.

BELOW: Ourense's Puente Romano.

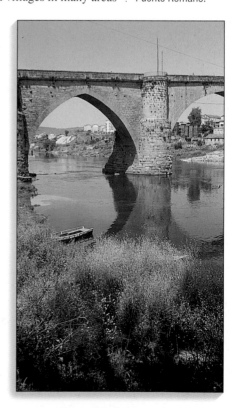

"Cradle of sailors"

From the ancient city of **Pontevedra**  ❽, 105 km (65 miles) west of Ourense on the N-541, you can visit most of the impressive Rías Baixas with relative ease by car. According to legend, the city was founded by Teucer, half-brother of Ajax. But historians say the town probably dates from the Roman period and its name from the Latin "*Pons Vetus*" (Old Bridge) that described the 11-arch span over the Río Lérez.The trading port had a brilliant life during the Middle Ages and Columbus's *Santa María* was built in its shipyards. But after the harbour silted up, a new port built at Marín surpassed it in importance.

Pontevedra preserves the charm of an old country town with fine examples of *cruceiros*, the stone crosses marking crossroads, in its streets. The **Santa María La Mayor** Plateresque church (open daily 9am–2pm, 5–8.30pm; free), nestled among the alleyways in the fishermen's quarter, was built late in the 15th century by the mariners' guild. Its interior features an impressive mix of Gothic notched arches, Isabelline twisted columns and ribbed vaulting in the Renaissance style. Close by in Praza de la Leña is the small but stunning **Museo de Pontevedra** (open Mon–Sat 9am–1pm and 5–7.30pm, Sun 11am–1.50pm), with Bronze Age jewellery and paintings by Zurbarán and Goya. A whole floor is devoted to the work of Alfonso Castaleo, a 20th-century Galician artist. His images of the Civil War are particularly moving.

Witchcraft

Galicians are renowned for their belief in magic, witches and superstition. In many cases this almost pagan belief in the spirit world has grafted itself on to Christianity. In the municipality of **As Neves** in southern Pontevedra province,

Pontevedra is the birthplace of great sailors, including the explorer Pedro Sarmiento de Gamboa, a skilled 16th-century navigator and cosmographer who wrote "Voyage to the Straits of Magellan".

BELOW:
Galician women preparing octopus.

every year on 29 July, people whose lives have been saved in one manner or another during the previous year gather to thank St Marta for her saving grace; the "saved" people dress up in funeral clothes and get inside coffins which are then paraded around the church of **Ribarteme** by their families. Much more widely, too, Carnival is a hedonistic week of revelling with a mass of medieval rituals, fancy-dress, eating and drinking.

Map on page 318

Water and wine

The coastal highway C-550 zigzags north from Pontevedra. The Salnés peninsula running round to Padrón has grown wealthy on tourism, intensive fish farming, smuggling and vineyards. A great variety of fish and shellfish changes hands at morning auctions on local wharves and a number of excellent seafood restaurants line the coast. Round a cape on the southern side of the **Ría de Arosa** is the extraordinary **La Lanzada beach**. In summer hundreds camp out on this long, picturesque strand which shines like a white clam shell. At the far end is a nature reserve with protected dunes and marshland. Further north is the island of **La Toja**, where Galicia's beach tourism began. A sick donkey was the first creature to benefit from the mineral waters of a spring here. Now a luxury hotel offers everything from blackjack to beauty treatments.

A satisfying stop on this highway is the smuggling town of **Cambados** ❾. Savour the strong Albariño varietal wine produced nearby which goes so well with seafood. A 17th-century church and the adjoining **Fefiñanes Pazo** (mansion), along with a row of arcaded houses, form the attractive **Plaza de Fefiñanes** at the town's north entrance. A little further down the highway is a lovely promenade overlooking the bay.

BELOW: the *horreo*, or Galician granary, is built on stilts to keep out vermin.

Rosalía de Castro's penetrating studies of country folk sparked a new interest in Galician culture. Her "Cantares Gallegos" (Galician Songs, 1863) is one of the greatest works of Spanish literature.

BELOW:
view of Galicia's Rías Baixas.

The northern section of the Atlantic coastline, known as the Coast of Death, leads out to Cabo Finisterre – literally the end of the earth to the Romans – via a stunning 8-km (5-mile) virgin beach at **Carnota**.

Rosalía de Castro

Padrón ❿ is said to be the town where the boat bearing the body of St James arrived in Spain. The boat's mooring stone can be seen under the altar in the local church beneath the bridge over the **Río Sar**. Galicia's most famous poet, Rosalía de Castro (1837–85) lived for many years in a stone house near the Sar that is now a **museum** (open Tues–Sun; free). She and her husband, the historian Manuel Murguía, formed the nucleus of a group of enthusiastic poets and writers who stimulated a *Rexurdimento* (renaissance) in Galician letters. The *Rexurdimento* stirred latent nationalist sentiment, and by the early 20th century several nationalist parties had been formed.

Rosalía de Castro identified with the tribulations of the poor of rural Galicia because of the pain in her own life. The illegitimate daughter of a priest, she was rejected by family and society, lived for many years in an unhappy marriage and in old age was racked by cancer. She is a universally revered figure for Galicians, who know her poetry well. More recently, Padrón was the birthplace of the Nobel-prizewinning novelist Camilo José de Cela.

Riches old and new

Vigo ⓫, Galicia's largest and most industrialised city, dates back to Roman times, although almost no buildings from that era remain. It became a rich port after Charles V authorised commercial trade with America in 1529. In 1702, a

Spanish treasure convoy was intercepted and destroyed by the British in Vigo Bay. To this day, it is believed that tons of gold lie at the bottom of the bay in the hold of lost galleons. More recently, Vigo's wealth has been based on fish-canning, car manufacturing, shipbuilding and the sleepless port, which is home to one-half of Spain's fishing fleet, the fourth largest in the world. Although not a traditionally beautiful city, the old quarter and Modernist buildings give it character; and the Galician art collection in the **Pazo de Quiñones**, a 17th-century manor-house set in the peaceful Parque de Castrelos, is unmissable.

Above all, Vigo is a city for sea-lovers. Enjoy the sun at one of several sparkling beaches, including **Samil, Alcabre** and **Canido**. Or take a ferry ride from the port to the charming fishing village of **Cangas** on the north side of the *ría* or to the **Islas Cíes**, small isles in the mouth of Vigo Bay.

To see the port where Columbus's *Pinta* docked in 1493 with news of the discovery of the New World, drive south for an hour on coastal highway C-550 to **Baiona**, a chic resort with smart yachts bobbing in the bay. **Castelo de Monterreal** ⑫, a massive castle fortress with a long defence wall, was built on this promontory rock in about 1500. It later became the governor's residence and has now been converted to the *parador* **Conde de Gondomar**. It is surrounded by pine and eucalyptus woods, and has a commanding vista of the Atlantic, the **Islas Estelas** in the mouth of the bay and the coast south to **Cabo Silleiro**.

Here, the crowds drop away for the final stretch of coastline running down to Portugal. The climate in the Miño estuary has a mild, tropical quality; kiwis, vines and subtropical flowers flourish. **A Guarda**, the border town, is an unspoiled fishing port with fine beaches and panoramic views from the Celtic **Museo de Monte de Santa Tecla** (open daily; free), south of the town centre. ❑

Map on page 318

Seafood is abundant and super fresh along this southern stretch of coast. Try fried shrimp with garlic, hake, scallops, raw oysters with lemon, boiled lobster or clams.

BELOW: Vigo's deep-water bay.

THE CANARY ISLANDS

*This isolated archipelago is often forgotten in any survey of
Spain. Yet seven million tourists a year come here, lured by the
continuous sunshine, endless beaches and volcanic landscapes*

Map
on pages
334–5

The Canary Islands offer some remarkable contrasts. Here you'll find one of the highest mountains in Europe, often capped by snow; beaches of black sand and seas of volcanic lava that are still hot; and moss-cloaked and mist-shrouded forests which have survived from the tertiary era. Some of the islands in this archipelago are razor-sharp, steep and volcanic, their tops in cloud; a couple of them are slivers of sand, like slices cut at a stroke from nearby mainland Africa and rolled flat by blistering sunshine.

This archipelago, marooned out in the Atlantic Ocean, is perhaps better known to Europeans escaping the mid-winter blues than to Spaniards. At the height of the season, tourists outnumber the locals by five to one. They are attracted by a remarkably consistent climate: the average temperature of 17°C (65°F) in winter increases to 24°C (75°F) in summer, with a cooling offshore breeze.

The Canaries have been transformed by tourism from an isolated cul-de-sac of Spain into a diverse, multicultural society. The seas are covered in sails and condominiums cling to the slopes. The well-equipped resorts are little cities in themselves, with a babel of different languages filling the streets and bars: there are whole districts that are almost entirely British, Dutch, French, German, Scandinavian and of course Spanish; you can buy genuine fish and chips made by a man from Macclesfield, or genuine sauerkraut made by a man from Stuttgart.

Islands of the "dogs"

And yet, despite this annual invasion, there are still plenty of surprises on the islands. Even the origin of the name is unexpected: it is not the sweet-singing birds that are celebrated, but dogs – *canes* in Latin – which the islands' conquerors discovered roaming wild in great numbers. Some historians suggest that these islands were virtually unpopulated when the Spanish first arrived in the 1400s; a more likely story is that the unfortunate Guanches, the original islanders, were all but wiped out. Their language has gone – unless you count *silbo*, the whistling language still practised on La Gomera, which supposedly developed after the conquistadors cut off the survivors' tongues, although it more likely developed simply as a way of communicating across deep ravines.

Since then, all sorts of other things have happened on these shores: Columbus supposedly interrupted his momentous voyage of discovery here to lie awhile in the arms of the Countess of Gomera; Nelson hoped to take the port of Santa Cruz and lost his arm here trying to capture a Mexican treasure-fleet; and General Franco launched the Civil War from here.

There are seven main islands in the Canaries: Gran Canaria, Fuerteventura and Lanzarote in Las Palmas

PRECEDING PAGES:
sunbathing on Gran
Canaria **LEFT:** Las
Teresitas beach,
Tenerife. **BELOW:**
working partnersip.

The promenade at Playa del Inglés, the largest resort on the south coast of Gran Canaria. It has a long white-sand beach stretching for 10 km (6 miles).

Province, and Tenerife, La Palma, La Gomera and El Hierro in Santa Cruz Province. Only a couple of centuries ago the Spaniards believed there were eight; they even mapped the eighth, which they called San Borondon, and visited it regularly. The myth continues, but the elusive San Borondon has not yet been picked up on any satellite picture. There are also four uninhabited islets, and countless reefs and rocks in the archipelago.

The eastern Canaries

Although Tenerife and Gran Canaria share equal status within the autonomous region of the Canary Islands, the latter is the seat of local government, and the main commercial and communications centre. **Gran Canaria** is the third largest island (1,532 sq. km, 592 sq. miles) and has a population of 700,000. Its capital, **Las Palmas de Gran Canaria ❶** (pop. 360,000), covers its northern tip.

Las Palmas manages to be both aristocratic and seedy. It has a long seafrontage, the largest port in Europe in terms of sheltered water, and was once a major stepping stone on the long haul to South America. In addition, Las Palmas has one of the best downtown beaches of any city in the world; you can emerge dripping from the surf on Playa de las Canteras one moment, and be inside a Las Palmas department store the next. La Vegueta, the old quarter to the south, is built in Spanish colonial style. The gothic **Catedral de Santa Ana,** with its adjacent museum (open Mon–Sat; entrance fee) is located here, as is the **Casa de Colón** (open daily; free), home of the island's governors and now containing a museum dedicated to Columbus's exploits.

The south of the island is the main tourist destination, with more hours of guaranteed sunshine and huge, strident resorts such as **Playa del Inglés** and

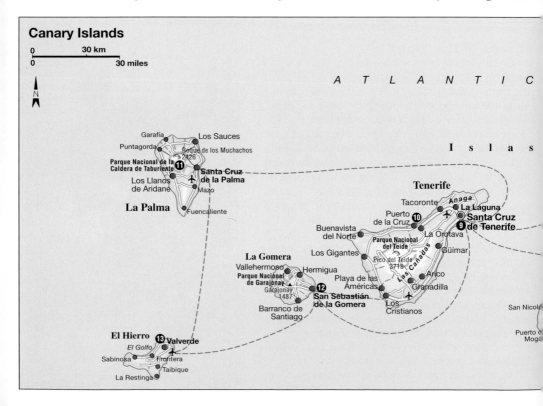

Canary Islands

0   30 km
0   30 miles

N

ATLANTIC

Islas

Garafía · Los Sauces
Puntagorda · Roque de los Muchachos △2426
Parque Nacional de la Caldera de Taburiente ⓫
Los Llanos de Aridane · Santa Cruz de la Palma
La Palma · Mazo
Fuencaliente

Tenerife
Tacoronte · Anaga · La Laguna
Puerto de la Cruz ⓾ · Santa Cruz ❾ de Tenerife
Buenavista del Norte · La Orotava
Parque Nacional del Teide · Güímar
Los Gigantes · Pico del Teide △3718 · Las Cañadas
La Gomera · Arico
Vallehermoso · Hermigua · Granadilla
Parque Nacional de Garajonay · Playa de las Américas
Garajonay △1487 · San Sebastián de la Gomera ⓬ · Los Cristianos
Barranco de Santiago

San Nicolá

El Hierro ⓭ Valverde
El Golfo · Frontera
Sabinosa · Taibique
La Restinga

Puerto d Moga

Maspalomas ❷ with its famous sand dunes. Until the 1950s the south was a remote, arid spot; now the southern shoreline is virtually one continuous urbanisation. Beyond the more upmarket resort of **Puerto de Mogán** ❸, the coast returns to its semi-wild state, with locals still pursuing their livelihoods of fishing or agriculture. In the northwest are the attractive towns of **Agaete,** built around a picturesque rocky bay, and **Gáldar,** both rich in Guanche remains.

Gran Canaria has a wild, steep and scenic interior, rising to 1,949 metres (6,395 ft) at the **Pico de las Nieves** ❹. There is an excellent view of the central summits from Cruz de Tejeda, where a restaurant-only parador is situated. The inland areas, notably the villages of Artenara and Atalaya, still have inhabited caves. The island's most famous ravine, the Barranco de Guayadeque, has cave restaurants.

A land without rain

The second largest of the Canary Islands at 1,668 sq.km (652 sq. miles), **Fuerteventura** also has one of the smallest populations (30,000). Like neighbouring Lanzarote and not-so-distant Africa only 96 km (60 miles) away, Fuerteventura doesn't have the height to prod the passing clouds into letting go some of their water. The island is consequently very barren and sandy, and its fragile economy is based on goats, tourists and the military (there's a Spanish Foreign Legion base here). The main town of **Puerto del Rosario**, which surrounds the port, is straggling and unattractive. The old capital city of **Betancuria**, now little more than a hamlet, is a pretty spot in the centre of the island.

Fuerteventura has the Canaries' best beaches. Most of the resort areas are either on the northern tip at **Corralejo** ❺, where there are two large hotels, or on the southern **Península de Jandía** ❻. The latter was at one time separated

Map
below

Before the arrival of the Europeans, several indigenous tribes, known collectively as Guanches, lived on the Canary Islands. Examples of stone and bone implements, and other Guanche artefacts, can be seen in museums all over the islands.

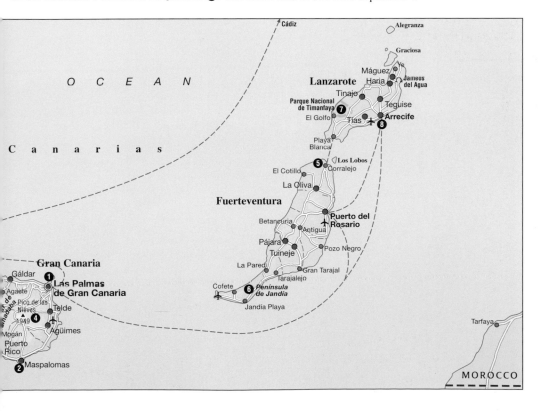

Demonstration of volcanic heat at the Parque Nacional de Timanfaya.

BELOW: lighthouse on Tenerife.

from the rest of the island by a wall, La Pared, erected by the original Guanche kings. This southern part of the island was isolated again during and after World War II, when it was given to a German by General Franco.

Volcano island

The fourth largest of the seven islands **Lanzarote** (795 sq. km, 307 sq. miles) has a population of 60,000. At the wrong time of year, when the light is sluggish and the ground unproductive, the island looks like what it is – the scab on a volcanic wound, still bubbling hot, red and raw underneath. At other times there are moments of rare beauty in this landscape, whose sparse, minimal features can come together in a memorable way. They say that the islanders paint their windows and doors green to compensate for the lack of green in their landscape.

Lanzarote's **Parque Nacional de Timanfaya** ❼ (tel: 928-80 15 00; open daily; entrance fee) is a massive volcanic wasteland of mangled rock and twisted lava created by eruptions between 1730 and 1736. Tours of the park include a visit to the Islote de Hilario in the Montañas de Fuego (Fire Mountains). Park rangers give dramatic demonstrations of the continuing power of the earth, and the park's El Diablo restaurant cooks with volcanic heat. Elsewhere on the island the prickly pear cactus is widespread, either growing wild or hosting colonies of cochineal beetle, which are used to make an edible dye.

Most tourist developments on Lanzarote are tastefully done, and the majority are no more than two storeys high. **Arrecife** ❽, the capital, is a modern town, though the waterfront promenades and pleasant beach add charm. Housed in the **Castillo de San José** (open daily; free) is a small but interesting contemporary art museum which includes a painting by César Manrique.

The western Canaries

The western islands – Tenerife, La Palma, La Gomera and El Hierro – are taller and more beautiful than the eastern group; the last three could together compete for the title of European Bali, with craggy *campesinos*, lush valleys, weird fiestas, a mixture of sunshine, cloud and mist, and deep and ancient forests.

The largest of the islands (2,057 sq. km or 794 sq. miles), **Tenerife** has a population of 760,000 and boasts the highest mountain in the whole of Spain (El Teide). In fact, the majority of the island's bulk is the volcanic Teide, which rises to 3,718 metres (12,198 ft), with forests, villages, lush valleys and finally beaches on its lower skirts. Tenerife's main town, **Santa Cruz de Tenerife ❾**, is a more pleasant but rather smaller place than Las Palmas. Worth visiting is the **Museo Arqueológico** (open Tues–Sun; entrance fee) on Calle Fuentes Morales; one of its most notable exhibits is the cannon reputed to have removed the arm of British admiral Nelson in the 18th century. The town lies in the shadow of the Anaga mountains, which form the northern part of the island, and conceal remarkable and rugged scenery and tiny hidden villages in their folds.

The largest tourist resorts on Tenerife (**Los Cristianos** and **Playa de las Américas**, for example) are in the south of the island, where the sunshine is guaranteed and where the main airport is now located. The original airport, west of Santa Cruz was the site of the world's worst air disaster when two Jumbo jets collided on the runway. International flights now arrive in the south.

The history of tourism here began in 1850, with the first steamship service between the islands and Cádiz. In those days, of course, only gentry could afford to travel. They came in particular to **Puerto de la Cruz ❿** and **La Orotava** in the fertile Orotava Valley on the northwestern coast, seeking the health

Local architect César Manrique designed many memorable cave conversions in Lanzarote, notably the Jameos del Agua complex on the northeast coast which includes a nightclub, restaurant and formal gardens.

Map on pages 334–5

BELOW: La Orotava during the flower festival.

benefits of the mid-Atlantic climate. The lush valley is still known for its banana plantations. Mainland Spain takes 95 percent of the crop and the characteristically small Canary bananas are now being promoted in Europe's supermarkets.

Both towns, with their elegant colonial-style mansions and narrow cobbled streets, still have some of the gentility bestowed on them by the early travellers. However, because the sea of this northern coast is rough and wild, Puerto lacks one major feature that the modern tourist expects – a sandy beach. This problem has been circumvented by the elegant Lago Martiánez, a series of swimming pools sculpted out of the rock at sea level by Lanzarote architect César Manrique. Canarian ingenuity doesn't stop there; 8 km (5 miles) north of Santa Cruz a beach has been created at Las Teresitas with 3½ million cubic feet of sand.

Tenerife's **Parque Nacional del Teide** (tel: 922-29 01 29; open daily; free) encompasses las Cañadas, the area left by the collapse of the ancient crater around El Teide, which has been dormant since 1798. The park is easily reached by good roads, although you are not allowed to climb right to the top of the peak because of erosion; instead you can take a cable-car, which stops 160 metres (525 ft) short of the summit. The area contains some unusual rock formations as well as a parador and visitors' centre.

The best of the rest

La Palma is the greenest and fifth largest of the islands (728 sq. km, 280 sq. miles), and has retained much of its population of 75,000 thanks to its suitability for agriculture. The island is very steep, rising to 2,426 metres (7,959 ft) at the **Roque de los Muchachos**, and falling away sharply to the sea most of the way around the rocky coast, thus denying mass tourism much of a foothold.

In the 1880s, Mrs Olivia Stone, a formidable Victorian traveller, toured the Canary Islands on donkey-back. Visitors began pouring into the islands after her book, "Tenerife and its Six Satellites", was published.

BELOW: balconies in La Palma.

Map
on pages
334–5

Much of the northern part of the island is occupied by the **Parque Nacional Caldera de Taburiente ⑪**, with its massive volcanic crater 9 km (5½ miles) in diameter. On the rim of the volcano is the Observatorio de Astrofisica, one of the largest telescopes in Europe.

Distinguished by being Columbus's chosen stepping-off point for the New World in 1492, things have changed little in **La Gomera** since then; this, the sixth largest island (378 sq. km or 146 sq. miles), has a population of 20,000, with tourism increasing. Gomera's main town of **San Sebastián ⑫** is linked to the south of Tenerife 32 km (20 miles) away by a regular shuttle ferry service. The parador here is one of the finest in Spain.

Gomera's limited tourist areas are the Valle Gran Rey, a deep and luxuriant valley on the southeastern corner of the island, which attracts young and longer-staying backpackers, and **Barranco de Santiago**, the site of the island's main resort development around the Hotel Tecina. Beach areas are limited: the island rises steeply to its highest point (Mount Garajonay 1,487 metres/4,879 ft) and the centre of the **Parque Nacional de Garajonay**, which is notable for its ancient tertiary-era forest made up of moss-cloaked laurel and cedar trees.

The smallest of the islands at 277 sq. km (107 sq. miles), **El Hierro** is also the least developed and least populated (6,000 inhabitants). Cattle and livestock farming are the mainstay of the community, and wine and excellent cheese are still made on the island. The principal town, **Valverde ⑬** (literally "green valley") is the only island capital situated inland, indicative of the fact that Hierro lays greater stress on agriculture than on seaborne trade. The island also has its own massive volcanic crater, although one side has collapsed into the sea; the result is **El Golfo**, a calm, wide gulf, and the island's most peaceful spot. ❏

La Palma was the scene of the most recent volcanic activity in the Canaries, when an eruption in the side of the old volcano of San Antonio in 1971 formed a new cone.

BELOW: El Teide's summit.

THE BALEARIC ISLANDS

Map on page 344

Writers and artists have long flocked to Mallorca, Menorca and Formentera, finding inspiration in the idyllic climate, the magnificent landscapes and, above all, the peace and quiet

With approximately 3,600 sq. km (1,400 sq. miles), Mallorca is the largest of the Balearic Islands, which lie in the Mediterranean Sea some 92 km (57 miles) off the coast of Alicante. Menorca is next in size, followed by Ibiza, the island closest to the Spanish mainland. The smallest, Formentera, which is visible from Ibiza, has just 82 sq. km (30 sq. miles).

Slingshots and talaiots

These islands make up the autonomous region of the Balearics (Balears). Their name comes from the Greek word for sling, *ballo.* So famous were the ancient natives of the Balearics for their skill in hurling deadly lead pellets with slings that the Romans called the two larger islands *Balear Maior* and *Balear Minor.*

Skeletal remains indicate that the islands were inhabited as early as 4000 BC but the oldest architectural ruins date from the 3rd millennium BC. The Talyotic Age, which extended from 1000 BC to the Roman conquest, left the most archaeological testimonies; stone structures called *talaiots,* believed to have been built by a people who came from the Eastern Mediterranean. The Carthaginians, whose occupation dated from the middle of the 7th century BC, recruited Balearic mercenaries whose slings were the terror of the Romans. It was not until 20 years after the destruction of Carthage (146 BC) that Rome was able to subjugate the islands.

PRECEDING PAGES: St John Festival on Menorca. **LEFT:** the coastline of Mallorca. **BELOW:** tower at Banyalbufar.

Conquest and Reconquest

As the Roman Empire was falling apart, the Vandals swept into the islands in AD 426 and remained until they were driven out by the Byzantines 100 years later. The three centuries of Muslim domination of the Balearics, made tributary to the Emirate of Córdoba in 848, left a heritage of Moorish place-names (beginning with "Bin") and whitewashed architecture.

The Christian Reconquest took place in Mallorca in 1229 under King James of Aragón. The event proved decisive in the final evolution of the islands' culture. They fell under the influence of Catalonia, and to this day each island speaks its own variant of Catalan. In the 13th century the Balearic Islands became important stops on the trade route between northern Italy and northern Europe. Mallorca produced great artists and craftsmen whose work may be seen in Palma's cathedral and the Castel de Belver.

With the rise of the Turkish Empire in the 16th century, the Balearic Islands became a bastion of the expanding Spanish Empire. Watchtowers or *talaies* throughout the islands testify to the constant need to keep watch against sudden raids of Muslim corsairs in search of booty and slaves. Ibiza city's magnificent walls date from this period.

With the resurgence of Mediterranean commerce in the middle of the 17th century, Mallorcan merchants once again began to benefit from the islands' strategic location. Many of the country mansions or *possessions* which grace the countryside date from this period, and their Italian-inspired architecture illustrates the strong links between Mallorca and Italy. In 1708 the British seized Menorca during the War of the Spanish Succession. They remained, except for a brief occupation by the French, until 1781.

Artists' colony

In Palma the sky is turquoise, the sea is blue, and the mountains are emerald. The air is just as blue as the sky. In a word, life here is delicious.

—FRÉDÉRIC CHOPIN

In the mid-19th century, foreign tourists began to discover the delights of the Balearics. A five-month stay by Aurore Dupin, Baroness Dudevant, better known by her pen name of George Sand, and the pianist and composer, Frédéric Chopin, inaugurated a whole era of tourism.

George Sand's book, *A Winter in Mallorca*, was the first of what is now an extensive travel literature on the islands. Writers such as Charles Wood, Gaston Vouillier and the eccentric Archduke Louis Salvador of Habsburg Bourbon followed. This descendant of Europe's oldest royal families discovered Mallorca in 1867. He returned five years later to settle down and acquired the estate of Miramar. He maintained a large household presided over by a Mallorcan peasant girl, Catalina Homar, the great love of his life. Archduke Louis Salvador was not an idle aristocrat; he wrote a total of 60 books headed by his seven-volume work, *Die Balearen – The Baleares Described in Words and Images*.

A steady stream of writers and artists looking for out-of-the-way picturesque places continued to visit Mallorca and Ibiza. Some, like Robert Graves, settled down to stay permanently.

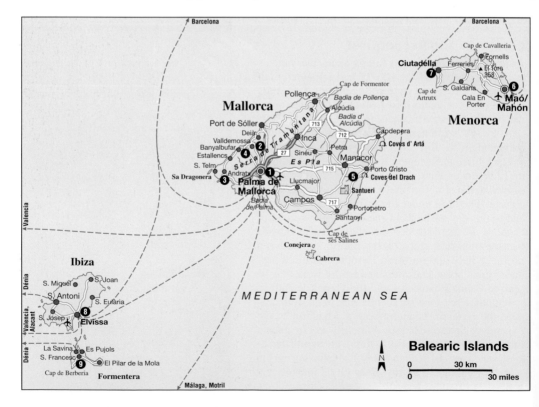

Mallorca

The tourist boom of the 1960s turned Mallorca into the most advanced holiday centre of the Mediterranean, providing accommodation and diversions for both monied jet-setters and economy-minded package-holiday tourists from France, Germany, Scandinavia and the UK. Palma is now the busiest airport in Europe during high season, and the economy of the Balearics is primarily based on tourism. Each summer, members of the Spanish royal family spend their holidays in the Marivent Palace near Palma.

The most impressive way to arrive at the island is by regularly scheduled boat service from either Barcelona or Valencia. From a distance **Palma de Mallorca's** ➊ medieval masterpiece of Gothic, the **catedral** (open Mon–Sat; entrance fee), stands out like a huge, rose-coloured, craggy rock. Work on the cathedral began in the 13th century and finished in the 16th century. The number and size of its windows make it the most luminous of Mediterranean cathedrals. A small but worthwhile museum displays precious gold and silver artefacts.

As the boat draws closer, the city's profile is crowned by other ancient monuments. **Castel de Belver** (open daily; entrance free), perched on a high hill, was a prison until early in the 20th century, although it was originally built as a summer palace. The 13th-century **Palau de l'Almudaina** (open Mon–Sat; entrance fee), set beside the cathedral on the foundations of an Arab *alcàsser* or fortress, is used for official functions by the Royal family and has some interesting Royal portraits. In the courtyard is the Gothic Capilla de Santa Ana.

The area around the cathedral was the site of the Arab city known in the Muslim world as *Medina Mayurka*. The only architectural remnants are an arch on Carrer Alumudaina and the two small chambers of the **Banys Arabs** (open

For a lively (and loud) night out, the old quarter of Palma has the best selection of bars. Head for Plaça Drassana and Carrer Apuntadors.

BELOW. Palma's Gothic *catedral*.

Ramon Llull, a 13th-century Christian monk, wrote 500 books including poetry, allegorical novels and works of medicine and mathematics. At the age of 80 he was stoned to death, while trying to convert Muslims.

BELOW: nets drying in the sun at Sóller.

daily; entrance fee) in Carrer Serra. This neighbourhood is especially interesting for wandering about, poking into ancient churches and admiring the houses of wealthy noblemen and merchants. The nearby streets of **Almudaina**, **Zanglada** and **Morey** have noble houses dating from the 16th through to the 18th century. On the **Plaça San Francesc** is a church of the same name built during the 14th century, although its present façade dates from the end of the 18th century. One of its eight-sided chapels, all of which are decorated with Renaissance and baroque art, contains the 15th-century sarcophagus of Ramon Llull.

A symbol of Palma's prosperous past is the magnificent 15th-century building known as **La Llotja** (open Tues–Sun; free), which used to house the merchants' stock exchange. Its four crenellated, octagonal-cornered towers and galleried windows serve as a counterweight to the majestic cathedral. The 17th-century Consolat de Mar next door has an impressive Renaissance-style gallery.

About 5 km (3 miles) southwest of the old town at Carrer Joan de Saridakis 29, the **Fundacío Pilar i Joan Miró** (open Tues–Sun, entrance fee) is worth a visit, if only to admire the architecture of the modern building, which was designed by Rafael Moneo. Inside, there is a permanent collection of Miró's work and a good souvenir shop.

Scenic drives

Inland, Mallorca divides into two: the Serra de Tramuntana which runs along the northern coast, and the fertile plain which makes up the bulk of the rest. The bays of **Alcúdia** and **Pollença,** on the northern tip of the island, are particularly attractive. Most heavy tourist urbanisation is within the Bay of Palma and out along the coves of the eastern coast.

If time is short, head straight towards **Valldemossa** ❷, about 25 km (15 miles) north of the capital, to see the **Carthusian Monastery** (open Mon–Sat; entrance fee), where George Sand and Chopin spent a winter. In spite of having a rather primitive piano to work with, Chopin composed some of his most beautiful pieces here, including the *Raindrop Prelude*.

The monastery was originally built as a palace by the Mallorcan King Sanç over the site of a former Moorish one. The neoclassical monastery chapel has frescoes on the ceiling painted by Goya's brother-in-law, Fray Miguel Bayeu. The owners of the well-kept houses of this village make a point of keeping their front doors open for passers-by to admire the decor of their entrance halls.

Closer to Palma, take the C-719 to **Andratx** ❸. This town's port is one of the most enchanting spots on the island. Despite tourist-oriented development, Port d'Andratx has kept its colour as a fishing village. Like many towns in the Balearics, the main town of Andratx was built some miles inland for protection from pirates and was surrounded by *talaies* or watchtowers. The fortified **church**, like many on the islands, was once surrounded by a moat. From Andratx, it is a short drive to the beach. The **Cala Sant Telm** affords a striking view of the island of **Sa Dragonera**. Nearby is the abandoned monastery of **Sa Trapa**. Local fishermen may be hired for a trip around Sa Dragonera, believed to be the beachhead of the Christian expedition which conquered Mallorca in 1229.

The northwest coast route

The C-710 coastal road from Andratx follows one of the world's most breathtaking routes, hugging the mountainside high above the sea. The village of **Estellencs**, which steeply straddles the side of **Mount Galatzó**, boasts a defen-

Map on page 344

BELOW: terraced fields overlooking the sea at Banyalbufar.

For additional rugged countryside next to the sea, visit the northern peninsula of Formentor. On the way, you'll pass the lovely town of Pollença, which has a Roman bridge on its outskirts.

sive tower used in the days when pirates were a menace. A little further along this road is the village of **Banyalbufar** ❹, set amid terraced gardens which have been carved out of the mountain and shored up with meticulously set stone walls. The terraces are irrigated by a network of flowing and glistening canals. The town still has half of the dozen fortified towers built as a defence against the marauding Turks of the 16th and 17th centuries. Below, a stony beach is made especially inviting by a cascade.

About 5 km (3 miles) past Valldemossa is the estate of **Miramar**, once the nucleus of various properties owned by the Archduke Louis Salvador. The most notable of these is the *possessió* **Son Marroig**, on the way to Deià. This splendid mansion built around an ancient defensive tower has a museum of Mallorcan folklore and collections of the Archduke (open daily; entrance free).

Deià has kept much of its original architecture. It has resisted the ravages of hotel complexes and tourist shops thanks largely to the efforts of its artists' colony led by Robert Graves, who first settled here in 1929 at Gertrude Stein's suggestion. "It's paradise, if you can stand it," she is reported to have told him. The Archduke Louis Salvador set up an inn on the road to Deià called the Ca Madò Pilla where visitors were allowed to stay free of charge for three nights.

The east coast

The extensive **Coves del Drach** ❺ and **Artà** (both open daily, entrance fee) in the eastern part of the island are worth seeing. A chamber-music ensemble performs in the largest of the subterranean lakes of the Coves del Drach, near Porto Cristo. You can also walk along the 2-km (1¼-mile) route. **Capdepera**, which has an impressive walled citadel, lies just to the north of the Coves d'Artà.

BELOW: Georgian town house in Maó.

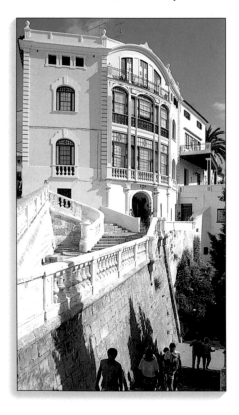

PREHISTORY IN MENORCA

Three different types of prehistoric constructions exist in Menorca. *Talaiots* are usually round, conical stone towers, two or three storeys high. Satisfactory explanations for the purpose of *talaiots* have yet to be given, although it is clear that they were useful for defence and as dwellings. A *naveta*, has the shape of an upside-down hull of a ship and was used as a mausoleum. The most fascinating and puzzling of the prehistoric monuments to be found in Menorca are called *tales,* from the Catalan word for table. A *taula* is one multi-ton megalith balanced on top of another in the form of a "T". About 30 have been identified, but only seven are still standing. They were most likely religious in purpose.

Another prehistoric wonder can be seen in **Cales Coves**, a network of some 140 man-made caves, most dating from the 9th century BC. In one of them there are Latin inscriptions from the 2nd century BC. In the two main Menorcan cities of Maó and Ciutadella, bars and discotheques have been installed in caves. The most spectacular discotheque on the islands is located in **Cala'n Porter**, set in a series of natural caves overlooking the sea.

Petra, located in the agricultural heartland of the island, is just a few kilometres from the C-715 running between the capital and the east coast. Father Junípero Serra, the founder of California's first missions, was born in this town in 1713. The state of California has set up a **museum** (open Tues–Sun; entrance fee), in Carrer Barracar Alt, with scale models of Serra's missions in California and Mexico as well as maps, letters and coins. The house adjacent to it in which the missionary was brought up has been preserved and furnished much as it was.

Menorca

The island of **Menorca** has an abundance of prehistoric structures. The people who built them are thought to be responsible for similar structures in Sardinia and at Stonehenge, England. Menorcan culture was also heavily influenced by British occupation in the 18th century and is most clearly seen in and around **Maó** ❻. Nowhere else in Spain are sash windows a regular feature of the architecture as they are here. The city, which the English made the island's capital, is situated at the end of a 5-km (3-mile) fjord, the only geological formation of its kind in the Balearics.

Outside the city are a number of Georgian mansions. At the seaside end of the fjord is the town of **Villa Carlos**, founded and named Georgetown by the British. Menorcan gin, introduced by Englishmen, has a distinctive taste and is popular throughout Spain. The Menorcan dialect has even assimilated a number of English words from that period of occupation.

Menorca's other large town, **Ciutadella** ❼, is situated at the western extreme of the island. It was the capital under Muslim rule and after the Christian conquest. Its Gothic **cathedral** has a tower built on the foundations of the minaret

Map on page 344

TIP

The best time to visit Ciutadella is during the Fiesta de Sant Joan, 23–24 June. Horsemen in medieval costume parade their horses while crowds gather round.

BELOW: sunbathing on Ibiza.

Map on page 344

Ibiza is a very popular destination among British ravers. This is one of the places where acid-jazz began and a haven for anyone wanting to experience club culture at its best.

BELOW: boating in the Balearics.
RIGHT: sunny islander.

of a mosque which used to stand in the same place. The stately houses of the nobility, dating from the 16th to the 19th century, give Ciutadella a dignified air.

Ibiza

Founded as *Ibosim* by the Carthaginians in the middle of the 7th century BC, **Eivissa (Ibiza City)** ❽ developed a flourishing economy, based on the export of salt, ceramics, glassware and agricultural products. Testimony of this prosperity are the Ibizan coins found throughout the Mediterranean.

But if Ibiza had a flourishing ancient past, its present is no less prosperous. For some 20 years it has been a mecca for jet-setters and trendy young travellers in search of not only sun, sand and surf but of a highly sophisticated nightlife, a nightlife often beginning in fashionable bars near the port and ending up near dawn in some of the world's most exotic discotheques.

In contrast to the hustle and bustle around the port is the dignified serenity of the oldest part of Eivissa, **Dalt Vila**, enclosed within a complete ring of walls. Crowning the hill of Dalt Vila, the sombre-looking **catedral** (open daily; free) is built on truly holy ground since its predecessors on the spot were a mosque, a palaeo-Christian church, a Roman temple dedicated to Mercury and a Carthaginian temple. The basic street plan of this part of Eivissa has changed little since it was first laid out by the Carthaginians. There are archaeological relics of this period at the **Museu Arqueologic** (open Tues–Sun; entrance fee) in Plaça Catedral. The museum has one of the best collections of Punic articles in the world. **Puig des Molins** (open Sun; entrance fee), on Via Romana at the foot of the hill, is a huge necropolis with more than 400 Carthaginian tombs.

Formentera

The island of **Formentera** is separated from Ibiza by 7 km (4 miles) of straits and islets. A regular boat service links Ibiza's port to Formentera's port of **La Savina**. This limited access is an advantage for those who want to get away from the hordes of tourists on Ibiza. Besides peace and quiet, Formentera offers the visitor the superb, long beaches of **Illetes** and **Levant**, in the far north of the island, and **Migjorn** along the south coast. There are also the package-tour-oriented beach of **Es Pujols** and a number of small *cales* or coves. **Sant Francesc** ❾, the island's capital, is 3 km (2 miles) south of La Savina. The agricultural character of the island is reflected in its name, which is derived from the Latin word for grain.

The best way to get around the island is by motorscooter, which may be rented at La Savina. On a scooter the island can be crossed in 40 minutes. The drive up to the plateau on the far eastern side of the island known as **La Mola** is recommended. The winding road to the top affords incomparable views of the island and of Ibiza. At the end of the road a lighthouse presides over sheer cliffs and a plaque commemorates the fact that Jules Verne chose this spot for the blast-off for his novel, *From the Earth to the Moon*. In summer Formentera attracts young people from all over Europe and North America. Since nightlife is limited to a few clubs, it is a friendly and intimate island. ❏

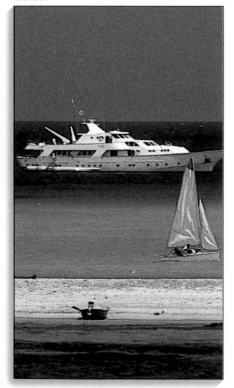

INSIGHT GUIDES
TRAVEL TIPS

New Insight Maps

Maps in Insight Guides are tailored to complement the text. But when you're on the road you sometimes need the big picture that only a large-scale map can provide. This new range of durable Insight Fleximaps has been designed to meet just that need.

Detailed, clear cartography
makes the comprehensive route and city maps easy to follow, highlights all the major tourist sites and provides valuable motoring information plus a full index.

Informative and easy to use
with additional text and photographs covering a destination's top 10 essential sites, plus useful addresses, facts about the destination and handy tips on getting around.

Laminated finish
allows you to mark your route on the map using a non-permanent marker pen, and wipe it off. It makes the maps more durable and easier to fold than traditional maps.

The first titles
cover many popular destinations. They include Algarve, Amsterdam, Bangkok, California, Cyprus, Dominican Republic, Florence, Hong Kong, Ireland, London, Mallorca, Paris, Prague, Rome, San Francisco, Sydney, Thailand, Tuscany, USA Southwest, Venice, and Vienna.

℞ INSIGHT GUIDES
The world's largest collection of visual travel guides

CONTENTS

Getting Acquainted

The Place

Area 504,880 sq. km (194, 885 sq. miles).
Capital Madrid.
Population 39,670,000.
Language Spanish (Castilian), plus Catalan, Basque and Galician.
Religion Roman Catholic.
Time zone One hour ahead of Greenwich Mean Time (GMT).
Currency Peseta.
Weights and measures Metric.
Electricity 220 volts.
International dialling code 34.

The Climate

Spain's climate ranges from the snow to almost desert and the high central plain can bake in summer. In general terms, the climate is cooler and wetter to the north and warmer and drier to the south.

See indvidual regions for more detail on climate.

Government

The Kingdom of Spain is a constitutional monarchy under King Juan Carlos I of the House of Bourbon, who has been on the throne since the death of Franco in 1975. Parliament (the Cortes) consists of a Senate and a Chamber of Deputies. Elections are held every four years.

The country is divided into 17 autonomous regions, each with its own legislature, and each of the mainland regions elects four senators. The Deputies in the lower house are elected by proportional representation. Regional parties, such as the Catalan Convergència i Unió, hold decisive votes in government-making, as well as in policy-making.

Spain is a member of the European Union, the North Atlantic Treaty Organisation and the Organisation for Economic Cooperation and Development.

Economy

Spain's economy has largely followed the pattern of western Europe, and has slowed after flying high up until the early 1990s. In the last years of the 13-year socialist government, voted out of office in 1996, privatisation and other non-socialist policies were introduced to combat the flagging economy. Manufacturing industries are very important but have declined in recent years, as have the coal and steel works of the north. There is a healthy financial sector, and the fishing industry is remains importan, with Spain running one of the largest fishing fleets in Europe. Tourism is an important earner, with more than 50 million visitors a year.

Population

Three-quarters of the 39½ million population lives in urban areas, in particular Madrid and Barcelona. About 10 percent of the workforce lis employed in agriculture.

Planning the Trip

Entry Regulations

Visas & Passports: Visitors from EU countries require only a valid National Identity Card from their home state to enter Spain. Citizens of Andorra, Austria, Liechtenstein, Monaco and Switzerland enjoy a similar privilege.

US citizens, Australians and New Zealanders require a valid passport and are automatically authorised for a three-month stay, which can be renewed for another three. Visitors from elsewhere must obtain a visa from the Spanish Consulate in their own country before setting off.

Useful Addresses

If you want to stock up on information before you leave home, here are a few of the Spanish Tourist Information Offices abroad:
● **New York:** 665 Fifth Avenue, New York, 10022, tel: 212 759 8822/28.
● **Chicago:** 845 N. Michigan Avenue, Suite 915, Chicago, Illinois 60611, tel: 312 944 0215/16.
● **Los Angeles:** 8383 Wilshire Blvd, Suite 960, 90211 Beverly Hills, California, tel: 213 658 7188/93.
● **Houston:** 5085 Westheimer, Suite 4800, 77056 Houston, Texas, tel: 713 840 7412/13.
● **Toronto:** 60 Bloor Street West, Suite 201, Toronto, Ontario M4W 3B8, tel: 416 961 3131.
● **London:** 22/23 Manchester Square, London W1M 5AP, tel: 020-7486 8077; fax: 020-7486 8034.

Europeans can prolong a three-month stay for an additional three months by applying for a *permanencia* in Madrid at the Comisaría de Policía, Sección de Extranjería, Calle Los Madrazo, 9, Madrid, tel: (91) 521 9350.

However, in order to reside in Spain for any extended period of time a *Visado de Residencia* must be applied for in one's country of origin. These formalities do not apply to members of the EU who can live and work freely in Spain.

A *Tarjeta de Estudiante* or Student Card can be applied for at District Police Stations or at Calle Los Madrazo, 9, by presenting a valid passport, an ordinary visa (from the Spanish Consulate in the country of origin), proof of financial means to cover one's stay, medical insurance and proof of enrolment in an officially recognised school.

All official documents must be accompanied by a corresponding photocopy (two are necessary if a work permit is also requested). Three passport-size photographs are needed for each application.

Health

No special inoculations are required for entering Spain, unless you are visiting from an area where there has been a recent outbreak of smallpox, cholera or yellow fever.

Tap water can be drunk without reservations and bottled water is available everywhere.

Unfortunately the phrase "Spanish tummy" can still prove accurate: food hygiene has improved enormously in recent years but you should nevertheless be a little cautious. In modest establishments avoid seafood on Sunday and Monday (it may not be as fresh as it should be) and be wary too of dishes containing raw egg, such as mayonnaise.

In summer, come prepared with a sun hat and protective suncreams.

Bring with you any prescription medicine you require. Although Spanish pharmacies are amply stocked with medicines made by international companies and many

Customs

Visitors can bring the following items into the country duty-free: Any personal effects, such as jewellery, a portable typewriter, cameras, film, portable video and sound equipment, musical instruments, sports equipment, camping material, etc. Visitors from outside the EU can also bring the following items duty-free (duty-free allowances for EU residents travelling within the EU ended in June 1999):

–Up to 200 cigarettes or 100 small cigars or 50 cigars or 250g of tobacco

–Up to 1 litre of alcohol of 22°

–Limited amounts of perfumes, coffee and tea.

If your camera, portable typewriter or whatever is new and you do not have the purchase receipt, it would be wise to ask a customs official to certify that you brought it with you.

Pets may be taken into Spain as long as you have a suitable Health Certificate for the animal signed by an officially recognised vet from the country of origin. This should indicate the dates of the last vaccines and, in particular, the date of an anti-rabies shot.

drugs can be purchased without prescription, your particular medication may not be available. Chemists in Spain do not honour foreign prescriptions.

Money

The peseta is the official Spanish currency. It comes in coins of 5, 25, 50, 100, 200 and 500 and notes of 1,000, 2,000, 5,000 and 10,000 denominations. On 1 January 1997 all coins bearing the image of Franco ceased to be legal tender, as well as the larger coins (the old 5, 25 and 50 peseta coins).

Best rates for travellers' cheques and foreign currency are obtained at banks (*see Banking, below*), but you can also change money in Madrid at

currency exchange shops (*Oficinas de Cambio*, of which one is at Calle Alcalá, 20 – you'll also find many in the Gran Vía, especially in the Callao area), the American Express Office (Plaza de las Cortes, 2), hotels (where the rates are lower), major department stores and shops frequented by tourists. We recommend you shop around.

Banks

Practically all Spanish banks will change foreign currency and travellers' cheques, for a fee. It is also possible to obtain pesetas in cash at any bank against your Visa or Mastercard credit card. However, visitors should be aware that personal cheques are not readily accepted in shops or other establishments as they are in other countries, even though they may be drawn on local banks. Always carry ID with you when you go to the bank.

Banking hours vary slightly from one bank to another. Most are open 8.30am–2.30pm weekdays, and some are open Saturday until 1pm or on Thursday afternoons until 7.30pm. All are closed on Sunday and holidays (and that includes Madrid fiestas in May – *see Public Holidays*). Several banks keep their major branches in the business districts open until 6pm or later.

Value Added Tax (VAT)

In order to be eligible, as a tourist, for a refund of the Spanish IVA (Value Added Tax), you must spend 15,000 pesetas or more on one item. This tax can range from 6 to 12 percent on the item, although on certain luxury goods it may be as high as 33 percent. The refund procedure is awkward and there are usually long waits at the department store offices which process the requests.

In any event, this is how it is done: first, you must obtain a triplicate form from the shop, indicating your purchase, its cost and the incorporated tax. If you are a citizen of the EU, show all copies of the form to your local customs, together with the goods, and in due course you should receive a cheque from the shop for the tax.

If you are not an EU citizen, turn the form over to Customs officials before you leave Spain. If you go from Madrid Barajas or any of the other major international airports, you can present the validated blue copy of the form at the Banco Exterior de España and they will refund the sum of the tax to you in the currency you wish.

If you leave the country from another Customs post, get them to validate your form and then send the blue copy back to the shop.

What to Wear

If you go sightseeing in shorts and miniskirts you may discover you are not admitted to churches and religious sites. The Ecumenical Council also requires that shoulders be covered.

Public Holidays

The following are national holidays:
● 1 January
● 6 January (Epiphany)
● 19 March (Saint Joseph; Father's Day)
● Holy Thursday and Good Friday
● 1 May (Labour Day)
● 15 August (Assumption Day)
● 12 October (Columbus Day or *Día de la Hispanidad*)
● 1 November (All Saint's Day)
● 8 December (Immaculate Conception)
● 25 December (Christmas Day).
Each town is also entitled to two local holidays in honour of its patron saints. Madrid celebrates 2 May, *Fiesta de la Comunidad de Madrid*, 15 May, *Día de San Isidro*, and 9 November, *Día de la Almudena*.

There are actually so many holidays, what with national and local fiestas, that it's said there is no one week in the whole year when all of Spain is working – although this is a slight exaggeration!

Practical Tips

Getting There

For information on getting to Spain, please see the *Getting There* information relating to individual regions. Information on getting to Madrid can be found on page 374.

MOTORING ADVICE

Foreign motorists in Spain must have either an international driving licence or a valid licence from their country of origin, the car's registration papers and valid insurance. Those who are not nationals of a European Community country will also require a *Carta Verde* or Green Card, which can be purchased at the border.

Spain has 317,000km (195,850 miles) of highway but only a few thousand miles are fast, convenient and relatively safe motorways. **Toll Fees** are payable on the modern motorways, which have rest areas, bars and service stations. Roadside telephones are also placed at convenient intervals, to call for assistance in case of emergency or breakdown.

The **speed limit** is 120kph (75mph) on motorways, 100kph (60mph) on all other roads and 60kph (35mph) going through cities and towns. **Seatbelts** must be worn by the driver and front-seat pasenger, and the car should be equipped with a spare set of head and rear-light bulbs or you could be fined.

Business Hours

Although many **offices** are adopting a standard 8 or 9am–5pm work day, shops usually have a morning and afternoon schedule, with a break at midday for the long lunch and

When to Shop

Shops are open 9.30 or 10am–1.30 or 2pm and then reopen again in the afternoon from 4.30 or 5–8pm, or a little later in summer. Most are closed on Saturday afternoons and all day Sunday. However, the major department stores like El Corte Inglés and the FNAC centre, and most shops in the Sol/preciados area (clothes shops, some shoe shops, etc) are open without interruption six days a week, 10am–9pm, and frequently on Sunday, despite the protests of small shopkeepers.

Panaderías (bakeries) open on Sunday mornings and are usually well stocked with other food staples and canned items which can prove useful at weekends.

siesta which are still very much a part of Spanish life, especially in summer. As a result, many Spaniards return home for lunch, which is the major meal of the day, while supper is light.

Religious Services

● **British Embassy Church of St George**, Anglican/ Episcopalian, Nuñez de Balboa, 43, tel: (91) 576 51 09. Sunday services at 8.30, 10 and 11.15am and Friday at 10.30am.
● **Catholic Masses** held in English (Sun 11am) in the **Capilla de Nuestra Señora de la Merced**, Avda Alfonso XIII, 165, tel: (91) 350 2909.
● **Synagogue**, Balmes, 3, tel: (91) 445 9843. Prayers at 8am and 8pm most days, Fri 7.30pm, Sat 9.15pm. July–Sept no evening services.
● **Islamic Centre**, Calle Alonso Cano, 3, tel: (91) 448 0554.
● The **Centro Cultural Islámico** (Islamic Mosque), tel: (91) 326 2610, rising above the M-30 highway on Calle Salvador de Madariaga, 4, is a splendid building of Moorish architecture, featuring a large auditorium, library and several exhibition halls.

Media

TELEVISION & RADIO

There are two nationwide television channels in Spain, TVE 1 and TVE 2, and each region has one or more local stations. In Madrid, you can also watch Telemadrid, which is run by the local Autonomous Community, as well as the local channels Canal 7, Canal 33 and Telemadroño, and three private networks Antena 3, Tele 5 and Canal Plus.

Canal Plus, which is a private pay channel (unlike Antena 3 and Tele 5) offers many new "undubbed" films (in "*Versión Original*"). Check press for details and look for "V.O."

Local stations in Catalonia (TV3 and Canal 33), the Basque country (ETB–1 and ETB–2), Galicia (TVG) and Valencia (Canal 9) have programming in the regional languages, while Canal Sur is the local Andalucían network.

The better hotels have access to satellite programming which includes a variety of channels, several of which broadcast in English (Super Channel, Sky Movies, Eurosport, BBC, CNN, Lifestyle etc.)

MAGAZINES & NEWSPAPERS

The Spanish daily papers are *El País*, *ABC*, *Ya*, *Diario 16* and *El Mundo*, and they provide full local information on cinema, theatre, regular and satellite television programming, and which chemist shops are open late at night. *El País*, *El Mundo* and *Diario 16* put out very handy supplements with their Friday editions, which give complete listings on all the activities, exhibitions, art shows and movie schedules being presented in Madrid that week, along with lists of restaurants, entertainment, television, etc. They are much on the lines of the weekly, all-encompassing *Guía del Ocio* (Guide to Leisure).

You will also be able to find the *International Herald Tribune* and *Time* and *Newsweek* magazines at major newsstands in most major cities and other papers such as the *The Times*, *The Guardian* and the *Wall Street Journal* can be purchased at larger stands.

There are a few magazines about Spain, printed in English, which you can buy – *Lookout* and *In Spain* are both published monthly; you can also pick up free English magazines with articles, events, reviews, listings and classified ads in most Irish pubs, bookshops, universities, language schools and tourist offices. *In Madrid* and *The Broadsheet* are the most popular and useful for the Madrid area. there is also a free music mag which you can find in pubs and record shops call *Mondo Sonoro*, which is good for gig listings. The major newspapers also have regional editions, and regions have their own dailies.

Postal Services

The district post offices are only open 9am–2.30pm on weekdays, and some close on Saturday mornings. All post offices close on Sunday. Principal post offices are open 9am–2pm and 4–7pm for general services, including preparation and postage of packages. Stamps can be purchased from 9am–10pm every day and telex and fax services are also available within these hours.

Stamps can also be bought in *estancos* or tobacconists, which are distinguishable by their brown and gold sign with the word *Tabacos*. The *estancos* are useful establishments, for in addition to selling tobacco, they can provide you with everything you need for writing home – paper, pens, envelopes and postcards – and will even weigh your letter to tell you what postage it requires.

Telephones

Coin and card operated telephone booths are everywhere. Wait for the tone, deposit a 25-peseta piece (the one with the hole in it) or 5 duros (the small golden coins) and dial the number. It is possible

Telephone Contacts

The following numbers may be helpful – though in some cases you'll need good Spanish.
003 Telephone info (Spain)
008 Operator Assistance for Europe
005 Operator Assistance for the rest of the world
091 National Police
080 Fire Department
092 Municipal Police
093 The Time
095 News in Spanish
096 Wake-up service (automatic)
061 Emergency medical attention
097 Sports Information
010 Citizen's Information
Everything you need to know about the city and its government. Extremely helpful staff. Open 8am–9pm Mon–Fri, except public holidays.

to place a **long-distance call** by depositing a handful of 100-peseta coins. Most bars have coin-operated or meter telephones available for public use as well. You can also purchase phonecards for 1,000 or 2,000 pesetas at any tobacconists.

For **overseas calls**, it's probably better to go to the offices of Telefónica (the Spanish telephone company), or to privately-run telephone shops where one can talk first and pay later and not have to worry about having enough coins. (Although it is convenient to ring from your hotel room, and all top hotels have direct-dialling facilities, you will be charged much more than you would on a public phone – at least 16 percent VAT will be added to the cost of your calls.)

To make a direct overseas call, first dial 00 and then wait for another dial tone before dialling the country and city codes. It is cheaper to call before 8am and after 10pm. There are no additional discounts at weekends. Recently, Retevision, the only alternative company to Telefónica, has started functioning in Spain. If the hotel or private number is registered with them, you have to dial 050 00 plus the country and city codes. In this case, you don't have to wait for a tone.

Please note: as from April 1998, all telephone numbers in Spain begin with 9 for both local and international calls.

Babysitting

Spaniards love children and, on the whole, won't frown at or object to their presence. However,in Madrid if you wish to leave your child under experienced supervision, you can do so in places such as "Descanso de mamá: hotel-guardería infantil", tel: (91) 574 3094, and Centro Infantil Nenos, tel: (91) 416 98. The latter is used by a lot of resident English speakers and they also offer a list of reliable babysitters.

For English-speaking babysitters, you can also check the classified ads in *Lookout* magazine, a good quality English language magazine sold throughout Spain. For short-term needs, many hotels offer babysitting services.

Embassies and Consulates in Madrid

Australia: Plaza Descubridor Diego de Ordás, 3, tel: (91) 441 9300.
Canada: Núñez de Balboa, 35, tel: (91) 431 4300.
Ireland: Paseo de la Castellana, 46, tel: (91) 576 3500.
United Kingdom: Fernando el Santo, 16, tel: (91) 319 0200.
United States: Calle Serrano, 75, tel: (91) 577 4000.

Emergencies

Spain these days is no more dangerous than any other cosmopolitan community, but it is no longer the haven of peace and safety it used to be. A high unemployment rate, an increasingly alarming drug problem and perhaps even freedom from authoritarian rule have changed all this, so it makes sense to take a few elementary precautions.

Emergency numbers

● **National Police**, tel: 091
● **Municipal Police**, tel: 092
● **Emergency Medical Care**, tel: 061
● **Fire Department**, tel: 080
● **Red Cross Emergency**, tel: (91) 522 2222 in Madrid.

For **lost or stolen Credit Cards**:
● **American Express**, tel: (91) 572 0303
● **Diner's Club**, tel: 547 4000
● **Eurocard, MasterCard**, tel: (91) 519 2100
● **Visa**, tel: (91) 362 6200
● **Tarjeta 4B**, tel: (91) 362 6200 or 902 114400
● **Red 6000**, tel: (91) 596 5300

Bag-snatching and pick-pocketing are probably the worst problems, so don't allow yourself to be distracted and take care in crowds and busy tourist areas. Avoid ostentation with money. Keep valuables in the hotel safe and don't carry large sums of money or your passport (take a photocopy instead), unless you are going to exchange money.

In the event of being robbed, contact the local Police Station or phone **Police Emergency** at 091.

Medical Services

Should you become seriously ill, go to the nearest major hospital. In Madrid, all of the following have 24-hour emergency rooms: La Paz Hospital in the north, Doce de Octubre in the south and the Gregorio Marañón Hospital in the centre of the city, on Calle Dr Esquerdo.

If you are an EU national, your state health insurance will cover your care. You can pick up an E111 form from any post office in your home country before travelling abroad. There is also a reciprocal arrangement with many foreign medical insurance companies.

Also available is a Spanish insurance policy, ASTES, which will cover any medical or hospital care if you fall ill or have an accident

during your stay in Spain. This Spanish Tourist Insurance, created and promoted by the Spanish state and backed by a group of 80 private insurance companies, covers full medical and hospital care, hotel lodging if an extension of your stay is recommended by a physician, repatriation and even lost luggage.
● The ASTES **Insurance Group** is located at Calle Diego de León, 44, 1˚izq., Madrid, tel: (91) 562 2087.

The Official Association of Dentists has opened a 24-hour, seven-day-a-week Dental Clinic for emergencies at Calle Padilla 68,5˚D., Madrid, tel: (91) 402 6421.

PHARMACIES

Spain has countless chemist shops or *farmacias*, each identifiable by a big, white sign with a flashing green cross. They are open from approximately 9.30am–1.30pm and 5–8pm Mon–Fri; 9am–1.30pm Sat. In most towns an effective system of rotation operates whereby there is always one chemist open round the clock in each area. An illuminated sign posted in front of each should indicate which chemists are on duty from 10pm–10am that day, and which is closest to where you are.

You can also consult the daily newspapers for a list of chemists on duty or telephone 010. Most chemist shops also have a list of the nearest clinics and hospitals posted in their windows.

Tipping

Service is not usually included in restaurants, so it is customary to leave the spare change (50–100 pesetas per person) in the dish when eating at a modest restaurant and a few duros (5-peseta coins) at a bar. When dining at an averagely smart restaurant, 10 percent of the bill is appropriate, unless you're charged for service. A 25-peseta tip is fine for an average taxi ride, and bathroom attendants expect between 10–25 pesetas per person.

Getting Acquainted

Geography

The huge plateau of Central Spain ranges from 600–1,000 metres (2,000–3,000 ft) high. The northern Meseta, the Castilla y León region, is dominated by cereal crops, the southerrn meseta, Madrid, Castilla-La Mancha and Extremadura,also features olive groves and vineyards, and, in Extremadura, sheep-grazing.

The city of **Madrid** is the highest capital city in Europe (650 metres/2,130 ft), sitting in a dish in the central Iberian plateau, flanked to the north and east by the sierras of Somosierra and Guadarama, and to the southeast by those of Toledo.

Climate

Central Spain has a continental climate, withbaking hot summers and cold winters. The southern Meseta is also exceedingly dry, Madrid has a relatively temperate climate. In autumn and spring, both extremely pleasant seasons, average temperatures range from 12–15°C (54–60°F), with a spread of 6°C (43°F) minimum to 21°C (70°F) maximum.

Summer and winter are more extreme. In summer, the temperature rises as high as 40°C (104°F) although mountain breezes can make the evenings slightly cooler.

The average winter temperature is 5°C (41°F), although it can drop below 0°C (32°F) in January, the most unsettled month of the year. You'll need to bring your winter coat and although it does not rain often (with an annual rainfall of about 438 mm per year), the wettest months are January–April.

Planning the Trip

Getting There

BY AIR

Madrid's Barajas airport, just 16 km (10 miles) out of the city, is one of Europe's six leading airports for passenger traffic. Many airlines fly direct to England (BA, Iberia, Spainair, Debonair) and the United States (Iberia, TWA, Delta, Virgin, United and American Airlines).

Iberia, whose main offices in Madrid are at Calle Velázquez, 130, operates all regular Spanish carrier flights abroad and domestic connections, the latter jointly with its subsidiaries Aviaco (headquarters at Maudes, 51) and Viva Air (Zurbano, 41).

● **Iberia information and reservations**: Serviberia, tel: (91) 400 500. However, Iberia is usually more expensive than other companies, so shop around. Halcón Viajes, a chain of travel agents, is popular and offers competitive prices (tel: 91 300 600 to find your nearest office); Viajes Marsans, tel: 91 115 947, is also good, and runs special offers.

From the Airport

To get into the city from the airport, there is a regular **bus service** which runs regularly (depending on the time of day) to the underground bus terminal at the Plaza Colón. The Aeropuerto-Colón bus operates from 4.45am through the day until 1.30am. From 4.45–5.45am the buses are hourly, after that they are every 15 minutes until 7am; from 7am–10pm, they are every 10/11 minutes, and then every 15 minutes until 1.30am.

● **Bus information**, tel: (91) 431

6192. Easy connections can be made at Colón to the Madrid Metro (or Underground), buss and taxis.

If taking a **taxi** from the airport into Madrid, avoid unofficial cab drivers. Official Madrid taxis are white with red stripes painted transversally across the doors. An additional 350 pesetas will be added to the fare as an airport surcharge, and 50 pesetas more can be included for each large piece of luggage. On Sunday, holidays and after 11pm, there is a further 150 peseta surcharge.

Tourist Offices

Madrid
Plaza Mayor, 3, tel: (91) 566 5477
Castilla-La Mancha
Albacete: Tinte, 2, tel: (967) 580 522.
Ciudad Real: Avda Alarcos, 21, tel: (926) 212 925.
Cuenca: Glorieta Gonzalez Palencia 2 – 3, tel: (969) 178 800.
Guadalajara: Plaza de las Caidos, 6, tel: (949) 216 26.
Toledo: Puerta de Bisagra, s/n, tel: (925) 220 843.
Castile-León
Avila: Plaza de la Catedral, 4, tel: (920) 211 387.
Burgos: Plaza Alonso Martínez 7, tel: (947) 203 125.
León: Plaza de la Regla, 3, tel: (987) 237 082.
Palencia: Mayor, 105, tel: (979) 740 068.
Salamanca: Compañía, 2, (Casa de las Conchas), tel: (923) 268 571.
Salamanca: Plaza Mayor, 14, tel: (923) 218 342.
Segovia: Plaza Mayor, 10, tel: (921) 460 334.
Soria: Plaza Ramon y Cajal s/n, tel: (975) 212 052.
Valladolid: Plaza de Zorrilla, 3, tel: (983) 351 801.
Zamora: Santa Clara, 20, tel: (980) 531 845.
Extremadura
Cáceres: Plaza Mayor, 33, tel: (927) 246 347.
Badajoz: Plaza de la Libertad, 3, tel: (924) 222 763.

Getting Around

By Air

Iberia is Spain's national airline, servicing both national and international routes. Its main offices are at Calle Velázquez, 130, 28006 Madrid.
● **Flight information and reservations**: Serviberia, tel: (91) 400 500. Iberia has ticket offices at Calle Velázquez 130, or you can buy an air ticket at any travel agency.

Aviaco, Iberia's subsidiary airline, only services domestic flights, while **Viva Air** covers international routes. The planes are generally older and smaller and fly less-frequented routes. Aviaco is at Maudes, 51 in Madrid, tel: (91) 554 3600; and Viva Air at Zurbano, 41, tel: (91) 349 0600. However, Iberia is usually more expensive than other companies, so we recommend you shop around.

Halcón Viajes, a chain of travel agents, is very popular and offers competitive prices (tel: 91 300 600 for information about your nearest office). **Viajes Marsans**, tel: 91 115 947, is also very good, and there are always good offers in the national press.

No point on mainland Spain is more than 55 minutes' flying time from Madrid, although travelling to and from airports can be quite time-consuming in the big cities. Approximate flying times are as follows:
Madrid–Barcelona: 55 minutes.
Madrid–Valencia: 30 minutes.
Madrid–Bilbao: 50 minutes.
Madrid–Seville: 50 minutes.
Madrid–Palma de Mallorca: 1 hour.
Madrid–the Canary Islands: 2 hours and 30 minutes.

By Rail

Madrid has two main train stations: Chamartín, in the north of Madrid, and Atocha, near the centre. Chamartín is an entire complex featuring the station itself, amply furnished with bars, restaurants, a self-service cafeteria and a shopping area and, across the driveway, a car park, cinemas, bowling alley, skating rink and discotheque.

The Cercanías lines, which go to Ávila, Sigüenza, El Escorial, Soria, Toledo, Segovia, Cercedilla and Navacerrada go from Atocha. This station has been renovated in recent years and is now a modern commercial complex handling all the retail traffic to the south (Andalucía, Extremadura) and Levante, among other areas. It also houses the terminal for the new, superfast AVE trains, which connect Madrid with Seville in a little over 3 hours.

The Estación del Norte "Príncipe Pío" previously handled all traffic to the north of the country but now it only services Alcalá de Henares, 3 Cantos and the Villalba areas, among others.

You can obtain **train information from RENFE**, the state-owned Spanish railway system, from information and reservations, tel: (91) 328 9020. Tickets can be delivered to you for a small fee. They can also be purchased at the RENFE offices (Alcalá, 44, and Paseo de Recoletos and Nuevos Ministerios RENFE stations, among others), the stations themselves or from most travel agencies.

There are many ways to save money on rail travel in Spain. Ask at a travel agent about Eurailpass, Blue Days (*Días Azules*) and the *Tarjeta Turística* offers.

A lovely trip, if you are planning a jaunt to Aranjuez, is to take the antiquated, coal-burning **Tren de la Fresa** which leaves from Atocha every Saturday, Sunday and public holiday at 10am from mid-April–Sept (no service in August). Return fares: Adults 2,900 pesetas, under-12s and over-65s 1,800 pesetas. Very popular in May and June, but you can book in advance at RENFE offices and travel agents, or at the railway museum in P° Delicias, 61.
● **RENFE information and bookings**, tel: (91) 328 9020. Traditionally-dressed stewardesses present travellers with souvenirs of their journey, and the famous fare of Aranjuez: fresas (strawberries).

Other train excursions are organised every year to the North or South of Spain, Wine Routes, Pilgrimage to Santiago de Compostela, etc.
● For further information, tel: IBERAIL (91) 571 6692.

By Bus

Bus travel has improved considerably in Spain. Buses covering the inter-city routes are air-conditioned, with video entertainment to pass the time and sometimes restrooms. Buses may take longer but are cheaper than trains. They make frequent stops at rest areas, giving passengers a chance to eat something and stretch their legs.

Trainspotting

Spanish trains have two classes: First (*Primera* or 1ª) and Second (*Segunda* or 2ª), and a variety of train categories which vary considerably in terms of comfort. The **Talgo** is a fast, comfortable train with video entertainment to while away the hours; the TERS and **Electrotrens** also have similar distractions. The

Expresos are the night trains, on which one can usually get a *cama* (small, private compartment) or an inexpensive *litera* (a couchette in a compartment shared with five other passengers). The **Rapidos** are local day trains, which should be avoided other than for short journeys.

There are several bus companies in Madrid which service specific areas of the country. Most leave from the **Estación Sur de Autobuses**, at Calle Méndez Alvaro esquina Calle Retama. For information, tel: (91) 468 4511/468 4200.

Auto Res, Calle Fernández Shaw, 1, near Plaza Conde de Casal, has a large network of bus lines which includes the entire Levante coast (Valencia and Castellón), Extremadura (Badajoz and Cáceres), Zamora, Cuenca, Valladolid, Salamanca and Palencia. For information, tel: (91) 551 7200.

The Continental bus line at Avenida de América, 34, tel: (91) 533 0400/3711, covers local routes, including Alcalá de Henares, Torrejón de Ardoz, Guadalajara, and also Burgos, San Sebastián, Vitoria, Santander, Soria, Logroño and Pamplona. Buses for Toledo leave from the Estación Sur, Calle Méndez Alvaro esquina Calle Retama, tel: (91) 468 4511/4200.

Enatcar buses leave from the Estación Sur de Autobuses, Calle Méndez Alvaro esquina Calle Retama, tel: (91) 468 4511/4200, for Orense, Pontevedra, Barcelona, Alicante and Levante, Granada, Algeciras, Huelva and the Costa del Sol. For information, tel: (91) 467 3577.

Car Rental

To rent a car in Spain you have to be at least 19 years of age with either an international licence or a valid licence from your own country.

It is usually necessary to pay for the car rental with a major credit card, such as Visa, MasterCard, American Express, Diner's Club, or you might have to leave a large deposit. You also need insurance.

Cars can be rented per day with an additional fee according to mileage, or in package deals, available for a set number of days, at unlimited mileage; consider which will be most advantageous for your purpose. You might also be interested in picking the car up in Madrid and leaving it in another city.

Madrid

Metro System

The Madrid underground or Metro system is the fastest, cheapest and most efficient way of getting around the city. (If you are claustrophobic, avoid rush hours: 8–9.30am, 1.30–2.30pm and 8–9pm).

The Metro is the second oldest in Europe – it was opened by King Alfonso XIII in 1919, and today has 165 stations, which will take you to just about every corner of the city. It operates from 6am–1.30am in the morning and is used by over 1 million people daily. Fortunately, most trains are air-conditioned. The ticket that used to known as the Bono is now called Metrobús and is valid on buses and metros. It costs 670 pesetas and can be used for 10 journeys. A single ticket (regardless of your destination) costs 130 pesetas.

For Metro information, tel: (91) 552 5909.

City Buses

The Madrid bus system might not be as fast or as comfortable as one would like, due to traffic conditions, but then again, Madrid is a small, rather compact city. Tickets cost 130 pesetas regardless of length of journey. You enter from the front and pay the driver preferably with change, or at the most with a 1,000 peseta note. Press the buzzer to tell him to let you out at the stop you want. Leave by the rear door. The Bonobús is now called Metrobús and is valid both on buses and metros. It costs 670 pesetas and can be used for 10 journeys. It can be purchased from the bus information booths at Puerta del Sol, Plaza Callao, Plaza Cibeles, Plaza de Castilla, etc., all newspaper stands and estancos. There is a slotted box behind the driver and when you insert your Metrobús it automatically registers your journey.

Buses are in service 6am–midnight. There are also Night Buses (Búhos – owls) which operate from 12am–6am. They all depart from Plaza Cibeles. For municipal

Car Rental in Madrid

It is unlikely that you will want to hire a car in Madris, as there are much better ways of getting around the city. However, it is a good idea to hire a car to explore the surrounding countryside of Central Spain. There are many car hire agencies, including the following

● **American Express**, Plaza de las Cortes, 2, tel: (91) 322 5424.

● **Atesa**, several branches in and around Madrid. Calle Mauricio Lejendre, 4, tel: (91) 314 3535. Airport branch, tel: (91) 393 7232.

● **Avis**, several branches in and around Madrid. Gran Vía, 60, tel: (91) 547 20 46/548 4203. Airport branch, tel: (91) 369 7222.

● **Europcar**, several branches in and around Madrid. Calle Orense, 29, tel: (91) 555 9931. Airport branch, tel: (91) 393 7235.

● **Hertz**, several branches in and around Madrid. Edificio España, local 18, tel: (91) 542 5803. Airport branch, tel: (91) 393 7228.

bus information (EMT), tel: (91) 401 9900 or 401 3100 (offices).

If you are planning an extended period of time in Madrid and doing a lot of bus and Metro travelling, it might be a good idea to purchase an Abono. This card can be applied for at any estanco by filling out a form and providing a passport-size photograph and a photocopy of your passport or national identity document.

Taxis

Compared with those of other cities, taxis in Madrid are an inexpensive way of getting around and are plentiful (except perhaps when it is raining). They are white, bear a transversal red stripe on the sides and the Madrid coat of arms. They are available if they are displaying a green libre ("free") sign on the windscreen or at night have a little green light on. If a red sign with the name of a Madrid neighbourhood is displayed, it means they are on their way home and are not obliged to pick you up unless you are on their route.

A meter on the dashboard will indicate the fare. When you flag a taxi, the meter starts off at a minimum fee and automatically increases every kilometre. If you ask the driver to wait, he can charge you by the hour. Additional supplements can be added to the meter price, so don't think the driver is trying to "take you for a ride". Prices are also constantly going up.

If you have serious reason to believe that the driver is over-charging you, ask for a receipt from his official note pad, which is perforated with his taxi licence number. Ask him to write down the starting point of the journey, the conclusion, date and time (there are spaces for these on the receipt) and sign it. Then send or present the receipt to: Sección de AutoTaxi y Vehículos de Alquiler, Ayto de Madrid, Calle Vallehermoso, 1, 28015 Madrid, tel: (91) 447 0714/15. A complaints form is included in the Taxi Information leaflet available from tourist offices.

Taxis can be hailed with relative ease in main thoroughfares, found at a *Parada de Taxi* (taxi stand, indicated by a large white "T" against a dark blue background) or requested by phone. For taxi pick-up, call Radio-Teléfono Taxi, tel: (91) 547 8200; Radio-Taxi Independiente, tel: 405 1213 or 405 5500; or Teletaxi, tel: (91) 371 2131; Radio Taxi Asociación Gremial, tel: (91) 447 5180.

Where to Stay

Choosing a Hotel

With over 50,000 beds, Madrid has accommodation to meet every need and wallet. Hotels are classified in five categories, reflected in the number of stars they have been awarded. *Hoteles-residencias* are also classified according to quality and services. These do not have a restaurant, but often have bar and cafeteria facilities. *Hostales* are more modest, and classified according to only 1, 2 or 3 stars. *Pensiones* or guesthouses are also useful for those on limited budgets. Most *pensiones* are run by a family. Rooms can be rented with home cooking included, and there is usually a family room which is shared with the other guests for watching television or reading.

An official notice should be posted behind the door, indicating the daily price of the room, although the rate can vary according to season. Breakfast is not included in the room rate and is often continental: coffee, tea or hot chocolate and toast or buns. Remember that 7 percent VAT (IVA) will be added to your bill, except for those of the Grand Luxury category, which charge 15 percent VAT.

Another possibility for longer stays is to rent a furnished apartment, an increasingly popular idea.

If planning excursions out of Madrid, probably your best bet would be to make a reservation at any of the *paradors* (state-run inns) on your route. The *parador* system, first planned in 1926, was started in the 1970s by the Ministry of Information and Tourism. Run-down castles and palaces were taken over and converted into charming and luxurious hotels at affordable prices.

Paradors relatively close to Madrid are: the Parador of Chinchón, Parador Conde de Orgaz of Toledo, Parador Raimundo de Borgoña of Avila, Parador of Salamanca, San Marcos Parador of León, Parador of Segovia, Zurbarán Parador of Guadalupe, Castle Parador of Sigüenza, Parador of Oropesa and the Parador of Gredos (which is noted for its magnificent natural mountain setting). Reservations can be made at the central office: Calle Requena, 3, tel: (91) 516 6666. Open: Mon–Fri 9am–2pm and 3pm–7pm, Sat 9am–2pm. By phone: Mon–Fri, Sat 9am–2pm. Note: s/n in an address signifies *sin número* (no number); ctra means carretera (highway).

The price guide given below refers to a standard double room. Most five-star (deluxe) hotels offer up to 50 percent discounts at weekends. Reserve well in advance. This also applies to many hotels in the expensive and moderate categories, although discounts are less spectacular. Add 7 percent IVA (VAT) to all prices.

MADRID

Ritz Deluxe
Plaza de la Lealtad, 5
tel: (91) 521 2857
One block away from the Prado Museum, offers luxury in the old style. $$$$
Santa Mauro Deluxe
Zurbano, 36
tel: (91) 319 6900
An old palace converted into a posh hotel with a quiet atmosphere. $$$$
Villamagna Deluxe
Paseo de la Castellana, 22
tel: (91) 576 7500
Grand luxury in modern style. $$$$
Palace
Plaza de las Cortes, 7
tel: (91) 360 8000.
A comfortable, classic hotel, with a fine cultural/political/international ambience, across the street from the Parliament. $$$$
Barajas
Avda Logroño, 305
tel: (91) 747 7700
14 km (9 miles) from the capital

and close to the airport, ideal for those seeking a quiet ambience. Swimming pool and gym. **$$$$**

Eurobuilding
Padre Damián, 23
tel: (91) 345 4500
In the heart of the business district of northern Madrid. Has many facilities including shops, restaurants, swimming pool. **$$$$**

Gran Hotel Reina Victoria
Plaza Santa Ana, 14
tel: (91) 531 4500
Remodelled and upgraded hotel which maintains its old-world atmosphere. **$$$$**

Melià Castilla
Capitán Haya, 43
tel: (91) 571 3311
Well suited for those on a business trip. **$$$$**

Suecia
Marqués de Casa Riera, 4
tel: (91) 531 6900
Centrally located beside the Fine Arts Circle. Its restaurant is noted for the typical Swedish smorgasbord served on Thursday and Friday evenings. **$$$$**

Wellington
Velázquez, 8
tel: (91) 575 4400
An old-fashioned, stylish hotel. Traditional meeting place for the bullfighting crowd. Close to good shops. Small outdoor swimming pool and a fine restaurant. **$$$$**

Emperador
Gran Vía, 53
tel: (91) 547 2800
Rooftop pool open June–Sep. **$$$–$$$$**

Holiday Inn Madrid
Plaza Carlos Trías Bertrán, 4
tel: (91) 456 8000.
It is representative of the US chain. Swimming pool. Fine restaurant. **$$$–$$$$**

Alcalá
Alcalá, 66
tel: (91) 435 1060
Across the street from the Retiro Park and near good shops. It has a fine Basque restaurant. **$$$**

Chamartín
Agustín de Foxá, s/n
tel: (91) 323 3087
Situated near the Chamartín railway station. **$$$**

Gran Hotel Conde Duque
Plaza Conde del Valle Suchil, 5
tel: (91) 447 7000
In the Argüelles area. **$$$**

Prado
Prado, 11
tel: (91) 369 0234
Recently remodelled and centrally located hotel. **$$$**

Las Alondras Sol
José Abascal, 8
tel: (91) 447 4000
A comfortable hotel. **$$–$$$**

Alameda
Avda Logroño, 100
tel: (91) 747 4800
Near the airport, 14 km (9 miles) from the city. Courtesy service for clients to the airport. Swimming pool. **$$**

Colón
Dr Esquerdo, 117
tel: (91) 573 5900
In a residential area. **$$**

Claridge
Plaza Conde de Casal, 6
tel: (91) 551 9400
On the outskirts of the city at the start of the Madrid-Valencia highway. **$$**

Inglés
Echegaray, 8
tel: (91) 429 6551
Cosy hotel in a busy area, close to the Puerta del Sol. Good value. **$$**

Madrid
Carretas, 10
tel: (91) 521 6520
An older hotel, a block away from the Puerta del Sol. **$$**

Puerta de Toledo
Glorieta Puerta de Toledo, 4
tel: (91) 474 7100
Located in old Madrid, near the Rastro flea market and the Puerta de Toledo Market complex. **$$**

Regina
Alcalá, 19
tel: (91) 521 4725
Centrally located. **$$**

Pensiones

Astoria, Carrera de San Jerónimo, 32
tel: (91) 429 1188
Across the street from the Palace Hotel and the Parliament building. (4,500–5,500 pesetas).
Avenida, Gran Vía, 15
tel: (91) 522 6360

(3,500–5,500 pesetas).
Continental, Gran Vía, 44
tel: (902) 521 4640
(4,000–5,600 pesetas).
Fuente Sol, Victoria 2, 3rd floor left
tel: (91) 521 6674
Just off the Puerta del Sol.
(2,500–4,500 pesetas with bath, TV)
Gravina, Gravina, 4
tel: (91) 522 3862
(2,000 pesetas).
La Perla Asturiana, Plaza de la Cruz, 3
tel: (91) 366 4600
Near Plaza Mayor. (3,600 pesetas).
Los Ángeles, Artistas, 18
tel: (91) 533 0375
Near the Plaza Tirso de Molina.
(4,300–6,500 pesetas).
Persal, Plaza del Angel, 12
tel: (91) 369 4643
(4,900–8,900 pesetas).

Price Guide

For a standard double room
$$$$ = Over 20,000 pesetas
$$$ = 15–20,000 pesetas
$$ = 15,000 pesetas
$ = Under 8,000 pesetas

Apartments

All apartments are in the moderate category, i.e. one night for two people costs around 15–20,000 pesetas, and four to six people can sleep for around 30,000 pesetas per night.
Centro Colón, Marqués de la Ensenada, 16, tel: (91) 349 0000.
Foxá 25/32, Agustín de Foxa, 25 and 32, tel: (91) 323 1119 and 733 1060, respectively.
Goya 75, Goya, 75, tel: (91) 435 6346.
Los Jerónimos, Moreto, 9, tel: (91) 420 0211.
Muralto, Tutor, 37, tel: (91) 542 4400.
Recoletos, Villanueva, 2, tel: (91) 431 9640.

CASTILLA-LA MANCHA

Alarcon
Parador de Alarcón
Amigos de los Castillos, 3
tel: (969) 330 315
fax: (969) 330 303
Built into a cliff overlooking the
Júcar river, this is one of Spain's
best castle-paradors. The roast
lamb is also excellent. **$$$$**

Albacete
Parador de la Mancha
Apdo 384, Route N 301
tel: (967) 245 321
fax: (967) 243 271
Just outside of Albacete, this rangy
ranch-like parador is elegant and
comfortable. **$$$$**

Almagro
Parador de Almagro
Ronda de San Francisco, 31
tel: (926) 860 100
fax: (926) 860 150
This 16th-century convent is
thought by many to be Spain's most
beautiful parador, with circular
stone and brick floor designs copied
from the nearby castle of Calatrava
and more than a dozen interior
patios. **$$$$**

Ayna – Sierra de Alcaraz
Felipe II
Avda Manuel Carrera, 9
tel: (967) 295 083
fax: (967) 295 083
This otherwise undistinguished
modern building has spectacular
views into the surrounding hills. **$$**

Riopar – Sierra de Alcaraz
Hotel Riopar
Calle Choperas, s/n
tel: (967) 435 377
fax: (967) 436 154
This new hotel near the source of
the Mundo river is tastefully
constructed in local wood and
stone; a good place to stay for
fishing the Mundo. **$$**

Beteta
Hotel Los Tilos
Extrarradio, s/n
tel: (969) 318 097
fax: (969) 318 299
This northern Cuenca base camp

for exploring the Beteta and
Tragavivos gorges has comfortable
rooms and serves hearty mountain
dishes, game in season, and
morteruelo, a country pâté. **$$**

Cuenca
Posada de San Jose
Julián Romero, 4
tel: (969) 211 300
fax: (969) 230 365
Built into a 16th-century convent with
rooms overlooking the Huécar canyon
in the old part of Cuenca. **$$$**

Daimiel
Las Brujas
Antigua Ctra De Madrid, km 1.7
tel: (926) 852 289
This handy hotel and restaurant is a
good jumping-off place for an
excursion through the wetlands of
Tablas de Daimiel. Simple
accomodation and fine regional
cuisine. **$$**

Price Guide

For a standard double room
$$$$ = Over 20,000 pesetas
$$$ = 15–20,000 pesetas
$$ = 15,000 pesetas
$ = Under 8,000 pesetas

Oropesa
Parador de Oropesa
Plaza del Palacio, 1
tel: (925) 430 000
fax: (925) 430 777
This feudal stronghold with the
Sierra de Gredos in the distance to
the northwest well merits a trip just
to stay within its medieval walls in
modern comfort. It's also the best
restaurant around. **$$$**

Pastrana
Colegio de San Buenaventura
Adolfo Martin-Gamero 20
tel/fax: (949) 370 021
Once a 16th-century music
academy, this hostel still resonates
with good vibrations. **$$**

Puerto Lápice
Aprisco de Puerto Lápice
Ctra Madrid-Cadiz, Ciudad Real
tel: (926) 576 150
This ancient building was once a
shelter for livestock. The circular
dining room has an open wrought-
iron fireplace in the centre under a
conical roof. Unique. **$$**

Sigüenza
Parador de Sigüenza
Plaza del Castillo
tel: (949) 390 100
fax: (949) 391 364
Elegant and comfortable medieval
castle overlooking the town. **$$$**

Toledo
La Almazara
Ctra Toledo-Arges
tel: (925) 223 866
fax: (925) 250 562
A country farmhouse-inn with
commanding views of Toledo. **$**
Parador Nacional Conde de Orgaz
Paseo Emperador, s/n
tel: (925) 221 850
fax: (925) 225 166
A splendid hotel, which also has
good views of Toledo. **$$$$**
Pintor El Greco
Alamillos des Tránsito, 13
tel: (925) 214 250
Next to the painter's house-
museum in what used to be a 17th-
century bakery. **$$$**

Tragacete
Hospedería Real del Jucar
Muñoz Grandes, 7
tel: (969) 289 205
fax: (969) 289 204
The best hotel in this town in the
Cuenca highlands, this is a good
base camp for excursions to the
waterfalls and the source of the
Cuervo river. **$$$**

CASTILE-LEÓN

Ávila
Palacio de Valderrábanos
Plaza de la Catedral, 9
tel: (920) 211 023
fax: (920) 251 691
Smartly furnished-traditional hotel
in historic mansion next to the
cathedral. Good restaurant. **$$$**

Parador de Ávila
Marqués Canales de Chozas, 2
tel: (920) 211 340
fax: (920) 226 166
Charming hotel set in the 15th-century Palacio de Benavides. **$$$**

La Hostería de Bracamonte
Bracamonte, 6
tel: (920) 251 280
A 16th-century mansion-cum-restaurant with typical decor.

Burgos
Del Cid
Plaza Santa Maria, 8
tel: (947) 208 715
Superbly placed opposite the cathedral, a stylish hotel with an excellent restaurant and useful garage parking. **$$$**

Fernán González
Calera, 17
tel: (947) 209 441
Comfortable, traditional hotel on the south bank of the river, with an elegant restaurant. **$$$**

Norte y Londres
Plaza de Alonso Martínez, 10
tel: (947) 264 125
Quiet, inexpensive hotel with genteel furnishings, handily placed for the tourist office and main sights. **$$**

León
Parador San Marcos
Plaza de San Marcos, 7
tel: (987) 237 300
fax: (987) 233 458
Top-class parador in one of Spain's most palatial Renaissance buildings. Magnificent public rooms, acclaimed restaurant and luxurious bedrooms. **$$$$**

Conde Luna
Independencia, 7
tel: (987) 206 600
fax: (987) 212 752
With a garden and pool. **$$$**

Quindos
Avda José Antonio, 24
tel: (987) 236 200
Clean, modern hotel on a fairly busy central corner. Quiet, stylish interior with a useful, separately-managed restaurant next door. **$$**

Palencia
Castilla la Vieja
Avda. Casado del Alisal, 26
tel: (979) 749 044
fax: (979) 747 577
Central. **$$**

Rey Sancho
Avda Ponce de León, s/n
tel: (979) 725 300
fax: (979) 710 334
A comfortable hotel with a large garden, pool and tennis court. **$$$**

Salamanca
Parador de Salamanca
Teso de la Feria, 2
tel: (923) 192 082
fax: (923) 192 087
This modern building is located on the Tormes River and offers a spectacular panorama of the city and especially of the cathedral. **$$$**

Rector
Paseo del Rector Esperabé, 10
tel: (923) 218 482
Beautifully furnished coverted mansion. Family-run, small and personal. No restaurant. **$$$**

Emperatriz
Compañía, 4
tel: (923) 219 156
Quaint medieval building near university quarter, with clean, simple rooms (mostly showers only). Dining room rather dark. **$$**

Gran Hotel
Plaza del Poeta Iglesias, 3–5
tel/fax: (923) 213 500
A classic hotel, popular with the bullfighting crowd and complete with a "feudal restaurant". **$$$**

Las Torres
Concejo, 4
tel: (923) 212 100
fax: (923) 212 101
Overlooking the Plaza Mayor, this modest, modern hotel lacks much character but is well equipped and handily placed for sightseeing. **$$**

Segovia
Parador de Segovia
Apartado de Correos, 106
tel: (921) 443 737
A modern, slightly institutional parador, some way out of town, but with a magnificent view of it. Comfortable and well equipped. **$$$$**

Acueducto
Padre Claret, 10
tel: (921) 424 800
fax: (921) 428 446
Outside the walls in the lower town, but reasonably convenient for sightseeing. Modern facilities. Rather noisy location. **$$**

Infanta Isabel
Isabel la Católica, 1
tel: (921) 461 300
fax: (921) 433 240
Elegant B&B hotel just off the main square, with cosy, comfortable rooms. Good value. **$$$**

Los Linajes
Dr Velasco, 9
tel: (921) 460 475
fax: (921) 460 479
Traditional hotel in a quiet spot by the city walls. Excellent views from some rooms. Parking is tricky. **$$**

Soria
Parador de Soria
Parque del Castillo
tel: (975) 240 800
Spacious, stylish, modern interior. Hilltop location, with excellent views over the park and the Duero valley. Dedicated to the poet Antonio Machado, who made Soria his home and immortalised it in his work. **$$$**

Valladolid
Olid Meliá
Plaza San Miguel, 10
tel: (983) 357 200
fax: (983) 336 828
This hotel, with modern installations, is nicely situated in the old part of town. **$$$**

Felipe IV
Gamazo, 16
tel: (983) 307 000
fax: (983) 308 687
A comfortable, centrally located hotel. **$$**

Lasa
Acera de Recoletos, 21
tel: (983) 390 255
fax: (983) 302 561
Renovated 19th-century apartment block on the Campo Grande towards the southern end of town. **$**

Meliá Parque
Joaquin García Morato, 17 bis
tel: (983) 220 000
fax: (983) 475 029
With a restaurant. **$$**

Zamora
Parador de Zamora
Plaza Viriato, 5
tel: (980) 514 497
fax: (980) 530 063
Installed in a 15th-century palace
with a splendid Renaissance
cloister, situated in the heart of
town. **$$$**
Hostería Real de Zamora
Cuesta de Pizarro, 7
tel/fax: (980) 534 545
Beautiful 16th-century mansion
near river and city walls. Cloister
and fountain courtyards in Moorish
style. **$$**
Hostal Rey Don Sancho
Ctra Villacastín-Vigo, km 276
tel: (980) 523 400
fax: (980) 519 760
With a restaurant. **$$**

Price Guide

For a standard double room
$$$$ = Over 20,000 pesetas
$$$ = 15–20,000 pesetas
$$ = 15,000 pesetas
$ = Under 8,000 pesetas

EXTREMADURA
Cáceres
Parador de Turismo de Cáceres
Ancha, 6
tel: (927) 211 759
Installed in the 14th-century Palacio
del Comendador, it is situated in
the heart of the restored
monumental quarter. **$$$$**
Extremadura
Avda de Virgen de Guadalupe, 5
tel: (927) 221 600
A reasonably priced, comfortable
hotel, with a swimming pool and
garden. **$$**
Parador de Turismo de Guadalupe
Mques de la Romana, 10
tel: (927)367 075
Opposite the monastery, with
rooms overlooking a magical
mudejar patio. **$$$$**

Parador de Turismo de Trujillo
Santa Beatriz de Silva, 1
tel: (927) 321 350
Good regional cooking marks out
this parador built within a converted
convent. **$$$$**

Badajoz
Gran Hotel Zurbarán
Paseo de Castelar, s/n
tel: (924) 223 741
A classic, centrally located hotel
with a swimming pool and fine
restaurant. **$$$$**
Parador de Turismo Via de la Plata
Plaza de la Constitución, 3
tel: (924) 313 800
Gracious 18th-century building with
garden. **$$$$**
Emperatriz
Plaza de España, 19
tel: (924) 313 111
Charmingly eccentric, slightly worn
hotel. **$$**

Eating Out

What to Eat

In Spain, restaurants, like hotels,
are classified into five categories,
this time symbolised with forks. In
addition to *restaurantes*, there are
bares, or all-purpose drinking
establishments, where one can
have anything from a coffee or a
coke to a whisky and a *bocadillo* (a
sandwich on crusty fresh bread) or
a sandwich (on toasted white
bread); *mesones*, which are typical
taverns with appropriate fare;
modern cafeterias or coffee shops
where you can get toasted
"sandwiches", or meals throughout
the day; and of course, the
"imported" hamburger and pizza
parlours.

Spanish eating hours are
different, the main meal being a
hearty, three-course affair served
between 2 and 4pm, while dinner is
light and eaten after 10pm.

Tapas are also an important part
of the programme. These small,
varied snacks help one get through
the long gaps between meals.

Spaniards tend to have a light
breakfast before going to work and
then a coffee break at mid-morning
when they indulge in pastries,
churros (fried dough rings) or a
pincho de tortilla (a wedge of potato
omelette served with crusty bread).
One o'clock is aperitife time, when
a vast array of *tapas* are laid out
along the bar counters. It is tapa
time again at 8pm and the idea is
to go from one bar to the next,
sampling the specialities proffered
at each.

Spaniards usually wash down
their *tapas* with draught beer (*una
caña de cerveza*), a *botellín* (a
small bottle of beer), or a small
glass of wine (*un chato de vino*),

tinto being red and *blanco*, white. One should sample the dry sherry, *vino fino* or simply *fino* or *jerez*, which comes from the southern grape-growing region around Jerez de la Frontera.

Spanish wine, like the food, is reasonable in price and very good besides. The country is particularly proud of its Riojas from the north, the different varieties of sherry from Jerez, and the champagnes or *cavas* (sparkling wines) from Catalonia. Inexpensively-priced, ordinary table wines from the Valdepeñas region can also be pleasant.

Although you can find just about every alcoholic beverage in Madrid, the country also has an interesting selection of after-dinner drinks: the famous *anisette* of Chinchón, the *pacharán* of Pamplona, the herbal brandies of Galicia and assorted *eaux de vie* and *ponches* from diverse regions of the country.

Despite the wide availability of alcohol in Spain and its relatively low price, you will rarely see anyone drunk.

Should you have any serious problems with the food, service or bill in a restaurant request the *hojas de reclamación*, the complaint forms. When they are filled out, the proprietor is obliged to send one copy to the local police station, which will look into the complaint.

Where to Eat

MADRID

Spanish

Alkalde
Jorge Juan, 10
tel: (91) 576 3359
Basque cooking. A charming, cosy restaurant, offering traditional specialities, located off the Calle Serrano. **$$$**

Botín
Cuchilleros, 17 (Plaza Mayor)
tel: (91) 366 4217
Famous for its roast pig and lamb prepared in an old wood-burning oven. **$$$**

Brasserie de Lista
José Ortega y Gasset, 6

tel: (91) 435 2818
A charming, old-fashioned restaurant with a turn-of-the-century flavour, though it is fairly new. **$$$**

Casa Lucio
Cava Baja, 35
tel: (91) 365 3252
Good food, wine, service and frequented by top celebrities including the Spanish royal family. Call for reservations. Closed August. **$$$**

Casa Paco
Puerta Cerrada, 11 (Plaza Mayor)
tel: (91) 366 3166
Fine sirloin steaks, among the best in the city. Closed Sunday **$$$**

Horcher
Alfonso XII, 6
tel: (91) 522 0731
International and Central European cuisine, specialising in game. One of the best restaurants in Madrid. Closed Saturday lunchtime and Sunday. **$$$**

Price Category

The approximate cost per person, including house wine, is coded in the following way:
$$$ = over 5,000 pesetas
$$ = between 2,500 – 4,500 pesetas
$ = less than 2,500 pesetas

Taberna del Alabardero
Felipe V, 6
tel: (91) 547 2577
Basque cooking. Near the Royal Palace and the Opera (Teatro Real). It now has a branch in Washington, DC. **$$$**

La Trainera
Lagasca, 60
tel: (91) 576 8035
Specialises in seafood. One Michelin star. Closed Sunday. **$$$**

Zalacaín
Alvarez de Baena, 4
tel: (91) 561 5935
Specialises in Basque cooking. One of the best restaurants in Madrid. Three Michelin stars. **$$$**

Casa Patas
Cañizares, 10
tel: (91) 369 0496
Home cooking and evening flamenco performances. **$$–$$$**

Hogar Gallego
Plaza del Comandante de las Morenas, 3
tel: (91) 559 6404
Galician cooking and seafood, and outdoor tables in summer. Closed Sunday evening. **$$–$$$**

Artemisa
Ventura de la Vega, 4
tel: (91) 429 5092
Tres Cruces, 4
tel: (91) 521 8721
Vegetarian restaurant. Good, imaginative cooking. Closed Sunday evening. **$$**

La Bola
Bola, 5 (Centre)
tel: (91) 547 6930
Home cooking and famous for its Madrid cocido (stew). Closed Sunday, Christmas Eve, the month of July, and Saturday evenings in August. **$$**

Boñar
Cruz Verde, 16 (Centre)
tel: (91) 531 0030
Cooking from León, fine meats and fish. Open until 3am. **$$**

Casa Ricardo
Fernando el Católico, 31
tel: (91) 447 6119
Typical Madrid cooking including *callos* (tripe), squid in its own ink and home-made sausage. Closed Sunday. **$$**

Las Cuevas de Luis Candelas
Cuchilleros, 1 (Plaza Mayor)
tel: (91) 366 5428
A typical restaurant located below the Plaza Mayor. Famous for its roasts and as the erstwhile hideway of a legendary "Robin Hood" style bandit, Luis Candelas. **$$**

Horno de Santa Teresa
Santa Teresa, 12
tel: (91) 308 6698
Asturian cooking, including *fabada* stew and fresh salmon. **$$**

Malacatín, Ruda, 5
tel: (91) 365 5241
Tavern-style restaurant, located in the Rastro flea market. The speciality Madrid *cocido* stew. Closed Sunday and holidays. **$$**

American
Hollywood
Magallanes, 1
tel: (91) 445 6110
Apolonio Morales, 3
tel: (91) 345 1036
Velázquez, 80
tel: (91) 435 6128
Plaza del Sagrado Corazón de
Jesús, 2
tel: (91) 546 6650
Princesa, 13
tel: (91) 559 1914
Castellana, 116
tel: (91) 564 6308
Plaza Isabel II, 3 (opposite the
Teatro Real)
tel: (91) 542 3045
Hamburger haven. **$$**
Rancho Texano
Ctra de Barcelona, km 12
tel: (91) 747 4736/44
Nice steaks. **$$$**

French
La Botella de Pepe
Padre Damián, 47
tel: (91) 350 7255
Pretty interior, outdoor tables in
summer. **$$$**

German
Edelweiss
Jovellanos, 7
tel: (91) 521 0326
Very popular so you might have to
wait for a table. Closed Sunday
evening. **$$**

Indian
Adrish
Calle San Bernadino, 1
tel: (91) 542 9498/9374
Interesting Indian dishes in this
restaurant near the Plaza España.
Closed Monday. **$$**
Annapurna
Zurbano, 5
tel: (91) 319 8716 and 308 3249
Elegant interior and fine cooking.
Closed Saturday lunchtime, Sunday
and holidays. **$$$**

Italian
Il Pastaio del Vecchio Mulino
Calle Ríos Rosas, 49
tel: (91) 554 2925
This extremely popular restaurant
offers home-made pasta to eat in or

take away. Traditional but
innovateive. Italian wines available.
Closed Monday. **$–$$**

Nouvelle Cuisine
El Cenador del Prado
Calle Prado, 4
tel: (91) 429 1561
Considered one of the best
restaurants in Madrid. One Michelin
star. **$$$**
Las Cuatro Estaciones
General Ibáñez Ibero, 5
tel: (91) 553 6305
Gourmet dining and seasonal
dishes. Closed Saturday lunchtime
and Sunday. Parking. **$$$**
Viridiana
Juan de Mena, 14
tel: (91) 523 4478
Very imaginative dishes. Closed
Sunday. **$$$**

Vegetarian
La Galette
Calle Conde de Aranda, 11
tel: (91) 576 0641
Plush vegetarian restaurant with
international dishes. Closed Sunday
lunchtime, and two weeks in
August. **$$**
El Granero de Lavapiés
Calle Argumosa, 10
tel: (91) 467 7611
Very popular. Simple, unfussy style.
Attractive tiled dining room. Open
for lunch Sun–Fri. **$**

CASTILLA-LA MANCHA
Almagro
Mesón El Corregidor
Jerónimo Ceballos, 2
tel: (926) 860 648
This onetime medieval inn is
famous for its rustic elegance and
offers excellent value besides. **$$**

Almansa
Mesón del Pincelín
Las Norias, 10
tel: (967) 340 007
Arranged around a roaring fire, this
typical manchego spot is well
known for its excellent local dishes
such as *gazpacho manchego*, a
soup served hot and including
pigeon, rabbit or partridge meat. **$$**

Brihuega
Asador El Tolmo
Avda de la Constitución, 26
tel: (949) 280 476
A perfect Castilian setting for fine
Manchego dining in the heart of
partridge country. The roasts are
peerless. **$$**

Cuenca
Plaza Mayor
Plaza Mayor, 5
tel: (969) 211 496
This traditional Castilian spot in the
heart of Cuenca's old town is a
local favourite for quality, value and
gazpacho pastor (a hearty stew) or
morteruelo (pâté). **$**
Meson Casas Colgadas
Canónigos, s/n
tel: (969) 223 509
This minimalist white dining room is
next to the Museum of Abstract Art
in one of Cuencas emblematic
Casas Colgadas (hanging houses)
perched on the cliff over the Huécar
gorge. Fine regional cuisine. A
must. **$$$**

Guadalajara
Amparito Roca
Toledo, 19
tel: (949) 214 639
One of the two top spots in
Guadalajara (the other is Miguel
Angel, Alfonso Lopez de Haro, 4,
tel: (949) 212 251. **$$$**), the
restaurant, named for a famous
pasadoble written for the
eponymous singer by the composer
Maestro Teixidor, specialises in
cabrito (roast kid) in *breve*, a sauce
composed of aromatic herbs.

Puerto Lápice
Venta del Quijote
This is a stop that should not be
missed, the legendary *venta* (inn)
where Don Quijote is thought to
have pledged allegiance to Dulcinea
and justice, love and truth. The
Manchegan cuisine is excellent. **$$**

Sigüenza
El Doncel
Paseo de la Alameda, 3
tel: (949) 390 001
fax: (949) 390 080
This inn and restaurant named for

the slain pageboy of Isabela la Católica prepares the typical roasts and stews of the region as well as international specialities. **$$**

Talavera de la Reina
Anticuario
Avda de Madrid, 1
tel: (925) 807 600
fax: (925) 815 808
The restaurant for the hotel Beatriz, locally considered the best in town, specialises in dishes based on game, and particularly partridge. **$$**

Toledo
Hostal del Cardenal
Paseo Recaredo, 24
tel: (925) 224 900
fax: (925) 222 991
This excellent spot appears near the top of any list of Toledo dining and lodging choices. The restaurant's wood ovens prepare roast suckling pig and lamb to perfection. **$$$**
Asador Adolfo
La Granada, 6
tel: (925) 227 321
The 14th 15th-century decor in this traditional gem deep in the Jewish quarter is no less impressive than the fresh local produce served here, including game in season. **$$$**
Hierbabuena
Cristo de la Luz, 9
tel: (925) 223 463
The dining room here is on an interior Moorish patio. The cuisine is simple, changing with the market and easy on the pocket as well. **$**

Tragacete
El Gamo
Plaza de los Caidos, 2
tel: (969) 289 008
fax: (969) 289 228
For both dining and lodging, this little hotel and restaurant in the mountains of Cuenca is a perfect hideout to keep in mind. **$**

Villalba de la Sierra
Mesón Nelia
Ctra De Cuenca, s/n
tel: (969) 281 021
This rustic spot on the banks of the Júcar river is a good place to try

different kinds of game on your way to explore Ciudad Encantada (Enchanted City) with its fantastic rock formations and pine forest. **$$**

Los Yébenes
Los Montes de Toledo
Carretera, s/n, 401, km 110
This hotel and restaurant overlooking olive groves and the Alberquillas mountains is the best place around for both dining and lodging. **$$$**

CASTILE-LEÓN

Avila
El Molino de la Losa
Bajada de la Losa, 12
tel: (920) 211 101
Housed in a 15th-century mill, the restaurant offers classic Castilian cuisine, including homemade sausage, roast pig and lamb, as well as salmon and hake. Closed Monday 15 Oct and 15 March. **$$$**

Price Category

The approximate cost per person, including house wine, is coded in the following way:
$$$ = over 5,000 pesetas
$$ = between 2,500 – 4,500 pesetas
$ = less than 2,500 pesetas

León
Casa Pozo, Plaza de San Marcelo.
tel: (987) 223 039
Specialities include crayfish with clams, *morcilla* (blood pudding made with rice and onions), and San Marcos pie. Closed Sunday, July, and Christmas. **$$$**
Mesón Leones del Racimo de Oro
Caño Vadillo, 2
tel: (987) 257 575
This former 16th-century stable serves game when in season, roasts and hearty leonés specialities. **$$$**

Palencia
Casa Damián
Ignacio Martínez de Azcoitia, 9
tel: (979) 744 628
Specialities include vegetable stew, fried hake and cooked partridge, followed by home-made desserts.

Closed Monday, and from 25 July–25 Aug. **$$$**
Lorenzo
Avda Casado del Alisal, 10
tel: (979) 743 545
Popular, offering simple dishes and special desserts. Closed Sunday, and 7 Sept–7 Oct. **$$**

Salamanca
Chez Victor
Espoz y Mina, 16
tel: (923) 213 123
Nouvelle cuisine. Specialities include leek and aubergine mousse, duck and, for dessert, crepes. **$$$**
El Candil
Ventura Ruiz Aguilera, 14–16
tel: (923) 217 239
Castilian cuisine. Specialities include roast piglet and flan. Closed Thursday and June Aug. **$$$**
Río de la Plata
Plaza del Peso, 1
tel: (923) 219 005
Castilian cuisine. Specialities include clams, the meats and fish of the region, and rice pudding. Closed Monday and July. **$$-$$$**

Segovia
Casa Amado
Fernandez Ladreda, 9
tel: (921) 432 077
Castilian cuisine. Frequented by the locals, good quality *casera*. Specialities include garlic soup, fried hake, frogs legs, lamb, suckling pig. Closed Wednesday, and October. **$$-$$$**
Mesón de Cándido
Azoguejo, 5
tel: (921) 425 911
Castilian cuisine. Always crowded, and full of ambience. The speciality is its collection of photos of famous people tasting the suckling pig. Certain tables overlook the 2,000-year-old aqueduct. **$$-$$$**

Valladolid
La Fragua
Paseo de Zorrilla, 10
tel: (983) 338 785
A culinary institution of the city, this restaurant's dishes rely on quality local produce and excellent meat and fish. Closed Sunday evening. **$$$**

Mesón Cervantes
Rastro, 6
tel: (983) 306 138
A family-run establishment, it specialises in rice with hare, fresh vegetable stew, stuffed partridge, venison with sweet and sour sauce and roast pig and lamb, among other succulent dishes. Closed Sunday, and August. **$$**

Zamora
Hostería Real de Zamora
Cuesta de Pizarro, 7
tel: (980) 534 545
Housed in a 16th-century mansion, it features both Castilian and Basque cooking. **$$$**
París
Avda de Portugal, 14
tel: (980) 514 325
Typical Castilian cuisine including ox-tail stew. **$$**

EXTREMADURA
Badajoz
Los Monjes
Paseo de Castelar, s/n
tel: (924) 223 741
Situated in the Hotel Zurbarán. Typical cuisine, including partridge salad, pork sirloin, lamb stew and excellent cheeses. **$$–$$$**
Mesón El Tronco
Muñoz Torrero, 16
tel: (924) 222 076
Local dishes, with excellent cured hams and cheeses, typical *caldereta* lamb stew and walnut croquettes. Closed Wednesday night, and Sunday. **$$$**

Cáceres
Atrio
Avda de España, 30
tel: (924) 242 928
Creative modern cooking based on regional specialities accompanied by excellent desserts. Closed Sunday evening. **$$$**
Figón de Eustaquio
Plaza de San Juan, 12–14
tel: (924) 248 194
Traditional regional cooking. **$$**

Nightlife

Concerts, Ballet & Opera

Concerts and recitals can be enjoyed throughout the year in Madrid. Main venues are the recently-opened **Teatro Real**, Madrid's opera house (Plaza de Isabel II, tel: 91 516 0600; information, tel: 91 516 0660; box office, tel: 91 516 0606); the **Auditorio Nacional de Música** (Príncipe de Vergara, 146, tel: 91 337 0100), the home of the National Orchestra; the **Teatro Monumental** (Atocha, 65, tel: 91 429 8119), the official concert hall for the National Radio and Television Orchestra; the **Teatro de la Zarzuela** (Jovellanos 4, tel: 91 429 8225) and the **Centro Cultural de la Villa** (Plaza Colón, tel: 91 575 6080).

The Teatro Real reopened recently after many years of renovations and is now on a par with all the major opera houses in Europe. It has a capacity for 1,800 spectators, a high-tech stage and brand new rehearsal facilities. Here you can see opera and ballet companies from around the world. You can also see concerts, opera and ballet at the other venues mentioned above. Zarzuela is a Spanish genre (light operetta) which you can see in the Auditorio Nacional and the Teatro de la Zarzuela, and other Madrid theatres (check press for details of productions). In the summer (late July–end Aug) you can watch Zarzuela in the traditional open-air setting of **La Corrala** (Calle Tribulete, 12, and Calle Sombrerete 13 – no phone. Shows every night at 10.15pm except Monday – check press for details).

There are several festivals which feature visiting theatre and dance companies and orchestras – the main ones are **Veranos de la Villa** (music festival, July–mid-Sept), **Festival de Otoño** (theatre and dance festival, October) and **Festival Mozart** (classical music, June–July). See press for details or tel: 010 (Mon–Fri 8am–9pm, except holidays).

You can puchase tickets at the venues themselves (check press for opening hours of box offices, as they may vary), in the FNAC building, Calle Preciados, 28, tel: 91 595 6100, open all day; or by phone in Tel-Entradas, Pº Recoletos,15, tel: 91 538 3333.

Flamenco

You can watch flamenco dancers at tablaos flamencos or watch the expert cante flamenco singers at other venues. But be warned that the prices in tablaos will probably be high.

Tablao Flamenco shows
Al Andalús
Calle Capitán Haya, 19
tel: (91) 556 1439
Open 11pm–6am Mon–Sat.
Café de Chinitas
Torija, 7
tel: (91) 547 1501
Open 9pm–2am Mon–Sat.
Corral de la Morería
Morería, 17
tel: (91) 365 8446
Open 9pm–3am daily.

Flamenco Venues
Casa Patas
Calle Cañizares, 10
tel: (91) 369 0496
Open midnight–3am daily. Performances 1am Mon–Sat. Madrid's most important flamenco venue. Bar-restaurant. You can also check listings for Suristán (see Live Music, above), which holds flamenco nights once a week, usually Wednesday. A good place to catch the nuevo flamenco artists.

Clubs with Live Music

Café Central
Plaza del Angel, 10
tel: (91) 369 4143
Open 1pm–1.30am; Fri–Sun close
2.30am. Live jazz.

Café del Foro
Calle San Andrés, 38
tel: (91) 902 445 3752
Open daily 7pm–2am, Fri–Sat close
4am. Live acts, magicians, salsa.

Café Jazz Populart
Huertas, 22
tel: (91) 429 8407
Open: 6pm–3am daily. Live jazz,
blues, salsa, etc.

Chesterfield Cafe
Calle Serrano Jover, 5
tel: (91) 542 2817
Open daily 1–5pm and 8pm–3am.
Live show Wed–Sun at 11.30pm.
Blues, soul, new country, rock and
pop. American restaurant and bar.

Clamores
Calle Alburquerque, 14
tel: (91) 445 7938
Open 7pm–3am approx. Mainly a
jazz venue, also with pop, blues,
soul, reggae and latin live music.

El Sol
Calle Jardines, 3
tel: (91) 532 6490
Open 11.30pm–5am Mon–Sat. Pop,
funk, rock, live bands.

Honky Tonk
Covarrubias, 24
tel: (91) 445 7938
Open 8pm–5am daily. Wednesday
night is Magic Night. Wide selection
of country, blues and rock.

Moby Dick
Avda de Brasil, 5
tel: (91) 556 7281
Open 10pm–dawn daily. Live pop,
blues and rock.

Suristán
Calle de la Cruz, 7,
tel: (91) 532 3909
Open 10pm–5am, Fri–Sat. Closed
Monday. Every night a different
style – African, Latin, reggae,
flamenco. Live bands most nights.

Irish Pubs

Irish pubs have sprouted
everywhere in Madrid. Here are
some of the most popular ones:

Casinos

Spaniards are among the world's
most enthusiastic gamblers.
The Casino Gran Madrid is at
Ctra de la Coruña, km 28.3 near
the town of Torrelodones, tel:
(91) 856 1100. Open
4.30–11.30pm daily, but phone
first to check. To be admitted,
you have to be over 18, carry
proper identification and be
correctly dressed (for men this
means a tie, except in the
month of August). A free bus
service is provided from Plaza
de España and Plaza de Colón.

Moore's
Calle Felipe III, 4
tel: (91) 365 5802
Open 10am–2am daily.

O'Connor's
Calle Almagro, 3
tel: (91) 902 310 4435
Open 9am–1am, Fri–Sat closes 3am.

O'Donnell's
Calle Barceló, 1
tel: (91) 532 6331
Open 10am–2am daily.

O'Neill's
Calle Príncipe, 12
tel: (902) 521 2030
Open daily from midday–late. Next
to Plaza Santa Ana.

The Irish Rover
Avda de Brasil, 7
tel: (91) 555 7671
Open 11am–2.30am, Fri–Sat closes
4am.

The Quiet Man
Calle Valverde, 44
tel: (91) 523 4689
Open 1pm–1am, Fri–Sat close 3am;
July–Aug 5pm–2am, Fri–Sat closes
3.30am.

Triskel Tavern
Calle San Vicente Ferrer, 3
tel: (91) 523 2783
Open 10am–3am, August 6pm–3am.

Clubs and Discos

Bali Hai
Calle Flor Alta, 8
Open 12.30pm–5.30am Thur–Sat.
Latest dance and techno sounds.

But
Calle Barceló, 11
tel: (91) 448 0698
Madrid's only full-time dance hall –
waltz, tango, rock'n'roll, pasodoble.

Joy Eslava
Arenal, 11
tel: (91) 366 3733
Open Fri–Sun 7pm–5am,
Mon–Thurs 11.30pm–5.30am.
A real disco with velvet décor.

Kingston's
Calle Barquillo, 29
tel: (91) 521 1568
Open 10pm–5am daily. Reggae,
soul and funk.

La Comedia
Calle Principe, 16
tel: (91) 521 5164
Open approx. midnight–4am
Thur–Sat, but changes so check
listings or phone. Rock, rap, funk.

Morocco
Calle Marqués de Leganés, 7
tel: (91) 531 3177
Open 11pm–5am Thur–Sun. Techno
disco, trendy crowd, funky décor.

Soul Kitchen
Calle Mesonero Romanos, 13
tel: (91) 532 1524
Soul, funk, rap, reggae, R&B, hip-
hop on Wed–Fri and Sat. Open
midnight–approx 5am. After-hours
techno and trance club Goa, Fri–Sat
6am–10am.

Villa Rosa
Plaza de Santa Ana, 15
tel: (91) 521 3689
Open 10pm–5am daily. Very popular
late-night dance bar. Ttiled interior.

Nightclubs with Shows

Florida Park
P° de coches del Retiro, s/n (in
Retiro Park)
tel: (91) 573 7805
Open 9pm–3am (shows at
10.30pm). Dinner is also served.

Scala Melià Castilla
Rosario Pino, 7
tel: (91) 571 4411
Open 9/10pm–3am daily, but
changes so phone first. A fine Las
Vegas-style show.

Check listings in Friday's
newspaper supplements and in the
In-Madrid English magazine.

Shopping

Madrid, as the capital, offers the visitor the whole range of shopping possibilities found in the different regions of Spain.

Spain has always been noted for the variety and quality of its craftwork from colourful hand-sewn, embroidered Manila shawls, leather and suede goods, to its internationally exported footwear and furniture.

The major department stores and tourist shops are to be found in the centre of Madrid between the Puerta del Sol and the Plaza Callao, and along the Gran Vía. The more select shops and international boutiques line Calle Serrano and its adjoining streets in the Salamanca area, while the most avant-garde designers have their shops in Calle Almirante, just off the Paseo de Recoletos.

There are also possibilities for antique shopping in Madrid: the Calle del Prado is a good hunting ground. Madrid Rastro, the open-air flea market, operates on Saturday, Sunday and holiday mornings, and you can find everything and anything there from valuable antiques, second-hand clothing and old books, to souvenirs, toilet articles and live canaries. Watch out for pickpockets.

The main department-store chain is El Corte Inglés (branches at Preciados, 3; Princesa, 41; Goya, 76; and Raimundo Fernández Villaverde, 1).

Shopping Centres

ABC Serrano, Calle Serrano, 61. A mall in the chic Salamanca area. More than 100 shops in a beautiful building, which boasts a rooftop summer terrace bar.

Galeria del Prado, Plaza de las Cortes, 7, is probably the most elegant of the Madrid shopping complexes. On the ground floor of the Palace Hotel, with its main entrance on the Carrera de San Jerónimo, this lavishly-decorated centre contains 38 exclusive shops and boutiques, together with a very pleasant, stylish restaurant.

Madrid 2, La Vaguada, Avda Monforte de Lemos, 36, in the north of Madrid. An ultra-modern, multi-level shopping centre with shops, supermarkets, bars, restaurants and cinemas.

Mercado Puerta de Toledo, Ronda de Toledo, 1. A former fish market transformed into a bright, spacious shopping centre where the best shops in town are to be found alongside exhibition and cultural areas, restaurants and bars.

Moda Shopping, in the Azca complex off the Paseo de La Castellana, is one of the newest centres with 100 shops and an atmosphere designed to induce a feeling of relaxation.

Multicentros, Serrano, 88 (the smallest of the Multicentros with 30 top boutiques); Princesa, 47 (due to its location in the university quarter of Argüelles, this offers the best in youthful trends); and Orense, 6.

Corner Shops

Recently, many small **corner shops**, run mainly by Chinese families, have sprung up around Madrid. Apart from a large selection of alcohol and crisps, you can also find some basic items there, such as bread and milk – the prices are higher, but the shops are open until very late. VIPS and 7–11 are also open late, and on Sunday; you'll find many of these stores in the city centre.

Sports and Leisure

Participant Sports

GOLF

Madrid's golf courses include:
Club de Camp, Ctra de Castilla, km 3, tel: (91) 357 2132.
Nuevo Club de Golf de Madrid, Las Matas. Ctra de La Coruña, 26, tel: (91) 630 0820. Open summer 9am–8pm, winter 9am–7pm. Closed Monday.

TENNIS

Tennis can be played at:
Club de Campo, Ctra de Castilla, km 3, tel: (91) 357 2132.
Club de Tenis Chamartín, Calle Federico Salmón, 2, tel: (91) 345 2500.
Real Club Puerta de Hierro, Avda. de Miraflores, s/n, tel: (91) 316 1635. Open all day.

SKIING

The nearest ski slopes are found at:
Navacerrada, only 50 km (30 miles) from Madrid along the N-6012 highway. It has five chair-lifts and three button-lifts.
The **Valcotos** ski resort is 65 km (40 miles) along the N-601 road and has two chair-lifts and five button-lifts.
Valdesquí is 70 km (40 miles) further on and has three chair-lifts and seven button-lifts.
The **La Pinilla** resort, 120 km (70 miles) from Madrid, at Cerezo de Arriba in the province of Segovia, has one telecabin, three chair-lifts and eight button-lifts. Information: (921) 550304.

For recorded information on snow conditions, call the AUTDEM Phoneline, tel: (91) 350 20 20.

HORSE RIDING

Stables are located at:
Club de Campo, Ctra de Castilla, km 3, tel: (91) 357 2132.

Spectator Sports

FOOTBALL

Madrid has several football stadiums, the most important being the **Estadio Santiago Bernabéu**, Calle Concha Espina, 1, tel: (91) 344 0052, (metro: Lima) in the north of the city, home of the Real Madrid team; and the **Estadio Vicente Calderón**, P° de la Virgen del Puerto, 67, tel: (91) 366 4707; shop, tel: (91) 365 3831 (metro: Pirámides) in the south beside the Manzanares river, belonging to the Atlético de Madrid team. These are, for the moment, Madrid's two First Division teams.

HORSE RACING

This can be enjoyed at the **Hipódromo de la Zarzuela**, Ctra de La Coruña, Km 7.8, tel: (91) 307 0140. Admission: adults 700 pesetas, children under 15 and adults over 65 300 pesetas, depending on the month of the year. Buses leave for the racetrack from Moncloa.

JAI-ALAI

This fast and exciting Basque sport can be seen at **Frontón Reyzabal** Avda Moratalaz, 40, tel: (91) 439 9131.

BULLFIGHTS

These are held in the **Las Ventas** bullring, Calle Alcalá, 237, tel: (91) 726 4800 and 365 2200 (Metro stop: Las Ventas). Box Office: Thur–Sun 10am–2pm and 5–8pm. The season begins in mid-March

and ends in mid-October, with bullfights scheduled for every Sunday and holiday, and on Thursday evenings during the summer months.

Tickets for the bullfights can be purchased a day in advance of the fight at Las Ventas.

The big **San Isidro Festival**, over three weeks of daily bullfights featuring top matadors and bulls from the best ranches, starts mid-May into June (check localy for exact dates). The autumn fair is held at the end of September.

During San Isidro Festival, the corrals at **El Batán** in the Casa de Campo park exhibit the bulls due to be fought and for a modest admission fee you can take a closer look at these impressive animals. There is also a pleasant outdoor bar and restaurant overlooking the corrals.

Children's Activities

Some suggestions for family entertainment in Madrid:
The Casa de Campo Park has a swimming pool at the Lago Metro stop, near the lake, where boats and canoes can be rented.

The park is also the setting for the modern **Madrid Zoo**, tel: (91) 711 9950/5416, with its Children's Zoo where it is possible to feed and pet the goats, sheep, deer, squirrels and pigeons. The zoo, home to over 3,000 animals, is located near the Batán Metro stop. Open 10.30am–8.30pm weekdays, and Sat until 9pm. T.

Also in the Casa de Campo is the **Parque de Atracciones** or Amusement Park, tel: (91) 463 2900/ 6433. A wide variety of rides and, in summer, performances by top Spanish and international singers. Near the Batán Metro stop and can be reached by buses 33 and 65. Hours vary from month to month, but usually from 12–7pm Nov–Jan; 12–8pm Feb; 12–10pm; Apr–Oct. Closing time varies.

The Casa de Campo can also be reached by way of a soaring

cross-town ride on the **Teleférico Cable Car** which can be boarded at the Paseo Pintor Rosales, tel: (91) 541 7450. Open 11am–3pm and 4.30–8pm or later (depending on sunset). Sat–Sun until 9pm.

In **Retiro Park** there are marionette shows at 6pm on Sat, Sun and public holidays, all year round, and in August the puppet festival **Titirilandia** brings puppets from around the world – shows on Fri and Sat at 7.30pm and 10.30pm. Children can also enjoy the playgrounds or go boating.

Other possibilities are:
● the **Aquarium** at Calle Maestro Vitoria, 8, off the Plaza de Callao, tel: (91) 531 8172.
● **Acciona** – Museo Interactivo de la Ciencia (Interactive Science Museum), Pintor Murillo, s/n, Parque de Andalucía, Alcobendas, tel: (91) 661 3909. Chemistry, optics, paleontology, energy. Exhibitions in which children can participate are staged in this new museum. Open 10am–6pm daily. Bus: Interbus 151, 152, 153, 154 from Plaza Castilla.
● The **Planetarium** in the Tierno

Galván Park, tel: (91) 476 3898. Open: Tues–Fri 9.30am–1.45pm and 5–7.45pm, Sat–Sun and public holidays 11am–1.45pm and 5–8.45pm. Closed Mon and public holidays. Shows: weekdays 5.30pm and 6.45pm, Sat and Sun 11.30am, 12.45pm, 5.30pm, 6.45pm and 8pm. Metro: Méndez Alvaro; bus: 148. There is a nice playground outside.
● **Safari Park**, tel: (91) 862 2314, is a wild animal reserve located in the town of Aldea del Fresno, on National Highway V near Navalcarnero about 40 km (25 miles) from Madrid. Open Mar–Nov 10.30am–sunset. It also has a museum, trained animal shows, a boating lake, miniature golf, swimming pools and restaurants.
● **Aquópolis**, tel: (91) 815 6911/6986. In Villanueva de la Cañada, km 25, on the La Coruña Highway (N–VI). Open June–Sept 12–8pm daily. Bus: Autoperiferia 581 from Estación Sur.
● **Aquasur**, tel: (91) 891 6034. Ctra de Andalucía, km 44, on the way to Aranjuez. Open mid-June –mid-Sept 10am–8.30pm daily.

Getting Acquainted

Economy

Andalucía is Spain's most important agricultural region and agriculture continues to play a vital part in the economy. Traditional products such as olive oil, cereals and grapes have lost ground to new crops and methods. Irrigation has been extended.

Cotton, sunflowers, citrus fruits, sugar beet and rice are the major crops of the region. Strawberries have become a money-spinning export from Huelva and along the sheltered Mediterranean coast avocados, sweet potatoes, kiwi fruit and custard apples flourish. Fish-farming is also a fast-expanding industry.

The mining of copper, lead, silver and gold, which dates from ancient times, is declining but service industries are growing and the regional authorities are striving to attract high-tech industry.

Since the 1960s there has been phenomenal growth in tourism, which has brought undreamed-of wealth to one of Spain's poorest areas. Apart from the annual influx of package-tour visitors, several hundred thousand northern Europeans have permanent or semi-permanent residences on or near the Mediterranean coast.

Geography & Population

Andalucía covers 87,000 sq. km (34,700 sq. miles), 17 percent of Spain's total area. Most of approximately 7 million inhabitants live on the coast or along the Guadalquivir river valley. The 660-km (410-mile) long Guadalquivir is the backbone of the region, draining a vast basin and providing water for power and irrigation as well as drinking. The alluvial sediments bordering the river provide fertile soil for crops.

North of the Guadalquivir, the hills of the Sierra Morena are a barrier to easy communication between Andalucía and the rest of Spain. To the south, the Cordillera Baetica runs from Gibraltar to Murcia, forming another higher barrier between the Guadalquivir basin and the Mediterranean coast.

Mulhacén in the Sierra Nevada is the peninsula's highest mountain at 3,478 metres (11,402 ft) and the ranges bristle with dramatic crags. These sierras shield the coasts of Almería, Granada and Málaga from frost and snow.

Climate

Andalucía's position at the southern edge of Europe gives it a privileged climate. Summers are hot and winters generally mild. However, there are considerable variations due to the size of the region, its mountainous character and the fact that it is bordered by both the Atlantic and Mediterranean.

Summers can be extremely hot in the interior with temperatures rising to 45°C (113°F) and even higher in the provinces of Seville and Córdoba. Almería has an extremely arid, desert-like climate. Snow covers the Sierra Nevada from November to June and frost is common in upland areas.

The Levante wind has considerable influence, often blowing hard for days on the Cádiz coast and creating a persistent cloud over the Rock of Gibraltar. June to October are usually dry, except for sporadic torrential downpours. Heavy rain in the winter months is usually interspersed with brilliant sunshine. The best months to tour the region are in spring and autumn.

Planning the Trip

Getting There

BY AIR

Southern Spain has frequent air links with the rest of Europe and North Africa, as well as direct flights to North America. It is within 2½ hours' flying time of London. Málaga and Seville airports have daily scheduled connections with international destinations, but in addition large numbers of visitors arrive by charter flights. Jerez airport has connections to London, and Almería and Gibraltar are also important entry points.

The colossal growth of the Costa del Sol tourist industry has converted Málaga into Spain's sixth busiest airport, with 5 million passenger arrivals annually. Scheduled services are available from the major airlines, including Iberia, British Airways, KLM, Lufthansa, Sabena, SAS, and Royal Air Maroc.

BY SEA

Few liners call at Southern Spain ports, apart from those on cruises. Trasmediterránea vessels, carrying passengers and vehicles, ply between Almería, Málaga, Algeciras, Cádiz and Seville and ports on the African coast and on the Canary Islands.

There are frequent services across the Straits of Gibraltar, both by ferry and hydrofoil, from Algeciras to Ceuta and Tangier.

BY RAIL

Since 1992, a high-speed rail service, the AVE, has linked Seville to Madrid, reducing travelling time to just over two hours. The fast Talgo service between Madrid and

Málaga takes just over four hours. Otherwise, train services between Barcelona and Madrid and Southern Spain have often been slow, partly due to the inadequate tracks. The most comfortable way to travel south is by Talgo trains, smooth-running expresses which travel from Madrid to major Andalucían cities.

BY ROAD

Road access to Southern Spain has improved dramatically in the past few years, as the network of four-lane routes has been extended. The Autopista del Mediterráneo (toll) runs all the way from the French border at La Junquera along the coast to Alicante: from there, fourlane freeways take travellers direct to Almería or to Granada and Seville. Madrid is also connected by a four-lane freeway to Seville (via Bailén and Córdoba) and Málaga (via Jaén and Granada).

An international bridge across the Guadíana river at Ayamonte was completed in 1991, allowing easy access to Andalucía from Portugal's Algarve coast.

Practical Tips

Media

A number of English-language publications serve the large number of expatriates living along the Mediterranean coast. Of the magazines, the longest established is *Lookout*, a glossy, Fuengirola-based monthly featuring practical information and articles about life in Spain. *Absoluto Marbella* is devoted to the glitzy lifestyle of the famous resort. *SunGolf* is a monthly magazine devoted to the golfing scene. Several free papers come out weekly, with details of doings in the expatriate community. They include *Sur in English* and *The Entertainer*. German publications include the monthly *Aktuelle*, and the monthly *Solkysten* caters for Scandinavians. There are also several radio stations broadcasting in English; the longest established is OCI (FM 101.6).

Telephone

In tourist areas in season you will find temporary structures housing small telephone exchanges. These are handy for long-distance calls as instead of fumbling with change you pay the operator afterwards. Restrict your calls from hotels as they often treble the charge.

Local Tourist Offices

Almería
Regional tourist office: Parque Nicolás Salmerón, Almería, tel: (950) 274 355.

Cádiz
Regional tourist office: Calderón de la Barca, 1, Cádiz, tel: (956) 211 313.

Jerez de la Frontera: Calle Large 39, tel: (956) 331 150.
Puerto de Santa María: Guadalete 1, tel: (956) 542 413.

Córdoba
Regional tourist office: Torrijos, 10 (Palacio de Congresos), tel: (957) 471 235.

Granada
Regional tourist office: Plaza Mariana Pineda, 10, bajo, tel: (958) 225 990.

Huelva
Regional tourist office: Avenida de Alemania 12, tel: (959) 257 403

Jaén
Regional tourist office: Arquitecto Berges, 1, Jaén, tel: (953) 222 737.
Baeza: Plaza del Pópulo s/n, tel: (953) 740 444;
Ubeda: Plaza del Ayuntamiento 2, tel: (953) 750 897.

Málaga
Regional tourist office: Pasaje de Chinitas, 4, tel: (95) 2213 445
Municipal tourist office: Avda Cervantes, 1, Paseo del Parque, tel: (95) 2604 410; also at airport, tel: (95) 2240 000.
Antequera: Palacio de Najera, tel: (95) 2842 180.
Benalmádena-Costa: Avda Antonio Machado, 14, tel: (95) 2442 494.
Estepona: Paseo Marítimo Jorge Manrique, s/n, tel: (95) 2800 913.
Fuengirola: Avda Jesús Santos Rein, tel: (95) 2467 457.
Marbella: Glorieta de la Fontanilla, tel: (95) 2822 818.
Nerja: Puerta del Mar, 2, tel: (95) 2521 531.
Ronda: Plaza de España, 1, tel: (95) 2871 272.
Torremolinos: Plaza Pablo Picasso, tel: (95) 2371 159.

Seville
Tourist office: Avda de la Constitución, 21, tel: (95) 4221 404.
Municipal tourism office: Paseo de las Delicias, 9, tel: (95) 4234 465.

Emergencies

SECURITY & CRIME

Thefts from tourists and their cars have become common in recent years. Common-sense precautions should prevent your holiday being spoiled in this way. Cities are black spots. Never leave anything of value in your car, including when parking near a beach. Don't leave cash or valuables unattended while you are swimming. When staying overnight, take all baggage into the hotel. If possible, park your car in a garage or a guarded car-park.

Particularly when driving into Seville, do not leave anything of value within sight. When walking, women should keep shoulder bags out of view if possible. Avoid badly-lit back streets at night in such quarters as Santa Cruz in Seville. Police patrols have been stepped up, but this area is a magnet for muggers, often working in twos and threes. Carry photocopies of your passport and other documents and leave the originals in the hotel safe.

If confronted do not resist, as thieves often carry knives. If robbed, remember thieves usually want easily disposable cash. Check the nearest gutters, rubbish containers and toilets for your personal possessions: thieves swiftly dispose of unwanted items.

Emergency Numbers

National Police: 091
Local Police: 092
Medical emergencies: 061
Fire brigade: 080

Getting Around

By Rail

Unlike the new national services, the regional trains between cities tend to be slow. The Costa del Sol between Málaga and Fuengirola is served by an efficient commuter service, every 20 minutes. A train ride in the grand style of the Orient Express is offered by the Al-Andalus Expreso. Operating May–October, this deluxe train visits Seville, Córdoba, Granada and Málaga, with option of a visit to Jerez .

Car Rental

International chains have airport offices, and offer collect and deliver services. Local companies are cheaper and will arrange to meet you on arrival if you book.

Avis airport offices
Almería, tel: (950) 224 126
Granada, tel: (958) 446 455.
Jerez de la Frontera, Cádiz, tel: (956) 150 005
Málaga, tel: (95) 2048 483/2048 518
Seville, tel: (95) 4449 121/4254 298.
Europcar airport offices
Almería, tel: (950) 292 934.
Granada, tel: (958) 245 275.
Jerez de la Frontera, tel: (956) 150 098.
Hertz airport offices
Almería, tel: (950) 292 500.
Córdoba (railway station), tel: (957) 402 060.
Granada, tel: (958) 252 419.
Jerez de la Frontera, tel: (956) 150 038.
Málaga, tel: (95) 2233 086.
Seville, tel: (95) 4449 125.

Where to Stay

Accommodation

Paradors charge between a luxury and moderate hotel double room rate. Prices are less costly for a double room if you use other types of accommodation. In a *pensión*, expect to pay about 3,000 pesetas; in 1 and 2-star *hostales*, prices will range from 3,000 to 7,000 pesetas.

ALMERÍA

Gran Hotel Almería
Avda Reina Regente, 8
tel: (950) 238 011
Almería's top class hotel, recently renovated, with good views over the harbour and the bay of Almería. **$$$**

Near El Ejido
Golf Hotel Almerimar
Urb. Almerimar
tel: (950) 497 050
Modern and conformable resort hotel in a holiday complex with golf course and yachting marina. **$$$**

Mojácar
Parador Reyes Católicos
Playa de Mojácar
tel: (950) 478 250
A splendid beachside location is the main attraction of this modern parador. **$$$**
El Moresco
Avda Encamp
tel: (950) 478 025
A good choice for those who want to stay in Mojácar itself, rather than on the beach 3 km (2 miles) below the village, with good views of the surrounding countryside. **$$**

San José
Hotel San José
Calle Correos
Sán José

tel: (950) 380 116
Small hotel with eight large rooms overlooking a secluded cove in the relatively unspoilt Cabo de Gata. Closed Nov–Jan. **$$$**

Pechina
Sierra Alhamilla
Pechina
tel: (950) 317 413
A pleasant small hotel in Pechina, 10 km (6 miles) north of Almería, built over old Moorish baths, next to a thermal spring. **$**

CÁDIZ
Atlántico
Avda Duque de Nájera, 9
tel: (956) 226 905
State-run hotel in a modern but stylish building, the best bet in its category if you want to stay in the picturesque old part of the city. **$$$**

Algeciras
Reina Cristina
Paseo de la Conferencia
tel: (956) 602 622
Surrounded by luxuriant gardens, this British-style stately turn-of-the-century hotel is a classic. **$$$$**

Arcos de la Frontera
Parador Casa del Corregidor
Plaza de España, s/n
tel: (956) 700 500
The splendid views from this hotel, perched on a cliff at the very top of the village, are worth a visit in their own right. The rooms are very large, furnished in typical *parador* style. The best ones look out over the cliff. **$$$**
Los Olivos
Paseo Boliches, 30
tel: (956) 700 811
Small hotel in an old Andalucían town house, its rooms arranged around a courtyard. Good value. **$$**

Grazalema
Villa Turística de Grazalema
El Olivar
tel: (956) 132 136
Part of the Andalucían "Villa Turística" network, with self-catering units (perfect for small groups), in addition to a small hotel. **$$**

Jerez de la Frontera
Jerez
Avda Alvaro Domecq, 35
tel: (956) 300 600
In the pleasant, leafy residential part of town, the classic Jerez hotel, recently renovated. Swimming pool and tennis courts. **$$$$**
Montecastillo Hotel and Golf Resort
Ctra de Arcos
tel: (956) 151 200
A few kilometres outside Jerez, near the motor-racing track, a sprawling and luxurious neo-Moorish palace adjoining a top class golf course designed by Jack Nicklaus. **$$$$**

Puerto de Santa María
Monasterio de San Miguel
Larga, 27
tel: (956) 540 440
Tasteful and comfortable, installed in a former 18th-century monastery which still retains the original cloisters, chapel and enclosed garden. **$$$**

Price Guide

For a standard double room
$$$$ = Over 20,000 pesetas
$$$ = 15–20,000 pesetas
$$ = 15,000 pesetas
$ = Under 8,000 pesetas

CÓRDOBA
Amistad Córdoba
Plaza de Maimónides, 3
tel: (957) 420 335
One of the best options in its range if you want to be close to the sights. Comfortable rooms in two former mansions looking over the Plaza Maimónides. **$$$**
Parador de Turismo La Arruzafa
Avda de la Arruzafa, 33
tel: (957) 275 900
Modern establishment in the parador network offers fine views from a hill on the outskirts of the city. **$$$**
Albucasis
Buen Pastor 11
tel: (957) 478 625
Family-run hostelry offering good value and clean, comfortable lodgings around a central courtyard in the heart of the old town. **$$**

Palma del Río
Hospedería San Francisco
Avda Pío X11, 35
tel: (957) 710 183
Renowned for its fine food, the hotel is installed in a former 15th-century Franciscan monastery. **$$**

GRANADA
Parador de Turismo de San Francisco
Real de la Alhambra
tel: (958) 221 440
Reservations are essential to get into the most sought-after rooms in the *parador* network, in a converted 15th-century Francisco monastery within the Alhambra gardens themselves. **$$$$**
Alhambra Palace
Peña Partida, 2
tel: (958) 221 408
At the foot of the Alhambra walls, an ochre-coloured neo-Moorish fantasy with good views over the city. The hotel bar and terrace are a popular meeting place. **$$$$**
Triunfo
Plaza del Triunfo, 19
tel: (958) 207 444
Off the main thoroughfare of Granada, the Gran Vía de Colón, a small and comfortably-appointed hotel, convenient for shopping and sights in the centre of the city. **$$$**
Hostal América
Real de la Alhambra, 53
tel: (958) 227 471
A small and intimate family-run hotel in an enviable location within Alhambra grounds. **$$$**
Juan Miguel
Acera del Darro, 24
tel: (958) 521 111
Reasonably-priced, comfortable option in the busy central district of Granada. **$$**

Almuñecar
Los Fenicios
Paseo de Andrés Segovia
La Herradura
tel: (958) 827 900
A bright, modern hotel right on the beach in the quiet fishing village of La Herradura, next to Almuñecar, with good views of the coast. **$$$**

Bubión (Alpujarras)
Villa Turística de Bubión
Barrio Alto
tel: (958) 763 111
The first, and still the best, of the Andalucían regional "Villas Turisticas" network, with modern self-catering apartments of various sizes, built in the traditional Alpujarras style. **$$**

Loja
La Bobadilla
Ctra Loja-Seville
tel: (958) 321 861
Super-deluxe hotel resort, built in palatial Andalucían country palace style, in the heart of the countryside. Top-rated restaurant, champagne for breakfast, and prices to match. **$$$$**

Sierra Nevada Ski Area
Melia Rumaykiyya
Dehesa de San Jerónimo
tel: (958) 481 400
Comfortable modern hotel offering good services to skiers. **$$$**
Ziryab
Plaza Andalucía
tel: (958) 480 512
Conveniently close to the ski lifts and reasonably priced, the newest hotel in Granada's ski resort. **$$**

HUELVA
Tartessos
Avda Martín Alonso Pinzón, 13
tel: (959) 282 711
Good location in a quiet residential area of the city. **$$**

Ayamonte
Parador Costa de la Luz
El Castillito
tel: (959) 320 700
Modern parador in a superb situation on a hill overlooking the village of Ayamonte, the Guadiana river, and Portugal on the farther shore. **$$**

La Rabida
Hostería de la Rábida
La Rábida, Palos de la Frontera
tel: (959) 350 312
A simple but comfortable 8-room *hostal*, next door to the 15th-century Franciscan monastery

where Columbus first called when he arrived in Spain. **$**

Mazagón
Parador Cristobal Colón
Ctra Matalascañas
tel: (959) 536 300
A modern *parador* in a tranquil, pine-shaded spot overlooking a sandy beach, with rooms opening out onto a garden. **$$$$**

Matalascañas
Tierra Mar
Matalascañas Parc, 120 Sector M
tel: (959) 440 300
Matalascañas, a vastly overbuilt beach resort, has little to recommend it... except that it is next to Doñana. This beachside hotel is a good base for exploring the national park. **$$**

JAÉN
Parador Castillo de Santa Catalina
tel: (953) 230 000
Situated on a hill overlooking the city, right next to Jaén's Moorish castle and built in the same style, with magnificent views of the sierra. **$$$**

Cazorla Park
Parador El Adelantado
Sacedo (26 km, 16 miles from Cazorla)
tel: (953) 727 075
In the heart of the sierra, a modern *parador* which is a good base from which to explore the 214,000 hectare (528,805 arce) wilderness of Cazorla park. **$$$**
Sierra de Cazorla
Ctra Sierra de Cazorla, La Iruela
tel: (953) 720 015
Functional but comfortable small hotel just outside the village of La Iruela, at the main entrance to the Cazorla park. **$**

Ubeda
Parador Condestable Dávalos
Plaza Vázquez Molina, 1
tel: (953) 750 345
One of the oldest hotels in the *parador* chain, installed in a 16th-century palace in the centre of Ubeda's old Renaissance section, with large rooms. **$$$**

Baeza
Casa Juanito
Avda Arca del Agua, s/n
tel: (953) 740 040
Simply appointed and inexpensive, on the main road at the exit of town, a central position for the whole province. The restaurant is considered one of Jaén province's best. **$**
Fuentenueva Hospedería
Paseo Arca del Agua
te: (953) 743 100
Friendly, nicely decorated small hotel installed in what used to be the town's women's prison. **$**

MÁLAGA
Parador de Turismo Gibralfaro
Monte de Gibralfaro
tel: (95) 2221 903
Recently renovated, this small (reservations are a must) *parador* is on the hill overlooking the city, next to an old Moorish fortress. It is not convenient for those without a car. **$$$**
Larios
Marqués de Larios, 2
tel: (95) 2222 200
Modern new hotel in a convenient location in the centre of the city, installed in a restored old building. **$$$$**
Las Vegas
Paseo de Sancha, 22
tel: (95) 2217 712
Near the Málaga bullring and next to the city's seafront promenade, with a pool and a large garden. **$$**

Antequera
Parador de Antequera
Paseo García del Olmo, s/n
tel: (95) 2840 261
Airy, spacious modern parador with good views of the sweeping plain of Antequera. **$$$**

Benalmádena-Costa
Alay
Puerto Deportivo
tel: (95) 2446 000
A modern hotel situated right next to the lively Benalmádena yacht harbour, one of the nightlife centres of the Costa del Sol. **$$$**

Estepona

Las Dunas
La Boladilla Baja, Ctra N-340, km 163
tel: (95) 2794 354
Luxurious spa hotel, split into several Andalucían-style buildings next to the beach east of Estepona, with large, sumptuously decorated rooms. **$$$$**

El Paraíso
Urb. El Paraiso, Ctra N340, Km 167
tel: (95) 2883 000
Modern hotel on a hill east of Estepona, next to a golf course and with views of the Straits of Gibraltar. **$$$$**

Caracas
Avda San Lorenzo, 50
tel: (95) 2800 800
Comfortable and reasonably priced, a good choice in the centre of the relatively quiet seaside town of Estepona. **$**

Fuengirola

Florida
Paseo Marítimo
tel: (95) 2476 100
Comfortable and unostentatious lodgings on the seafront, close to the main shopping and nightlife spots in the town, with a pleasant leafy garden and pool, and convenient for the beach. **$$**

Mijas

Byblos Andaluz
Urb. Mijas Golf (near Fuengirola)
tel: (95) 2473 050
A super-deluxe spa hotel adjoining a golf course 5 km (3 miles) inland from Fuengirola. Top-class restaurant and stylish atmosphere. **$$$$**

Hotel Mijas
Urb. Tamisa
tel: (95) 2485 800
Modern, airy hotel with ample gardens at the entrance to the postcard village of Mijas, offering fine views of the coast. **$$$**

Marbella

El Fuerte
Avda El Fuerte
tel: (95) 2861 500
Among the most professionally-run establishments on the Costa del Sol, and the best option in the centre of Marbella, at the end of the town's seafront promenade, with a tropical garden and rooms with views of the sea. **$$$**

Los Monteros
Ctra N340, km 187
tel: (95) 2771 700
Exclusive luxury resort hotel adjoining a golf course near the beach 5 km (3 miles) east of Marbella. **$$$$**

Puente Romano
Ctra N340, km 176,7
tel: (95) 2820 900
A landmark on the "Golden Mile" west of the town, a palatial hotel designed like a Moorish-Andalusian pueblo, with gardens and trickling fountains and, within, marble and carpeted sumptuousness. **$$$$**

Marbella Club
Ctra N340, km 1170,2
tel: (95) 2822 211
This classy hotel founded in the 1950s was the birthplace of the Marbella legend. Bungalow-style accommodation set among gardens which spread down to the beach. **$$$$**

Nerja

Parador de Nerja
Almuñécar, 8
tel: (95) 2520 050
Modern *parador* on a cliff overlooking the beach, with rooms arranged around a pleasant garden. **$$$**

Ronda

Parador de Ronda
Plaza de España
tel: (95) 2877 500
The newest of Spain's *paradors*, spectacularly perched on a cliff in the best possible position next to the famous gorge, the restored façade of an old building concealing a striking modern interior design. **$$$$**

Polo
Mariano Souviron, 8
tel: (95) 2872 447
Comfortable, friendly, and reasonably priced, with a pleasant atmosphere, in the centre of the town. **$**

Torremolinos

Aloha Puerto
Salvador Allende, 45, Montemar
tel: (95) 2387 066
Large and modern, in a good location next to the beach. **$$$**

Cervantes
Las Mercedes
tel: (95) 2384 033
Large, modern hotel, the best option for those who want to stay close to the centre of Torremolinos. **$$$**

Tropicana
Trópico, 6
tel: (95) 2386 600
A good choice right on the beach at the western end of Torremolinos's popular fish-restaurant quarter, La Carihuela. Fun atmosphere. **$$$**

Miami
Aladino, 14
tel: (95) 2385 255
Inexpensive, friendly, informal, small family-run hotel in a traditional Spanish villa next the Carihuela beach. No credit cards. **$**

Price Guide

For a standard double room
$$$$ = Over 20,000 pesetas
$$$ = 15–20,000 pesetas
$$ = 15,000 pesetas
$ = Under 8,000 pesetas

SEVILLE

Alfonso XIII
San Fernando, 2
tel: (95) 4222 850
Old-style elegance in this all-time classic hotel of Seville, built in Neo-Mudéjar style in the 1920s. **$$$$**

Hotel Casa Imperial
Imperial, 29
tel: (95) 4500 300
One of Seville's newest hostelries is in a restored 16th-century palace behind the Casa de Pilatos, with four inner patios. 24 suites, each decorated differently, with enormous bathrooms. **$$$$**

Inglaterra
Plaza Nueva, 7
tel: (95) 4224 970
Comfortable and friendly, overlooking the Plaza Nueva, a convenient location for touring the city. **$$$$**

Las Casas de la Judería
Callejón de Dos Hermanas
tel: (95) 4415 150
Three old palaces in the Santa Cruz quarter were restored and converted into this maze-like hotel, with a number of inner courtyards. **$$$**

Doña María
Don Remondo, 19
tel: (95) 4224 990
Close to the Seville cathedral, with rooms in various sizes, some furnished with antiques, and a roof-top swimming-pool. **$$$**

Murillo
Lope de Rueda, 7
tel: (95) 4216 095
Simple but comfortable and reasonably-priced, with a friendly, informal atmosphere, in the heart of Santa Cruz quarter. **$$**

Simon
García de Vinuesa, 19
tel: (95) 4226 660
One of the best-value choices in the centre of the city, not far from the cathedral, offering pleasant no-frill lodgings in an 18th-century house around an Andalucían patio. **$**

Carmona

Casa de Carmona
Plaza Lasso, Carmona (33 km-20 miles east of Seville)
tel: (95) 4143 300
One of Andalucía's most stylish hotels, installed in a 16th-century aristocratic mansion, exquisitely decorated. **$$$$**

Parador Alcázar del Rey Don Pedro Carmona
tel: (95) 4141 010
A Mudéjar-style building on a hill overlooking the town, completely renovated in 1998, with spacious rooms. **$$$**

Eating Out

Where to Eat

It is not necessary to step into a restaurant to eat well in Andalucía. Fast food was a part of Spanish culture when the hot dog was hardly more than a puppy. *Tapas*, tasty snacks varying from grilled birds to stewed tripe and chick peas, are served in many bars. Sometimes they come free with the drinks; sometimes you have to order them and pay extra. If you want more, you can ask for a *ración* (plateful), or *media ración* (half plateful).

In bars calling themselves cafeterias, you can order a *plato combinado*. This is usually a variation on pork chop, fried eggs, ham, salad and chips. Even the smallest village usually has a bar serving *tapas* or a *fonda* (inn) serving set meals at budget prices.

Restaurants usually offer a *menú del día*, a three-course meal, including wine, at an economical price. Note also that on the Atlantic and Mediterranean coasts you can eat well on the beaches in restaurants known as *chiringuitos* and *merenderos*. Some of these have become quite sophisticated, with prices to match. Others remain simple, with the best bet probably being "fish of the day".

Restaurants in inland cities keep Spanish hours (lunch at 2.30 or 3pm, dinner at 9pm onwards), but those on the Costa del Sol make more allowances for foreign tourists, serving lunch from 1pm and dinner from 7pm.

Moderate to Expensive restaurants usually accept at least one of the credit cards; Mastercard and Visa are more widely accepted than Amex or Diners. Cheaper establishments prefer cash.

ALMERÍA

Club de Mar
Muelle de las Almadrabillas
tel: (950) 235 048
Recently moved to a modern new location by the beach, this classic Almería restaurant has built a solid reputation on its fresh seafood dishes. CC: Amex, Mastercard, Visa. **$$$**

La Gruta
Ctra N-340, km 436
tel: (950) 239 335
Inside a cave overlooking the sea between Almería and Aguadulce. Grilled meat is the speciality. Closed Sunday; November. CC: Amex, Diners, Mastercard, Visa. **$$$**

Mojácar area

Terraza Carmona
Manuel Giménez, 1, Vera
tel: (950) 390 188
Located in the beachside community of Vera, north of Mojácar, long-established restaurant offers a good combination of local dishes (mainly fish) and international fare . Closed Monday, September 1–15. CC: Amex, Mastercard, Visa. **$$**

Price Guide

$$$$ = more than 4,000 pesetas
$$$ = 1,500–4,000 pesetas
$$ = under 1,500 pesetas
Prices are per person for a three-course meal, not including wine

CÁDIZ

El Faro
San Felix, 15
tel: (956) 211 068
The best-known of Cádiz's restaurants, in the old quarter of town, and renowned for its seafood served in its wood-beamed dining room. There's also a large *tapas* bar. CC: Amex, Mastercard, Visa. **$$$**

Ventorillo del Chato
Ctra de San Fernando, km 647
tel: (956) 250 025
In an 18th–century inn standing on the sandy isthmus that joins Cádiz to the mainland, specialising in

seafood, although good meat too.
Closed Sunday. CC: Amex,
Mastercard, Visa. **$$$**

San Roque
Los Remos
Finca Villa Victoria, Ctra La Linea-
Gibraltar km 2, Campamento San
Roque
tel: (956) 698 412
Delicious seafood served in style in
a magnificent colonial house
surrounded by gardens. Best to
reserve. Closed Sunday. CC: Amex,
Mastercard, Visa. **$$$$**

Arcos de la Frontera
El Convento, Marqués de
Torresoto, 7
tel: (956) 703 222
Dining area decorated in Seville
tiles and potted plants arranged
around interior courtyard in a 17th-
century palace. Menu features
some unusual regional dishes for
the more daring. CC: Amex,
Mastercard, Visa. **$$$**

Jerez de la Frontera
La Mesa Redonda
Manuel de la Quintana, 3
tel: (956) 340 069
A small, 8-table restaurant, serving
impeccable Jerez dishes, most
based on recipes from aristocratic
sherry families. One of the best
restaurants in Andalucía.
Reservations essential. Closed
Sunday, holidays, and August. CC:
Amex, Visa. **$$$$**
Venta Antonio
Ctra Jerez-Sanlúcar, km 5
tel: (956) 140 535
Five km (3 miles) outside Jerez on a
country road, Venta Antonio started
out as a modest roadside inn, but
has earned an enviable reputation
for its fresh seafood. CC: Amex,
Diners, Mastercard, Visa. **$$$**

Puerto de Santa María
El Faro del Puerto
Crta El Puerto-Rota
tel: (956) 858 003
Sister restaurant to the famous El
Faro of Cádiz, run by young chef-
proprietor Fernando Córdoba, with
equally fresh seafood, but a more
imaginative approach, set in a

pleasant villa outside the town
centre. Best to reserve. Closed
Sunday dinner. CC: Amex, Diner,
Mastercard, Visa. **$$$$**
El Patio
Misericordia, 1
tel: (956) 540 506
Near El Puerto's Ribera del Marisco
(shellfish wharf), in an old house
with a cool interior courtyard,
serving local seafood and classic
Andalucían meat dishes such as
Rabo de Toro (ox tail). CC: Amex,
Diners, Mastercard, Visa. **$$$**

CÓRDOBA
El Caballo Rojo
Cardenal Herrero, 28
tel: (957) 478 001
Near the mosque, the longest
established and best-known of
Córdoba's restaurante is still a
good bet. Aside from traditional
Spanish dishes, the menu
incorporates some unusual Moorish
preparations, based on medieval
recipes, such as *Cordero a la Miel*
(lamb in honey). Reservations
essential. CC: Amex, Diners,
Mastercard, Visa. **$$$$**
El Churrasco
Romero, 16
tel: (957) 290 819
The name suggests grilled meats (a
speciality here), but there is much
more besides. A good place to try
Salmorejo, a thick Córdoba version
of *gazpacho*. Also worth checking is
the wine museum and wine cellar
housed in an annex. Best to
reserve. Closed August. CC: Amex,
Diners, Mastercard, Visa. **$$$**
La Almudaina
Campo Santo de los Mártires, 1
tel: (957) 474 342.
Installed in a 15th-century house
near the Alcázar gardens, serving
local recipes based on fresh
produce. Seven different dining
areas, around a central courtyard.
Closed Sunday dinner, all day
Sunday in summer. CC: Amex,
Diners, Mastercard, Visa. **$$$$**

Palma del Río
Hospedería San Francisco
Avda Pío X11, 35
tel: (957) 710 183
Restaurant in the hotel of the same

name, in a restored 17th-century
monastery, famous for its
combination of Basque and
Andalucían flavours. Closed Sunday
evening, and 1–15 Aug. CC:
Mastercard, Visa. **$$$$**

Montilla
Las Camachas
Ctra Córdoba-Málaga km 48
tel: (957) 650 004
A rambling old roadside restaurant
where the landed gentry of the wine
district dine out. Sturdy, good food,
and local Montilla wines on sale.
CC: Amex, Mastercard, Visa. **$$$**

GRANADA
Ruta del Veleta
Ctra Sierra Nevada, km. 5.4, Cenes
de la Vega
tel. (958) 486 134
On the old road to the Sierra
Nevada, 5 km (3 miles) from the
city, it has served consistently good
food for decades. Spacious, well
decorated dining rooms, and an
outdoor terrace. Classic Spanish
food is the speciality. Best to
reserve. Closed Sunday dinner. CC:
Amex, Diners, Mastercard, Visa.
$$$$
Galatino
Gran Vía, 29
tel: (958) 800 803
Newish restaurant in the centre of
the city, Striking modern decor, and
a creative cuisine that has already
earned an enviable reputation. Best
to reserve. CC: Amex, Diners,
Mastercrd, Visa. **$$$$**
Sevilla
Oficios, 12
tel: (958) 221 223
This Granada classic close to the
cathedral is a good place to sample
traditional Granada dishes such as
Jamon con Habas (cured ham with
broad beans) or *Tortilla Sacromonte*
(omelette with lambs brains, ham
and vegetables). Closed Sunday
dinner, Mon. CC: Amex, Diners,
Mastercard, Visa. **$$$**

Almuñécar
Jacqui-Cotobro
Edificio Río, Playa Cotobro
tel: (958) 631 802
The simple dining room with bare

brick walls gives little indication that this restaurant by the beach is famous all over Spain for its French cuisine. The best plan is to order the *Menu Degustacion*, including a wide choice of three different courses, plus dessert. Best to reserve. Closed Monday, last week November and first week December. CC: Mastercard, Visa. **$$$**

HUELVA

Las Candelas
Avda Huelva, Aljaraque
tel: (959) 318 301.
6 km (4 miles) from the centre, Huelva's best-known restaurant offers good value and quality fresh seafood and fish stews. Closed Sunday. CC: Amex, Mastercard, Visa. **$$$**

Aracena
Jose Vicente
Avda Andalucía, 53
tel: (959) 128 455.
In an unassuming location on the outskirts of the village, this small restaurant is a true gem in the heart of Huelva's northern Sierra. The best place to try fresh pork. Closed June 1–15. CC: Amex, Mastercard, Visa. **$$$**

JAÉN

Mesón Vicente
Francisco Martín Mora, 1
tel: (953) 232 222
Popular restaurant next to the cathedral, serving traditional Jaén dishes and game. There is also a good *meson* (tavern) serving *tapas*. Closed Sunday dinner. CC: Amex, Mastercard, Visa. **$$$**

Baeza
Juanito
Paseo Arca del Agua
tel: (953) 740 040
Spacious and friendly, one of the best known restaurants in Andalucía on account of its owner's missionary zeal in recovering traditional recipes, in which the virgin olive oil of Jaén plays a key role. Closed Sunday dinner, Monday dinner. CC: Visa. **$$$**

Cazorla
Cueva de Juan Pedro
Plaza de Santa María Church
tel: (953) 721 225
Literally a hole in the wall, this tiny, informal cave-restaurant specialises in grilled meat. **$$**

MÁLAGA

Café de Paris
Velez Málaga, 8
tel: (95) 2225 043
On a back street near the lighthouse, this is Málaga's most sophisticated restaurant, serving imaginative dishes in an elegant atmosphere. Reservations are essential. Closed Sunday.
CC: Amex, Diners, Mastercard, Visa. **$$$$**

Escuela de Hostelería
Finca La Consula, Churriana
tel: (95) 2622 562
Málaga's official hotel and catering school, located 8 km (5 miles) west of the city, serves some of the best food on the Costa del Sol. Reservations essential. Lunch only. Closed Sat–Sun. CC: Amex, Mastercard, Visa. **$$$$**

Casa Pedro
Quitapenas, 121, El Palo
tel: (95) 2290 013
In the fishing district of El Palo at the eastern end of Málaga, this beachside restaurant is a favourite with Málaga families for its fried fish. Very crowded on Sundays. Closed Monday dinner. CC: Amex, Diners, Mastercard, Visa. **$$$**

Antequera
La Espuela
Plaza de Toros
tel: (95) 2703 424
Beneath the grandstand in the town's bullring. Andalucían specialities such as *Porra Antequerana* (a thick *gazpacho*) and rabbit in almond sauce. CC: Diners, Mastercard, Visa. **$$$**

Ronda
Pedro Romero
Virgen de la Paz, 18
tel: (95) 2871 110
Unabashedly touristy, but serving good traditional Andalucían fare. It is located across from the Ronda

bullring, is named after the "father of bullfighting", and the taurine theme prevails in the decor (bull's heads, posters) and the menu (*Rabo de Toro*) is the speciality. CC: Amex, Diners, Mastercard, Visa. **$$$**

COSTA DEL SOL

Estepona
Alcaría de Ramos
Ctra N340, km 167
tel: (95) 2886 178
Located in an Andalucían-style house with good views east of the town, serving very well prepared classic Spanish dishes. Closed Sunday dinner. CC: Mastercard, Visa. **$$$**

Costa del Sol
Calle San Roque
tel: (95) 2801 101
A small French bistro on a side street near the main bus station in Estepona, offering excellent value. The menu of the day is a bargain. Closed Monday. CC: Amex, Diners, Visa, Mastercard. **$$$**

Fuengirola
El Bote
Paseo Marítimo, Torreblanca del Sol
tel: (95) 2660 296
Spacious and popular, right next to the beach at the eastern end of Fuengirola's seafront promenade, serving fresh fish dishes. Closed Wednesday. CC: Amex, Mastercard, Visa. **$$$**

Portofino
Paseo Marítimo, 29
tel: (95) 2470 643
Friendly and lively Italian-owned restaurant on the seafront in central Fuengirola, enormously popular, and serving consistently good international dishes, with a few Italian specialities as well. Best to reserve. Closed Monday, and no lunch in summer, CC: Amex, Diners, Mastercard, Visa. **$$$**

Marbella
La Hacienda
Urb. Las Chapas,
tel: (95) 2831 267
Pleasantly set in a villa in the hills east of Marbella, this restaurant, started in the 1960s, was among

the first truly top-class international dining spots on the Costa del Sol. Its French-Belgian cuisine adapted to local recipes set a model for others. Best to reserve. Closed Monday, Tuesday and mid-Nov – mid-Dec. CC: Amex, Diners, Mastercard, Visa. **$$$$**
La Meridiana
Camino dc la Cruz
tel: (95) 2776 190.
Near the gleaming modern Marbella mosque, this elegant dining spot is a favourite among the famous resort's glitterati. Fresh ingredients are given imaginative treatment. Reservations essential. Closed January, no dinner in summer. CC: Amex, Diners, Mastercard, Visa. **$$$$**

Price Guide

$$$$ = more than 4,000 pesetas
$$$ = 1,500–4,000 pesetas
$$ = under 1,500 pesetas
Prices are per person for a three-course meal, not including wine

Nerja
Casa Luque
Plaza Cavana, 2
tel: (95) 2521 004
Authentic Spanish food in an old Andalucían house, near Nerja's main landmark, the Balcón de Europa. Pleasant patio for al fresco dining, and a good selection of dishes with a northern Spanish accent. Closed Monday. CC: Amex, Diners, Mastercard, Visa. **$$$**

Torremolinos
Frutos
Ctra de Cádiz, km 235 (next to Los Alamos petrol station)
tel: (95) 2381 450
Midway between Torremolinos and the airport, a spacious restaurant which for decades has been known for its hearty helpings of traditional Spanish fare, with excellent meat and fish. Closed Sunday dinner. CC: Amex, Mastercard, Visa. **$$$**
El Roqueo
Carmen, 35, La Carihuela
tel: (95) 2384 946.

In Torremolinos's fishing quarter, La Carihuela, it's hard to go wrong: every other house is a seafood restaurant, and they're all good. This one, facing out onto the seafront promenade, is among the longest established and the best known. Closed Tuesday and November. CC: Amex. Mastercard, Visa. **$$$**

SEVILLE
Egaña-Oriza
San Fernando, 41
tel: (95) 4227 211
The Basque inspired cuisine of this attractive restaurant, near the Murillo gardens facing the old tobacco factory, is acclaimed as among the best in Andalucía. Imaginative presentations in an elegant, modern setting. Best to reserve. Closed Sunday, Saturday lunch and August. CC: Amex, Diners, Mastercard, Visa. **$$$$**
La Albahaca
Plaza Santa Cruz, 12
tel: (95) 4220 714
A pretty restaurant in the heart of Seville's Barrio Santa Cruz, in a turn-of-the-century town house. The accent is on the decor – three stylish dining rooms, each with a different colour scheme – as well as on the food, an imaginative mixture of Andalucían, French and Basque influences. Best to reserve. Closed Sunday. CC: Amex, Diners, Mastercard, Visa. **$$$$**
Mesón Don Raimundo
Argote de Molina, 26
tel: (95) 4223 355
Near the Seville cathedral, this large, popular restaurant, decorated with assorted bric a brac, offers a classic Sevillano dining experience. The speciality is meat and game, and the portions are large. Closed Sunday dinner. CC: Amex, Diners, Mastercard, Visa. **$$$**
Hostería del Laurel
Plaza de los Venerables, 5
tel: (95) 4220 295
On a small square in the Barrio de Santa Cruz, popular, both as a good-value dining spot and a tapas venue. Traditional Andalucían cuisine, informal atmosphere. CC: Amex, Diners, Mastercard, Visa. **$$**

Culture

Diary of Events

The following is a list of some of the more important or interesting festivals and events in the region. Exact dates tend to change from yer to year, so you should always consult the tourist office for details.

THROUGHOUT ANDALUCÍA
January: Three Kings Parades, on the eve of the Epiphany (Jan 5)
March/April: Semana Santa processions, from Palm Sunday to Easter Sunday
June: Noche de San Juan, midsummer bonfires lit at midnight June 23 in many Andalucían towns
July: Virgen del Carmen, patroness of fishermen, honoured with seaborne processions in fishing communities along the whole coast in mid July.

CÁDIZ
February: Cádiz city hosts one of Spain's best Carnival celebrations.
March/April: coinciding with Holy Week, running of bulls in Vejer de la Frontera and Arcos de la Frontera
May: Jerez, World Motorcycling Championship at Jerez race track. Jerez Horse Fair: display of horses and horsemanship.
August: Sanlucar de Barrameda: horse races along the beach. Sotogrande, international polo matches throughout the month.
September/October: Jerez, Fiesta de Otoño (Autumn Festival), including Sherry harvest festival.

CÓRDOBA
May: Córdoba, Festival of the Patios (first week of month) and annual fair (last week of month).

June: Romeria de los Gitanos – pilgrimage of the gypsies – in Cabra.
July: International Guitar Festival at the Gran Teatro in Córdoba.

GRANADA

March: Espárrago Rock, Andalucía's biggest outdoor rock festival, in Granada.
May: Cruces de Mayo festival in Granada.
June/July: Granada, International Festival of Music and Dance. One of Spain's leading festivals offers a varied programme of music and dance by national and international companies. Concerts in the Auditorio Manuel de Falla and the Palacio Carlos V in the Alhambra, dance in the Generalife.
November: Granada International Jazz Festival.

HUELVA

May: Romeria del Rocío, Spain's biggest pilgrimage, to the shrine of the Virgin in El Rocio (Doñana).

JAÉN

February: International chess tournament in Linares.
April: Romeria de la Virgen de la Cabeza, a major pilgrimage in Andújar.

MÁLAGA

July: International Music and Dance Festival in the caves of Nerja.
August: Málaga fair, the second biggest in Andalucía.

Bullfighting

Andalucía is the cradle of bullfighting, the controversial struggle between man and beast, and the town of Ronda is regarded as the cradle of modern bullfighting. Many of Spain's top matadors come from the region and many of the most-respected fighting bulls. There are occasional charity fights in winter, but the season really gets under way at Easter and with the series of *corridas* during the Seville Fair in April.

Seville's Maestranza bullring is

Events Guide

Granada's events guide, *Guía Cultural y de Ocio*, published fortnightly in Spanish and English, gives useful information about cultural events. Seville has a useful entertainment guide, *El Giraldillo*. On the Costa del Sol, numerous publications, some free, offer information about what's on. The weekly *Sur in English* has details about theatre, sport, films in English, and club events.

September: Goyesca Fair in Ronda, with carriage displays and bullfight.
October: Fuengirola, Fiesta del Rosario, the Costa del Sol's biggest annual fair.
December: Festival of Verdiales, a primitive mountain music, in Málaga (Dec 28).

SEVILLE

April: Seville, Spring Fair or Feria. The biggest Andalucían festival. Seville, Antiques fair.
July: Italica, International Festival of Theatre and Dance. Contemporary dance and classical ballet by prestigious international companies. Held in the Roman amphitheatre.
September: Biannual Flamenco Festival. Held every two years (1998, 2000, etc). Represents the best in flamenco.

the most important arena. Daily fights are held during the fairs in other towns, throughout the summer. Six bulls are killed during a *corrida*, which usually starts at 6pm.

Tickets are expensive, particularly if you want to be in the shade (*sombra*) and near the *barrera*, the ringside. Cheaper tickets are sold for *Sol*, the seating on the sunny side of the arena. In some communities, bull-runs are held in the streets during local festivities.

Nightlife

Seville has a lively nightlife. The **Santa Cruz area** is favoured by the young, as are the newer bars along **El Torneo,** running parallel to the Guadalquivir river, across from La Cartuja. Lively terrace bars include the **Babaloo**, sometimes featuring live music, and the **Barqueta** (both near Puente la Barqueta bridge). A few streets in from El Torneo, on **Plaza de la Niña de los Peines**, is the trendy and not at all expensive **XL**. There's a good ambience around the **Alameda de Hércules** square and in **La Macarena** district.

Seville also has a number of live music bars, the best of which is **Blue Moon** (Calle Juan Cavestany), featuring live jazz. In summer, there are free concerts staged at night in the **Puerta de Triana**.

Granada knows how to fill the evening hours, thanks to its large student population. Students tend to gravitate to the **Plaza del Principe**. Other favourite hangouts are the maze-like **Albaicin district** and the **Plaza Nueva**. In summer, a good place for bars is the **Paseo de los Tristes** (Sad People's Promenade), below the Alhambra.

Andalucía's nightlife centre is the Costa del Sol, especially Marbella during summer. The best action revolves around the bustling **Puerto Banús yacht harbour** – the **Sinatra bar** is the traditional meeting place. Other classic watering holes include **Joe's Bar**, **Crescendo**, **La Comedia**, and **Mambo**. There are also swank discos nearby, including **Regine's** (Puente Romano) and the palatial **Olivia Valere** (Ctra de Istan, near the mosque), locked in an unending battle to see which can attract the most celebrities. Also near the mosque is the art deco **La Notte**.

Flamenco

There are a number of venues offering live flamenco performances. Purists insist that by its very nature flamenco cannot be restrained to a staged act, and dismiss these establishments as tourist traps, but some of the better clubs offer solid entertainment that fairly closely approximates the genuine article. The best places to see flamenco are Seville and the Santiago district in Jerez. Most venues open around 10pm and stay open until very late. A few recommended venues:

● **El Arenal**, Calle Rodo, 7, Seville, tel: (95) 4216 492
● **Tablao Los Gallos**, Plaza Santa Cruz, 11, Seville, tel: (95) 4228 522
● **Peña Antonio Chacón**, Calle Salas, 2, Jerez de la Frontera (Cádiz), tel: (956) 347 472
● **Peña La Buena Gente**, Plaza de San Lucas, 9, Jerez de la Frontera (Cádiz), tel: (956) 338 404
● **Meson La Bulería**, Calle Pedro Lopez, 3, Córdoba, tel: (957) 483 839
● **Tablao Cardenal**, Calle Torrijos, 10, Córdoba, tel: (957) 483 112
● **Jardines Neptuno**, Calle Arabial, Granada, tel: (958) 251 112

The best flamenco is to be seen in the flamenco festivals and contests held between the end of June and the middle of September in small towns and villages – there's one, or more, every Saturday, somewhere in Andalucía. The best known are the **Potaje in Utrera** (Seville) at the end of June, **La Caracolá** in Lebrija (Seville) in mid-July, the festival in **Mairena del Alcor** (Seville) at the beginning of September, and **Fiesta de la Bulería** held in the Jerez bullring in mid-September. In true flamenco tradition, these events tend to start late and be drawn-out affairs, lasting far into the wee hours.

Shopping

ALMERÍA

Principal buys are in handicrafts: **ceramics and pottery** from Albox, Níjar, Sorbas and Vera; **basketwork** from Almería, Alhabía and Níjar; *jarapas*, rugs made with rags and strips of cotton from Nijar, Huercal Overa and Berja; **bedspreads and blankets** from Albox, Berja and Macael; **marble objects** from Macael.

CÁDIZ

Sherry from Jerez and Puerto de Santa María (such as Harveys, Williams and Humbert, Pedro Domecq and Osborne, well known to the British market); fine **leather** from Ubrique; **carpets** from Arcos de la Frontera; **capes and ponchos** from Grazalema; **guitars** from Algodonales; **wickerwork** from Jerez; **saddlery** from Olvera.

CÓRDOBA

Silver filigree jewellery, for which Córdoba is particularly noted; **Montilla wines** (bodeges in Montilla, 46 km/28 miles from Córdoba); **anís liquor** from Rute; **ceramics**, Lucena pottery with geometric green and yellow design, and *botijos* (two-spouted drinking pitchers) from La Rambla; **leatherwork**; **decorative metalwork** in copper, bronze and brass from Espejo and Castro del Río.

GRANADA

Cured mountain hams from the Alpujarras; **pottery**, most typical is Fajalauza with distinctive blue and green design originally from the Albaicín; **leather**, especially embossed leatherwork; **marquetry** (technique of inlaying wood with bone, ivory, mother of pearl and other woods) **chests**, **chess boards**,

small tables; metal craftwork, **lanterns** made to traditional Moorish designs; **rugs, cushions** and **bedspreads** from the Alpujarras; **hand-made guitars**, several workshops on the Cuesta de Gomerez leading to the Alhambra; **silver filigree jewellery**.

HUELVA

Cured hams from Jabugo; **white wine** from the Condado de Huelva; **pottery** from Aracena and Cortejana; **rugs** from Ecinasola; **embroidery** from Aracena, Alonso and Puebla de Guzmán; **handmade leather boots** Valverde de Camino.

JAÉN

Glass and ceramics from Andújar, Bailén and Ubeda; **carpets** and **wickerwork** from Ubeda, Jaén and Los Villares; **forged iron objects** and **lanterns** from Ubeda; **guitars** from Marmolejo.

MÁLAGA

The towns along the Costa del Sol also offer a variety of **street markets**, colourful though not necessarily the place to find a bargain. Market timings are as follows: Monday Marbella; Tuesday Fuengirola and Nerja; Wednesday Estepona; Thursday Torremolinos and San Pedro de Alcántara; Friday Arroyo de la Miel and Benalmádena pueblo; Sunday Estepona port and Málaga (by the football stadium).

SEVILLE

Antiques around the streets Mateos Gago, Placentines and Rodrigo Caro; **ceramics** and **tiles** from Santa Ana (factory in Triana) and La Cartuja de Sevilla (factory at Ctra de Mérida); **saddlery** and **leather items**, **boots** and **chaps**; **fashion**, Seville's own designers Victorio and Lucchino have showroom at Sierpes, 87; **fans** and **castanets**.

Getting Acquainted

The Place

Eastern Spain comprises Catalonia, Valencia and Murcia. Most of this section deals with Catalonia, the most popular of the regions. For further regional detail, contact the tourist office in Barcelona, Centro de Informació Turística de Catalunya, Passeig de Gràcia, 107, tel: (93) 2384 000.

Government

Catalonia, the most unified region of eastern Spain, is a self-governing community governed by the Generalitat in Barcelona. Since it gained its autonomous status in 1977, the Convergencia i Unió (centre-right) party has been in power, though Barcelona has a socialist mayor. Catalonia's provinces – Barcelona, Girona, Lleida and Tarragona – are divided into 41 *comarques*.

Economy

Some 25 percent of Spain's industry is in Catalonia, mainly textiles, chemicals and mechanical equipment. Thirty-five percent of the population is engaged in industry, 60 percent in services and only 5 percent in agriculture, which nevertheless flourishes, with olives, grapes, apples and pears as the basic crops. The Olympic Games in Barcelona in 1992 were also a benefit to the economy.

Geography

Catalonia covers an area of approximately 32,000 sq. km (12,355 sq. miles)The Catalan Pyrenees are snow-covered for many months of the year, some up to 2,950 metres (9,700 ft) high.

The Vall d'Aran in Lleida and the Cerdanya in Girona are typified by green, rolling foothills and broad, fertile valleys; the comarca of La Garrotxa is a volcanic region and a swathe of wooded hills follows the coast down to Barcelona.

The coast is more than 580-km (350-miles) long and is divided into four main parts: the Costa Brava, from the border to Blanes, mainly an area of rocky coves; the Costa del Maresme, to the north of Barcelona, with long sandy beaches; the shorter Costa Garraf, reaching as far south as Cubelles and often included in the Costa Daurada (Dorada) which stretches the length of Tarragona province.

In the Empordà, in the province of Girona, and the Ebre delta, in Tarragona, there are extensive marshlands, important for migratory birds and areas of rice cultivation. The Alt Penedès, in Tarragona, is a big wine-producing region and the plain of Alcanar at the southern end of the Costa Daurada is covered with citrus groves.

Population

Catalonia has a population of just over 6 million, of which 1.7 million live in Barcelona and 1 million more in the industrial suburbs.

Climate

Catalonia has a climate as varied as its geography. In Andorra and the Pyrenees the temperature can drop to below freezing in winter. In the north of the Costa Brava winds whip up apparently out of nowhere and last for several days. But a little further south the climate is more reliable, with little rain in summer.

The average temperature in coastal resorts is 25°C (77°F) in summer and 11°C (52°F) in winter. Inland it can be much hotter and spring and autumn may be preferred by visitors.

Planning the Trip

Getting There

CATALONIA

By air: Barcelona airport (tel: 298 3838) is 12km (7 miles) south of the city at El Prat. Iberia runs a shuttle service between Barcelona and Madrid.

By road: The French border is 149km (92 miles) north of Barcelona at La Jonquera on the A7 motorway.

By rail: Through-services connect Paris to Barcelona.

VALENCIA & MURCIA

By air: There are international airports at Valencia (Manises Airport) and Alicante (El Altet Airport). A few international flights go to San Javier airport which serves Murcia.

By sea: Ferries connect the port of Valencia with the Balearic islands.

By road: Good roads link Madrid to the three main cities: the NIII (mainly dual carriageway or *autovía*) to Valencia; the N330 *autovía* to Alicante and the N301 to Murcia. The A7 motorway links the region to Barcelona and Andalucía.

By rail: Main rail lines run from Valencia to both Madrid and Barcelona. Alicante and Murcia also have services to Madrid.

Local Tourist Offices

CATALONIA

Lleida: Oficina d'Informació Turistica, Arc del Pont, 25007, tel: 973 270 997.

Andorra: Sindicat d'Iniciativa, Carrer Dr Vilanova, Andorra La Vella, tel: 376 827 117; Oficina de Turisme del Principat d'Andorra, Carrer Marià Cubí, 159, 08021 Barcelona.

Puigcerdà: Oficina de Turisme del C.I.T., Carrer Querol, tel: 972 880 542.
La Jonquera: Oficina de Turisme, Porta Catalana, A7 motorway, tel: 972 554 050.
Portbou: Oficina d'Informació Turística, Estació RENFE, 17497, tel: 972 125 161.
Girona: Oficina de Turisme, Rambla Libertat, 1, 17004; Oficina Municipal de Turisme, Estació (Station) RENFE, 17007, tel: 972 226 575.
Barcelona: Patronat Municipal de Turisme, Estació (Station) de Rodales, 08003; Oficina de Turisme, Plaça Catalunya, tel: (933) 189 505; Patronat Municipal de Turisme, Estació (Station) de Sants, 08014, tel: (933) 257 331.
Reus: Oficina de Turisme, Plaça Libertat, tel: (977) 773 715.
Tarragona: Oficina de Turisme, Carrer Fortuny, 4, 43001, tel: (977) 233 415; Patronat Municipal de Turisme, Carrer Major, 39, 43003, tel: (977) 245 203.

Regional offices

Government regional tourist services (Servei Territorial de Comerç, Consum i Turisme): for registering complaints, etc.
Lleida: Avinguda Prat de la Riba, 76, 25004.
Girona: Travessia de la Creu, 1, 17002.
Barcelona: Centro d'Informació Turística de Catalunya, Palau Robert, Passeig de Gràcia, 107, tel: (93) 2384 000.
Tarragona: Rambla Vella, 7, 43003.

VALENCIA

Comunidad Valenciana: Calle de la Paz, 46, Valencia, tel: (96) 3986 422.
Valencia city: Ayuntamiento, 1, tel: (96) 3525 478.
Alicante: Explanada de España, 2, tel: (96) 5200 000.
Castellón: Plaza María Agustina, 5, tel: (96) 4221 000.

MURCIA

Calle San Cristóbal, 5, tel: (96) 8366 130.

Practical Tips

Media

Television: There are seven television channels. TVE 1 and TVE 2 are national, the first broadcasting almost exclusively in Castilian, the second mostly in Catalan. The two Catalan channels supported by the Generalitat are TV3, a popular channel, and Canal 33, which is slightly more high-brow, covering the arts, sports and minority interests. There are three private channels: Antena 3 and Tele 5, both Madrid based, and Canal Plus, a subscription-only channel linked to its French counterpart. French television can be seen in some northern areas and people in Tarragona can pick up Valencian television, which is on the same wavelength as Canal 33. There is also a useful device available which allows viewers the choice of watching some films either in their dubbed version or in their original language.
Radio: Between 9.30am and 4.30pm on weekdays during July and August Rádio Associació de Catalunya broadcasts an hour each of Catalan, English, German, Italian and French (105 MHZ on FM). There are local radios in every town and in summer foreign languages burst through the Catalan to advertise shops, discos and events. The most popular radio station is Cadena SER, a national radio with high local input (828 kHZ MW). Radio 2 national radio is a very good classical music station.
Print: Catalonia's two main daily newspapers are El Periódico, in Catalan and Castilian, and La Vanguardia, in Castilian. The popular Madrid daily, El País, has a large Barcelona staff producing a

Festivals in Catalonia

There are numerous colourful national and local festivals, especially in spring and early summer. Important ones are:
Carnival: on Shrove Tuesday, celebrated everywhere, particularly in Roses, Sitges and Vilanova i la Geltrú.
Semana Santa: Holy Week, religious processions in most towns.
St George's Day, Sant Jordi: 23 April, day of books and roses – lovers' day.
Festival of the Virgin of Montserrat: 27 April, at the monastery.
Corpus Christi: flower carpets in several towns, including Sitges.
St John's Eve: 23 June, bonfires and other pyrotechnics.
Vendimia: the wine harvest festivals are in mid-September.
Verge Mercè festival: 24 September, Barcelona's biggest festival.

Catalonia edition which alters about six news and features pages plus the sport. Avui (Today) is the only Catalan region-wide daily, but there are a number of local daily papers such as the Diari de Barcelona, El Nou in Vic, and the Diari de Girona.

Getting Around

CATALONIA

By Rail

There are four main rail links in and out of Barcelona:

R1: Portbou-Girona-Barcelona. This is the main line down from Paris. An additional line operates north of Barcelona in summer: the Vapor de la Costa goes up the Maresme coast to Blanes then picks up the R1 at Massanet.

R2: Puigcerdà-Ripoll-Vic-Barcelona. This is the link-up to Toulouse in France, and a good way into the Pyrenees.

R3: Barcelona-Manresa/Reus/Valls-Lleida. This line continues to Zaragoza, and Madrid. From Lleida a line goes up to Pobla de Segur, half way to the Aigüestortes national park.

R4: Barcelona-Tarragona. The Costa Daurada train continues down the coast to Valencia.

Trains to France and certain other destination leave from the Estació de França, near the harbour, refurbished in the late 1980s as a major national and international terminus.

Trains up the coast as far as Blanes leave from the RENFE station in Plaça Catalunya, on the corner of Ronda de la Universitat. Connections to France from Blanes can be made by the SARFA bus company, tel: (93) 2651 158.

Trains to the southeast run from the Passeig de Gràcia and from the central station, Sants, in Plaça Països Catalans, from which connections can be made to any part of Spain. Stations are marked with the national railways acronym RENFE (Red Nacional de Ferrocarriles Españoles).

Further information: RENFE,

Taking taxis

There are prominently-marked ranks in central areas and fares are very reasonable (a 10 percent tip is usual, though in no way required or expected). Although public transport is adequate and you won't need a car for visiting any of the major towns, to make the most of the country you really do need private transport.

Estació Central Barcelona de Sants, Plaça Països Catalans s/n, 08014 Barcelona, tel: (93) 3224 141. **Barcelona** also has a suburban line, run by the Ferrrocarils de la Generalitat de Catalunya, tel: (93) 2051 515. From Estació Plaça d'Espanya trains go to Montserrat, Igualada and Manresa. Get off at Santa Coloma de Cervelló to see Gaudí's Colònia Güell. From Plaça Catalunya they go to Sabadell, Terrassa and Sant Cugat.

By Road

Catalonia is well served by motorways: the A7 runs from the border towards Valencia, becoming the A17 briefly before it reaches Barcelona, and the A2 for a short while to the south of the city. The A19 motorway, which runs north from Barcelona almost to Blanes, and a new ring-road, known as the "Ronda", have greatly improved city's severe traffic problems.

The new "eix transversal" (transversal axis) cuts directly from Girona via Vic to Lleida for travellers who prefer to bypass Barcelona y. The E-9, C1411 now connects Barcelona with the Cerdanya valley in 2 hours, via Manresa, Berga and the Tunel del Cadí.

The N11 (N roads are main, single-lane, national highways) shadows the motorway from the border down to Exit 9. It then follows the coast down to Barcelona, emerging to the south of the city and turning inland towards Lleida. For much of its length the N11 has a fairly light traffic flow, although its coastal stretch becomes

congested in the summer months and should be avoided if possible. From Barcelona the Autovia 152 (a two-lane highway) goes to Vic and on to Puigcerdà; the 240 links Tarragona and Lleida; and the 141 goes from Lleida to join the 152 just below Vic.

In between these main routes, Catalonia is criss-crossed by a network of regional and local roads, mainly going north-south, following the rivers coming down from the Pyrenees and making hard work of east-west journeys. The roads themselves are of varying quality, some of which more than compensate, by scenery and lack of traffic, for what they may lack in width or smoothness.

Hitchhiking

There are two organisations in Barcelona which organise lifts at low prices. These are: Barnastop, Pintor Fortuny, 21, 08001 Barcelona, tel: (93) 3182 731; and Comparco, Ribes, 31, 08013 Barcelona, tel: (93) 2466 908.

VALENCIA & MURCIA

By Public Transport

Coaches are generally more direct and more frequent than trains. There are coach stations in the cities and coach services linking the towns of the region. Narrow gauge rail lines run along the Costa Blanca (more scenic than practical), between the Mar Menor and Cartagena, and around the outskirts of the city of Valencia.

By Road

The A7 motorway runs along or near the coast from Catalonia to Andalucía. North of Alicante, except for a stretch circumnavigating Valencia, it is a toll road (*autopista*); south of Alicante it is toll free (*autovía*). The old main roads, N340 and N332, provide alternatives to it but they can be slower and congested. Other main (N) roads are good. Inland, however, many smaller roads wind tortuously around the contours.

Where to Stay

Hotels

CATALONIA

Barcelona City

Barcelona's Olympic hotel-building boom added many lodging facilites to the city's supply. Nevertheless, better class hotels should be booked, as conventions can fill them up. Middle-priced hotels particularly can be in short supply during peak periods.

Condes de Barcelona
Passeig de Gràcia, 75
tel: (93) 4882 200
fax: (93) 4871 442
Top of the range hotel in a converted Modernist mansion. Colón $$$$

Avinguda Catedral, 7
tel: (93) 3011 404
fax: (93) 3172 915
In the Gothic quarter, though the cathedral bells may keep you awake. $$$

Hotel Gran Via
Gran Via de les Corts Catalanes, 642
tel: (93) 3181 900
fax: (93) 3189 997
Near the Plaça Catalunya and has a brocaded, Regency feel. $$

Hotel España
Sant Pau, 9 i 11,
tel: (93) 3181 758
fax: (93) 3171 134
A Modernist extravaganza from Domènech i Montaner and, though the bedrooms are plain, its public rooms maintain a sense of the belle époque. $$

Neutral
Rambla de Catalunya, 42
tel: (93) 3187 370
Just two of a clutch of pleasant, low-priced hotels on or near Rambla de Catalunya. $$

There are lots of inexpensive

pensiones and hostales on the roads and lanes leading off both sides of the Rambla, and they are generally progressively more seedy towards the port. Near Plaça Catalunya at the top there are 1- and 2-star hotels on Carrer de Santa Anna: the **Cortes**, tel: (93) 317 91 12, fax: (93) 3027 870; and the **Nouvel**, tel: (93) 3018 274, fax: (93) 3018 370. Further down off to the right on Carrer del Carme, there are four pensiós: the **Carmen**, tel: (93) 3171 076; **Aneto**, tel: (93) 3019 989, fax: (93) 3019 862; **Selecta**, tel: (93) 3014 484; and the **Mare Nostrum**, tel: (93) 3185 340, fax: (93) 4123 069. The **Sant Agustí**, Plaça Sant Agustí, 3, tel: (93) 3172 882, fax: (93) 3172 928, is pleasantly situated in a quiet square behind the market; on the opposite side of Rambla is the **Hotel Jardí $$**, Plaça St Josep Oriol, 1, tel: (93) 3015 900, fax: (91) 3183 664, overlooking two attractive squares.

Price Guide

For a standard double room
$$$$ = Over 20,000 pesetas
$$$ = 15–20,000 pesetas
$$ = 15,000 pesetas
$ = Under 8,000 pesetas

Barcelona Province

Balneario Termes Victòria
Carrer Barcelona, 12, 08140 Caldes de Montbui
tel: (93) 8650 150
fax: (93) 8650 816
A spa hotel which is now becoming trendy. $$$

Sant Bernat
Finca el Cot, 08460 Montseny
tel: (93) 8473 011
fax: (93) 8473 220
A pleasant small hotel situated near the forest and mountains of the natural park. $$$

Parador Nacional
08500 Vic, 15 km (10 miles) northeast of Vic off the N153
tel: (93) 8122 323
fax: (93) 8122 368
Very popular and very beautiful. A relatively new building for a parador,

it is wonderfully set in a pine forest overlooking the Sau reservoir. The restaurant serves good traditional Vic dishes. $$$$

Monistrol
Ctra Abrera-Manresa (C1411), km 13
tel: (93) 8350 477
fax: (93) 8284 421
Overshadowed by mountains and is an alternative to a cell in the monastery. $

El Bruc
Ctra Nacional II, Km 570, 08194 El Bruc
tel: (93) 7710 061
fax: (93) 7710 086
This is a well-appointed hotel set in this legendary valley. It also has an excellent restaurant: listen out for the mythical drummer boy while you eat traditional Catalan cuisine. $$$

Parador Nacional Duques de Cardona
08261 Cardona
tel: (93) 8691 275
A hilltop castle overlooking the town and salt mines, authentically complete with squeaking floorboards. The restaurant in the baronial hall is on the pricey side but the food is fine and the portions large. $$$

Lleida/Lérida Province

Residència Principal
Plaça de la Paeria, 8, Lleida
tel: (97) 3230 800
fax: (97) 3230 803
A comfortable, medium-priced hotel in the heart of the old town. $$$

Gran Sol
Ctra Manresa s/n, Solsona
tel: (97) 3480 975
fax: (97) 3481 000
Just a kilometre from Solsona, this hotel and restaurant is better known for its cuisine than for lodging. $$$

Hotel Terradets
Ctra C147 s/n (the main Balaguer-Tremp road), Cellers (Sellés)
tel: (97) 3651 120
fax: (97) 3651 304
Situated in a beautiful setting by a lake. The hotel also has a good, inexpensive restaurant serving local dishes as well as a surprisingly good paella. $$$

Hotel Manantia
25528 Caldes de Boi, (on the Val de Boí side)
tel: (97) 3696 210
fax: (97) 3696 220
This spa hotel is worth the extra for a luxury stay and has a good restaurant. **$$$$**

Parador Nacional
Carrer Sant Domènec, 6, La Seu d'Urgell
tel: (97) 3352 000
fax: (97) 3352 309
The menu is excellent. **$$$$**

Hotel Andria
Passeig Joan Brudieu, 24
tel: (97) 3350 300
fax: (97) 3351 425
Comfortable hotel that's half the price of the *parador*. **$$**

Vall D'Aran

Parador Nacional Gaspar de Pórtola
Ctra Baqueira, s/n, Arties
tel: (97) 3640 801
fax: (97) 3641 001
A 16th-century house, once home to an explorer who went to California, now converted into an intimate inn, which caters for skiiers. **$$$$**

Hostal Valarties
Carrer Major, 3, Arties
tel: (97) 3644 364
fax: (97) 3642 174
Has a dozen rooms and a lounge with open fireplace and is attached to the renowned restaurant run by Irene España Plagues. **$$$**

Girona Province

La Torre del Remei
Camí Reial s/n, Cerdanya
Bolvir de Cerdanya, 17463
tel: (972) 140 182
fax: (972) 140 449
The most luxurious spot in the Pyrenees, José and Lola Boix have created a masterpiece of fine cuisine and elegant hospitality. Exceptional. **$$$$**

Can Ventura
Plaça Mayor, 1, Cerdanya
tel: (972) 896 178
Excellent and hearty fare in a 17th-century farmhouse of unusual charm in the Spanish "enclave" of Llívia, just 6 km (4 miles) northeast of Puigcerdà. **$$**

Hotel Llívia
Avenida de Catalunya, s/n, Cerdanya
tel (972) 896 000
fax: (972) 146 000
Excellent and friendly clubhouse for exploring the Cerdanya. **$$**

Hotel del Lago
Avenida Dr. Piguillem, 7, Cerdanya
tel: (972) 881 000
fax: (972) 141 511
This cosy spot next to Puigcerdà's fabled lake is elegant, comfortable, quiet and just a couple of minutes' walk from the centre of town. **$$$**

Mulleras
Can Mulleras, s/n, Olot
17176 Sant Privat d'En Bas
tel: (972) 693 257
Pretty country *pensión* only a couple of miles outside Olot in the Val d'En Bas. Its walls are covered with local paintings. Bread and tomato with ham for breakfast and an inexpensive evening set menut. **$$**

Güell
Plaça Espanya, 8, Camprodón
tel: (972) 740 011
fax: (972) 741 112
An elegant and inexpensive hotel in the centre of town. **$$**

You will eat heartily, especially meat dishes such as beef with prunes, at any of the restaurants in the rural village of Setcases, 13 km (8 miles) to the north.

Durán
Lasauca, 5, Figueres
tel: (972) 501 250
fax: (972) 210 492
Has a traditional interior of tiles and high-backed chairs and a *porró* of Muscatel does the rounds at the end of the meal of Empordà dishes. **$$**

Hotel Ampurdán
Ctra Nacional N11, km 763, Figueres
tel: (972) 500 562
fax: (972) 509 358
Was one of Josep Pla's favourites, and is often credited as the birthplace of the "new" Catalan cuisine. **$$$**

Peninsular
Carrer Nou, 3, Girona
tel: (972) 203 800
fax: (972) 210 492
Well-established hotel, just over on the new side of town. **$$$**

Llitonia
Gran Via de Jaume I, 22, Girona
tel: (972) 203 850
fax: (972) 203 334
In the centre of town with modern, renovated rooms. **$$**

Costa Brava

Hotel Portlligat
17488 Portlligat, Portlligat
tel: (972) 258 162
fax: (972) 258 643
The only commercial establishment in Dalí's bay, with a salt-water swimming pool alongside it. The sort of place to go for a treat, either staying overnight or just for a meal in the well-appointed dining room overlooking the bay. **$$$**

Hostal Ampurias
17130 L'Escala, Empúries
tel/fax: (972) 770 207
Out of town, right by the ruins and right on the beach. **$$**

Aiguablava Hotel
17255 Platja de Fornells
tel: (972) 622 058
fax: (972) 622 112
The classic Costa Brava hotel, beautifully situated in Fornells Bay. **$$$**

Parador Nacional Costa Brava
17255 Platja d'Aiguablava
tel: (972) 622 162
fax: (972) 622 166
Modern *parador* with good local dishes. **$$$**

Sant Sebastià
Santuari de Sant Sebastià, s/n, Palafrugell
tel: (972) 301 639
Spectacularly placed hotel, above a lighthouse at the top of cliffs. The hotel, built around a courtyard, has character and there is a bar and restaurant attached. **$$**

Trias
Passeig del Mar, s/n, Palamós
tel: (972) 601 800
fax: (972) 601 819
Rather pricey, but another of the coast's well-known hotels which has been going for years. **$$$**

La Gavina
Plaça de la Rosaleda, s/n, S'Agaró
tel: (972) 321 100
fax: (972) 321 573
The only 5-star hotel on the coast. **$$$$**

Sant Pol
Platja de Sant Pol, 125, S'Agaró
tel: (972) 321 070
fax: (972) 822 378
Less expensive than the nearby La
Gavina. **$$**

Costa Daurada
Rey Don Jaime
Avinguda de l'Hotel, s/n,
Castelldefels
tel: (93) 6651 300
fax: (93) 6651 801
This is expensive, but worth it for
the beautiful hilltop view of the
costa as far as Barcelona. Fine
food. **$$$**
Rancho
Passeig de la Marina, 212,
Castelldefels
tel: (93) 6651 900
fax: (93) 6360 832
Quieter than the beach-front hotels
and has good quality cuisine. **$$$**
Nàutic
Passeig Marítim, 374, Castelldefels
tel: (93) 6650 174
Facing the beach, the superior
seafood is served in quaint
surroundings. **$$$**
Calípolis
Passeig Marítim, s/n, Sitges
tel: (93) 8941 500
fax: (93) 8940 764
A fairly large hotel situated just a
few hundred metres from the
church and museums on the
seafront. **$$$**
Terramar
Passeig Marítim, s/n, Sitges
tel: (93) 8940 054
fax: (93) 8945 604
An older style establishment facing
the beach with gardens and good
sports facilities. **$$$**

Tarragona Province
España
Rambla Nova, 49, Tarragona
tel: (977) 232 712
fax: (977) 232 079
A small, old-fashioned hotel right in
the middle of town, reasonably
priced.
Torreblanca
Carrer Josep M Fàbregas, 1, Valls
tel: (977) 601 022
fax: (977) 606 323
Attractive *pensión*. **$**

Residència-Casa de Pagès la Carrerada
Carrer Carrerada, 8, Priorat
43739 Porrera
tel: (977) 828 021
Fax: (977) 828 021
One of the first of several *casas de
pagès* supported by the Generalitat
to supply accommodation on a
small scale. It is an old house,
beautifully converted in a modern
abstract style, and designed for
only a dozen guests. **$$**

Price Guide

For a standard double room
$$$$ = Over 20,000 pesetas
$$$ = 15–20,000 pesetas
$$ = 15,000 pesetas
$ = Under 8,000 pesetas

VALENCIA
Valencia (Capital)
Astoria Palace
Plaza Rodrigo Botet, 5
tel: (96) 3526 737
Centrally located, luxury hotel with
good service.
Reina Victoria
Barcas, 4
tel: (96) 3520 487
A stylish old-fashioned hotel built in
1913, close to the main square of
the city. **$$$**
Inglés
Marqués de Dos Aguas, 6
tel: (96) 3516 426
Historic building, recently
refurbished, next to the Palacio del
Marqués de Dos Aguas (Ceramics
Museum). **$$**
Ad Hoc
Boix 4
tel: (96) 3919 140
A small hotel, centrally located, with
more character than the city's large
chain hotels. **$$**

Valencia Province
L'Estació
Parc de L'Estació, s/n, Bocairent
tel: (96) 2905 211
This is actually the town's former
railway station, which has been
rehabilitated as a small, modern
hotel. **$**

Sidi Saler Palace
Playa del Saler, s/n, El Saler
tel: (96) 1610 411
A comfortable hotel with swimming
pool and beauty centre, situated
beside the beach a few kilometres
outside Valencia. **$$$$**
Monte Picayo
Urb. Monte Picayo, s/n, Puçol
tel: (96) 1420 100
This is a luxurious complex within
reach of Valencia. Some bedrooms
have their own pool and garden.
$$$
Hostería de Mont Sant
Subida al Castillo, Xátiva
tel: (96) 2275 081
A very small, welcoming hotel
occupying a restored Cistercian
monastery. **$$**

Alicante (Capital)
Hotel Sidi San Juan
La Doblada, s/n, Plaza de San Juan
tel: (96) 516 13 00
fax: (96) 516 33 46
A fine hotel with excellent
installations, restaurants,
swimming pools, etc., situated on
the beach. **$$$$**
Meliá Alicante
Playa Postiguet
tel: (96) 5205 000
fax: (96) 5204 756
A very comfortable hotel with a
swimming pool and restaurant. **$$$**
Palas
Cervantes 5
tel: (96) 5209 211
A characterful old mansion located
near the seafront and the
Explanada. **$$**

Alicante (Province)
Huerto del Cura
Porta de la Morera, 14, Elx
tel: (96) 5458 040
Located across the road from the
beautiful gardens of the same
name, the hotel enjoys a similarly
lovely situation in Elx's extensive
palm groves. **$$$**
El Montiboli
Partida Montiboli, s/n, La Vila
Joiosa
tel: (96) 5890 250
A seaside hotel perched on a low
cliff outside a small resort south of
Benidorm. **$$$**

Parador de Javea
Avda Mediterráneo, 7, Jávea
tel: (96) 5790 200
A purpose-built parador with beautiful gardens beside the beach. **$$$**

Castellón
Palau del Ossets
Plaza Mayor, 16, Forcall
tel: (964) 177 524
An attractively restored 16th century palace on the main square of the village. **$**

Fábrica de Giner
Ctra Morella-Zorita del Maestrazgo, Morella
tel: (964) 173 142
A modern hotel in an old textile factory 4.5 km (3 miles) from Morella with a duck pond in the grounds. **$**

Cardenal Ram
Cuesta Suñer, 1
tel: (964) 173 085
Handsome 16th-century mansion which dominates the porticoed main street of Morella. **$**

Hostería del Mar
Avda Papa Luna, 18, Peñíscola
tel: (964) 480 600
A modern hotel with an interior in a mock-medieval style, across the road from the beach.

MURCIA

Murcia (Capital)
Conde de Floridablanca
Princesa, 18
tel: (968) 214 626
This hotel, which is decorated with stained glass, antiques and crafts, is across the river from the city centre but within walking distance of the main sights. **$$**

Arco de San Juan
Ceballos, 10
tel: (968) 210 455
Regarded as one of the best hotels in Murcia, the hotel is a modern building behind an old façade. It stands on one of the main squares of the city. **$$**

MURCIA PROVINCE

Termas de Archena
Balneario de Archena
tel: (968) 670 100
A spa hotel decorated in a superb Mozarabic style with domes, patios

and ornate plasterwork. **$**
Los Habaneros
San Diego, 60, Cartagena
tel: (968) 505 250
A modest and functional hotel with rooms at reasonable prices. **$**

Príncipe Felipe
Los Belones, La Manga del Mar Menor
tel: (968) 137 234
The hotel is part of the luxurious complex La Manga Club, built in the style of a Spanish village. Among its many facilities are golf courses, swimming pools, tennis courts and a health centre. **$$$**

Amaltea
Ctra de Granada, s/n, Polígono de los Peñones, Lorca
tel: (968) 40 65 65
A modern hotel with attractive gardens planted with palm trees. **$$**

Where to Eat

Where to Eat

CATALONIA
Barcelona
Barcelona's restaurants are nearly too numerous and mouth-watering to begin to describe or recommend. Gourmet options might begin with **Jean Luc Figueres**, Santa Teresa, 10, tel: (93) 4152 877, arguably the city's finest cuisine. Next, consider **Tram-Tram**, Major de Sarrià, 121, tel: (93) 2048 518, up in the pleasant village-like Sarrià, easily reached on the Sarrià train. **Set Portes**, Passeig Isabel II, 14, tel: (93) 3193 033, serves fine fare in old-world elegance from 1pm–1am, while **Los Caracoles**, Escudellers, 14, tel: (93) 3023 185, is excellent, though crammed with tourists. **Cal Pep**, Plaça de les Olles, 8, tel: (93) 3196 183, serves the best, hottest, freshest *tapas* in Barcelona. If there are people waiting , don't hesitate to join them – it's worth it. **Botafumeiro**, Carrer Gran de Grácia, 81, tel: (93) 2184 230. An excellent Galician seafood restaurant and oyster bar, offering continual service from 1pm–1am.

Passadís D'en Pep, Plaça de Palau, 2, tel: (93) 3101 021, is a small but "in" restaurant that's expensive but excellent, where most diners are happy to eat what they are given. **El Raïm**, Carrer Pescaderia, 6, tel: (93) 3192 998, has been "in" for bygone literati and is still a pleasant, informal place. To get an artistic flavour, visit **Els Quatre Gats**, Carrer Montsío, 3, tel: (93) 3024 140. The building itself is spectacular. The paintings on the walls are copies, but one really does have to sit in the same place that Rusiñol, Casas, Picasso and the rest did.

Other characterful spots include **El Gran Café**, Carrer de Avinyó, 9, tel: (93) 3187 986. A turn-of-the-century sewing machine premises, which nostalgically retains its decor and serves good Catalan dishes bistro style. Try one of the two **Eqipte** restaurants, the latest opened on the Rambla, at 79 Rambla; the one at the back of the market is fun: Carrer Jerusalem, 12, tel: (93) 3177 480.

Lleida/Lérida province

La Huerta restaurant
Avinguda de Tortosa, 9, Lleida
tel: (973) 242 413
Typical Lleidan food and wines. **$$**
Solterra
Plaça de Sant Roc, 2, Solsona
tel: (973) 480 627
Local cheeses, wines and dishes. **$$**
Can Ton
Carrer de la Font, La Seu d'Urgell

tel: (973) 352 719
Very cheap – and very popular. **$**
Casa Irene
Carrer Major, 3, Arties
tel: (973) 640 900
Exceptional cooking – dishes include home-smoked salmon with crab sauce, duck with truffles; green walnut liqueur is the house speciality. **$$$**

Girona

Can Borrell
High in the hills at Meranges, Cerdanya. For years a leader of Catalan nouvelle cuisine, Can Borrell is an excellent restaurant. The drive up is spectacular, the cuisine superb, and the restaurant is chic rustic. **$$$**
La Tieta
Carrer de las Ferrers, 20, Cerdanya
tel: (972) 880 156
Built into a restored 16th-century

townhouse, once part of Puicerdà's ramparts. Excellent fare. **$$$**

Costa Brava

La Xicra
Estret, 17, Palafrugell
tel: (972) 305 630
Fine local specialities. Closed Tuesday pm and Wednesday (except August) and November. **$$$**
Maria de Cadaqués
Notaries, 39, Palamós
tel: (972) 314 009
Serves Empordà dishes, fish and seafood specialities. **$$**
Plaça Murada
Plaça Murada, 5
tel: (972) 315 376
Excellent seafood and upland combinations. **$$**
 Just two of a number of good fish restaurants around the port.
Taverna del Mar
S'Agaro
Try on a pot of fish (*olla pescadors*) at this up-market beach café. **$**

Costa del Maresme

Emma
Baixada de l'Estació, 5, Caldes d'Estrac
tel: (93) 7911 305
Cosy little restaurant for fresh fish and local cuisine. **$$**
Arenys de Mar
There are good fish restaurants in the port, such as the **Posit de Pescador**. The **Hispania** in Reial, 54, tel: (93) 7910 306, is celebrated for its Catalan cuisine.

Costa Daurado

Vivero
Passeig Balmins, Sitges
tel: (93) 8942 149
A basic place with tables outside overlooking the small beach and serving mainly seafood. **$**
Els 4 Gats
Carrer Sant Pau, 13, Sitges
tel: (93) 8941 915
A reasonably priced, quality restaurant located on a narrow street descending to the sea. **$$**
Can Gatell-Rodolfo
Carrer Miramar, 27, Cambrils
tel: (97) 7360 106
One of three restaurants in the town owned by the Gatell family. All

Catalonian Wine Routes

Wine producers, co-operatives and *bodeges* are hospitable places, and at most of them you will be able to taste the wine before buying.
Empordà-Costa Brava: In the most northeasterly corner of the region, this stretches between Figueres and the French border to the sea. There are co-operatives at Roses, Pau, Vilajuïga, Garriguella, Mollet de Peralada, Capmany, Sant Climent Sescebes, Rabós and Espolla, a village whose wines Catalan writer Josep Pla thought the best. The centre for the local *cava* industry is Peralada, a delightful medieval town worth a visit.
Penedès: Catalonia's largest and best-known wine region, just west of Barcelona, centres on the towns of Vilafranca del Penedès and Sant Sadurní d'Anoia. The famous high-tech Torres Bodega is in Carrer Comercio, Vilafranca (closed August). There is a good selection of the local producers' wines in the shops, plus the excellent Museu del Vi (closed Sunday). Sant Sadurní is the *cava*

town, home of Catalonia's two top producers of this *méthode champenoise* wine, Codorníu and Freixenet. Caves Codorníu on the edge of the town is a fine Modernist building restored by Puig i Cadafalch and worth a visit.
Priorat: Perhaps the most charming of the regions, where small villages make wine in small quantities. The precipitous slopes are attractive to look at but hard to work, and few young people remain at home to help out on the land. There are co-operatives at Bellmunt del Priorat, Lloà, Gratallops, Porrera, Torroja del Priorat, La Viella Alta, La Viella Baixa, Pobleda and La Morera de Montsant. The most modern wine makers are at Scala Dei.
Tarragona: De Müller, supplier of altar wine to the Vatican, is the surviving grand old wine maker in Tarragona, in the Carrer Reial, open during weekday office hours. There are several cavernous *bodeges* in the town. Outside Tarragona, on the N240 towards Valls, there is the modern Lopez Bertrán wine producer.

are famous for their classic Tarragona fish dishes (*romesco, àrros a banda, suquet,* etc.) but this one is the most traditional. **$$$**

Tarragona province
Les Coques
Baixada Nova del Patriarca, 2, Tarragona
tel: (977) 228 300
Serves good regional dishes. **$$**
La Rambla
Rambla Nova, 10, Tarragona
tel: (977) 238 729
Rather smart and it serves what some consider to be the best and most authentic *romesco* with two courses of different kinds of fish. Pau Aquilo is an old-fashioned owner who is always around and running everything with amazing precision. **$$$**
Les Voltes
Carrer Trinquet Vell, 12, Tarragona
tel: (977) 230 651
Built into the Roman amphitheatre, this is a local favourite. **$$**

Price Guide

$$$$ = more than 4,000 pesetas
$$$ = 1,500–4,000 pesetas
$$ = under 1,500 pesetas
Prices are per person for a three-course meal, not including wine

Restaurant Pi
Rambla, 2, El Vendrell
tel: (977) 660 002
A café-restaurant done in a rather overblown Modernist style. It serves local dishes, such as *xató* slad and its own version of *calçots*. **$$**
Restaurant Masía Bou
Ctra de Lleida, s/n, Valls
tel: (972) 600 427
This is the place to eat *calçots*. There are countless photos of celebrities, from Dalí to Suarez, wearing bibs and wolfing down their onions. It is smart and on the pricey side, but the *calçots* are the real thing, grown at the back of the restaurant, cooked in the backyard and followed by the traditional meal of spicy sausage and lamb. **$$$**

Restaurant Piro
Carrer Piro, 21, Gratallops, Priorat
tel: (977) 839 004
Serves really good *platos típicos* with a menu which changes daily according to local ingredients (they collect their own rovellon mushrooms). **$$**

VALENCIA
Valencia Capital
Eladio
Chiva, 40
tel: (96) 3842 244
A classic restaurant in Valencia, particularly noted for its fish dishes and desserts. Closed Sunday, and August. **$$**
Marisquería Civera
Lleida, 11
tel: (96) 3475 914
Fresh seafood, paella and vegetables. Closed Sunday evening; Monday and August. **$$**

A line of restaurants at Las Arenas Beach, near the port, specialise in *paellas*, rice dishes and great seafood:
L'Estimat
Avda Neptuno, 16
tel: (96) 3711 018
Closed Sunday and Monday evening. **$$**
La Rosa
Avda Neptuno, 70, 46011
tel: (96) 3712 076
Closed winter evenings and from 15 Aug–15 Sept. **$$**
La Marcelina
Avda Neptuno, 8
tel: (96) 3712 025
Closed Monday and from 7–31 January. **$$**
La Pepica
Avda Neptuno, 6
tel: (96) 3710 366
Closed from 15–30 Nov. **$$**
Valencia Province
Venta L'Home
Autovía Madrid-Valencia, km 294, Bunyol
tel: (96) 2503 515
On the main road between Madrid and Valencia. Specialities include Mediterranean salad. **$$**

Racó de L'Olla
Carretera del Palmar, s/n, El Palmar
tel: (96) 1620 172
In a village beside the Albufera and its paddy fields, just outside Valencia. It specialises in rice dishes and *all i pebre de anguilas* (eels in a garlic and pepper sauce). Closed Monday from Sept–June and Sunday in July and August; 10 days in January. **$$**

Alicante Capital
Dársena
Club Nautico, Levante, 6
tel: (96) 5207 589
Unbeatable for rice dishes and for fish. More relaxed at dinner than lunch. Closed Sunday evening, and Monday in summer. **$$$**

Alicante Province
La Lubina
Avda de Bilbao, 3, Benidorm
tel: (96) 5853 085
Specialities include sea bass cooked in the oven, encrusted with salt. Closed 25 Oct–15 Mar. **$$**
L'Obrer
Ctra de Alcoy, 27, Benimantell
tel: (96) 5885 088
Known for its local delicacies, including *olleta de blat* (mountain stew), roast lamb and almond and chocolate pie. Closed Friday and from 23 Jun–31 Jul. **$$**
L'Escaleta
Avda del País Valenciá, 119, Cocentaina
tel: (96) 5592 100
Restaurant in a town near Alcoi which serves exquisite food, elegantly presented. Closed Sunday evening, Monday, Easter Week and last fortnight in August. **$$**
El Trampolí
Ctra de Las Rotas-La Recona, 83, Denia
tel: (96) 5781 296
Excels in seafood and *Arroz a Banda* (rice cooked in a fish stock). Closed 20 Jan–23 Feb. **$$$**
El Girasol, Ctra Moraria-Calpe, km 1.5, Moraira
tel: (96) 5744 373
Star-chef cooking aiming at Parisian standards. Tables must be reserved. Gastronomic menu.

Closed Monday, except in summer; November. **$$$**
Ca L'Angeles
Gabriel Miró, 16, Polop de la Marina
tel: (96) 5870 226
A simply furnished village house, with a menu varying according to season and based on fresh produce. Closed Tuesday and from 16 June–16 July. **$$**

Castellón
Mesón del Pastor
Cuesta Jovani, 7, Morella
tel: (96) 4160 249
Restaurant in the centre of a historic town which specialises in local dishes including *Sopa de Pastor* (shepherd's soup). Closed Wednesday, except in summer. **$$**
Hostería del Mar
Avda Papa Luna, 10, Peñíscola
tel: (96) 4480 600
Belonging to the hotel of the same name, this restaurant specialises in rice dishes. Medieval banquets are staged at weekends. **$$**

Murcia Capital
El Rincón de Pepe
Apóstoles, 4
tel: (968) 212 239
Highly recommended, with an extremely varied menu. Closed Sunday. **$$$**
Hispano
Radio Murcia, 3
tel: (968) 216 152
A classic restaurant serving local cuisine. Closed Saturday; July and August. **$$$**

Murcia Province
Mesón de la Huerta
Avda del Príncipe, s/n, Alcantarilla
tel: (968) 802 390
Echoing a traditional inn next door to the Museo de la Huerta with excellent *tapas* and full meals based on the surrounding huerta's vegetable dishes. Desserts include *Papajarotes*, double-sized pancakes fried on lemon leaves, with a sweet liqueur sauce. **$$–$$$**

Nightlife

Clubs & Discos
CATALONIA
The brightest night spots tend to be in the kind of crowded resorts one wants to avoid: the spectacular razzmatazz of the **Grand Palace** in Lloret de Mar or the Galas in Salou; or the **laser shows** of La Platja d'Aro, which boasts the greatest concentration of discos on the coast.

In the summer months discos spring up in all the resorts, charging perhaps 2–3,000 pesetas to get in and adding several hundred pesetas to the price of a drink. With meals eaten late, nightlife doesn't begin to get going until after midnight, continuing until around 5am when the tradition is to have fresh *churros* (doughnuts) dunked in hot chocolate.

Many of the late drinking places in Barcelona have no entrance fee: they just demand a lot of money for their drinks. Others, such as *Otto*

Casinos
Catalonia
There are three casinos in Catalonia. They open from around 7pm–4am. There is a small entry fee of around 600 pesetas and you must take your passport.
Peralada: The casino is part of the castle. Though the gaming rooms are hung with tapestries, the hostesses in glittering top hats and tails look a little out of place, tel: (972) 538 125.
Lloret de Mar: Part of the Hotel Casino de Lloret, it has all the usual games, plus a slot machine room, restaurant, disco and pool. Carrer de Tossa, s/n, tel: (972)

Zutz, like you to queue up so they can then refuse you entrance if they disapprove of you in one way or another. It is hard to recommend any of these, not least because they come in and out of fashion so fast. At the moment, **Otto Zutz**, Lincoln 15, appears to be here to stay, as do **Luz de Gas**, Muntaner 246, **Jamboree**, La Banto 264, **La Boite**, Diagonal 477, **Bikini**, Deu Imata 105, **Luna Mora**, and **Nick Havanna**, Rossello 208.

VALENCIA & MURCIA
Nightlife in the largest cities of the region revolves around *pubs* which are not to be confused with British and Irish public houses. These late-night bars strive to create atmosphere by providing few places to sit, attractive bar staff, loud music, and often but not always a dance floor. Few people go out before midnight and many pubs do not come alive until around 2am. It is common to go around several pubs before going on to a disco. Many people finish the night with breakfast and then go to bed. Valencia, in particular, has an immense choice of pubs and discos grouped in areas serving subtly different clientele. These areas go in and out of fashion – ask around if you want to find the latest places. In the summer, there is also plenty of nightlife in the larger resorts.

366 116.
Sant Pere de Ribes: Called the Gran Casino de Barcelona, this is actually 42 km (26 miles) from the city on the outskirts of Sitges. In addition to the usual range of attractions there is a dance hall with an orchestra on Friday and an open-air concert theatre. Tel: (938) 933 666.

Valencia & Murcia
There are casinos at Monte Picayo (near Valencia), between Benidorm and La Vila Joiosa on the Costa Blanca and at La Manga on the Mar Menor.

Shopping

CATALONIA

Leather goods are very good value, as are kitchen, garden and decorative **ceramics** available in small shops, at markets and in huge roadside emporiums. La Bisbal is the largest Catalan ceramic centre. Miravet, in Tarragona is also an important pottery town, as is Verdu in the Urgell (Lleida) where most of the ceramic ware is black.

Hand-made lace can be bought, especially in L'Arboç in Baix Penedès, Tarragona.

Olive oil and **wine vinegar** are good value, and wine and spirits are still cheap. A good Rioja or Valdepeñas can be had for less than 600 pesetas and good Spanish brandies 1,200 pesetas a litre.

VALENCIA & MURCIA

Valencia and Murcia are rich in crafts. In particular, you will see a wide variety of **ceramics** on sale. Manises, near Valencia, is known for its colourful tiles. Lladró porcelain figures are made in Tabernes Blanques near Valencia where you can visit the factory and make purchases in its on-site shop.

Traditional **blankets** are made in Morella, in the Maestrazgo and **recycled glassware** with an attractive green tinge, is manufactured in L'Ollería. Fine **lacework** is on sale in Guadalest, Beniardá, Callosa d'Ensarriá and Jalón Valley. The city of Valencia has a **fan** making tradition and in Murcia you can buy Christmas **crib figures**.

One interesting place to shop for presents is Gata de Gorgos, near Jávea, whose main street is lined with shops selling **basketry, olive wood bowls** and other local crafts.

Sport

Sailing

CATALONIA

There are 36 marinas along the 580 km (360 miles) of Catalonia's coast. Even though facilities have been expanding since the mid-1980s, berths can still be hard to come by in summer. There are some anchorage points along the rockier northern coast, and temporary berths on public jetties or in harbours are either very cheap or free. See the port authorities on arrival. A helmsman's certificate is required for any boating activity.

VALENCIA & MURCIA

There are a great many sailing clubs and marinas all along the coast. Some of them offer sailing courses and have yachts for hire. They can usually provide **windsurf** boards too.

Sporting climate

The climate of Valencia and Murcia is ideal for a range of sports, particularly water sports. Most beaches are safe and suitable for **swimming**. Many have a blue flag. Normally it is warm enough to swim between June to September. The rockier parts of the Costa Blanca are good for **snorkelling** or **scuba diving** and equipment can be easily hired from all the major resorts.

Most cities have **tennis** courts, like Club Tenis Valencia, Botánico Cavanilles, 7, tel: (96) 3690 658. There are also excellent courts, with instructors available, in La Manga Club, tel: (968) 564 511.

Golf

CATALONIA

There are over 40 golf courses active year round in Catalonia, including pitch and putts.

Club de Golf Costa Brava, La Masía, 17246 Santa Cristina d'Aro, province of Girona, tel: (972) 837 150. Just inland between Sant Feliu de Guíxols and La Platja d'Aro, this course has some narrow doglegs. Open all year round. Closed Wednesday Oct–May.

Club de Golf Pals, Platja de Pals, 17256 Pals, province of Girona, tel: (972) 636 006. Finely set among pine woods beside the beach at Pals, the main hazard is the Tramuntana wind. Open all year round. Closed Tuesday between 1 September–30 June.

Golf Fontanels de Cerdanya, Soriguerola, 17538 Fontanels de Cerdanya, Girona. This spectacular course, across and down river from the Reial Club de Golf de Cerdanya, takes full advantage of the broad Cerdanya valley. 18 holes, many water hazards.

Reial Club de Golf de Cerdanya, Apartat de Correus, 63, 17520 Puigcerdà, province of Girona, tel: (972) 881 338. The green fees are modest, but the course has many championships, particularly in August and September as well as at Easter. The clubhouse complex includes a hotel. Open all year unless snowed off.

Club de Golf Sant Cugat, 08190 Sant Cugat del Vallès, province of Barcelona, tel: (93) 6743 958. Just inland from Barcelona city. Where Severiano Ballesteros made his professional debut. Open all year except Monday.

Club de Golf Vallromanes, Apartat de Correus, 43, 08170 Montornès del Vallès, province of Barcelona, tel: (93) 5680 362. Behind Mataró on the Maresme coast, the first half of the course is flat, the second half on a hilly slope. Open all year round. Closed Tuesday.

Reial Club de Golf El Prat, Apartat de Correus, 10, 08820 El Prat de Llobregat, province of Barcelona, tel: (93) 3790 278. Open all year.

VALENCIA & MURCIA

Valencia and Murcia have a range of golf courses. Well-known are:
El Saler, outside Valencia, Ctra Saler, km 18, tel: (96) 1611 186.
La Manga Club, Los Belones, La Manga, tel: (968) 564 511
There are also golf courses at Jávea, Calpe, Altea and Torrevieja.

Walking

CATALONIA

You can walk your boots off in Catalonia. Some 3,000 km (1,875 miles) of footpaths have been mapped out by trail-blazing Catalans.

Mos footpaths are marked with red-and-white stripes painted on rocks and trees. If they are accompanied by an arrow it shows a change of direction. If the two lines are crossed it shows you where not to go.

There are some long-distance "GR" (*gran recorrido* or long distance) routes, which have small signposts with the numbers of the routes and the names of the next village. These are ambitious walks. The GR 92 stretches the whole length of the coast from Portbou to Ulldecona; the GR 11 covers the entire Catalan Pyrenees, from Cap de Creus to Aragónt.

VALENCIA & MURCIA

An increasing number of maps and guides, as well as better signposting, has opened up the inland areas of the region for **hiking** and **hill walking**. Suitable areas include the Maestrazgo, the Upper Turia region of Valencia province, the hills behind the Costa Blanca, and the area around Alcoy. These and other areas also offer **rock climbing**, **cycling** and **horse riding**.

Skiing

CATALONIA

There are 17 resorts in the region, including Alpine and Nordic skiing, all in the Pyrenees. Their season extends from the beginning of December to the end of April.

The main Alpine ski resorts:
Baqueira-Beret, 43 pistes from 1,500–2,500 metres (4,820–8,200 ft). Where the royal family go.
Tuca-Mall Blanc, 20 pistes from 1,000–2,250 metres (3,280–7,380 ft). Also in the Vall d'Aran, this is 2 km (1 mile) from the region's main town of Vielha. It has some tricky trails and a slalom stadium.
Boí-Taüll, 14 pistes from 2,010–2,455 metres (6,685–8,060 ft). Its lack of sophistication is compensated for by the fine Romanesque villages.
Super Espot, 24 pistes from 1,490–2,320 metres (4,890–7,610 ft). At the entrance to the Aigüestortes Park, Surrounded by magnificent scenery.
Llesui, 22 pistes from 1,445–2,430 metres (4,740–7,970 ft). Just north of Sort. The bare slopes of the mountains make it obstacle-free.
Port Ainé, 18 pistes from 1,650–2,440 metres (5,410–8,000 ft). Begun in 1986, this resort is also near Sort, 6 km (4 miles) north of Rialp. It has slopes suitable for beginners.
Port del Comte, 31 pistes from 1,690–2,400 metres (5,545–7,870 ft). Actually in the pre-Pyrenees. There are meadow and woodland trails and a slalom stadium.
Rasos de Peguera, 9 pistes from 1,895–2,050 metres (6,215–6,725 ft). South of the great Cadí range and 13 km (8 miles) north of Berga, this is Barcelona's closest resort.
La Molina, 29 pistes from 1,590–2,465 metres (5,215–8,085 ft). Always popular, sometimes full.
Masella, 88 pistes from 1,600–2,530 metres (5,248–8,300 ft). Next to La Molina, on the north face of Tossa d'Alp. Most of its trails go through pine woods.
Vall de Núria, 9 pistes from 1,965–2,270 metres (6,440–7,440 ft). Inaccessible by road, skiiers must take the "zip" train up the Freser Valley from Ribes. Uncomplicated slopes, plus ice skating on the lake.
Vallter 2000, 16 pistes from 2,010–2,500 metres (6,595–8,201 ft). The most easterly resort.

Language

Catalan

Catalonia, and to a much lesser extent Valencia, is bilingual in Castilian (Spanish) and Catalan or Valenciano. Everybody speaks Spanish, but Catalans generally prefer to speak Catalan.

Catalan is a fully fledged Romance language, derived more closely from Provençal French and Occitanian or Langue d'Oc than from the Iberian language group, which includes Spanish, Portuguese and Gallego. Its teaching and publication were banned during the Franco era and it has since undergone a great resurgence. It is used in conversation, in schools, in businesses, in the media. Most books, including guide books, are in Catalan. All street and place names have been changed and any remaining notice in Spanish may well have *En Català* scrawled across it, for language is a vital part of Catalan nationalism.

Here are a few basic words and phrases, in Catalan:
Good morning Bon dia
Good evening Bona tarda
Hello/Goodbye Hola/Adéu
Please Si us plau
Thank you Gracie/Merci
You're welcome De res
How much is? Quant val?
Where is? On es?
At what time? A quina hora?
How do you say? Com es diu?
Open/Closed Obert/Tancat
Where can I change money? On puc canviar moneda?

Getting Acquainted

The Place

Area: Northern Spain includes the Basque Country, Galicia, Cantabria, Asturias and Navarre (often known as "Green Spain"), La Rioja and Aragon. There is a great deal of variation in climate, both regionally and seasonally, so pack for all eventualities.
Language: Spanish (Castilian – *castellano*) throughout, in addition to Basque (*euskera*) being spoken in the Basque Country, and Galician (*gallego*) in Galicia.

Government

The degree of devolution between the Comunidades is not at all consistent, and the Basque Country and Catalonia have the greatest autonomy, including the ability to raise taxes.

Economy

Northern Spain has Europe's largest fishing fleet in Vigo. It's known for being the industrial area of Spain, with industries based around Bilbao and Barcelona. The Basque Country is also a financial centre – the Banco de Bilbao is one of the nation's leading banks.

There is poverty in the remoter hills and valleys. Galicia is the poorest region of Spain, its agricultural land divided into small uneconomic strips

Climate

In Northern Spain, there is a great deal of variation in climate (both regionally and seasonally). Green Spain, which stretches from the

Basque Country along the Atlantic seaboard through Cantabria and Asturias to Galicia, is obviously so named because it rains a lot, so take waterproofs, umbrellas and suitable footwear – even in summer. Bilbao and Santiago are renowned for being very rainy and the pasture-clad hills are often swathed in mist.

Winters in the north and northwest can be very wet, and it may snow. Summers, on the contrary, have lavish measures of sunshine and warmth everywhere, increasing in intensity as you travel inland and cross the mountains of the Cordillera Cantábrica.

The north is, therefore, an ideal destination for a summer beach holiday. There are hundreds of beautiful coves and beaches (many sheltered and backed by green fields), as well as seaside resorts that have long been popular among Spaniards in the hot season.

Planning the Trip

Getting there

From Great Britain, Northern Spain is well served by airports, if speed is of the essence. Fly-drive is a good option, as the country is best explored by car.

BY AIR
From the UK

Iberia, Spain's national airline, operates direct, non-stop flights from London Heathrow to Bilbao and Santiago de Compostela, as well as flights to Santander (via Barcelona), Vitoria (via Madrid or Barcelona), San Sebastián (via Barcelona), Vigo (via Madrid) and La Coruña (via Madrid). Visitors can also fly direct, non-stop to Oviedo from London Gatwick or continue on the same plane to La Coruña.

Iberia also flies from Manchester and Dublin to Barcelona and Madrid, where you can pick up connections to the destinations in the north detailed above.

For further information, telephone Iberia's London enquiry/reservations service on 020-7830 0011.

British Airways operates one direct, non-stop service to Northern Spain – from Heathrow to Bilbao. La Coruña, Santander, Vitoria, San Sebastián, Bilbao, Vigo, Santiago de Compostela, Gijón and Avilés can be reached by flying BA to Barcelona or Madrid and then transferring to a domestic carrier, or catching a train.

For information and reservations on all its flights, telephone British Airways in the UK on 0345-222 111.
Charter flights
From the UK there are charter flights to Santiago de Compostela and Bilbao, and to Girona.

Local tourist offices

These tourist offices (*oficinas de turismo*) are open all year:
Catalonia Rambla de la Libertat, 1, Girona.
Aragón General Las Heras, 5, Huesca.
Tomás Nogués, 1, Teruel.
Torreón de la Zuda, Glorieta Pio XII, s/n, Zaragoza.
Andorra Andorra la Vella.
Navarre Calle Duque de Ahumada, 3, Pamplona.
Rioja Calle Miguel Villanueva 10, Logroño.
Basque Country Plaza Arriaga, s/n. Fueros, 1, San Sebastián.
Asturias Plaza de Alfonso II El Casto, 6, Oviedo.
Cantabria Plaza Velard, 1. Municipal information: Jardines de Pereda.
Picos de Europa Casa Dago, 33550 Cangas de Onís, Asturias.
Galicia Dársena de la Marina, La Coruña
.Rúa del Villar, 43, Santiago de Compostela.
Estación Maritima de Translatlánticos, Vigo.

From the USA
If you are visiting from North America, **Iberia**, tel: (800) 892-4141, flies from Los Angeles, New York, Montreal and Miami to Barcelona; and from Los Angeles, New York, Montreal, Toronto and Chicago to Madrid. From these two destinations, you can then make a connection to any of the cities in Northern Spain mentioned above.
TWA, tel: (800) 892-4141, or Delta airlines, tel: (800) 241-4141, have direct flights to Barcelona, some stopping in Lisbon. Continental, tel: (800) 231-0856, also fly to Madrid and Barcelona.

BY SEA
Brittany Ferries operates from Plymouth to Santander, Cantabria (24 hours' sailing time) from March–November; and from Poole to Santander (28 hours) or Portsmouth to Santander (30

hours) from November–March. Call Brittany Ferries in the UK on 0990-360 360 for details.
P&O European Ferries runs a year-round service from Portsmouth to Bilbao. Telephone them in the UK on 0990-980 555 for more information.

BY RAIL
The main rail crossing points from France to Spain are Portbou on the Mediterranean coast and Irún at the Atlantic end of the Pyrenees (the line continues to Bilbao with serpentine branches to Pamplona, Vitoria-Gasteiz and Logroño). Lesser crossings are Puigcerdà, a little to the east of Andorra (the line continuing on to Barcelona), and Puerto de Somport in the central Pyrenees (continuing to Jaca, Huesca and Zaragoza).

BY CAR
From Calais in France to the eastern Spanish border, La Junquera, takes around 13 hours on the motorway (French tolls amount to around £40 each way), and about 15 hours to Hendaye in the west. The Pyrenees and the Cordillera Cantábrica often make travel slow.

Distances

Bilbao – Barcelona:
607 km/377 miles (6 hr).
Bilbao – Madrid:
397 km (4 hr).
San Sebastián – Madrid:
488 km/303 miles (5 hr).
Santander – Madrid:
393 km/244 miles (4 hr).
Oviedo – Madrid:
445 km/276 miles (5 hr).
Gijón – Madrid:
474 km/294 miles (5 hr 30 min).
Santiago de Compostela – Madrid: 613 km/381 miles (7 hr).

Getting Around

The region is adequately served by both bus and train services, but nless you are travelling on the new, high-speed trains (TALGO or AVE) between major cities, trying to go cross-country by train can involve long-winded journeys, so if you don't have your own transport you may be better off travelling by coach.

Bus stations

Girona: Plaza de España, s/n tel: (972) 212 319
Jaca: Plaza Biscos, s/n tel: (974) 355 060
Huesca: Avda del Parque, s/n tel: (974) 210 700
Logroño: Avda dc España, 1 tel: (974) 235 983
Pamplona: Calle Conde Oliveto, 8, tel: (948) 223 854
Bilbao: Calle Gurtubay, 1 tel: (94) 4395 077
San Sebastián: Calle Sancho el Sabio, 33, tel: (943) 463 974
Santander: Calle Navas de Tolosa, s/n, tel: (942) 211 995
Gijon: Calle Llanes, 2 tel: (98) 5342 711
Oviedo: Plaza Primo de Rivera, 1 tel: (98) 5281 200
Santiago de Compostela: San Cayetano, s/n, tel: (981) 587 700
La Coruña: Calle Caballeros, s/n (next to the Corte Inglés) tel: (981) 239 099
Vigo: Avda de Madrid, s/n tel: (986) 373 411

Train Stations

Girona: Plaza de España, s/n tel: (972) 207 093
Jaca: Calle Ferrocarriles, s/n tel: (974) 361 332

Huesca: Avda de Zaragoza ,s/n
tel: (974) 242 159
Logroño: Plaza de Europa, s/n
tel: (941) 240 202
Pamplona: Ctra San Sebastián
tel: (948) 130 202
Bilbao: Estación de Abando, Calle
Hurtado de Amezaga
tel: (94) 4238 623
San Sebastián: Estación del Norte,
Ctra. Francia, tel: (943) 283 089
Santander: Calle Rodríguez, s/n
tel: (942) 210 211
Gijon: Calle Juan Carlos I, s/n
tel: (98) 5170 202
Oviedo: Calle Urías, s/n
tel: (98) 5250 202
Santiago de Compostela: Calle
Hórreo, s/n, tel: (981) 520 202
La Coruña: Avda Joaquín Planelles,
s/n, tel: (981) 150 202
Vigo: Calle Urzaiz, s/n
tel: (986) 431 114

Where to Stay

Hotels

Following is our selection of hotels
in the Northern Spanish regions of
Aragón, Asturias, Cantabria, the
Basque Country, Galicia and
Navarre.

ARAGÓN

Huesca
Pedro I de Aragón
Del Parque, 34
tel: (974) 220 300
fax: (974) 220 094
Elegant, modern hotel with good
facilities in a pleasant area west of
the old town. **$$$**
Sancho Abarca
Plaza de Lizana, 13
tel: (974) 220 650
fax: (974) 225 169
Situated in the centre of town, with
a restaurant. **$$**

Jaca (Huesca)
Conde Aznar
Paseo de la Constitución, 3
tel: (974) 361 050
fax: (974)360 797
Simple hotel in a fine house on the
same smart street as the Gran
Hotel. Good local cuisine. **$$**
Gran Hotel
Paseo de la Contitución, 1
tel: (974) 360 900
fax: (974) 364 061
Modern, central hotel near a park,
convenient for skiers. **$$$**

Teruel
Parador de Teruel
Ctra N234 (Sagunto-Burgos)
tel: (978) 501 800
Attractive, upbeat *parador* on the
city outskirts, with Moorish details
and secluded grounds. Good
restaurant. **$$$**

Zaragoza
Conde Blanco
Predicadores, 84
tel: (976) 441 411
fax: (976) 280 339
Modern, good-value hotel in a quiet,
attractive street on the north-west
side of town. Excellent service. **$$**
Hotel Don Yo
Bruil, 4–6
tel: (976) 226 741
fax: (976) 219 956
A very nice hotel with pleasant
staff. **$$$**
Hotel Palafox
Casa Jiménez, s/n
tel: (976) 237 700
fax: (976) 234 705
Modern hotel with rooftop pool. **$$**
Meliá Zaragoza Corona
Avda César Augusto, 13
tel: (976) 430 100
fax: (976) 440 734
Luxurious hotel in the centre of the
city with a good restaurant. **$$$$**
Orus
Escoriaza y Fabro, 45
tel: (976) 536 660
fax: (976) 536 163
One-time chocolate factory, now an
elegant hotel. **$$$**
Tibur
Plaza de la Seo, 2
tel: (976) 202 000
Conveniently located on the
cathedral square, with the recently
excavated Roman forum outside the
front door, this well-equipped hotel
offers a comfortable stay. **$$$**

Price Guide

For a standard double room
$$$$ = Over 20,000 pesetas
$$$ = 15–20,000 pesetas
$$ = 15,000 pesetas
$ = Under 8,000 pesetas

ASTURIAS

Gijón/Xijon
Parador Molino Viejo
Parque de Isabel la Católica
tel: (98) 5370 511
fax: (98) 5370 233
The only *parador* in Asturias, the
Molino Viejo (Old Mill). Near the end
of the Playa de San Lorenzo. **$$$**

Rural Asturias

For information about country houses and other accommodation in Asturias, tel: (901) 300 600.

Principe de Asturias
Calle Manso, 2
tel: (98) 5367 111
fax: (98) 5334 741
This excellent hotel overlooks the beach and Bay of Gijón, with the majority of the rooms enjoying spectacular ocean views. **$$**

Oviedo
Hotel NH Principado
Calle San Francisco, 6
tel: (98) 5217 792
fax: (98) 5213 946
This hotel is good value and pleasant, offering friendly service at half the price of the Reconquista. **$$**
Hotel de la Reconquista
Calle Gil de Jaz, 16
tel: (98) 5241 100
fax: (98) 5241 166
This spectacular 17th-century building houses what is universally considered to be Oviedo's finest hotel. **$$$$**

Taramundi
La Rectoral
La Villa
tel: (98) 5646 767
fax: (98) 5646 777
A typical 17th-century country house – rustic, romantic and surrounded by one of the most character-filled towns in Asturias; don't miss a stopover here. **$$$**

BASQUE COUNTRY
Bilbao (Bilbo)
Carlton
Plaza Federico Moyúa, 2
tel: (94) 4162 200
fax: (94) 4164 628
Orson Welles, Ernest Hemingway, Ava Gardner, and many great bullfighters have stayed here. The Republican Basque government headquarters were here, and later, Franco's general staff. The place breathes history. **$$$$**

Ercilla
Ercilla, 37–39
tel: (94) 4102 000
fax: (94) 4439 335
A highly popular hotel and the centre of bullfighting and theatrical activity of the city. A fine restaurant, the Bermeo. **$$$$**
Nervión
Paseo Campo Volantín, 11
tel: (94) 4454 700
fax: (94) 4455 608
Located beside the estuary. **$$**
Villa de Bilbao
Gran Vía, 87
tel: (94) 4416 000
fax: (94) 4416 529
Centrally located with excellent service. **$$$$**

Rural Basque Country

Staying on farms is a popular way to visit the Basque Country. For information, contact: Office for Agrotourism, 48200 Garai (Biskaia); tel/fax: (946) 211 188.

San Sebastián/Donostia
Avenida
Paseo de Igueldo, 55
tel: (943) 212 022
fax: (943) 212 887
On the road up to one of San Sebastián's mountains overlooking the sea. **$$**
Londres y de Inglaterra
Zubieta, 2
tel: (943) 426 989
fax: (943) 423 914
Lovely hotel by the beach, across from the old part of town. **$$$$**
María Cristina
Plaza República Argentina, 4
tel: (943) 424 900
fax: (943) 423 914
Originally opened in 1912, it has been entirely remodelled and is again the top hotel in the city. **$$$$**
Monte Igueldo
Monte Igueldo, s/n
tel: (943) 210 211
fax: (943) 215 028
With a scenic view. **$$**
Niza
Zubieta, 56
tel: (943) 426 663
fax: (943) 426 663

A centrally located hotel with a scenic view. Coffee-shop. **$$**
Parma
Paseo de Salamanca, 10
tel: (943) 428 893
fax: (943) 424 082
In the city's old section. **$$**

CANTABRIA
Santander
Bahia
Alfonso XIII, 6
tel: (942) 221 700
Close to the picturesque port. **$$**
NH Ciudad de Santander
Menéndez Pelayo, 13–15
tel: (942) 227 965
fax: (942) 217 303
Centrally located with parking. **$$**
Real
Perez Galdos, 28
tel: (942) 272 550
fax: (942) 274 573
Dating back to the beginning of the century, this elegant hotel is very close to Santander's beaches. **$$$$**
Rhin
Avda Reina Victoria, 155
tel: (942) 274 300
fax: (942) 278 653
In a pretty area close to the sea. **$$**
Santemar
Joaquín Costa, 28
tel: (942) 272 900
fax: (942) 278 604
Centrally located. **$$$**
Sardinero
Plaza de Italia, 1
tel: (942) 271 100
fax: (942) 271 698
Right on Sardinero beach. **$$**

GALICIA
A Coruña
Finisterre
Paseo del Parrote, 22
tel: (981) 205 400
fax: (981) 208 462
Imposing central hotel in key downtown location. **$$$**
Riazor
Avda. Barrié de la Maza, 29
tel: (981) 253 400
fax: (981) 253 404
City-centre hotel with sea views. **$$**

Rural Galicia

Turgalicia operates a well organised network of tourist accommodation in country houses ranging from vineyard homes to pazo manor houses, tel: (981) 542 527.

A Guarda
Convento de San Benito
Plaza de San Benito
tel: (986) 611 166
Overlooking the port, this converted convent is a perfectly placed base for exploring the Miño estuary. **$$**

Lugo
Hotel Mendez Nuñez
Reina, 1
tel: (982) 230 711
fax: (982) 229 738
A classic 19th-century hotel in the centre of the old town. **$$**
Hostal Piornedo
Piornedo de Ancares, Cervantes
tel: (982) 368 319
Rustic hotel and an ideal base to explore Os Ancares sierra. **$$**

Ourense
Parador de Verín
Monterrei, Verín
tel: (988) 410 075
Handy stop off the Madrid road, overlooking Monterrei castle. **$$$**

Pontevedra
Parador Casa de Barón
Barón, 19
tel: (986) 855 800
Old manor house-turned-state-owned parador with good regionally inspired cooking. **$$$$**

Santiago de Compostela
Hogar San Francisco
Campillo de San Francisco, 3
tel: (981) 581 600
fax: (981) 571 916
A historic hotel in an old friary school in the Cathedral quarter. **$$**
Parador Los Reyes Católicos
Plaza de Obradoiro, 1
tel: (981) 582 200
fax: (981) 563 094
Luxury hotel near Cathedral of Santiago, with all the creature comforts a weary pilgrim deserves. One of Europe's great historic hotels. **$$$$**

Sansexo
Hotel Rotilio
Avda. del Puerto
tel: (986) 720 200
A family hotel in a fishing village with views of the port and sea, and an excellent restaurant. **$$**

Vigo
Bahia de Vigo
Canovas del Castillo, 5
tel: (986) 226 700
fax: (986) 437 487
Suites available. In-house restaurant. **$$$**
Ciudad de Vigo
Concepción Arenal, 5
tel: (986) 435 233
fax: (986) 439 871
Centrally located. **$$$**
Ensenada
Alfonso XIII, 35
tel: 226 100
fax: (986) 438 972
Near the train station. **$$**

Price Guide

For a standard double room
$$$$ = Over 20,000 pesetas
$$$ = 15–20,000 pesetas
$$ = 15,000 pesetas
$ = Under 8,000 pesetas

NAVARRE
Pamplona
Ciudad Pamplona
Iturrama, 21
tel: (948) 266 011
fax: (948) 173 626
In the heart of the city. **$$**
NH El Toro
Ctra Guipúzcoa, km 5
tel: (948) 302 211
fax: (948) 302 085
A few km outside town, with a swimming pool. **$$**
HUSA Iruña Park
Arcadio María Larraona, 1
fax: (948) 172 387
A large hotel with restaurant. **$$$**
Iruña Palace-Los Tres Reyes
Jardines de la Taconera
tel: (948) 226 600

fax: (948) 222 930
A beautiful hotel. During the running of the bulls (6–15 July), this is an oasis of peace a step away from the action. **$$$$**
La Perla
Plaza del Castillo, 1
tel: (948) 227 706
fax: (948) 211 566
The oldest hotel in town – and the best in value for romantics. From these balconies, Hemingway witnessed his first *encierro*. **$$**
Leyre
Leyre, 7
tel: (948) 228 500
fax: (948) 228 318
Located near the bull ring. **$$**
Maisonnave
Nueva, 20
tel: (948) 222 600
fax: (948) 220 166
Central, with good service. **$$**
Yoldi
Avda. de San Ignacio, 11
tel: (948) 224 800
fax: (948) 212 045
Has its own restaurant. **$$**

Villaviciosa
La Casona de Amandi
Villaviciosa.
tel: (985) 890 130
fax: (985) 890 129
Officially rated three stars but barely costing two, this graceful mansion is surrounded by fields just outside Villaviciosa. There is much to explore in the area. **$$**

Ribadesella
Hotel Rural l'Alceu
Camango
tel/fax: (985) 858 343
One of the Casonas Asturianas network of inns, it lies 4 km (2 miles) outside Ribadesella, in the town of Camango at the mouth of the River Sella. A 16th-century ecclesiastical house with a perfect *hórreo* (raised granary) next to it. **$**

Where to Eat

Where to Eat

ARAGÓN

Zaragoza

Los Borrachos
Paseo de Sagasta, 64
tel: (976) 275 036
Specialities include patés, fresh fish, wild boar, venison and homemade ice-cream and sherbert. Closed Sunday, and August. **$$$**

Mesón del Carmen
Hernán Cortes, 4
tel: (976) 232 373
Aragonese cuisine. Specialities include chicken in *chilindrón* (tomato-based sauce), lamb, cod and, for dessert, peaches with wine. **$$$**

Huesca

Las Torres
María Auxiliadora, 3
tel: (974) 228 213
Imaginative cooking, including cod with black noodles, hake *al chilindrón*, pig's feet, and licorice ice cream. Closed Sunday, and 16–30 August. **$$$**

Navas
San Lorenzo, 15
tel: (974) 224 738
Three forks. Traditional dishes which feature brains with thyme, tuna with herbs, cod with red peppers and a variety of home-made desserts. **$$$$**

Jaca

La Cocina Aragonesa
Cervantes, 5
tel: (974) 361 050
Excellent Aragonese fare in a rustic setting with a roaring fire in winter. Roasts, stews and game specialities. **$$$**

NAVARRE

Pamplona

Josetxo
Estafeta, 73
tel: (948) 222 097
Navarrese cuisine. Located on the street where the running of the bulls takes place, the restaurant's specialities are dishes typical of the region: artichokes and asparagus of Tudela, cod, lamb *al chilindrón*, and flounder in champagne. Closed Sunday, and August. **$$$**

Rodero
Arrieta, 3
tel: (948) 228 035
Navarrese cuisine. Specialities include croquettes, mixed vegetables in the spring, jewfish *a la donostiarra*, and hake *a la navarra*. **$$$**

Price Guide

$$$$ = more than 4,000 pesetas
$$$ = 1,500–4,000 pesetas
$$ = under 1,500 pesetas
Prices are per person for a three-course meal, not including wine

THE BASQUE COUNTRY

San Sebastián

Akelarre
Paseo Padre Orcolaga, 56
tel: (943) 212 052
Barrio Igueldo. Basque cuisine. Specialities include asparagus spears in hollandaise sauce, endive salad with apples and walnuts, sea bass with green pepper, flounder, and strawberry cake. Closed Sunday, Monday afternoon, and first two weeks of October. **$$$**

Arzak
Alto del Miracruz, 21
tel: (943) 278 465
Basque cuisine. Specialities include baby squid in their ink, flounder in champagne, and exceptional vegetable dishes. Closed Sunday, and Monday afternoons, and during the first two weeks of June. **$$$**

Bilbao

Gorrotxa
Alameda Urquijo, 30 (Gallery)
tel: (94) 4220 535
Exquisite cuisine featuring *vieiras* (local shellfish) with mushrooms, foie gras pastry with peregourdine sauce, lobster, turbot with onions and wine, steak Wellington, and excellent desserts. Closed Sunday, and 25 July–15 August. **$$$$**

Guria
Gran Vía, 66
tel: (94) 4410 543
Known as the home of the Codfish Wizard, although it offers many other dishes. Closed Sunday. **$$**

CANTABRIA

Santander

Gran Casino del Sardinero
Plaza de Italia
tel: (942) 276 054
International cuisine. Specialities include, hake, filet mignon and apple tart. **$$**

Chiqui
Avda de García Lago
tel: (942) 282 700
Cantabrian cuisine. Specialities include roasted brill, *tocino del cielo* (a sweet flan). **$$**

El Molino
En Puente Arce, Ctra N-611, km 12
tel: (942) 575 055
Cantabrian cuisine. Specialities include *pastel de setas* (a pastry with wild mushrooms), sea bass salad, and between courses, celery sherbert. Closed Monday. **$$–$$$**

ASTURIAS

Oviedo

El Raitán
Plaza de Trascorrales, 6
tel: (98) 5214 218
Waiters in regional costume serve a lunchtime taster menu of nine traditional local dishes – a crash course in Asturian cuisine. **$$**

Casa Fermín
Calle San Francisco, 8
tel: (98) 5216 452
One of Oviedo's most famous gourmet spots, and a favourite among local food lovers. Be sure to reserve in advance. **$$**

Gijón

Bella Vista
Avda Garcia Bernardo, 8
tel: (98) 5367 377
Known for its fish and seafood, this

local favourite has its own live tank where you are welcome to select your own crustacean. **$$**

Casa Víctor
Calle Carmen, 11
tel: (98) 5348 310
Victor Bango's original approach to traditional seafood dishes fills this place with excited diners, which is always a good sign. **$**

Taramundi
El Mazo
Calle Cuesta de la Rectoral
tel: (98) 5646 760
Set in a restored rectory, serving good mountain cuisine and specialising in beef, lamb, goat and game when in season. Try the local *caldo de Taramundi* soup. **$$**

GALICIA

La Coruña
Coral
Callejón de la Estacada, 9
tel: (981) 202 569
Galician cuisine. Specialities include hake, seafood soup and *bonito* in tomato sauce. **$$**

Pardo
Novoa Santos, 5
tel: (981) 280 021
Seafood croquettres, monkfish stew, Galician cuisine. Closed Sunday; 15–30 June. **$$**

Santiago de Compostela
Don Gaiferos
Rua Nueva, 23
tel: (981) 583 894
Galician specialities, including flounder stuffed with seafood, seafood brochette, hake in cider, *caldo gallego* (a light broth). **$$$**

Casa Vilas
Rosalía de Castro, 88
tel: (981) 592 170
Galician cuisine. Specialities

include octopus with potatoes, lamprey in red wine, and the native *tarta de Santiago*, a moist almond cake. Closed Sunday. **$$$**

Vigo
El Mosquito
Plaza de la Pedre, 4
Specialities include flounder, roast kid and grilled meats. Closed Sunday; and 15 Aug–15 Sept. **$$**

Puesto Piloto Alcabre
Avda Atlántida, 98
tel: (986) 297 975
Galician cuisine. Specialities include *arroz de vieiras* (rice with a shellfish) and *tarta de yema*, a cake made with egg yolk. Closed Sunday night; two weeks in November. **$$$**

Pontevedra
Doña Antonia
Soportales de la Herería, 4–1°
tel: (986) 847 274
Galician specialities include *tosta de vieiras* (shellfish on toast). **$$$**

Casa Solla
Ctra La Toja, km 2
tel: (986) 872 884
Galician specialities include flounder with clams. Closed Thursday, and Sunday night. **$$$**

Shopping

The most rewarding souvenirs will be in **traditional art and craftwork**. The many woodlands make carved objects and utensils abundant. In Galicia, Camariñas is still a centre for **lace making**, Noya for **black banded straw hats**. Sargadelos is a centre for **black Asturian pottery**. **Wooden clogs** are still made in Carmiona, Cantabria. The ubiquitous **beret** comes from Tolosa. The Basque country's specialities are **tapestries** and **white pottery**. **Woollen blankets** come from Ezcaray in Navarra. Every town has a morning market.

Sport

Football

First division football matches are a Sunday afternoon ritual across northern Spain – matches are usually played in Santiago de Compostela, La Coruña, Santander, Bilbao, San Sebastián, Logroño and Pamplona. Check with tourist office for dates and ticket information.

Jai-Alai

For jai-alai matches in Bilbao, try the Club Deportivo de Bilbao, Alameda Rekalde 28, tel: (94) 4231 109. In San Sebastián, *cesta punta* is played at Galarreta (on the Hernani road south of town), tel: (943) 551 023. In Pamplona, try Euskal Jai Berri in Huarte, 10 km (6 miles) west of Pamplona, tel: (948) 331 160.

Local Sports

Ox-pulling, scything, stone-lifting and many other variations of rural sporting events are held during the fiestas in the Basque Country.

Bilbao's mid-August Semana Grande features Basque sports as well as *trainera* (whale boat) racing in the Nervión. The whale boat races in San Sebastián draw the province of Guipúzcoa to the beach in mid-September. July in Oviedo is when the cider-pouring contests are held, with contestants judged by the amount of cider they spill.

Horse Racing

San Sebastián's racetrack at Zubieta (Paseo del Hipódromo s/n, Zubieta, tel: 943 371 690) has meetings between June and September.

Getting Acquainted

The Place

The Canary Islands form an archipelago made up of seven major islands and several small islets in the Atlantic Ocean.

TENERIFE

This is the largest island. Its topography is varied, with an impressive mountain range, including the gigantic natural crater of the Cañadas del Teide, rising over 2,000 metres (6,500 ft) above sea level. The capital of the island is Santa Cruz de Tenerife.

GRAN CANARIA

Gran Canaria is the third largest island with landscape ranging from mountains, sharp ravines and cliffs to deserts and tropical forests. The capital is Las Palmas.

LANZAROTE

The volanic island of Lanzarote is the result of major eruptions taking place as recently as the 18th and 19th centuries. Its terrain is often compared to a lunar landscape.

Climate

The major islands of the archipelagoenjoy a subtropical climate and mild temperatures all year round. Winter/summer temperatures range on average from 17–23˚C (64– 74˚F) in Tenerife, or 16–22˚C (62–72˚F) in Gran Canaria. The more mountainous zones on Tenerife, La Palma and Gran Canaria result in abundant rain in winter, which is responsible for the lush landscape, in direct contrast to the other drier and more desert-like islands.

Planning the Trip

Getting there

The Canary Island archipelago is situated 115 km (71 miles) off the African coast, while the nearest point on the Spanish Peninsula, Cádiz, is 700 km (435 miles) away.

BY AIR

The archipelago is served by the main airlines and direct flights from Madrid take a little over two hours. Most planes land at the international airports of Las Palmas on Gran Canaria or at Santa Cruz on Tenerife. Most visitors arrive on one of the many charter flights from Europe. Very good deals are often available on these, so shop around.

BY SEA

The only passenger and vehicle shipping line to operate a regular service between mainland Spain and the Canary Islands is the ferry compnay Trasmediterranea, which runs a once-a-week service from Cadiz to Gran Canaria, Lanzarote and Tenerife, departing from Cadiz on Saturday.

Tourist Offices

Gran Canaria: Parque de Santa Catalina, tel: (928) 264 623
Tenerife: Palacio Insular, Plaza de España, s/n, tel: (922) 239 897
Lanzarote: Parque Municipal, tel: (928) 801 517
Fuerteventura: Tourist office: Avda Constitución, 5, tel: (928) 538 44
La Palma: O'Daly, 22, tel: (922) 412 106
La Gomera: Real, 4, tel: (922) 140 147
El Hierro: Licenciado Bueno, 1, tel: (922) 550 302

Calendar of Events

5 January: Parade of the Three Kings in Santa Cruz de Tenerife and Las Palmas de Gran Canaria.
February: The very popular and colourful Carnivals of Santa Cruz de Tenerife and Las Palmas de Gran Canaria.
May: Santa Cruz festivities in Tenerife, including the celebration of the founding of the capital on 3 May.
20 May: The Romería or Pilgrimage of San Isidro the Farmer in Los Realejos (Tenerife), also declared of Special Touristic Interest.
June: Corpus Christi Day. Flower carpets are woven along the streets in Villa de Mazo (La Palma). Processions in Las Palmas de Gran Canaria and La Laguna (Tenerife). Fiestas of Special Touristic Interest.
June: Octava de Corpus. Held eight days after Corpus Christi Day in La Orotava on Tenerife, including a pilgrimage to the San Isidro Sanctuary.
25 July: Fiesta of Santiago Apóstol (St James' Day). Santa Cruz de Tenerife commemorates the heroic defence of the city against Lord Nelson's naval attack.
16 August: San Roque pilgrimage in the town of Garachico (Tenerife), which has been declared of Special Touristic Interest.
25 August: San Ginés fiestas celebrated in Arrecife (Lanzarote), also of Special Touristic Interest.
17 September: Fiestas of Special Touristic Interest in honour of Cristo del Calvario in Icod de los Vinos (Tenerife).
October (second Saturday): Pilgrimage of Nuestra Señora de la Luz in Las Palmas de Gran Canaria including a procession of boats.

Where to Stay

Hotels

GRAN CANARIA

Meliá Las Palmas
Gomera, 6
tel: (928) 268 050
Modern installations with a pool and an international atmosphere and situated right on Las Canteras beach. **$$$$**

Sansofé Palace
Portugal, 68 and Playa Canteras, 78
tel: (928) 224 282
It is located right on the beach and has a restaurant. **$$**

Maspalomas

Maspalomas Oasis
Plaza Las Palmers, s/n
tel: (928) 141 448
An elegant top-class luxury hotel in secluded subtropical gardens by the beach. **$$$$**

Ifa-Faro Maspalomas
Plaza del Faro, 1
tel: (928) 142 214
Open-plan design using wood finishes and arched balconies. Giant chess and freeform pool. Quiet and upmarket. **$$$$**

Apolo
Avda Estados Unidos, 28
Playa del Inglés
tel: (928) 760 058
A smallish 1970s block in a fairly quiet hilly central location 250 metres from the beach. Indoor waterfall. **$$$$**

Price Guide

For a standard double room
$$$$ = Over 20,000 pesetas
$$$ = 15–20,000 pesetas
$$ = 15,000 pesetas
$ = Under 8,000 pesetas

Orchidea
Playa de Tarajillo
tel: (928) 764 600
A village-like Moorish-looking complex 3 km (2 miles) from the resort centre, with its own facilities and a nice beach. Friendly and good for families. **$$$**

Parque Tropical
Avda de Italia, 1
tel: (928) 774 012
One of the most attractive hotels in this bustling resort, in traditional Canarian style with a pagoda entrance feature and lovely water-gardens. It also has direct access to beach. **$$$$**

Sandy Beach
Menceyes, s/n
tel: (928) 772 726
Pleasant, imaginatively-designed complex in Andalucían style with large pools and sundecks. Spacious bedrooms, attractive gardens; some nightlife but not rowdy. **$$$**

TENERIFE

Santa Cruz

Mencey
Dr José Naveiras, 38
tel: (922) 276 700
Deluxe hotel on central tree-lined boulevard. Very good facilities and helpful staff. **$$$$**

Atlántico
Castillo, 12
tel: (922) 24 63 75
Pleasant, inexpensive hotel on pedestrianised shopping street near Plaza de España. Terrace café-bar on first floor. **$$**

Puerto de la Cruz

Meliá Botánico
Richard J. Yeoward, s/n
tel: (922) 381 400
Luxury rooms near the Botanical Gardens with magnificent views of Teide. Quiet, exclusive atmosphere. Lovely grounds. **$$$$**

Tenerife Playa
Avda de Colón, 16
tel: (922) 383 211
Well-equipped and stylish, with good sea views, opposite the Lido. Rooftop solarium. **$$$**

Monopol
Quintana, 15
tel: (922) 384 611

Beautiful Canarian mansion in heart of old quarter, with plant-filled atrium and wooden balconies. **$$**

Teide National Park

Parador Cañadas del Teide
Las Cañadas del Teide
tel: (922) 386 415
Spectacularly located in the National Park overlooking strange rock formations. Good Canarian restaurant and self-service café. Visitor centre. **$$$**

Playa de las Américas

Jardín Tropical
Urb. San Eugenio
tel: (922) 746 000
Beautifully designed luxury hotel in Moorish style, overlooking the sea. Romantic terrace restaurant and tranquil gardens. **$$$$**

LANZAROTE

Arrecife

Lancelot
Avda Mancomunidad, 9
tel: (928) 805 099
Attractive seafront hotel opposite a sandy beach and coral reefs. Stylish facilities for the price. **$$**

Costa Teguise

Melia Salinas
Playa de Las Cucharas
tel: (928) 590 040
Innovative contemporary hotel (another Manrique design), relaxing and spacious. Huge plant-filled atrium and luxurious bedrooms. Attractive beaches. **$$$$**

Playa del Carmen

Los Fariones
Roque del Oueste, 1
Urb. Playa Blanca
tel: (928) 510 175
Secluded upmarket hotel on private cove beaches offering good facilities and a traditional air. Apartment complex adjacent. **$$$**

LA GOMERA

Parador de San Sebastián de la Gomera
Balcón de la Villa y Puerto
tel: (922) 871 100
Hilltop country house hotel with gorgeous views and gardens,

traditional Canarian architecture and regional food. **$$$**

LA PALMA

Parador de Santa Cruz de la Palma
Avda Marítima 34
tel: (922) 412 340
Attractively placed along the seafront in La Palma's elegant capital port, this parador is simple but pleasing, a good base for exploring the island. **$$**

La Palma Romántica
Las Llanadas, Barlovento
tel: (922) 186 221
On the northern tip of the island, this peaceful, well-equipped hotel functions as a mini-resort. Good views, and an indoor pool (it's chillier here). **$$**

EL HIERRO

Parador del Hierro
Las Playas, Valverde
tel. (922) 558 030
Low-slung, pantiled hotel on seafront by lonely cliffs. Attractive, rustic decor and a homely atmosphere. **$$$**

FUERTEVENTURA

Parador de Fuerteventura
Playa Blanca, Puerto del Rosario
tel: (928) 851 150
A mile or two outside the main town. in a majestic beachfront setting. Handy for the airport. **$$**

Where to Eat

What to Eat

The local cooking obviously features a lot of fish and seafood dishes, although the local specialities are the *papas arrugadas* (small, tasty, boiled potatoes), served with spicy *mojo sauce*, rabbit in *salmorejo* (another savoury dressing), *sancocho* (stew with meat, yucca and banana), sweet *morcillo* (blood) sausage, etc.

The Canary archipelago is a major producer of bananas, although the subtropical climate is also ideal for cultivating other crops, such as tomatoes, avocados, papayas, corn and tobacco.

With the influx of tourists, there are many international restaurants in all the major cities.

Where to Eat

GRAN CANARIA

Orangerie
Hotel Palm Beach, Avda Oasis, s/n, Playa de Maspalomas
tel: (928) 140 806
Acclaimed hotel restaurant amid lush subtropical gardens. Stuffed sea urchins a speciality. Dinner only. Closed Thursday and Sunday and from Jun–Aug. **$$$$**

Churchill
León y Castillo, 274, Las Palmas,
tel: (928) 249 192
An original menu which varies greatly according to the quality produce available. Specialities are *carpaccio* fish, patés, salads, duck, tropical fruit desserts and *charlota de chocolate*. Closed Saturday midday, Sunday and holidays.

La Parrilla
(Hotel Reina Isabel), Alfredo L. Jones, 40, Las Palmas
Good service and local wines.

Specialities such as the fish soup, *cherne al cilantro*, hake gratiné with lobster, sirloin, steak, papaya cocktail. **$$$**

Mesón La Cuadra
General Mas de Gaminde, 32, Las Palmas
tel: (928) 243 380
Combined Castilian-Canary cooking, specialising in the typical roasts of the mainland. Closed Monday. **$$$**

Tenderete II
Avda de Tirajana, 3 (Edificio Aloe), Playa del Inglés
tel: (928) 761 460
Typical Canary Island restaurant, Try fish baked in salt, *sancocho, papas* with *mojo, bienmesabe* ice cream, cheese and island wines. **$$$**

Price Guide

$$$$ = more than 4,000 pesetas
$$$ = 1,500 4,000 pesetas
$$ = under 1,500 pesetas
Prices are per person for a three-course meal, not including wine

TENERIFE

Café del Príncipe
Plaza del Príncipe, Santa Cruz
tel: (922) 278 810
Typical Canary Island cooking. Closed Monday, and Easter week.

Los Menceyes (Hotel Mencey)
Dr José Naveiras, 38, Santa Cruz
tel: (922) 276 700
Charming decor and quality food, including avocado with shrimp, baked turbot with saffron and special house desserts. Closed lunchtime in August. **$$$$**

LANZAROTE

El Diablo
Islote de Hilario, Montañas de Fuego
tel: (928) 840 057
Watch your steaks sizzling on a volcanic barbecue while you admire the views. **$$**

Getting Acquainted

The Balearic archipelago, located between the mainland of Spain and the North African coast, consists of the principal islands of Mallorca, Menorca, Eivissa (Ibiza) and Formentera, with surrounding and outlying smaller islands, very few of them populated.

The islands have a population of some 800,000, in a combined area of 5,000 sq. km (1,936 sq. miles). **Formentera**: With a pop. of 5,000, covers 82 sq. km (31 sq. miles), receives 15,000 visitors annually. **Eivissa**: With a total of over 60,000 residents (about 5,000 are foreigners) and an area of 572 sq. km (220 sq. miles), receives over 1 million annual visitors. **Menorca**: With 62,000 residents and 699 sq. km (270 sq. miles), gets visited annually by some 600,000 people. **Mallorca**: With near to 600,000 residents and a surface 3,640 sq. km (of 1,405 sq. miles), receives over 5,600,000 annual visitors.

In total, the Balearics receive in excess of 7 million mainland visitors annually.

Climate

The three main islands enjoy more or less the same weather conditions, with local variations caused by phenomena such as Mallorca's mountain ranges. The Balearics' average high temperature is 21.2°C (70°F), average low 13.8°C (57°F) and the sun shines annually to an average 59 percent. Rainfall in Mahon (Menorca) is 580 mm (23 in) a year, while that in Palma (Mallorca) only reaches 480 mm (19 in).

Planning the Trip

Getting There

BY AIR

The Balearic islands of Mallorca, Menorca and Eivissa, off the eastern coast of Spain, are served regularly by both scheduled international and charter flights. Scheduled services operate from several Spanish mainland cities, and these are flown by both Iberia, Aviaco and Spanair, among others. The renovated and enlarged Son Sant Joan airport in Mallorca caters to the millions of year-round visitors. A recent increase of companies has led to competitive prices for flights within Spain.

BY SEA

Services by sea to the Balearic Islands are provided by convenient ferry routes, primarily from Barcelona and Valencia. Visitors to Formentera, must make their connections in Eivissa from where frequent ferries, including car ferries, cross to the port of La Sabina. In summer, there are also services to Alcudia, in Mallorca. Ferries operate from Alicante and Denia to Eivissa and Formentera. There are also inter-island ferries, and a fast hydro-jet (2 hours) runs between Palma and Eivissa.

The main operator of services is Transmediterránea.

Useful numbers

Transmediterránea
tel: (971) 405 014
Flebasa (inter-island ferry service), tel: (971) 405 360
Palma de Mallorca airport, tel: (971) 789 000.

Practical Tips

Tourist Offices

MALLORCA

Consell de Mallorca, at airport arrivals building, tel: (971) 789 556.
Govern Balear Tourist Office, Jaime III, 10, Palma, tel: (971) 712 216 and 712 744.
Fomento del Turismo de Mallorca, Constitución, 1, 1st floor, Palma, tel: (971) 715 135 and 725 396.
Palma Municipal Tourist Offices are located at Santo Domingo, 11, tel: (971) 724 090 and Plaza España, in Palma, tel: (971) 711 527.

Other municipalities, such as Calviá, have local tourist offices. Some of these offices are seasonal only, mounted on trailers, and located strategically.

MENORCA

Consell de Menorca, Camí del Castell, 28, Mahón, and on the central Plaza Esplanada, 40, Mahón, tel: (971) 360 793.

EIVISSA

Consell de Eivissa, Vara de Rey, 13, Eivissa (Ibiza town), tel: (971) 301 900.
Fomento de Turismo de Ibiza, Historiador José Clapés, 4, Ibiza town, tel: (971) 302 490.
Municipality of San Antonio, Passeig de ses Fonts, San Antonio, tel: (971) 343 363.
Municipality of Santa Eulàlia, Mariano Riquer Wallis, Santa Eulàlia, tel: (971) 330 728.

FORMENTERA

Municipality of San Francisco Javier, Port de la Sabina. (At the ferry terminal), tel: (971) 322 057. It is often difficult to get through on this number, try calling the Govern

Balear in Palma, tel: (971) 712 216 for information.

Business Hours

The islands have traditionally observed the noon-time siesta, with businesses and shops generally open from 8.30 or 9am–1 or 1.30pm, and 4 or 4.30pm–7 or 7.30pm. As an exception, shops and businesses in Menorca tend to re-open after lunch at a later hour, around 5pm.

In certain sectors of business, these traditional hours are changing. For example the big department stores such as El Corte Inglés, and the out-of-town hypermarkets generally open all day, from 10am–9pm, but close on Sunday.

Other businesses, related to organisations in other countries and different time-zones, will also sometimes have differing hours.

Emergencies

The local emergency number to call the **police** (Policia Nacional) in Palma, Eivissa and in Mahon is 091. In Ciudadela (Menorca), tel: (971) 381 095 and in Manacor, Mallorca, tel: (971) 550 044.

For the **Fire Service** in Palma dial 080, and for the rest of Mallorca and the rest of the islands dial 085.

Ambulances are operated by the Spanish Red Cross as well as by private operators. For the Red Cross, in Mallorca tel: (971) 202 222; Eivissa tel: (971) 390 303; and Mahón (Menorca) tel: (971) 361 180 and (971) 361 200.

All the emergency numbers are found in the first few (green) pages of the telephone directory.

For emergency ambulance:
Palma, tel: (971) 202 222.
Eivissa, tel: (971) 390 303.
Mahon (Menorca), tel: (971) 361 200.
Ciutadella (Menorca), tel: (971) 381 993.

Shopping

The islands all produce good **leatherware**, with footwear factories in Mallorca and Menorca, and nicely designed leather clothing everywhere.

Mallorca has **artificial pearl** and glass-blowing factories. Menorca has a well-developed **costume jewellery** industry, and produces excellent **cheeses** and **gin**. Eivissa is known for its **fashion**, and has a large cottage-industry making **jewellery**

Locally-produced **pottery** and **ceramics**, particularly cooking-vessels, are a good buy on all islands, and there is a choice of good **embroidery** and **basketwork**. **Paintings** by local artists are also worth looking at, and these can be seen in galleries, or at lower prices in the flea and hippy markets.

Media

Newspapers: There are several Spanish-language newspapers published in the islands. Some of these are the *Diario de Ibiza, Diario de Mallorca, Última Hora,* and *Diario Insular de Menorca.*

English-speakers in Mallorca have the *Majorca Daily Bulletin.* Otherwise known as the *Daily Bee,* the newspaper has something for everyone. World news sometimes appears with a delay of a day as it often needs to be translated from Spanish parent-paper *Última Hora.*

Radio stations are varied in both quality and content, and more than one of the Spanish stations broadcast continuous music. The English-speaking station in Palma has local news, music, interviews, quizzes, etc. Radio 103.2 FM, as it is called, also carries advertising and is a good source of information about the island.

In Eivissa, two local stations carry about one hour a day of English broadcasting, one being on Radio Popular on FM 89.1.
In Menorca, there is also an English programme on the local station.

Where to Stay

Hotels

MALLORCA
Palma

Son Vida Hotel
Urb. Son Vida
tel: (971) 790 000
Overlooking Palma and its Bay. Grand Deluxe. Two golf courses, tennis, many other facilities. **$$$$**

Valparaíso Palace
Francisco Vidal, La Bonanova
tel: (971) 400 411
Overlooking Palma, views of harbour and Bay, set in lush gardens. Indoor and outdoor pools, separate health clubs for men and women. **$$$$**

Meliá Victoria
Joan Miró, 21
tel: (971) 734 342
Reigning over the Palma harbour front, the Meliá Victoria has its main entrance close to the nightlife around Plaza Gomila, and its lower, harbour exit leads directly to the centre of the night's activities on the Paseo Marítimo. **$$$$**

Meliá Confort Bellver
Paseo Marítimo, 11
tel: (971) 735 142
Faces out over the harbour front, close to the centre of town. **$$$$**

Nixe Palace Hotel
Joan Miró, 269, Palma
tel: (971) 700 888
A seaside hotel, which has a small beach, sun-terraces and other facilities. Good hotel for the business traveller who wants to be away (10 minutes) from downtown. **$$$**

Costa Azul
Paseo Marítimo, 7
tel: (971) 73 19 40
Only a 3-star hotel, but listed as an old favourite with families and business travellers over the years. Right on the harbour front. **$$$**

Saratoga
Paseo de Mallorca, 6
tel: (971) 727 240
The Saratoga is convenient for the business traveller on a tight budget, close enough to be able to walk to most lawyers, banks, businesses and shops downtown. **$$**

Outside Palma
Hotel Formentor
Playa de Formentor
tel: (971) 899 100
Overlooking the beach, this peaceful traditional hotel is family-run and many of the staff have spent their entire career here. Surrounded by pine trees and gardens. **$$$$**

La Residencia
Son Moragues, Deià
tel: (971) 639 011
Individually designed and decorated rooms, quiet luxury in this hill town, home to artists and poets. Famous for excellent cuisine. **$$$$**

Bonanza Playa
Ctra de Illetes
tel: (971) 401 112
Built into a cliff at the sea's edge, the lobby area is at street level on the top floor, with rooms and extensive facilities below. Family-run, with year-after-year repeat clients. **$$$$**

The Villamil
Ctra de Andratx, km 22, Paguera
tel: (971) 686 054
A member of the Forte Group chain. Overlooks the beach, and has gardens and sun-terraces to relax in. **$$$$**

Hotel Bendinat
Urb. Bendinat
tel: (971) 675 725
A family-run hotel. Only some 30 rooms, ensuring individual attention for clients. Located on a small point, with good sea swimming right at the end of the garden. **$$$**

MENORCA
Maó
Port Mahón Hotel
Paseo Marítimo
tel: (971) 362 600
The Port Mahón overlooks the fjord-like port, once the Mediterranean base for Nelson's Royal Navy.

Quiet, almost sedate, it makes a good base for a business or holiday visit. **$$$$**

The Hotel del Almirante
Ctra Villacarlos, near Maó
tel: (971) 362 700
Interesting and charming conversion of British admiral Collingwood's residence, good views of Maó harbour, hacienda-style accommodation around swimming pool. **$$**

Ciutadella
The Almirante Farragut
Avda de los Delfines
tel: (971) 382 800
A very large hotel, built on a promontory over the sea, with a small beach on one side. In summer, tour-operators from all over Europe keep the Farragut fully-booked. **$$$**

Price Guide

For a standard double room
$$$$ = Over 20,000 pesetas
$$$ = 15–20,000 pesetas
$$ = 15,000 pesetas
$ = Under 8,000 pesetas

EIVISSA
Although there are city-centre hotels in Eivissa (Ibiza town), the level of activity and noise is high. As distances around the island are relatively short, it is best to stay outside and make trips into town for shopping or nightlife.

Pike's
Ctra Sa Vorera, km 12, C'an Pep Toniet
tel: (971) 342 222
Classified as a 2-star *pension*, Pike's is really difficult to grade, being nearly unique. Owned and run by Australian yachtsman Tony Pikes, the hotel has less than 10 rooms, and provides a relaxing retreat for well-known actors, etc. Set in a restored farmhouse, there is a pool and garden, and a good restaurant. Children aren't welcome. **$$$$**

Les Jardins de Palermo
near Es Cubells
tel: (971) 800 318
In the same genre as Pike's, Les

Jardins is unclassifiable although listed as a *pension*. Self-described as "a little piece of Paradise", it is the ideal hideaway for lovers or honeymooners, and children aren't encouraged. Operated by jack-of-all-trades René Wilhelm, a Swiss former Formula III driver, decorator, fashion designer, boutique owner, etc. Excellent *nouvelle cuisine* restaurant, pool, gardens, in this 10-room retreat. **$$$$**

Hotel Resaurante Village
Urb. Caló de'n Real
San José
tel: (971) 808 001
This hotel perches over the sea, surrounded by pine forest and gardens, with a stairway down to the beach. A tennis-players' paradise, with four courts and coaching. Pool, sauna, whirlpool and a good restaurant. **$$$$**

Ca's Català
Calle del Sol
Santa Eulàlia
tel: (971) 331 006
Classified as a Residence Hostal, the Ca's Català offers nicely furnished single and double rooms, a pool and garden. Breakfast only is served, but non-residents drop in for this and also for mid-morning coffee and pastries. **$$**

FORMENTERA
Platja de Mitjorn
Club La Mola
tel: (971) 328 069
In a picturesque setting, with a pool, tennis, mini-golf, children's playground and cafeteria. **$$$**

Hotel Formentera Playa
tel: (971) 320 000
Located in a scenic area, with a pool, playground and cafeteria. Closed: winter, opens in April. **$$**

Platja Es Pujols
Hotel Roca Bella
tel: (971) 328 130
Situated near the beach, with a swimming pool. **$$$**

Where to Eat

What to Eat

Although there is no menu visible at local bars, you can generally ask what they have to eat and you could be pleasantly surprised with a thick homemade stew or a fresh salad with grilled seafood.

There are all sorts of typical foods on the islands, from *paella* and *arroz brut*, through suckling pig and tender lamb, to *caldereta de langosta* and *tumbet*, or elvers in garlic-oil, or *calamares en su tinta* (squid in inky sauce – it sounds better in Spanish, and tastes great).

Where to Eat

MALLORCA

Porto Pi
Joan Miró, 174, Palma
tel: (971) 400 087
Near Club de Mar and Rififi seafood restaurant. Serves gourmet Basque and nouvelle cuisine. **$$$**

Bodega Santurce
Concepción, 34, Palma
Basque food in this family-run hole in the wall. No reservations, no coffee, open only lunchtime, uncomfortable seating, but unbeatable value. **$$**

Caballito de Mar
Paseo Sagrera, 5, Palma
tel: (971) 721 074
Fish cooked in sea-salt, expensive and takes time to cook, but must be tried once, with al-i-oli. **$$**

Casa Gallega
Pueyo, 2, Palma
tel: (971) 714 377
Try the *salpicón, pulpo a banda* or fresh salmon. **$$**

Mesón Tio Pepe
Pont d'Inca, Palma
tel: (971) 600 880
Bodega atmosphere, enormous

T-bones, selected suckling pig and a mixed-grill so big you'll have a problem finishing it. Avoid Sunday lunchtime. **$$**

Punta de Son Gual
Ctra Palma-Manacor, km 11
Excellent shoulder or leg of lamb, other choices. Avoid Sunday lunchtimes. **$$**

Rancho Picadero
Flamenco, 1, Ca'n Pastilla
tel: (971) 261 002
Indoor barbecue. Suckling pig, other choices. **$$**

Bar Carlos
Joan Miró, Palma
Opposite Hotel Borenco. Typical Mallorquín food by Rafa Bonet, smoky and crowded, evenings only, good value. **$$**

Celler Montenegro
Calle Montenegro, Palma
Behind Plaza de la Reina, downtown Palma. Good Mallorquín home cooking. **$$**

Es Salé
Joan Miró, Palma
Near Plaza Gomila. **$$**

Price Guide

Price guide
$$$ = over 4,500 pesetas
$$ = between 1,500 and 4,500 pesetas
$ = less than 1,500 pesetas

EIVISSA

El Brasero
Barcelona, 4, Eivissa
tel: (971) 311 469
Duck, salmon. German owned. **$$**

El Shogun
Pasadis, 5, Eivissa
Sushi, Sashimi, Sukiyaki. **$$$**

Es Pi D'or
Cala Gració, San Antonio
tel: (971) 342 872
Salmon, fish soup and more. **$$**

Helmut's
Ctra a San José
German home-cooking. **$$**

Pike's
Ca'n Pep Toniet, San Antonio
tel: (971) 342 222. **$$**

Rincón de Pepe
San Vicente, 53, Santa Eulàlia
Tapas, snacks.

Sa Capella
Ctra a Ca'n Germá, San Antonio,
tel: (971) 340 057
Pork of all kinds.

Sa Soca
Ctra a San Antonio.
Ibicenco cooking.

Sausalito
Plaza Sa Riba, Eivissa
Swordfish, lamb. French owner.

MENORCA

Cap Roig
Near San Mezquida
Great view, seafood. **$$**

Ca's Quintu
Plaça Alfonso III, 4, Ciutadella
tel: (971) 381 002
Menorquín and other dishes. **$$**

Pan Y Vino
Torret
Small, atmospheric restaurant, popular with the resident population of expatriates. **$$**

Pilar
Cardona y Orfila, 61, Maó
tel: (971) 366 817
Local Menorquín cuisine, evenings only. **$$**

La Tropical
Luna, 36, Maó
tel: (971) 360 556
Budget-priced Menorquin food. **$**

FORMENTERA

Bergantín
Port de la Sabina
tel: (971) 341 461
International menu. **$$**

Capri
Es Pujols
tel: (971) 328 352
Seafood. **$$**

Taberna La Formentereña
Platja Mitjorn, km 9
Excellent *Espinacas Balear*, seafood, meats with irresistible sauces in this beach restaurant. **$$**

Truy
Es Pujols
tel: (971) 325 073
International menu. **$$**

Language

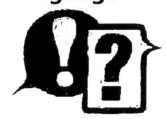

Although Spanish (or Castilian) is the national language, the Balearic people speak a variant of Catalan, which in Mallorca is known as *mallorquí*, in Menorca as menorquí, and in Eivissa as *eivissenc*. These dialects differ slightly from one another in accent, local vocabulary and expressions. Their source language, Catalan, is a Romance language similar to Provençal. Interesting left-overs from the time when Britain's Royal Navy had its Mediterranean base in Menorca are words and expressions used by modern-day Menorquins in every day conversation.

Examples:
A bow-window is called a *boinder*
A screwdriver is a *tornaescru*
A bottle becomes *bòtil*
Marbles are *mervils*
A leg of pork (shank) is *un xenc*
A black eye is *un ull blec* (*ull* is eye in *menorquí*)
To rap a door with your knuckles is to *toc de necles*

Spanish – like French, Italian and Portuguese – is a Romance language, derived from the Latin spoken by the Romans who conquered the Iberian peninsula more than 2,000 years ago. The Moors who settled in the peninsula centuries later contributed a great number of new words (*see panel*). Following the discovery of America, Spaniards took their language with them to the four corners of the globe. Today, Spanish is spoken by 250 million people in north, south and central America and parts of Africa.

In addition to Spanish, which is spoken throughout the country, some regions have a second language. Catalan (spoken in Catalonia), Valenciano (Valencia), Mallorquín (the Balearics) and Gallego (Galicia) are all Romance languages, unlike Euskera, the language of the Basques, which is notoriously complex and difficult – it is unrelated to any other European tongue, and experts are not even sure what its origins are.

Unlike English, Spanish is a phonetic language: words are pronounced exactly as they are spelt, which is why it is somewhat harder for Spaniards to learn English than vice versa (although Spanish distinguishes between the two genders, masculine and feminine, and the subjunctive verb form is an endless source of headaches for students). The English language is one of Britain's biggest exports to Spain. Spaniards spend millions on learning aids, language academies and sending their children to study English in the UK or Ireland, and are eager to practise their linguistic skills with foreign visitors. Even so, they will

Moorish Connections

The Moors arrived in Spain in 711, and occupied parts of the peninsula for the next eight centuries. They left behind hundreds of Arabic words, many related to farming and crops, as well as place names including those of towns (often identified by the prefix Al-, meaning "the" or Ben-, meaning "son of") and rivers (the prefix Guad- means "river"). Some of these Arabic words passed on to other languages, including French, and from there into English.

Among those present in both Spanish and English are:

sugar (*azúcar*), coffee (*café*), apricot (*albaricoque*), saffron (*azafrán*), lemon (*limón*), cotton (*algodón*), alcohol (*alcohol*), karat (*kilate*), cipher (*cifra*), elixir (*elixir*), almanac (*almanaque*), zenith (*cenit*), and zero (*cero*).

The Alphabet

Learning the pronunciation of the Spanish alphabet is a good idea. In particular, learn how to spell out your own name. Spanish has a letter that doesn't exist in English, the ñ (pronounced "*ny*").
a = *ah*, **b** = *bay*, **c** = *thay* (strong th as in "thought"), **ch** = *chay*, **d** = *day*, **e** = *ay*, **f** = *effay*, **g** = *hay*, **h** = *ah-chay*, **i** = *ee*, **j** = *hotah*, **k** = *kah*, **l** = *ellay*, **u** = *ell-yay*, **m** = *emmay*, **n** = *ennay*, **ñ** = *enyay*, **o** = *oh*, **p** = *pay*, **q** = *koo*, **r** = *erray*, **s** = *essay*, **t** = *tay*, **u** = *oo*, **v** = *oovay*, **w** = *oovay doe-blay*, **x** = *ek-kiss*, **y** = *ee gree-ay-gah*, **z** = *thay-tah*

be flattered and delighted if you make the effort to communicate in Spanish. You should beware, however, of some misleading "false friends" (*see panel*).

Basic Rules

English is widely spoken in most tourist areas, but even if you speak no Spanish at all, it is worth trying to master a few simple words and phrases.

As a general rule, the accent falls on the second-to-last syllable, unless it is otherwise marked with an accent (´) or the word ends in D, L, R or Z.

Vowels in Spanish are always pronounced the same way. The double LL is pronounced like the y in "yes", the double RR is rolled, as in Scots. The H is silent in Spanish, whereas J (and G when it precedes an E or I) is pronounced like a guttural H (as if you were clearing your throat).

When addressing someone you are not familiar with, use the more formal "usted". The informal "tu" is reserved for relatives and friends.

Words & Phrases

Hello *Hola*
How are you? *¿Cómo está usted?*
How much is it? *¿Cuánto es?*
What is your name? *¿Cómo se llama usted?*

My name is... *Yo me llamo...*
Do you speak English? *¿Habla inglés?*
I am British/American *Yo soy británico/norteamericano*
I don't understand *No comprendo*
Please speak more slowly *Hable más despacio, por favor*
Can you help me? *¿Me puede ayudar?*
I am looking for... *Estoy buscando*
Where is...? *¿Dónde está...?*
I'm sorry *Lo siento*
I don't know *No lo se*
No problem *No hay problema*
Have a good day *Que tenga un buen día, or Vaya con Diós*
That's it *Ese es*
Here it is *Aquí está*
There it is *Allí está*
Let's go *Vámonos*
See you tomorrow *Hasta mañana*
See you soon *Hasta pronto*
Show me the word in the book *Muéstreme la palabra en el libro*
At what time? *¿A qué hora?*
When? *¿Cuándo?*
What time is it? *¿Qué hora es?*
yes *sí*
no *no*
please *por favor*
thank you (very much) *(muchas) gracias*
you're welcome *de nada*
excuse me *perdóneme*
hello *hola*
OK *bién*
goodbye *adiós*

Slang

¡Guay! **Swell!**
Bocata **Sandwich**
Litrona **a litre-bottle of beer**
Guiri **foreigner**
Kilo **one million pesetas**
Duro **five pesetas (eg. veinte duros is 100 pesetas)**

good evening/night *buenas tardes/noches*
here *aquí*
there *allí*
today *hoy*
yesterday *ayer*
tomorrow *mañana (note: mañana also means "morning")*
now *ahora*
later *después*
right away *ahora mismo*
this morning *esta mañana*
this afternoon *esta tarde*
this evening *esta tarde*
tonight *esta noche*

On Arrival

I want to get off at... *Quiero bajarme en...*
Is there a bus to the museum? *¿Hay un autobús al museo?*
What street is this? *¿Qué calle es ésta?*
Which line do I take for...? *¿Qué línea cojo para...?*
How far is...? *¿A qué distancia está...?*

airport *aeropuerto*
customs *aduana*
train station *estación de tren*
bus station *estación de autobuses*
metro station *estación de metro*
bus *autobús*
bus stop *parada de autobús*
platform *apeadero*
ticket *billete*
return ticket *billete de ida y vuelta*
hitch-hiking *auto-stop*
toilets *servicios*
This is the hotel address *Ésta es la dirección del hotel*
I'd like a (single/double) room *Quiero una habitación (sencilla/doble)*
... with shower *con ducha*
... with bath *con baño*
... with a view *con vista*
Does that include breakfast? *¿Incluye desayuno?*
May I see the room? *¿Puedo ver la habitación?*
washbasin *lavabo*
bed *cama*
key *llave*
elevator *ascensor*
air conditioning *aire acondicionado*

Emergencies

Help! *¡Socorro!*
Stop! *¡Alto!*
Call a doctor *Llame a un médico*
Call an ambulance *Llame a una ambulancia*
Call the police *Llame a la policia*

Numbers, Days and Dates

NUMBERS				DAYS OF THE WEEK	MONTHS
0	*cero*	15 *quince*	500 *quinientos*	Monday *lunes*	January *enero*
1	*uno*	16 *dieciseis*	1,000 *mil*	Tuesday *martes*	February *febrero*
2	*dos*	17 *diecisiete*	10,000 *diez mil*	Wednesday	March *marzo*
3	*tres*	18 *dieciocho*	1,000,000 *un millón*	*miércoles*	April *abril*
4	*cuatro*	19 *diecinueve*		Thursday *jueves*	May *mayo*
5	*cinco*	20 *viente*		Friday *viernes*	June *junio*
6	*seis*	21 *veintiuno*	SAYING THE DATE	Saturday *sábado*	July *julio*
7	*siete*	30 *treinta*	20 October 2000,	Sunday *domingo*	August *agosto*
8	*ocho*	40 *cuarenta*	*el veinte de*		September
9	*nueve*	50 *cincuenta*	*octubre del año*		*septiembre*
10	*diez*	60 *sesenta*	*dos mil* (no capital	SEASONS	October *octubre*
11	*once*	70 *setenta*	letters are used for	Spring *primavera*	November
12	*doce*	80 *ochenta*	days or months)	Summer *verano*	*noviembre*
13	*trece*	90 *noventa*		Autumn *otoño*	December
14	*catorce*	100 *cien*		Winter *invierno*	*diciembre*
		200 *doscientos*			

Call the fire brigade *Llame a los bomberos*
Where is the nearest telephone? *¿Dónde está el teléfono mas próximo?*
Where is the nearest hospital? *¿Dónde está el hospital más próximo?*
I am sick *Estoy enfermo*
I have lost my passport/purse *He perdido mi pasaporte/bolso*

On the Road

Where is the spare wheel? *¿Dónde está la rueda de repuesto?*
Where is the nearest garage? *¿Dónde está el taller más próximo?*
Our car has broken down *Nuestro coche se ha averiado*
I want to have my car repaired *Quiero que reparen mi coche*
It's not your right of way *Usted no tiene prioridad*
I think I must have put diesel in my car by mistake *Me parece haber echado gasoil por error*
the road to... *la carretera a...*
left *izquierda*
right *derecha*
straight on *derecho*
far *lejos*
near *cerca*
opposite *frente a*
beside *al lado de*
car park *aparcamiento*
over there *allí*
at the end *al final*
on foot *a pie*
by car *en coche*
town map *mapa de la ciudad*
road map *mapa de carreteras*
street *calle*
square *plaza*
give way *ceda el paso*
exit *salida*
dead end *calle sin salida*
wrong way *dirección prohibida*
no parking *prohibido aparcar*
motorway *autovía*
toll highway *autopista*
toll *peaje*
speed limit *límite de velocidad*
petrol station *gasolinera*
petrol *gasolina*
unleaded *sin plomo*
diesel *gasoil*
water/oil *agua/aceite*
air *aire*

puncture *pinchazo*
bulb *bombilla*

On the Telephone

How do I make an outside call? *¿Cómo hago una llamada exterior?*
What is the area code? *¿Cuál es el prefijo?*
I want to make an international (local) call *Quiero hacer una llamada internacional (local)*
I'd like an alarm call for 8 tomorrow morning *Quiero que me despierten a las ocho de la mañana*
Hello? *¿Dígame?*
Who's calling? *¿Quién llama?*
Hold on, please *Un momento, por favor*
I can't hear you *No le oigo*
Can you hear me? *¿Me oye?*
He/she is not here *No está aquí*
The line is busy *La línea está ocupada*
I must have dialled the wrong number *Debo haber marcado un número equivocado*

Shopping

Where is the nearest bank? *¿Dónde está el banco más próximo?*
I'd like to buy *Quiero comprar*
How much is it *¿Cuánto es?*
Do you accept credit cards? *¿Aceptan tarjeta?*
I'm just looking *Sólo estoy mirando*
Have you got...? *¿Tiene...?*
I'll take it *Me lo llevo*
I'll take this one/that one *Me llevo éste/ese*
What size is it? *¿Que talla es?*
size (clothes) *talla*
small *pequeño*
large *grande*
cheap *barato*
expensive *caro*
enough *suficiente*
too much *demasiado*
a piece *una pieza*
each *cada una/la pieza/la unidad (eg. melones, 100 ptas la unidad)*
bill *la factura (shop), la cuenta (restaurant)*
bank *banco*
bookshop *librería*
chemist *farmacia*
hairdressers *peluquería*

post office *correos*
department store *grandes almacenes*

MARKET SHOPPING

Supermarkets (*supermercados*) are self service, but often the best and freshest produce is to be had at the town market (*mercado*) or at street markets (*mercadillo*), where you place you order with the person in charge of each stand. Prices are usually by the kilo, sometimes by gramos (by the gram) or by unidad (by the piece).

fresh *fresco*
frozen *congelado*
organic *biológico*
flavour *sabor*
basket *cesta*
bag *bolsa*
bakery *panadería*
butcher's *carnicería*
cake shop *pastelería*
fishmonger's *pescadería*
grocery *verdulería*
tobacconist *estanco*
market *mercado*
supermarket *supermercado*
junk shop *tienda de segunda mano*

Sightseeing

mountain *montaña*
hill *colina*
valley *valle*
river *río*
lake *lago*
lookout *mirador*
city *ciudad*
small town, village *pueblo*
old town *casco antiguo*
monastery *monasterio*
convent *convento*
cathedral *catedral*
church *iglesia*
palace *palacio*
hospital *hospital*
town hall *ayuntamiento*
nave *nave*
statue *estátua*
fountain *fuente*
staircase *escalera*
tower *torre*
castle *castillo*
Iberian *ibérico*
Phoenician *fenicio*
Roman *romano*

Moorish *árabe*
Romanesque *románico*
Gothic *gótico*
museum *museo*
art gallery *galería de arte*
exhibition *exposición*
tourist information office *oficina de turismo*
free *gratis*
open *abierto*
closed *cerrado*
every day *diario/todos los días*
all year *todo el año*
all day *todo el día*
swimming pool *piscina*
to book *reservar*

Dining Out

In Spanish, *el menú* is not the main menu, but a fixed menu offered each day at a lower price. The main menu is *la carta*.

breakfast *desayuno*
lunch *comida*
dinner *cena*
meal *comida*
first course *primer plato*
main course *plato principal*
made to order *por encargo*
drink included *incluida consumición/bebida*
wine list *carta de vinos*
the bill *la cuenta*
fork *tenedor*
knife *cuchillo*
spoon *cuchara*
plate *plato*
glass *vaso*
wine glass *copa*
napkin *servilleta*
ashtray *cenicero*
waiter, please! *camarero, por favor*

Liquid Refreshment

coffee *café*
　black *sólo*
　with milk *con leche*
　decaffeinated *descafeinado*
sugar *azúcar*
tea *té*
herbal tea *infusión*
milk *leche*
mineral water *agua mineral*
fizzy *con gas*
non-fizzy *sin gas*
juice (fresh) *zumo (natural)*

Table Talk

I am a vegetarian *Soy vegetariano*
I am on a diet *Estoy de régimen*
What do you recommend? *¿Qué recomienda?*
Do you have local specialities? *¿Hay especialidades locales?*
I'd like to order *Quiero pedir*
That is not what I ordered *Ésto no es lo que he pedido*
May I have more wine? *¿Me da más vino?*
Enjoy your meal *Buen provecho*

cold *fresco/frío*
hot *caliente*
beer *cerveza*
　bottled *en botella*
　on tap *de barril*
soft drink *refresco*
diet drink *bebida "light"*
with ice *con hielo*
wine *vino*
red wine *vino tinto*
white *blanco*
rosé *rosado*
dry *seco*
sweet *dulce*
house wine *vino de la casa*
sparkling wine *vino espumoso*
Where is this wine from? *¿De dónde es este vino?*
pitcher *jarra*
half litre *medio litro*
quarter litre *cuarto de litro*
cheers! *salud*
hangover *resaca*

Menu Decoder

BREAKFAST AND SNACKS
pan bread
bollo bun/roll
mantequilla butter
mermelada jam
confitura jam
pimienta pepper
sal salt
azúcar sugar
huevos eggs
　cocidos boiled, cooked
　con beicon with bacon
　con jamón with ham
　fritos fried
　revueltos scrambled
yogúr yoghurt

tostada toast
sandwich sandwich in square slices of bread
bocadillo sandwich in a bread roll

MAIN COURSES
Meat/Carne
buey beef
carne picada ground meat
cerdo pork
chivo kid
chorizo sausage seasoned with paprika
chuleta chop
cochinillo suckling pig
conejo rabbit
cordero lamb
costilla rib
entrecot beef rib steak
filete steak
abalí wild boar
jamón ham
jamón cocido cooked ham
jamón serrano cured ham
salchichón sausage
lomo loin
morcilla black pudding
pierna leg
riñones kidneys
sesos brains
solomillo fillet steak
ternera veal or young beef
lengua tongue
a la brasa charcoal grilled
al horno roast
a la plancha grilled
asado roast
bién hecho well done
en salsa in sauce
en su punto medium
estofado stew
frito fried
parrillada mixed grill
pinchito skewer
Poco hecho rare
relleno stuffed

Fowl
codorniz quail
faisán pheasant
pavo turkey
pato duck
perdiz partridge
pintada guinea fowl
pollo chicken

Fish/Pescado
almeja clam
anchoas anchovies

anguila **eel**
atún **tuna**
bacalao **cod**
besugo **red bream**
bogavante **lobster**
boquerones **fresh anchovies**
caballa **mackerel**
calamar **squid**
cangrejo **crab**
caracola **sea snail**
cazón **dogfish**
centollo **spider crab**
chopito **baby cuttlefish**
cigala **Dublin Bay prawn/scampi**
dorada **gilt head bream**
fritura **mixed fry**
gamba **shrimp/prawn**
jibia **cuttlefish**
langosta **spiny lobster**
langostino **large prawn**
lenguado **sole**
lubina **sea bass**
mariscada **mixed shellfish**
mariscos **Shellfish**
mejillón **mussel**
merluza **hake**
mero **grouper**
ostión **Portuguese oyster**
ostra **oyster**
peregrina **scallop**
pescadilla **small hake**
pez espada **swordfish**
pijota **hake**
pulpo **octopus**
rape **monkfish**
rodaballo **turbot**
salmón **salmon**
salmonete **red mullet**
sardina **sardine**
trucha **trout**

VEGETABLES/CEREALS/ SALADS

vegetables **verduras**
ajo **garlic**
alcachofa **artichoke**
apio **celery**
arroz **rice**
berenjena **eggplant/aubergine**
cebolla **onion**
champiñon **mushroom**
col **cabbage**
coliflor **cauliflower**
crudo **raw**
ensalada **salad**
espárrago **asparagus**
espinaca **spinach**
garbanzo **chick pea**
guisante **pea**

haba **broad bean**
habichuela **bean**
judía **green bean**
lechuga **lettuce**
lenteja **lentil**
maíz **corn/maize**
menestra **cooked mixed vegetables**
patata **potato**
pepino **cucumber**
pimiento **pepper**
puerro **leek**
rábano **radish**
seta **wild mushroom**
tomate **tomato**
zanahoria **carrot**

FRUIT AND DESSERTS

fruta **fruta**
aguacate **avocado**
albaricoque **apricot**
cereza **cherry**
ciruela **plum**
frambuesa **raspberry**
fresa **strawberry**
granada **pomegranate**
higo **fig**
limón **lemon**
mandarina **tangerine**
manzana **apple**
melocotón **peach**
melón **melon**
naranja **orange**
pasa **raisin**
pera **pear**
piña **pineapple**
plátano **banana**
pomelo **grapefruit**
sandía **watermelon**
uva **grape**
Postre **Dessert**
tarta **cake**
pastel **pie**
helado **ice cream**
natilla **custard**
flan **caramel custard**
queso **cheese**

Further Reading

GENERAL

Los Andaluces. Madrid: Ediciones Istmo, 1980. Collection of wide-ranging essays on the people, their history, economy and culture to the present day.**The Art of Flamenco**, by D.E. Pohren. Musical New Services Ltd, 1984. The *aficionado's bible*.

A Way of Life. Madrid: Society of Spanish Studies, 1980. Colourful, humorous account of a disappearing Andalucían lifestyle.

As I Walked Out One Midsummer Morning, by Laurie Lee. Penguin, 1983. Romantic young man's vision of pre-Civil War Spain.Also by Lee **A Rose for Winter**. Penguin, 1983. Lee's post-war return to Andalucía.

The Assassination of Federico García Lorca, by Ian Gibson. Penguin, 1983. Banned in Franco's Spain because it revealed the truth about Lorca's death.

Federico García Lorca: A Life. Faber & Faber, 1989. Award-winning, biography.

The Bible in Spain, by George Borrow. First published 1842. Eccentric, opinionated and entertaining.

La Civilización hispano-árabe by Titus Burckhardt. (Original title: *Die maurische Kultur in Spanien*. Munich: Verlag Georg D.W. Callwey, 1970.) Madrid: Alianza Editorial, 1977. Examination of Moorish culture.

Cooking in Spain, by Janet Mendel. Fuengirola, Málaga: Lookout Publications. Details of many typical Andalucían dishes.

Los Curiosos Impertinentes, by Ian Robertson. Published in Spanish by Serbal, 1988. English travellers' adventures in and comments on Spain between 1760 and 1855.

Death in the Afternoon, by Ernest Hemingway. (1932).

Death's Other Kingdom, by Gamel Woolsey. Virago Press, 1988. Vivid account of outbreak of Civil War by this American poet, the wife of Gerald Brenan.

Handbook for Travellers in Spain, by Richard Ford. Centaur Press, 1966; and *Gatherings from Spain*. Dent Everyman, 1970. Classic 19th-century travels.

Here in Spain, by David Mitchell. Fuengirola, Málaga: Lookout Publications. Views of foreign travellers through the centuries.

Histoire de l'Espagne Musulmane, by Évariste Lévi-Provencale. III volumes. Erudite history of Spain under the Moors.

Further reading

Although Spain did not figure in the Grand Tour of the early tourists, from the 19th century it attracted a succession of foreign travellers in search of the "exotic" such as Henry Swinburne, Joseph Townsend, and Richard Ford. Ford did the most to awaken interest in the region with witty and shrewdly-observed accounts of his travels between 1830–1833.

This century Gerald Brenan, who lived much of his life in Andalucía, stands out as a writer whose great affection for the region did not diminish his critical faculties.

In Hiding: The Life of Manuel Cortes. Penguin, 1982. How a village mayor stayed hidden for 30 years for fear of execution.

Inside Andalusia – A Travel Adventure in Southern Spain, by David Baird. Fuengirola, Málaga: Lookout Publications, 1988. Informative account of Andalucía and its people, well illustrated.

Los Moriscos del Reino de Granada, by Julio Caro Baroja. Madrid: Ediciones Istmo, 1985. One of Spain's foremost historians relates the last days of the Moors of Granada.

The Modern State of Spain, by J.-F. Bourgoing. (1808).

Or I'll Dress You in Mourning, by Larry Collins and Dominique Lapierre. Simon & Schuster. Brilliantly documented insights into Spain's post-Civil War hardships which moulded the Andalucían matador El Cordobés.

The People of the Sierra, by Julian A. Pitt-Rivers. Weidenfield & Nicolson, 1954. Social anthropologist's dissection of a remote mountain community.

The Pueblo: A Mountain Village in Spain, by Ronald Fraser. Pantheon. Villagers of Mijas tell their own story.

The Presence of Spain, by James Morris. (1964, reissued as Spain by Jan Morris).

The Road from Ronda, by Alastair Boyd. Collins, 1969. Vivid account of a horse-ride through the Serranía de Ronda.

A Romantic in Spain, by Théophile Gautier. (1926, first published 1845 as *Voyage en Espagne*).

South from Granada, by Gerald Brenan. Cambridge University Press, 1988. Classic account of life in a remote Granada village. Also by Brenan **The Face of Spain**. Penguin, 1987. Brenan's grim view of an impoverished post-war Spain.

The Spaniards: *A Portrait of the New Spain*, by John Hooper. (1986).

A Spanish Raggle-Taggle, by Walter Starkie. (1934).

Tales of the Alhambra, by Washington Irving. Granada: Miguel Sánchez. Legends and colourful view of Granada's last century.

Tartessos, by Adolph Schulten. Madrid: Espasa-Calpe. Controversial attempt to establish the site of Tartessos near the mouth of the Guadalquivir.

Travels into Spain, Mme d'Aulnoy. (1930, first published 1691).

White Wall of Spain, by Allen Josephs. Iowa State University Press. Fascinating examination of Andalucía's roots and the creation of a unique culture.

Other Insight Guides

Other Insight Guides which highlight destinations in this region include:

Insight Guide: Southern Spain is your key to Andalucía, often regarded as the soul of the country.

Insight Guide: Northern Spain Discover "Green Spain", including the Pyrenees, Galicia, Asturias and the Basque Country.

Insight Guide: Catalonia The Costa Brava and Spain's unique Catalan culture.

Insight Guide: Barcelona explores the trendy cosmopolitan city, which is the largest in the Mediterranean.

Insight Guide: Madrid covers Spain's big city and its cultural capital, in glorious colour.

Insight Pocket Guides

Insight Pocket Guides will take you straight to the best of the Spanish cities in day-by-day itineraries specially created by local hosts. They include a full-size fold-out map which can be used independently of the book. Titles in this series include: **Madrid, Barcelona, Costa Brava, Mallorca, Gran Canaria and Tenerife**.

Insight Compact Guides

Insight Compact Guide: Barcelona and **Insight Compact Guide: Costa Brava** are just two titles taken from Apa Publications' third series of guidebooks. The mini-encyclopedias are packed with facts, photographs and maps, all carefully cross-referenced, and are the ideal easy-reference books for practical use on the spot.

ART & PHOTO CREDITS

AGE Fotostock 52R, 52L, 77, 103, 130T, 257, 259, 340/341
AKG 193T
AISA 4/5, 87, 142, 144, 153, 200, 280, 281, 304, 308, 311, 325, 328T, 329
Oriol Alamany 94
Fernando Alvira 234, 246, 247
M Angeles Sanchez 109, 167, 240, 241
Archivo Océano 215
Gonzalo M Azumendi 6/7, 68/69, 151, 157, 172, 179, 284/285, 286, 289, 290, 291, 292, 293, 294, 295, 299, 300, 305, 306, 307, 310, 312
David Baird 104
G Barone 198, 201, 213, 267
F Lisa Beebe 102, 105, 196, 214, 228, 240T
Dani Codina 250
Cover/Santos Cirilo 75
Cover/X. Gómez 177, 256L
Cover/Sofia Moro 61
Doug Corrance 224T
Courtesy of Instituto Geografico Nacional 16/17
J D Dallet 56, 106, 130, 148, 162T, 171, 178, 184, 188/187, 195, 223, 226, 232/233, 235, 237, 242, 242T, 245T, 287, 294T, 317, 319, 320, 324
Courtesy of Pedro Domecq 222
Gustave Dore 101
Andrew Eames 35, 44
Annabel Elston 251, 252, 252T, 253, 255L, 255R, 255T, 260, 261, 261T, 262, 263, 263T
Europa Press Reportajes 53
Expo Tenerife 333, 337
Muriel Feiner 78, 82, 83
Albert Fortuny 174
Wolfgang Fritz 140T
Jaume Gual 127
Glyn Genin 342, 343, 345, 347, 348T
Blaine Harrington 71, 72, 79, 80, 120, 163, 165, 180, 302
Dallas & John Heaton 197
Dave G Houser 14
Imagen 3 22, 28, 29, 32, 59, 62, 327
Imagen MAS 149, 150, 152T, 156, 161, 175, 176, 181, 182, 183, 185, 282, 282T, 283, 301, 313, 314, 315
Nick Inman/Images of Spain 238L,

238R, 239, 244, 245
Index 116/117, 339
Veronica Janssen 1, 326
Michael Jenner 134
Jean Kugler 116/117, 162, 205, 211
Rita Kummel 81, 269, 298
Antonio Lafuente 108
Lyle Lawson 65, 158, 158T, 160T, 288T, 292T, 300T, 303, 304T, 308T, 313T, 314T, 316, 322, 322T
Alain Le Garsmeur 95, 219
Jose Lucas 190
M+W Fine Arts/New York/José Martin 24, 37, 40
Fiona MacGegor 131, 133
José Martin 23, 25, 30, 38, 41, 43, 45, 46/47, 48, 49, 54, 55, 84/85, 86, 90, 91, 93, 129T, 134, 134T, 143L, 143R, 145, 145T, 147, 149T, 159, 279T, 321
Mike Mockler 96, 98, 99
Robert Mort 107, 109
Museu d'Art Modern 92
National Maritime Museum 39
Gary John Norman 334T, 336T
Richard Nowitz 164
Oronoz Archivo Fotografico 34, 58
Patronat de Catalunya 276
Andrea Pistolesi 146, 169, 279
Jens Poulsen 57
Carl Purcell 26, 100, 128, 129, 140, 155
Mark Read 8/9, 76, 114/115, 194T, 196T, 199T, 200T, 204, 204T, 206T, 207T, 211T, 212T, 214T, 222T, 225, 227T, 229, 229T, 230T
Jörg Reuther 336, 338
Martin Rosefeldt 137T, 138T
Servei Fotografic M.A.C 88
Jeroen Snijders 268T, 270T, 272, 272T, 274, 274T, 275, 275T
Spectrum 330/331
Martinez Tajadura 154L, 154R, 163, 271, 346
Roger Tidman 97
Klaus Thiele 195T
Topham Picturepoint 64, 135, 290T, 302T
Robin Townsend 21, 255L, 255R, 267
Bill Wassman 2/3, 10/11, 12/13, 20, 27, 66/67, 73, 75, 112/113, 126, 132, 134L, 136, 137, 138, 139, 140,

141, 147T, 170, 191, 193, 194, 199, 201, 203, 205, 207, 209, 218, 221, 227, 230, 231, 254, 256T, 266, 273, 323, 328, 332, 348, 349, 351
Roger Williams 50, 258
George Wright 207, 212

Picture Spreads

Pages 110/111 : Top row left to right: J D Dallet, Gonzalo M Azumendi, M Angeles Sanchez, Ellen Rooney; Centre row: AISA, M Angeles Sanchez, Imagen MAS; Bottom row: Imagen MAS, AISA
Pages 186/187: Top row left to right: Imagen MAS, AISA, Andrea Pistolesi, Imagen MAS; Centre row: J D Dallet, Imagen MAS; Bottom row: Imagen MAS, Imagen MAS, AISA
Pages 216/217: Top row left to right: Mark Read, AISA, Jose Lucas, Jose Lucas; Centre row: Jose Lucas; Bottom row: Jose Lucas, Jose Lucas, Mark Read, Jose Lucas, Mark Read
Pages 264/265: Top row left to right: AR/Gau, AISA, J D Dallet, AR/Gau; Centre row: J D Dallet; Bottom row: AR/Gau, J D Dallet, AR/Gau, Ellen Rooney
Pages 296/297: Top row left to right: Inaki Andres, Guggenheim Bilbao/Erika Barahona Ede, Mitxi-Miguel Calvo, Roger Williams; Centre row: Inaki Andres; Bottom row: Carlos Garcia, Mitxi-Miguel Calvo, Inaki Andres

Maps Colourmap Scanning Ltd
© 1999 Apa Publications GmbH & Co. Verlag KG (Singapore branch)

Cartographic Editor **Zoë Goodwin**
Production **Stuart A. Everitt**
Design Consultants
Carlotta Junger, Graham Mitchener
Picture Research
Monica Allende, Hilary Genin

Index

Numbers in italics refer to photographs

☀ INSIGHT GUIDES
The world's largest collection of visual travel guides

A range of guides and maps to meet every travel need

Insight Guides
This classic series gives you the complete picture of a destination through expert, well written and informative text and stunning photography. Each book is an ideal background information and travel planner, serves as an on-the-spot companion – and is a superb visual souvenir of a trip. Nearly 200 titles.

Insight Pocket Guides
focus on the best choices for places to see and things to do, picked by our local correspondents. They are ideal for visitors new to a destination. To help readers follow the routes easily, the books contain full-size pull-out maps. 120 titles.

Insight Maps
are designed to complement the guides. They provide full mapping of major cities, regions and countries, and their laminated finish makes them easy to fold and gives them durability. 60 titles.

Insight Compact Guides
are convenient, comprehensive reference books, modestly priced. The text, photographs and maps are all carefully cross-referenced, making the books ideal for on-the-spot use when in a destination. 120 titles.

Different travellers have different needs. Since 1970, Insight Guides has been meeting these needs with a range of practical and stimulating guidebooks and maps

> **"** I was first drawn to the Insight Guides by the excellent "Nepal" volume. I can think of no book which so effectively captures the essence of a country. Out of these pages leaped the Nepal I know – the captivating charm of a people and their culture. I've since discovered and enjoyed the entire Insight Guide series. Each volume deals with a country in the same sensitive depth, which is nowhere more evident than in the superb photography. **"**

Sir Edmund Hillary

☀ INSIGHT GUIDES

The world's largest collection of visual travel guides

Insight Guides – the Classic Series
that puts you in the picture

Alaska	China	Hong Kong	Morocco	Singapore
Alsace	Cologne	Hungary	Moscow	South Africa
Amazon Wildlife	Continental Europe		Munich	South America
American Southwest	Corsica	Iceland		South Tyrol
Amsterdam	Costa Rica	India	Namibia	Southeast Asia
Argentina	Crete	India's Western	Native America	Wildlife
Asia, East	Crossing America	Himalayas	Nepal	Spain
Asia, South	Cuba	India, South	Netherlands	Spain, Northern
Asia, Southeast	Cyprus	Indian Wildlife	New England	Spain, Southern
Athens	Czech & Slovak	Indonesia	New Orleans	Sri Lanka
Atlanta	Republic	Ireland	New York City	Sweden
Australia		Israel	New York State	Switzerland
Austria	Delhi, Jaipur & Agra	Istanbul	New Zealand	Sydney
	Denmark	Italy	Nile	Syria & Lebanon
Bahamas	Dominican Republic	Italy, Northern	Normandy	
Bali	Dresden		Norway	Taiwan
Baltic States	Dublin	Jamaica		Tenerife
Bangkok	Düsseldorf	Japan	Old South	Texas
Barbados		Java	Oman & The UAE	Thailand
Barcelona	East African Wildlife	Jerusalem	Oxford	Tokyo
Bay of Naples	Eastern Europe	Jordan		Trinidad & Tobago
Beijing	Ecuador		Pacific Northwest	Tunisia
Belgium	Edinburgh	Kathmandu	Pakistan	Turkey
Belize	Egypt	Kenya	Paris	Turkish Coast
Berlin	England	Korea	Peru	Tuscany
Bermuda			Philadelphia	
Boston	Finland	Laos & Cambodia	Philippines	Umbria
Brazil	Florence	Lisbon	Poland	USA: Eastern States
Brittany	Florida	Loire Valley	Portugal	USA: Western States
Brussels	France	London	Prague	US National Parks:
Budapest	Frankfurt	Los Angeles	Provence	East
Buenos Aires	French Riviera		Puerto Rico	US National Parks:
Burgundy		Madeira		West
Burma (Myanmar)	Gambia & Senegal	Madrid	Rajasthan	
	Germany	Malaysia	Rhine	Vancouver
Cairo	Glasgow	Mallorca & Ibiza	Rio de Janeiro	Venezuela
Calcutta	Gran Canaria	Malta	Rockies	Venice
California	Great Barrier Reef	Marine Life ot the	Rome	Vienna
California, Northern	Great Britain	South China Sea	Russia	Vietnam
California, Southern	Greece	Mauritius &		
Canada	Greek Islands	Seychelles	St. Petersburg	Wales
Caribbean	Guatemala, Belize &	Melbourne	San Francisco	Washington DC
Catalonia	Yucatán	Mexico City	Sardinia	Waterways of Europe
Channel Islands		Mexico	Scotland	Wild West
Chicago	Hamburg	Miami	Seattle	
Chile	Hawaii	Montreal	Sicily	Yemen

Complementing the above titles are 120 easy-to-carry Insight Compact Guides, 120 Insight Pocket
Guides with full-size pull-out maps and more than 60 laminated easy-fold Insight Maps